This is
Scotland
Highlands
& Islands

13/2/20

15/7/23

- You can return this item to any Bournemouth library but not all libraries are open every day.

- Items must be returned on or before the due date. Please note that you will be charged for items returned late.

- Items may be renewed unless requested by another customer.

- Renewals can be made in any library, by telephone, email or online via the website. Your membership card number and PIN will be required.

- Please look after this item - you may be charged for any damage.

ALAN

630005800 M

Every self-respecting Scot comes over all proprietorial when introducing the glories of their country to a friend or loved one for the first time. So much so, you'd think they'd designed the whole place themselves. As if the jaw-dropping scenery of Wester Ross or the Trossachs was some kind of DIY makeover. The Scots have every right to be proud, for when the rain stops falling and the mist clears, there is, quite simply, no more beautiful place on Earth. If there is a heaven, it must surely look like the Highlands and Islands, but let's hope the petrol's cheaper.

Scotland is one of the least densely populated countries in Europe. Not much smaller than its southern neighbour, England, it has only a tenth of its population; and most of those are crammed into the narrow central belt, leaving two-thirds of the country virtually empty. This is Europe's last great wilderness; one of the few places in this increasingly cluttered continent where you can really get away from it all.

Best of
Scotland
Highlands &
Islands

❶ Islay's distilleries

The Isle of Islay is famous the world over for its distinctive single malt whiskies and after a visit here to sample the peaty delights of its eight distilleries you'll soon be planning to turn a single into a return trip. Page 100.

❷ Corryvreckan

The world's second largest whirlpool, between the islands of Jura and Scarba, is officially unnavigable but intrepid visitors can take a white-knuckle RIB ride across its crashing waters while looking out for porpoises, seals and other wildlife. Page 104.

❹ Glen Coe

Haunting and dramatic Glen Coe is one of Scotland's most evocative places, with a blood-soaked history that is made all the more poignant by the jaw-droppingly beautiful scenery all around. Page 203.

❺ West Highland Railway

All aboard the West Highland Railway! This 164-mile trip runs from Glasgow to Mallaig and is widely acknowledged as one of the world's great rail journeys. Page 218.

❸ Lairig Ghru

Take on the challenge of this famous long-distance trail that runs for 25 miles from Aviemore over the spectacular Lairig Ghru Pass to the welcoming sight of Braemar, nestled in Royal Deeside. Page 145.

⑥ Bealach na Ba

The 'Pass of the Cattle' on the Applecross Peninsula is one of the highest roads that can be negotiated in the UK and the views from the top are out of this world, as is the seafood on offer at the wonderful Applecross Inn. Page 232.

⑦ Sandwood Bay

The northwest coast can boast many fine beaches but this one is very special indeed. Come here with a loved one – and a bottle of your favourite single malt – and watch the sun set in splendid isolation. Page 253.

⑧ Calanais

Uncover the mystery of these 5000-year-old standing stones. No fences, security guards or hordes of tourists to deal with here; just you, the stones and an ethereal quiet and stillness. Page 332.

⑨ Barra

Wee Barra has it all: beaches, machair, peat-covered hills, tiny crofting communities and Neolithic remains. 'Barradise' indeed, and if you fly in, there's the added thrill of landing on the world's only beach runway. Page 358.

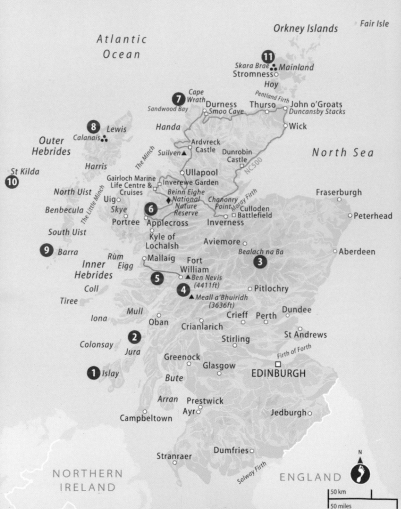

⑩ St Kilda

Voyage across perilous seas to the mysterious haunted islands of St Kilda. Spectacular and isolated, and home to the largest colony of seabirds in Europe, these islands capture the imagination in a way that few other places do. Page 364.

⑪ Skara Brae

Be blown away at the best-preserved Stone Age village in northern Europe. Set amongst the dazzling white sands of the Bay of Skaill and battered by ferocious and relentless Atlantic gales, it's hard to imagine humans living here 5000 years ago. Page 382.

⑫ Hermaness National Nature Reserve

Explore the 2422 acres of dramatic coastal landscape and wild moorland of this remote Shetland outpost. Home to more than 100,000 nesting seabirds, including gannets, puffins and great skuas, this is a place that feels like the very edge of the world. Page 426.

Route planner

The Highland Boundary Fault is the geographical division running northeast from Helensburgh (west of Glasgow) to Stonehaven (south of Aberdeen). To the north of this line lie the Highlands and Islands, which comprise roughly two-thirds of Scotland. This is an area of high mountain ranges punctuated by steep-sided valleys, or glens, and deep lochs. The northwest coastline is indented by numerous steep, fjord-like sea lochs, and offshore are some 790 islands, around 130 of which are inhabited. These are grouped into the Outer Hebrides, or Western Isles, the Inner Hebrides, and, to the north, the Orkney and Shetland Islands.

One week

Highlands circuit

Just north of Glasgow is Loch Lomond and the Trossachs National Park, gateway to the Western Highlands. From here, drive north through atmospheric Glen Coe to Fort William, the self-proclaimed outdoor capital of the UK, which lies in the shadow of Ben Nevis, Britain's highest peak.

From Fort William, you could hop aboard the West Highland Railway for a spectacular journey to Mallaig, where you can board a ferry for Skye, although you'll need several days properly to explore the Isle's glens, mountains and clan sites. Instead, travelling northeast from Fort William, stop in Fort Augustus to marvel at the Caledonian Canal, before driving along the west side of Loch Ness. Be sure to pause at impressive Urquhart Castle and consider a detour to hike the remote and wildlife-rich country of Glen Affric.

Pressing north into Inverness, hop aboard a dolphin cruise in the Moray

Right: Ben Nevis
Opposite page: Red deer, Trossachs National Park

Firth or visit the Culloden battlefield site. There's also the option to drive one hour northwest to spend a day enjoying the scenery and seafood around Ullapool.

From Inverness, drive south down the A9 into the Cairngorms National Park, briefly stopping at the Tomatin malt whisky distillery and at Carrbridge for the kids to let off steam at Landmark. Then travel up the funicular railway at Cairngorm to dine in Britain's highest restaurant. From Aviemore, pass through highland Perthshire, with the chance to visit Scone Palace, before returning to Glasgow via the Trossachs.

Two to three weeks

Inner Hebrides and the Western Highlands

From Glasgow, head west to the Kintyre Peninsula for great scenery, wildlife and windsurfing, the continue west to the Isle of Islay for pristine beaches, clan history and whisky distilleries. Back on the mainland, drive north to Oban, stopping en route to explore the Neolithic remains around Kilmartin.

The Isle of Mull is easily accessible from Oban. Spend a few days on the island to see its birds of prey and to visit atmospheric Duart Castle. You could also head out to Staffa and the holy island of Iona. Tuck into fresh seafood in picturesque Tobermory before departing Mull for the wild Ardnamurchan Peninsula; you may spot minke whales from the lighthouse. Head northwest past the silver sands of Morar to Mallaig and catch a boat to Skye for castles, mountains and Highland hospitality.

From Skye, cross back onto the mainland at Kyle of Lochalsh and head east for Fort Augustus and Loch Ness, stopping to admire the majestic scenery at Eilean Donan Castle. From Fort Augustus head south, then east along Loch Laggan to the distillery at Dalwhinnie. Joining the A9, make a final stop at Blair Atholl Castle before returning to Glasgow.

One month or more

From Glasgow, take in Loch Lomond, Loch Fyne and Inverary Castle en route to Oban. After sampling seafood on the quay, board the ferry for Barra, with views of Mull and Ardnamurchan.

On Barra, visit formidable Kisimul Castle. The deserted beaches of neighbouring Vatersay deserve your attention before you sail north for Eriskay from where Bonnie Prince Charlie launched his campaign for the Scottish crown. Explore the Gaelic-speaking isles of South and North Uist, with their windswept beaches and slower pace of life.

Moving on from North Uist, spend time enjoying the excellent food, stunning coastlines, authentic tweed and superb surfing on Harris and Lewis. Then sail from Lochmaddy to Uig on the Isle of Skye for several days of castles and mountain scenery.

From Skye, spend a week winding north through the picturesque coastal villages and starkly beautiful landscapes of the remote northwest, including the mountains of Torridon and Assynt, and enchanting Sandwood Bay. Enjoy wildlife-spotting and hillwalking, fabulous game and seafood. When you reach Durness, press eastwards to the seabird-peppered cliffs at Dunnet Head, the mainland's most northerly point. Consider a boat ride to explore the many Neolithic wonders on Orkney before making your way south towards Inverness. En route, stop for a dolphin cruise off Cromarty.

Head inland to explore the west side of Loch Ness, visiting the ruin of Urqhhart Castle. Hikers should make a detour into Glen Affric before continuing southwest to Fort William and Ben Nevis. Further south, pass through dramatic Glen Coe and enjoy the scenery of the Trossachs on your way back to Glasgow.

Above: Tobermory
Opposite page: Duart Castle

North Coast 500

The USA has Route 66, Australia the Great Ocean Road and South Africa the Garden Route. Now Scotland has its very own epic road trip in the shape of the North Coast 500.

The official route begins and ends at Inverness Castle. From there it goes across to Kyle of Lochalsh, the gateway to Skye, up the magnificent west coast to Durness, along the north coast to John o'Groats then down the east coast to Inverness again.

Here we list some of the top sights to make your North Coast 500 tour a memorable experience.

Culloden Battlefield

It was here on April 16, 1746, that the Hanoverian army crushed the Jacobites in what was the last battle to be fought on mainland Britain. Page 171.

Beinn Eighe National Nature Reserve

With its cluster of mountain peaks and ancient pinewoods, and the prospect of seeing golden eagles soaring above, it's clear why Beinn Eighe was chosen as Britain's first National Nature Reserve. Page 236.

Inverewe Garden

This is one of Scotland's greatest botanical attractions. It was created out of bare rock and a few scrub willows in 1862 by Osgood Mackenzie and is full of exotic plants from around the world. Page 240.

Bealach na Ba

The 'pass of the cattle' on the Applecross Peninsula is one of the highest roads that can be negotiated in the UK and offers breathtaking views from the summit. Page 232.

Suilven

Rising out of the ancient Assynt landscape, Suilven is a stunning sight with its distinctive two peaks. The climb to Caisteal Liath – the Grey Castle – is steep and unrelenting, but

you are rewarded with an awesome view of the lochans and moors far below. Page 240.

Handa Island
Uninhabited Handa Island is one of Britain's most important breeding grounds for a range of seabirds including puffins, guillemots, fulmars, razorbills and skuas. Page 252.

Sandwood Bay
There are superb, unspoilt beaches along Sutherland's west, north and east coasts, but one of the very best is at Sandwood Bay. Page 253.

Cape Wrath
From Durness, the most northwesterly village in mainland Scotland, take a short ferry trip across to the peninsula of Cape Wrath, home to an operational lighthouse built in 1828 and an abundance of wildlife. Page 258.

Duncansby Stacks
Take a walk across Duncansby Head to see jagged sea stacks, deep caves and natural arches. It's an ideal location for whalewatching and the red sandstone cliffs are packed with seabirds during the breeding season. Page 263.

Dunrobin Castle
Resembling a French chateau with its conical spires, Dunrobin stands above a magnificent garden that took its inspiration from the Palace of Versailles. Page 268.

Dolphin watching
If you're lucky, you may be able to see the wild bottlenose dolphins of the Moray Firth. There are several boat trips or you can opt to stay on dry land and watch from Chanonry Point. Page 278.

Opposite page: Beinn Eighe
Above left: Handa Island puffin
Above right: Duncansby Stacks

Highland cow

When to go

Climate

The high season is from May to September, and this is when Scotland receives the vast majority of its visitors. Though the weather tends to be better during the summer months, prices for accommodation are higher, and hotels and guesthouses in the most popular places need to be booked in advance. It's also a good idea to make reservations on ferries to the islands during this period, especially to Skye and Mull. A major advantage to visiting in the summer months are the long hours of daylight, especially in the far north, where the sun doesn't set till around 2300 or later in June and July.

From October to Easter, many sights are closed, and travelling around the Highlands and Islands can be difficult, as public transport services are limited. Many of the smaller tourist offices are also closed during the low season. Although some hotels and guesthouses close too, the majority are now open all year round, as are most restaurants. Taking everything into consideration, May and September are probably the best months for a visit to the Scottish Highlands and Islands. These are also good months to avoid the dreaded midge (see box on page 475) at its bloodthirsty worst during June, July and August, and the scourge of many a Highland holiday.

Weather Inverness

January	February	March	April	May	June
5°C	6°C	8°C	10°C	13°C	15°C
1°C	1°C	2°C	3°C	6°C	9°C
50mm	40mm	30mm	30mm	40mm	40mm

July	August	September	October	November	December
17°C	17°C	14°C	11°C	7°C	6°C
11°C	11°C	8°C	6°C	3°C	2°C
60mm	70mm	50mm	60mm	60mm	50mm

The Scottish climate is notoriously unpredictable, especially on the west coast, where a bright, sunny morning can turn into a downpour in the time it takes to butter your toast. Predicting the weather is not an exact science and tables of statistics are most likely a waste of time. There's an old saying in Scotland that if you don't like the weather, then wait 20 minutes, and this just about sums it up. The west coast receives far more rain than the rest of the country and the east coast gets more sunshine. The west coast is also milder in the winter due to the relatively warm waters of the Gulf Stream. Winters in the north can be very harsh, especially in the mountains and glens, making hiking conditions treacherous. Winter storms also make it difficult to travel around the islands as ferry services are often cancelled.

Generally, May to September are the warmest months, with an average summer high of around 18-19°C and, though they are often the driest months, you can expect rain at any time of the year. Remember the old hikers' adage that there's no such thing as bad weather, only inadequate clothing.

Festivals

There is a huge range of organized events held throughout Scotland every year, ranging in size and spectacle from the Edinburgh Festival, the largest arts festival in the world, to more obscure traditional events featuring ancient customs dating back many centuries. A couple of good general websites for all events in Scotland are www.visitscotland.com and www.scotlandinfo.eu. The most popular tourist events are the **Highland Games** (or **Gatherings**), a series of competitions involving lots of kilts, bagpipes and caber-tossing, which are held across the Highlands and Islands, the northeast and Argyll from June to September. The best known is the **Braemar Gathering**, see box, page 150, which is attended by various members of the royal family. Those at Oban and Dunoon are large events, but smaller gatherings are often more enjoyable and 'authentic'. Details of Highland Gatherings can be obtained through the Scotland Highland Games Association, www.shga.co.uk.

Folk festivals take place all over the country, from Arran to Shetland, and are great fun. Musicians from all over Scotland gather to play the tunes, sing the songs and maybe, just maybe, drink the odd beer or two. Among the best of the folk festivals is the **Shetland Folk Festival**, usually held over a long weekend in April or early May. Also recommended are those held in Inverness, Islay and Skye. All are usually held during the summer months, but check in advance for dates. Details of these festivals, and many others, are available from the regional **iCentres**. Details of local festivals are given in the listings sections of individual town and cities.

January New Year's Day A variety of ancient local celebrations take place, including the Kirkwall Ba' Game, a mixture of football and mud wrestling.

Up-Helly-Aa Re-enactment of the ancient Viking fire festival held on Shetland on the last Tuesday in January, see page 411.

Burns Night Burns suppers held on 25 January all over the country to celebrate the poet's birthday. Lots of haggis, whisky and poetry.

May Spirit of Speyside Whisky Festival Held on Speyside in May.

September Braemar Highland Gathering, www.braemargathering.org.

Attended by the royal family, the first Saturday in September.

October National Mod Competitive Gaelic music festival held at various locations.

Tour of Mull Rally The highlight of the Scottish rally season, run over the island's public roads (no wonder they're in such appalling condition) in October.

31 December Hogmanay Old year's night, and the most important national celebration. Possible derivations of the word include Holag Monath, Anglo Saxon for 'holy month', and Hoog min dag, which is Dutch for 'great love day'. Edinburgh's huge street party is the largest in the northern hemisphere.

What to do

from skiing and surfing to hiking and climbing

Blessed with wild, rugged mountains, windswept lochs, idyllic islands and miles of remote coastline, Scotland is paradise for the visitor who comes to unwind or in search of adventure amidst breathtaking scenery. Indeed, enlightened access legislation, www.outdooraccess-scotland.com, now provides almost limitless opportunities for the responsible tourist to roam freely through the countryside, cycle through miles of forest, paddle down tumbling rivers or scramble up mountains to bag Munros (mountains over 3000 ft). Furthermore, come rain, hail or shine, tour operators now offer a variety of thrilling, adrenalin-packed activities from canyoning, funyakking and whitewater rafting, to telemark skiing, skydiving and surfing, demonstrating that Scotland's growing reputation as an adventure sports mecca is no idle boast.

Birdwatching

ⓘ **Royal Society for the Protection of Birds**, T0131-317 4100, www.rspb.org.uk. **Scottish Ornithologists Club**, Waterstone House, Aberlady, East Lothian, EH32 0PY, T01875-871330, www.the-soc.org.uk. **Scottish Wildlife Trust**, Harbourside House 110 Commercial Rd, EH6 6NF, www.scottishwildlifetrust.org.uk, which owns and runs over 100 nature reserves.

Scotland is great for birdwatching. Over 450 species have been recorded, including vast colonies of seabirds, birds of prey and many rare species. Among the best places in Scotland to see birds are Handa Island off the coast of Sutherland, and the Treshnish Islands, off Mull, where you'll see colonies of shags, razorbills, guillemots and puffins. Another excellent place for birdwatching is Loch Garten by Boat of Garten, where you can see ospreys. Many of the Hebridean islands, such as Islay, Mull and Tiree, are home to a rich variety of seabirds and you can also see golden eagles here. Orkney and Shetland are famous for their rich variety of birdlife and are home to large colonies of seabirds and migratory birds. There are puffins, kittiwakes, fulmars, shags, razorbills, guillemots and even auks. A more unusual and rare resident of Shetland is the snowy owl.

Canoeing, kayaking and rafting

ⓘ **Scottish Canoe Association**, T0131-317 7314, www.canoescotland.org. **National Kayak School**, 8 Argyll St, Oban, T01631-565310, www.nationalkayakschool.com.

Scotland's rivers, lochs and deeply indented coastline offer great opportunities for canoeing, surf kayaking,

ON THE ROAD

Mountain safety

Visitors to Scotland should be aware of the need for caution and safety preparations when walking or climbing in the mountains. The nature of Scottish weather is such that a fine sunny day can turn into driving rain or snow in a matter of minutes. Remember that a blizzard can be raging on the summit when the car park at the foot of the mountain is bathed in sunshine. It is essential to get an up-to-date weather forecast before setting off on any walk or climb. Whatever the time of year, or conditions when you set off, you should always carry or wear essential items of clothing. A basic list for summer conditions would be: boots with a good tread and ankle support, and a thick pair of socks; waterproof jacket and trousers, even on a sunny day; hat and gloves are important if the weather turns bad; warm trousers should be worn or carried, tracksuit bottoms are okay if you also have waterproof trousers; a spare woolly jumper or fleece jacket will provide an extra layer; a map and compass are essential to carry and to know how to use. Other essentials are food and drink, a simple first-aid kit, a whistle and a torch. A small 25-30 litre rucksack should be adequate for carrying the above items. Also remember to leave details of your route and expected time of return with someone, and remember to inform them on your return.

In the winter extra warm clothing is needed, as well as an ice axe and crampons, and the ability to use them. The skills required for moving over ice or snow should be practised with an experienced and qualified mountain guide or instructor.

sea kayaking and careering down rivers in inflatable two-man fun yaks and whitewater rafts. Perthshire, served by the Tummel, Garry and Tay rivers is arguably Scotland's kayaking hub and the place to find adventure operators such as **Nae Limits** and **Splash**. However, whilst legions of river kayakers head for the slalom gates of Grandtully, it's the azure waters of the Inner and Outer Hebrides, that have helped establish Scotland as one of Europe's top sea kayaking destinations.

Canyoning

ⓘ **Nae Limits**, T08450-178177, www. naelimits.co.uk; **Vertical Descents**, T01855-821593, www.verticaldescents.com. **The Canyoning Company**, T07725-813729, www.thecanyoningcompany.co.uk.

This involves heading downriver in a gorge and dropping several hundred feet by swimming, jumping into plunge pools, sliding down log flumes and abseiling. In Perthshire and Lochaber you can go cliff-jumping from heights of up to 60 ft into rock pools, combined with head-first descents of waterfalls. If that's too tame try the Tyrolean Traverse, crossing a gorge at 300 ft.

Climbing

ⓘ **Mountaineering Council of Scotland**, The Old Granary, West Mill St, Perth, T01738-493942, www.mountaineering.scot.

With hundreds of summer and winter climbing routes, rock climbers and winter mountaineers alike are spoilt for choice. From Glencoe and Lochaber to the Cuillin ridge on Skye, the Cairngorms and majestic hills of Torridon and Assynt, there's no lack of opportunity to test one's nerve. Scotland is a great place to try rock climbing and its arduous winter cousin, ice climbing. The Cairngorms and Cuillins offer the most challenging climbing, as do Glencoe and Torridon. Most mountaineering clubs have regular weekend meets in the hills as well as social gatherings closer to home.

Cycling

ⓘ **Cyclists' Touring Club (CTC)**, www. cycling.org/scotland, is the largest cycling organization in the UK. **SUSTRANS**, T0131-346 1384, www.sustrans.org.uk, is the UK's leading sustainable transport charity. See www.visitscotland.com for maps and details of cycle routes in their area. Visit Scotland also publishes *Cycling in Scotland* (free), listing bike repair shops and operators. See also **www.spokes.org.uk**.

The bicycle was invented in Scotland, so it seems appropriate that travelling by on two wheels is one of the best ways to explore the country. Thanks to SUSTRANS and other hard-working voluntary organizations, Scotland boasts a growing number of traffic-free cycle routes.

Scotland's miles of rural roads are a delight to explore, with routes using disused railway tracks and upgraded canal towpaths, including the dedicated tracks on the Isle of Arran. The wild and remote Highlands are very popular with cycle tourers. Routes such as Torridon and Applecross provide challenging climbs and exhilarating descents. However, some routes are shared with walkers and horse-

riders so caution and consideration should be exercised at all times.

You can cut down on the amount of pedalling you have to do by transporting your bike by train. Bikes can be taken free on all ScotRail services including the sleeper rail services on a first-come, first-served basis (call **ScotRail** bookings, T0344-811 0141, www.scotrail.co.uk). However, check with **Virgin Rail** and **GNER** for their conditions of carriage. Regardless, space is always limited on trains so it's a good idea to book as far in advance as possible. With a few exceptions, such as the Durness Bus between Ullapool, Durness, Thurso and Inverness, buses are unable to carry bikes unless they are dismantled and boxed. Ferries transport bikes for a small fee and airlines will often accept them as part of your baggage allowance. Check with the ferry company or airline about any restrictions.

Diving

ⓘ **The Puffin Dive Centre**, see page 52, T01631-566088, www.puffin.org.uk, based in Oban, is the UK's most comprehensive diving facility and runs intensive PADI courses.

Scotland may not have the Great Barrier Reef but it does have some of the finest dive locations in the world, featuring shipwrecks, reefs, sheer underwater cliffs, soft corals and abundant sea life. The west coast offers the best diving, as the water is warmed by the effects of the Gulf Stream and is not as cold as you might expect, even without a dry suit. Among the best sites are the west coast of Harris, the Summer Isles and the remote island of St Kilda. There are lots of wrecks in the Sound of Mull, and the chance to find a Spanish Galleon off Tobermory. Scapa Flow in Orkney is world-renowned as the burial site of the German First World War fleet. For details on PADI courses and dive trips in Orkney check out www.scapascuba.co.uk.

Fishing

ⓘ **Scottish Federation of Sea Anglers**, T01592-591882, www.scottishfederation ofseaanglers.wordpress.com, provides comprehensive information on the main species to fish for and advice on where to fish. See also **www.visitscotland.com** or **www.fishpal.com**, for a complete listing and key information about locations in Scotland.

Scotland's rivers, streams, lochs and estuaries are among the cleanest waters in Europe and are filled with salmon, trout (sea, brown and rainbow) and pike. Not surprisingly, fishing (coarse, game and sea) is hugely popular in Scotland.

There is no close season for coarse fishing or sea angling. For wild brown trout the close season is early October to mid-March (see also under South Uist, page 357). The close season for salmon and sea trout varies from area to area and between net and rod fishing. It is generally from late August to early February for net fishing, and from early November to early February for rod fishing. No licence is required to fish in Scotland, but most of the land and rivers are privately owned so you must obtain a permit from the owners or their agents. These are often readily available at the local fishing tackle shop and usually cost from around £15, though some rivers can be far more expensive.

Golf

ⓘ **VisitScotland**, www.visitscotland.com. VisitScotland's *Golfing in Scotland* brochure provides a comprehensive break-down of prices and courses across the country, plus lists of accommodation providers. See also www.scottishgolfcourses.com. To arrange golfing holidays, visit **www.golfbreaks.com**.

Scotland has over 400 golf courses, with more being built all the time, and therefore has more courses per head of population than any other country in the world. Any decent-sized town in Scotland will have a golf course nearby and most, if not all, are available for play. There are many public courses, which tend to be both cheap and extremely busy, and often have excellent layouts. The majority of private clubs allow visitors, although many have restrictions as to what days these visitors can play. Weekends are usually reserved for club competitions for the members, so it is best to try to play on a weekday. All private clubs have a dress code and it is inadvisable to turn up in a T-shirt and jeans. These minor caveats aside, you are likely to receive a warm, courteous welcome.

Many clubs offer a daily or weekly ticket with the cost depending on the course and area.

Hillwalking

ⓘ **Forestry Commission Scotland**, https://scotland.forestry.gov.uk. **Scottish Rights of Way Society**, www.scotways.com. **Woodland Trust**, www.woodlandtrust.org.uk.

Five great short walks

Scotland is a walker's paradise. Whether you are looking for family strolls on the beach, a challenging 3000-ft mountain hike or an adventure on one of Scotland's numerous long-distance trails, you are spoilt for choice. Wherever you choose to roam ensure you dress appropriately, for the weather conditions on Scotland's hills and mountains are notoriously fickle.

Sandwood Bay (Blairmore)

Scotland's coastline is peppered with beaches but Sandwood Bay, 10 miles south of Cape Wrath is arguably one of the best (see page 258). This vast stretch of golden, deserted sand is accessed over peatland from Blairmore via a four-mile track. At Sandwood, look south for the magnificent Am Buachaille sea stack that rises over 30 yds out of the waves. The whole area sits within a protected 11,490-acre estate of crofting land managed by the John Muir Trust. Enjoy your picnic but don't overstay your welcome. It's rumoured that ghosts of shipwrecked mariners roam the deserted dunes.

Reinigeadal to Tarbert (Isle of Harris)

Of the five walks, this seven-mile hike across the rugged eastern hills of Harris to Tarbert is the most challenging and exposed. The sea views are spectacular, but spare a thought for the hardy kids who, for generations, could only reach school via this tortuous track above the sea. Cloaked in silence, the trail winds through deer-inhabited wilds managed by the North Harris Community Land Trust. The ruins of long-abandoned crofts poke through the heather as you walk west over Beinn a' Chaolais. On skirting high above the remote sea loch of Trollamarig, look for the abandoned hamlet of Molingeanais.

Scotland is a walker's paradise. Throughout the country there are numerous marked trails, ranging from short walks to long-distance treks from one side of the country to the other. Whatever your taste or level of fitness and experience, you'll find plenty of opportunities to get off the beaten track and explore the countryside.

The best time for hiking in the mountains depends solely on the weather and your experience. Mountain weather conditions change so fast that one moment it can be a clear, crisp day in November and the next a blizzard. So,

though April to October is arguably the 'safest' period for the less experienced, always carry clothing that will keep you warm should conditions deteriorate. Winter walking in the Highlands requires technical equipment such as ice axes and crampons, and a lot of experience. June to August are the busiest times, though only the most popular routes, such as Ben Nevis, get really crowded. Another problem during these months are midges, see box, page 475. May to mid-June is probably the most pleasant time overall, as the weather can often be fine and the midges have yet to appear.

Sanna Bay (Ardnamurchan)

The wildlife and rugged scenery of the Ardnamurchan Peninsula, barely scratched by the human hand, remains one of Scotland's best-kept secrets. On a fine day, pack a picnic and head for the remote village of Sanna – the westernmost point on the British mainland. Here, a beautiful expanse of fine golden sand caressed by turquoise waters will convince you that this is the Caribbean, until you dip your toe in the chilly water. As you walk the two miles south to the hamlet, gaze seaward for a breathtaking panorama of the Small Isles and the distant peaks of Skye. Keep a look out for seals, dolphins and basking sharks.

Glenmore Forest (Cairngorm)

Glenmore Forest Park (est 1948) offers an invigorating 4½-mile hike from above the shores of Loch Morlich to the tranquil waters of An Lochan Uaine (the Green Lochan) and beyond to the rustic, simple shelter of Ryvoan Bothy. This walk is ideal for a family outing on a well-marked path. Aside from views of the Cairngorms, it's a rare opportunity to hike through remnants of ancient Caledonian pinewood and juniper that long ago covered the landscape. Look out for red squirrels, pine marten and red deer.

Conic Hill (Loch Lomond)

It's a short, sharp 45-minute climb from the car park at Balmaha on the southeastern shores of Loch Lomond. However, on reaching the rounded summit of Conic Hill (1115 ft) you are rewarded with magnificent views across the forested islands of the southern part of Loch Lomond – at over 22 miles long, it's the largest stretch of fresh water in the UK and the hub of the Loch Lomond and Trossachs National Park. Further westward enjoy the jagged peaks of the Arrochar Alps, whilst to the northeast lies the magnificent heather- and forest-strewn hills once roamed by the 17th-century clansman and folk hero, Rob Roy MacGregor. See page 135.

September is also a good time, though it can be a lot colder.

Scotland has a long tradition of enabling access to mountain and moorland. This free access, of course, relies on walkers behaving responsibly and recognizing that the countryside is a place of work as well as recreation. It's the Land Reform (Scotland) Act 2003 that underpins one's right to roam in Scotland but with the proviso that it's undertaken responsibly and in accordance with the Outdoor Access Code. In particular, it's the walker's responsibility to ensure he or she doesn't damage fences, crops or worry livestock. By adhering to these common-sense rules, all who come to enjoy Scotland's countryside will be helping to maintain access that is the envy of every other country in the UK. However, most land in Scotland remains privately owned and at certain times of the year, such as the main shooting seasons, walkers may be asked to respect certain restrictions on access. The main deer stalking season runs from mid-August to mid-October and the grouse shooting season is between 12 August (referred to as the 'Glorious Twelfth') and 10 December. There may also be restricted access during the lambing season from March to May.

Kitesurfing and windsurfing

ⓘ **Scottish Power Kite Association (SPKA)**, www.spka.org; **Wild Diamond**, Tiree, T07712-159205, www.wilddiamond.co.uk, offers lessons and hire. See www.thebeachguide.co.uk for a list of the beaches in the north of Scotland; also www.windsurf.co.uk.

Kitesurfing is growing in popularity in Scotland with Tiree a popular location for 'grabbing air'. Windsurfing and particularly wave-sailing amidst the powerful surf of Tiree and Machrihanish on the Kintyre peninsula are extremely popular, with the former hosting the annual Tiree Wave Classic every October.

Mountain biking

ⓘ A good resource hub is **www.dmbins.com** (**Developing Mountain Biking in Scotland**); https://scotland.forestry.gov.uk has details of Forestry Commission Scotland sites with mountain biking trails; **www.visitscotland.com/adventure**, provides a good description of the key mountain bike centres and trails across Scotland. It's also worth picking up a copy of the *Scottish Mountain Biking Trails Guide*.

Cross-country and downhill mountain biking has really taken off in Scotland over the past decade, with more than a dozen purpose-built trail centres now established in forests around the country. Indeed, today Scotland is regarded, by no less than the **International Mountain Biking Association**, as one of the world's top mountain-biking destinations. This country boasts no less than a dozen dedicated mountain bike trail centres, including the Wolf Trax mountain bike trail centre by Laggan, and Learnie Forest in the Black Isle, www.himba.org.uk. These are hot mountain bike destinations but arguably the most famous is to be found at Fort William where the 'Witch's Trail' and nerve-wracking 1½-mile 'Black Run' downhill track annually attracts the world's best riders for a stage of the **UCI MTB World Cup**, www.ridefortwilliam.co.uk. The Fort William downhill track (May to September) is accessed by the gondola system (1000-1700). See page 197 for prices and details of bike hire in Fort William.

Pony trekking and horse riding

ⓘ **British Horse Society Scotland (BHS)**, Woodburn Farm, Crieff, T01764-656334, www.bhs.org.uk, the BHS website provides a full listing of all BHS-approved riding schools in Scotland and details of forthcoming major events. **Trekking and Riding Society of Scotland (TRRS)**, Bruaich-Na-H'Abhainne, Margowan, Killin, Perthshire, KF21 8TN, T01567-820909, www.ridinginscotland.com.

Pony trekking is a long-established activity in Scotland and miles of beautiful coastline, lochsides, and moorland are accessible on horseback. There are numerous equestrian centres around the country catering to all levels of riders. **VisitScotland** produces a 'Riding Scotland' brochure listing riding centres around the country, all of them approved by the **Trekking and Riding Society of Scotland (TRSS)** or the **British Horse Society (BHS)**. Centres offer pony trekking (leisurely strolls at walking pace for novices), hacks (short rides at a fast pace for experienced riders) and trail riding (long-distance rides at no more than a canter). For general information contact the TRSS.

Skiing

ⓘ **Snowsport Scotland**, T0131-625 4405, www.snowsportscotland.org, for information on all aspects of Scottish skiing and snowsports; also useful is **www.visitscotland.com**.

Conditions in Scotland are not as reliable as the Alps, but with short, steep descents off-piste, dozens of beginner/intermediate groomed pistes and breathtaking mountain scenery, snowboarders, skiers and telemark skiers are handsomely rewarded when the snow falls and the sun shines. The core season is from January to April, but it is possible to ski from as early as November to as late as May. Ski packages and lessons are available, though it's easy to arrange everything yourself. There's plentiful accommodation in and around the ski centres.

There are five ski centres in Scotland and the largest are Glenshee, which has the most extensive network of lifts and selection of runs, and Cairngorm, which has over 30 runs spread over an extensive area. Glencoe is the oldest of the ski resorts, and with runs like the 'flypaper', offers tremendous skiing for experts. Nevis Range Aonach Mor near Fort William, has the highest ski runs and the only gondola in Scotland. The Lecht is ideal for beginner and intermediate skiers or boarders and also has a 'tubing' piste.

Details for each of the five resorts, including phone numbers and websites,

are given in the appropriate place in the main text. For further general information contact **VisitScotland** for its 'Ski Scotland' brochure and accommodation list, or visit their website, www.visitscotland.com/adventure, which is updated daily. Or you can contact **Snowsport Scotland** (see above). During the ski season, resort websites publish up-to-date snow and weather conditions, and outline which pistes are open. To hire, buy or seek advice when ski touring and ski mountaineering in Scotland, it's recommended that you contact **Mountain Spirit** in Aviemore, T01479-811788, www.mountainspirit.co.uk.

Surfing

ⓘ **Scottish Surfing Federation**, www.thessf.com. Useful websites are **www.sas.org.uk** and **www.hebrideansurf.co.uk**.

Scotland has some of the best surfing beaches in Europe, a fact recognized by its hosting of a **World Pro Surf Tour** (qualifying) competition in 2006. But despite the clean coral and beach breaks, powerful waves and pristine (island) beaches, this is no sun-drenched Hawaii. Surfing in Scotland is decidedly chillier with temperatures in the spring and autumn as low as 4-5°C! However, you could be pleasantly surprised at the temperature between July and October, but remember a good wetsuit is essential.

The best beaches on the West Coast are to be found at the northern tip of the Isle of Lewis, on North and South Uist, the north coast of Scotland (including Thurso), Machrihanish at the southwestern tip of the Mull of Kintyre and all along the coast east of Edinburgh. On the north coast the top spot is Thurso, home to the world-class Thurso East break (strictly for experts). In recent years, a host of reputable surf schools have sprung up, also try the surf shops, which sell equipment and provide information on the best breaks.

From the famous Thurso East break and surf competitions in northeast Scotland, to the massive waves on the Isle of Lewis and Tiree, to instruction and hire on a string of beaches, Scottish surfing is really taking off.

Whale and dolphin watching
ⓘ **Hebridean Whale and Dolphin Trust**, T01688-302620, www.whaledolphintrust.

Shopping tips

Scottish textiles, especially the **tartan** variety, are popular and worth buying. You can get hold of everything from a travelling rug to your own kilt outfit. Shops up and down the country, and especially in Inverness, can tell which clan your family belongs to and make you a kilt in that particular tartan. For the full outfit, including kilt, sporran, jacket, shoes and *skeann dhu* dagger, expect to pay in the region of £600, or more if you want elaborate accessories. **Harris Tweed** is also a good buy and you can watch your cloth being woven on the Hebridean islands of Harris and Lewis.

Knitwear is also good value and sold throughout Scotland. Shetland is a good place to find high-quality wool products. **Jewellery** is another popular souvenir and there are many excellent craft shops throughout the Highlands and Islands making beautiful jewellery with Celtic designs. **Glassware** is also popular, particularly Edinburgh crystal and Caithness glass, as well as pottery. You can order Scottish crafts at www.papastour.com.

Food is another good souvenir and not just the ubiquitous shortbread sold in tartan tins. If you haven't far to travel home, smoked salmon, or any other smoked product, is good value. One of the best islands for food products is Mull, where you can buy delicious smoked fish and game, and cheeses. And, of course, there's **whisky**. Most distilleries will refund the cost of their guided tour in the form of a discount voucher on a bottle of their brand whisky.

Shop hours in Scotland are generally Monday to Saturday 0900-1730 or 1800. In larger towns and cities, many shops also open on Sundays and late at night, usually on a Thursday and Friday. Large supermarkets and retail complexes found outside large towns are open till 2000 or later Monday to Saturday and till 1600 on Sunday. There are some 24-hour superstores in and around major cities. In the Highlands and Islands, few shops are open on Sunday, most notably in the Outer Hebrides. Also note that in many rural areas there is an early-closing day when shops close at 1300. This varies from region to region, but the most common day is Wednesday.

co.uk; **Sea Watch Foundation**, www.seawatchfoundation.org.uk. Also try www.outdooraccess-scotland.com for further details on wildlife watching.

Almost anywhere around the western and northern coasts of Scotland there is a chance to see bottlenose dolphins, white-beaked dolphins, Risso's dolphins, common dolphins, white-sided dolphins, pilot whales, minke whales, porpoises, seals and, occasionally orcas (killer whales). The best places to see bottlenose dolphins are at Cromarty and Chanonry Point, both on the Moray Firth. Other good places to catch glimpses of bottlenose and other dolphins, as well as porpoises and minke whales, are the westerly tip of Ardnamurchan, Mull, Neist Point on Skye, Gairloch and Rubha Reidh Lighthouse, Stoer Head, Handa Island, Cape Wrath, Strathy Point, Dunnet Head, Duncansby Head, Lybster, Brora and Golspie, Tarbat Ness and off the Isle of Mull. The Generally speaking, the best time to see the various species of marine mammal (cetaceans) is late summer, from late July to early September.

Seals can be seen in abundance, particularly on the rocks around the wonderfully serene Lochranza Bay in the north of Arran. From Harris to Plockton and Oban, there are plenty of seal-spotting boat trips on offer from spring to autumn. To be guaranteed to spot seals visit the **Scottish Sea Life Sanctuary**, T01631-720386, www.visitsealife.com, north of Oban. Otters are more elusive. They tend to live on undisturbed remote stretches of the seashore or quiet areas of a river. If you are determined to spot the creatures, contact **Skye Environmental Centre**, home to the International Otter Survival Fund, T01471-822487, www.otter.org, who can provide more information.

Improve your travel photography

Taking pictures is a highlight for many travellers, yet too often the results turn out to be disappointing. Steve Davey, author of Footprint's *Travel Photography*, sets out his top rules for coming home with pictures you can be proud of.

Before you go

Don't waste precious travelling time and do your research before you leave. Find out what festivals or events might be happening or which day the weekly market takes place, and search online image sites such as Flickr to see whether places are best shot at the beginning or end of the day, and what vantage points you should consider.

Get up early

The quality of the light will be better in the few hours after sunrise and again before sunset – especially in the tropics when the sun will be harsh and unforgiving in the middle of the day. Sometimes seeing the sunrise is a part of the whole travel experience: sleep in and you will miss more than just photographs.

Stop and think

Don't just click away without any thought. Pause for a few seconds before raising the camera and ask yourself what you are trying to show with your photograph. Think about what things you need to include in the frame to convey this meaning. Be prepared to move around your subject to get the best angle. Knowing the point of your picture is the first step to making sure that the person looking at the picture will know it too.

Compose your picture

Avoid simply dumping your subject in the centre of the frame every time you take a picture. If you compose with it to one side, then your picture can look more balanced. This will also allow you to show a significant background and make the picture more meaningful. A good rule of thumb is to place your subject or any significant detail a third of the way into the frame; facing into the frame not out of it.

This rule also works for landscapes. Compose with the horizon two-thirds of the way up the frame if the foreground is the most interesting part of the picture; one-third of the way up if the sky is more striking.

Don't get hung up with this so-called Rule of Thirds, though. Exaggerate it by pushing your subject out to the edge of the frame if it makes a more interesting picture; or if the sky is dull in a landscape, try cropping with the horizon near the very top of the frame.

Fill the frame

If you are going to focus on a detail or even a person's face in a close-up portrait, then be bold and make sure that you fill the frame. This is often a case of physically getting in close. You can use a telephoto setting on a zoom lens but this can lead to pictures looking quite flat; moving in close is a lot more fun!

Interact with people

If you want to shoot evocative portraits then it is vital to approach people and seek permission in some way, even if it is just by smiling at someone. Spend a little time with them and they are likely to relax and look less stiff and formal. Action portraits where people are doing something, or environmental portraits, where they are set against a significant background, are a good way to achieve relaxed portraits. Interacting is a good way to find out more about people and their lives, creating memories as well as photographs.

Focus carefully

Your camera can focus quicker than you, but it doesn't know which part of the picture you want to be in focus. If your camera is using the centre focus sensor then move the camera so it is over the subject and half press the button, then, holding it down, recompose the picture. This will lock the focus. Take the now correctly focused picture when you are ready.

Another technique for accurate focusing is to move the active sensor over your subject. Some cameras with touch-sensitive screens allow you to do this by simply clicking on the subject.

Leave light in the sky

Most good night photography is actually taken at dusk when there is some light and colour left in the sky; any lit portions of the picture will balance with the sky and any ambient lighting. There is only a very small window when this will happen, so get into position early, be prepared and keep shooting and reviewing the results. You can take pictures after this time, but avoid shots of tall towers in an inky black sky; crop in close on lit areas to fill the frame.

Bring it home safely

Digital images are inherently ephemeral: they can be deleted or corrupted in a heartbeat. The good news though is they can be copied just as easily. Wherever you travel, you should have a backup strategy. Cloud backups are popular, but make sure that you will have access to fast enough Wi-Fi. If you use RAW format, then you will need some sort of physical back-up. If you don't travel with a laptop or tablet, then you can buy a backup drive that will copy directly from memory cards.

Available in both digital and print formats, Footprint's Travel Photography by Steve Davey covers everything you need to know about travelling with a camera, including simple post-processing. More information is available at www.footprinttravelguides.com

Where to stay

B&Bs, bothies and boutique hotels

Staying in the Highlands and Islands of Scotland can mean anything from being pampered to within an inch of your life in a baronial mansion to roughing it in a tiny island bothy with no electricity. If you have the money, then the sky is very much the limit in terms of sheer splendour and excess. We have listed many of the top-class establishments in this book, with a bias towards those that offer that little bit extra in terms of character. Those spending less may have to forego the four-posters and Egyptian cotton sheets but there are still many good-value small hotels and guesthouses with that essential wow factor – especially when it comes to the views. At the bottom end of the scale, there are also some excellent hostels in some pretty special locations.

Price codes
Where to stay

££££ £160 and over	£££ £90-160
££ £50-90	£ under £50

Accommodation prices in this book are based on the cost for two people sharing a double room with en suite bathroom during the high season. Cheaper rooms with shared bathrooms are available in many hotels, guesthouses and B&Bs. Many places, particularly larger hotels, offer substantial discounts during the low season and at weekends. All places listed are recommended as providing good quality and value within their respective price category. Note that outside the major cities, the vast majority of youth hostels and backpackers cost less than £20 per night.

Restaurants

£££ over £30	££ £15-30	£ under £15

The price ranges in this book are based on a two-course meal for one person (main course plus starter or dessert) without drinks. All places listed are recommended as offering relatively good value, quality and standards of service within their respective price category.

We have tried to give as broad a selection as possible to cater for all tastes and budgets but if you can't find what you're after, or if someone else has beaten you to the draw, then the tourist information centres (or iCentres) will help find accommodation for you. They can recommend a place within your particular budget and give you the number to phone up and book yourself, or will book a room for you. Some offices charge a small fee for booking a room, while others ask you to pay a deposit of 10% which is deducted from your first night's bill. Details of town and city iCentres are given throughout the guide. There are also several websites that you can browse and book accommodation. Try www.visitscotland.com.

Accommodation in Scotland will be your greatest expense, particularly if you are travelling on your own. Single rooms are in short supply and many places are reluctant to let a double room to one person, even when they're not busy. Single rooms are usually more than the cost per person for a double room and in some cases cost the same as two people sharing a double room.

Hotels, guesthouses and B&Bs

Area tourist boards publish accommodation lists that include campsites, hostels, self-catering accommodation and VisitScotland-approved hotels, guesthouses and bed and breakfasts (B&Bs). Places participating in the VisitScotland system will have a plaque displayed outside which shows their grading, determined by a number of stars ranging from one to five. These reflect the level of facilities, as well as the quality of hospitality and service. However, do not assume that a B&B, guesthouse or hotel is no good because it is not listed by the tourist board. They simply don't want to pay to be included in the system, and some of them may offer better value. If you'd like to stay in a Scottish castle as a paying guest of the owner, contact **Scotts Castle Holidays** ① *T01208-821341, www.scottscastles.com.*

Hotels

At the top end of the scale there are some fabulously luxurious hotels, often in spectacular locations. Many of them are converted baronial mansions or castles, and offer a chance to enjoy a taste of aristocratic grandeur and style (at a price, some charge in excess of £250 per night). At the lower end of the scale, there is often little to choose between cheaper hotels and guesthouses or B&Bs. The latter often offer higher standards of comfort and a more personal service, but many smaller hotels are really just guesthouses, and are often family-run and every bit as friendly. Note that some hotels, especially in town centres or in fishing ports, may also be rather noisy, as the bar can often be the social hub.

Rooms in most mid-range to expensive hotels almost always have bathrooms en suite. Many upmarket hotels offer excellent room-only deals in the low season. An efficient last-minute hotel booking service is www.laterooms.com, which specializes in weekend breaks. Also note that many hotels offer cheaper rates for online booking through agencies such as www.lastminute.com.

Guesthouses

Guesthouses are often large, converted family homes with up to five or six rooms. They tend to be slightly more expensive than B&Bs, charging anywhere between £35 and £65 per person per night, and though they are often less personal, usually provide better facilities, such as en suite bathroom, colour TV in each room and private parking. In many instances they are more like small budget hotels. Many guesthouses offer evening meals, though this may have to be requested in advance.

Bed and breakfasts (B&Bs)

B&Bs provide the cheapest private accommodation. At the bottom end of the scale you can get a bedroom in a private house, a shared bathroom and a huge cooked breakfast for around £30-40 per person per night. Small B&Bs may only have one or two rooms to let, so it's important to book in advance during the summer season and on the islands where accommodation options are more limited. More upmarket B&Bs have en suite bathrooms and TVs in each room and usually charge from £40-45 per person per night. In general, B&Bs are more hospitable, informal, friendlier and offer better value than hotels. Many B&B owners are also a great source of local knowledge and can even provide OS maps for local walks. B&Bs in the Outer Hebrides and other remote locations also offer dinner, bed and breakfast, which is useful as eating options are limited, especially on a Sunday.

Some places, especially in ferry ports, charge room-only rates, which are slightly cheaper and allow you to get up in time to catch an early morning ferry. However, this means that you miss out on a huge cooked breakfast. If you're travelling on a tight budget, you can eat as much as you can at breakfast time and save on lunch as you won't need to eat again until evening. This is particularly useful if you're heading into the hills, as you won't have to carry so much food. Many B&B owners will even make up a packed lunch for you at a small extra cost.

For those travelling on a tight budget, there is a large network of hostels offering cheap accommodation. These are also popular centres for backpackers and provide a great opportunity for meeting fellow travellers. Hostels have kitchen facilities for self-catering, and some include a continental breakfast in the price or provide cheap breakfasts and evening meals. Advance booking is recommended at all times, particularly from May to September and on public holidays, and a credit card is often useful.

Scottish Youth Hostel Association (SYHA)
The **Scottish Youth Hostel Association** (**SYHA**) ① *T0345-293 7373, www.syha. org.uk*, is separate from the YHA in England and Wales. It has a network of over 60 hostels, which are often better and cheaper than those in other countries. They offer bunk-bed accommodation in single-sex dormitories or smaller rooms, kitchen and laundry facilities. The average cost is around £12-25 per person per night depending on what kind of accommodation you want. Though some rural hostels are still strict on discipline and impose a 2300 curfew, those in larger towns and cities tend to be more relaxed and doors are closed as late as 0200. Some larger hostels provide breakfasts for around £4-5 and three-course evening meals for £10-15. For all EU residents, adult membership costs £15 (£6 for under 25s), and can be obtained at the SYHA National Office (T01786-891400), or at the first SYHA hostel you stay at. SYHA membership gives automatic membership of Hostelling International (HI). The SYHA produces a handbook (free with membership) giving details of all their youth hostels, including transport links. This can be useful as some hostels are difficult to get to without your own transport. You should always phone ahead, as many hostels are closed during the day and phone numbers are listed in this guide. Many hostels are closed during the winter, details are given in the SYHA Handbook. Youth hostel members are entitled to various discounts, including 20% off Edinburgh bus tours, 20% off Scottish Citylink tickets and 33% off the Orkney Bus (Inverness–Kirkwall).

Independent hostels
Details of most independent hostels (or 'bunkhouses') can be found in the annual **Independent Hostel Guide**, www.independenthostelguide.com. The **Independent Backpackers Hostels of Scotland** is an association of nearly 100 independent hostels/bunkhouses throughout Scotland. This association has a programme of inspection and lists members in their free 'Blue Guide'. Independent hostels tend to be more laid-back, with fewer rules and no curfew, and no membership is required. They all have dormitories, hot showers and

Wild camping

The Land Reform (Scotland) Act 2003, which together with the Scottish Access Code came into effect in February 2005, ensures Scotland offers walkers, canoeists, cyclists and campers some of the most liberal land access laws in Europe. Technically it means you have the 'right to roam' almost anywhere, although the emphasis is on 'responsible access' (see www.outdooraccess-scotland.com).

self-catering kitchens. Some include continental breakfast, or provide cheap breakfasts. All these hostels are listed on their excellent website, www.hostel-scotland.co.uk. Also try www.independenthostels.co.uk. In the Outer Hebrides a few hostels are run by the **Gatliff Trust** (see box on page 331) and in Shetland there is also the option of staying in camping böds (see box on page 416).

Campsites and self-catering

Campsites

There are hundreds of campsites around Scotland. They are mostly geared to caravans, and vary greatly in quality and level of facilities. The most expensive sites, which charge up to £15-20 to pitch a tent, are usually well-equipped. Sites are usually only open from April to October. If you plan to do a lot of camping, you should check out www.scottishcamping.com, which is the most comprehensive service with over 500 sites, many with pictures and reviews from punters. North Americans planning on camping should invest in an international camping carnet, which is available from home motoring organizations, or from **Family Campers and RVers (FCRV)** ① *4804 Transit Rd, Building 2, Depew, NY 14043, T1-800-245 9755, www.fcrv.org.* It gives you discounts at member sites.

Self-catering

One of the most cost-effective ways to holiday in the Highlands and Islands is to hire a cottage with a group of friends. There are lots of different types of accommodation to choose from, to suit all budgets, ranging from luxury lodges, castles and lighthouses to basic bothies with no electricity.

The minimum stay is usually one week in the summer peak season, though many offer shorter stays of two, three or four nights, especially outside the peak season. Expect to pay at least £300-500 per week for a two-bedroom cottage in the winter, rising to £600-1000 in the high season, or more if it's a particularly nice place. A good source of self-catering accommodation is the VisitScotland's guide, which lists over 1200 properties and is available to buy from any tourist office, but there are also dozens of excellent websites to browse. Amongst the best websites are the following: www.cottages-and-castles.co.uk, www.scottish-country-cottages.co.uk, www.cottages4you.co.uk, www.ruralretreats.co.uk, www.unique-cottages.co.uk and www.assc.co.uk. If you want to tickle a trout or feed a pet lamb, www.farmstay.co.uk, offers over a thousand good-value rural places to stay around the UK, all clearly listed on a clickable map.

The **National Trust for Scotland** ⓘ *28 Charlotte Sq, Edinburgh, T0844-493 2100, www.nts.org.uk*, owns many historic properties which are available for self-catering holidays, sleeping between two and 15 people. Prices start at around £500 per week in high season rising to £1500 for the top of the range lodges.

Food
& drink

Aberdeen Angus beef, Loch Fyne oysters and Islay malts

While Scotland's national drink is loved the world over, Scottish cooking hasn't exactly had good press over the years. This is perhaps not too surprising, as the national dish, haggis, consists of a stomach stuffed with diced innards and served with mashed tatties (potatoes) and neeps (turnips/swedes). Not a great start. And things got even worse when the Scots discovered the notorious deep-fried Mars bar.

However, Scottish cuisine has undergone a dramatic transformation in the last few decades and Scotland now boasts some of the most talented chefs, creating some of the best food in Britain. The heart of Scottish cooking is local produce, which includes the finest fish, shellfish, game, lamb, beef and vegetables, and a vast selection of traditionally made cheeses. What makes Scottish cooking so special is ready access to these foods. What could be better than enjoying an aperitif whilst watching your dinner being delivered by a local fisherman, knowing that an hour later you'll be enjoying the most delicious seafood?

Modern Scottish cuisine is now a feature of many of the top restaurants in the country. This generally means the use of local ingredients with foreign-influenced culinary styles, in particular French. International cuisine is also now a major feature on menus all over the country, influenced by the rise of Indian and Chinese restaurants in recent decades. In fact, so prevalent are exotic Asian and Oriental flavours that curry has now replaced fish and chips (fish supper) as the nation's favourite food.

Food

Fish, meat and game form the base of many of the country's finest dishes. Scottish beef, particularly Aberdeen Angus, is the most famous in the world. This will, or should, usually be hung for at least four weeks and sliced thick. Game is also a regular feature of Scottish menus, though it can be expensive, especially venison (deer), but delicious and low in cholesterol. Pheasant and hare are also tasty, but grouse is, quite frankly, overrated.

Fish and seafood are fresh and plentiful, and if you're travelling around the northwest coast you must not miss the chance to savour local mussels, prawns, oysters, scallops, langoustines, lobster or crab. Salmon is, of course, the most famous of Scottish fish, but you're more likely to be served the fish-farmed variety than 'wild' salmon, which has a more delicate flavour. Trout is also farmed extensively, but the standard of both remains high. Kippers are also a favourite delicacy, the best of which come from Loch Fyne or the Inverawe smokery, see page 61. Proper fish and chips in Scotland are made with haddock; cod is for Sassenachs (the English) and cats.

Haggis has made something of a comeback, and small portions are often served as starters in fashionable restaurants. Haggis is traditionally eaten on Burns Night (25 January) in celebration of the great poet's birthday, when it is piped to the table and then slashed open with a sword at the end of a recital of Robert Burns' *Address to the Haggis*. Other national favourites feature names to relish: cock-a-leekie is a soup made from chicken, leeks and prunes; cullen skink is a delicious concoction of smoked haddock and potatoes; while at the other end of the scale of appeal is hugga-muggie, a Shetland dish using fish's stomach. There's also the delightfully named crappit heids (haddock heads stuffed with lobster) and partan bree (a soup made form giant crab's claws, cooked with rice). Rather more mundane is the ubiquitous Scotch broth, made with mutton stock, vegetables, barley, lentils and split peas, and stovies, which is a hearty mash of potato, onion and minced beef.

Waist-expanding puddings or desserts are a very important part of Scottish cooking and often smothered in butterscotch sauce or syrup. There is a huge variety, including cranachan, a mouth-watering mix of toasted oatmeal steeped in whisky, cream and fresh raspberries, and Atholl Brose, a similar confection of oatmeal, whisky and cream.

Eaten before pudding, in the French style, or afterwards, are Scotland's many home-produced cheeses, which have made a successful comeback in the face of mass-produced varieties. Many of the finest cheeses are produced on the islands, especially Arran, Mull, Islay and Orkney. Caboc is a creamy soft cheese rolled in oatmeal and is made in the Highlands.

Anyone staying at a hotel, guesthouse or B&B will experience the hearty Scottish breakfast, which includes bacon, egg, sausage, 'tattie scone' and black pudding (a type of sausage made with blood; the Stornoway variety is the best), all washed down with copious quantities of tea. Coffee is readily available everywhere, with most places now offering a selection of cappuccinos and café lattes. You may also be served kippers (smoked herring) or porridge, an erstwhile Scottish staple. Made with oatmeal and with the consistency of Italian polenta, it is traditionally eaten with salt, though heretics are offered sugar instead. Oatcakes (oatmeal biscuits) may also be on offer, as well as potato scones, baps (bread rolls) or bannocks (a sort of large oatcake). After such a huge cooked breakfast you probably won't feel like eating again until dinner.

Beer

Beer is the alcoholic drink of choice in Scotland. The most popular type of beer is lager, which is generally brewed in the UK, even when it bears the name of an overseas brand, and is almost always weaker in both strength and character than the lagers in mainland Europe. However, examples of the older and usually darker type of beers, known as ales, are still widely available, and connoisseurs should try some of these as they are far more rewarding. Indeed, the best of them rival Scotland's whiskies as gourmet treats.

Traditionally, Scottish ales were graded by the shilling, an old unit of currency written as /-, according to strength. This system is still widely used by the older established breweries, though many of the newer independents and 'micros' have departed from it. 70/- beers at around 3.5% ABV (alcohol by volume), known as 'heavy', and 80/- beers (4.5% sometimes known as 'export'), are the most popular, while 60/-, 'light' (3-3.5%) is harder to find. Very strong 90/- beers (6.5% + ABV), known as 'wee heavies', are also brewed, mainly for bottling.

The market is dominated by the giant international brewers: Scottish Courage with its McEwans and Youngers brands; Interbrew with Calders and Carslberg; and Tetley with Tennents lagers. Tennents was the first British brewery to produce a continental-style lager commercially back in the 19th century, and, despite a competitive marketplace, remains a favourite for many Scots.

Much better are the ales from smaller independent breweries. Edinburgh's Caledonian is a world-class brewer producing many excellent beers, including a popular 80/- and a renowned golden hoppy ale, Deuchars IPA. Belhaven, an old, established family brewery in Dunbar, has some superb traditional beers including a malty 80/-, once marketed as the Burgundy of Scotland. Broughton, a microbrewery in the Borders, produces the fruity Greenmantle and an oatmeal stout. Another micro, Harvieston of Clackmannanshire (once an important brewing country) offers a wide and adventurous range of specialities, including Ptarmigan 80/- and a naturally brewed cask lager, Schiehallion. The Heather Ale Company, near Glasgow, has the spicy and unusual Fraoch (pronounced 'Frooch'), which is flavoured with real heather as well as hops.

Draught beer in pubs and bars is served in pints, or half pints, and you'll pay between £3.50 and £4.50 for a pint (unless you discover a 'Happy Hour' offering good deals on drinks, usually for much more than one hour! Happy hours usually apply in late afternoon or early evening). In many pubs the basic ales are chilled under gas pressure like lagers, but the best ales, such as those from the independents, are 'real ales', still fermenting in the cask and served cool but not chilled (around 12°C) under natural pressure from a handpump,

Turn water into whisky

Malt whisky is made by first soaking dry barley in tanks of local water for two to three days. Then the barley is spread out on a concrete floor or placed in cylindrical drums and allowed to germinate for between eight and 12 days, after which it is dried in a kiln, heated by a peat fire. Next, the dried malt is ground and mixed with hot water in a huge circular vat called a 'mash tun'. A sugary liquid called 'wort' is then drawn from the porridge-like result and piped into huge containers where living yeast is stirred into the mix in order to convert the sugar in the wort into alcohol. After about 48 hours the 'wash' is transferred to copper pot stills and heated till the alcohol vaporizes and is then condensed by a cooling plant into distilled alcohol which is passed through a second still. Once distilled, the liquid is poured into oak casks and left to age for a minimum of three years, though a good malt will stay casked for at least eight years.

electric pump or air pressure fount. All Scottish beers are traditionally served with a full, creamy head.

Whisky

No visit to the Scottish Highlands would be complete without availing oneself of a 'wee dram'. There is no greater pleasure on an inclement evening than enjoying a malt whisky in front of a roaring log fire whilst watching the rain outside pelt down relentlessly. The roots of Scotland's national drink (*uisge beatha*, or 'water of life' in Gaelic) go back to the late 15th century, but it wasn't until the invention of a patent still in the early 19th century that distilling began to develop from small family-run operations to the large manufacturing business it has become today. Now more than 700 million bottles a year are exported, mainly to the United States, France, Japan and Spain.

There are two types of whisky: single malt, made only from malted barley; and grain, which is made from malted barley together with unmalted barley, maize or other cereals, and is faster and cheaper to produce. Most of the popular brands are blends of both types of whisky – usually 60-70% grain to 30-40% malt. These blended whiskies account for over 90% of all sales worldwide, and most of the production of single malts is used to add flavour to a blended whisky. Amongst the best-known brands of blended whisky are Johnnie Walker, Bells, Teachers and Famous Grouse. There's not much between them in terms of flavour and they are usually drunk with a mixer, such as water or soda.

Single malts are a different matter altogether. Each is distinctive and should be drunk neat to appreciate fully its subtle flavours, though some believe that the addition of water helps free the flavours. Single malts vary enormously. Their distinctive flavours and aromas are derived from the peat used for drying,

Opinions vary as to what are the best single malts and as to when you should drink them. As a rough guide, we would recommend a Speyside malt such as Glenmorangie or Glenlivet before dinner and one of the Islay malts – Ardbeg, Bowmore, Bunnahabhain (pronounced 'bun-a-haven'), Lagavulin, or the very wonderful Laphroaig (pronounced 'la-froig') – after dinner.

If the Islays are not to your taste, then you could try instead the versatile Highland Park from Orkney or perhaps Tamdhu or Aberlour from Speyside. Those eternal favourites, Glenfiddich and The Macallan, can be enjoyed at any time.

the water used for mashing, the type of oak cask used and the location of the distillery. Single malts fall into four groups: Highland, Lowland, Campbeltown and Islay. There are over 40 distilleries to choose from, most offering guided tours. The majority are located around Speyside, in the northeast. The region's many distilleries include that perennial favourite, Glenfiddich, which is sold in 185 countries. Recommended alternatives are the produce of the beautiful and peaceful Isle of Islay, whose malts are lovingly described in terms of their peaty quality and the produce of the island known as 'Scotland in Miniature', Arran, whose 10-year-old malt, distilled in Lochranza, has won recent international acclaim. Scots tend to favour the 10-year-old Glenmorangie, while the most popular in the USA is The Macallan.

Gin

Less well known is Scotland's long association with gin (or 'Mother's ruin' as it used to be known). It all began back in the 1700s when bottles of Dutch Jenever (named after the juniper berries used in its creation) were traded in the Port of Leith in Edinburgh. This drink became so popular that Scottish distilleries soon started making their own. Some 70% of all gin produced in the UK is made in Scotland, including some of the world's leading brands: Gordon's; Tanqueray and Hendricks. Now there are over 50 producers up and down the country. In 2010, distilleries on Speyside and Islay produced Caorunn and The Botanist and every year sees the introduction of new craft brands as the country's artisanal gin industry goes from strength to strength. For a list of the various gin distilleries see **VisitScotland**'s gin map (www.visitscotland.com) or visit the website of **Gin Club Scotland** (www.ginclubscotland.com).

Restaurants

There are places to suit most tastes and budgets. In the large towns you'll find a reasonable selection of eating places, including Indian, Chinese, Italian, Thai and French restaurants, and, of course Scottish, but beyond the main tourist centres choice is much more limited. More and more restaurants are moving away from national culinary boundaries and offering a wide range of international dishes and flavours, so you'll often find Latin American, Oriental and Pacific Rim dishes all on the same menu. This is particularly the case in more continental-style bistros, brasseries and café-bars, which now offer a more informal alternative to traditional restaurants. Vegetarians are increasingly well catered for, and though in more rural parts vegetarian restaurants are thin on the ground, better-quality eating places will normally offer a reasonable vegetarian selection.

For a cheap meal, your best bet is a pub, hotel bar or café, where you can have a one-course meal for around £10. The best value is often at lunchtime, when some restaurants offer three-course set lunches or business lunches for less than £20. You'll need a pretty huge appetite to feel like eating a three-course lunch after your gigantic cooked breakfast, however. Also good value are the pre-theatre, or 'early-bird' dinners offered by many restaurants in the main towns. These are usually available from around 1730-1800 until 1900-1930, so you could get away with just a sandwich for lunch. At the other end of the price scale are many excellent restaurants where you can enjoy the finest of Scottish cuisine, often with a continental influence, and these are often found in hotels. You can expect to pay from around £30-40 a head up to £60-70 and more (excluding drinks) in the very top establishments.

The biggest problem with eating out in Scotland, as in the rest of the UK, is the limited serving hours in some pubs and hotels, particularly in more remote locations. In small places especially, it can be difficult finding food outside the hours of 1200-1400 and 1800-2100. Places that serve food all day till 2100 or later are restaurants, fast-food outlets and the many bistros and café-bars, which can be found not only in the main cities but increasingly in smaller towns. The latter often offer very good value and above-average quality fare.

Argyll

beautiful islands, romantic castles and whisky distilleries

Stretching north from the Mull of Kintyre almost to Glencoe and east to the shores of Loch Lomond, Argyll marks the transition from Lowland to Highland. The region is less dramatic than the northwest but it has its own special beauty.

It's a region of great variety, with all the ingredients of the classic highland holiday: lush, wooded glens, heather-clad mountains, charming fishing ports, romantic castles and majestic sea lochs.

Oban is also the main ferry port for the Inner Hebrides, the group of islands lying off the coast of Argyll. The most accessible and most popular is Mull, a short ferry ride from Oban. The variety of scenery on offer is astounding and its colourful capital, Tobermory, is the most attractive port in western Scotland. A stone's throw from Mull is tiny Iona, one of the most important religious sites in Europe, with some divine beaches. Boat trips can be made to the dramatic island of Staffa, rearing out of the sea like a giant pipe organ. Further west, windswept Coll and Tiree offer miles of unspoilt beaches, plenty of sunshine and great windsurfing. Those who enjoy a good malt whisky should head for Islay, famed for its distilleries, while neighbouring Jura is a wild and beautiful place, perfect for some off-the-beaten-track hiking. If you're after some peace and quiet on Jura then you're in good company, for this is where George Orwell came to write *Nineteen Eighty-Four*.

Best for
Whisky ▪ Wildlife ▪ Remote island beaches

Oban & around 48
Mid-Argyll, Kintyre, Cowal
  & Bute 59
Mull & Iona 77
Coll, Tiree & Colonsay 90
Islay & Jura 96

Footprint
picks

★ **Loch Etive**, page 60

Take a boat trip into the heart of one of Scotland's hidden treasures.

★ **Kilmartin Glen**, page 63

Once part of the ancient Kingdom of Dalriada, this is an area of Neolithic and Bronze Age cairns, stone circles, rock carvings, Iron Age forts and medieval castles.

★ **Mount Stuart**, page 74

This Victorian Gothic house on the aptly named Isle of Bute is a magnificent architectural fantasy.

★ **Iona**, page 87

This tiny island, the birthplace of Christianity in Scotland, is a little piece of heaven with its pristine alabaster beaches washed by an azure sea.

★ **Islay**, page 97

It's whisky-a-go-go on this wild and windswept island, famed for its world-leading single malts.

★ **Corryvreckan Whirlpool**, page 104

The world's second largest whirlpool can be crossed by RIB with a local tour operator; but it's not for the faint-hearted.

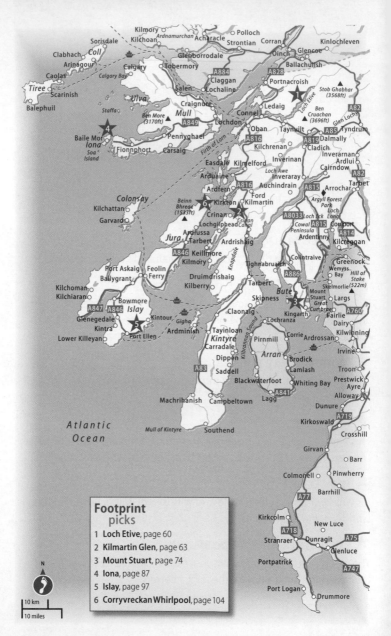

Footprint
picks

1 **Loch Etive**, page 60
2 **Kilmartin Glen**, page 63
3 **Mount Stuart**, page 74
4 **Iona**, page 87
5 **Islay**, page 97
6 **Corryvreckan Whirlpool**, page 104

10 km
10 miles

Finding your feet

There are daily direct flights from Glasgow to Islay's Glenegedale airport and Tiree with **Loganair** and **Flybe**. **Flybe** also have flights from several UK and European airports but not all are direct.

There are plenty of buses and trains from Glasgow and Fort William to Oban. For details of bus connections, contact **Scottish Citylink**, www.citylink.co.uk, or the **Oban iCentre**, T01631-563122. Bus, train and ferry times can be found in Argyll and Bute Council's free *Area Transport Guides* to Lorn, Mull and Islay and Jura, available at the Oban tourist office.

CalMac car and passenger ferries sail to Mull, Islay, Coll, Tiree, Colonsay and Gigha, and passenger-only ferries sail to Iona (and to the Small Isles, see page 307). The departure point for ferries to Mull, Coll, Tiree and Colonsay is Oban. Ferry times change according to the day of the week and time of year. Services listed in the Transport sections for each separate island are for the summer period (March-October). For full details of timetables and prices visit www.calmac.co.uk. The departure point for ferries to Islay (and on to Jura), and some ferries to Colonsay, is Kennacraig. For further details, see the Transport sections: Mull, page 86; Coll, page 92; Tiree, page 93; Colonsay, page 95; Islay, page 103; and Jura, page 105.

Getting around

There are regular ferry sailings to the islands and a car or bicycle is best for exploring. Away from the main roads a car or bike is essential. Most ferries to the islands and remote peninsulas are run by **CalMac**. The Island Hopscotch ticket (see Tip, above) can be used on a variety of route combinations and is valid for a month from the date of your first journey. It requires advance planning but is better value than buying single tickets. Another excellent option is the **Island Rover** ticket, which is valid for all routes over an eight- or 15-day period. During the peak

Tip...
If you're planning on taking more than a couple of ferries, especially with a car, it may be more economical to buy an **Island Hopscotch** ticket.

summer months it's essential to book ferry tickets in advance. **Highland Air Services** (obanandtheislesairports.com) operate several flights between Oban, Islay, Tiree, Coll and Colonsay on alternate weekdays.

Public transport is steadily improving across much of Argyll, though don't expect the same frequency of bus services as in the main towns. The main bus operator is **West Coast Motors** (www.westcoastmotors.co.uk). The Oban to Glasgow rail line passes through the northern part of the region. Times of local buses and trains can be checked at local tourist offices and at www.argyll-bute.gov.uk. For further details, see the Transport sections, pages 86, 92, 93, 95, 103 and 105.

When to go

Spring or early summer are the best times as accommodation is easier to find, most places are open and the weather can be reasonably good. Also the dreaded midges are not at their worst. September is also a good time. In the winter months some tourist facilities are closed.

Time required

Mainland Argyll, Mull and Iona, and Islay and Jura all require a week each. In two weeks you could cover the mainland plus one or two islands.

Tourist information

There are **VisitScotland** iCentres in Oban, Craignure (Mull), Bowmore (Islay), Inveraray, Dunoon, Rothesay, Tarbert (Loch Fyne) and Campbeltown. Oban **iCentre** has information on all the islands covered in this chapter. For details, see listings under each destination. The **Oban & Lorn Tourism Alliance** have a useful website: www.oban.org.uk.

Oban
& around

Oban is Argyll's tourist hub, the largest west coast port north of Glasgow and the main departure point for ferries to the Inner and Outer Hebrides. Not surprisingly, it gets very crowded in summer, with passing traffic and people using it as a base for exploring the region. A working port, Oban's main streets narrowly avoid the excesses of tourist kitsch and offer visitors a wide range of hotels, guesthouses, B&Bs, restaurants and shops. There are also several tourist attractions of note if stuck here in bad weather. The town itself lies in the beautiful setting of a wide, crescent-shaped bay backed by steep hills, with the tiny, idyllic island of Kerrera, just offshore, providing a natural shelter. Oban is at the centre of the northerly part of Argyll known as Lorn, which comprises several relatively peaceful islands including Lismore, Kerrera, Seil and Luing.

With a population of 8000, Oban's great landmark is McCaig's Tower, an incongruous structure that resembles Rome's Coliseum and which dominates the skyline. The tower was built by local banker John Stuart McCaig in the late 19th century, as a means of providing work for unemployed stonemasons. Unfortunately, McCaig died before the project was complete, and to this day no one is quite sure of his intentions. There's not much to see, apart from the exterior walls, but the views of the town and bay are quite magnificent and well worth the climb. There are various routes on foot, but the most direct is to go up Argyll Street and on the left beside the church climb the set of steps known as Jacob's Ladder, which lead to Ardconnel Terrace. Turn left and the tower soon comes into view and is well signposted.

Another good walk is to the ruins of seventh-century **Dunollie Castle**, north of town on the Corran Esplanade towards Ganavan, from where there are also wonderful views. The castle was built on the site of an ancient stronghold of the King of Scots, and was then taken over in the 13th century by the MacDougalls, Lords of Lorn. Continue round the corner to **Ganavan Sands**, a long, safe sandy beach about 1½ miles north of the town, for a romantic west coast sunset.

If the weather's bad take a tour round the excellent **Oban Distillery** ⓘ *Stafford St, opposite North Pier, T01631-572004, www.discoveringdistilleries.com; Jan-Feb daily 1230-1630; Mar-Jun daily 0930-1700; Jul-Sep Mon-Fri 0930-1930, Sat and Sun 0930-1700; Oct and Nov daily 0930-1700; Dec daily 1200-1630; 1-hr tour costs £10, child (8-17) £5, includes £5 off bottle of whisky in shop,* which dates back to 1794

The **War and Peace Museum** ⓘ *T01631-570007, May-Oct Mon-Thu 1000-1800, Fri-Sun 1000-1600; Mar, Apr and Nov daily 1000-1600, free,* on the Esplanade near North Pier is worth a look. Staffed by enthusiastic volunteers, it tells the story of Oban's role in the Second World War through a display of old photos and memorabilia. **Dunstaffnage Castle** ⓘ *T01631-562465 (HES), Apr-Sep daily 0930-1730, Oct-Mar daily Sat-Wed 1000-1600, castle grounds open all year, £6, concessions £4.80, children (5-15) £3.60, under 5s free, 3 miles north of Oban, off the A85,* is an impressive 13th-century fort that was a stronghold of the MacDougalls until captured by Robert the Bruce in 1309. Much of its towering curtain wall is still intact. The ruins of the little chapel nearby are worth a look. Long before this castle served as a temporary prison for Flora MacDonald, it's believed the site was used to keep the original Stone of Destiny.

Essential Oban

Finding your feet

Oban, the 'gateway to the isles', is reasonably well served by buses and trains from Glasgow, Fort William and Inverness, and there are a number of west coast local bus services to and from Lochgilphead and Kilmartin. There are regular local buses around town and around Lorn, including to Ellenabeich and North Cuan on Seil, Isle of Luing, North Connel, Dalavich, Bonawe and Ganavan Sands. These are mostly operated by **West Coast Motors** (T01586-552319). **CalMac Ferry Terminal** (T0800-066 5000) is on the Railway Pier, to the south of the town centre, and the train station is opposite the bus terminal on Station Square. **Oban airport** (T01631-572910) is six miles northeast of town, near the village of North Connel. See also Transport, page 52.

Tourist information

iCentre
North Pier, T01631-563122. End Jun-end Aug Mon-Sat 0900-1900, Sun 1000-1700; end Aug-end Oct Mon-Sat 0900-1800, Sun 1000-1700; Nov-May Mon-Sat 1000-1700, Sun 1100-1600.
Has a foreign exchange bureau and a huge choice of maps to buy or pick up among the scores of leaflets. It's very busy but the staff are extremely helpful.

Where to stay

As the main ferry port for the islands, Oban gets busy in the summer with traffic. Book well in advance or get the tourist office to find you a bed. As well as those listed below, there are many cheaper options. See page 483 for useful websites.

££££ Dungallan House Hotel
Gallanach Rd, T01631-563799, www.dungallanhotel-oban.co.uk.
Built in 1870 by the Duke of Argyll, this tastefully refurbished residence is a great Oban establishment that offers fine dining on locally sourced produce, over 100 malts and excellent views on the road south to the Kerrera ferry.

££££ Manor House Hotel
Gallanach Rd, T01631-562087, www.manorhouseoban.com. Open year-round.
11 rooms. A beautiful stone house in a secluded location overlooking the bay, about ¼ mile south of the ferry terminal. Style and comfort assured and with a reputation for fine food.

££££-£££ Greystones
1 Dalriach Rd, T01631-358653, www.greystonesoban.co.uk.
Grand baronial house overlooking the town and harbour. 5 stylish and elegant rooms, each priced differently. Lovely touches such as wine glasses, corkscrew and wine cooler in

rooms, also guest sitting rooms and library, wonderful breakfasts. Highly recommended place to stay.

£££ Glenburnie House
Corran Esplanade, T01631-562089, www.glenburnie.co.uk. Apr-Oct.
Victorian house on the seafront, highly rated B&B. Tasteful rooms and excellent breakfasts, including fresh fruit salad and salmon with scrambled eggs. Rooms with sea views are more expensive.

£££-££ Dunheanish Guest House
Ardconnel Rd, T01631-566556, www.dunheanish.com.
6 rooms. Very friendly and welcoming guesthouse perched above the town with wonderful views across the bay. Rooms are tastefully decorated and some have king-size 4-poster beds. Vegetarian breakfasts available. Note no children under 14. Off-street parking.

Camping

Oban Caravan & Camping Park
Gallanach Rd, 2 miles south of town beyond the Kerrera ferry, T01631-562425. Apr to mid-Oct.
Beautiful setting looking out to Kerrera. Camping pods available for those who like a little more comfort.

Roseview Caravan and Camping
On the Glenshellach Rd, 1½ miles south of the ferry terminal, T01631-562755. Mar-Nov.
Very good campsite with facilities for kids.

Restaurants

Note that many restaurants stop serving by 2200.

£££ Waterfront Fishhouse Restaurant
1 Railway Pier, T01631-563110, www.waterfrontfishhouse.co.uk. Daily 1200-1400, 1730-2100.

Great views across the bay while you tuck into fantastic seafood at this perennial local favourite. Fish and seafood is the main event here but there's a good selection of non-piscine dishes.

£££-££ Coast
104 George St, T01631-569900,
www.coastoban.co.uk.
Daily 1200-1400, 1730-2100.
An imaginative menu in a stylish setting. Mouth-watering vegetarian, meat and

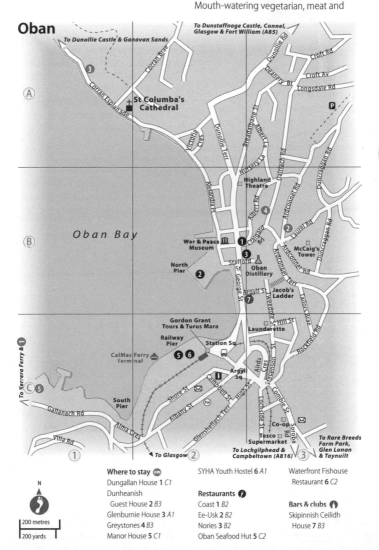

Oban

To Dunollie Castle & Ganavan Sands

To Dunstaffnage Castle, Connel, Glasgow & Fort William (A85)

Corran Brae
Corran Esplanade
Croft Rd
Croft Av
Dunollie Rd
Deanery Br
Longsdale Rd

St Columba's Cathedral

Breadalbane St
Dunollie Terr
Victoria Cres
Dalriach Rd

Nursery La
Albert Rd
Highland Theatre
Laurel Rd
Ardconnel Rd
Duncraggan Rd

Oban Bay

War & Peace Museum
Stafford St
Craigard Rd
McCaig's Tower
Ardconnel Terr

North Pier
Oban Distillery
Jacob's Ladder
Tailor's Brae

George St
Breadalbane St
Argyll St

Gordon Grant Tours & Turus Mara
Hill St
Launderette
Rockfield Rd

Railway Pier
Station Sq

CalMac Ferry Terminal
To Kerrera Ferry
Airds Cres

South Pier
Shore St
Albany St
Campbell St
High St
Argyll Sq
Lochside St
Combie St
Stevenson St

Gallanach Rd
Alma Cres
Villa Rd
Glenshellach Terr
Soroba Rd

Co-op
Tesco Supermarket
To Rare Breeds Farm Park, Glen Lonan & Taynuilt

To Glasgow

To Lochgilphead & Campbeltown (A816)

N

200 metres
200 yards

Where to stay
Dungallan House **1** *C1*
Dunheanish
 Guest House **2** *B3*
Glenburnie House **3** *A1*
Greystones **4** *B3*
Manor House **5** *C1*
SYHA Youth Hostel **6** *A1*

Restaurants
Coast **1** *B2*
Ee-Usk **2** *B2*
Nories **3** *B2*
Oban Seafood Hut **5** *C2*
Waterfront Fishouse
 Restaurant **6** *C2*

Bars & clubs
Skipinnish Ceilidh
House **7** *B3*

seafood dishes served with a smile. Good-value set lunch for £14.50 a head.

£££-££ Ee-Usk
North Pier, T01631-565666, www.eeusk.com. Daily 1200-1500, 1745-2130.
Busy, glass-fronted fish restaurant, which isn't cheap but prides itself on the quality of its seafood. Service with flair. Good-value 2-course set lunch and early-evening special for £15 a head. Note that no children under 12 after 1745. Before you ask, *ee'usk* is Gaelic for fish and is pronounced 'iasg'.

£ Oban Seafood Hut
By the ferry terminal. Daily 0900-1800.
This bustling green wooden shed remains Oban's best takeaway seafood haunt and is outstanding value. For an inexpensive quality snack try a pot of squat lobster tails, a fresh crab sandwich or the mouth-watering scallops in garlic.

There are also several good fish and chip shops in town, including **Nories (£)** at 86 George St.

Bars and clubs

Skipinnish Ceilidh House
George St, T01631-569599.
Oban is no party town, but for an unrivalled taste of high-energy and informal live ceilidh music head for **Skipinnish Ceilidh House**. Get there in time for the dancing lessons and you'll enjoy it even more. DJ spins tunes later in the evening.

Entertainment

The Highland Theatre
North end of George St, T01631-562444.

This is, confusingly, the local cinema. It shows most of the popular current releases.

Festivals

To check for major events in the area, visit www.eventscotland.org.
Apr-May Highlands & Islands Music & Dance Festival for Children, held at the end of Apr/beginning of May.
Aug Argyllshire Gathering (Oban Games), held during the 4th week of Aug in Mossfield Park, www.obangames.com.
Sep World Stone-skimming Championships, held on Easdale in late Sep, www.stone skimming.com. Drinking and merriment.

What to do

Boat trips
Boat trips can be made from Oban to Mull, Iona, Staffa and The Treshnish Islands with a variety of companies, including:
Gordon Grant Marine, *T07831-885985, www.staffatours.com*. Various boat tours from Oban to Staffa, Treshnish Isles, Iona and Mull. Tours cost from £30 up to £60.
Argyll Sea Tours, *T07900-605245, www. argyll-seatours.co.uk*. Wildlife boat trips and also fishing trips, 3-hr mackerel fishing trip £35/15.

Diving
Puffin Dive Centre, *Gallanach Port, Gallanach Rd, T01631-566088, www. puffin.org.uk*. Diving trips and courses.

Swimming
Atlantis Leisure, *Dalriach Rd, T01631-566800, www.atlantisleisure.co.uk*. Sports and leisure centre with pool.

Transport

Bus
There are regular daily buses to and from **Glasgow** (2½ hrs), **Inverness** (4 hrs), via **Fort William** (1¼ hrs), **Benderloch** and **Appin** with **Scottish Citylink**, www.citylink.

co.uk. **West Coast Motors** run buses to **Fort William** and **Inverness**, to **Ardrishaig**, via **Kilmartin** and **Lochgilphead** (Mon-Sat), to **Ellenabeich** and **North Cuan** (Mon-Sat), and regular daily buses to **Dalmally**, via Cruachan Power Station, **Lochawe** and Taynuilt Hotel.

The **West Highland Flyer** minibus, T07780-724248, Easter-end Oct, links the Oban (Mull) and **Mallaig** (Skye) ferries. It will take you just 2½ hrs to do this route and the minibus will also carry your bike. Departs Oban 0945 and arrives in Mallaig at 1215. Travels via Fort William and the Glen Nevis Youth Hostel on request.

Car hire
Flit Van & Car Hire, 2 Glencruitten Rd, T01631-566553. **Hazelbank Motors**, Lochavulin Rd, T01631-566476, www.obancarhire.co.uk.

Cycle hire
There are numerous cycling routes and walks in Argyll. Ask at the **iCentre** for the leaflet, *Cycle the Forests of North Argyll,* or visit https://forestry.gov.uk/mtbscotland.

Oban Cycles, 87 George St, T01631-566033, www.obancyclescotland.co.uk, Tue-Sat 1000-1700, for cycle hire, sales and repairs.

Ferry
Oban is the main ferry port for many of the Hebridean islands, for details of the **CalMac** ferry terminal, see page 47.

The departure point for ferries to **Kerrera** is 1½ miles along the Gallanach Rd.

A passenger ferry leaves to **Lismore island** Mon-Sat 4 times daily, twice on Sun, 50 mins. A tiny passenger ferry sails from **Ellenabeich** on Seil to **Easdale** (see page 55). A daily car ferry to **Luing** (South Cuan) sails from North Cuan on Seil, see page 55 for details.

Train
There are 3 trains daily to **Glasgow**, via **Crianlarich**, where the Oban train connects with the Mallaig/Fort William to Glasgow train.

Isle of Kerrera *Colour map 3, B5/C5.*
Boasting one of the best short (six-mile) coastal walks in the UK, the tranquil Isle of Kerrera, lying half a mile offshore and a five-minute ferry ride ① *daily, every 30 mins 1030-1700 Jul-Oct, from Gallanach Rd, 2 miles south of town, for more details visit www.calmac.co.uk,* is well worth visiting. The island supports just 35 inhabitants; walkers or cyclists may spot wild goats, otters, sea eagles and seals or even porpoises offshore. Five minutes' walk south of the welcoming Kerrera bunkhouse and tearoom, visitors are rewarded with the imposing ruins of Gylen Castle and views across to Mull, the Slate Islands, Lismore and Jura. Built by the MacDougalls in 1587, **Gylen Castle** sits proudly on a clifftop looking down the Firth of Lorn. A mile northwest of the ferry jetty is **Slatrach Bay**, a sandy beach providing a terrific place for a family picnic. There are no shops so arrive with provisions. However, at the **Oban Marina**, located at the northeastern end of Kerrera, you'll find the excellent **Waypoint Bar and Grill**, see under Restaurants, page 57.

Connel to Oban Sealife Centre *Colour map 3, B5.*
Five miles north of Oban an impressive steel cantilever bridge carries the A828 across the mouth of Loch Etive at Connel. It's worth stopping here to see the **Falls of Lora**, a wild tide-race created by the narrow mouth of the sea loch and the reef that spans most of it, thus restricting the flow of water. The result is the impressive rapids, which are best seen from the shore in the village or from halfway across the bridge.

Some 10 miles north up this road on the shore of Loch Creran, 16th-century Barcaldine Castle offers a luxurious B&B option (see Where to stay, page 56). **Oban Sealife Centre** ① *T01631-720386, www.visitsealife.com, summer daily 1000-1700, winter 1100-1600, £13.40, children (3-14) £11, family of 4 £45, book online for 30% discount,* is enormous fun. This environmentally friendly facility rescues seals and other aquatic creatures, which are then released back into the wild at the end of the season. Aside from over 30 displays, there's a touch pool, an underwater observatory and a terrific forest adventure trail. Parents can rest their tired feet in the coffee shop. Bus No 405 runs regularly from outside Oban train station to the Sealife Centre.

Appin *Colour map 3, B5.*

The road runs around Loch Creran and enters the district of Appin, made famous in Robert Louis Stevenson's *Kidnapped*, which was based on the 'Appin Murder' of 'The Red Fox – Campbell of Glenure' in 1752. The prominent Jacobite James Stewart was tried by a 'kangaroo court' of Campbells and subsequently hung in Ballachulish with his body left to rot for three years. A road turns southwest off the main Fort William road to **Port Appin**, on the western tip of the peninsula, the departure point for the passenger ferry to Lismore (see below). To the north of Port Appin is the irresistibly photogenic **Castle Stalker** ① *T01631-730354, www.castlestalker.com, 1 guided tour per day Apr-Oct, allow 2 hrs including boat trip there and back, maximum 12 people at a time so need to book in advance, £20, children £10, family £50.* Standing on its own tiny island with a background of islands and hills, it's probably second only to the famous Eilean Donan in its portrayal of Scotland's romantic image. It was built upon the remnants of a previous MacDougall stronghold built in the 15th century by the Stewarts of Appin before falling into Campbell hands after the ill-fated 1745 rebellion. **Castle Stalker View Café** overlooks the castle from the north and is a great place to eat and photograph the ancient site (see Restaurants, page 57).

Isle of Lismore *Colour map 3, B5.*

The island of Lismore lies only a few miles off the mainland, in Loch Linnhe, yet feels a world away. It makes an ideal day trip and offers great opportunities for walking and cycling, as well as wonderful views across to the mountains of Morvern and Mull, the Paps of Jura to the south and Ben Nevis to the north. It's a fertile little island (the name *leis mór* is Gaelic for the big garden) that once supported a population of 1400, though the present population is only 176. Lismore has a long and interesting history as outlined by the award-winning, wood-clad **Gaelic Heritage Centre (Ionad Naomh Moluag)** ① *T01631-760030, www.lismoregaelicheritagecentre.org,uk, café and centre open daily Apr-Oct 1100-1600,* which has a café and gift shop. Lismore was the ecclesiastical capital of Argyll for several centuries and the **Cathedral of St Moluag** was founded here in the 12th century, just north of Clachan. All that remains is the choir, which is now used as the parish church. The cathedral occupies the site of a church founded by the Irish saint, who established a religious community on the island about the same time as St Columba was busy at work in Iona. Legend has it that the two saints were racing to the island, in an attempt to be the first to land and found a monastery. Such was Moluag's religious zeal that he cut off his finger and threw it on to the shore, thus claiming possession. Not far from the church is the 2000-year-old **Broch of Tirefour**, one of the best-preserved prehistoric monuments in Argyll, with surviving circular walls up to 16 ft high. Other sights include **Castle Coeffin**, a 13th-century fortress built by the MacDougalls of Lorn on the site of an earlier Viking settlement. In the southwest of the island lies the 13th-century **Achadun Castle**, built for the Bishops of Argyll. It's a short walk from here to **Bernera Island**, which can be reached at low tide (but don't get stranded). For a selection of recommended walking routes on the island visit www.walkhighlands.co.uk. Bikes can be hired at **Lismore Bike Hire** (T07376-425996). Ferries to Lismore leave from Oban (50 minutes) or Port Appin (10 minutes). See www.calmac.co.uk for times and prices.

South Lorn and the Slate Islands *Colour map 3, C4/5.*

Eight miles south of Oban the B884 turns west off the A816 and wriggles its way round glassy lochs and knobbly, green hills studded with copper-coloured cattle to the tiny Slate Islands, so called because in the mid-19th century the island's slate quarries exported millions of roofing slates every year. The quarrying industry has long since gone, leaving the area dotted with pretty little villages of whitewashed cottages.

The most northerly of the Slate Islands is **Seil** (or Clachan Seil), which is reached from the mainland across the seriously humpbacked **Clachan Bridge**. Better known as the 'Bridge over the Atlantic', it was built in 1792, with its high arch allowing ships to pass beneath. Beside the bridge is an old inn, **Tigh an Truish**, or 'House of the Trousers', where islanders once swapped their kilt for trousers in order to conform to the post-1745 ban on the wearing of Highland dress. There's also a petrol pump and souvenir shop here. Two miles south, at **Balvicar** (where there's a bank in the grocery store) the road turns right and climbs up and over to the harbour and the attractive village of **Ellenabeich**, which is also, rather confusingly, known by the same name as the nearby island of Easdale. Ellenabeich has been home to the Isle of Seil microbrewery (reputedly Scotland's smallest) since 2004. Before sinking a pint of their Corryveckan Ale, try the 130-yd, 12-hole Isle putting green. Apparently, if you beat the course par of 24, a bottle of Oban whisky is yours. The village is also the base for the excellent **Seafari Adventures** (see What to do, page 58), and here too you'll find the **Scottish Slate Islands Heritage Trust Centre** ⓘ *T01852-300307, www.slateislands.org.uk, Apr-Oct daily 1030-1300, 1400-1700*, with its insight into the area's history.

The tiny, car-free island of **Easdale** is separated from Seil by a 200-yd-wide channel which has to be dredged to keep it open. The island, only 800 yds by 700 yds, was the centre of the slate industry and, between 1842 and 1861 produced over 130 million roof slates. Now inhabited by around 60 residents, the island once supported over 450 people before the quarries were flooded in the great storm of 1881 and the industry collapsed. A few minutes' walk from the ferry pier you'll find the delightful folk museum run by island volunteers. If the museum is closed, wander past the whitewashed former slate workers' cottages to seek out island information over a pint at the cosy **Puffer Bar**. The island's lively social life also revolves around the community hall with one of the highlights of the year being the keenly contested **World Stone-skimming Championships**, see Festivals, page 52. For more information on the island, visit www.easdale.org. To get there, park in the car park at Ellenabeich and sound the klaxon in the tiny waiting room on the pier.

Another road runs south from Balvicar to **North Cuan**, from where the car ferry sails across the treacherous Cuan Sound to the long, thin island of **Luing** (pronounced 'Ling'). The island once had a population of around 600, which was drastically reduced during the Clearances to make way for cattle. Luing is still well known for its beef, and is the home of a successful new breed named after it. The island is small, six miles by two miles, and mostly flat, making it ideal for exploring by bike. Bikes can be hired just 50 yds from the ferry slipway at the **Sunnybrae Caravan Park** ⓘ *T01852-314274*, from where static caravans can be hired (see Where to stay). A mile or so further south is the village of **Cullipool** where you'll find the **Atlantic Islands Centre** ① *T01852-314096, www.atlanticislandscentre. com*, which is the island's social hub as well as a heritage centre, gift shop and reastaurant. The only other village is Toberonochy, three miles from Cullipool. Wildlife abounds with sightings of otters, seals, eagles and buzzards, whilst visitors can also enjoy a breathtaking panorama of the outlying isles of Mull, Shuna and Scarba. A car ferry sails to Luing every half hour Monday-Saturday and a passenger ferry run in the evenings and on Sundays. See www.calmac.co.uk for times and prices.

South of the turn-off to the Slate Islands is **Arduaine Gardens** ① *T01852-200366, gardens open daily 0930-sunset, £6.50, concessions £5, family £16.50*, a beautiful place and an absolute must for all gardening enthusiasts. Gifted to the National Trust for Scotland in 1992, this 20-acre oasis boasts spectacular rhododendrons in early summer, Himalayan lilies, blue Tibetan poppies, a woodland garden, sweeping lawns and inspirational views across to Jura and the Slate Islands.

This is serious boating country, and just south of Arduaine, on the northern coast of the Craignish Peninsula, is surreal **Craobh Haven**, a yachting marina built in the style of a reproduction 18th-century fishing village. South of Craobh Haven is another yachting marina at **Ardfern**, where the **Galley of Lorne Hotel and pub** is invariably packed with yachties. You can arrange boat trips from Ardfern around Loch Craignish and to the offshore islands, see What to do, page 57.

Listings Around Oban

Where to stay

££££ Airds Hotel & Restaurant
Port Appin, T01631-730236,
www.airds-hotel.com.
One of Scotland's finest family-run hotels. The owners, Shaun and Jenny McKivragan, ensure a personal touch pervades this classy establishment, which boasts exquisite views, superb cuisine and 11 delightful rooms, also 2 luxury self-catering cottages. Recommended.

££££ Barcaldine Castle
Benderloch, 9 miles north of Oban and the A828, T01631-720598, www.barcaldinecastle. co.uk. Open year-round.
5 rooms. This is a rare opportunity to stay in a 17th-century castle, home of the Campbells of Barcaldine. The castle was built in 1609 on the shores of Loch Creran by 'Black' Duncan Campbell. A wonderful experience for those who can afford it.

££££ Loch Melfort Hotel
Arduaine, T01852-200233, www.lochmelfort. co.uk. Open all year.
8 rooms and 2 suites in the main house and 20 rooms in the sea-view lodge. Enjoy supreme comfort and top-quality food in a spectacular location on Asknish Bay, right next door to Arduaine Gardens. The **Asknish Bay** restaurant boasts 2 AA rosettes and serves exquisite food with stunning views over Asknish Bay, while the more informal **Chartroom II Bistro** offers a more informal atmosphere with an emphasis on local seafood. The hotel has good disabled access. Dogs can stay for a £9 supplement.

££££-£££ Pierhouse Hotel and Seafood Restaurant
Port Appin, T01631-730302, www. pierhousehotel.co.uk. Open all year.
Looking out to the tiny pier and over Loch Linnhe, this stylish little hotel offers very comfortable and uncluttered accommodation in 12 en suite rooms over 2 floors. The restaurant serves outstanding

food. There is also a guests' snug and the **Ferry Bar** for an informal drink. The hotel will arrange day trips or you can relax in the Finnish sauna.

£ Kerrera Bunkhouse
Isle of Kerrera, T01631-566367, www.kerrera bunkhouse.co.uk. Open year-round.
Impossibly cute and cosy accommodation for up to 7 people in this lovely wee bunkhouse, complete with tea garden which is open Easter-Sep daily 1030-1630. Dog friendly.

Camping

North Ledaig Caravan and Motorhome Site
By Connel, 12 miles north of Oban, T01631-710291. Apr-Oct.
Clean and friendly, great location by the beach.

Sunnybrae Caravan Park
South Cuan, Isle of Luing, T01852-314274.
To enjoy fabulous sunsets towards Jura and an away-from-it-all escape. There are 8 4-berth static caravans for rent for around £500 per week in high season.

Self-catering

Willowburn Cottages
Seil, T01852-300276, www.willowburn.co.uk.
2 luxury self-catering cottages. Just past the 'Bridge over the Atlantic' on Seil island, they enjoy a delightful, peaceful setting with views over Sound of Seil. An absolute gem. Recommended.

Restaurants

See also Where to stay, above.

£££-££ Waypoint Bar and Grill
Isle of Kerrera, T01631-565333, www.obanmarina.com.
In addition to great seafood, this restaurant at Oban Marina runs a complimentary ferry boat service for guests dining at the restaurant (boat leaves Oban's North Pier every few hours from 0810, last boat back to Oban at 2220, £5 pp, must be booked in advance).

££ Hawthorn Restaurant
Keil Crofts, Benderloch, T01631-720777, www.hawthorn-restaurant-co.uk. May-Nov Tue-Sun 1730-2100, Fri-Sun 1200-1400.
About 8 miles north of Oban is this unassuming whitewashed cottage serving the most delicious local seasonal produce at reasonable prices. Well worth the trip from Oban.

££-£ Castle Stalker View
Appin, T01631-730444. Feb-Oct daily 0930-1700, Nov-Dec Thu-Sun 1000-1600, closed Jan.
On the hillside overlooking the castle and directly off the Oban to Ballachulish main road, is this gift shop and excellent café. Tuck into the likes of Inverawe smoked salmon, freshly baked cakes and coffee. Panoramas down the sea lochs to Oban and unrivalled views over the castle. There are also information boards outlining the history of the castle and the infamous Appin murder. Outside, there's a path down to a viewpoint. Highly recommended.

£ Poppies Garden Centre & Restaurant
Saulmore Shore, Connel, T01631-565718, www.poppiesgardencentre.co.uk. Daily 0900-1700.
A few miles north of Oban is this garden centre tearoom and restaurant which makes a perfect spot for a light lunch or tea and cakes. Try their award-winning meringues.

Bars and clubs

You'll always find a pint and warm welcome at the **Galley of Lorne Hotel** in Ardfern; the **Puffer Bar** in Easdale; and the **Oyster Brewery Bar and Restaurant** in Ellenabeich.

What to do

Boat trips
Etive Boast Trips, *Dunstaffnage Marina, Dunbeg, T07900-253585, etiveboattrips.co.uk.* Offer a variety of boat trips, from a 2-hr trip around Oban Bay (£20/15) up to a full-day

cruise to the head of spectacular Loch Etive, £60/45, which is well worth it.

Seafari Adventures, *Ellenabeich, Seil (also book at Oban iCentre), T01852-300003, www. seafari.co.uk.* Their 300 hp RIBS take you on a thrilling ride across the Corryvreckan whirlpool, with opportunities to spot seals, porpoises and lots of seabirds, £42, children £32. They also run a new Easdale to Iona and Staffa day trip (departs 1030 and returns 1630 Wed only), £80, under 16s £59. Travel to Iona to see the Abbey, with ample time ashore, includes non-landing trip to Staffa to view puffin colony. Recommended.

Transport

See Oban Transport, page 52.

Cycle hire
Isle of Luing Bike Hire, Isle of Luing, T01852-314274. Hires bikes for £15 per day from Sunnybrae Caravan Park (see Isle of Luing, above).

Mid-Argyll, Kintyre, Cowal & Bute

Further south from Oban the long finger of Mid-Argyll extends past the offshore 'whisky isles' of Islay and Jura, pointing southwards into the remote Kintyre Peninsula where rolling hills protect the Isle of Arran from the wrath of the Atlantic Ocean. This area is packed with history. Winding roads take visitors on a journey past attractive sea lochs and huge forests, revealing at Kilmartin Glen one of Europe's most important prehistoric sites. Mull of Kintyre is the lonely tip, a stone's throw from Northern Ireland. On the other side of Loch Fyne is the walking haven and giant claw of Cowal Peninsula, looking as if it's about to crush in its grasp the aptly named Isle of Bute, home to one of Scotland's most fantastical stately homes.

Loch Awe is the longest freshwater loch in Scotland and, further north, is the beautiful Loch Etive. Between the two lochs runs the River Awe, which squeezes through the dark and ominous Pass of Brander. It is so steep and narrow that, according to legend, it was once held against the army by an old woman brandishing a scythe. There's enough to see here to justify a couple of days' exploration, particularly the little-visited west shore of Loch Awe, and there are plenty of other places to visit around Inveraray to the south.

At the northeastern tip of Loch Awe, between the villages of of **Dalmally** and **Lochawe**, is the romantic ruin of 15th-century **Kilchurn Castle** ⓘ *HES, free,* on a promontory jutting out into the loch. Access is on foot from the A85 under the nearby railway viaduct. The lochside floods periodically so caution is advised. Also worth a look around here is the lovely, and rather bizarre, **St Conan's Church** ⓘ *free, donation requested,* just off the A85 by Lochawe village. Built in the late 19th century but not used until 1930, the church's serene atmosphere is striking. Inside is an effigy of Robert the Bruce, with one of his bones buried underneath. The exterior, especially the south side overlooking the loch, is a riot of eccentric detail. You can buy fishing permits from the **Tight Line Bar** in the village.

Four miles west of Lochawe, and almost a mile inside Ben Cruachan (3695 ft) is the underground attraction of the **Cruachan Power Station** or **'Hollow Mountain'** ⓘ *Apr-Oct daily 0930-1645, Nov-Mar Mon-Fri 1000-1545, 30-min guided tour £7.50, child 6-16 £2.50, under 6 free.* From the visitor centre on the shores of Loch Awe, a bus trip takes you into the heart of the mountain through tunnels until you reach the giant steel doors and generating room. Whilst exploring this Bond-like subterranean warren, it's impossible to forget the millions of tons of rock above your head. Pray Loch Awe doesn't spring a leak!

Further west, and 12 miles east of Oban, is the tiny village of **Taynuilt**, near the shore of Loch Etive. Just before the village, at Bridge of Awe, is a sign for **Inverawe Smokehouses** ⓘ *T03448-475490, www.smokedsalmon.co.uk, Mar-Dec daily 0900-1700,* where you can take fishing lessons, learn about traditional smoking techniques, or wander along a series of nature trails. If the weather's fine, you can buy some of their delicious smoked products and have a picnic, see box, opposite. If you fancy some smoked salmon delivered to your home, make sure you sign up for their mailing list.

One mile north of the village on the shores of Loch Etive is **Bonawe Iron Furnace** ⓘ *HES, T01866-822432, Apr-Sep daily 0930-1730, £5, concessions £4, children £3.* Founded in 1753 by a group of Cumbrian ironmasters, Bonawe used the abundant woodlands of Argyll to make charcoal to fire its massive furnace. At its height, it produced 600-700 tons of pig-iron a year and provided cannonballs for Admiral Nelson at the Battle of Trafalgar. Iron production ceased at Bonawe in 1876 and it has now been restored as an industrial heritage site, with displays explaining the whole production process.

Running south from the village is the very lovely and very quiet Glen Lonan. Three miles along the Glen Lonan road, at **Barguillean Farm**, is **Angus Garden** ⓘ *T01866-822335, daily 0900 till dusk,* one of Argyll's youngest and smallest gardens, but also one of the most peaceful and evocative, set around the shores of little Loch Angus. It was created in 1957, in memory of Angus MacDonald, a journalist and writer killed in Cyprus in 1956.

Piscine cuisine

At **Inverawe Fisheries and Smokery,** near Loch Etive, see below, they buy smaller farmed salmon because they believe the lower fat content makes them tastier than larger ones. Traditional curing methods prevail here. The fish are dry salted, washed, smoked over oak logs for anything from 16 to 24 hours, depending on conditions, and then they are hand-sliced. The result is smoked salmon with a rich and freshly oaky taste. From a 100 g smoked salmon pack to a 750 g pre-sliced side of salmon, as well as gravadlax, smoked trout, eel and halibut, there's a diverse range to choose from.

Walks around Loch Awe and Loch Etive

A single-track road runs southwest of Kilchrenan along the shores of Loch Awe to the tiny villages of **Dalavich** and **Ford**, through the very beautiful Inverinan Forest, a Forestry Commission property which has a series of undemanding marked trails running through the hills overlooking the loch. The first walk starts out from the little hamlet of **Inverinan**. Red waymarkers lead you from the car park into the woods surrounding the gorge of the River Inan. Part of the route follows the old drove road along which cattle were driven from the Highlands down to the markets in south and central Scotland. The walk is three miles long and should take around 1½ hours. Further along the road, half a mile north of Dalavich, is a car park at **Barnaline Lodge**, the starting point for a nine-mile bike route, a way-marked walk through the Caledonian Forest Reserve, and a couple of other woodland walks. The longest of the walks is the five-mile route that leads along the **River Avich**, then along the shores of **Loch Avich** before returning to the lodge. Some 2½ miles south of Dalavich is a car park, which marks the starting point for a blue waymarked walk along the shores of **Loch Awe**. The route passes through **Mackenzie's Grove**, a sheltered gorge containing some of the largest conifers on the west coast. The route then runs along the shores of the loch, from where you can see the remains of a crannog, one of over 40 of these Iron Age settlements on Loch Awe. The route then heads back to the car park; about three miles in total. These routes are all outlined, with accompanying maps, in the Forestry Commission Scotland leaflet, *A Guide to Forest Walks and Trails in North Argyll,* available at tourist offices. Alternatively, visit https://forestry.gov.uk/recreation.

Listings Loch Awe and Loch Etive

Where to stay

££££ Ardanaiseig Hotel
3 miles east of Kilchrenan village (12 miles from Taynuilt) on an unclassified road, T01866-833333, www.ardanaiseig.com.
16 rooms. This impossibly romantic getaway, owned by a former antiques dealer and filled with flamboyant and quirky paintings and ornaments, is one of Scotland's finest hotels.

The luxurious Highland retreat also boasts one of the best hotel restaurants in Scotland (**£££**). With such outstandingly delicious food, a delightful ambience (including drinks by the fire in the library bar) and even private boat trips to atmospheric Kilchurn Castle, hotel breaks don't come any better than this.

£££ Blarcreen House
Ardchattan Estate, T01631-750272, www.blarcreenhouse.com. Mar-Dec.

3 rooms. A mile past Ardchattan Priory on the road from Oban to Bonawe. Elegant, Victorian farmhouse standing on its own surrounded by lovely countryside. Individually styled rooms, homely ambience and 3-course dinner available for £30 pp.

What to do

Fishing
Lochawe Boats, *Arbrecknish by Dalavich, off the B840, T01866-833256. All year.* £25 per day for rowing boat or canoe. £45 per day for outboard motor boat. Loch Awe fishing permits from £8 per day.

Inveraray and around

stone circles, burial cairns and forts from an ancient kingdom

Inveraray *Colour map 3, C6.*

Inveraray is the classic 18th-century planned town (don't call it a village), with its straight, wide streets and dignified Georgian houses, and enjoys the most stunning of settings, on the shores of Loch Fyne. It was rebuilt by the third Duke of Argyll, head of the Campbell clan, at the same time as he restored the nearby family home, which now attracts hordes of summer visitors. As well as its natural beauty and elegance, and fine castle, Inveraray has several other attractions that make an overnight stay in the town worthwhile. The sweet-toothed shouldn't walk past the door of **Sweet Memories** on Main Street East (open all year) where shelves are packed with jars of Scottish old world confectionery, including humbugs, aniseed balls and cough candy.

One of Argyll's most famous castles, **Inveraray Castle** ① *T01499-302203, Apr-Oct, daily 1000-1745 (last admission 1700),* £11, *concessions* £10, *children* £8, *under 5s free,* has been the clan seat of the Campbells for centuries and is still the family home of the Duke of Argyll. The present neo-Gothic structure dates from 1745, and its main feature is the magnificent armoury hall, whose displays of weaponry were supplied to the Campbells by the British government to quell the Jacobite rebellion. The elaborately furnished rooms are also on display, as is the fascinating and troubled family history in the Clan room. Several walks around the estate are described on the website. **Inveraray Jail** ① *T01499-302381, Apr-Oct 0930-1800, Nov-Mar 1000-1700,* £11.50, *senior* £10.45, *children* £6.95, the Georgian prison and courthouse in the centre of the town has been brilliantly restored as an interesting museum that gives a vivid insight into life behind bars from medieval times up until the 19th century. You can sit in on an 1820 courtroom trial, then visit the cells below and learn all about some of the delightful prison pursuits, such as branding with a hot iron, ear nailing and public whipping. The whole experience is further enhanced by the guides, who are dressed as warders and prisoners. Makes you want to stay on the right side of the law, although, thankfully, conditions have improved – as you will see for yourself.

A few miles southwest of town, on the A83 to Lochgilphead at Dalchanna Farm, is **Argyll Adventure**, see page 65.

Three miles beyond Argyll Adventure is **Auchindrain Township** ① *T01499-500235, www. auchindrain.org.uk, Apr-Oct daily 1000-1700 (last admission 1600), Nov-Mar check times,* £7.50, *concessions* £6.50, *children* £5, a restored and authentic West Highland farming village with parts dating to the 1700s. Features include two perfectly restored thatched cottages and barns, furnished and equipped with dairy and household items to give a real insight into what rural life must have been like in centuries past. There's also an informative visitor centre and tearoom.

Four miles further down the A83 is **Crarae Gardens** ① *T01546-886614, visitor centre Apr-Aug daily 1000-1700, Sep-Oct Mon-Thu 1000-1700, gardens open all year daily*

0930-sunset, £6.50, concessions £5, family £16.50, one of Scotland's very best public gardens, dramatically set in a deep wooded glen on the shores of Loch Fyne. Initiated by Lady Campbell in 1912, there are marked woodland walks winding their way through a spectacular array of rhododendrons, azaleas and numerous other exotic plants towards the tumbling waterfalls of the 'Himalayan Gorge'. Any time of year is rewarding to visit including autumn when foliage is resplendent in rich tints.

★ Kilmartin and around *Colour map 3, C5.*

Much of this region was once part of the ancient Kingdom of Dalriada, established by the Irish Celts (known as the *Scotti*, hence Scotland) who settled here in the fifth century. North of Lochgilphead, on the A816 to Oban, is **Kilmartin Glen**, an area of Neolithic and Bronze Age chambered and round cairns, stone circles, rock carvings, Iron Age forts and duns, Early Christian sculptured stones and medieval castles. Indeed, there are more than 350 ancient monuments within just a few miles radius of **Kilmartin Museum** ① *T01546-510278, www.kilmartin.org, Mar-Oct 1000-1730, Nov-Dec 1100-1600, £6.50, concessions £5.50, children £2.50, family £14*. Housed in the old manse next to the parish church in the tiny village of Kilmartin, the 15-minute audio-visual display and imaginative exhibits provide an invaluable insight into the surrounding landscape. It's worth staying to have lunch in the excellent museum café (open 1000-1700). Next door in the church graveyard are the Kilmartin crosses, dating from as far back as the ninth and 10th centuries. Also within the graveyard is one of the largest collections of medieval grave slabs in the West Highlands.

Two miles north of Kilmartin, sitting high above the A816, is **Carnasserie Castle** ① *free, it's a little way from the car park*, an imposing 16th-century tower house built by John Carswell, Bishop of the Isles, who translated *The Book of the Common Order* in 1567, the first book to be printed in Gaelic.

Most notable of all Kilmartin's monuments is the **linear cemetery**, a line of burial cairns that stretch southward from Kilmartin village for over two miles. The largest and oldest of the group is the Neolithic cairn, Nether Largie South, which is over 5000 years old and big enough to enter. The other cairns, Nether Largie North, Mid Nether Largie and Ri Cruin, are Bronze Age, and the huge stone coffins show carvings on the grave slabs. Nearby are the **Temple Wood Stone Circles**, where burials took place from Neolithic times to the Bronze Age.

On the other side of the A816, and visible from the road, is a group of monuments which can all be reached from **Dunchraigaig Cairn**. This is a huge Bronze Age cairn with some of the covering stones removed to reveal three stone coffins. From here a path is signed to **Ballymeanoch Standing Stones**, the tallest of which is 12 ft high. Two of the stones are decorated with cup marks, prehistoric rock carvings that can be found at numerous locations throughout the Kilmartin area. There's also a henge monument in the same field. These were generally round or oval platforms with an internal ditch, and it's thought they were used for ceremonial purposes. The best example of rock carvings is at Achnabreck, near Cairnbaan village, the largest collection anywhere in Britain. The purpose and significance of these cup- and ring-marked rocks is still a matter of debate.

A few miles south of Kilmartin village is the Iron Age hill fort of **Dunadd**, which stands atop a rocky outcrop and dominates the surrounding flat expanse of **Moine Mhór** (Great Moss), one of the few remaining peat bogs in the country and now a nature reserve. **Dunadd Fort** became the capital of the ancient kingdom of Dalriada around AD 500 and is one of the most important Celtic sites in Scotland. The views from the top are wonderful and worth the visit alone, but you can also see carved out of the exposed rock, a basin and footprint, thought to have been used in the inauguration ceremonies of the ancient kings of Dalriada.

Crinan Canal *Colour map 3, C5.*

Kilmartin Glen is bordered to the south by the Crinan Canal, a nine-mile stretch of waterway linking Loch Fyne at Ardrishaig with the Sound of Jura. It was designed and built by Sir John Rennie in 1801, with the assistance of the ubiquitous Thomas Telford, to allow shipping to avoid the long and often hazardous journey round the Mull of Kintyre and to help stimulate trade in the islands. These days you're more likely to see pleasure yachts and cruisers sailing on the canal than the cargo vessels that once transported coal and other goods to the islands and returned with livestock. You don't need to come in a boat to appreciate the canal. You can walk or cycle along the towpath that runs the entire length of the canal, from Ardrishaig to Crinan, and watch boats of all shapes and sizes negotiating a total of 15 locks. The best place to view the canal traffic is at **Crinan**, a pretty little fishing port on Loch Crinan at the western end of the canal.

Knapdale *Colour map 5, A2.*

Running south from the Crinan Canal down to Kintyre is Knapdale, a forested, hilly area that gets its name from its Gaelic description, *cnap* (hill) and *dall* (field). It's an area worth exploring, for there are many walking and cycling trails and superb views from the west coast across to the Paps of Jura. Immediately south of the canal is Knapdale Forest, which stretches from coast to coast over hills dotted with tiny lochs. Forestry Commission Scotland has marked out several trails. Three fairly easy circular routes start from the B8025 which runs south from **Bellanoch**, just east of Crinan.

One trail sets out from the car park at the unmanned Barnluasgan Interpretation Centre and runs up to a point beyond **Loch Barnluasgan**, with great views over the forest and the many lochs. It's a mile in total. A second trail, also a mile long, starts from a car park a little further along the B8025 and heads through the forest to the deserted township of **Arichonan**. The third trail starts out from the car park between the starting points for the first and second trails. It runs right around **Loch Coille-Bharr** and is three miles long. A more strenuous walk starts from a car park about 100 yds into the forest, off the B841, about half a mile west of Cairnbaan, and climbs up to the peak of **Dunardy** (702 ft).

At the Barnluasgan Interpretation Centre a little side road turns south down the eastern shore of beautiful Loch Sween, past the village of Achnamara, to the 12th-century **Castle Sween**. First impressions of the castle, situated on the shores of the lovely loch with the forested hills all around, are tainted by the sprawling caravan park and self-catering chalets on a nearby 15,000-acre estate. Three miles south is the ruined 13th-century **Kilmory Knap Chapel**. A new glass roof protects the carved stones inside. Here, visitors will find an 8-ft-high, 15th-century **MacMillan's Cross**, which shows the Crucifixion on one side and a hunting scene on the other. There are also several unmarked graves, believed to be those of 13th-century Knights Templar who fled from France.

Lochgilphead *Colour map 5, A3.*

The main town in the area of Mid-Argyll, and administrative centre for the entire Argyll and Bute region, is Lochgilphead, a sleepy little place at the head of Loch Gilp, an arm of Loch Fyne. Lochgilphead started life as a planned town, but the industries came and went, leaving it with the customary grid plan of wide streets but little else. Today it serves as a useful base for exploring the area, with accommodation options, a bank and a supermarket. There's a nice easy walk from the car park at Kilmory Castle Gardens, about a mile east of town, up to Kilmory Loch. It takes about an hour there and back and is well marked. The gardens also make a pleasant stroll and there are other marked walks, including up to **Dun Mór** (360 ft).

Tourist information

Inveraray iCentre
Front St, T01499-302063.

Where to stay

££££ Crinan Hotel
T01546-830261, www.crinanhotel.com.
Nestled on the shores of Loch Crinan and by the famous Crinan Canal, guests are assured of fine dining and luxury in this acclaimed retreat. Fantastic views, pampering on a majestic scale and a sensational restaurant make a stay here well worthwhile.

£££-££ George Hotel
Main St, T01499-302111,
www.thegeorgehotel.co.uk.
17 rooms. Enjoy genuine hospitality and tasty local produce (see Restaurants, below) in this atmospheric, late 18th-century hotel with cosy bar, real ales and a resident ghost. Some rooms with double jacuzzi are at the very top end of this price band. There are a further 8 rooms in the adjacent **First House**, another 4 rooms in **The Barn**, as well as 2 self-catering cottages (breakfast £10 pp extra).

£££-££ Newton Hall Guest House
Shore Rd, T01499-320244, www.
newtonhallguesthouse.co.uk.
Converted Victorian church in a lochside setting a short walk from town. 7 tastefully furnished rooms. Hosts Bruce and Pam ensure a warm welcome, a comfortable and relaxing stay and a wonderful breakfast with a view.

££ Kilmartin Hotel
Opposite the church in Kilmartin village,
T01546-510250.
6 rooms, 4 en suite. Handy, comfortable stop whilst exploring historic Kilmartin Glen. Good value but the food on offer is variable.

£ Inveraray Youth Hostel
Dalmally Rd, T01499-302454. Apr-end Oct.

The perfect budget base from which to explore the nearby castle and town.

Restaurants

£££-££ Loch Fyne Oyster Bar
At Cairndow on the A83 near Clachan,
T01499-600482. Daily 0900-1100,
Sun-Thu 1200-1745, Fri-Sat till 1830.
Book ahead at this famous seafood restaurant known to attract politicians and celebrities as well as discerning gastronomes. All the seafood is from sustainable stock. There's also an excellent delicatessen to further tempt your tastebuds, though we doubt you'll have room after gorging on a seafood platter.

££-£ The George Hotel
Main St, T01499-302111.
Real ales on tap, hearty bar meals and reasonably priced dinners using locally sourced meats and seafood. If staying, try the home-made jams.

££-£ Kilmartin Museum Café
Kilmartin Museum, see page 64. Mar-Oct
daily 1000-1700 and Thu-Sat evenings for
dinner, Nov-Dec 1100-1600.
Superb cooking, much better than you should expect, and a lesson to many other visitor attractions in how to do things well. Wholesome and healthy soups, snacks, home made bread and excellent coffee. Book ahead if planning on dinner.

What to do

Adventure and horse riding
Argyll Adventure, *T01499-302611, www.*
argylladventure.com. Apr-Oct daily 1000-1700,
from £8 per activity. A horse riding and activity centre by the banks of Loch Fyne. As well as lessons and horse and pony treks, there are also various activities such as crossbow shooting, Laser Quest, and paintballing. Call ahead to book pony treks/riding.

Boat trips

Craignish Cruises, *Ardfern by Lochgilphead, T01852-500247, T07747-023083, www.craignish cruises.co.uk*. Runs private charters and fishing trips to the Sound of Jura, Corryvreckan and Garvellachs, from £38 for a 3-hr Corryvreckan wildlife trip.

Venture West, *Dunrostan Farm, Achnamara, T07789-071188, www.venture-west.co.uk*. Day trips to Islay, Jura, Colonsay, Iona and Staffa, also 2-hr trips across the Corryvrechan whirlpool (£35/25) and to the Garvellach islands.

Bus

West Coast Motors (T01586-552319, www.westcoastmotors.co.uk) run buses throughout Argyll several times daily Mon-Fri. There are **Citylink** buses between **Glasgow** and **Campbeltown** that pass through **Lochgilphead**, **Tarbert** and **Inveraray**, and to and from **Oban**. For timetables visit the **West Coast Motors** website.

Cycle hire

Crinan Cycles (34 Argyll St, Lochgilphead, T01546-603511, Mon-Sat 0930-1730), bikes for rent, also parts and repairs and will advise on routes and provide maps. **Rusty Cycle Shed** (Barr Bheag, Taynuilt, T07791-974152, www.rcscycles.co.uk, Apr-Oct). Bike hire and shop.

Kintyre *Colour map 5, A2/3 and B2.*

stunningly beautiful garden on 'God's island'

The long peninsula of Kintyre is probably best known as the inspiration for Paul McCartney's phenomenally successful 1970s dirge, *Mull of Kintyre*, but don't let that put you off. Historic Kintyre may be isolated but it's also packed with great scenery, wildlife and beaches, which attract the experienced surfer and windsurfer alike.

Hardy walkers also have the opportunity to explore the 100-mile **Kintyre Way** ⓘ *www. kintyreway.com*, stretching from Tarbert harbour to Dunaverty in the south. The peninsula would be an island, were it not for the mile-long isthmus between West and East Loch Tarbert, a fact not lost on King Magnus Barefoot of Norway. In the 11th century he signed a treaty with the Scottish king, Malcolm Canmore, giving him all the land he could sail round, and promptly had his men drag his longboat across the narrow isthmus, thus adding Kintyre to his kingdom.

Tarbert *Colour map 5, A3.*

The fishing village of Tarbert sits at the head of East Loch Tarbert, in a sheltered bay backed by forested hills, and is one of the most attractive ports on the west coast. Tarbert (the name derives from the Gaelic *An Tairbeart*, meaning 'isthmus') has a long tradition of fishing, and in the 18th and 19th centuries was a major herring port. Today, prawns and other shellfish are the main catch and though there is still a sizeable fleet, fishing has declined in importance to the local economy. Tourism is now a major source of income, with yachties in particular swelling local coffers when the **Scottish Series**, the second largest yacht race in the UK, sails into the picturesque natural harbour in late May.

Overlooking the harbour is the dramatically sited ruin of Robert the Bruce's 14th-century **castle**. There's not much left to see, other than the five-storey 15th-century keep. It's unsafe to investigate the ruins too closely, but the view alone is worth the walk. There are steps leading up to the castle, next to the **Loch Fyne Gallery** on Harbour Street. Behind the castle there are several marked trails leading up into the hills, with great views over Loch Fyne and the islands. Less strenuous is the short walk at the end of Garvel Road, on the north side of the harbour, which leads to the beach. At the end of East Pier road, beyond the Cowal Ferry, is yet another good walk, to the **Shell Beaches**. One mile south, you can also explore the lovely gardens at **Stonefield Castle Hotel**, see Where to stay, page 69.

Gigha *Colour map 5, A2. www.gigha.org.uk.*
The small island of Gigha (pronounced *Gee-a* with a hard 'g') translates from Norse as 'God's Island'. A grand claim, perhaps, but there's no question that this most accessible of islands is also one of the loveliest (and it's pretty much midge-free). It's only a 20-minute ferry ride away, and is only seven miles by one mile, so it can be visited easily in a day, which is just about enough time to appreciate why the Vikings loved it so much. Like so many of the Hebridean islands, Gigha has had a long list of owners, including various branches of the MacNeils and, more recently, in 1944, Sir James Horlick, he of bedtime drink fame. Now, though, the islanders are the proud owners of their own little piece of paradise, thanks to a successful buy-out in 2001.

It was Horlick who created the islanders self-proclaimed 'Jewel in the Crown'; the wonderful **Achamore Gardens** ⓘ *1 mile south of the ferry terminal, T01583-505275, www.achamoregardenstrust.co.uk, daily 0900-dusk, £3*. Thanks to Gigha's mild climate, the 50-acre woodland garden has an amazing variety of tropical plants, including rhododendrons, azaleas and camellias. The sight of albino peacocks and palm trees may have you doubting this is a Scottish island at all. There are two marked walks, starting from the walled garden. Managed by the Isle of Gigha Heritage Trust, a three-year, £600,000 garden restoration project has ensured Gigha's 'jewel' continues to shine for years to come.

The island's other delights include some good walks, white sandy beaches and fantastic views across to Jura on one side and Kintyre on the other. One of the best walks is to take the path left after the nine-hole golf course, signed Ardaily, past Mill Loch to the **Mill** on the west shore. The views from here are just magnificent. Another good idea is to walk, or cycle to the peninsula of **Eilean Garbh** at the north of the island. About half a mile beyond Kinererach Farm a path leads left to the peninsula where two crescent-shaped beaches are separated by a thin spit of land. And if the weather's good enough for a picnic, make sure you try some of the island's famously distinctive cheese. For details on ferries, see Transport, page 70.

Essential Kintyre

Finding your feet

There is at least one flight daily (35 minutes) from Glasgow to Campbeltown. The airport is at Machrihanish, three miles west of the town. For times and reservations and for transport details to and from the airport, T01586-553797, or visit the **Flybe** website www.flybe.com. There are several daily **Citylink buses** (www.citylink.co.uk), from Glasgow to Campbeltown (4½ hours) via Inveraray, Lochgilphead, Kennacraig and Tarbert.

Getting around

Public transport on Kintyre has improved, though still requires patience. On the west coast there's a regular (daily) bus service running between Campbeltown, Tarbert, Lochgilphead and Glasgow that also stops at the Kennacraig ferry terminal (for crossings to Islay). From Tarbert to Claonaig (for ferries to Lochranza on Arran) and Skipness there are buses Monday to Saturday. A bus also covers the quiet east route between Campbeltown and Carradale. Details are available from **Argyll & Bute Council** (T01546-602127), or **Tarbert** (Centre, Harbour Street, T01880-739138, open April to October). See Transport, page 70.

Campbeltown and around *Colour map 5, B2.*

At the southern end of the Kintyre Peninsula is Campbeltown, once home to 34 whisky distilleries and a large fishing fleet. Still the largest town in Kintyre, the two remaining distilleries hint at the town's decline in fortune, though the **Campbeltown Heritage Centre** ⓘ *Big Kiln St, T01586-551400, www.campbeltownheriatgecentre.co.uk, May-Sep Mon-Thu 1130-1630, £2*, richly documents its history. Six miles west lies **Machrihanish** and until recently a secretive military airbase beyond which miles of golden sands and gigantic Atlantic breakers beckon beachcombers and experienced wave-sailors alike. Nearby is a dramatic 18-hole championship golf course. The beach can be approached either by walking north from the village, or south from the car park on the main A83 to Tayinloan and Tarbert, where it leaves the coast.

If the weather's good, it's worth taking a walk up to **Beinn Ghulean**, which overlooks the town and loch. Follow the signs for the A83 to Machrihanish until you reach Witchburn Road. After passing the creamery on your left, turn left into Tomaig Road and continue until you come to a wooden gate. Cross over the stile and follow the track through the fields, crossing two more stiles, before you reach the Forest Enterprise sign which marks the start of the walk. It's about four miles there and back from the end of Tomaig Road.

One of the most popular day trips is to the uninhabited **Davaar Island**, connected to the peninsula by a tidal breakwater. Here you can see the cave painting of the Crucifixion, completed in secret by a local artist in 1877. The island can be visited at low tide from Kildalloig Point, a couple of miles east of town. Check tide times at the tourist office before setting out.

It's only a short drive south from Campbeltown to the tip of the peninsula, the **Mull of Kintyre**. There's nothing much to see in this bleak, storm-battered place, apart from the coast of Ireland, a mere 12 miles away and clearly visible on a good day. The road out to the lighthouse, built in 1788 and remodelled by Robert Stevenson, grandfather of Robert Louis, is both twisty and spectacular. Above the lighthouse is a small poignant cairn in memory to military personnel killed when their helicopter crashed in bad weather two decades ago on the remote hillside. It's possible to walk from here up to Machrihanish (about 10 miles), past the ruined township of **Balmavicar** and the **Largiebaan Bird Reserve**. The views are great and there's a chance of seeing golden eagles.

The southernmost village on Kintyre is **Southend**, a bleak, windswept place with a wide sandy beach. At the east end of the beach, jutting out on a rocky promontory, are the scant remains of **Dunaverty Castle**, once a MacDonald stronghold, where 300 Royalists were brutally massacred in 1647 by the Covenanting army of the Earl of Argyll, despite having already surrendered. To the west of Southend, below the cliffs, is the ruined 13th-century **Keil Chapel**, which is said to mark the spot where St Columba first set foot on Scottish soil, before heading north to Iona. Close by is a pair of footprints carved into the rock, known as Columba's footprints.

The slow and winding single track B842 meanders up the east coast from Campbeltown to Skipness and Claonaig, departure point for the ferry to Arran. The scenery en route is gentle and pleasant, with nice views of Arran, and there are some worthwhile places to stop.

Some 10 miles further up the coast are the idyllic ruins of **Saddell Abbey**, a Cistercian establishment founded by Somerled in 1160. The abbey fell into ruin in the early 16th century and much of the stone was used in the building of 18th-century Saddell Castle for the Bishop of Argyll. Though little remains, there are some impressive medieval grave slabs, depicting knights, monks, ships, animals and other images.

A few miles further north is the village of **Carradale**, the only place of any size on the east coast, nestling in the sandy sweep of beautiful Carradale Bay. There are several pleasant marked walks through the woods between the B842 and the shore. The shortest of these walks (with green waymarkers) starts from the Network Centre (see below) and is a mile long. There's a three-mile walk with red waymarkers which starts at the **Port Na Storm** car park and follows the forest road to the left. After 150 yds the route turns left again at the road junction. A mile further on, you turn right off the road and follow the track up to the summit of **Cnoc-nan Gabhor**, from where there are great views of Kintyre and across to Arran. A third walk (six miles; blue waymarkers) also starts from the Port Na Storm car park. This time the route heads right at the junction 150 yds beyond the car park and then runs north along the shore, with a chance of seeing dolphins and basking sharks. The path then swings west towards the road, then turns south with views of Carradale Glen.

About 12 miles north of Carradale the B842 ends at **Claonaig**, which is actually nothing more than a slipway for the ferry to Arran. From here the B8001 heads west to meet the A83 near the Kennacraig ferry pier. A dead-end road runs north for a few miles to the tiny village of **Skipness**, where you can visit the substantial ruins of the 13th-century Skipness Castle and nearby chapel.

Listings Kintyre

Tourist information

Tarbert

Tarbert iCentre
Harbour St, T01880-739138.

Campbeltown

Campbeltown iCentre
Makinnon House, The Pier, T01586-556162.

Where to stay

There are dozens of good B&Bs around Tarbert. Call the local **iCentre** for details (see above). There are several self-catering options run by the **Heritage Trust** on Gigha island. Visit www.gigha.org.uk for further details.

££££ Kilberry Inn
West of Tarbert on the B8024, T01880-770223, www.kilberryinn.com. Easter-Oct and at weekends in the winter.
5 rooms. The restaurant with rooms offers superb Scottish meat and seafood dishes (**£££**), and cosy comforts including a roaring log fire. Has a glowing reputation for serving fabulous food, especially seafood and locally sourced beef and lamb that has won the restaurant plaudits by national newspaper food critics. Dogs and children over 12 are welcome. Note that internet and phone reception is very poor, which adds to the feeling of being remote.

££££-£££ Stonefield Castle Hotel
2 miles north of Tarbert, on the A82 to Lochgilphead, T0843-1787141, www.bespokehotels.com.
36 rooms. Dating from 1837, this impressive former castle is a fine example of Scottish baronial architecture and provides guests with comfort, eye-catching views of Loch Fyne and 60 acres of woodland garden to walk off the delicious 4-course dinner.

£££ Anchor Hotel
By the harbour, T01800-552319, www.lochfyne-scotland.co.uk.
Very friendly and comfortable hotel well situated on the harbourfront. Accommodation in double, twin and family rooms or indulge yourself in the luxurious barge for something a bit different (and more expensive **££££**). Good food in the

hotel restaurant. No car park but plentiful parking on the street outside.

£££-££ Gigha Hotel
Isle of Gigha, T01583-505254,
www.gighahotel.co.uk.
Comfortable, friendly hotel with double/twin rooms and some looking out over the sea. Offers very good food in the dining room or less formal bistro. Also has 2 self-catering cottages.

Camping

££ The Isthmus Camping Pods
Just outside Tarbert off the A83 heading west,
T01880-821554, www.theisthmus.co.uk.
Sitting back off the road between Kennacraig ferry and Tarbert are these wonderful wooden camping pods offering more comfort for those who prefer their camping to come with heating and proper insulation from the heat and cold. Pods sleep up to 5 and this price is based on 2 adults with extra small people £10 each per night and dogs can stay too for £8. Good café-bistro on site with pizza oven.

£ Muasdale Holiday Park
T01583-421559, www.muasdale holidays.com.
22 miles south of Tarbert, off the A83 at the tiny village of Muasdale is this lovely site beside a glorious white-sand beach with stunning views of Islay and Jura. There are 8 beachside tent pitches, plus 'micro chalets' for those who prefer more comfort and also 2 self-catering apartments.

Festivals

Aug Mull of Kintyre Music Festival. If you're around Campbeltown in mid-Aug don't miss 3 days of the best in traditional Celtic music. **Sep Gigha Music Festival**, held early in the month.

Transport

Air
There is at least 1 flight daily (35 mins), all year round from Campbeltown airport (at Machrihanish) to and from **Glasgow** with **Flybe** (T01586-553797, www.flybwe.com).

Bus
There are 5 buses a day daily from Campbeltown to **Machrihanish** (for airport), **Saddell**, 25 mins; **Carradale**, 45 mins, and to **Southend**, 25 mins. Ask at the **iCentre** in Campbeltown.

Ferry
There is a car and passenger ferry from **Portavadie** on the Cowal Peninsula to **Tarbert**, daily every hour Apr-Oct, 25 mins, less frequent departures in winter.

Ferries leave from **Kennacraig**, 5 miles south of Tarbert, to **Colonsay** (see page 94) and **Islay** (see page 97).

A small car and passenger ferry leaves from **Tayinloan** to the ferry pier at Ardminish on **Gigha**, Mon-Sat 0800-1800, Sun 1100-1700, 20 mins. For times and fares visit www.calmac.co.uk.

Cowal Peninsula and the Clyde Coast *Colour map 3, C6.*
hiking and biking through mountain forests

The Cowal Peninsula reaches out into the Firth of Clyde, framed by Loch Fyne and Loch Long. This is the most visited part of Argyll due to its proximity to Glasgow, but, despite the summer hordes, many of whom come for the **Cowal Highland Gathering** in late August, much of it is undisturbed. Most people head straight for the rather drab main ferry port and traditional Clyde seaside resort of Dunoon. More adventurous souls enjoy the forests and mountains of Argyll Forest Park in the north or the peace of the southwest coastline.

Argyll Forest Park

The northern part of the peninsula is largely covered by the sprawling Argyll Forest Park which extends from Loch Lomond south to Holy Loch. This area contains the most stunning scenery in Cowal, and includes the **Arrochar Alps**, a range of rugged peaks north of Glen Croe which offer some of the best climbing in Argyll. The most famous of these is anvil-like Ben Arthur (2891 ft), better known as **The Cobbler**. Less imposing are the hills south of Glen Croe, between Loch Goil and Loch Long, in an area known as Argyll's Bowling Green (not because it's flat, but an English corruption of the Gaelic *Baile na Greine*, meaning 'sunny hamlet'). There are many footpaths and cycle tracks threading their way through the park. Details of five are outlined in the excellent *Argyll Forest Park Guide*, which is available to download from the Forestry Commission website, https://scotland.forestry.gov.uk.

Arrochar to Dunoon

The gateway to Cowal, Arrochar sits at the head of Loch Long on the main A83, only a few miles west of Tarbet and the shores of Loch Lomond. It's a small, uninspiring place but the setting is dramatic, with The Cobbler towering overhead. A few miles beyond Arrochar, on the shores of Loch Long, is **Ardgarten**, which is an excellent base for walking and mountain biking around the many trails through Argyll Forest Park and a start-point for climbing The Cobbler (seven hours return trip). From Ardgarten, the A83 climbs steeply up Glen Croe to reach one of Scotland's classic viewpoints at the top of the pass, the **Rest and Be Thankful** (built under Major Caulfeild after the '45). The hordes of like-minded tourists, eager for that memorable photograph, cannot detract from the majestic views of the surrounding craggy peaks. If you want to spend more time exploring the park, stay at the excellent Forestry Commission cabins.

The road forks at the viewpoint. The A83 continues towards **Inveraray**, see page 62, and the single-track B828 heads southwest to meet the B839, which runs down to the village of **Lochgoilhead**, in a beautiful setting on Loch Goil. There are several hotels and B&Bs as well as an unsightly village of self-catering holiday chalets next door. At the end of the road, several miles down the west side of Loch Goil, are the ruins of 15th-century **Carrick Castle**.

The A83 meanwhile runs down through **Glen Kinglas** to reach the village of **Cairndow**, at the head of Loch Fyne. Here, gastronomes must decide whether to drive south down the A815 and east side of Loch Fyne for Inver Cottage, by Castle Lachlan, or continue towards Inveraray and **Clachan**, to dine in the ever-popular **Loch Fyne Oyster Bar**, see page 65. At the southern end of Loch Eck, at Benmore, is **Benmore Botanic Garden** ⓘ *T01369-706261, Apr-Sep daily 1000-1800, Mar and Oct 1000-1700, £6.50, concessions £5.50, children free*, a lovely woodland garden and offshoot of the Royal Botanic Garden in Edinburgh. Its 120 acres are laid out with over 300 species of rhododendron and feature an avenue of giant redwoods.

Dunoon

The largest town in Cowal, with around 8000 inhabitants, is Dunoon, one-time favourite holiday destination for Glaswegians, who came in their hordes on board the many paddle steamers that sailed "doon the watter" from Glasgow. Dunoon still attracts many visitors, but the town's economy has suffered following the closure of the Holy Loch US nuclear submarine in the 1990s. Nevertheless, Dunoon still comes to life during the **Cowal Highland Gathering**, see page 73. There's not much to detain you here, although the **Castle House Museum** ⓘ *Easter-Oct Mon-Sat 1000-1600, £3, concessions £2.50, children free*, on Castle Hill overlooking the town offers an insight into clan history and the role of the Clyde in wartime, and allows you to bone up on Cowal's often grisly past.

The southwest

One of the most beautiful parts of Argyll is the southwest of Cowal, particularly the route down to the little village of **Tighnabruaich**. The A8003 runs down the west side of Loch Riddon and there are few lovelier sights than the view from this road across the **Kyles of Bute**, the narrow straits that separate Cowal from the island of Bute. Tighnabruaich gets busy in the summer with visitors who come here to enjoy the best sailing on the west coast. A few miles southwest of Kames is **Portavadie**, on the west coast of Cowal. A CalMac car and passenger ferry sails from here to Tarbert, on the Kintyre Peninsula, saving a lot of time if you're heading for the islands of Islay, Jura or Colonsay.

Helensburgh

Overlooking the Clyde is the town of Helensburgh, its wide, grid-plan streets lined with elegant Georgian houses. The town is most famously known for its connection with the great Glasgow architect, **Charles Rennie Mackintosh**. In the upper part of the town is **Hill House** ① *Upper Colquhoun St, T01436-673900, Apr-Oct daily 1130-1700, £10.50, concessions £7.50, family £24.50, tearoom open 1330-1630*, one of the best examples of Mackintosh's work. The house was designed for Glasgow publisher Walter Blackie in 1902-1904, and is managed by the National Trust for Scotland. In accordance with Blackie's wish to have a house with an individual feel, it is a masterpiece of balanced perfection and artistry with great attention to detail. The use of light and dark, and the symbolism of the floral patterns – hallmarks of his personal art nouveau style – are in evidence. After exploring the house, visit the cosy tearoom in the converted kitchen. Trains run from Glasgow Queen Street station to Helensburgh Central.

Listings Cowal Peninsula and the Clyde Coast

Tourist information

Dunoon

Dunoon iCentre
*7 Alexandra Parade, T01369-703785.
Open all year.*

Where to stay

£££ Royal An Lochan
*Tighnabruaich, T01700-811239,
www.theroyalanlochan.co.uk.*
This elegant hotel with its own moorings boasts exquisite dining (**£££**), beautiful decor and many a fine dram in the snug bar. Rooms at the front with views across the Kyles of Bute are a wee bit more expensive.

£££-££ Kames Hotel
Kames, T01700-811489, www.kames-hotel.com.
Offers 10 en suite rooms, terrific views down the Kyles and delicious food. The hotel bar is a great place to enjoy a drink and can be very lively.

Self-catering

Portavadie
*Loch Fyne, T01700-811075,
www.portavadie.com.*
On the shores of Loch Fyne near the ferry crossing to Tarbert is this stunning new marina/luxury spa with self-catering accommodation and restaurants. Accommodation ranges from luxury apartments to cosy cottages. The £10 million spa and leisure complex features indoor pool, saunas, gym, outdoor spa pools and Scotland's largest outdoor heated infinity pool. Also has an excellent fine dining restaurant and **Kitchen & Bar** for more humble fare.

Camping

Glendaruel Caravan/Campsite
T01369-820267.
Terrific secluded location, well maintained and close to amenities.

Restaurants

£££-££ Inver Restaurant
Strathlachlan on B8000, past Strachur, T01369-860537, www.inverrestaurant.co.uk.
Mouth-watering starters, succulent game and hand-dived scallops, to-die-for desserts and homely ambience. A gem so book ahead. Recommended.

£££-££ Royal An Lochan
Tighnabruaich, T01700-811239 (see Where to stay, above).
Seafood is a speciality at this very fine hotel restaurant but there are also Scottish classics such as game terrine, venison with red onion marmalade and cranachan.

Festivals

Aug Cowal Highland Gathering, held on the last weekend of the month. The world's largest gathering culminates in a spectacular march of massed pipes and drums through the streets of Dunoon.

Oct Cowalfest (www.cowalfest.org). An action-packed week-long walking and arts festival in early Oct.

Transport

Bus
West Coast Motors, T01586-552319, run 3 (No 386) buses Mon-Sat from the Dunoon ferry terminal to **Inveraray** via **Benmore Gardens**, **Strachur** and **Cairndow**. The 1st bus leaves at 0850. Alternatively, there are at least 5 buses daily (No 484) Mon-Sat from Dunoon ferry terminal to **Lochgoilhead**.

Ferry
Ferries from **Gourock** to **Dunoon** are operated by **Argyll Ferries** (www.argyllferries.co.uk), with train connections from Glasgow Central. There is also a ferry service from **McInroy's Point**, 2 miles from Gourock, with **Western Ferries**, www.western-ferries.co.uk. It leaves every 15-20 mins during peak times and runs daily 0730-2400.
   West Coast Motors buses No 477/478/479 run several times daily (Mon-Sat) from Dunoon to the **CalMac** ferry terminal at Portavadie via **Tighnabruaich** and **Kames**. The same buses also go to the **CalMac** ferry at **Colintraive** for the crossing to **Rhubodach** (**Bute**) and then continue into **Rothesay**, 1 hr 40 mins.

Isle of Bute

picturesque island that's best explored on foot or on two wheels

Barely a stone's throw off the south coast of Cowal is the island of Bute, another favourite holiday destination for people from Glasgow and Ayrshire, who come here in droves during the busy summer months. But though the island is small (15 miles long by five miles wide), it's deceptively easy to escape the hordes, who tend to congregate around the east coast resort of Rothesay, leaving the delights of the sparsely populated west coast free for those who enjoy a bit of peace and quiet.

Rothesay
The sole town on Bute is Rothesay, with its handsome period mansions lining the broad sweep of bay, its elegant promenade lined with palm trees and the distinctive Art Nouveau former **Winter Gardens**, now refurbished and renamed the Bute Discovery Centre, complete with a cinema, restaurant and the island's iCentre. **Rothesay Castle**

Essential Isle of Bute

Finding your feet

West Coast Motors run buses to Rothesay from Tighnabruaich in southwest Cowal at least once a day from April to October, the journey takes one hour. Timetables for all routes can be downloaded from their website, www.westcoastmotors.co.uk. Bute is easily accessible from Glasgow. Take a train from Glasgow Central to the ferry terminal at Wemyss Bay, and from there it's a 35-minute crossing to Rothesay. The ferries leave every 45 minutes from 0715 until 1945 (later on Friday, Saturday and Sunday). For times and fares see www.calmac.co.uk. A **CalMac** car/passenger ferry also makes the five-minute crossing from Colintraive to Rhubodach, at the northern end of Bute, daily every 30 minutes or hour from Easter until the end of August (Monday-Saturday 0530-2055 and Sunday 0830-2055).

Getting around

The bus service provided by **West Coast Motors** is good, though limited on Sunday. There is an excellent bus service from Rothesay to Mount Stuart. Passengers coming into Rothesay can take the No 90/490 (or on Sundays the No 493) **West Coast Motors** service to Kilchattan Bay leaves from a stop just outside the ferry terminal.

Tip...

The best way to see Bute is still by bike, with roads fairly quiet and in good condition beyond Rothesay.

ⓘ *T01700-502691, Apr-Sep daily 0930-1730, Oct daily 1000-1600, Nov-Mar Sat-Wed 1000-1600, £5, concessions £4, children £3.* One thing men must do before leaving Rothesay is visit the palatial **Victorian public toilets** ⓘ *Easter-Sep daily 0800-2100, Oct-Mar daily 0900-1700.* This architectural gem enables gents to 'spend a penny' in style.

★ Mount Stuart

T01700-505808, www.mountstuart.com. House and grounds open Apr to end Oct daily 1200-1700, grounds 1000-1800. House and grounds £11.50, concessions £9.50, children £6.75; grounds only £6.50, concessions £5, children £3.50. Tickets include 1-hr guided tour, book in advance.

One of Bute's main attractions is Mount Stuart, a unique Victorian Gothic house set in 300 acres of lush woodland gardens, three miles south of Rothesay. This magnificent architectural fantasy reflects the Third Marquess of Bute's passion for astrology, astronomy, mysticism and religion, and the sheer scale and grandeur of the place almost beggars belief. This is truly one of the great country houses of Scotland and displays breathtaking craftsmanship in marble and stained glass, as well as a fine collection of family portraits and Italian antiques. Much of the existing house dates from 1877, and was built following a terrible fire which destroyed the original, built in 1719 by the Second Earl of Bute. Equally impressive are the landscaped gardens and woodlands, established by the Third Earl of Bute (1713-1792), who advised on the foundation of Kew Gardens in London, and the stunning visitor centre complete with audio-visuals and restaurant. The present owner is Johnny Dumfries (only the Daily Mail calls him the Seventh Marquess of Bute), former racing driver who won Le Mans in 1988 and who, famously, gave up his house for the wedding of Stella McCartney, daughter of Paul, in 2003. It's worth spending a whole day here in order to take in the splendour of the house and to explore the beautiful gardens. And if the weather's fine, why not bring a picnic and enjoy the wonderful sea views.

Other places around the island

Just before Mount Stuart is the tidy little village of **Kerrycroy**, designed by the wife of the Second Marquess of Bute and featuring an interesting mix of building styles. South of Mount Stuart and the village of Kingarth is **Kilchattan Bay**, an attractive bay of pink sands and the start of a fine walk down to Glencallum Bay, in the southeastern corner of the island.

Southwest of Kilchattan Bay, **St Blane's Chapel** is a 12th-century ruin in a beautifully peaceful spot near the southern tip of the island. The medieval church stands on the site of an earlier monastery, established in the sixth century by St Blane, nephew of St Catan, after whom Kilchattan is named. The ruin can be reached by road from Rothesay, or as part of the walk from Kilchattan Bay. Four miles north of St Blane's, on the west coast, is **Scalpsie Bay**, the nicest beach on the island and a good place for seal spotting. A little further north is **St Ninian's Point**, looking across to the island of **Inchmarnock**. At the end of the beach are the ruins of a sixth-century chapel, dedicated to St Ninian.

The Highland–Lowland dividing line passes through the middle of Bute at Loch Fad, which separates the hilly and uninhabited northern half of the island and the rolling farmland of the south. The highest point on the island is **Windy Hill** (913 ft) in the north, from where there are great views across the island. A less strenuous walk is up **Canada Hill**, a few miles southwest of Rothesay, above Loch Fad. Walk along Craigmore promenade and turn off at the old pier to **Ardencraig Gardens**. Then continue uphill along the golf course to the top of the hill for great views of the Firth of Clyde.

Bute

Kilchattan Bay to Glencallum Bay walk

A longer walk is the circular route from Kilchattan Bay south to Glencallum Bay and back, via St Blane's chapel (see above). The bay was once a final staging point for boats bound for overseas. The walk is five miles in total. Allow about four hours. There are buses to and from Rothesay. The route is waymarked, but if you want to take a map, it's OS Landranger sheet 63 or Explorer 362. The Rothesay Discovery Centre (iCentre) carries a full stock of maps (see page 76).

Follow the signpost for 'Kelspoke Path' beside Kiln Villas and take the track, which climbs steadily before turning sharply back on itself. Go through a gate and shortly before the next gate turn right. Follow the rough track, which swings right, then left over open ground to the ruins of Kelspoke Castle.

Continue along the grassy path, past a reservoir on your right, then cross the stile and go down and across a small burn. Turn left and follow the burn, before heading right to join the shore path and follow this past the lighthouse on your left and around the headland to **Glencallum Bay**. Continue round the shoreline and at the far end of the bay follow the waymarks as the path climbs to cross the headland. The path then levels out and from here there are great views across to the mountains of Arran.

The path then reaches the col above **Loch na Leighe**. Drop down to the loch and follow the waymarks south over open ground. Before reaching a farm called The Plan, go right over two footbridges, then left below a low ridge. Keep to the right of the buildings, following the waymarks across open ground to the stile that crosses to the ruins of **St Blane's Chapel** (see above). Leave the chapel by the gap in the boundary wall and go through a gate, turning left on a clear track which climbs steadily to a stile. Cross the stile and turn right, following the edge of the field down to a gate. Walk uphill on the left side of the field to **Suidhe Hill**. At the top of the field, cross the fence and keep going, turning right at the corner of the fence. Go through a gate at the next corner and look for a waymark about 100 yds downhill. Follow the path steeply downhill, passing through a kissing gate and staying close to the wall. You then reach a drying green at the foot of the hill; turn left and follow a path around the buildings and back onto the road at **Kilchattan**.

Listings Isle of Bute *maps page 75.*

Tourist information

Rothesay iCentre
Isle of Bute Discovery Centre, Victoria St,
T01700-507043. Open all year.

Where to stay

There is plentiful accommodation in Rothesay, much of it similar in price and quality. Ask at the **iCentre** (see above).

£££ Chandlers Hotel
Ascog, T01700-505577,
www.visitchandlers.com.
9 spacious and tastefully furnished rooms and very good food in the restaurant, staff are very friendly and helpful, all making for a comfortable and relaxing stay.

££ Kingarth Hotel
Kingarth, in the south of the island, T01700-
831662, www.kingarthhotel.co.uk.
Quiet, cosy 1782 inn offering genuine hospitality, terrific seafood or steak platters (**££-£**) and the chance to banter with the locals. A wonderful place to enjoy the food and ambience.

Restaurants

£ West End Café
1-3 Gallowgate, Rothesay, T01700-503596.
Tue-Sun.
It is a must while you are on Bute to sample the fish and chips at this award-winning chippy. Phone ahead to avoid the massive queues in summer.

Festivals

May Isle of Bute Jazz Festival, held during the May Bank Holiday weekend.
Jul Isle of Bute Dunoon Sheepdog Trials and **Inveraray Highland Games**.

Transport

Bus and ferry
Bus Nos 477/478/479 (Mon-Sat) travel to the ferry terminal at **Rhubodach** and on crossing, stops in **Kames** and **Tighnabruaich** before reaching **Dunoon**, 1 hr 40 mins.

Mull
& Iona

Whether bathed in sunshine or shrouded in mist, each of Scotland's isles possesses a magical quality. The Isle of Mull, a 50-minute sail from Oban and the third largest of the Hebridean islands, is no different. Teeming with wildlife and a gateway to the tiny and spiritual isle of Iona, Mull (derived from the Norse meaning 'high, bold headland') supports 2800 inhabitants and remains one of Scotland's most popular Hebridean isles. Indeed, Mull, just 26 miles east to west and 24 miles north to south, has enough going for it to appeal to most tastes: spectacular mountain scenery, 300 miles of wild coastline, castles, a narrow-gauge railway, fine cuisine and, in Tobermory, one of Scotland's prettiest coastal villages, which also served as the main setting for the cult children's TV series, *Balamory*.

Craignure to Tobermory *Colour map 3, B4.*
The arrival point for visitors is the village of Craignure. Some 1½ miles south of here is **Torosay Castle and Gardens**. The castle has been closed to the public since 2011 but there is a lovely walk from Craignure.

A couple of miles east of Torosay is **Duart Castle** ① *T01680-812309, www.duartcastle. com, Apr Sun-Thu 1100-1600, May to mid-Oct daily 1030-1700, £6.50, concessions £5.80, children 5-14 £3.25.* The 13th-century ancestral seat of the Clan Maclean stands imperiously at the end of a promontory, commanding impressive views over Loch Linnhe and the Sound of Mull. Every five years (the next is in 2022) the castle and Mull host the Clan Maclean Gathering. The castle's main feature is the tower house, built in the late 14th century when it became the main residence of the Macleans of Duart. Today it's a fascinating place to visit, with many relics and artefacts on display. There's also a tearoom serving home-baked goodies and lunches.

Midway between Craignure and Tobermory, on the main A849, is the pretty village of **Salen**, where a fantastic culinary experience awaits at **Mediterranea** (see Restaurants, page 84). Salen, situated at the narrowest point on the island, has several sites of interest on its doorstep. Two miles south is Mull's tiny and only airfield, adjacent to which is the excellent **Glenforsa Hotel** (see Where to stay, page 83) where majestic views down the Sound of Mull can also be enjoyed. One mile north of Salen, overlooking the bay, is the ruin of **Aros Castle**, built in the 14th century and one of the strongholds of the Lords of the Isles. Tradition holds that the treasure of the Spanish galleon sunk in Tobermory Bay in 1588, was recovered by the Macleans and lies buried beneath Aros Castle.

Four miles southwest of Salen, near Gruline and Loch Ba, is the **MacQuarrie Mausoleum**, which houses the remains of Major-General Lachlan MacQuarrie (1761-1824). He took over as Governer-General of New South Wales from the unpopular William Bligh, formerly of the *Bounty*, and became known as the 'Father of Australia'. The mausoleum is maintained by the NTS, on behalf of the National Trust of Australia.

Essential Mull and Iona

Finding your feet

Mull is served by regular car/passenger ferry services, mostly from Oban (45 minutes) but also from Kilchoan on the Ardnamurchan Peninsula and Lochaline on the Morvern Peninsula. Once on the island you can get to most places by bus. Buses on Mull are operated by **West Coast Motors**, www.westcoastmotors.co.uk, and their website lists all timetables. Services given in the Transport section are for April to October. Winter services are less frequent. There are regular five-minute sailings to Iona from Fionnphort. For ferry times and fares, see www.calmac.co.uk. See Transport, page 86.

Tobermory *Colour map 3, B4.*
There is surely no prettier or distinctive port in the west of Scotland than Tobermory, Mull's main town and setting for the popular children's TV series *Balamory*, which was produced until 2005. Tobermory got its name from a small settlement once situated northwest of the current town where there's a spring known in Gaelic as *Tobar* (well) *Mhoire* (Mary). The brightly painted houses that line Tobermory's harbourfront date from the late 18th century when the British Fisheries Society built Tobermory as a planned herring port. During the Second World War, Tobermory was the home of

the naval training base HMS Western Isles, which became the Royal Navy's anti-submarine training school, under the leadership of the much-feared Gilbert Stephenson. Nowadays, a few remaining fishing boats, plus dozens of yachts, bob at anchor in the protected waters of the natural harbour. Lying at the bottom of the harbour is a galleon of the Spanish Armada, which sank in mysterious circumstances, along with its treasure of gold doubloons. Remnants of a Spanish galleon can be seen on Main Street in the wonderful **Mull Museum** ① T01688-301100, Easter-Oct Mon-Fri 1000-1600, free, housed in an old bakery. Raining or not, it's worth visiting to get an insight into the island's fascinating and tragic history.

Best boat trips
Mull Charters
Sea Life Surveys
Turus Mara
See page 86

The harbourfront (Main Street) is where you'll find most of what you want: tour agencies, hotels, guesthouses, restaurants, pubs and the award-winning baker. Mercifully, though, it's free from the tartan tat that blights so many other tourist hot-spots. At the foot of the main road down to the harbour is the tiny **Tobermory Distillery** ① T01688-302647, www.tobermorydistillery.com, Mon-Fri 1000-1700, Sat-Sun 1000-1600, tours every hour £8-10 pp, which offers a guided tour rounded off with a sampling of one or more of the island's single malts. At the top of Back Brae, on Argyll Terrace, is **An Tobar** ① T01688-302211, www.comar.co.uk, café open Apr-Oct Mon-Sat 1000-1700, Oct-Feb Tue-Sat 1100-1600, an excellent arts centre housed in the old school and featuring a varied programme of exhibitions,

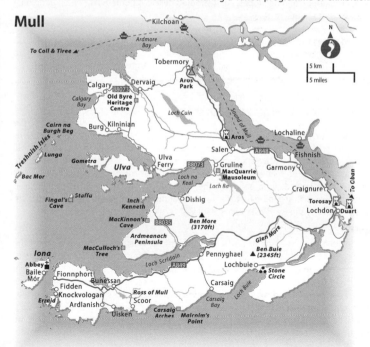

Mull

music and workshops. The café serves hot drinks, soups, toasties and home-baking, as well as daily specials and special pre-show suppers at 1830 in July and August. The famous touring **Mull Theatre** ① *T01688-302828*, has its main venue and administration office at Druimfin, a mile or so south of Tobermory. The theatre company and An Tobar (see above) merged in 2011 to form Comar, a multi-arts organization that presents around 100 events a year across live music, theatre, visual arts, dance, film, literature and comedy.

West coast Mull *Colour map 3, B3.*

Mull's west coast is where you'll find some of the island's most stunning scenery. The B8073 winds its way anti-clockwise from Tobermory in a series of twists and turns as it follows the contours of the coastline. The road climbs west from Tobermory then makes a dramatic descent, with hairpin bends, to Dervaig.

Dervaig is a lovely village of whitewashed cottages, beautifully situated at the head of Loch Cuin. Here sits **Kilmore Church**, with its unusual pencil-shaped spire. Until its closure in 2006, Dervaig was also the home of the smallest professional theatre in Britain. One mile beyond Dervaig take the turn-off to Torloisk to reach Glen Bellart and the highly informative **Old Byre Heritage Centre** ① *T01688-400229, www.old-byre.co.uk, Easter-Oct Mon-Fri 1030-1830, £4, concessions £3, children £2.* There are dozens of exhibits of the island's history, geology and flora and fauna, as well as a couple of films that highlight the history of Mull through the ages and its varied wildlife. Ask about the location of the nearby Neolithic standing stones. The tearoom's delicious home-baking is an additional treat, see Restaurants, page 84.

Five miles west of Dervaig is **Calgary Bay**, Mull's most beautiful beach ringed by steep wooded slopes with views across to Coll and Tiree. Calgary in Alberta, Canada, was named after the former township. Many emigrants were forcibly shipped to Canada from here during the Clearances. There are some wonderful paths through Calgary Wood, just past **Calgary Farmhouse Hotel**, including a half-hour circular walk.

Isle of Ulva *Colour map 3, B3.*

If you have the time and need to escape the hectic bustle of Mull, then take a day out on idyllic Ulva (meaning 'wolf island' in Norse), just off the west coast. You won't see any wolves around, but you're almost guaranteed to spot deer, golden eagles, buzzards and seals offshore. There are several woodland and coastal trails across the island, including one to the southwest where there are basalt columns similar to those on Staffa. Alternatively, you can follow the trail to the top of the hill for views across to the Cuillins on Skye (on a clear day), or else cross the causeway to Ulva's even smaller neighbour **Gometra**. It's worth stopping for a meal at the wonderful **Boathouse**, a licensed tearoom close to the ferry slip (see Restaurants, page 84).

Staffa *Colour map 3, B3.*

The tiny uninhabited island of Staffa, five miles off the west coast of Mull, is one of the most spectacular sights not just in Scotland but anywhere in the world. It consists of immense hexagonal, basalt pillars, which loom up out of the sea like a giant pipe organ. Staffa was formed 60 million years ago by the slow cooling of Tertiary basalt lavas. These have been carved by the pounding sea into huge cathedral-like caverns such as the mightily impressive **Fingal's Cave**. The sound of the sea crashing against the black crystalline columns made such an impression on Felix Mendelssohn in 1829 that he immortalized the island in his *Hebrides Overture*. The composer was obviously aware of its original name in Gaelic, which means 'the melodious cave'. You can land on the island –

if the weather is good enough – and walk into the cave via the causeway; an experience not be missed. But even if the seas are too rough, it's worth making the 90-minute boat trip just to witness the columns and cave.

South Mull *Colour map 3, B2/3 and C2/3.*

From Ulva ferry the B8073 heads east along the north shore of **Loch na Keal** then enters a wide flat valley, where the road forks east to Salen and west along the south shore of Loch na Keal. This part of Mull is dominated by **Ben More** (3170 ft), the island's highest mountain. All around is a spectacular region of high jutting mountains and deep glens, extending west to the **Ardmeanach Peninsula**. The peninsula may look impenetrable, but with the proper walking gear can be explored on foot. On the north coast, about a mile from the road, is the massive entrance to **MacKinnon's Cave**, which runs for about 100 yds back under the cliffs. Make sure to visit only at low tide. The area around the headland, now owned by the National Trust for Scotland, is known as **The Wilderness**. Near the headland is **MacCulloch's Tree**, a fossilized tree 40 ft high and thought to be 50 million years old, which was discovered in 1819. The tree is only accessible by a seven-mile footpath which begins at Burg Farm. You should have a map of the area and also time your arrival with low tide.

Mull's southernmost peninsula stretches west for 20 miles from the head of Loch Scridain as far as Iona. Most visitors use it merely as a route to Iona but there are a couple of interesting little detours along the way. A twisting side road leads south from Pennyghael over the hills and down to **Carsaig Bay**, from where you can head east or west along the shore for some dramatic coastal scenery. Two roads lead south from Bunessan. One leads to **Scoor**, near where is a great beach at Kilveockan. The other road splits near the coast: the left branch leads to **Uisken Bay**; the right-hand branch leads to **Ardlanish Bay**, each with a good beach.

The road ends at **Flonnphort**, the departure point for the small passenger-only ferry to Iona, just a mile across the Sound of Iona. The village is little more than a car park, a row of houses, a pub and a shop, but there are several inexpensive B&Bs for those arriving too late to make the crossing.

A road runs south from Fionnphort to **Knockvologan**, opposite **Erraid Island**, which is accessible at low tide. The island has literary connections, for it was here that Robert Louis Stevenson is believed to have written *Kidnapped*. **Balfour Bay** on the south of the island is named after the novel's hero who was shipwrecked here. The beach at Knovologan is a real find and there's a good chance you'll have it all to yourself. Park your car at Knovologan Farm, a few miles beyond Fldden Farm, and the stunning beach is a 10-minute walk. Even better, camp at the gloriously sited **Fidden Farm campsite** (T01681-700427).

Walks on Mull

Mull presents numerous walking opportunities, ranging from gentle forest trails to wild and dramatic coastal routes, or even a spot of Munro-bagging for the more intrepid. With the exception of the Cuillins on Skye, Mull's highest peak, **Ben More** (3170 ft) is the only Munro not on the mainland.

The trail starts at a lay-by on the B8035, at Dishig, and is fairly clear, though it can be tricky near the top. Return the same way, or more experienced climbers could continue down the narrow ridge to the eastern summit, **A'Chioch**, then descend the eastern face to the road that skirts **Loch Ba**. The views from the top

Tip...
OS Landranger maps 47, 48 and 49 cover the entire island.

are magnificent, across the other Hebridean islands and even as far as Ireland. If it's a cloudy day, it's worth postponing the ascent until there's clear weather. Allow around six hours for the round trip.

There are a couple of excellent coastal walks which start out from Carsaig Bay. A good path heads west along the shore to **Carsaig Arches** at Malcom's Point. The path runs below the cliffs out to the headland and then around it, and after about a mile reaches **Nun's Cave**, a wide and shallow cave where the nuns of Iona took refuge after being expelled during the Reformation. The path continues for another mile or so, but becomes a bit exposed in places and traverses a steep slope above a sheer drop into the sea. The famous arches are columnar basalts worn into fantastic shapes. One is a free-standing rock stack and another is a huge cave with two entrances. You'll need to allow about four hours in total plus some time at the arches.

Heading east from Carsaig Bay is a spectacular 4½-mile walk to **Lochbuie**, past **Adnunan stack**. It starts out through woodland, then follows the shore below the steep cliffs, with waterfalls plunging straight into the sea. It's easy at first but then gets very muddy in places and there's quite a bit of wading through boggy marsh, so make sure you've got good walking boots. Allow about five to six hours in total.

A shorter walk takes you to the Bronze Age Lochbuie Stone Circle at the foot of **Ben Buie**. Leave your car at the stone bridge before you reach the village. Look for the green sign on the gate to your left and follow the white marker stones across the field. The stone circle is hidden behind a wall of rhododendrons, so follow the marker stones across the plank bridge until you see it. It takes about 30 minutes.

There are several marked trails through Forestry Commission land on Mull. The first walk is to **Aros Park**, on the south side of Tobermory Bay. Start out from the car park near the distillery in Tobermory and follow the shoreline for about a mile to Lochan a'Ghurrabain, which is good for trout fishing. From here there is also a marked path around the loch (one mile). A longer walk is to **Ardmore Bay**, three miles north of Tobermory. The trail/cycle path starts at the car park by the road that runs northwest from Tobermory. From here, it runs out almost to Ardmore point and back again, passing a couple of ruined villages on the way. There's a good chance of seeing seals and sea birds in Ardmore Bay. The trail is four miles in total.

Four miles north of Craignure is the car park and picnic site at **Garmony Point**, where a two-mile trail leads to the ferry terminal at **Fishnish**, hugging the shore all the way. Another trail (four miles) runs out to Fishnish Point and back through the forest to the car park.

Listings Mull *map page 79.*

Tourist information

Craignure

Craignure iCentre
Opposite the pier in the same building as the CalMac office, T01680-812377. Daily all year round.

Tobermory

Visitor information service
Ledaig car park, T01688-302875, www.exploremull.co.uk. Mon-Sat 0900-1700, Sun 1000-1700.

Where to stay

Craignure to Tobermory

£££ Glenforsa Hotel
2 miles south of Salen, T01680-300377,
www.glenforsa.com. Easter-Oct.
Delightful hotel built from Norwegian
wood and run by friendly hotelier and
aviator above whose reception hangs a
propeller off a First World War aircraft.
14 tasteful, wood-furnished twin and
double rooms plus self-catering lodge,
beautiful views down the Sound of Mull
and a lovely restaurant serving wild
salmon, Mull oysters (**££**) and real ales.

££ Craignure Inn
Craignure, T01680-812305,
www.craignure-inn.co.uk.
This 18th-century inn, complete with an
interior of rough-hewn stone walls, wooden
floor and open fire, has an atmospheric cosy
bar serving real ales and food that includes
Hebridean lamb (**££**). Has 3 rooms available.

££-£ Arle Lodge
Aros, T01680-300299, www.arlelodge.co.uk.
Friendly, self-catering accommodation
in 10 rooms sleeping up to 31 guests in
family en suite rooms, doubles and twins,
continental breakfast included. Also self-
catering cottage for up to 5. Good value.

Tobermory

££££-£££ Western Isles Hotel
T01688-302012, www.westernisleshotel.com.
Open all year.
The new owners are proud that this grand,
sandstone hotel with commanding views
over Tobermory harbour is no longer part of
a chain. Step inside and it's clear the family
are on a mission to transform this 26-room,
Victorian-era hotel back to its former glory.
The Master Seaview rooms are worth the
additional pounds for the breathtaking view
but whatever room you choose, expect
great food and a warm welcome.

£££ Brockville B&B
Raeric Rd, T01688-302741,
www.brockville-tobermory.co.uk.
2 rooms. Set on the hillside above the
harbour and 5 mins' walk away is this 4-star
B&B offering comfortable rooms and a very
friendly welcome from hosts Helen and
Gordon, also nice touches such as dressing
gowns and iPod dock.

£££ Highland Cottage
Breadalbane St, T01688-302030,
www.highlandcottage.co.uk.
6 rooms. Stylish and very comfortable
boutique B&B set high above the harbour
but within easy walking distance. Guests can
eat in the dining room or the staff will advise
on places to eat out in town. Well-stocked
bar and 2 guest lounges, also pet friendly.

££ Lonan B&B
Off Western Rd, T01688-302082. Easter-Oct.
Welcoming, small B&B with lovely garden,
terrific breakfasts and only 5 mins' walk
from Main St. Landlady Jean bends over
backwards to ensure an enjoyable stay.

£ Tobermory SYHA
Main St, T01668-302481.
Terrific harbourfront location. Always busy so
book ahead.

Self-catering

Isle of Mull Cheese
On the edge of town, 500 yds off the Dervaig
Rd, at Sgriob-Ruadh Farm, T01688-302627,
www.isleofmullcheese.co.uk.
They have 4 cottages for rent on their
working dairy farm (see also Shopping,
page 85) with use of the a heated indoor
pool and sauna.

West coast Mull

£££-££ Druimard Country House Hotel
Dervaig, T01688-400345, www.druimard
mull.co.uk. End Mar-Oct.
Beautifully restored Victorian country house
owned by artists Sally and Graham Bruve-

Richards. 2 tastefully furnished rooms in garden annexe with its own entrance and views to Glen Bellart. Good breakfast with vegetarian and child-friendly options.

£ Dervaig Hostel
6 miles from Tobermory, in tiny Dervaig, T01688-400411.
Hostel in village hall, sleeps up to 10 in 2 en suite rooms, one for 6 and the other 4. Great for families and guests are welcome to join in ceilidhs and various other community events. A terrific budget option.

South Mull

£££ Pennyghael Hotel
In Pennyghael, overlooking the loch, T01681-704288, www.pennyghaelhotel.com.
6 comfortable en suite rooms with great loch views and restaurant serving locally farmed meats and seafood (**£££-££**). Also has 2 self-catering cottages in the grounds from Apr-Sep. Wildlife tours with Bryan Rains of **Wild About Mull** can be arranged with pick-up from the hotel, and owners can also book boat trips to Iona and Staffa.

Restaurants

Craignure to Tobermory

££ Mediterranea
Salen, T01680-300200, www.mull-cuisine. co.uk. Apr-Oct daily from 1730.
An island gem serving Sicilian classics. Beyond the bright yellow door awaits mouth-watering seafood and pasta creations, delightful staff and a cosy ambience. Book ahead.

Tobermory
The best-value fish and chips are sold nightly by the mobile vendor at the harbourfront.

£££-££ The Café Fish
Right on the pier, T01688-301253, www. thecafefish.com. Mon-Sat from 1100, lunch 1200-1500, dinner from 1730, last orders 2200.

Superb fish and seafood dishes in this island favourite. Choose the cosy interior or al fresco for dining on the freshest seafood, be it scallops, langoustines, oysters, lobsters, mussels or crab. If you can't decide then why not attempt the gargantuan shellfish platter (£35). A real delight.

£££-££ Western Isles Hotel
See Where to stay, above.
Tasty menu with local seafood and game on the menu. 3 options for eating depending on how intimate you want to be, but all have fantastic views and attentive service.

££-£ Mishnish Hotel
T01688-302500, Main St.
An island institution and, despite its makeover, 'the Mish' retains an element of charm and serves up hearty meals to accompany your real ale. You can choose between more traditional fare or pizza and pasta in the Italian restaurant. The hotel has 12 en suite rooms upstairs.

West coast Mull

££ Am Birlinn
At Penmore, just off the Derviag–Calgary road, T01688-400619, www.ambirlinn.com. Wed-Sun 1200-1430 and 1700-2100.
This is a great place to enjoy delicious fish and locally sourced meats in an informal atmosphere. Has outdoor play area so you can enjoy an aperitif while the little terrors let off steam.

£ The Boathouse
On Ulva, T01688-500241, www.theboathouse ulva.co.uk. Mon-Fri 0900-1700, lunch served 1200-1600, also open Sun Jun-Aug.
This is wonderful place for lunch is run by Emma and Rebecca who use only the finest local seafood, including their own oysters, also home-based goodies and Fairtrade teas and coffees. Highly recommended.

£ Old Byre Heritage Centre
Dervaig, see page 80. Apr-end Oct.
Simple, home-made delights offered all day. Not a huge menu but a worthwhile lunch stop.

Entertainment

Tobermory

The legendary **Mishnish Hotel** (see Restaurants, above) wins over **MacGochan's** for its ambience. Both pubs run live music events and attract a healthy numbers of revellers. There are also music events at **An Tobar**, see page 79.

Festivals

Apr Mull Music Festival, known as the **Whisky Olympics**, for details T01688-302383. Held on the last weekend of the month, it is a great time to be on Mull. You can enjoy a feast of Gaelic folk music and, of course, whisky. The focus of the festival is the bar of the **Mishnish Hotel**, Tobermory.

Jul Mendelssohn on Mull Music Festival, held over 10 days in early Jul, is another great festival. It commemorates the famous composer's visit here in 1829. **Tobermory Highland Games**, is held annually on the 3rd Thu of the month.

Sep Mull and Iona Food Festival. This mid-Sep festival showcases the wealth of outstanding produce cultivated on the island.

Oct Tour of Mull Rally, held in early Oct for over 30 years. This should not be missed by rally enthusiasts, though book early as the island becomes extremely busy.

Shopping

Tobermory

From the local butcher and baker to the chocolate-maker, Tobermory is foodie-heaven. It's also where to pick up fishing tackle, camping and bike spares.

Brown's Tobermory, *21 Main St, T01688-302020*. 1st opened in 1897, this shop is now under new ownership, but rest assured it has everything. In addition to trout-fishing permits, this is where to stock up on everything from camping gas to tent pegs. They'll even change your watch battery. Also hires mountain bikes.

Island Bakery, *Main St, T01688-302223*. Try their award-winning organic lemon melts, oat crumbles and chocolate gingers with huge pieces of stem ginger.

Isle of Mull Cheese, *on the edge of town, 500 yds off the Dervaig Rd, at Sgriob-Ruadh Farm, T01688-302627, www.isleofmullcheese.co.uk. Apr-Sep Mon-Fri 1000-1600*. Here you can savour their award-winning, traditionally made cheese and admire their wonderful glass barn.

Mull Pottery, *southern edge of Tobermory en route to Salen, T01688-302347*. Tasteful hand-thrown pots in different shapes and sizes. Good café-bistro upstairs with views. There is also a shop at 46 Main St in Tobermory.

Tobermory Chocolates, *57 Main St, T01688-302526, www.tobermorychocolate.co.uk. Mon-Sat 0930-1700, Sun 1000-1600*. A chocolate-lover's heaven. Here you can try out their speciality – chocolate made with the local whisky and delicious Staffa cake.

What to do

Boat/wildlife trips

You can find out about the sealife around Mull by visiting the **Hebridean Whale and Dolphin Trust** (28 Main St, Tobermory, T01688-302620, www.hwdt.org, Apr-Oct daily 1000-1700, Nov-Mar Mon-Fri 1100-1600). This charity aims to protect the marine environment through education.

Alternative Boat Hire, *Mark Jardine, Sailing Trips & Boat Hire, Lovedale Cottage, Isle of Iona, T01681-700537, www.boattripsiona.com*. Trips around the coastline and handline fishing on a traditional wooden boat. You can hire by the hour or for an afternoon, May-Oct, from Fionnphort and Iona.

Island Encounters, *Salen, T01681-7000090, www.mullwildlife.co.uk*. Have been running wildlife tours for 25 years with Richard Atkinson and now also Nigel Shannon. You'll see golden eagles, white-tailed sea eagles, hen harriers, divers, merlins, peregrine falcons, seals and porpoises, to name but a few.

Isle of Mull Wildlife Expeditions, *Ulva Ferry, T01688-500121, www.torrbuan.com*.

Experienced and highly acclaimed wildlife guide David Woodhouse runs these excellent day-long tours with the chance to spot golden eagles, otters, seals and porpoises. If you really want to spoil yourselves spend a night or 2 in **Torr Buan House**, the stunning home of David and wife Joy. Guests have their own suite with fantastic views of Iona, Ulva, Ben More and the sea cliffs of Gribun and a chance to see golden and sea eagles, hen harriers and owls from your very own windows. **££££-£££** for dinner B&B. Highly recommended.

Mull Charters, T01680-300444, www.mull charters.com. Run by Judith and Martin Keivers from Salen. Wildlife and fishing trips depart from the ferry slip for Ulva. Their popular 3-hr 'Sea Eagle Adventure' trip is £40/25. Booking essential. Trips run daily from Apr-Oct.

Sea Life Surveys, Ledaig, Tobermory, beside McGochan's pub, T01688-302916, www.sealifesurveys.com. Excellent whale-watching and wildlife tours, including 4-hr **Whalewatch** (£50 pp) and full-day Whalewatch Explorer (£70 pp).

Turus Mara, Penmore Mill, Dervaig, T01688-400242, www.turusmara.com. Birdwatching and wildlife trips from Ulva Ferry, also depart from Oban (see page 53). Chance to spot seals, puffins and visit the classic Fingal's Cave on Staffa.

whalewatchwithus.com, Ledaig car park, Tobermory, T01688-302875. Wildlife cruises (£30/20 for 2-hr wildlife cruise, £50 for 4-hr whale watching), not recommended for children under 12.

Transport

Craignure to Tobermory
Bus
There are daily buses from Craignure, which coincide with ferry arrivals. There's a bus from Craignure to **Fionnphort** (for Iona) 4 times a day Mon-Fri, 3 times on Sat and 1 on Sun. Bus 495 runs from Craignure to Tobermory, 496 goes from Craignure to **Fionnphort** and 494 from Tobermory to Dervaig and **Calgary**. Buses are operated by **West Coast Motors**.

Car
Tobermory is a 30- to 40-min drive (2-hr cycle) north from the ferry pier at Craignure.

Cycle hire
On Yer Bike, Salen, T01680-300501. Rents bikes Apr-Oct. Also has a shop by the ferry terminal in Craignure, T01680-812580.

Ferry
To **Oban** from Craignure, Mon-Sat 5-7 times daily, 5 times on Sun, 45 mins. To **Lochaline** on the Morvern Peninsula from **Fishnish**, Mon-Sat every 45 mins, 9 times on Sun, 15 mins. For times and fares visit the **CalMac** website.

Tobermory
Cycle hire
Brown's Tobermory, Main St, T01688-302020, hires bikes. See also Shopping, above.

Ferry
Ferries to **Kilchoan** on the Ardnamurchan Peninsula, 7 times daily Mon-Sat and 5 times daily on Sun (May-Aug).

West coast Mull
Ferry
A small bicycle/passenger-only ferry, makes the 2-min crossing to Ulva on demand from **Ulva Ferry**, all year for Mon-Fri sailings 0900-1700, Sun sailings Jun-Aug only. From Easter-Sep show signal at the pier to cross. Oct-Easter best to call the ferryman on T01688-400352, or T01688-500241. Note there's no bus to Ulva Ferry. Either cycle or take the bus to **Salen** and jump on a pre-booked bike, see Cycle hire, above, or book a taxi, details from Craignure **iCentre**.

South Mull
Ferry
To **Iona**, a passenger-only ferry leaves from **Fionnphort** on Mull frequently Mon-Sat 0815-1815, and Sun hourly 0845-1800, 5 mins.

important religious site and home to some heavenly beaches

Iona (population 130) is a small island – barely three miles long and a little over a mile wide – but its importance to Christianity is out of all proportion to its size. Iona's place in religious history was guaranteed when St Columba arrived in the land of the Gaels with his 12 disciples and founded a monastery there in AD 563. The Irish monk then set about converting a large part of pagan Scotland (for the head-hunting Picts to the north and east followed the teachings of Druids) and much of northern England. Iona went on to become the most sacred religious site in Europe and has been a place of pilgrimage for several centuries. Today that pilgrimage has turned into more of an invasion, with day-trippers making the five-minute ferry trip from Mull to visit the abbey. Few, however, venture beyond the main village, Baile Mór, and it's easy to find a quiet spot, particularly on the west coast with its sparkling silver beaches washed by turquoise sea. It's worth spending a day or two here to soak up the island's unique spiritual peace so well conveyed in the words of Dr Johnson: "that man is little to be envied whose … piety would not grow warmer among the ruins of Iona".

Iona Abbey and Nunnery
T01681-700512, www.historicenvironment.scot, Apr-Sep daily 0930-1730; Oct-Mar 1000-1600. £7.50, concessions £6, children £4.50.

The present abbey dates from around 1200, though it has been rebuilt over the centuries and was completely restored in the 20th century. The oldest part is the restored **St Oran's Chapel**, to the south of the abbey on the right, which is plain and unadorned save for its splendid 11th-century Norman doorway. You get a good view of the whole complex from the top of the small grassy knoll opposite the abbey entrance. It is said that Columba was prevented from completing the building of the original chapel until a living person had been buried in the foundations. His friend Oran volunteered and was duly buried. Columba later asked for the face to be uncovered so that he could bid a final farewell to his friend, but Oran was found to be alive and claimed he had seen Heaven and Hell, describing them in such blasphemous terms that Columba ordered he be covered up immediately!

Surrounding the chapel is the **Reilig Odhrain**, the sacred burial ground, which is said to contain the graves of 48 Scottish kings, including Macbeth's victim, Duncan, as well as four Irish and eight Norwegian kings. The stones you see today are not the graves of kings but of various important people from around the West Highlands and Islands, including that of John Smith, leader of the British Labour Party from 1992 until his death in 1994.

Beside the Road of the Dead, which leads from the abbey church to St Oran's Chapel, stands the eighth-century **St Martin's Cross**. This is the finest of Iona's Celtic high crosses and is remarkably complete, with the Pictish serpent-and-boss decoration on one side and holy figures on the other. Standing in front of the abbey entrance is a replica of **St John's Cross**, the other great eighth-century monument. The restored original is in the Infirmary Museum, at the rear of the abbey, along with a fine collection of medieval gravestones.

No part of St Columba's original buildings survives, but to the left of the main entrance is **St Columba's Shrine**, the small, steep-roofed chamber which almost certainly marks the site of the saint's tomb. This is **Torr an Aba**, where Columba's cell is said to have been. The

Iona is known as the 'Cradle of Christianity in Scotland', and was once a centre of the arts. The monks produced elaborate carvings, manuscripts, ornate gravestones and Celtic crosses. Their greatest work was the beautiful *Book of Kells*, which dates from AD 800, and which is now on display in Dublin's Trinity College. This proved to be the high point of the church's history. Shortly after came the first of the Viking raids, in AD 806, when many monks were slaughtered at Martyrs' Bay, followed by another in AD 986 which destroyed the work of many years. The relentless pressure from the established church ended with the suppression of the Celtic Church by King David in 1144.

In 1203 Iona became part of the mainstream church with the establishment of a nunnery for the Order of the Black Nuns, as well as a Benedictine Abbey by Reginald of the MacDonalds of the Isles. Iona became overshadowed by the royal city of Dunfermline, and its final demise came with the Reformation when buildings were demolished and all but three of the 360 carved crosses destroyed.

The abbey lay in ruins until, in 1899, the island's owner, the eighth Duke of Argyll, donated the buildings to the Church of Scotland on condition that the abbey church was restored for worship. Then, in 1938, the Reverend George Macleod founded the Iona Community as an evangelical Church of Scotland 'brotherhood', with the abbey buildings as its headquarters, and by 1965 had succeeded in rebuilding the remainder of the monastic buildings. Now the abbey complex has been completely restored and the island of Iona, apart from the abbey buildings, is owned by the National Trust for Scotland.

abbey itself has been carefully restored to its original beautiful simplicity and inside, in a side chapel, are marble effigies of the eighth Duke of Argyll and his third wife, Duchess Ina.

Baile Mór

The passenger ferry from Fionnphort on Mull lands at Baile Mór, Iona's main village, which is little more than a row of cottages facing the sea. There are over a dozen places to stay but, as demand far exceeds supply during the busy summer season, it's best to book in advance at one of the tourist offices on Mull or in Oban. There's also a post office, a very good craft shop and general store in the village. Just outside the village, on the way to the abbey, are the ruins of the **Augustinian nunnery**. To the north, housed in the parish church manse, built by Thomas Telford, is the **Iona Heritage Centre** ① *T01681-700576, Apr-Oct Mon-Sat 1030-1630, £2.20*, which features displays on the island's social history. There's also a shop and tearoom. Nearby stands the intricately carved 15th-century **Maclean's Cross**.

Around the island

On the west coast are some lovely beaches of white sand and colourful pebbles. The best of the lot is the **Bay at the Back of the Ocean**, beside the golf course, and only a 1½-mile walk from the ferry. This was one of John Smith's favourite places and it's easy to see why. At the southern tip of the island is another sandy beach at **St Columba's Bay**, believed to be the spot where the saint first landed. Another good walk is to the top of **Dun I**, the only real hill, which rises to a height of 300 ft. To get there, continue on the road north

The story of St Columba

St Columba (Colum Cille in Gaelic), a prince of Ireland and grandson of the Irish King, Niall of the Nine Hostages, came to Scotland not as a missionary, but as an act of self-imposed penance for his actions. He stubbornly refused to hand over his copy of the Gospels, illegally copied from St Finian's original, which led to a bitter dispute with the king. This ended in a pitched battle in which Columba's supporters prevailed, but he was so overcome with remorse at the bloodshed he had caused that he fled Ireland, finally settling on Iona as it was the first place he found from where he couldn't see his homeland. Columba, however, was not retiring into obscurity. His missionary zeal drove him to begin building the abbey. He banished women and cows from the island, declaring that "where there is a cow there is a woman, and where there is a woman there is mischief". Workers at the abbey had to leave their womenfolk on nearby Eilean nam Ban (Women's Island). Not content with that, he also banished frogs and snakes from Iona, though there are plenty on Mull. He is even said to have pacified the Loch Ness Monster during a visit to Inverness. He went on to found the Celtic Church, or the Church of the Culdees, with centres throughout Scotland, which differed in many ways from the Church of Rome.

from the abbey, past MacDougal's Cross, then go through a gate to the right of Bishop's Walk Farm and follow the fence up to where you join a footpath to the top. It's only about half an hour up and down and there are great views from the top of the entire island and the coastline of Mull.

Listings Iona

Where to stay

££££-££ Argyll Hotel
T01681-700334, www.argyllhoteliona.co.uk. Apr-Oct.
The better of the island's 2 upmarket hotels with 17 rooms, an excellent restaurant serving the best of local produce. The luxury sea-view suite is **££££** but the other rooms are **£££-££**. They will organize tours.

£ Iona Hostel
T01681-700781, www.ionahostel.co.uk.
A fabulous hostel with views to the Treshnish Islands. 25-min walk north from the village and ferry. It's best to book ahead in summer. A wee gem of a hostel with impeccable green credentials and that also promises the best duck eggs this side of heaven.

Festivals

See page 85.

What to do

Boat/wildlife trips
See also page 85.
Alternative Boat Hire, *Mark Jardine, Sailing Trips & Boat Hire, Lovedale Cottage, T01681-700537, www.boattripsiona.com.*
Trips around the coastline and handline fishing on a traditional wooden boat. You can hire by the hour or for an afternoon, May-Oct, from Fionnphort and Iona.
Turus Mara, *see page 86.*

Coll, Tiree & Colonsay

The trickle of visitors who come to explore low-lying, windswept Coll step onto one of the best-kept secrets in Scotland. Here, on lands where the likes of the mysterious Na Sgeulachan standing stone has stood for over 3000 years, tourism remains almost invisible, the 150 islanders enjoying a natural playground where families can picnic on deserted pearl-white beaches with views towards Mull and the Inner Hebrides. Idyllic neighbouring Tiree, or Tir-Iodh (land of corn), also boasts stunning beaches caressed by the waters of the Gulf Stream. Statistically one of the sunniest and windiest locations in the UK, Tiree's billiard-flat hinterland teems with rare birdlife and excited wildlife enthusiasts, whilst offshore, windsurfers, surfers and kitesurfers play in towering waves that since the 1980s have earned Tiree the nickname of 'mini-Hawaii' – in 2007 it even hosted a round of the PBA Windsurfing World Cup. Little wonder Tiree now offers a healthy number of B&Bs. Colonsay too is remote, tranquil and undemanding; an island brimming with wildlife, flowers and even a miniature mountain range. Like Tiree, Colonsay has steadily embraced tourism and in particular self-catering accommodation. It may not be the easiest island to reach but clearly its magic has already been discovered.

peaceful island with picture-perfect beaches

Coll is just 13 miles long and four miles wide, and the best of its 23 beaches are on the west coast, at **Killunaig**, **Hogh Bay** and **Feall Bay**. The latter is separated from nearby **Crossapol Bay** by giant sand dunes managed by the RSPB, the islands largest landowner, to protect the resident corncrake population. The **CalMac** ferry from Oban calls in at Coll's only village, **Arinagour**, where half of the island's population live and where you'll find the post office (and bike hire opposite), petrol station, general store and cosy **Island Café**. There's no public transport but a taxi is available. If it's not too windy, it's best to explore by bike. It's worth taking a walk up **Ben Hogh** (341 ft), the island's highest point, overlooking Hogh Bay on the west coast, to get a terrific view of the island. Tired of beaches? Try some fishing or the nine-hole golf course at **Cliad**, two miles west of Arinagour.

Listings Coll

Where to stay

£££ Coll Hotel
Arinagour, T01879-230334,
www.collhotelcom.
Run by the Oliphant family since the 1960s, the 'Scottish Island Hotel of the Year' does not disappoint. Supremely comfortable accommodation in 7 bedrooms and superb food on offer in the residents' dining room or the hotel bar (**££**). It's a particular treat if you're a fan of great seafood. Lots of nice, thoughtful extras such as pick-up from the ferry, free bikes and even teddy bears for children to borrow during their stay.

££ Caolas House
South of Arinagour, T01879-230438.
A friendly, cosy farmhouse B&B by the beach, with terrific home-cooking.

£ Coll Bunkhouse
Arinagour, T01879-230217,
www.collbunkhouse.com.
Modern hostel with excellent facilities, sleeps up to 16.

Restaurants

££-£ Island Café
Arinagour, T01879-230262. Wed-Sat 1100-1400 and 1700-2100, Sun 1200-1800.
Licensed and great for daytime snacks, coffee and soups. Its Sun lunch is popular, including a roast, shortbread, cheese and oatcakes (from £12.50). Whilst adults dine or laze on the sofas enjoying the sea view, there are toys, books and even table football for the kids.

What to do

Island tours are available on Tue and Fri with local guide, 2 hrs in a 4WD, T01879-230520. Sharks and wildlife boat trips on Thu with **Basking Shark Scotland** between Apr and Oct. For details visit www.baskingsharkscotland.co.uk. Kayak hire from Carol Flett, T01879-230436.

Transport

Air
There is also a flight from **Oban** with **Hebridean Air Services** (www.hebrideanair.co.uk) to **Tiree**, **Coll** and **Colonsay**.

Cycle hire
Book in advance at the **Post Office**, T01879-230395, Mon-Sat 0900-1300.

Ferry
CalMac car/passenger ferries leave for **Oban**, Mon, Wed, Fri-Sun, 2 hrs 40 mins, and to **Tiree**. For times and fares visit www.calmac.co.uk.

Taxi
Contact Val on T01879-230402.

Tiree *Colour map 3, B2.*

one of Britain's best surf spots

Tiree is a low, flat island, only about 11 miles long and six miles across at its widest, and is also known by the nickname 'Tir fo Thuinn', or 'Land below the waves'. It is one of the best places to surf in the British Isles. When seen from a distance most of it disappears below the horizon, save its two highest hills, Ben Hynish (462 ft) and Beinn Hough (390 ft), on the west coast. Though flat, remember that Tiree's fierce winds can make cycling hard work. Campervans laden with surf-gear are a reminder that this is a windsurfing paradise and each October Tiree hosts the week-long Tiree Wave Classic. Scores of world-class windsurfers come to compete and party, putting accommodation at a premium.

The ferry port is at **Scarinish**, at the western edge of the sweep of **Gott Bay**. The main village of Scarinish is also where to find the Co-op supermarket, the post office and the bank, there's also a garage at the pier head. About four miles from Scarinish, is Vaul Bay, where, aside from golf, there are the well-preserved remains of **Dun Mor**, a Pictish broch built around the first century AD and standing on a rocky outcrop to the west of the bay.

Essential Tiree

Finding your feet

CalMac car and passenger ferries sail to the island from Oban, via Coll once daily. The **ferry port** (T01879-220337), is at Scarinish. From 0700-1800 (Monday-Saturday) the whole island is covered by a **Ring n' Ride service** (T01879-220419), a bus/taxi service which operates standard fares and is ideal for exploring the island. Pick up a copy of the *Area Transport Guide to Tiree and Coll* from Oban **iCentre** (see page 50). **Tiree Airport** (T01879-220456), where flights from Glasgow and Oban arrive, is at The Reef. See Transport, page 93.

The island's main road runs northwest from Scarinish, past the beautiful beach at **Balephetrish Bay** to **Balevullin**, where you can see some good examples of restored traditional thatched houses. Just to the south, at Sandaig, is the **Sandaig Museum** ⓘ *open all year around, but the summer exhibition is open Jul-Sep, Tue and Sat afternoon*, a thatched croft inside which displays tell of the island's social history.

In the southwestern corner of the island is the spectacular headland of **Ceann a'Mara**, or Kenavara. The massive cliffs are home to thousands of sea birds. East from here, across the golden sands of **Balephuil Bay**, is the island's highest hill, Ben Hynish, topped by a radar-tracking station resembling a giant golf ball. It's worth the climb to the top for the magnificent views over the island and to the distant Outer Hebrides.

Below Ben Hynish, to the east, is the village of **Hynish**, where you'll find the **Signal Tower Museum**, which tells the story of the building of the **Skerryvore Lighthouse** (1840-1844) by Alan Stevenson, an uncle of Robert Louis Stevenson. This incredible feat of engineering was carried out from Hynish, where a dry dock/reservoir was built for shipping materials by boat to the Skerryvore reef, 11 miles to the southwest.

Listings Tiree

Where to stay

££ Scarinish Hotel
Scarinish, T01879-220308,
www.tireescarinishhotel.com.
10 rooms, 6 en suite. Located right by the old harbour, this modest hotel has fabulous views across the bay from its **Old Harbour** restaurant where the simply served local beef, lamb and shellfish will tickle your tastebuds. Also has pizza menu and the **Lean To Bar** is a popular place for a drink. Dogs welcome (£5 a night).

£ Mill House Hostel
Cornaigmore, T01879-220892,
www.tireemillhouse.com.
Fantastic hostel accommodation in converted barn and farmhouse close to Loch Bhasapol. Choice of 6-bed dorms or twin/double rooms. Bike hire available.

Restaurants

££ Ceabhar Restaurant and Cottage
Sandaig T01879-220684, www.ceabhar.com.
Tue-Sat 1700-2100.
Delicious dinners and Sun lunch. Also self-catering cottage for rent (sleeps up to 8, dog friendly) and has its own microbrewery.

£ The Cobbled Cow
In the Rural Centre at Crossapool by the airport. Closed Mon.
Terrific home-baking, good for a snack, lunch or evening meals.

What to do

Skipinnish Tours, *Skipinnish, Ruaig, T01879-220009, www.skipinnish-sea-tours.co.uk.* From £15-40 pp for trips (Apr-Oct) that include shark and whale spotting and trips to Staffa, Lunga and out to Skerryvore Lighhouse (4 hrs).
Wild Diamond Watersports, *Burnside Cottage, Cornaig, T01879-220399, www. wilddiamond.co.uk.* Offers surfing, wind-surfing, kitesurfing, sand yachting and kayaking equipment hire and courses.

Transport

Air
Tiree has an airport (T01879-220456) with 1 flight to **Glasgow** daily Mon-Sat, all year round, 45 mins. There is also a flight from **Oban** with **Hebridean Air Services** (www.hebrideanair.co.uk) to Tiree, Coll and Colonsay.

Car hire
MacLennans, T01879-220555.

Cycle hire
Millhouse Hostel, Cornaigmore, T01879-220435.

Ferry
CalMac car/passenger ferries sail to **Oban**, once daily, 3 hrs 50 mins.

Taxi
John Kennedy Taxis, T01879-220419. Shared and private taxi hire.

home to one of Scotland's finest beaches

Colonsay's population of around 120 lives in the three small villages, the largest of which is Scalasaig, the ferry port.

A few miles north of the ferry, in the middle of the island, is **Colonsay House**, dating from 1772. It was sold, along with the rest of the island, in 1904 to Lord Strathcona, who had made his fortune in Canada with the Hudson Bay Company and went on to found the Canadian Pacific Railway. The house is not open to the public but the lovely **gardens** ⓘ *Wed and Fri 1200-1700, £2, children £1*, and woods, full of rhododendrons, giant palms and exotic shrubs, are worth a stroll. There's also the chance to buy home-baking and a cup of coffee near the house.

There are several standing stones, the best of which are **Fingal's Limpet Hammers**, at **Kilchattan**, southwest of Colonsay House. There are also Iron Age forts, such as **Dun Eibhinn**, next to the hotel in Scalasaig. Colonsay is also home to a wide variety of wildlife and over 190 species of bird have apparently been recorded. You can see choughs, one of Britain's rarest birds, as well as corncrakes, buzzards, falcons, merlins and perhaps even the odd golden eagle or sea eagle. There are also otters, seals and wild goats (said to be descended from the survivors of the Spanish Armada ships wrecked in 1588). The jewel in the island's crown, though, lies six miles north of Scalasaig, past Colonsay House, at **Kiloran Bay**. The beach here is described as the finest in the Hebrides. Just a glimpse of this magnificent half mile of golden sands, backed by tiers of grassy dunes, with massive breakers rolling in off the Atlantic, is worth the two-hour ferry crossing alone.

Just off the southern tip of Colonsay is the island of **Oronsay**, two miles square with a population of six, and one of the highlights of a visit to Colonsay. The name derives from the Norse for 'ebb-tide island', which is a fitting description as Oronsay can be reached on foot at low tide, across the mud flats known as 'The Strand'. It takes about an hour to walk from the south end of Colonsay to the ruins of a 14th-century **Augustinian Priory**. This was home of some of the most highly skilled medieval craftsmen in the Western Highlands. A surviving example of their work is the impressive Oronsay Cross and the beautifully carved tombstones, on display in the **Prior's House**. Make sure you take wellies for the walk across the Strand and check on the tides. Tide tables are available at the hotel or shop. Spring tides (new and full moon) allow about three to four hours to walk across and back, which is just enough time to see the priory but little else. An alternative is to time one way to coincide with the postbus.

Essential Colonsay

Finding your feet

There are ferry sailings from Oban arriving at Scalasaig on the east coast. From Kennacraig and Port Askaig there is one sailing a week on Wednesday. Ferries need to be booked well in advance during the summer months. For those on the island without their own transport, there's a limited bus and postbus service from Monday to Saturday.

Where to stay

Accommodation on Colonsay is limited and must be booked well in advance. Even self-catering options are hard to come by, because the same families return year after year.

For details on 16 self-catering options see **Colonsay Holidays**, T01951-200312/6, www.colonsayholidays.co.uk. These are also the contact details for the hotel and lodge listed below.

£££ Colonsay Hotel
A few hundred yards from the ferry, T01951-200316.
A cosy 18th-century inn with 8 stylishly furnished rooms, a friendly bar, open fire and excellent food in the informal dining room. Staff are very friendly and helpful. They also arrange island tours.

£ Colonsay Backpacker's Lodge
2 km from the ferry, T01951-200316. Open all year.
A comfortable backpackers' hostel, which sleeps 16. Phone for a lift from the ferry.

What to do

For wildlife, archaeological and sightseeing tours of the island by bus or on foot, call Kevin Byrne (T01951-200320). On Wed there's also the chance to do a whistle-stop tour of the island before the ferry departs for Kennacraig, T01951-200141.

Transport

Air
There is a flight from **Oban** with **Hebridean Air Services** (www.hebridean air.co.uk) to Tiree, Coll and Colonsay.

Cycle hire
As the island is only 8 miles long by 3 miles wide, you might consider hiring a bicycle. Bike hire from **Archie's Bikes**, T01951-200355. They will deliver bikes to your accommodation.

Ferry
There are ferry sailings to **Oban**, once daily Mon, Wed, Thu, Fri and Sun, 2 hrs. To **Kennacraig**, 1 sailing on Wed, 3 hrs 35 mins. To **Port Askaig**, on Islay, 1 sailing on a Wed, 1 hr 15 mins. Ferries need to be booked well in advance during the summer months (Apr-Sep).

Islay
& Jura

Islay (pronounced eye-la), the most southerly of the
Hebridean islands and one of the most populous, with
around 4000 inhabitants, enjoys a rich farming and
crofting heritage but it has one particular claim to
fame – single malt whisky. Aside from whisky, people
also come here to watch birds. The island is something
of an ornithologists' wonderland, and from October to
April plays host to migrating barnacle and white-fronted
geese flying down from Greenland in their thousands
for the winter. The short ferry crossing from Islay takes
you to Jura, a primeval and uncompromising place; a
lost world, pervaded by an almost haunting silence.
The words 'wild' and 'remote' tend to get overused in
describing the many Hebridean islands, but in the case
of Jura they are, if anything, an understatement. Jura has
one road, one hotel, six sporting estates and 5000 red
deer, which outnumber the 117 people by 25:1, the
human population having been cleared to turn the island
into a huge deer forest. Rather appropriately, the name
Jura derives from the Norse 'dyr-ey', meaning deer island.
Yes, Jura is beautiful – but arguably at a price. For whilst
it may be heaven for the landed gentry who control the
vast estates, the distinct lack of development ensures
affordable housing for the locals remains beyond the
grasp of many.

In addition to innumerable tea shops, Islay offers the unique opportunity to visit several of Scotland's most impressive distilleries in one day. The island has eight working distilleries in total (see box, page 100) and their distinctive peaty malts are considered to be among the finest. At the end of May each year, the island hosts the **Islay Malt and Music Festival**, for which the distillers produce their special edition malts (see Festivals, page 102).

Port Ellen and around

Port Ellen is the largest place on Islay and the main ferry port, yet it still has the feel of a sleepy village. There are many day trips from Port Ellen. A road runs east out to **Ardtalla**, where it ends. Along the way, it passes three distilleries, first **Laphroaig**, then **Lagavulin** and lastly **Ardbeg**, all of which offer guided tours, see box, page 100. Between the Lagavulin and Ardbeg distilleries is the dramatically sited 16th-century ruin of **Dunyvaig Castle**, once the main naval base and fortress of the Lords of the Isles. Five miles further on is the impressive **Kildalton Cross**, standing in the graveyard of the ruined 13th-century chapel. The eighth-century cross is well preserved and is one of Scotland's most important Early Christian monuments, and the carvings depict biblical scenes.

Southwest of Port Ellen a road runs out to a small, rounded peninsula known as **The Oa**, an area of varied beauty, both wild and pastoral, and with a wonderful coastline. The road runs as far as **Upper Killeyan**, from where it's about a mile uphill to the spectacular headland at the **Mull of Oa**. Here you'll see the strange-looking **American monument**. The obelisk commemorates the shipwrecks offshore of two US ships, the *Tuscania* and the *Ontranto*, both of which sank in 1918 at the end of the First World War. There's a great walk north from the Mull of Oa up to Kintra, but it's best to start out from Kintra.

A turn-off from the road to The Oa leads north to **Kintra**, at the south end of The

Essential Islay

Finding your feet

Islay can be reached by air from Glasgow. There are two flights daily with **Loganair/ Flybe** (40 minutes). For reservations visit www.loganair.co.uk. There is also a flight from to and from Oban via Colonsay on Tuesday and Thursday with **Hebridean Air Services**. The airport (T01496-302361) is at Glenegedale, about five miles north of Port Ellen on the road to Bowmore. The ferry from Kennacraig to Port Ellen sails twice daily on Mondays, Tuesdays, Thursdays, Fridays and Saturdays and once on Wednesdays and Sundays. A ferry also sails from Kennacraig to Port Askaig once daily on Monday, Wednesday and Friday. The ferry from Oban to Port Askaig sails on Wednesdays. For those without their own transport, there's a regular bus service around Islay, with **Islay Coaches** (T01496-840273). There are buses from Portnahaven to Port Ellen, via Port Charlotte, Bridgend, Bowmore and the airport; from Port Askaig to Port Ellen via Ballygrant, Bridgend, Bowmore and the airport; from Port Ellen to Ardbeg, Bowmore, Port Askaig and Portnahaven; and also a postbus to Bunnababhain. Buses run regularly from Monday to Saturday, but only once on Sunday.

Islay & Jura

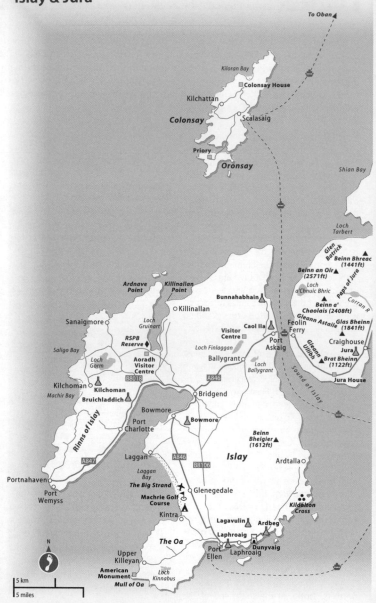

To Oban

Kiloran Bay

■ **Colonsay House**

Kilchattan

Colonsay

Scalasaig

■ **Priory**

Oronsay

Shian Bay

Loch Tarbert

Glen Batrick

▲ **Beinn Bhreac (1441ft)**

Beinn an Oir ▲ (2571ft)

Loch a Chnuic Bhric

Paps of Jura

Beinn a' Chaolais (2408ft)

Glas Bheinn (1841ft)

Gleann Astaile

Corran R

Gleann Uillsh

Craighouse

Jura ▲

Brat Bheinn (1122ft)

Bunnahabhain

Ardnave Point

Killinallan Point

○ **Killinallan**

Visitor Centre ☐

Caol Ila ▲

Feolin Ferry

Sanaigmore ○

RSPB Reserve ◆

Loch Gruinart

Port Askaig

Loch Finlaggan

Aoradh Visitor Centre ☐

Ballygrant

Loch Ballygrant

Sound of Islay

Saligo Bay

B8018

Loch Gorm

A846

Jura House

Kilchoman ○ ▲

Machir Bay

Bruichladdich ▲

Bridgend ○

Bowmore

Bowmore ▲

Port Charlotte ○

Rinns of Islay

Islay

A846

Laggan ○

B8106

Beinn Bheigier (1612ft) ▲

A847

Ardtalla ○

Portnahaven ○

Laggan Bay

The Big Strand ✈

Machrie Golf Course ⛳

Glenegedale ○

Port Wemyss ○

Kildalton Cross ✝

Kintra ○

Lagavulin ▲

Ardbeg ▲

The Oa

Laphroaig ▲ 🏰

Dunyvaig

Upper Killeyan ○

Port Ellen ○

Laphroaig

■ **American Monument**

Loch Kinnabus

Mull of Oa

N

5 km

5 miles

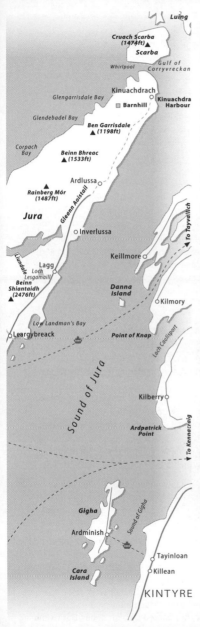

Big Strand at Laggan Bay, with five miles of sands and dunes. There's a restaurant and accommodation here, and it's a great place for camping. The restaurant is at the end of the road, with the beach on one side and, on the other, a wild and spectacular coastal walk incorporating caves and the impressive **Soldier's Rock** sea-stack. Ask at the iCentre (see page 101) for the *Explore Islay* walking trail leaflet. Just to the north of Kintra is the **Machrie golf course**, a golfing experience not to be missed.

Bowmore and the Rinns of Islay

The A846 runs north from Port Ellen, straight as a pool cue, to Bowmore, the island's administrative capital and second largest village. Founded in 1768 by the Campbells, it retains a sleepy air. The village is laid out in a grid plan with the main street running straight up the hill from the pier to the unusual round church, designed to ward off evil spirits, who can hide only in corners. Thankfully, the good spirit stayed behind and can be found at the **Bowmore Distillery**, just to the west of Main Street. This is the oldest of the island's distilleries, founded in 1779.

North of Bowmore, **Bridgend** is the site of the tiny **Islay Ales Brewery**. Here too the A846 joins the A847 which runs west to the hammerhead peninsula known as the **Rinns of Islay** (*rinns* is derived from the Gaelic for 'promontory'). A few miles west of Bridgend the B8017 turns north to the **RSPB Reserve** at **Loch Gruinart**. The mudflats and fields at the head of the loch provide winter grazing for huge flocks of barnacle and white-fronted geese from Greenland, arriving in late October. There's an excellent RSPB visitor centre at **Aoradh** (pronounced *oorig*), which houses an observation point with telescopes and CCTV, and there's a

ON THE ROAD
Islay's malts distilled

Ardbeg, T01496-302244, www.ardbeg. com. Describes itself as the peatiest malt whisky in the world. Malt was first distilled within these whitewashed walls in 1815. The distillery closed in 1981 but was bought and reopened by Glenmorangie in 1997.
Bowmore, T01496-810441, www.bowmore.com. Established in 1779, Bowmore is the oldest distillery on Islay. Its flagship is the 12-year-old single malt. The Craftsman's Tour is highly recommended and offers the chance to savour many a single malt. It has a visitor centre with additional information on the history of the distillery and also rents luxuriously appointed former workers' cottages just yards from the shore and distillery. Call for details.
Bruichladdich, T01496-850190, www.bruichladdich.com. Produces a range of innovative malts including Mood Malts, Multi-Vintage and Single Vintage. Claims to produce different Bruichladdich's by drawing upon its maturing stocks that date back to 1964 (pronounced 'brook-laddie').
Bunnahabhain, T01496-840557, www.bunnahabhain.co.uk. Started in 1881 (and pronounced 'bun-a-havan'), this is known as the 'gentle giant' of Islay because it's the least peaty of the Islay malts. The distiller produces a 12-, 18- and 25-year-old malt and also a 34-year-old malt.
Caol Ila, T01496-302769, www.malts.com. Pronounced 'coal-eela', this distillery was founded in 1846 and lies close to Port Askaig, with great views across the Sound of Islay to Jura. Unlike most of its island peers, this single malt is best before dinner.
Kilchoman, Rockside Farm, Bruichladdich, T01496-850011, www.kilchoman distillery.com. Islay's newest distillery (established 2005). It already produces almost 100,000 litres of alcohol per year. Kilchoman claims to be one of only half-a-dozen distilleries in Scotland that carries out traditional floor maltings. All its barley is grown in the fields next door.
Lagavulin, T01496-302749, www.malts.com. Their 16-year-old single malt is one of the classics and also makes the ideal after-dinner tipple. A very interesting tour.
Laphroaig, T01496-302418, www.laphroaig.com. Its wonderful setting is summed up by its name, meaning 'The beautiful hollow by the broad bay' in Gaelic. According to many this is the ultimate in malt whisky and is at its best after dinner. This distillery has a reputation for one of the best whisky tours on Islay.

Check the distillery websites for tour times as these vary according to the time of year. Most basic tours last about an hour and cost £6 or £7, though the Laphroaig tour is £10. The ticket includes a dram at the end or a discount voucher off the price of a bottle.

hide across the road. There are about 110 species of bird breeding on Islay, including the rare chough and corncrake.

The coastal scenery around the Rinns is very impressive, particularly at **Killinallan Point**, a beautiful and lonely headland at the far northeast of Loch Gruinart. Also impressive is **Ardnave Point**, west of Loch Gruinart, and further west along the north coast, **Sanaigmore**. The best beaches are at **Saligo** and **Machir Bay** on the west coast, past Loch Gorm. Both are lovely, wide, golden beaches backed by high dunes, but swimming is ill-advised due to dangerous undercurrents. Less than a mile behind Machir Bay you'll also find **Kilchoman Distillery and Visitor Centre** (see box, opposite), the isle's newest working distillery and the first on the island for some 125 years. If you fancy a canter along the sands, this is also where to find the Rockside Farm Trekking Centre ① T01496-850231.

Port Charlotte is without doubt the most charming of Islay's villages, with rows of well-kept, whitewashed cottages stretched along the wide bay. Here, below the comfortable youth hostel is the **Islay Natural History Trust** ① *T01496-850288, www.islandnatural history.org, Easter-Oct, Mon-Fri 1030-1630, £3, concessions £2, children £1.50; all tickets are valid for a week.* It's a must for anyone interested in flora and fauna, with good displays on geology and natural history, a video room and reference library. Housed 300 yds away in a former Free Church, the compact **Museum of Islay Life** ① *T01496-850358, www. islaymuseum.org, Apr-end Oct Mon-Fri 1030-1630, £3.50, concessions £2.50, children £1,* is especially worth a visit, with photographs and over 1600 exhibits, including an illicit still found on the island, highlighting the rich past and culture of the native Ileach's (*ee-lach's*). Close-by there's bike hire, whilst just south of the village you'll find the pleasant **Port Mor Campsite**. At the southern end of the Rinns, seven miles south of Port Charlotte, is the picturesque fishing and crofting village of **Portnahaven**, its Hebridean cottages rising steeply above the deeply indented harbour and where the cosy **An Tigh Seinsse bar** by the harbour serves delicious meals including Queen scallops and mains of Islay beef.

Port Askaig and around

Port Askaig is Islay's other ferry port, with connections to the mainland and to the islands of Jura and Colonsay. It's little more than a dock, a car park and a pub huddled at the foot of a steep, wooded hillside. A short walk north along the coast is the **Caol Ila Distillery**, and a couple of miles further north, at the end of the road which branches left before you enter Port Askaig, is the beautifully situated **Bunnahabhain Distillery**.

The A846 runs east from Bridgend out to Port Askaig passing through **Ballygrant**, just to the south of **Loch Finlaggan**. Here, on two crannogs (artificial islands), were the headquarters of the Lords of the Isles, the ancestors of Clan Donald. The MacDonalds ruled from Islay for nearly 350 years, over a vast area covering all of the islands off the west coast and almost the whole of the western seaboard from Cape Wrath to the Mull of Kintyre. To the northeast of the loch, there's the **Finlaggan Centre** ① *T01496-840644, www.finalggan.org, Apr-end Oct Mon-Sat 1030-1630, donations welcome,* which has been expanded to accommodate more objects from the ancient site. You can walk across the fen to **Eilean Mor**, where you'll find a medieval chapel and several ornately carved gravestones. On neighbouring **Eilean na Comhairle** (The Council of the Isle) the Lords of the Isles decided policy.

Listings Islay *map page 98.*

Tourist information

Islay iCentre
Bowmore, T01496-305165. Apr-Jun Mon-Sat 1000-1500, Sun 1200-1500, Jun-Aug Mon-Sat 0900-1730, Sun 1200-1500, Sep-Oct Mon-Sat 1000-1700, Oct-Mar Mon-Fri 1000-1500.

They will find accommodation for you. A useful website is www.islayinfo.com.

Where to stay

££££ Port Charlotte Hotel
On the seafront, Port Charlotte, T01496-850360, www.portcharlottehotel.com.

10 rooms. Restored Victorian inn with gardens and conservatory, serving excellent food (see Restaurants, below). Expensive but one of the best small hotels around. The hotel bar is a great place to relax and enjoy one of the island's famous single malts.

£££ Glenegedale
Port Ellen, T01496-300400,
www.glenegedalehouse.com.
4 rooms. The owners of this guesthouse have every right to be proud of their luxurious accommodation. No stone has been left unturned in their determination to provide a memorable stay, hence the award of the most hospitable B&B in the West of Scotland by VisitScotland. From the roaring peat fire to the complimentary tea and home-baking on your arrival day, hosts Graeme and Emma have thought of everything. Warmly recommended.

£££ Harbour Inn
Main St, Bowmore, just yards from the shore,
T01496-810330, www.bowmore.com.
7 tastefully furnished en suite bedrooms, but the real treat is the fabulous restaurant complete with cosy bar (see Restaurants, below).

£££ Kilmeny
Ballygrant, 4 miles from Port Askaig,
T01496-840668, www.kilmeny.co.uk.
With wonderful views, this is a stylish, rural option with 4 comfortable rooms and a self-contained suite all situated in 300 acres of farmland. Recommended.

££ Sornbank
Bridgend, T01496-810544,
www.sornbank.co.uk.
2 en suite rooms. B&B close to amenities, with excellent breakfast. Lets 2 self-contained flats on a weekly or fortnightly basis, 1 sleeps 2 and the other 4.

£ Port Charlotte Youth Hostel
Port Charlotte, T01496-850385. Apr-Oct.
This very comfortable, spacious SYHA hostel is close to the ales, malts and tasty meals served by the **Port Charlotte Hotel** and **Lochindaal Hotel**. Highly recommended.

Self-catering

Coull Farm Cottage
Bruichladdich, T01496-850317,
www.coull-farm-holidays.co.uk.
Sleeps 5 in a cosy cottage with panoramic views and excellent nearby walks.
£300-500 per week.

Drumlanrig
Carnduncan, Gruinart, T7710-187975,
www.islay-drmlanrig.co.uk.
Sleeps up to 6 people in a well-equipped farmhouse cottage, located close to the renowned RSPB birdspotting reserve and handy for the likes of beaches and pony trekking. From £550-750 per week.

Restaurants

£££ Harbour Inn
See Where to stay, above.
Serves outstanding seafood in a stylish setting.

£££ Kilmeny Country House
See Where to stay, above.
Serves locally caught shellfish and reared beef in a friendly atmosphere. Highly rated food. Recommended.

£££ Port Charlotte Hotel
See Where to stay, above.
Also serves outstanding, locally sourced dishes.

££ Lochindaal Hotel
Port Charlotte T01496-850202,
www.lochindaalhotel.co.uk.
You'll find locally caught shellfish, including mussels and scallops on the menu, and beef or lamb sourced from Hebridean farms. Try their gargantuan seafood platter for 2-3 people (£100).

Festivals

May Islay Festival of Malt and Music, www.feisile.org. Annual folk music festival, for which the distillers produce their own special edition malts.

Sep Islay Jazz Festival, www.islayjazz festival.co.uk.

What to do

Wild Islay Birding, *Ballygrant, contact Gary Turnbull, T01496-840725, www. wildislaybirding.co.uk.* Full day (£45 pp) and half-day tours.

Islay Sea Adventures, *Lagavulin, T01496-300129, www.islay-sea-adventures.co.uk.* Wildlife-spotting boat trips starting from Port Ellen marina. Also Corryvreckan trips from Port Askaig.

Venture West *(see page 66).* Boat trips from Crinan (near Lochgilphead, see page 64) to Corryvreck and Jura. They offer a sea taxi drop-off and pick-up from various points.

Transport

Air

There are daily direct flights from **Glasgow** to Islay's **Glenegedale airport** (T01496-302361). For full details of flight times and prices see **Flybe** (www.flybe.com) and **Loganair** (www.loganair.co.uk) websites.

Cycle hire

Islay Cycles, Port Ellen, T07760-196592, www.islaycycles.co.uk. From £20/15 per day.

Ferry

There are **CalMac** offices in Port Ellen and Port Askaig, T0800-066 5000. Ferries depart daily from Port Ellen (2 hrs 20 mins) and Port Askaig (1 hr 55 mins) to **Kennacraig**; and from Port Askaig to **Oban**, via **Colonsay** on Wed, 4 hrs 15 mins. For ferries to **Jura**, see below.

Jura *Colour maps 3, C4 and 5, A1.*

great walking and wildlife in this remote island wilderness

Three things bring people to sparsely populated Jura, where in early August locals and visitors participate in the open-water rowing competitions of the grandly titled Jura Regatta.

First there's the scenery. This is one of the last true wildernesses in the British Isles and perfect for some real off-the-beaten-track walking. The appealingly named **Paps of Jura**, are three breast-shaped peaks that dominate not only the island itself but also the view for miles around. From Kintyre, Mull, Coll and Tiree, and from the mountains of mainland Scotland from Skye to Arran, they can be seen on the horizon. The Paps provide some tough hillwalking and require good navigational skills, or a guide. It takes a good eight hours to cover all three peaks, though during the Paps of Jura fell race they are covered in just three hours. A good place to start is by the three-arch bridge over the Corran River, north of Leargybreack. The first pap you reach is **Beinn a'Chaolais** (2408 ft), next is the highest, **Beinn an Oír** (2575 ft) and the third is **Beinn Shiantaidh** (2476 ft). To find out about guides, ask at **Jura Stores** ① *T01496-820231*, in Craighouse that has provided much-needed provisions since the 1890s.

Next there's wildlife. Aside from the thousands of red deer, there are sea eagles and golden eagles in the skies above and the surrounding seas are full of seals, dolphins and porpoises, with the elusive otter making an occasional appearance.

And finally, there's whisky. The island's only road leads from the ferry to the only village, **Craighouse**, eight miles away on the southeast coast. Here you'll find the **Jura Distillery** ① *T01496-820385, www.jurawhisky.com, Apr-Oct tours Mon-Sat at 1100 and 1400, Nov-Mar Mon-Fri at 1100 and 1400, £6*, which produces 1½ million litres annually and offers a snifter of the stuff at the end of a friendly and informative 45-minute tour.

Essential Jura

Finding your feet

A small car and passenger ferry makes the regular five-minute crossing daily from Port Askaig on Islay. For times and fares visit www.calmac.co.uk. There's also a handy passenger-only ferry between Tayvallich and Craighouse that runs from June to the end of September; details at www.jurapassengerferry.com. There is a bus service on Jura, which runs from Feolin Ferry to Craighouse several times a day, Monday to Saturday. A few buses continue to Lagg and Inverlussa and return to Craighouse. Note that some journeys are by request only and must be booked the day before. Buses are operated by **Garelochhead Coaches**, T01496-810200, www.garelochheadcoaches.co.uk. See also Transport, page 105.

Another of the island's draws is the ★ **Corryvreckan whirlpool** at the very northern tip, between Jura and the uninhabited island of **Scarba**. The notorious whirlpool, the second largest in the world, is in fact a tidal race that creates an action like a gigantic washing machine. It is seen at its awesome best during spring tides, especially with a westerly gale, when this most treacherous stretch of water creates waves of over 30 ft (9 m) and the terrible roar can be heard from up to 10 miles away. A two-hour tidal difference between the sound on the east and the Atlantic flood tides combine with the gulf of Corryvreckan's steep sides and underwater pinnacle, the Hag, to create the vortex. The Royal Navy officially says it's unsailable, but that doesn't stop several local boat tours actually going over the top of it. It is named after a Viking, Bhreacan, who anchored his boat here for three days and nights with a rope woven from the hair of virgins. Unsurprisingly, the rope parted under the strain, casting doubt on the status of one of the contributors, and Bhreacan drowned. To get there, follow the rough track from **Ardlussa** to **Kinuachdrach** (about 8 miles), or get someone to drive you, then it's a two-mile walk. Before setting out, ask at the hotel for information and directions.

In 1947, the Corryvreckan nearly claimed the life of one Eric Arthur Blair – aka George Orwell – who had come to Jura to finish the novel that would later become *Nineteen Eighty-Four*. Despite being diagnosed with tuberculosis, Orwell went to live on Jura with his three-year-old adopted son, Richard, in spartan conditions at **Barnhill**, a cottage in the middle of nowhere and 25 miles from the nearest doctor. That summer he invited his niece and nephew to stay, and one day took them out into the Corryvrekcan in a tiny boat. When the outboard motor was ripped off by the force of the tide and the boat capsized, Orwell and the others only just escaped with their lives by clambering onto a small island; they were later rescued by a passing lobster boat. Today, Barnhill attracts literary pilgrims and, though closed to the public, can be rented for a week's stay (see Where to stay, below).

Also on the island, three miles south of Craighouse village, at **Ardfin**, is the beautiful walled garden at **Jura House**, which is filled with wild flowers and Australasian plants and trees. The garden is now inaccessible to the public as the Ardfin Estate was bought by an Australian multi-millionaire who is currently building a luxury golf course and hotel complex.

Where to stay

£££ Jura Hotel
Craighouse, T01496-820243, www.jurahotel. co.uk. Open all year.
18 bedrooms. The island's one and only hotel, overlooking the Small Isles Bay. The hotel bar is the island's social hub, and hosts Steve and Fiona Walton, who have been here for 25 years, can provide information on walks as well as arranging tours to the Corryvreckan and fishing trips. The restaurant serves good food, see Restaurants, below. Great place to relax after a hike and enjoy banter with the locals. Gets very busy in summer. Camping is also possible in the hotel grounds.

Self-catering
There are several cottages for rent, contact www.juraholidaycottage.co.uk for full details. For more ascetic souls, and devotees of George Orwell, you can rent **Barnhill**, the house where he wrote *1984*. Contact Damaris Fletcher, T01786-850274. Sleeps 8, £1000 per week. Very remote – 14 miles north of the nearest pub and shop.

Restaurants

££ Jura Hotel
See Where to stay, above.
Currently the only option for either a bar meal or evening dining. Try the fresh langoustines or famed venison pie.

Festivals

Aug Jura Regatta. See page 103.

What to do

See also What to do, Islay, page 103.

Alex Dunnachie, *T01496-820314 or 07884-024777, or email at jurabus@yahoo.com.*
Runs guided tours of Jura, or can drive you from A to B.

Transport

Cycle hire
Jura Bike Hire, Keils, just beyond Craighouse, T07768-450000.

Ferry
A small car and passenger ferry makes the regular 5-min crossing daily from **Port Askaig** on Islay to **Feolin Ferry**. For times and prices see www.calmac.co.uk. There's also a passenger-only ferry between **Craighouse** and the mainland, **Tayvallich** (off B841), that runs daily except Wed Jun-Sep, £20 one-way with bus connections. For bookings T07768-450000.

Central
Highlands

rugged mountains, remote glens and mysterious lochs

The vast swathe of Central Highlands is not a distinct region but rather the sum of disparate parts of other regions, including Perthshire, the Trossachs, Angus Glens, part of Deeside, the Grampians, Strathspey and Loch Lomond.

The historically important regions of Perthshire and Stirling straddle the Highland Boundary Fault, the dividing line between the heavily populated Central Lowlands and the wild and empty Highlands. Just across this 'border' is the Trossachs, a picture-postcard area of mountains, forests and lochs that stretches west from Callander to the eastern shore of Loch Lomond, and the glens of Perthshire, whose atmospheric lochs and mountains are rich in history.

The spectacular and varied landscape ranges from the gentle pleasures of Loch Tay to the rugged peaks of the Grampian Mountains, where there are Munros aplenty for the bagging and all manner of adventure activities, including some of Scotland's best winter skiing. On the eastern shores of Loch Lomond is the West Highland Way, Scotland's most popular long-distance hike and, in the northeast, is Deeside, home to many of Scotland's most notable castles, one of which is the holiday home of the most famous family in the UK.

Best for
Castles ▪ Mountain biking ▪ Walking ▪ Whisky

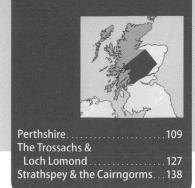

Perthshire......................109
The Trossachs &
    Loch Lomond.................127
Strathspey & the Cairngorms...138

Footprint
picks

★ **Scone Palace**, page 111

The ancient crowning place of Scottish kings, including Macbeth and Robert the Bruce, with magnificent 100-acre gardens.

★ **Fortingall**, page 123

This idyllic little Perthshire village is home to the oldest living thing in Europe (a yew tree) and is the birthplace of one Pontius Pilate.

★ **Glen Lyon**, page 124

One of the loveliest glens in the whole country and barely another soul in sight. The perfect place for a summer picnic.

★ **Queen Elizabeth Forest Park**, page 129

This vast, spectacular wilderness of 75,000 acres is waiting to be explored by adventurous walkers and cyclists.

★ **Duke's Pass**, page 129

The road north from Aberfoyle to Callander passes through the spectacular Duke's Pass as it snakes through the heart of the beautiful Trossachs.

★ **Abernethy Forest RSPB Reserve**, page 146

Home to breeding pairs of the rare osprey as well as the Scottish crossbill, capercaillie and red squirrels.

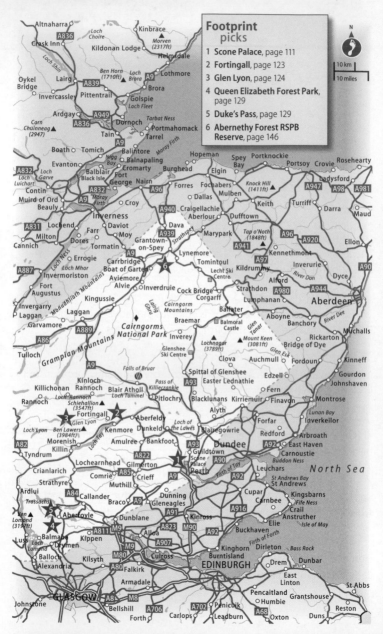

Footprint
picks

1 **Scone Palace**, page 111
2 **Fortingall**, page 123
3 **Glen Lyon**, page 124
4 **Queen Elizabeth Forest Park**, page 129
5 **Duke's Pass**, page 129
6 **Abernethy Forest RSPB Reserve**, page 146

N

10 km
10 miles

Perthshire

Perth, where the rural and urban intertwine, is the main gateway to the eastern side of the Highlands and the A9, the road north, is a gentle introduction to the wild northern reaches of Scotland. The Perthshire Highlands may lack the sheer magisterial grandeur of the northwest but they have their own serene beauty. Numerous remnants from the Highland's troubled past are scattered around the glens of Perthshire, including Blair Castle and Scone Palace.

Essential Central Highlands

Getting around

Most of the major tourist centres around Perthshire and Strathspey can be reached by bus or train but to explore more thoroughly and to get around the Trossachs easily you'll need your own transport.

Time required

A week would be enough time to see the best of Perthshire, the Trossachs and Loch

Best walks

Pass of Killiecrankie, page 118
Schiehallion, page 119
Blair Atholl to Glen Fincastle, page 119
Ben Lawers, page 124

Best views

Kinnoull Hill, page 111
The Hermitage, page 113
Ben y Vrackie, page 117
Falls of Moness, page 123
Ben Lawers, page 124

Lomond, plus another week to explore Strathspey and the Cairngorms.

When to go

Anytime from Easter through to the end of September is good but if you want winter sports don't come until December or January.

'The Fair City' of Perth is aptly named. Situated on the banks of Scotland's longest river, the Tay, Perth and its surrounding area boasts some of the most beautiful scenery in the country. It's a pleasant, compact town with a popular farmers' market (www.perthfarmersmarket.co.uk), on the first Saturday of every month, Perth was once the capital of Scotland. Awash with traditional traders like Kerrigan's Tobacconists, where you'll find old-world sweeties, and 'scone shops' of which Scottish comedian Billy Connolly would be proud, there are several notable sights to visit, from the ultra-modern, £20 million Concert Hall that stands on the site of a 17th-century horse market, to the fascinating jewel in Perth's crown, Scone Palace. For nearly 500 years Scone was the home of the Stone of Destiny and the site where every Scottish king was crowned. It's pleasant to stroll by the river, whilst the city is well placed for outdoor activities such as walking, fishing and cycling.

Sights

North of the High Street, on North Port, is the **Fair Maid's House** (closed to the public) the fictional home of Sir Walter Scott's virginal heroine in his novel, *The Fair Maid of Perth*. Close by, at the corner of Charlotte Street and George Street, is the **Museum and Art Gallery** ⓘ *T01738-632488, www.culturepk.org.uk, Tue-Sun 1000-1700 in summer, check for winter times, free*, with over 500,000 exhibits including displays on local history, art, archaeology, natural history and whisky.

In the 18th century the world-famous Black Watch regiment was raised in Perth, and the **Black Watch Museum** ⓘ *Hay St, T01738 638152, www.theblackwatch.co.uk, Apr-Oct daily 0930-1630, Nov-Mar 1000-1600, £7.50, concessions £6, children £3.50, under 5s free, guided tours £12.50/£10/7.50*, housed in the 15th-century Balhousie Castle, is well worth a visit even to the most un-military minded. The museum is on the edge of the North Inch,

Essential Perthshire

Finding your feet

Perth is accessible from almost anywhere in the country. It's only one to 1½ hours from Edinburgh or Glasgow, and half an hour from Dundee by road, and is on the main train lines to these cities, as well as on the main lines north to Aberdeen and Inverness. For further details, see Transport, page 116.

Getting around

Though the more remote northerly parts of Perthshire are difficult to reach by public transport, much of the region is easily accessible. The main road north to

Inverness, the A9, runs through the heart of the region. Dunkeld and Pitlochry are on the Perth–Inverness rail line and there are several daily trains to Perth. **Stagecoach Strathtay**, www.stagecoachbus.com, run hourly buses (less frequently on Sunday) from Perth to Blairgowrie and Glenshee on the A93.

Tourist information

The region, from Kinross in the south to Blair Atholl in the north and from Glenshee in the east to Rannoch Moor in the west, is covered by **VisitScotland Perthshire** (www.visit scotland.co.uk), with tourist offices in Aberfeldy, Blairgowrie, Dunkeld, Perth and Pitlochry.

to the north of the town centre. It's also worth perusing the work of the renowned Scottish colourist, John Duncan Fergusson, within the **Fergusson Gallery** ① *T01738-783425, Tue-Sat 1000-1700, Sun 12000-1630, free*, in Perth's historic Round House.

For those with more horticultural leanings, **Branklyn Garden** ① *116 Dundee Rd, T1737-625535 (NTS), Apr-Oct daily 1000-1700, £6.50, concessions £5, family £16.50*, has been described as "the finest two acres of private garden in the country". Started in 1922 and with an impressive collection of rare and unusual plants, it includes superb examples of Himalayan poppies and is well worth a visit at any time of year. Many of the plants grown there are on sale in the shop.

Kinnoull Hill Woodland Park is a beautiful wooded area on the outskirts of the city. The trip to the top of Kinnoull Hill itself (783 ft) affords an astounding view across Perth, down to the Tay estuary and through Fife to the Lomond hills. To the north, the views stretch from Ben More in the west to Lochnagar in the northeast. There are four walks through the Woodland Park – Nature Walk, Tower Walk, Jubilee Walk and Squirrel Walk – and each of these is graded according to how difficult it is and what type of conditions the walker can expect. However, none of the walks are extremely strenuous, though the Squirrel Walk is most suitable for the less able. If you're feeling particularly energetic, cycling and horse riding take place in specific zones in the park, principally in the Deuchny Wood area. There is a **Countryside Ranger Service** in the park; the rangers will be happy to answer any questions you may have about their work or the park itself. Also ask at the tourist office in town for details.

Huntingtower Castle ① *3 miles west of Perth on the A85 to Crieff, T01738-627231 (HES), Apr-Sep daily 0930-1730, Oct daily 1000-1600, Nov-Mar Sun-Wed 1000-1600, £5, concessions £4, children 5-15 £3, under 5s free*, is also worth a visit. It consists of two complete towers dating from the 15th and 16th centuries, linked by a 17th-century range, and features some fine 16th-century painted ceilings. The castle, once owned by the Ruthven family, has some interesting history of its own. Prior to the building of the range, a daughter of the house once leapt between the two towers to avoid being caught in her lover's bedroom.

The **Museum of Abernethy** ① *T01738-850889, www.museumofabernethy.co.uk, May-Sep Wed-Sun 1400-1700, free*, provides a further insight into Perthshire's history, including the ancient Picts. This museum is just seven miles south of Perth on the A912.

★ **Scone Palace**
T01738-552300, www.scone-palace.co.uk, May-Sep daily 0930-1700, grounds open till 1745, Apr and Oct 1000-1600. Palace and grounds £11.50, concessions £10.20, children £8, grounds only £6.80/6/5; Nov-Mar free access to grounds Fri-Sun 1000-1600. 'Scotland's Treasure Ticket' also covers admittance to Blair Castle and Glamis Castle, £28, concessions £25, children £17, family £85.

Essential Perth

Getting around

The train and bus stations are almost opposite each other at the west end of town, where Leonard Street meets Kings Place. The town centre is compact and easy to get around on foot, but Scone Palace and many B&Bs are on the eastern bank of the river, so you may wish to take a bus. Local buses are run by **Stagecoach Strathtay**. To reach Scone Palace take the No 3 Strathtay bus service from outside Mountain Supplies on South Street. This service runs every hour on the hour. For local bus timetables visit the Perth & Kinross Council website, www.pkc.gov.uk.

Three miles northeast of Perth on the A93 Braemar road, is the not-to-be-missed Scone Palace, one of the most historically important places in the country (though much of the present palace building only dates from the 19th century). The home of the Earls of Mansfield, Scone (pronounced 'scoon') has a long and fascinating history. It was the capital of the Pictish Kingdom in the sixth century and home of the Celtic church. Here, Kenneth MacAlpin united Scotland and, in AD 838, placed the stone of Scone (or 'Stone of Destiny') on Moot Hill, opposite the palace entrance. This became the ancient crowning

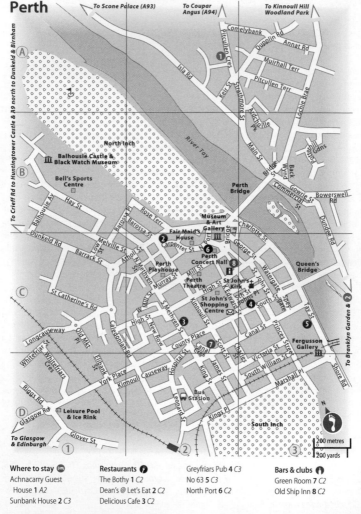

Perth

To Scone Palace (A93)
To Coupar Angus (A94)
To Kinnoull Hill Woodland Park
To Crieff Rd to Huntingtower Castle & A9 north to Dunkeld & Birnam
To Dunkeld & Birnam
To Glasgow & Edinburgh
To Branklyn Garden

Comelybank
Pitcullen Cres
Dupplin Rd
Annat Rd
Isla Rd
Kinfauns Rd
Muirhall Terr
Strathmore St
Pitcullen Terr
Lochie Brae
River Tay
Main St
Back Wynd
Gowrie St
Commercial St
Bowerswell Rd
Dundee Rd
North Inch
Balhousie Castle & Black Watch Museum
Bell's Sports Centre
Hay St
Rose Terr
Perth Bridge
Museum & Art Gallery
Charlotte St
Balhousie Av
Melville St
Barossa St
Barossa Pl
Fair Maid's House
Carpenter St
George St
Perth Bridge
Queen's Bridge
Dunkeld Rd
Barrack St
Atholl St
Murray St
Perth Playhouse
Mill St
Perth Concert Hall
Perth Theatre
St John's Kirk
Watergate
Tay St
St Catherine's Rd
Kinnoull St
North Methven St
High St
St John's Shopping Centre
St John's Pl
South St
Princes St
Caledonian Rd
County Place
Canal St
South St
Fergusson Gallery
Longcauseway
Old Mkt
High St
New Row
Hospital St
Canal St
Scott St
Whitefriars
Whitefriars Cres
Ellbank St
Methven St
York Place
Kinnoull Causeway
King St
James St
Victoria St
South William St
Marshall Pl
Shore Rd
Riggs Rd
Bus Station
Leonard St
Kings Pl
South Inch
Glasgow Rd
Leisure Pool & Ice Rink
Glover St
200 metres
200 yards

Where to stay 🛏
Achnacarry Guest
House **1** A2
Sunbank House **2** C3

Restaurants 🍴
The Bothy **1** C2
Dean's @ Let's Eat **2** C2
Delicious Cafe **3** C2

Greyfriars Pub **4** C3
No 63 **5** C3
North Port **6** C2

Bars & clubs 🍸
Green Room **7** C2
Old Ship Inn **8** C2

place of Scottish kings, including Macbeth and Robert the Bruce. The Royal City of Scone became the seat of government, and the kings of Scotland resided at the Palace of Scone before their coronation. The coronation stone was removed to Westminster by that most hated foe, Edward I, in 1296, and was only returned to Scotland in 1996 in an unsuccessful Conservative attempt to win back support north of the border. The famed stone currently resides in Edinburgh Castle. In 1651, the last coronation in Scotland took place when King Charles II was crowned by the Scots on Moot Hill. The ceremony was attended by Lord Stormont, forefather of the present occupier, Lord Mansfield. Part of the church where this took place still remains. Today, Scone Palace attracts over 100,000 annual visitors.

Aside from its impressive history, the palace also houses beautiful collections of porcelain, needlework, royal furniture, clocks, ivories and many other absorbing artefacts. You could also spend a few hours walking in the magnificent 100-acre gardens, filled with bluebells, rhododendrons, roses and rare trees, with strutting peacocks and Highland cattle roaming around. There's also a maze, picnic park and children's adventure playground, plus a gift shop and coffee shop with delicious home-baking.

Stanley Mills
T01738-828268, HES, Apr-Sep daily 0930-1730, Oct daily 1000-1600, £6, concessions £4.80, children £3.60.

Seven miles north of Perth off the A9 and on the banks of the River Tay stands the impressive Stanley Mills water mill complex. In 1786, the first water mill was constructed to harness the power of the Tay to support a thriving cotton spinning industry. Though commercial operations ceased in 1989, in 1995 Historic Scotland began the restoration of the mill complex. In 2008 and after a £4.6 million redevelopment, the complex reopened with the lovingly restored Bell Mill and Mid Mill forming a visitor attraction and education resource that through interactive displays, exhibits and even the 'voices' of the long-deceased workers reveals how the mill operated and how it impacted on the lives of the community, including its children.

Dunkeld and Birnam
Some 12 miles north of Perth is the attractive village of **Dunkeld**, standing right on the Highland line. It's definitely worth making a stop here, if only to admire the **cathedral** ⓘ *T01350-727249, www.dunkeldcathedral.org.uk, Apr-Sep daily 1000-1730, Oct-Mar daily 1000-1600, free*, in the most idyllic situation on the banks of the fast-flowing, silvery Tay. Half of it is still in use as a church and the other half is in ruins. The oldest part of the cathedral is the 14th-century choir, which now forms the parish church, while the 15th-century nave and tower are also still standing. Much of the original was damaged during the orgy of ecclesiastical destruction that accompanied the Reformation. It was damaged again in the Battle of Dunkeld in 1689, fought between supporters of the protestant William of Orange and the Stuart monarch James VII. Dunkeld offers excellent walking opportunities, details of which are available from the **iCentre** (see page 114).

Across the bridge from Dunkeld is **Birnam**, made famous in Shakespeare's *Macbeth*. Birnam was the inspiration for another famous literary figure, Beatrix Potter, who spent her childhood summers here. Visitors can explore the origins of Peter Rabbit at the **Beatrix Potter Exhibition** ⓘ *T01350-727674, www.birnamarts.com, daily 1000-1630 £3, free for under 3s*. There's also a lovely, child-friendly café.

A short distance north of Dunkeld on the A9 is the turning to **The Hermitage**. A marked woodland walk starts from the car park (£2) and follows the River Braan to the Black

Linn Falls, overlooked by Ossian's Hall, an 18th-century folly built by the Duke of Atholl. Surrounded by Douglas fir trees as high as 210 ft, it's a beautifully serene spot, which has inspired the likes of Wordsworth and Mendelssohn. Further on is **Ossian's Cave**. It's worthwhile purchasing a copy of the 'Dunkeld and Birnam' walking routes map (£1) from the **Dunkeld iCentre** and from where you can also walk to The Hermitage. Buses to Pitlochry (T01738-629339) will stop on request just south of The Hermitage.

A few miles northeast of Dunkeld, off the A923 to Blairgowrie, is the **Loch of the Lowes Visitor Centre** ① *T01350-727337, Mar-Oct daily 1000-1700, Nov-Feb Fri-Sun 1030-1600, £4, concessions £3.50, children 50p,* managed by the Scottish Wildlife Trust. There's a hide with binoculars for viewing a pair of breeding ospreys (early April to August), which can sometimes be seen over the loch. Woodpeckers and red deer are also among the wildlife on the reserve with its 'nest-cam' and shop.

Listings Perth and around *map page 112.*

Tourist information

Perth iCentre
45 High St, Perth, T01738-450600. Apr-Jun and Sep-Mar Mon-Sat 0930-1700, Sun 1100-1600; Jul-Aug Mon-Sat 0900-1830, Sun 1100-1700.

Dunkeld iCentre
The Cross, Dunkeld, T01350-727688. Jul-Aug Mon-Sat 0900-1730, Sun 1030-1630; Sep-Oct Mon-Sat 1000-1630, Sun 1100-1600; Nov-Mar Fri-Sun 1100-1600; Apr-Jun Mon-Sat 1000-1630, Sun 1100-1600.

Where to stay

££££ Ballathie House Hotel
Kinclaven, near Stanley, 9 miles north of Perth, just off the A9, T01250-883268, www.ballathiehousehotel.com.
43 rooms. An elegant, 19th-century former hunting lodge serving up delicious traditional Scottish cuisine in beautiful surroundings. Renowned as a base for traditional field sports, the estate also offers self-catering and B&B options in its **Sportsman's Lodge**.

££££ Dunkeld House Hotel
Dunkeld, T01796-727771, www.dunkeldhousehotel.co.uk.
Luxurious former summer residence for the wife of the 7th Duke of Atholl, now an impressive hotel with full leisure and outdoor activity facilities. Accommodation in rooms, suites, a self-contained lodge (sleeps up to 9) or cottage (sleeps up to 4). The dinner, bed and breakfast option is the best value.

£££ Huntingtower Hotel
1 mile west of Perth off the A85 to Crieff, T01738-583771, www.huntingtowerhotel.co.uk.
Elegant Tudor-style country house hotel in landscaped gardens, with 34 rooms. Serves good food and is able to organize many outdoor activities.

£££-££ Sunbank House Hotel
50 Dundee Rd, Perth, T01738-624882. 10 rooms, 2 with disabled access.
A traditional Victorian sandstone hotel overlooking the Tay set in ½ acre of gardens, 10 mins' walk from the city centre and close to Branklyn Garden and Kinnoull Hill. Spacious and comfortable bedrooms. Italian owners will provide dinner and also picnics on request.

££ Achnacarry Guest House
3 Pitcullen Cres, on the A94 Coupar Angus road, 10 mins' walk from Perth town centre, T01738-621421, www.achnacarry.co.uk.
6 rooms. Comfortable and friendly B&B, 10 mins from town centre.

££ Tormaukin Inn
Glendevon, 10 miles south of Crieff. T01259-781252, www.tormaukinhotel.co.uk.
Atmospheric 250-year-old drover's inn with lots of rustic charm and comfortable rooms, real ales in the cosy bar and a terrific restaurant (££), serving steak and ale pie and baked hare. Family rooms available and dogs welcome in stable block. Great value.

££-£ Comrie Croft
Comrie Rd by Crieff, T01764-670140, www.comriecroft.com. Open all year.
Award-winning green campsite/backpackers' hostel, with accommodation in the farmhouse, steading bunkhouse, eco-camping or Norwegian katas (complete with wood-burning stoves), which also offers mountain bike hire, walking trails and wildlife viewing.

£ Wester Caputh Independent Hostel
Caputh, 5 miles east of Dunkeld, on the A984 to Coupar Angus, T01738-710449. Open all year.
17 beds and a log stove. A 3-mile walk to the pub but 300 yds from public transport.

Camping

Scone Palace Camping & Caravan Club Site
5 miles north of Perth, T01738-552323. Apr-Oct.
Located within the picturesque estate. 120 pitches and good amenities, including showers.

Restaurants

£££-££ Dean's @Let's Eat
Kinnoull St, T01738-643377. Tue-Sat 1200-1430, 1800-2100.
Still one of the best places to eat in Perth with contemporary Scottish cuisine, cooked fresh to order with a smile. Bargain 2-course set lunch for £12.50.

£££-££ No 63
63 Tay St, T01738-441451. Tue-Sat 1200-1400, 1830-2100, pre-theatre menu 1745-1930.
Stylish restaurant down by the river with a thoughtful dinner and lunch (££) menu that includes crab and Carnoustie pork.

£££-££ North Port
8 North Port, T01738-580867. Tue-Sat 1200-1430, 1700-2130.
An excellent addition to Perth's culinary scene. Serves the finest ingredients from all over Scotland, from Isle of Skye crab to Cupar venison, and the finest of Scottish cheeses, if you have any room left. Good-value 2-course lunch and pre-theatre dinner menus (£13.95 and £16.95).

££ The Bothy Restaurant and Bar
33 Kinnoull St, T0845 659 5907.
Pleasant ambience with tasty steaks and duck amongst the treats. Good brunch menu.

£ Delicious Café
46 South Methven St, T01738-451617. Mon-Sat 1000-1700.
Child friendly and great range of fresh filled sandwiches, wraps, toasties, coffees and smoothies.

£ Greyfriars Pub
15 South St, T01738-633036.
Cosy pub serving hearty lunches, daily 1200-1430, with great selection of real ales including 'Piddle in the Cellar!'

Bars and clubs

Some pubs are listed under Restaurants, above. There are many drinking establishments in the town but 2 of the best are the **Old Ship Inn** (31 Hight St, T01738-624929) and the **Green Room** (97 Canal St, T01738-248121), which is also a live music venue.

Entertainment

Perth Theatre and Concert Hall, *Mill St, T0845-621031, www.horsecross.co.uk.* The old theatre has now been transformed into a striking £20 million arts and music venue with daily music and theatre events and 2 excellent cafés and bar.

Playhouse, *6 Murray St, T01738-623126*. Offers a dose of escapism on the big screen.

Festivals

May Atholl Highlanders Parade Watch soldiers in full highland regalia and as part of Britain's only private army march at Blair Atholl Castle.

Jun Perthshire Archaeology Month Participate in excavations, guided walks, talks and exhibitions held on the subject throughout Perthshire.

Aug Perth Highland Games Held on the 2nd Sun in Aug (1030-1730) the week after the **Perth Show**, which also take place in South Inch.

What to do

Cycling
3 national cycle routes pass through Perthshire using quiet country roads and off-road track. Ask at the local tourist office or see www.sustrans.org.uk for details.

Fishing
Details of all the Perthshire fisheries are available from the **Perth iCentre**, or visit www.gordonianfishings.co.uk.

Golf
See www.perthshire.co.uk, for a full list of the area's many courses.
King James VI Golf Club, *Moncreiffe Island, T01738-632460*. An 18-hole golf-course near the town centre.

Horse racing
Perth Racecourse, *near Scone Palace, T01738-551597, www.perth-races.co.uk*. Has regular jump racing events during the summer.

Leisure centres
Bell's Sports Centre, *Hay St, T01738-454647. Daily 0900-2200*. Covers virtually every sport and leisure activity imaginable.
Dewar's Centre, *Glover St and next door to the pool, T01738-454700. Sun-Thu 0900-2330, Fri-Sat 0900-0030*. Where you can curl, ice skate or bowl.
Perth Leisure Pool, *Glasgow Rd, T01738-454654, www.liveactive.co.uk. Daily 1000-2200*.

Transport

Bus
Regular buses to **Blairgowrie**, **Dunkeld** (No 23), **Aberfeldy** (No 23), **Pitlochry** (No 27), **Alyth**, **Scone** (No 71), and **Kinloch Rannoch** (No 89), Stagecoach Strathtay, T0871-200 2233, www.stagecoachbus.com.

Citylink buses running between **Perth** and **Inverness** stop at the train station by **Birnam** several times daily. **Scottish Citylink buses**, www.citylink.co.uk, run frequently to **Glasgow** (1 hr 25 mins), **Edinburgh** (1½ hrs), **Dundee** (35 mins), **Aberdeen** (2½ hrs) and **Inverness** (2½ hrs).

Car hire
Arnold Clark, St Leonard's Bank, Perth, T01738-442202.

Train
There are hourly trains to **Stirling** (30 mins), **Dundee** (25 mins) and **Aberdeen** (1 hr 40 mins), and several daily to **Inverness** via **Pitlochry** (30 mins) and **Aviemore**. There's a train service daily to **Glasgow Queen St** (1 hr); and frequent trains to **Edinburgh** (1 hr 20 mins).

great walking and plenty of good pubs and restaurants

Despite being one of the busiest Highland tourist towns in the summer, Pitlochry's setting on the shores of the River Tummel, overlooked by Ben y Vrackie, makes it a pleasant enough base for exploring the area, especially out of season. The town also has a few attractions of its own.

Sights

Pitlochry's main attraction is the **fish ladder**, part of the power station and dam which formed man-made **Loch Faskally** when it was constructed on the River Tummel. The ladder allows salmon to swim up to their spawning grounds and you can watch them leaping spectacularly in the spring and summer. The best months are May and June. The fish ladder is across the river, a short distance from the **Pitlochry Festival Theatre**, see page 122.

Also here is the **Explorers Garden** ① T01796-484600, www.explorersgarden.com, Apr-Oct daily 1000-1700, £4, concessions £3.50, children 5-15 £1, under 5s free. This fascinating garden containing diverse plant species and trails pays tribute to the story of Scotland's 18th- and 19th-century botanists and explorers.

There are two whisky distilleries to visit. The larger, though less inspiring, of the two is Bell's **Blair Atholl Distillery** ① T01796-482003, www.malts.com, Apr-Oct daily 1000-1700, Nov-Mar daily 1000-1600, tours hourly between these times, standard tour £7.50, redeemable in shop, at the southern end of town, heading towards the A9 to Perth. A couple of miles east of town, on the A924, is the **Edradour Distillery** ① T01796-472095, www.edradour. com, Apr-Oct Mon-Sat 1000-1700, £7.50, children 12-17 £2.50. Producing just 12 casks of whisky a week, it remains the smallest distillery in Scotland – a blessing or a curse, depending on how busy it is.

Local walks

OS Landranger maps Nos 43 and 52 cover all the walks, and the OS Explorer map No 21 (Pitlochry and Loch Tummel) covers them in greater detail.

The tourist office sells a useful leaflet, *Pitlochry Walks* (£1), which describes several long local walks, and there are many other fine walks in the surrounding area. The greatest walking attraction is **Ben y Vrackie** (2758 ft), a steep six-mile walk (there and back) from the tiny hamlet of Moulin, a mile north of Pitlochry on the A924 (turn left at the **Moulin Inn**). The path is well trodden and the going is relatively easy, across bleak moorland, until the steep final ascent on scree. On a clear day the views across Perthshire and towards the Trossachs from the summit are wonderful. Don't attempt this on a cloudy day. In spite of its proximity to Pitlochry, you need to be properly equipped and take the usual safety precautions, see box, page 21.

Another excellent walk from Pitlochry, described in the tourist office leaflet, leaves town on the north road and turns left past the boat station. It then crosses the Cluanie footbridge and follows the road to Loch Faskally and up the River Garry to Garry Bridge over the Pass of Killiecrankie, see below. The path returns to Pitlochry along the west bank of the River Garry, before turning west up the River Tummel, passing close by the Linn of Tummel, then crossing the Tummel and following the west shore of Loch Faskally to the dam and fish ladder.

Pass of Killiecrankie

Four miles north of Pitlochry the A9 cuts through the Pass of Killiecrankie, a spectacular wooded gorge which was the dramatic setting for the Battle of Killiecrankie in 1689, when a Jacobite army led by Graham of Claverhouse, Viscount 'Bonnie Dundee', defeated the government forces under General Hugh Mackay. One government soldier allegedly evaded capture by making a jump of Olympic gold medal-winning proportions across the River Garry at **Soldier's Leap**. The **NTS Visitor Centre** ① *T01796-473233, Apr-Nov daily 1000-1700, free (honesty box £1 donation advised, parking £2)*, tells the story of the battle and features interactive displays on the area's natural history.

The 1½-mile waymarked trail from the centre through the ancient, native deciduous trees to the gorge and Leap is both rewarding and spectacular. There's also another three-mile waymarked trail around the **Killiecrankie Nature Reserve** that starts from the Balrobbie Farm car park and which may offer sightings of the great spotted woodpecker. Follow the signs for the reserve from Killiecrankie village, take the minor road over the River Garry, then take the left fork up a steep hill. Turn right at the sharp bend into the farm car park. Access to the reserve is free, but there's a cairn for donations and a parking charge.

Head down the driveway, then turn right along the road which climbs uphill below wooded crags. Turn right through a gate, opposite a cottage and follow a grassy track to a gate in a stone wall. Through the gate, the path climbs diagonally under the crags to an iron gate beside a bench. Go through the gate and the path zigzags steeply up to an area of open marsh. The path curves right and continues to climb across a heather moor and past a ruin.

At the crest of the hill, from where there are wonderful views down to Blair Atholl, go downhill, over a stile and enter woodland. Beyond the trees is another bench, then the trail turns to the right. After another two stiles the path heads left downhill, then zigzags down a rocky slope, before heading diagonally downhill to the right to an iron gate. Pick up the path again by a stone wall and follow it back to the car park.

Blair Castle

www.blair-castle.co.uk, T01796-481207, Apr-Oct daily 0930-1730, last admission 1630; house and gardens £11, concessions £9.50, children £7. Gardens only adult and concession £6.50, children £3. Note not all trains from Pitlochry stop at Blair Atholl.

Seven miles from Pitlochry, and a mile from the village of **Blair Atholl**, is Blair Castle, the traditional seat of the Earls and Dukes of Atholl. This whitewashed, turreted castle dates from 1269 and presents an impressive picture on first sight. This is the headquarters of Britain's only private army, the Atholl Highlanders. Thirty rooms in the castle are open for public viewing and are packed full of paintings, furniture, armour, porcelain and much else besides, presenting a startling picture of aristocratic Highland life in previous centuries. The surrounding landscaped grounds are home to peacocks and Highland cattle, and there are woodland walks, pony trekking, Land Rover tours and a walled Japanese water garden to enjoy. Every August, its grounds also host the internationally acclaimed **Blair Horse Trials** ① *www.blairhorsetrials.co.uk*. A handy camping site is immediately adjacent to the castle grounds. The castle also runs occasional 'Attic Tours', which give access to private areas including the highest vantage point in the castle. These are extremely popular and prior booking is essential.

Falls of Bruar

Eight miles from Blair Atholl, just off the A9, are the dramatic Falls of Bruar. A well-maintained path leads from the lower falls along the deep gorge of the Bruar River to the upper falls and back down the other side. It's a 1½-mile round trip.

From the House of Bruar (see below), turn right by the adventure playground, then left up the river bank. The path passes under a railway arch and through a kissing gate. It then heads through open forest to a rocky outcrop, from where you can see the lower falls. A series of wooden steps leads down from the outcrop, then a path climbs up until it forks. Go right, then cross the bridge, from where there's a good view of the lower falls. From here a clear path leads up the far side until it reaches a deer fence. Climb up to the gate, go through it and continue uphill through trees until the path levels out high above the gorge. Further on there's a picnic area, then the path curves left down to the upper bridge, which is a great vantage point from which to admire the stunning view. The path heads left through more trees. It then crosses a stream before descending to the lower bridge and then back to the car park. Take extreme care with children.

By the car park is the tourist-trap of the **House of Bruar**, a huge shopping emporium designed like a Victorian hunting lodge where you can buy the likes of fine country clothing, artwork and a wide range of Scottish food and drink products. There's also a good, if busy and somewhat pricey restaurant that serves lunches, home-bakes and coffee.

Blair Atholl to Kinloch Rannoch

The B8019 turns off the B8079 road from Pitlochry to Blair Atholl and runs west along the shores of beautiful lochs Tummel and Rannoch, best seen in the autumn when the trees change their colours. You may also spot caipercaillie and red squirrels in the area. At the eastern end of Loch Tummel is **Queen's View**, a spectacular viewpoint which looks down the loch and across to Schiehallion. Here, there's a **Forestry Commission Scotland Visitor Centre** ⓘ *T01796-474188, Apr-Oct daily 1000-1700, free, parking £2*, with displays and audio-visual programmes about the area and recently updated maps for sale outlining locals walks and climbs. There's also a tearoom (T01796-473133).

Schiehallion (3547 ft) is one of Scotland's best-loved mountains, whose distinctive conical peak made it ideal for use in early experiments in 1774 to judge the weight of the earth. These were not an unqualified success, but led to the invention of contour lines as an aid to surveying the mountain. The walk to the summit is fairly straightforward, except for the very rocky final half-mile stretch. You'll need to be properly clothed and equipped and take a map and compass. The route to the summit starts at the car park on the B846 Kinloch Rannoch to Aberfeldy road, near Braes of Foss; OS sheet No 51 covers the route.

Beyond Loch Tummel is the village of **Kinloch Rannoch**, where hikers can stock up on supplies before heading into the hills. Some 16 miles west of the village the road ends at the very remote Rannoch station, where tired hikers can catch trains north to Fort William or south to Glasgow.

Blair Atholl to Glen Fincastle walk

A lovely three-mile linear walk leads from Blair Atholl village to Glen Fincastle, passing through woodland and across moorland and pasture. Starting in the village, head down past the watermill and stay on the road until it ends at the river. Then follow a path left until it takes you to a footbridge over the River Garry. Cross the footbridge and then over two stiles until you reach the main A9. Cross the road, taking care as it's usually busy, to another stile, then continue through trees to a gate with a footprint sign. On the other side of the gate, the path zigzags up through a wood which thins out as you reach the top of the hill.

Here, the path fords a stream then continues across open moorland to the other side of the hilltop, where there's a gate. Go through the gate and follow the grassy track down to Tomanraid cottage. From here you can see down into Glen Fincastle. Before the cottage go left over a stile and then down to a gate. Through the gate, head straight along the track until you reach a junction. Go through the gate ahead and down a grassy lane to another gate. Then the path curves diagonally to the left down to a metal gate at the end of a public road. To return to Blair Atholl simply retrace your steps. It's worthwhile popping into the rustic 17th-century **Watermill Café** ① *T01796-481321*, in the village for a great coffee, freshly baked breads and bagels, or to purchase bags of oatmeal ground on the premises.

Blair Atholl to Glen Fincastle walk

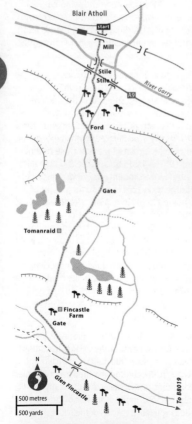

500 metres
500 yards

Where to stay

The tourist office, T01796-472215, can provide a full list of guesthouses and B&Bs.

££££ Killiecrankie Hotel
3 miles north of town, in the village of Killiecrankie, T01796-473220, www. killiecrankiehotel.co.uk. Mar-Dec.
10 rooms. A cosy country house, established in 1840 and renowned for the quality of its fine wines, malts and evening meals.

££££-£££ Knockendarroch Hotel & Restaurant
Higher Oakfield, Pitlochry, T01796-473473, www.knockendarroch.co.uk.
14 rooms. Luxurious and stylish accommodation in this charming Victorian mansion set in 2 acres of woodland garden in a quiet street, great views from the rooms, where you can take breakfast in privacy, 2 lounges and a restaurant (see Restaurants, below).

£££ Craigatin House & Courtyard
165 Atholl Rd, T1796-472478, www.craigatinhouse.co.uk.
14 rooms, 1 suitable for wheelchairs. This early 19th-century house offers stylish and contemporary accommodation in the house or converted stables. Also has a reputation for sublime breakfasts.

£££ Pine Trees Hotel
Strathview Terrace, T01796-472121, www.pinetreeshotel.co.uk.

29 rooms. Comfortable, large Victorian country house set in 10 acres of gardens away from the tourist bustle. Guests can enjoy a drink in one of 3 cosy lounges or a fine meal in the hotel's restaurant.

£££-££ East Haugh House
1 mile southeast of Pitlochry town centre, off the old A9, T01796-473121.
Set in beautiful gardens, this charming hotel offers a warm welcome and an excellent restaurant (**£££-££**). 12 rooms, 1 is disabled friendly, 5 in converted bothy plus 2-bed cottage, the suite (**££££**) has its own cinema room, open fire and spa bath. Can arrange outdoor sports.

£££-££ Fasganeoin Country House
Perth Rd, T01796-472387, www. fasganeoincountryhouse.co.uk.
A lovely 8-bedroom country house in a secluded setting with views towards Loch Tummel yet just mins away from the thoroughfare of town.

££ Old Stables
2 Losset Rd, Alyth, T01828-632547, www.oldstables.com.
Fabulous 3-bedroom B&B in a converted 19th-century steading, with cosy comforts like the log fire and sauna.

££ Roseburn
15 West Moulin Rd, Pitlochry, T01796-470002, www.roseburn.biz.
A classy guesthouse offering 3 delightful bedrooms and a tasty breakfast.

£ SYHA Youth Hostel
Knockard Rd, set amidst woodland, just a ½ mile from town, T1796-472308. Feb-Oct.
Great facilities.

Self-catering

Easter Dunfallandy Country House
T01796-474128, www.dunfallandy.co.uk.
There are many options in and around Pitlochry but this is one of the best. Sleeps up to 12 in 5 bedrooms.

Several of the town's top hotels serve excellent food in their restaurants and these are generally the best places to go for a culinary treat. Among the very best are:

£££ Killiecrankie Hotel
See Where to stay, above.
Excellent evening meals matched by an award-winning reputation for its fine wines.

£££ Knockendarroch Hotel & Restaurant
See Where to stay, above.
Superb modern Scottish cuisine.

£££-££ East Haugh Country House Hotel & Restaurant
1 mile south of Pitlochry on the old A9 road, T01796-473121, www.easthaugh.co.uk.
A 17th-century country house renowned for its dining and excellent seafood.

££ Fern Cottage Restaurant
Ferry Rd, Pitlochry, T01796-473840.
Within the walls of this lovely stone-walled cottage awaits mouth-watering, freshly prepared lunches (1200-1500) and dinners (1730-2100). The best local ingredients are cooked with a Mediterranean twist, offering something a wee bit different. 2-course set lunch is great value at £13.95. Recommended.

££ House of Bruar
See page 119.
A good if pricey place to stop along the A9 for a bowl of soup or some fudge.

££ The Loft
Golf Course Rd, Invertilt Rd, Birdge of Tilt, Blair Atholl, T01796-481377. Wed-Sun 1200-1500, 1700-2030.
Thoughtfully prepared and tasty menu. Lovely ambience and value for money.

£ Blair Atholl Water Mill
Ford Rd, Blair Atholl, T01796-481321. Mar-Oct.
Delicious home-bakes, sandwiches, coffee and even freshly milled oats in this charming and rustic tearoom. The mill dates back to 1613, £2 entry to view workings. Recommended.

£ Moulin Inn and Brewery
A few miles north of Pitlochry, Moulin on the A924, T01796-472196.
Aside from sampling the ales brewed next door, sit back and enjoy the ambience of a pub that opened its doors in 1695 and still serves up good-value, traditional Scottish bar meals.

Entertainment

Pitlochry Festival Theatre, *across the river from the town centre, T01796-484626, www.pitlochryfestivaltheatre.com.* Stages a different play every night, 6 nights a week May-Oct and other shows throughout the year.

What to do

Horse riding
Blair Castle Trekking Centre, *Atholl Estates, Blair Atholl, T01796-481568, www.atholl-estates.co.uk. Apr-Jun Tue-Sun, Jul-Sep Sun-Fri.* Offers short treks and longer ones for the more experienced.

Walking
Atholl Estates Ranger Service, *Atholl Estates Office, Blair Atholl, T01796-481355, www.atholl-estates.co.uk.* Advice, guided walks and leaflets on 9 waymarked walking and bike

trails (30 miles) in the Blair Atholl area. Also have information on Land Rover safaris and various other activities.

Transport

Bus
Elizabeth Yule Transport, T01796-472290, www.elizabethyulecoaches.co.uk, runs a Mon-Sat service between **Pitlochry** and **Calvine** via **Blair Atholl** and **Killiecrankie** with buses leaving Pitlochry at the following times: 0750, 1000, 1300, 1540, 1625 and 1740. On Wed there's also a No 89 service from **Perth** to **Kinloch Rannoch** via **Pitlochry** (2100) and **Killiecrankie** (2120).

Cycle hire
Blair Atholl Bike Hire, Blair Atholl Caravan Park, T0845-5482270, www.blairatholl bikehire.co.uk. **Escape Route**, 3 Atholl Rd, Pitlochry, T01796-473859, www.escape-route.co.uk. Mon-Sat 0900-1730, Sun 1000-1700. Friendly staff in well-stocked bike shop that hires kids' and adult mountain bikes (including child seat and tandems). Prices from £24 for a full day. Also has a good selection of waterproof maps of walking and cycle routes around Perthshire.

Aberfeldy and Loch Tay *Colour map 4, B2.*

stunning scenery, fascinating history and a major watersports centre

The quaint town of Aberfeldy, Scotland's first Fairtrade Town, stands on the banks of the River Tay, on the A827 which runs between the A9 and Loch Tay. Popular with kayakers who brave the rapids in nearby Grandtully, the village is well placed geographically for exploring the northern part of Perthshire and less crowded than Pitlochry. The 14-mile-long Loch Tay is surrounded by some of the loveliest scenery in Perthshire and is well worth exploring.

Aberfeldy

The River Tay is spanned by Wade's Bridge, built by General Wade in 1773 during his campaign to pacify the Highlands.

Dewar's Aberfeldy Distillery ⓘ *T01887-822010, www.dewars.com, Apr-Oct Mon-Sat 1000-1800, Sun 1200-1600, Nov-Mar Mon-Sat 1000-1600, tours from £9.50,* just outside Aberfeldy, is another of Scotland's many distillery visitor centres offering a tour, dram and history of the water of life.

A mile west of Aberfeldy, across the Tay at Weem, is **Castle Menzies** ⓘ *T01887-820982, www.castlemenzies.org, Apr-Oct Mon-Sat 1030-1700, Sun 1400-1700, £6.50, concessions £5.50, children £3*, an impressive, restored 16th-century 'Z-plan' fortified tower house, the former seat of the chief of Clan Menzies. For a great coffee or lunchtime bite, it's also worth popping into the nearby **House of Menzies** ⓘ *T01887-829666, www.houseofmenzies.com, Apr-Oct daily 1000-1700*, at Castle Menzies Farm. In Dull, three miles west you'll also find a fabulous café/delicatessen in the same building as **Highland Adventure Safaris** (see What to do, page 125).

A popular local walk is to the **Falls of Moness**, through the famous **Birks of Aberfeldy**, forever associated with the poet Robert Burns who in 1787 was inspired by the *birks* (birch trees) to write his eponymous song. It's a fairly easy walk along a marked trail lined with oak, elm, ash and birch trees up to the falls where there are lovely views of Strathtay and the surrounding hills. It's about four miles there and back.

Loch Tay and around

It's estimated that Scotland's landscape has over 190,000 known landmarks of archaeological significance. In the past decade divers discovered a 2000-year-old wooden canoe in the depths of Loch Tay. Who knows what other ancient artefacts remain to be discovered.

At the northeast end of the loch is **Kenmore**, a neat little village of whitewashed cottages dominated by a huge archway which stands at the gateway to Taymouth Castle, built by the Campbells of Glenorchy in the early 19th century. Whilst for several years the castle has been undergoing redevelopment (potentially into a luxury hotel) golfers can still enjoy a scenic round at the 18-hole **Taymouth Castle Golf Course** ⓘ *T01887-830234*. Half a mile from the village on the southern bank of the loch, is the informative **Scottish Crannog Centre** ⓘ *T01887-830583, www.crannog.co.uk, Apr-Oct daily 1000-1730, £10, concessions £9, children £7*, an authentic reconstruction of a 'crannog', a Bronze Age island dwelling that archaeologists believe was built for both defensive and food storage purposes. There are apparently over a dozen ancient crannogs in Loch Tay. At the Crannog Centre experts reveal how our ancestors ate and slept whilst there's also the opportunity to try and make fire with just wood and flint.

For those with their own transport, two of the least-known and loveliest routes in the country are at hand. The first is the spectacular road which winds its way south from Kenmore high up into the mountains, across a bleak and barren plateau and down the other side to the tiny hamlet of **Amulree**. This road and ancient drovers' route is often closed in the winter and there are gates at either end. From Amulree you can continue south to Crieff, through the gentler, but equally stunning scenery of the **Sma' Glen**. Alternatively, you could head north to Aberfeldy and then complete the circuit back to Kenmore. Some 10 miles from Crieff, near the village of Comrie, is the, **Auchingarrich Wildlife Centre** ⓘ *T01764-679469, www.auchingarrich.co.uk, daily 1000-1800, £8.45, children and concession £6.95*, an award-winning, family-orientated wildlife centre with Highland cattle, falconry centre, playbarn and rare animals to observe within 100 acres of Perthshire countryside.

A few miles west of Kenmore a minor road turns off the A827, which runs along the north bank of the loch, and heads to ★ **Fortingall**, a tiny village of classic beauty which features on many a calendar. It's little more than a row of thatched cottages which wouldn't even get a mention were it not for two amazing claims. The 3000-year-old yew tree in the churchyard is said to be the oldest living thing in Europe. Even more astonishing is the claim that this is the birthplace of Pontius Pilate, said to be the son of a Roman officer who was stationed here. Furthermore, it is believed that Pilate returned here to be buried, and a gravestone in the churchyard bears the initials 'PP'. If you have your own transport, make a detour up ★ **Glen Lyon**, one of the most beautiful of all Scottish glens. On a summer's day there can be few lovelier places on earth, as the River Lyon tumbles through corries and gorges and through flowering meadows, with high mountain peaks on either side and eagles soaring overhead. It's no surprise that Wordsworth and Tennyson waxed lyrical over its qualities. The road from Fortingall runs all the way to the head of the glen, at Loch Lyon. This is walking and fishing paradise. There are several Munros to 'bag' and fishing permits are available at the **Fortingall Hotel**, see Where to stay, below.

Ben Lawers *OS sheet No 51 covers the area.*

The highest mountain in Perthshire, Ben Lawers (3984 ft), dominates the north side of Loch Tay. Its massif of seven summits includes six Munros which are linked by an eight-mile ridge which can be walked in one day by fit and experienced hillwalkers. The best access to the ridge is from Glen Lyon. The trek to the main summit starts from the **NTS Visitor Centre** ⓘ *T01567-820988, Apr-Sep daily 1000-1700*, two miles along a track which turns off the main A827 about halfway between Kenmore and Killin. This track continues over a wild pass to Bridge of Balgie in Glen Lyon. Leaflets describing the climb are available from the visitor centre. It's a seven-mile walk there and back, and though the route is straightforward and easy to follow, it's a very steep, tough climb of 2700 ft from the centre to the summit. Allow five to six hours. You should be fit, properly clothed, see box, page 21, and have some previous hillwalking experience; but the views from the top on a clear day are amazing, across to the North Sea in the east and the Atlantic Ocean in the west. Information about an easier one-mile nature trail and the flora and fauna in the area is available from the visitor centre.

Listings Aberfeldy and Loch Tay

Where to stay

££££-£££ Ardeonaig House Hotel
South Loch Tay by Aberfeldy, T01567-820351,
www.ardeonaig.com.
Halfway between Killin and Kenmore on the southern shores of Loch Tay is this wonderful and charming hotel offering the very best in pampering in beautiful surroundings. Accommodation ranges from standard doubles to superior loch views and the luxurious garden bothies and lodges with lovely touches such as champagne and handmade chocolates on arrival. The hotel restaurant boasts a terrific wine list and food to die for (see Restaurants, below). Recommended.

££££-£££ Fortingall Hotel
Next to the churchyard, Fortingall,
T01887-830367, www.fortingall.com.
Peaceful, relaxing and supremely comfortable hotel dating back to the Victorian era, with 10 tastefully refurbished en suite rooms and a choice of dining in the restaurant or less formal **Ewe Bar**.

£££ Kenmore Hotel
Kenmore, T01887-830205,
www.kenmorehotelcom.
40 rooms and 10 luxury lodges. Claims to be Scotland's oldest coaching inn, dating from 1572. True or not, the snug bar certainly oozes character and serves hearty meals. The modest bedrooms are reasonable, whilst the somewhat characterless main restaurant

(**££**) provides excellent views over the surrounding area.

£££-££ Ailean Chraggan
Weem, a mile or so west from Aberfeldy, T01887-820346, www.chraggs.co.uk.
Chraggs is a comfortable 5-bedroom family-run hotel serving good food in the perennially lively bar. Good value, just sneaks into the **£££** price band.

£££-££ Balnearn Guest House
Crieff Rd, Aberfeldy, T01887-472387.
This handsome Victorian-style house in its own attractive gardens offers very comfortable accommodation in 10 en suite rooms. Good base for exploring the area and only a 2-min walk from the Birks o' Aberfeldy.

£ Adventurer's Escape
Weem by Aberfeldy, T01887-820498.
Ideal for canoeing and mountaineering instruction.

Self-catering

The Bothy
Tullichettle, Comrie, T01764-670349. Mar-Dec.
Whitewashed 1840s stable converted into cottage with expansive rural views. Sleeps 4.

Mains of Taymouth Cottages
Kenmore by Aberfeldy, T01887-830226.
Acclaimed, luxury cottages set on a 120-acre rolling estate by the Tay, with facilities including hot tubs, barbecue and fishing.

Restaurants

£££ Ardeonaig House Hotel
South Loch Tay by Aberfeldy, T01567-820400, see Where to stay, above. Dinner served 1800-2100.
With Michelin and Inn of the Year Awards, this romantic small hotel also boasts a terrific South African wine list, great breakfast and 3 dinner menus, including the owner's Signature menu. A treat for the gourmet lover and romantic alike. Recommended.

£ The Taybank
Tay Terrace, Dunkeld, T01350-727340. Sun-Thu 1100-2300, Fri-Sat 1100-2400.
If you go to no other pub in Perthshire, make sure you come here for traditional stovies, real ale and a terrific atmosphere aided by its legendary spontaneous music sessions. Also regular sessions on Wed and Thu nights. Lovely riverside beer garden for those rare balmy summer evenings. Highly recommended.

£ The Watermill
Mill St, Aberfeldy, T01887-822896. Daily 1000-1700 (Sun from 1100).
Within this 18th-century former mill, you'll find second-hand books, artworks and terrific sandwiches and cakes to be savoured as you relax by the wood-fired stove.

What to do

Tour operators
Highland Adventure Safaris, *Aberfeldy, T01887-820071, www.highlandsafaris.net.*
Wildlife spot from landrovers, try your hand at gold panning or take to the wheel for some memorable off-road adventure. Also mountain biking, walking and Loch Tay boat cruises.
Loch Tay Boating Centre, *Kenmore, T01887-830379, www.loch-tay.co.uk. Apr-Oct daily 0900-1900.* Rents speedboats, fishing boats and canoes, as well as bicycles.

Watersports
Aberfeldy, Weem and Kenmore boast several notable centres offering river kayaking, whitewater rafting and canyoning.
Nae Limits, *3 miles south of Pitlochry, T01796-482600, www.nae limits.com.* Offer a whole host of water-based adventure sports including whitewater rafting, canyoning and tubing as well as quad biking. Also caters for thrill-seeking kids with 'Wee Limits' for 5-12s.
Splash White Water Rafting, *Dunkeld Rd, Aberfeldy, T01887-829706, www.rafting.co.uk.* Offer a range of whitewater rafting packages on some of Perthsire's wildest rivers.

The other major road running north from Perth is the A93, soon reaching the respectable town of **Blairgowrie**, or Blairgowrie and Rattray to give it its full title. It lies amidst the raspberry fields of Strathmore and is conveniently placed to serve as an accommodation centre for **Glenshee Ski Centre** (T01339-741320, www.ski-glenshee.co.uk), at the crest of the Cairnwell Pass (2199 ft). The most extensive ski area in Scotland, Glenshee is ideal for telemark and alpine skiing. Call the centre to check weather forecast. To get there by public transport, the **Heather Hopper Bus** runs in summer only. (For details, call **D&E Coaches**, T01463-222444.)

A quiet agricultural town, Blairgowrie boasts several good restaurants and tearooms including **Cargills** by the river and the **Ericht Alehouse**, whilst **James Crockart & Son** ⓘ *28 Allan St, T01250-872056, www.jamescrockartandson.co.uk*, will appeal to shooting and fishing fanatics. However, for many, Blairgowrie is a convenient sandwich stop before driving south towards Perth or following the twisty A93 road north to the Spittal of Glenshee, the ski centre and the stunning scenery of Braemar and Deeside beyond. For further information on skiing, see What to do, below.

Listings Blairgowrie and Glenshee

Tourist information

Blairgowrie

Blairgowrie iCentre
26 Wellmeadow, T01250-872960. Open daily.

What to do

Skiing
For **Glenshee Ski Centre**, see above.

Transport

Bus
There's a regular bus service from Blairgowrie to **Dundee** and **Perth** (No 57) and a fairly frequent service (No 71) to **Pitlochry**.

The Trossachs
& Loch Lomond

The Trossachs is a very beautiful and diverse area of sparkling lochs, over 20 craggy Munros (mountains of over 3000 ft) and deep, forested glens. For this reason, it's often called the 'Highlands in miniature', best visited in the autumn when the hills are purple and the trees are a thousand luminous hues, from lustrous gold to flaming scarlet and blazing orange.

West of the Trossachs is Loch Lomond, Britain's largest inland waterway, measuring 22 miles long and up to five miles wide. Though still 'bonnie', its western banks now reverberate to the noise of traffic heading north from nearby Glasgow (20 miles) to Fort William on the busy and notorious (for accidents) A82. Recent years have seen bylaws introduced to control the speed of jet skis and boats on the loch, which is part of the 720-square-mile Loch Lomond and The Trossachs National Park, Scotland's first. The eastern and northern shores are quieter, though on any given day of the year you'll find a hardy hillwalker high above the (eastern shores) road on the slopes of mighty Ben Lomond (Scotland's most southerly Munro) enjoying spectacular views down the loch.

Walking in the Trossachs *OS Landranger maps 56 and 57 covers these routes.*

Loch Lomond and The Trossachs National Park is superb walking country. East of Loch Lomond itself, the two most challenging peaks are Ben Venue and Ben A'an, respectively three and five miles north of Aberfoyle. **Ben Venue** (2392 ft) is a fairly strenuous climb that begins with a steady waymarked ascent (dress and equip yourself appropriately for the climb) from behind the **Loch Achray Hotel**. Allow about four hours for the return trip. Though **Ben A'an** (1489 ft) isn't a giant of a hill, it's a steep, unrelenting climb from the moment you begin at the car park on the north banks of Loch Achray. The woodland car park is located two miles west of the lochside **Harbour Café** ① *T01877-330011*, on the shores of Loch Venachar. You should reach the summit within 1½ hours. Whichever ascent you choose, spectacular views await westwards towards Loch Lomond and southwards to the Campsie Hills and Glasgow. Before you go, pack a picnic to enjoy the views over

Essential The Trossachs and Loch Lomond

Finding your feet

There are regular (Monday to Saturday) buses from Stirling to Aberfoyle and Callander. There are also daily services to Aberfoyle from Glasgow, via Balfron. There's a daily **Scottish Citylink** (www.citylink.co.uk), service between Edinburgh and the Isle of Skye, which stops in Callander and links with buses to Killin. Scottish Citylink buses also run regularly from Glasgow to Balloch, and on to Luss and Tarbet. Some buses go to Ardlui and on to Crianlarich. The Citylink Oban to Dundee bus runs twice daily through Perthshire villages. The same operator also runs a daily service from Edinburgh via Stirling to Fort William (for details of both services, see Transport, page 134). **First** buses run daily (No 10 and No 11A) between Glasgow and Aberfoyle via Drymen, and also operate a service to Balloch that stops in Drymen, and an Aberfoyle to Stirling service (No 11 and No 11A), which stops at Port of Menteith.

Tip...
Come in early autumn when the forests and mountains are a blaze of vibrant colours.

ScotRail runs a daily service every half hour from Glasgow to Balloch (50 minutes). ScotRail's West Highland line to Fort William and Mallaig, with a branch line to Oban, reaches Loch Lomond at Tarbet and there's another station further north at Ardlui.

Getting around

Options for getting around without your own transport are severely limited. Those who don't wish to drive should consider bringing a bike or hiring one here. **Caber Coaches** (T01887-820090), bus No 91 runs Monday to Saturday between Aberfeldy and Killin via Kenmore. For details of getting around the national park by public transport visit www.lochlomond-trossachs.org.

In addition to cruise companies, there are several small ferry operators, which provide a convenient means for (foot passengers only) to cross Loch Lomond. There's a **Waterbus service** (T01389-722600), which runs across the loch from several piers and pontoons on both sides. **Cruise Loch Lomond** crosses the loch between Tarbert, Luss, Rowardennan, Inveruglas and Inversnaid. For times and prices check www.cruiselochlomond.co.uk.

Loch Katrine. On a still day, it's possible to hear the commentary from the deck of the toy-like *SS Walter Scott* far below Ben A'an. All local iCentres sell detailed maps of the area (see page 131).

Both these mountains lie within the ★ **Queen Elizabeth Forest Park**. This vast and spectacular wilderness of 75,000 acres borders Loch Lomond to the west and incorporates Loch Ard, Loch Achray and Loch Lubnaig, as well as Ben Venue, Ben A'An and Ben Ledi, which overlooks Callander. The park is run by Forestry Commission Scotland and is criss-crossed by a network of less difficult waymarked trails and cycling paths which start from the **Lodge Forest Visitor Centre** ① *T0300-067 6615, daily Jan-Feb 1000-1500, Mar-Apr and Oct-Dec 1000-1600, May-Jun and Sep 1000-1700, Jul-Aug 1000-1800, parking £3, dogs welcome*, about a mile north of Aberfoyle at Duke's Pass on the A821. The centre incorporates audio-visual displays on the park's flora and fauna, information on the area's numerous walks and cycle routes, a café and gift shop, or you can visit the red squirrel hide or swing through the trees at **Go Ape**.

Aberfoyle *Colour map 4, C1.*

The sleepy village of Aberfoyle suddenly bursts into life in the summer with the arrival of hordes of tourists. It lies on the edge of the Queen Elizabeth Forest Park and, like Callander to the east, is a major tourist hub providing an ideal base for golf, walking and cycling in the surrounding hills. There's an abundance of guesthouse accommodation, though it's advisable to book ahead during the busy summer season.

Three miles east of Aberfoyle is the **Lake of Menteith**, the only lake in Scotland (as opposed to loch). On **Inchmahome Island** in the middle of the lake are the beautiful and substantial ruins of **Inchmahome Priory** ① *T01877-385294 (HES), Apr-Sep daily 1000 (1st outward sailing)-1615 (last outward sialing), Oct 1000-1515, £7.50, concession £6, children £4.50*, the 13th-century Augustinian priory where the four-year-old Mary, Queen of Scots was sent in 1547, safe from the clutches of Henry VIII. A ferry takes visitors over to the island from **Port of Menteith**.

To the north of Aberfoyle is Doon Hill, better known as the **Fairy Knowe**. The tree at the top is said to be the home of the 'People of Quietness', and in 1692 a local minister was less than discreet in telling the world of their secrets. As punishment he was taken away to fairyland, and his spirit has languished there ever since. If you go round the tree seven times, your wish will be granted, but go round it backwards and ... well, we won't be held responsible. It's about 1½ hours up and back. Follow the road across the bridge south of the car park by the visitor centre, then continue until it forks; take the left fork, a waymarked path, to the hilltop.

Aberfoyle to Callander

The A821 route north from Aberfoyle, through the spectacular ★ **Duke's Pass**, and then east past Loch Achray and Loch Vennachar, is a beautiful route and not to be missed. There are a couple of worthwhile diversions along the way. About five miles north of Aberfoyle, a forest track branches to the right and runs through Achray Forest and along the shores of **Loch Drunkie**, before rejoining the A821 further north. A few miles further on, a road turns left to **Trossachs Pier** on the southern shore of **Loch Katrine**. This is the departure point for cruises on the *SS Sir Walter Scott* between April and October (see What to do, page 134). It sails to the remote settlement of **Stronachlachar** on the far western shores of the loch and back. There is also a one-hour afternoon cruise at 1330 and 1500 that makes a short, non-stop loop of the southern section of the freshwater loch. There's a cycle path around the loch as far as Stronachlachar so it's possible to take the morning cruise and cycle back

ON THE ROAD
Better red than dead

As the tourist board never tires of reminding us, the Trossachs is Rob Roy country. Rob Roy ('Red Robert' in Gaelic) was one of Scotland's most notorious outlaws or one of the bravest Highland heroes, depending on your point of view. It is true that he was a freebooter, but he was also defending Highland clan culture and more specifically fighting for the very survival of his own clan against proscription and persecution by the government and its supporters.

Rob Roy MacGregor (1671-1734) was born in Glengyle, to the northwest of Loch Katrine. The MacGregors' lands included those previously owned by the rival Campbells but bestowed on the MacGregors for services rendered to Alexander II in his conquest of Argyll. For a long time the clan kept possession of their lands by right of the sword, but the constant attempts by neighbouring clans to displace them led to retaliation by the MacGregors and earned them a reputation for being aggressive. Rob Roy did little to change this image, and his bitter feud with the powerful Duke of Montrose led to his being outlawed and eventually captured and sentenced to transportation. He was pardoned and returned to Balquhidder, where he stayed for the rest of his life. He now lies buried in the churchyard.

The Rob Roy story was first popularized by Sir Walter Scott's eponymous 19th-century novel, and his life continues to be romanticized, most recently in the 1995 film starring Liam Neeson and Tim Roth. Like Robin Hood before him, his courage in refusing to bow to the forces of authority seems to strike a chord with people.

to the pier. The superb bike hire outfit **Katrine Wheelz** (page 134), by the pier, is the place to get the whole family on bikes.

Callander and around *Colour map 4, C2.*

At the eastern end of the Trossachs and 14 miles northwest of Stirling is Callander, a tourist honey-pot whose Main Street sadly includes a few too many tartan-tat shops. Yet look closely and you'll also find several excellent restaurants and delightful wee shops selling home-made fudge and other goodies. It's just as well there are many walks and cycling trails (including Route 7 to Balquhidder) to burn off those holiday calories. In Ancaster Square is the **Rob Roy and Trossachs Visitor Centre** ① *T01877-330342, Mar-May and Oct daily 1000-1700, Jun and Sep 09301800, Jul-Aug 0900-1900, Jan-Feb Sat and Sun 1100-1630, £4.50.* The interactive displays and two film clips provide an entertaining account of the life of Rob Roy MacGregor.

Opened in 1995, the **Hamilton Toy Collection** ① *111 Main St, T01877-330004, www. thehamiltontoycollection.co.uk, Apr-Oct Mon-Sat 1030-1700, Sun 1200-1700, £3, children £1,* is a true Aladdin's Cave, crammed with toys from the past 100 years. Step into the modest shop and, whatever your age, take a trip down memory lane. There are over 100 original Action Men, Victorian-era tin soldiers, Hot Wheels and Dinky Toys from the 1930s. You will also find bisque dolls dating back to the 1880s, 1930s dolls houses and over 100 vintage teddy bears, including the loveable Paddington Bear.

A recommended local walk is to **Bracklinn Falls**, reached by a woodland trail which leads from Bracklinn Road. At the time of writing this is not a circular walk as a wooden bridge has been washed away. Normally, it's about 30 minutes' walk each way. Another trail from Bracklinn Road leads up to **Callander Crags**, from where there are great views of the surrounding area. Allow 1½ hours there and back. The most challenging walk in the area is to the summit of **Ben Ledi** (2883 ft), but it's a tough climb and you'll need to be fit, experienced and prepared. Ask at the **iCentre** for further information and for maps.

Two miles north of Callander, on the A84 route to the Highlands, are the **Falls of Leny**, in the narrow and dramatic Pass of Leny. The falls are accessible from the car park by the roadside or via the **Callander to Strathyre Cycleway** (Route 7), which follows the old train line to Oban, from Callander north along the west bank of **Loch Lubnaig**. This forms part of the **Glasgow to Killin Cycleway**, which runs from the centre of Glasgow, via Balloch, Aberfoyle, Callander, Balquhidder and Lochearnhead, to Killin. For the fit, this is the best way to see the Trossachs.

The A84 heads north from Callander along the east bank of Loch Lubnaig, and beyond towards **Loch Earn**. A few miles further north, a side road branches left to the tiny village of **Balquhidder**, famous as the burial place of Rob Roy. His grave in the churchyard, by his wife and two of his sons, is thankfully understated. In the nearby converted village library, there's a cosy tearoom ⓘ *Mar-Oct, times vary*, with sandwiches and cakes.

North of Callander to Lochearnhead and Killin

A few miles north of the turning to Balquhidder, where the A84 meets the A85 from Crieff to Crianlarich, is **Lochearnhead**, at the western tip of Loch Earn. The loch is a highly popular watersports centre, see What to do, page 134. Lochearnhead is also a good base for walking in the surrounding hills. In the far northwestern corner of the Stirling region, just to the west of Loch Tay, is **Killin**, a pleasant little village which makes a good base for walkers wishing to explore the wild mountains and glens of the ancient district of **Breadalbane** (pronounced *Bread-albinn*). Killin's picture-postcard setting, with the beautiful **Falls of Dochart** tumbling through the centre of the village make it a popular destination for tourists.

Some 12 miles west of Killin is **Crianlarich**, at the crossroads of the A82 Glasgow–Fort William road and the A85 to Perth, and at the junction of the Glasgow to Fort William and Oban rail lines. It is a staging post on the West Highland Way. Six miles further north is tiny **Tyndrum**, which shot to prominence almost 20 years ago after the discovery of gold in the surrounding hills. There's a seasonal **iCentre** (see below) and, next door the **Real Food Café** ⓘ *open Mar-Oct Mon-Thu 0730-2030, Sat and Sun till 2100; Nov-Feb daily 0730-2100*, an award-winning organic fish and chip shop that's not cheap – but worth it.

Listings The Trossachs

Tourist information

Aberfoyle

Aberfoyle iCentre
Main St, T01877-381221, www.visitscotland.com. Apr-Oct daily 1000-1700, Nov-Mar 1000-1600.

Callander

Callander iCentre
52-54 Main St, T01877-330342. Apr-Oct daily 0930-1700, Oct-Mar daily 0930-1600.

Balloch

Balloch iCentre
Some 15 miles southwest of Aberfoyle. Daily Jul-Aug 0930-1800, Jun and Sep 0930-1730, Oct-May 1000-1700.
A large **VisitScotland iCentre** at the southernmost end of Loch Lomond. Can provide details about ferry and bus transport in the entire park area.

Tyndrum

Tyndrum iCentre
Main road, T01838-400246. Apr-Jun and Sep-Oct daily 1000-1700, Jul-Aug daily 1000-1800.

Where to stay

££££ MacDonald Forest Hills Hotel
Loch Ard, on the B829 from Aberfoyle, T0844-879 9057, www.macdonaldhotels.co.uk.
50 bedrooms. Graceful 19th-century country house converted into a family-friendly hotel, offering multitudinous facilities and activities including a luxury health spa with pool, sauna, steam room and fully equipped gym. There's also the chance to mountain bike, sail, hike and fish. There are lovely views over Loch Ard from the restaurant, where you can expect the menu to include a variety of delicious, locally sourced meats and fish (**£££-££**) or enjoy dining in the less formal **Rafters Restaurant**.

£££££-£££ Lake Hotel
Port of Menteith, on the lakeshore overlooking Inchmahome, T01877-385258, www.lake-hotel.com.
A discerning and multi award-winning hotel in a beautiful location. Named Scotland's 'Romatic Hotel of the Year' for 2017. The restaurant cooks up many memorable treats (3-course dinner **£££**).

££££-£££ Monachyle Mhor Hotel
Balquhidder, on the road to Inverlochlarig, T01877-384622, www.monachylemhor.net.
Renowned for its culinary delights and warm welcome, this family-run hotel boasts 16 wonderfully appointed, individually styled bedrooms in a serene, rural setting with terrific views over the loch, as well as an old ferry cabin, a reclaimed bothy (£140 per night, sleep up to 4) and a restored showman's wagon (£125). The hotel's organic garden provides fresh herbs for the restaurant, whilst much of the produce

is sourced in the local area. This is one of the UK's top eateries and its 5-course table d'hôte is not to be missed. Highly recommended if you can afford it.

££££-£££ Roman Camp Country House Hotel
Callander, T01877-330003, www.romancamphotel.co.uk.
15 rooms. An exquisite 16th-century former hunting lodge set in extensive grounds by the river, away from the hoi polloi. Oozes character and Queen Victoria was quite taken with the place. Good Scottish cuisine (**£££**).

£££ Creagan House
At the northern end of Loch Lubnaig, in Strathyre, T01877-384638, www.creaganhouse.co.uk.
5 rooms. An atmospheric family-run 17th-century farmhouse consistently providing award-winning service combined with fine food, an impressive wine list and over 50 single malts in its cosy restaurant.

£££ The Four Seasons
In the village of St Fillans, a few miles east of Lochearnhead, T01764-685333, www.thefourseasonshotel.co.uk.
Spectacular setting on the shores of Loch Earn, this refurbished 12-bedroom, 19th-century house is family- and dog-friendly and boasts 2 fine restaurants, including the **Meall Reamhar** where a 4-course extravaganza of fine Scottish cuisine will set you back £35 per person. There are also chalets (**£££-££**) sleeping up to 4) and a self-catering apartment (**££**) within the wooded grounds.

£££-££ Callander Meadows
24 Main St, Callander, T01877-330181, www.callandermeadows.co.uk.
Simplicity is the key to this 18th-century townhouse offering 4 delightful en suite bedrooms and a wonderful restaurant menu (**£££-££**), including desserts to die for. Recommended.

££ Mhor 84 Hotel
On A84 at the head of Balquhidder Glen, near Lochearnhead, T01877-384622, www.mhor84.net.
Wee sister to the spectacular **Monachyle Mhor Hotel** (see above), this small, 7-bedroom motel is the perfect pit-stop for travellers passing through. Also has a 2-bedroom cottage. Funky, minimalist design throughout and food served all day in its excellent restaurant (**££-£**). Live music on Thu. Rates are for room only but it's a real bargain at this price. Highly recommended.

£ Braveheart Backpackers
Lochay Lodge and Steading by the Killin Hotel, T01567-829089.
Basic 12-bed accommodation in this pretty village. Bike and canoe hire available.

Self-catering

Altskeith Country House
By Loch Ard, T01877-387387, www.altskeith.com.
Just 3 miles west of Aberfoyle, this historic, sandstone house, blessed with breathtaking views over Loch Ard towards Ben Lomond, promises and delivers a heavenly luxury stay for the discerning traveller and friends. A home from home: a huge rustic living room with roaring fire, gargantuan dining room, 10 tastefully appointed en suite bedrooms and a kitchen fit for Jamie Oliver. There are also endless outdoor pursuits to enjoy, from windsurfing, biking and kayaking to walking in the nearby Loch Ard Forest. Glasgow is 45 mins' drive away, Edinburgh 60 mins. Accommodates up to 22 people on an exclusive use basis.

Leny House
Callander, T01877-331078, www.lenyestate.com.
Stay in the baronial north wing of historic Leny House and enjoy 5-star self-catering or 4 guests can enjoy a luxurious stay in the estate cottages and chalets.

Camping

Cobeland Campsite
2 miles south of Aberfoyle on the edge of the Queen Elizabeth Forest Park, T01877-382392. Apr-Oct.

Trossachs Holiday Park
3 miles south of Aberfoyle, off the A81, T01877-382614. Mar-Oct.
An excellent site set in 40 acres, with mountain bike hire.

Restaurants

£££ Monachyle Mhor Hotel
See Where to stay, above.
This renowned restaurant makes stylish and imaginative use of superb local ingredients. Outstanding service and food, as you'd expect for a dinner that starts at £46 per head. Book ahead. Recommended.

£££ Roman Camp Country House Hotel
See Where to stay, above.
Excellent choice if you wish to push the boat out, with 4-course dinner at £55 a head and 3-course lunch at £30.

£££-££ Callander Meadows
See Where to stay, above.
Great restaurant that prides itself on its imaginative menu, fresh, locally sourced produce and irresistible desserts.

££ Brig O' Turk tea room
Brig O' Turk, 7 miles west of Callander on road to Aberfoyle, T01877-367283, www.brigoturktearoom.co.uk. Thu-Sat 1000-2100, Sun 1000-1700.
Look out for the green hut with hanging baskets outside. Inside it's like a scout hut with higgledy-piggledy chairs and mis-matching crockery and tablecloths. Informal and very good food, including burgers, schnitzel and a changing specials board. Excellent cakes and puds.

££ The Lade Inn
Kilmahog, 1 mile north of Callander, T01877-330152.

Enjoy the real ales from the microbrewery and delicious meals prepared using locally sourced produce including trout and beef. Terrific atmosphere.

£ Deli Ecosse
Callander, 10 Ancaster Sq, T01877-331220. Thu-Tue 0800-1700.
For a superb range of takeaway or eat-in Scottish and continental sandwiches, wines and fresh coffee.

£ Mhor Fish
75-77 Main St, Callander, T01877-330213. Tue-Sun (Wed-Sun in winter).
Fish and seafood lovers will find it impossible to walk past the door of this award-winning restaurant and takaway where you'll find the tastiest fish suppers, as well as fish chowder, burgers, oysters and mussels awaiting your plate or carry-out box.

What to do

For detailed advice on the many cycling, fishing, walking and hiking possibilities within the Loch Lomond and The Trossachs National Park, contact the national park website, www.lochlomond-trossachs.org, or call in at one of the visitor centres at Balmaha (T01389-722100, Sat-Sun 0930-1600), Tyndrum, Callander, Aberfoyle, Balloch, Glen Finglas or Duke's Pass.

Go Ape, *Lodge Forest Visitor Centre (see also page 129), 1 mile north of Aberfoyle on A821, T0845-643 9215, www.goape.co.uk.* Offers adrenalin junkies the opportunity to swing through the trees on a high-wire aerial course. Thrills include flying 150 ft above a waterfall.

Katrine Wheelz, *by the pier, Loch Katrine, T01877-376316. Apr-Oct daily 0900-1700.* Bike hire from £10 per day for a child's bike to £20 for an adult. Also by the hour. Recommended.

Lochearnhead Watersports,*Watersports Centre, Lochearnhead, T01567-830330, www.lochearnhead-water-sports.co.uk.* Offers waterskiing, canoeing, kayaking and wakeboarding on the loch.

SS Sir Walter Scott, *Loch Katrine, 5 miles north of Aberfoyle over the Duke's Pass, you'll find a turn-off to the Trossachs pier, T01877-376315/6, www.lochkatrine.com. Apr-Oct daily.* At 1030 the cruise boat sails to Stronachlachar and back, 2 hrs, £16.50 concessions £15, children £8.50. There is also a 1-hr afternoon cruise (£13.50, concessions £12, children £7) that makes a short, non-stop loop of the southern section of the freshwater loch. There are also 2 other boats, the *Lady of the Lake* and the new *MacGregor of Glengyle*.

Transport

Bus
The **Citylink**, www.citylink.co.uk, **Oban** to **Dundee** bus runs twice daily through Perthshire villages including **Comrie**, **St Fillans**, **Lochearnhead** and **Killin**. The same operator also runs a once-daily service (Mon-Sat) from **Edinburgh** via **Stirling** to **Fort William** that passes through **Callander**, **Strathyre**, **Lochearnhead**. Caber Coaches (T01887-820090) bus No 91 runs Mon-Sat between Aberfeldy and Killin via Kenmore.

Britain's largest inland waterway is one of Scotland's most famous lochs, thanks to the Jacobite ballad about its 'bonnie banks'. These same banks are now one of the busiest parts of the Highlands, due to their proximity to Glasgow (only 20 miles south along the congested A82). Since 2002, the loch has formed the natural 'hub' of the 720-square-mile Loch Lomond and The Trossachs National Park, a designation that by implementing much-needed controls has alleviated much of the disturbance by speedboats and jet skis over the summer months.

At the southern end of the loch is the resort town of **Balloch**, packed full of hotels, B&Bs, caravan parks and any number of operators offering boat trips around the loch's southern waters. At the northern end of the town is Loch Lomond Shores ① *T01389-751031, www. lochlomondshore.com, year-round daily 1000-1800*, a huge visitor centre-cum-shopping mall, adjacent to which is the **iCentre**, see page 136. Here you can pick up all the information you need on the national park, as well as book a loch cruise, hire bikes, kayaks or sailing dinghies, or simply enjoy the views from the café in the Drumkinnon Tower. The tower is home to **Sealife Loch Lomond** ① *T01389-721500, www.visitsealife.com, daily 1000-1700, door price £13.95 per person, under 3s free, online price £9.77, with otter feeding at 1100 and 1500, and rays at 1330*. It's a fun, educational experience that takes you on an 'underwater journey' to understand the abundant and diverse marine creatures that live in Loch Lomond, the Clyde Estuary and in the ocean. Giant fish tanks, touch pools, a sunken boat, rare otters and interactive displays are all part of the attraction. The west bank of the loch, from Balloch north to Tarbet, is one long, almost uninterrupted development of marinas, holiday homes, caravan parks and exclusive golf clubs. The most picturesque village here is **Luss**, though it is more of a theme park than a real village. It is to the genuine Highland experience what Homer Simpson is to philosophical debate. One-and-a-half-hour boat trips leave from Luss pier. Further north, things begin to quieten down a bit. At Tarbet, it's worthwhile jumping aboard one of the boats run by **Cruise Loch Lomond** ① *T01301-702356, www.cruiselochlomond.co.uk*. There are a number of options. There's a 90-minute circular cruise around the loch on board *Capercaillie* (£12.50/£11 concession/£7 for children) but surely the most innovative is The **West Highland Way Rambler** whereby hikers first enjoy a 45-minute cruise under Ben Lomond before disembarking on the east shore of the Loch at Rowardennan and hiking six miles north along the famous West Highland Way to Inversnaid before being picked up again by the boat. Still further north, the loch gets deeper and narrower en route to **Ardlui** and the famously cosy and rustic Inverarnan Inn, beyond which the A82 meets the A85 at **Crianlarich**.

The tranquil east bank of Loch Lomond is a great place for walking. The West Highland Way follows the east bank all the way from **Drymen**, through **Balmaha**, **Rowardennan** and **Inversnaid**. Beyond Rowardennan this is the only access to the loch's east bank, except for the road to Inversnaid from the Trossachs. From Rowardennan you can climb **Ben Lomond** (3195 ft), the most southerly of the Munros. It's deceptively long though not too difficult and the views from the top, in good weather, are astounding. An easier climb is **Conic Hill**, on the Highland fault line and very close to Glasgow. The route starts from the Forestry Commission interpretative and ranger post in the car park at Balmaha. It takes about 1½ hours to reach the top, from where the views of the loch are stunning. Across the road, it's worthwhile hopping aboard the MacFarlane & Son ① *T01360-870214,* *www.balmahaboatyard.co.uk*, to explore the beautiful isle of **Inchcailloch** with its nature trails and ancient ruins. In both cases, times vary so it's best to call ahead. There's also a Waterbus service to the island (see Getting around, page 128).

Listings Loch Lomond

Tourist information

iCentre
Balloch, T01389-751031.
Year-round daily 1000-1800.
All the information you need on the national park.

Where to stay

££££ Cameron House Hotel
2 miles north of Balloch, T01389-755565,
www.cameronhouse.co.uk.
Exclusive lochside hotel with spa, 3 restaurants and a marina. Includes every luxury you would expect at £300 plus per night.

£££ Rowardennan Hotel
Rowardennan, T01360-870273,
www.rowardennanhotel.co.uk.
18 rooms. Comfortable choice, with a cosy, old-world bar. Serves good-value food. Dog friendly.

£ Loch Lomond SYHA Youth Hostel
Arden, T01360-870259, www.syha.org.uk.
Grand 19th-century turreted mansion complete with obligatory ghost and outstanding lochside location close to Ben Lomond footpath.

Camping

Lomond Woods Holiday Park
Tullichewan, on the Old Luss Rd, T01250-878123, www.woodleisure.co.uk.
A good campsite where you can hire mountain bikes.

Milarrochy Bay
Balmaha, 5 miles north of Drymen, T01360-870236.
A very good camping and caravanning site with stunning views over Loch Lomond.

Restaurants

£££ Cameron House Hotel
See Where to stay, above.
3 lovely restaurants and a beautiful lochside setting. Dress to impress.

££ Oak Tree Inn
Balmaha, on the east side of the loch,
T01360-870357, www.oaktreeinn.co.uk.
Excellent pub food served with a touch of finesse. Busy in summer, great atmosphere. Has double rooms for B&B (**££**), should lunch become dinner. Also functions as a village shop, coffee bar and ice cream parlour. If you're in the vicinity the chances are you'll end up here.

£ Tarbet Tea room
Tarbet, T01301-702200. Daily 0830-1700.
Tucked just off the main road as the road forks to Arrochar, this humble dwelling that served as a school in the Second World War is where weekend walkers and cyclists still come in their droves for a hearty cooked breakfast, toasties or cream tea. Fantastic value and very friendly; just don't expect silver service. Recommended.

Bars and clubs

The Clachan Inn
Drymen, T01360-660824.
Established in 1734, this whitewashed, croft-like, cosy pub serving hearty bar meals (**££-£**) and fine ales may well be Scotland's oldest registered pub. It's certainly one of the friendliest.

Drover's Inn

Inverarnan, T01301-704234.
The famous Highland watering hole, with smoke-blackened walls, low ceilings, bare floors, open fires, a hall filled with stuffed animals, a barman in a kilt and a great selection of single malts. The perfect place for a wild night of drinking in the wilderness. This 300-year-old pub is now part of a hotel with 15 rooms (**£££-££**) offering quirky yet comfortable accommodation and even the chance to sleep in a 4-poster bed in the appealingly named 'Haunted Room', The **Drovers Lodge** (**£££**) opposite, has chalet-style rooms.

What to do

Cruise Loch Lomond, *Turbet, T01301-702356, www.cruiselochlomond.co.uk.* Operating from the Boatyard since 1973, its modern cruise boats run a host of excellent year-round excursions with commentary, including the **West Highland Way Rambler** (from £15), **Inversnaid Explorer** (from £13) and **Rob Roy Discovery** (from £15).

Loch Lomond Waterski Club, *by Balloch, T01436-860632.* Offers tuition and waterski hire (Apr-Sep).
Lomond Activities, *64 Main St, Drymen, T01360-660066, daily 0900-1700.* Individual and family bike hire, including child seats and helmets.
Paddle Power and Adventure, *T07500-470976, www.paddlepowerandadventure. co.uk.* Offers instruction and hire for kayaks and canoes as well as trips and rock climbing and walking in summer.
Sweeney's Cruises, *Balloch, T01389-752376, www.sweeneyscruiseco.com.* Runs cruises around the southern part of the loch several times a day Apr-Oct and twice daily Nov-Mar. Also runs a Waterbus service from from Balloch to Luss and Luss to Balmaha.

Transport

Bus

For further details on bus travel from Loch Lomond, see Essential The Trossachs and Loch Lomond, page 128.

Strathspey &
the Cairngorms

One of Scotland's busiest tourist areas is Strathspey, the broad valley of the River Spey, Scotland's second longest river, which rises high in the hills above Loch Laggan and flows northeast to its mouth on the Moray Firth. The lower reaches are famous for salmon fishing and whisky, while the upper reaches, covered here, attract outdoor sports enthusiasts. Hemmed in between the mighty Monadhliath Mountains to the north and the magnificent Cairngorms, Britain's second highest range, to the south, this is an area which offers excellent hiking, watersports, mountain biking and winter skiing. In September 2003, the Cairngorms were officially declared a national park, the largest in Britain.

Essential Strathspey and the Cairngorms

Finding your feet

This part of the Highland region is easily accessible by public transport as Aviemore is one of the main hubs, with regular buses and trains from Inverness, Perth, Edinburgh and Glasgow. There are several buses (Monday to Saturday) from Inverness to Grantown-on-Spey, Boat of Garten and Aviemore with **Stagecoach Highlands**. They also operate several buses a day from Inverness to Newtonmore via Carrbridge, Aviemore, Kincraig and Kingussie. For bus timetables visit www.bustimes.org.uk. For further details, see Transport, pages 144, 148, 153 and 154.

Aviemore and around *Colour map 4, A3.*

one of Scotland's great outdoor sports centres

The main focus of the area is the tourist resort of Aviemore, a name synonymous with winter sports. In the 1960s Aviemore was transformed from a sleepy Highland village into, until very recently, a jumble of concrete buildings, tacky gift shops and sprawling coach parks.

Today, the creation of the **Macdonald Aviemore Highland Resort** ① *www.aviemore highlandresort.com*, complete with retail complex, food court, restaurants, golf course, swimming pool and beauty spa, has significantly helped Aviemore rectify the worst excesses of its early mistakes. Still, Aviemore remains a 'tourist honey-pot' with a rash of contemporary bars that are a magnet for the stag, hen and après-ski crowds. It's certainly heaven for the outdoor enthusiast, discerning diner, whisky lover or real ale drinker, as this bustling town now boasts several notable restaurants and watering holes.

Unless you wish to soak up the luxury and leisure facilities of the Macdonald Aviemore Highland Resort, or hop on the Strathspey Railway (see page 143), you'll find Aviemore is merely a staging post for the places of interest in and around the surrounding mountains, forests, rivers and villages. The area around Aviemore is blessed with an abundance of craggy peaks, lochs, rivers and acres of forest, including pockets of the ancient and native Caledonian pine forest. Consequently, much of Speyside is home to rare wildlife including pine martens, wildcats, red squirrels, ospreys and capercaillie, and Britain's only herd of wild reindeer. A great place for kids is the **Cairngorm Reindeer Centre** ① *Glenmore Forest Park, on the road from Coylumbridge, 7 miles from Aviemore, T01479-861228, www. cairngormreindeer.co.uk, hill visits May-Sep 1100 and 1430, Jul-Aug also at 1530, Oct-Apr 1100, £14, children £8, concession £11, paddock visit daily 1000-1700, £3.50/2.50*, where you can observe reindeer at the centre (paddock visit) or walk (20-30 minutes) up to where the herd live on the hillside (hill visit), and even feed the stags and hinds of the glen.

Families will also enjoy the **Cairngorm Sled-dog Adventure Centre** ① *T07767-270526, www.sled-dogs.co.uk, year-round, kennel visit 1 hr, £8, children £4, 45-min sled-dog experience £60, children £40*, just three miles east of Aviemore on the 'ski road' and 500 yds past the Clay Pigeon Shooting range in Rothiemurchus Estate. A range of daily tours are offered, including a kennel visit where visitors can see the 30 huskies being fed and trained and also learn about the history of dog-sledding. There are short daytime and evening trips, where you can experience being pulled by the dogs, and for the more adventurous there's a three-hour sled-dog safari (£175 per person) that includes helping

Aviemore train station, **iCentre** (see below), banks, supermarket, restaurants, guesthouses and a couple of excellent outdoor shops are all to be found along the main thoroughfare of Grampian Road. Buses, including those to the ski centre and **Scottish Citylink**'s Inverness/Glasgow/Edinburgh services, stop here too.

to prepare the dogs, 'mushing' through the forest in a specially adapted buggy and enjoying a brew deep in the woods. Whichever you choose, prepare to get wet, muddy and/or snowy. It can be cold so wrap up warmly.

Rothiemurchus Estate

Most of upper Strathspey is owned by Forestry Commission Scotland and Rothiemurchus Estate, which has been in the possession of the Grant family since the 16th century. Fortunately, the owners enthusiastically support access to these lands that form part of the Cairngorms National Park and which, in addition to opportunities for outdoor adventure and inhaling fresh air, boast miles of waymarked trails. Thanks to an undulating forest cycle trail completed in 2008, it's now possible for families to pedal off the road from Aviemore all the way to Glenmore and picturesque Loch Morlich (nine miles east) at the bottom of the Cairngorm Mountain access road. The **Rothiemurchus Visitor Centre** ① *Inverdruie, www.rothiemurchus.net, T01479-812345, daily 0900-1730,* is definitely worth a visit. In addition to being packed with information on the walks, nature trails, stalking, fishing, pony trekking and cycling options on the huge estate, the centre boasts a fantastic delicatessen and high-quality arts and crafts shop, as well as the **Druie Café-Restaurant** for delicious lunches, dinners and day-time snacks.

An easy circular walk of about two hours around **Loch an Eilean** in Rothiemurchus Estate starts from the end of the side road which turns east off the B970, two miles south of Aviemore. From the car park at the end of the road head for the lochside. The route around the loch is clearly marked and it's difficult to lose your way as it follows the loch shore. It's a very pleasant walk through woodland with views of a 14th-century castle ruin on an island in the middle of the loch. The views and change of light here are breathtaking, whilst it's a magical experience to hear one's call echo across the loch and through the silent forest. It's a romantic spot too, highlighted by the fact locals sometimes marry in the forest by the lochside. You can extend the walk by around a mile by including the circuit around **Loch Gamhna**. The paths around Loch an Eilein are also connected with the massive network of trails around Rothiemurchus. OS Sheet 36 covers the route. There are toilets by the car park (£3), and in a small croft, postcards, ice cream and information about the walks and wildlife in the area are available.

Listings Aviemore and around

Tourist information

Aviemore

Aviemore iCentre
Grampian Rd, about 200 yds south of the train station, T01479-810930, www.visitscotland.com.

Sep-Jun Mon-Sat 0900-1700, Jul-Aug Mon-Sat 0900-1900, Sun 0900-1700, phone to check times.
Will book accommodation as well as provide free maps and leaflets on local attractions and change foreign currency.

Where to stay

As a major tourist resort, Aviemore boasts a vast range of accommodation, including top-class hotels, good-value B&Bs and guesthouses and hostels as well as countless self-catering options. Contact the local **iCentre** (see above) for details and availability or go to www.visitaviemore.com.

££££ Hilton Coylumbridge Hotel
Coylumbridge by Aviemore, T01479-810661, www.hiltonaviemore.com.
Set in 65 acres of woodland by Rothiemurchus Estate, the family-friendly credentials of this luxury hotel include a dedicated Fun House, dry-ski slope and climbing wall, whilst parents can relax by the pool and enjoy fine dining (**£££-££**). 15 mins' walk from Aviemore centre.

££££-£££ The Macdonald Aviemore Resort
T0344-879 9152 www.macdonaldhotels.com.
Huge leisure and conference complex featuring 4 hotel options: the luxurious **Macdonald Highland Hotel** (**££££**), the family-orientated **Aviemore Hotel** (**££££-£££**), the business-orientated **Morlich Hotel** (**££££-£££**) and **Luxury Woodland Cottages** (**£££**). The resort boasts several restaurants, see below. This Macdonald village within a village also comes complete with 1st-class leisure facilities, including the 18-hole **Spey Valley Golf Course**, and swimming pool. There are regular buses daily between Cairngorm Mountain and the resort, via Glenmore and Coylumbridge.

£££ Cairngorm Hotel
Grampian Rd, T01479-810233, www.cairngorm.com.
Slap bang in the midst of Aviemore, this is where to combine a comfortable stay with a lively hotel bar that's popular with the locals whilst dining on hearty bar meals and freshly prepared game and seafood in the restaurant (see below).

£££-££ Glenmore Lodge
Glenmore, T01479-861256, www.glenmorelodge.org.uk.
Britain's top outdoor training centre, patronized by many British Winter Olympians. Equipped with a pool, gym and even a roller-ski cross-country track within the forest. There's twin-room and chalet accommodation available and all facilities are included in the price. This is an ideal base for those seeking a rural retreat with top-class instruction in climbing, mountaineering and kayaking.

££ Rowan Tree Country Hotel
Overlooking Loch Alvie, 3 miles south of Aviemore on the B9152, T01479-810207, www.rowantreehotel.com.
12 rooms. Cosy, comfortable and friendly hotel that goes the extra mile for guests. One of the oldest hotels in the area, it also serves excellent food.

££-£ Aviemore Bunkhouse
Dalfaber Rd, T01479-811181, www.aviemore-bunkhouse.com.
Sleeps up to 41 people in en suite family rooms, double rooms and 6-bed rooms. Very cosy and high-quality facilities, with the excellent **Old Bridge Inn** pub and restaurant next door. Recommended.

£ SYHA hostel
Grampian Rd, T01479-810345. Open all year.
Very good hostel, just mins from all amenities and transport links.

Restaurants

£££-££ Aspects
The Macdonald Aviemore Resort, see Where to stay, above, T0344-879 9152. Daily 1930-2130.
Within the resort complex, Aspects prides itself on offering freshly produced Scottish-based cuisine in a stylish setting.

£££-££ Scottish Steakhouse
Spey Valley Golf & Country Club, T344-879 9100.

Less formal than **Aspects**, and the place to enjoy tender Scotch beef.

££ Cairngorm Hotel
See Where to stay, above.
Continues to deserve its reputation for serving up tasty Scottish dinner classics, as well as your favourite pub-grub.

££ Druie Restaurant-Café
At Rothiemurchus Estate, 2 miles off the A9, 5-min drive from Aviemore, T01479-812800, www.rothiemurchus.net. Daily 0930-1700.
This is where to bite into wonderfully fresh, appetizing daytime snacks or enjoy a tasty wholesome lunch with meats and fish sourced from the local area. There's also a deli and farm shop where you can buy some of the tasty local produce to take home. Recommended.

££ Mountain Café
111 Grampian Rd, Aviemore, T01479-812473. Daily 0830-1700.
It's not the cheapest breakfast or lunch in town but with choices like porridge (£5.50), fresh fruit and zuchini pancakes, and a menu to suit vegan, gluten free and vegetarian diners, this café combines memorable eating with style.

££ Old Bridge Inn
Dalfaber Rd, T01479-811137. Lunch served 1200-1430, dinner 1730-2100.
Tucked away on the old road below the main street, this atmospheric inn remains a high-quality eating establishment favoured by many a local. Ceilidhs and Highland dinner dances are hosted and, for less formal eating, diners can sit by the bar to enjoy a pint of real ale with some hearty pub-grub. Recommended.

££-£ The Winking Owl
123 Grampian Rd, T01479-812368. Mon-Thu 1200-2300, Fri-Sat 1100-0100, Sun 1230-2300.
The wooden interior, mountain views and good wholesome food make this a worthwhile stop for a drink or bite.

Bars and clubs

The bar of the **Cairngorm Hotel** is always lively, see Where to stay. The **Old Bridge Inn** and **Winking Owl** are also 2 good pubs, see Restaurants, above.

What to do

Fishing
Fishing is a major pursuit in the area. Armed with a permit, you can fish for trout and salmon on the River Spey. **Rothiemurchus Estate** also offers bait and fly fishing and equipment hire for its stocked loch (daily 0900-1700) at Inverdruie. There's even a 'novice loch' where, with rod and tackle provided, beginners can benefit from an hour's instruction with 1-hr's fishing. For further information about fishing at Rothiemurchus and on the Spey, call T01479-810703 or the local fishing secretary on T01479-831274. Alternatively, log onto www.fishpal.com or www.visitscotland.com/fish, for a full listing of stockists and hire outlets in the Speyside area.
Cairngorm Mountain Sports, *111 Grampian Rd, Aviemore, T01479-810903.* Permits, rods and tackle can be bought here.

Horse riding
Horse riding and pony trekking are on offer at various places throughout Strathspey.
Alvie Stables, *Alvie, near Kincraig, T01479-831409, T07831-495397.* Excellent, offering rides for adults and children (over 4 years). From 20-min mini-rides to 1½-hr hacks for the more experienced.
Carrbridge Trekking Centre, *Station Rd, Carrbridge, T01479-841602.* Offer 1- and 2-hr treks with 30-min treks for young children. Ideal for families, but advanced notice of arrival recommended.

Mountain biking
From Rothiemurchus Estate and Glenmore Forest to the tough 'Burma Road' connecting Carrbridge with Aviemore and

the Ryvoan route, Cairngorms National Park and outlying areas make perfect mountain-bike country for novices and experts. Strathspey is teeming with mountain bike routes for all levels.

The Laggan Wolftrax Centre, *on A86 between Spean Bridge and Newtonmore.* 1¾ miles west of Laggan village, has over 20 miles of purpose-built tracks ranging from fairly easy up to the most technically difficult single-treck in Scotland. The centre has a café which is open daily in summer (Fri-Mon in winter). The trails are open daily year-round.

Bothy Bikes, *5 Granish Way, Dalfaber, Aviemore, T01479-810111, www.bothybikes. co.uk. Daily 0900-1730.* Friendly, highly knowledgeable bike shop and rental. Will advise on routes and trails in the surrounding area. Also has shop at Laggan Wolftrax in the summer.

Skiing

For information on skiing in the Cairgorms, see page 144.

Aviemore & Glenmore Ski Shop, *Glenmore, by Loch Morlich and close to Glenmore Forest Park Visitor Centre (see page 145), T01479-861257, www.aviemoreski.co.uk.* This is the place to go for ski and snowboard hire, lift passes, ski and snowboard instruction, also has a café and après ski bar.

Steam train

Strathspey Steam Railway, *Aviemore Station, Dalfaber Rd, Aviemore, T01479-810725, www.strathspeyrailway.co.uk. £21.50, senior £18.45, child £10.15, under 5s free, family £54.* A round trip from Aviemore through Boat of Garten to Broomhill, 1½ hrs. A fabulous 'old world' experience. Apr-Oct and 'Santa' and 'New Year' (Mince Pie) specials. The station is just to the east of the main train station.

Tour operators

As one of Scotland's primary outdoor adventure locations, there are a host of operators offering all kinds of adrenalin activities and professional coaching.

G2 Outdoor, *The Hatchery, Alviwe Estate, near Aviemore, T01540-651784, www. g2outdoor.co.uk.* From gorge walking to mountaineering, telemark skiing and river kayaking, this is a highly professional, fun-orientated outfit.

Glenmore Lodge, *Aviemore, T01479-861256, www.glenmorelodge.org.uk.* Arguably Britain's top outdoor training centre with a rash of expert mountain and kayaking guides available to coach those who want to learn or improve their kayaking, winter mountaineering and/or rock climbing skills.

Highland Venture, *Rothiemurchus Estate, T01479-812345, www.quadtreksaviemore. co.uk.* Quad-biking treks for over 12s, £40 for 1 hr.

Highland Wildlife and Birdwatch Safaris, *Aviemore, T01479-811169, T07974-151503, www.highlandwildlifesafaris.co.uk.* Run great value guided wildlife tours in and around Cairngorms National Park.

Rothiemurchus Estate, *T01479-812345, www.rothiemurchus.net. Daily 0930-1730.* Runs a vast range of outdoor activities, including quad-bike treks, pony trekking, river tubing, family rafting, paddle boarding, etc. Amongst its host of outdoor activities, the estate runs an excellent 'Behind the Scenes' tour designed to provide photo opportunities and an insight into the wildlife, ancient Caledonian forest and history of the land as you explore the vast estate by 4WD.

Scot Mountain Holidays, *Fraoch Lodge, Deshar Rd, Boat of Garten, T01479-831331, www.scotmountainholidays.com.* Activity holidays arranged include walking, cycling, family adventures, volunteering, private guided trips and wildlife. Also has homestay accommodation at **Fraoch Lodge**.

Walking

The walks around Strathspey are covered by OS Landranger map No 36 (1:50, scale) or OS Outdoor Leisure Map No 3 (1:25,000 scale).

Watersports

In summer, the main activities are watersports, and there are 2 centres which offer sailing, canoeing and windsurfing tuition and equipment hire. **Loch Insh Watersports Centre**, *Kincraig by Kingussie, T01540-651272, www.lochinsh. com. Open year-round.* The centre has been running for 40 years and offers a host of activities, including kayaking, sailing and windsurfing in addition to mountain bike hire and boat trips to spot wildlife on the loch. There's also a fabulous boathouse café/ restaurant, a guesthouse and alpine-style self-catering chalets with loch views. **Loch Morlich Watersports Centre**, *8 miles east of Aviemore, T01479-861221, www. lochmorlich.com. Apr-Oct.* Windsurfing, kayaking and sailing.

Transport

Bus

To **Inverness**, 45 mins; **Kingussie**, 20 mins; **Pitlochry**, 1¼ hrs; **Perth**, 2 hrs; **Glasgow**, 3½ hrs; and **Edinburgh**, 3½ hrs. For **Aberdeen**, change at Inverness. **Scottish Citylink**, www.citylink.co.uk.

Car hire

Aviemore Car Hire, Station Sq, T01479-811700. All the main operators can also be found in Aviemore.

Train

There are direct trains to **Glasgow** and **Edinburgh**, 3 hrs; and **Inverness**, 40 mins.

Cairngorms National Park *Colour map 4, A3.*

hiking, climbing, mountain biking and rare wildlife

The area around Aviemore is only a small part of the Cairngorms National Park, whose boundaries extend from Grantown-on-Spey to the heads of the Angus Glens, and from Ballater on Deeside to Loch Laggan. Scotland's second national park is also the UK's largest at 1400 square miles. It is home to 25% of Scotland's native woodland and is a refuge for many rare plants and animals, including 25% of the UK's threatened species. Probably the most famous of the park's wild residents is the osprey, but you'll also see golden eagles, ptarmigan, the extremely rare crossbill, red deer, red squirrel and pine marten. As well as the park's natural attractions, there are also countless outdoor activities on offer, as the Cairngorms is one the UK's prime climbing and hiking areas and now home to an increasing number of outdoor adventure operators. Unsurprisingly, it's also where several of Scotland's most gifted Winter Olympic athletes train and whether you're looking for excellent mountain biking, watersports, winter sports (see page 143), horse riding, fishing or stalking, this is the place to come.

Cairngorm Ski Area

9 miles southeast of Aviemore, www.cairngormmountain.org.uk. Frequent buses Nos 34 and 36 from Aviemore.

Cairngorm is Scotland's longest-established ski resort and remains Scotland's largest ski area, with almost 30 runs and over 20 miles of pistes starting over 2500 ft above Loch Morlich. This is where many of Britain's leading ski racers have first learnt the arts of skiing and snowboarding. When the sun shines, the snowfall is good and the crowds are few it can be a very satisfying experience. The season normally runs from January till the snow disappears (which can be as late as May in some years). Visitors can rent skis and snowboards, book lessons and purchase day and half-day ski passes from the busy **Day Lodge** ① *T01479-861261*, at the foot of the ski area. Aside from dozens of pistes, Cairngorm also boasts Scotland's only **funicular mountain railway** ① *daily 1st train at 1000, last train down leaves at 1530, every 20 mins, £13.50, concessions £12.95, children £9, family £38.25*. This runs to the **Ptarmigan restaurant/café** and gift shop near the summit of Cairn Gorm. The **Aviemore iCentre** and the Cairngorm Day Lodge ticket office provide free piste maps of the Cairngorm ski area. The **Cairngorm Ranger Service** ① *T01479-861703*, by the Day Lodge, post up a daily mountain weather forecast, advise on the local wildlife and run occasional guided walks.

Walking in the Cairngorms

The Cairngorms provide some of Scotland's most challenging walking, with no fewer than 49 Munros and half of Britain's eight mountains over 4000 ft (Ben Macdrui, Braeriach, Cairn Toul and Cairn Gorm). These mountains come into their own in winter, providing experienced climbers with a wide range of classic ice climbs and fantastic opportunities for ski touring. However, in light of the sub-Arctic weather conditions, which can descend in minutes to produce frightening and disorientating white-outs, forays onto these summits should not be taken lightly. They require a high degree of fitness, navigational experience and preparation (see page 24).

The summit of **Cairn Gorm** (4081 ft) is readily accessible as you take the mountain railway up to the **Ptarmigan restaurant**. However, the railway cannot be used to access the high mountain plateau beyond the ski area and mountain walkers may not use the railway for their return journey.

There are over 50 miles of footpath through this area. In addition to peaceful trails and ranger-led walks through the Rothiemurchus Forest (see above), another good area for walking is around **Glenmore Forest Park**. The **visitor centre** ① *T01479-861220*, near Loch Morlich produces a very good *Glen More Forest Guide Map* which details the many local walks. The centre also has a lovely café, a great interpretative display about the wildlife, and panels/photographs that offer insights into the role Glenmore played in training the Norwegian resistance and commandos during the Second World War.

The best-known of the long-distance trails is the famous ★ **Lairig Ghru**, a 25-mile hike from Aviemore over the Lairig Ghru Pass to Braemar. The trail is well marked but can easily take over eight hours and is very tough in parts. Note that the weather in this part of the world can be very unforgiving for the ill-equipped and unprepared. Do not underestimate this walk. An easier proposition is a 12-mile loop which leads to the start of the Lairig Ghru Pass, starting from Loch Morlich. To reach **Loch Morlich** take the B970 east from the southern end of Aviemore, beyond Coylumbridge. The route starts at the western end of Loch Morlich where a forestry track runs south from the road. It leads to a bridge over the River Luineag. Cross the bridge and continue along the track, keeping straight on where another track heads off left. About a mile further on, another track heads off to the right, but keep to the left fork, signposted for **Rothiemurchus Lodge**.

The track climbs up towards the lodge. Just before it, turn right on to a clear track which leads up to a reservoir. Soon another track heads off to the right, signposted for the Lairig Ghru. Follow this path through heather moorland. The path then heads left, climbing up through open moorland to the lip of the glen. The entrance to the Lairig Ghru is straight ahead.

After about a mile, as the hills begin to encroach on either side, a rough path almost doubles back to the left. Follow this path up the slope to the gap between Creag a' Chalamain and Creag an Leith-Choin. The deep gully, the Chalamain Gap, is filled with huge boulders and requires great care when clambering through it. Beyond the gully a path leads through heather and pine saplings, dropping down to the side of a burn, then climbing up on its other side. Continue on this path, which then drops steeply down to the side of the burn. Cross the footbridge and climb the slope beyond to reach the main road. Turn left along the road to return to the start of the route.

East of Aviemore

rare birdlife, fishing and skiing

Boat of Garten *Colour map 4, A3.*

The most unusual way to get here is on the Strathspey Steam Railway (see page 143), which runs regularly Apr-Sep from Aviemore. Loch Garten is not easy to reach without your own transport, check with local iCentres for tours.

Eight miles northeast of Aviemore is the quiet village of Boat of Garten, home to breeding pairs of rare ospreys on Loch Garten, two miles east of the village. ★ **Abernethy Forest RSPB Reserve** ① *T01479-831476, www.nnr-scotland.org.uk, Apr-early Sep daily 1000-1800, £5, concessions £3, children £2*, on the shore of Loch Garten, can be visited during the nesting season when the RSPB opens an observation centre. This is also one of few places in the world to see Scottish crossbills. You may also see ospreys at the Rothiemurchus trout loch at Inverdruie, and maybe even on Loch Morlich and Loch Insh. The Abernethy reserve is home to several other rare species such as capercaillie, whooper swans and red squirrels. 'Caperwatch' takes place from April to mid-May (0530 to 0800).

Carrbridge *Colour map 4, A3.*

At Carrbridge, a pleasant little village seven miles north of Aviemore, is the **Landmark Forest Theme Park** ① *T01479-841613, www.landmarkpark.co.uk, Apr to mid-Jul daily 1000-1800, mid-Jul to Aug 1000-1900, Oct-Mar 1000-1700, £6.95, concessions/children £5.90*, a woodland park which combines entertainment, education and shopping. This is where kids can really let off steam as they explore the raised Treetop Trail for viewing wildlife, a maze, fire tower and the highly popular Water Coaster. It's far from tacky and it's great fun. In the village itself is the decidedly fragile-looking 17th-century stone arch of the **Bridge of Carr**, which is definitely not for vertigo sufferers. The nine-hole, 2623-yd **Carrbridge Golf Course** ① *T01479-841623*, is also worth a hit.

Grantown-on-Spey *Colour map 4, A3.*

This genteel Georgian holiday town is 15 miles northeast of Aviemore and attracts the more mature tourist by the coach load. Everything here is geared towards fishing, and anyone wishing to get kitted out should get themselves down to **Mortimers** on the High Street. For more information on the town, visit www.grantownonline.com.

Tomintoul *Colour map 4, A3.*

The A939 runs south and then east from Grantown-on-Spey to the little village of Tomintoul (altitude 1600 ft), the nearest settlement of any size to the Lecht ski resort and also the highest village in the Highlands.

On the village square is the **museum** ① *Apr-Oct daily 1000-1700, free*, which has a display of local history, wildlife, landscape and outdoor activities. Tomintoul is best known as the starting point of one of the most beautiful and notorious stretches of road in the country. In winter, the Tomintoul to Cock Bridge road is almost always the first road in Scotland to be blocked by snow.

Lecht Ski Centre *Colour map 4, A4.*
T01975-651440, www.lecht.co.uk. Phone or check website for latest weather conditions.

From Tomintoul the road rise steeply to The Lecht, a ski resort for all seasons. It offers dry-slope skiing throughout the year and its snowmaking facilities mean that the winter season can be extended beyond January and March. The Lecht's gentler slopes make it ideal for beginners and intermediates, and the emphasis is on family skiing. There's a snowboard fun park with half pipe, log slide, gap jump and table top. However, there are also more difficult runs for the more experienced skier, and extensive off-piste skiing. In addition, there's a summer activity area with quad bikes and fun-karts.

From the ski centre, the A939 drops dramatically to the hamlet of **Cock Bridge**. A few miles to the east is the austere **Corgarff Castle** ① *Apr-Sep daily 0930-1700, Oct 1000-1600, £6, concessions £4.80, children £3.60*, a 16th-century tower house, later turned into a garrison post, with an eventful and gruesome history. Here Margaret Forbes and her family were burned alive by the Gordons in 1571 during the bitter feud between the two families. In the wake of the ill-fated 1745 rebellion the government remodelled the castle, building a star-shaped defensive wall, and garrisoned 60 men to maintain order and communications in this part of the Highlands. Corgarff continued in use into the 19th century when English Redcoats were stationed here in order to try and prevent whisky smuggling.

A few miles east of Corgarff the A939 meets the A944 Tomintoul–Ballatar road. Five miles beyond the junction is the tiny village of Strathdon, famous for the **Lonach Highland Gathering**. Held on the third Saturday in August, it has a healthy blast of authenticity in comparison to the more glitzy affair in Braemar on Deeside.

Listings East of Aviemore

Where to stay

Grantown-on-Spey
As you'd expect, there's a wide range of upmarket accommodation. Some of the best places in town are on Woodland Terrace.

£££ Culdearn House
Woodlands Terrace, T01479-872106, www.culdearn.com.
With 6 beautifully appointed bedrooms, this country house is a fine place to stay, with roaring fires, fine dining (**£££-££**) and even finer collection of malt whiskies. A great choice if you're after some well-deserved luxury after a hard day's walking in the hills. The owners will even make you a packed lunch and dry your wet clothes. Recommended.

£££ The Garth Hotel
Castle Rd, T01479-872836, www.garthhotel.com.

18 en suite rooms. Hailed as the town's premier independent hotel, it's not difficult to see why. This is where to combine a comfortable stay with freshly prepared dinners (**££**) before choosing from among the cosy bar's excellent selection of real ales and whiskies.

£££ Muckrach Country House Hotel
A few miles southwest of town at Dulnain Bridge, T01479-851227, www.muckrach.com.
A delightful, high-class, small hotel and one that retains its reputation for fine cuisine (**£££-££**). 13 individually styled rooms including a dog-friendly room and suite.

£ Craggan Outdoors
Grantown-on-Spey, T01479-873283, www.craggan.co.uk.
Excellent budget accommodation in their: **Ardenbeg Bunkhouse** (Grant Rd) sleeps up to 23 in various-sized rooms; **Glenbeg**

Bunkhouse (1 mile south of town by the A95) sleeps up to 27; and **Glenbeg Bothy** (same directions) sleeps up to 6.

Self-catering

Muckrach Castle
3 miles from Grantown-on-Spey, T01343-823000, www.muchrackcastle.co.uk.
With views towards the Cairngorms, this provides a rare opportunity to relax in your own 15th-century castle. 5 bedrooms, sleeps 8-10.

Tomintoul

££ Argyle Guest House
7 Main St, T01807-580766.
6 rooms. Lovely, friendly B&B close to all amenities.

£ SYHA Hostel
Main St, T01807-580364, www.syha.org.uk. Apr-Sep.
20 beds. Handy for food, the pub, the bus and the Speyside Way.

What to do

See under Aviemore, page 142.

Transport

Bus
Bus No 32 runs from Carrbridge to Newtonmore and No 34 and 34X run from **Aviemore** to **Inverness** via Grantown **Boat of Garten** and **Nethy Bridge**. For times and prices see www.stagecoachbus.com.

Deeside *Colour map 4, A3/4.*

castles, mountain walks and a very famous family

The A939 runs south from the junction with the A944 to Ballatar, one of the main towns that line the popular tourist trail of Deeside, or rather Royal Deeside, for its connections with the royal family who have holidayed here, at Balmoral, since Queen Victoria first arrived in 1848.

Today, Deeside's royal associations have made it the tourist honeypot of the northeast, but the royal presence has also saved it from mass development. There's an air of understated affluence and refinement in the villages strung out along the A93 that runs along the north bank of the Dee and, as well as the obvious attraction of Balmoral, there are many other fine examples of baronial castles. Deeside is also a great area for outdoor activities, such as hiking in the surrounding mountains, fishing, stalking, mountain biking, canoeing and skiing.

Ballater and Balmoral *Colour map 4, A4.*
The neat little town of Ballater is proud of its royal connections. You can buy meat from the butcher with his 'By Royal Appointment' sign, or clothes from royal outfitters. Ever since Queen Victoria first arrived by train from Aberdeen in 1848, the royal family have been spending their holidays here in their summer residence, Balmoral. She was not amused at the prospect of having an unsightly rail station on her doorstep, so the line ended eight miles east, at Ballater. The line has been closed for some time and, unfortunately, the old train station was destroyed by fire in 2015.

The royals are not the only famous summer visitors. The poet Byron (who attended Aberdeen Grammar School) spent many childhood summer holidays at Ballaterach, a few miles east of Ballater. He had a narrow escape when he slipped and nearly fell into the fast-flowing stream at the Linn of Dee, beyond Braemar. He was rescued just in time and went on to wax poetic about the beautiful hills which are Ballater's other great attraction. The town makes the ideal base for hiking (see below) as well as a number of other outdoor activities. Many of the walks set off from within the 6000 acre Loch Muick (pronounced 'Mick') and Lochnagar Wildlife Reserve, nine miles southwest of Ballater, at the head of Glen Muick. There's a visitor centre and car park at Spittal of Glenmuick. From here a track leads along the west shore of the loch to the lodge where Queen Victoria met John Brown. You may spot birds of prey and deer. See also What to do, page 142.

Balmoral Castle *Colour map 4, A4.*

T01339-742534, www.balmoralcastle.com, Apr-end Jul daily 1000-1700, £11.50, concessions £10.50, children £6.

Eight miles west of Ballater is the area's main attraction, Balmoral Castle. The 16th-century tower house, formerly owned by the local Gordon family, was bought for Queen Victoria by Prince Albert in 1852 and converted into today's baronial mansion. It has been the royal family's summer retreat ever since. Only the ballroom and the grounds are open to the likes of you and me, and only for three months of the year. Pony trekking and pony cart rides are available around the grounds and are favourite ways of enjoying the wonderful scenery. Opposite the castle gates is **Crathie Church**, which is used by the family when they're in residence. There's a small souvenir shop next to the main gates and a visitor centre which gives a lot of information on the castle and its owners. If you want to soak up even more of the royal atmosphere there are cottages to rent year-round (see website for details).

Braemar *Colour map 4, A3.*

Nine miles west of Balmoral, is Braemar, the final town on Deeside, lying at the foot of the awesome, brooding **Cairngorm Massif**, which dominates the Eastern Highlands. Even at the height of summer you can see a dab of snow still lying in a hollow in the surrounding mountains, and Braemar is an excellent base for hiking, see below, and winter skiing at Glenshee, see page 126. It's an attractive little place, much loved by Queen Victoria and much visited during its annual Braemar Gathering (or games, see box, page 150), which attracts tens of thousands of visitors each year, amongst them members of the royal family. **Braemar Highland Heritage Centre** ① *Balmoral Mews by the tourist office, T01339-741944, Apr-Oct daily 0900-1700, Nov-Mar daily 1000-1600, free*, has a small exhibition including a 12-minute audio-visual presentation.

Just north of the village is **Braemar Castle** ① *T01339-741219, www.braemarcastle.co.uk, Apr-Jun, Sep and Oct Wed-Sun 1000-1700, Jul and Aug daily 1000-1700, £8, concessions £7 and children £4, dating from 1628.* This impressive fortress was used by Hanoverian troops after the Jacobite Rising of 1745. It is L-shaped, with a star-shaped defensive wall and a central round tower with a spiral stair. There are barrel-vaulted ceilings and an underground prison. Its owner also possesses the world's largest cairngorm – a semi-precious stone, a variety of quartz, which is yellow, grey or brown in colour – weighing 52 lbs. Thanks to an inspired restoration project spearheaded by the local community, it's now possible to visit this atmospheric castle.

A very scenic side trip from Braemar is to the **Linn of Dee**, six miles west of the village, at the end of the road. Here, the river thunders through a narrow gorge to spectacular effect. There are numerous walks from here along the river, or, for the more adventurous, the famous **Lairig Ghru**, which runs through the Cairngorms to Aviemore, see page 145. Between the Linn of Dee and the tiny settlement of **Inverey**, a mile to the east, there's a very basic youth hostel (open early May to end September), which has no showers and no

We are most certainly amused

There has been a gathering of some sort at Braemar for 900 years, ever since Malcolm Canmore set contests for the local clans so that he could pick the strongest and bravest of men for his army. These events take place up and down the country throughout the summer, but none is as famous, or well attended, as Braemar's. Queen Victoria attended in 1848 and the gathering is still patronized by the royal family. Crowds come from all over the world to proclaim the monarch as Chieftain of the Braemar Gathering.

At the gathering the visitor will see contests in traditional Scottish events, such as tossing the caber, Highland dancing and bagpipe competitions and displays. There is an inter-services tug o'war championship, a medley relay race and a hill race up Morrone. The sound of the massed pipes echoing around the encircling heather-clad hills and a plethora of tartan also help to make this a real tourist highlight. The royal connection (and the crowds) apart, many other local communities hold similar games.

phone, so book through **Braemar Youth Hostel**, see page 152. Unfortunately, there's now no postbus from Ballater post office for Linn of Dee so you'll need to walk or cycle. Some 15 miles south of Braemar on the A93, at Spittal of Glenshee, is the **Glenshee Ski Centre**, the largest in Scotland. See page 126 for details.

Walks in Deeside

Ballater and Braemar are ideal bases for walking in the surrounding Grampian Mountains, and if you feel like 'bagging a Munro' (ie climbing a mountain over 3000 ft), there are some close at hand. All of this area, that's also reportedly home to 25% of Britain's endangered species, is included in the **Cairngorms National Park** (www.cairngorm. co.uk), which opened in 2003. This is the largest national park in Britain, covering a vast 4500 sq km, from Aboyne in the east to Dalwhinnie in the west, and from Blair Atholl north to Grantown-on-Spey.

Lochnagar (OS Landranger No 44. Colour map 4, B4). The best walk in the area is to the summit of Lochnagar (3789 ft), made famous by Prince Charles in the book he wrote for his brothers when young, *The Old Man of Lochnagar*. The noble and mysterious mountain dominates the **Royal Forest of Balmoral** and takes its name from a small loch at its foot (it's also known as the White Mounth). This fine granite mass is approached from the car park by the Rangers' visitor centre at Spittal of Glen Muick. The path to the top is well trodden and well marked, though steep as you near the summit. It's 10 miles there and back, so allow a full day for the climb. You'll need to be properly equipped and take a map.

Cambus o' May and Morrone (OS Landranger No 43). An easier walk is to Cambus o' May, on the river, about four miles east of Ballater. It's a great spot for a picnic, or to swim in the river, or to enjoy a stroll along the riverbank. A good walk from Braemar is to the summit of Morrone (2818 ft), the mountain to the southwest. The walk takes about four hours in total.

Glen Tanar to Glen Esk (OS Landranger No 44. Colour map 4, A4-B5). Another good climb is the route up Mount Keen (3081 ft), the most easterly Munro, which lies between

Deeside and Glen Esk, the loveliest of the Angus glens. Again, you should allow a whole day for this expedition. It can be approached from the visitor centre in Glen Tanar, at the end of the little road that runs southwest off the B976, across the river from Aboyne. You can climb to the summit and return by the same route but, if your party has two cars, it is well worth walking over to Glen Esk, 14 miles away. Drive around to the Invermark car park at the head of Glen Esk and park your car there. From Glen Tanar follow the old drove road which at times runs with the Mounth road. Skirting the **Home Farm** with its Arboretum and its dammed lake, the fairly flat track winds along Glen Tanar through the forest for about four miles. Then comes the Halfway Hut, used for rest by former shooting parties. You pass shooting butts en route. The next stretch is through open country with the **Clachan Yell** (626 ft) on the left.

The walk proper then begins to take shape. Cross the stone bridge of **Etnach**, and then the path begins to lead up to the **Shiel of Glentanar**. The second bridge forks left and the track heads for the summit. The rough path continues along a ridge, the shoulder of Mount Keen. From the summit with its stone marker, **Dinnet** and its two lakes are visible to the north, and the River Esk glints its way down the valley to the south. Watch out for adders. On the descent, you'll pass the **Queen's Well**, used by Queen Victoria when she and her party went down to Fettercairn posing as a wedding party. The well is decorated with a graceful granite crown which was erected in 1861. The royal party covered much of the climb on hill ponies. The stone arch at Fettercairn commemorates this visit.

Listings Deeside

Tourist information

Ballater

Ballater iCentre
Cairngorms National Park authority office in the Albert Memorial Hall, Station Square (temporary accommodation while the Old Royal Station is being rebuilt), T01339-755306, www.visitscotland.com. Daily 1000-1700.

Braemar

Braemar iCentre
Balmoral Mews, Mar Rd, T01339-741600. Nov-Mar daily 0930-1630, Apr-Oct daily 0900-1700.

Where to stay

Ballater and Balmoral
There's plenty of accommodation in Ballater, from expensive hotels to reasonably priced B&Bs.

££££-£££ Hilton Craigendarroch
Braemar Rd, Ballater, T01339-755858, www3.hilton.com.
Victorian country house converted into a modern resort hotel with full leisure and sports facilities. Accommodation in luxurious suites or lodges. Excellent dining in the resort's restaurants.

£££-££ Deeside Inn
13-15 Victoria Rd, Ballater, set back from the A93 heading out of town towards Braemar, T01339-755413, www.crerarhotels.com.
Victorian-era hotel with comfortable contemporary rooms, friendly, good value and good food, with a terrific selection of malt whiskies.

£££-££ Glen Lui Hotel
Invercauld Rd, Ballater, T01339-755402, www.glen-lui-hotel.co.uk.
19 rooms. Comfortable hotel serving fine food and with good views over the golf course to Lochnagar.

££ Inverdeen House
11 Bridge Sq, Ballater, T01339-755759,
www.inverdeen.com.
Among the many B&Bs in town this one is
particularly recommended. Antiques in the
house, French, German and Polish spoken.
Great breakfasts.

Self-catering

Royal Deeside Holiday Cottages
Aboyne, near Ballater, T01339-885341,
www.royaldeesideholidaycottages.co.uk.
Managed by the Dinnet Estate, these
3 traditional stone cottages in peaceful
surroundings sleep up to 6. From
£675 per week in peak season.

Braemar
Accommodation is hard to find before and
during the **Braemar Gathering**, but at other
times of the year there's plenty to choose
from, including many B&Bs and guesthouses.

£££ Braemar Lodge Hotel
*On the outskirts of the village on the road
south to Glenshee and Blairgowrie, T01339-
741627, www.braemarlodge.co.uk.*
A lovely hotel with the option of log cabin
(££) in the grounds or a 12-bed bunkhouse
(£) that's a good choice for budget travellers.
Fine dining in the restaurant and over
200 whiskies to choose from in the Malt
Room. Transport, shops and a pub are just
500 m away.

££ Callater Lodge Hotel
Glenshee Rd, T01339-741275,
www.callatarlodge.co.uk.
Charming and comfortable 6-bedroom
guesthouse with a cosy and stylish guest
sitting room and breakfasts that are worth
staying here for on their own.

£ Rucksacks
15 Mar Rd, T01339-741517.
A cheap and friendly bunkhouse complete
with sauna that's popular with hikers and
those using the nearby **Glenshee Ski Centre**.

Also rents out mountain bikes. Sleeps up to
26 in 3 buildings.

£ SYHA Youth Hostel
Corrie Feragie Lodge, Glenshee Rd,
T01339-741659. Open all year.
Terrific former shooting lodge with good
range of facilities and reasonably close to
the shops and bus stop.

Camping

Invercauld Caravan Site
Glenshee Rd, T01339-741373. Dec-Oct.

Restaurants

Ballater and Balmoral
See also Where to stay, above.

££ India on the Green
9 Victoria Rd, Ballater, T01339-755701.
Open 1200-1400 and 1700-2300.
Since 2013 this has been an Indian restaurant,
and one of the best in the region. Well
worth it if you fancy a change from modern
Scottish cuisine. The food is thoughtfully
prepared and tasty to boot.

££-£ Rowan Tree
T01339-755191, Bridge St, Ballater.
Good coffee and fresh home-baking or pop
in for home-made soup, open sandwiches
and a range of mains, including locally
sourced beef. Good value.

Braemar
A quiet town, Braemar isn't teeming with
café-bars and restaurants.

£££-££ Braemar Lodge
See Where to stay, above.
Serves daily lunches and dinners, with the
dinner menu including staples such as
Aberdeen Angus beef and game.

££ The Gathering Place
7-9 Invercauld Rd, T01339-741234.
Tucked away off the main road, this lovely,
cosy restaurant boasts fine Scottish cuisine
with an emphasis on beef and game, a

roaring open fire and walls adorned with Scottish artwork. Good value.

£ Taste Coffee Shop and Deli
Airlie House, Chapel Brae, T01339-741425.
Tue-Sat 1000-1700.
Bright café/restaurant serving soup and sandwiches.

Festivals

Braemar
Sep Braemar Games, www.braemar gathering.org, or contact the Secretary, BRHS, Coilacreich, Ballater, T01339-755377. Held on the 1st Sat in Sep. Booking is highly recommended.

What to do

See under Aviemore, page 142.

Transport

Bus
There are regular services from Aberdeen to towns on Deeside. **Stagecoach Highland** bus No 504 runs from Ballater via **Strathdon** and **Tomintoul** to **Grantown-on-Spey** and on to **Aviemore**. There are regular buses from **Aberdeen** to Braemar via Ballater and Balmoral operated by **Stagecoach Bluebird** (T01224-212266, www.stagecoachbus.com).

West of Aviemore

step back in time at the Highland Folk Museum

Kingussie *Colour map 4, A2.*
The quiet village of Kingussie (pronounced *King-yoosie*) lies 12 miles southwest of Aviemore and makes a pleasant alternative as a place to stay. The main attraction here and in the village of **Newtonmore**, two miles south, is the excellent **Highland Folk Museum** ① *T01540-673351, www.highlifehighland.com, Apr-Aug daily 1030-1730, Sep-Oct daily 1100-1630, free*, which offers an insight into highland life in the 17th century. The traditional, re-created blackhouse and collection of highland artefacts is in Kingussie, whilst the 17th-century 'township' in Newtonmore includes actors in traditional dress 'working' on a farm, in an old smokehouse and a water mill. During the summer there are also demonstrations of spinning, woodcarving and peat-fire baking. Another worthwhile attraction is **Ruthven Barracks**, standing on a hillock across the river. This former barracks was built by the English Redcoats as part of their campaign to tame the Highlands after the first Jacobite rising in 1715. It was destroyed by the Jacobites in the wake of defeat at Culloden to prevent it from falling into enemy hands, and it was from here that Bonnie Prince Charlie sent his final order which signalled the end of his doomed cause. Access is free and the ruins are particularly attractive at night when floodlit.

At nearby Kincraig village, between Kingussie and Aviemore, is the **Highland Wildlife Park** ① *T01540-651270, www. highlandwildlifepark.org.uk, Apr-Oct daily 1000-1700, Jul and Aug 1000-1800, Nov-Mar daily 1000-1600, park tours £15.90, concessions £13.50, children £12*, which has a captive collection of rare native animals, including wildcat, European bison and over 60 red deer.

Essential Kingussie

Finding your feet

Kingussie is on the main Inverness to Perth/Glasgow/Edinburgh routes and all Perth to Inverness trains stop here as do most **Citylink** buses. There are also several services by **Stagecoach Highland** between Kingussie, Glenmore, Laggan Bridge and Dalwhinnie. For timetables, see https://:bustimes.org.uk.

Some 15 miles south of Kingussie down the A9 in the village of Dalwhinnie is the **Dalwhinnie Distillery** ① *T01540-672219, www.malts.com; Jan-Mar and Nov-Dec daily 1000-1545, Apr-May and Oct daily 0930-1645, Jun Mon-Fri 0930-1715, Jul-Aug daily 0930-1745; tours from £12, tasting only £6-18*, established in 1898. Take a tour and sample its 15-year-old malt.

Listings West of Aviemore

Where to stay

££-£ Happy Days Hostel
65 High St, Kingussie, T01540-661175, www.cairngormhighlandhostel.com.
A good budget option with its own café/diner next door for breakfast, lunches and snacks.

££-£ The Pottery Bunkhouse & Coffee Shop
Laggan Bridge T01528-544231, www.potterybunkhouse.co.uk.
Comfortable and well-equipped, 28-bed hostel-style accommodation in 6-bed dorms or family rooms for 5 (**££**). Great home-baked goodies in the coffee shop. Minimum booking is a group of 5.

£ Tipsy Laird Pub & Bunkhouse
68-70 High St, Kingussie, T01540-661708, www.thetipsylaird.co.uk.
A decent hostel next door to a cosy traditional village pub. See also Restaurants, below.

Restaurants

£££ The Cross
Tweed Mill Brae, a private drive leading off Ardbroilach Rd, Kingussie, T01540-661166, www.thecross.co.uk.
Quite simply, this is foodie heaven. Wonderful cooking using the very finest local meat, game and fish. It's not cheap but such quality is worth pushing the boat out for. 3-course dinner is £55 or opt for the extravagantly indulgent 6-course tasting menu at £65 with matching wines (an extra £35). The hotel has 8 very comfortable rooms

(**££££-£££**) and 2 cosy guest lounges. A must for gastronomes.

££ Boathouse Restaurant
At Loch Insh Watersports Centre, Kincraig, between Aviemore and Kingussie, T01540-651394.
Owned by the wonderfully named Freshwater family. A good lochside restaurant which doubles as a café during the day.

££-£ Glen Hotel
Main St, Newtonmore, T01528-673203.
Serves up great-value bar lunches and dinners. Huge portions for very hungry visitors.

£ The Pottery Bunkhouse & Coffee Shop
See Where to stay, above.
Serves up excellent home-baking, soup and filled sandwiches. You can also buy pottery and knitwear here.

£ Tipsy Laird
High St, Kingussie, see Where to stay, above.
Hearty bar meals and real ales, better than average for the region. Good service. Also has a beer garden.

What to do

See under Aviemore, page 142.

Transport

Bus
On schooldays, **Stagecoach Highland** runs several services between **Kingussie**, **Glenmore**, **Laggan Bridge** and **Dalwhinnie**. From **Kingussie**, at least 2 buses (No 35 and No 38) run Mon-Sat to **Aviemore** via **Kincraig**, 20 mins. On schooldays only, the

No 37 leaves Kingussie High School at 1535 and travels via **Insh**, Loch an Eilean Rd and **Rothiemurchus** to **Glenmore**, 1 hr 15 mins. The easiest way to head north from Kingussie to **Aviemore** and **Inverness** is by catching the M91 **Citylink** service that runs 4 times a day between **Edinbugh** and **Inverness**. Also catch this service to travel south from **Kingussie** to **Edinburgh** via **Dalwhinnie**, **Pitlochry** and **Perth**.

North & Northwest

This is the region that best reflects Scotland's romantic image. Wild, rugged and sparsely populated after the infamous 17th- to 18th-century Highland Clearances, this is the Scotland of mist-shrouded glens, towering mountain peaks, windswept purple heather hillsides, brooding lochs, ghostly ancient castles and quaint coastal ports.

Inverness is the 'Capital of the Highlands'. It lies at the northeastern end of the Great Glen, which cuts diagonally across the Southern Highlands to Fort William like a surgical incision, linking Loch Ness with the west coast. Still further south is Glencoe, another climber's paradise and one of the Highland's most evocative glens. The main town in Lochaber is Fort William, which lies in the shadow of Britain's highest mountain, Ben Nevis. Northwest from here stretches a dramatic shoreline of deep sea lochs and sheltered coves of pure white sand backed by towering mountains and looking across to numerous Hebridean islands. West of Fort William, via the lyrical Road to the Isles, is work-a-day Mallaig, the main departure point for ferries to Skye and the Small Isles. Further north is Ullapool, a key ferry port for the Outer Hebrides and the ideal base from which to explore Assynt and the wild and near-deserted far northwest.

Best for
Adventure sports ▪ Fantastic seafood ▪ Wildlife

Inverness. 160
Around Inverness 170
Loch Ness & around 178
Fort William & around. 191
Glen Coe 203
West of Fort William. 212
Great Glen to Kyle of Lochalsh. . 225
Wester Ross 232
Ullapool & around. 243
North coast 257
Northeast coast 266

Footprint picks

★ **The Moray Firth,** page 171

Fine beaches, clifftop walks and one of the best places in Europe to see bottlenose dolphins.

★ **Glen Coe**, page 203

Haunting, dramatic and jaw-droppingly beautiful, this is one of Scotland's truly special places.

★ **The Road to the Isles**, page 217

This evocatively named route runs along a coastline of vanilla beaches and sinuous bays backed by machair and washed by turquoise seas.

★ **West Highland Railway**, page 218

Running from Glasgow to Mallaig, this 164-mile trip is widely acknowledged as one of the world's great rail journeys.

★ **Glenelg**, page 226

The tiny village is home to Gavin Maxwell's famous otters, as well as wildcats, pine martens, golden eagles and sea eagles.

★ **Loch Kishorn to Applecross**, page 232

The views from the Bealach na Ba are out of this world and the seafood on offer at the end of the journey is equally spectacular.

Footprint
picks

1 **The Moray Firth**, page 171
2 **Glen Coe**, page 203
3 **The Road to the Isles**, page 217
4 **West Highland Railway**, page 218
5 **Glenelg**, page 226
6 **Loch Kishorn to Applecross**, page 232

Essential North and Northwest

Finding your feet

There are daily flights to Inverness airport from Edinburgh, Glasgow, London and most major UK airports. Inverness is linked to the south by the notorious A9 from Edinburgh and Perth, to Aberdeen by the A96 and to Fort William by the A82, and is well served by buses. Wick, Thurso, Ullapool, Portree (Skye), Fort William and Aberdeen all enjoy regular bus connections with Inverness. Daily trains from Glasgow and Edinburgh run to Inverness with subsequent connections north to Wick and Thurso, west to Kyle of Lochalsh and east to Aberdeen. Fort William is easily reached from Glasgow by bus, whilst the train (via Fort William) terminates at Mallaig for the ferry to Skye (Armadale). For further details, see Transport, page 168.

Getting around

Exploring the Northwest Highlands is undeniably easier if you have your own transport, though the main tourist centres, including Ullapool and Wick, are easily accessed by bus or train. Getting off the beaten track requires patience but is worthwhile and easily achieved with a little forward planning. Excellent online sources of travel information, including timetables and operators, are www.travelinescotland.com, and www.bustimes.org.uk. Tourist offices throughout the Highlands also carry leaflets on their local and regional transport network. Details of ferries from the mainland ports to Skye, the Outer Hebrides and Orkney are given in the respective island chapters, but by far the most scenic route to the Highlands is the spectacular West Highland

Railway, one of the world's great rail journeys, particularly the section from Fort William to Mallaig (see box, page 218).

Time required

You'll need at least two weeks to do justice to this fabulous region, and more if you want to do the NC500 in full.

When to go

Spring or early summer are the best times as accommodation is easier to find, most places are open and the weather can be reasonably good. Also the dreaded midges are not at their worst. September is also a good time. In the winter months some tourist facilities are closed and you need to be prepared for bad weather on the mountains.

Tip...
If you're cycling the NC500, it's best to do it in a clockwise direction to benefit from the wind direction for most of the route.

Tourist information

Roughly speaking, this chapter includes the northern half of mainland Scotland. It's covered by **VisitScotland**'s highland region whose tourist offices can provide free information and book local accommodation (for a small fee). From November to March smaller information centres (**iCentres**) may be closed or have restricted opening hours. For a list of all iCentres in this region, visit www.visitscotland.com.

Inverness

Inverness is the only city in the Highlands and, as the busy and prosperous hub of the region, its population (70,000) has trebled over the past 30 years. All main routes through the Highlands pass through here at some point, so it's a hard place to avoid. The town's position at the head of the Great Glen and on the shores of the Moray Firth have made it a firm favourite with tourists, who flock here in their legions during the summer months to look for the evasive Loch Ness Monster. Although Inverness city itself holds few major sights, it's a buzzing, attractive place to base yourself as you explore the other sights in the surrounding area, including the possibility of spotting pods of dolphins in the Moray Firth. The city, however, is not without its own appeal, particularly the leafy banks of the River Ness, which runs through its heart, linking Loch Ness with the Moray Firth, and its fair share of fine accommodation and restaurants.

The city is dominated by its red sandstone castle which now houses the Sheriff Court. Built in 1834, this Victorian edifice is very much the new kid on the block in terms of Scottish castles. The original castle dates from the 12th century and was built on a ridge to the east of the present structure. Nothing remains of the old castle, which is unsurprising given its bloody and eventful history. It was here that King Duncan of Scotland was slain by Macbeth, an event dramatically (and erroneously) portrayed in Shakespeare's eponymous work. The castle was occupied three times during the Wars of Independence in the 13th century, and when Robert the Bruce recaptured it in 1307 he destroyed it. In the mid-17th century Cromwell ordered his men to build a stone version on the same site. In 1715 James Francis Edward was proclaimed king there, but not long after it was destroyed by the Jacobites to prevent it from falling into enemy hands following the defeat of Bonnie Prince Charlie at Culloden, see box, page 172. On the castle terrace is a statue of Flora MacDonald, a poignant memorial to her role in helping the prince to escape. Directly across the road, is the Castle Tavern, beloved by real ale drinkers.

Below the castle, on Castle Wynd and near the iCentre is the **Inverness Museum and Art Gallery** ① T01463-237144, www.highlifehighland.com, Apr-Oct Tue-Sat 1000-1700, Nov-Mar Thu-Sat 1000-1700, free. In recent years this interesting museum, complete with café, has undergone a £1 million refurbishment and now includes a wealth of exhibits that outline the social history of the Highlands, its wildlife, and ancient artefacts from the times of the Vikings and the Picts. Among the interactive displays is an opportunity to try your hand at speaking Gaelic. Just around the corner, on High Street, is the Gothic-style **Town House**,

Essential Inverness

Finding your feet

There are daily flights from London Heathrow, Edinburgh, Stornoway and Kirkwall with British Airways (**Loganair**), and daily flights from London Gatwick, London Luton and Bristol with **easyJet**. There are regular flights from Birmingham, Exeter, Manchester, Southampton and Belfast with **Flybe**, whilst **Ryanair** flies from Nottingham (East Midlands) and **Aer Arann** from Dublin. The **airport** (T01667-464000, www. invernessairport.co.uk) is seven miles east of the town at Dalcross. There's a daily airport **JetBus** service operated by **Stagecoach** (www.stagecoachbus.com) every 30 minutes to the town centre, which takes 20 minutes

and costs £4.20 single and £7.20 return. A taxi from the airport costs around £21. The bus station (just off Academy St, T01463-233371) and the train station (east end of Academy St, T01463-239026) have left-luggage lockers charging a maximum of £5 per item per day. See also Transport, page 168.

Getting around

Inverness town centre is compact and easy to explore on foot, and most of the hotels and guesthouses are within a 15-minute walk of the **iCentre** (see page 164). Loch Ness is not within walkable distance, so you'll either need your own transport, or you'll have to book a tour. See What to do, pages 167 and 184.

Inverness

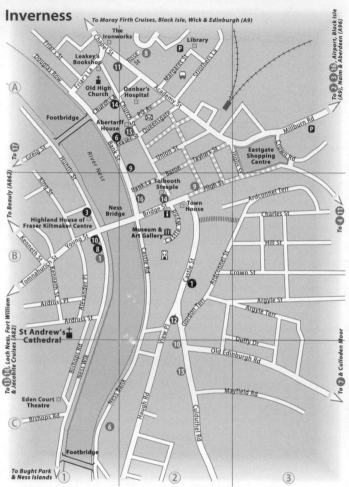

To Moray Firth Cruises, Black Isle, Wick & Edinburgh (A9)

The Ironworks
Chapel St
Rose St
Library
Friars' St
Douglas Row
Friars La
Leakey's Bookshop
Margaret St
Strothers La
Academy St
Old High Church
Dunbar's Hospital
PO Av
Queensgate
Abertarff House
Fraser St
Bank St
Union St
Baron Taylor's St
Eastgate Shopping Centre
Millburn Rd
To Beauly (A862)
River Ness
Greig St
Huntly St
King St
Bank La
Tolbooth Steeple
High St
Ardconnel Terr
Charles St
Ness Bridge
Bridge St
Town House
Hill St
Highland House of Fraser Kiltmaker Centre
Kenneth St
Young St
Museum & Art Gallery
Castle St
Crown St
Tomnahurich St
Kenneth St
Alexander Pl
Ardross Pl
Ardross St
Gordon Terr
View Pl
Crown St
Argyle St
Argyle Terr
To Beauly, Loch Ness, Fort William
St Andrew's Cathedral
Bishops Rd
Ness Wlk
Ness Bank
Haugh Rd
Duffy Dr
Old Edinburgh Rd
Culduthel Rd
Mayfield Rd
To Loch Ness, Fort William & Jacobite Cruises (A82)
Eden Court Theatre
Bishops Rd
Footbridge
To Bught Park & Ness Islands
To Airport, Black Isle (A9), Nairn & Aberdeen (A96)
To Culloden Moor

N

200 metres
200 yards

Where to stay
Columba **1** B1
Culloden House **2** A3
Glenmoriston Town House **6** C1
Glenruidh House **7** C3
Highland Backpackers Inverness Hostel **8** A2
Highlander Hostel **9** B2
Inverness Student Hotel **10** C2
Kingsmills Inverness **11** B3
Loch Ness Country House **13** C1
Macdonald Drumrossie **3** A3
Moyness Guest House **14** C1
Ness Guesthouse **4** B3
Rocpool Reserve & Chez Roux **15** C2
SYHA Youth Hostel **16** A3
Trafford Bank **17** A1

Restaurants
Café No 1 **1** B2
Kitchen Brasserie **3** B1
Leakey's Bookshop **4** A1
Mustard Seed **6** A1
Riva **8** B1
Riverside **9** A2

Rocpool **10** B1

Bars & clubs
Blackfriars **11** A1
Castle Tavern **12** B2
Gellions **14** B2
Hootananny **15** A2
Johnny Foxes & The Den **16** B2

One of the old town's first visitors was that much-travelled cleric, St Columba, who came in AD 565 to confront the Pictish King Brude, whose fortress was reputedly at Craig Phadraig, a few miles west of Inverness. Around the mid-12th century King David I built the original castle and made Inverness a royal burgh on the strength of its growing importance as a trading port. Furs, hides, wool and timber were all exported as far afield as the Mediterranean. The town's economic prosperity and status as the most important northern outpost, however, made it a prime target for marauding Highland clansmen, and during the Wars of Independence in the 13th century Inverness was also a regular target for both English and Scots armies.

The town's renaissance came with the completion of the Caledonian Canal and rail links with the south in the 19th century. These improved communications heralded something of a tourist boom amongst the wealthy and fashionable who came north to the Highlands to shoot anything that moved in the name of sport. In the mid-19th century Queen Victoria decided to embrace all things Scottish, which only boosted the town's popularity. Over recent decades Inverness has grown rapidly, not only as a prime base for visiting tourists, but also as the main administrative and commercial centre for the Highlands. Since being conferred city status in 2000, Inverness has seen the opening of the 750-seat Ironworks (see Entertainment, page 167), the Highland capital's first ever purpose-built live concert venue, and the beloved Eden Court Theatre reopened after a £23 million refurbishment.

where Prime Minister Lloyd George held an emergency cabinet meeting in 1921, the first ever to be held outside London.

Opposite, on the corner of Bridge Street and Church Street, is the **Tolbooth Steeple**, which dates from 1791 and which had to be repaired after an earth tremor in 1816. Apparently, a (now blocked off) tunnel once led from the castle to a prison located below the Tolbooth. Among the cafés and bars to be found on historic Church Street – a fascinating part of the city that local 'culture vultures' aim to steadily rejuvenate – is the town's oldest building, **Abertarff House**. Built around 1592, it is now a contemporary art and jewellery gallery. Almost opposite is the much-restored **Dunbar's Hospital**, built in 1688 as an almshouse for the town's poor. At the end of Church Street, where it meets Friar's Lane, is the **Old High Church** founded in the 12th century and rebuilt in 1772, though the 14th-century vaulted tower remains intact. In the adjoining atmospheric graveyard, prisoners taken at Culloden were executed, and you can still see the bullet marks left by the firing squads on some of the gravestones. At the far end of Church Street you'll also find **Leakey's Bookshop** (T01463-239947) housed within a former church. It's jam-packed with second-hand books and has a delightful café upstairs; the owners estimate their towering shelves contain over 100,000 books.

The **Highland House of Fraser Kiltmaker Centre** ⓘ *4-9 Huntly St, T01463-222781, www. highlandhouseoffraser.com. Factory tours take place daily May-Sep 0900-2200, Oct-Apr 0900-1800, min 10 people, £2.50, concessions and children £1.50,* still has a working kilt factory upstairs. In addition to watching kilts being made, two informative videos provide insights to the history of highland dress (including what Scotsmen wear under their kilts). In addition to mannequins dressed in period outfits, there are props used in the making of *Braveheart*. Nearby, directly opposite the castle, is the neo-Gothic **St Andrew's Cathedral** which dates from 1869 and is worth a peek if you're passing by. Continuing south along Ness Bank, past the impressive glass frontage of the refurbished **Eden Court Theatre** (see Entertainment, page 167) you reach **Bught Park**, which overlooks the Ness Islands, joined by footbridge to both banks. The islands are attractively laid out as a park and are a favourite with local anglers. This also happens to be a lovely place for a peaceful evening stroll.

Listings Inverness *map page 162.*

Tourist information

Inverness iCentre
36 High St, T01463-252401. Easter-Oct Mon-Sat 0900-1800, Sun 0930-1600, call for winter opening hours.
The very busy iCentre is a 10-min walk from the train station. It stocks a wide range of literature on the area, can book accommodation and transport, and gives out free maps of the town and environs. There's also a bureau de change and internet access. Information (and possibly tickets) for the tours listed above are available from here. It's also worth visiting www.inverness-scotland.com.

Where to stay

With an abundance of guesthouses, B&Bs and several good-quality hotels in and around Inverness, you shouldn't have much trouble finding somewhere to stay, though it does get very busy in Jul and Aug. Ideally, reserve ahead or consider booking through the **iCentre**.

The best places to look are along both banks of the river south of the Ness Bridge, Old Edinburgh Rd and Ardconnel St (east of the castle) and around Bruce Gardens, Ardross St, Kenneth St and Fairfield Rd (the west bank). There are also several budget hostels in and around the centre, and a couple of campsites.

££££ Culloden House Hotel
Milton of Culloden, 3 miles east of town near the A9, T01463-790461, www.cullodenhouse.co.uk.

28 rooms. Within this delightful Georgian mansion where Bonnie Prince Charlie prepared for battle at Culloden, you'll discover 1st-class accommodation and award-winning fine dining (**£££**).

££££ Loch Ness Country House Hotel
About 3 miles southwest of the town centre, just off the A82 Fort William Rd, T01463-230512, www.lochnesscountryhousehotel. co.uk.
11 rooms. An elegant Georgian mansion house within extensive gardens, with Victorian 4-poster beds, luxurious marble bathrooms and an excellent restaurant (see Restaurants, below). Can also arrange fishing, golf and riding.

££££ Rocpool Reserve Hotel
Culduthel Rd, T01463-240089, www.rocpool.com.
This boutique hotel, 10 mins' walk from the centre, offers a level of style and luxury that is unmatched in Inverness: hip, chic and decadent are very apt descriptions of the rooms here. For those with deep pockets, its **Chez Roux** restaurant, run by the acclaimed French chef, Albert Roux, offers exceptional food (**£££**), see Restaurants, below, and the **R Bar** is a stylish place for cocktails.

££££-£££ Columba Hotel
7 Ness Walk, T01463-231391, www. columbahotelinverness.com.
Overlooking the river, this hotel from 1881 has been refurbished, and offers 82 comfortable rooms in a very central location. Very friendly service and a fine restaurant.

££££-£££ Glenmoriston Town House Hotel
20 Ness Bank, T01463-223777,
www.glenmoristontownhouse.com.
With 30 individually styled rooms, this is a classy establishment. Its **Contrast Brasserie has** picked up notable awards and there are more than 260 malts and over 40 gins available in the piano bar.

££££-£££ MacDonald Drumossie Hotel
3 miles southeast of the town centre,
Old Perth Rd, T0344-879 9017,
www.macdonaldhotels.co.uk.
44 rooms. Views over the Moray Firth and handy for Culloden Moor, this is a deluxe hotel in a rural setting with all the creature comforts including the very fine **Grill Room** restaurant (**£££-££**).

£££ Kingsmills Hotel Inverness
Culcabock Rd, 1 mile south of the city centre near A9, T01463-237166,
www.kingsmillshotel.com.
Another higher-end hotel, with 82 rooms. Parts of the building date back to the 17th century. Comfortable rooms and superb leisure facilities, including spa and a guest discount at the adjacent Inverness Golf Club. 2 restaurants. Family suites available.

£££ Trafford Bank
96 Fairfield Rd, T01463-241414,
www.traffordbankguesthouse.co.uk.
5 en suite rooms. Owner Lorraine Feel continues to delight and win awards for this sumptuous guesthouse, which assures guests comfort, style and a very warm welcome. One of the best B&Bs in the entire country. Highly recommended.

£££-££ Glenruidh House Hotel
Old Edinburgh Rd South, 2 miles from the town centre and adjacent to Loch Ness Golf Course (phone for directions), T01463-226499,
www.cozzeenessie-bed.co.uk.
5 rooms. Packed with history and character, this peaceful, friendly 'boutique' hotel serves organic, fresh produce in a secluded setting and has over 40 species of bird in its garden.

£££-££ Moyness Guest House
6 Bruce Gardens, T01463-233836,
www.moyness.co.uk.
Fine Victorian villa in a quiet area near the theatre, with 7 very comfortable en suite rooms and nice touches like Botanics products in the bathrooms. During the 1920s this was the home of acclaimed Scottish author, Neil M Gunn.

£££-££ The Ness Guesthouse
48 Union Rd, T01463-559174,
www.thenessguesthouse.com.
Very friendly and welcoming guesthouse with 4 tasteful and comfortable rooms. Excellent breakfast. Offers everything you want from a B&B.

£ There are several hostels in Inverness, including: **Highlander Hostel** (23a High St, T01463-221225, www.highlanderhostel. com); **Highland Backpackers Inverness Hostel** (24 Rose St, 2 mins from bus station, T01463-241962, www.invernesshostel.com); **Inverness Student Hotel** (8 Culduthel Rd, at the top of Castle St, T01463-236556); and **SYHA Youth Hostel** (Victoria Drive, off Millburn Rd, T01463-231771).

Camping

Bught Caravan and Camping Site
Bught Park, on the west bank of the river near the Inverness Aquadome, T01463-236920. Easter-Oct.
The largest and most centrally located campsite, with good facilities.

Bunchrew Caravan and Camping Park
3 miles west of Inverness, T01463-237802. Mar-Nov.
Excellent campsite with views towards Ben Wyvis and the Beauly Firth and with good hot showers.

Restaurants

As you'd expect in a major tourist centre, there's the usual plethora of pubs, cafés and restaurants serving cheap and basic food for the non-discerning palate, but those looking for a high standard of cuisine won't be disappointed either.

Takeaways and chain restaurant options are plentiful, particularly on Academy St, Eastgate, around the train station and on Young St, just across the Ness Bridge.

£££ Chez Roux
In the Rocpool Reserve Hotel (see Where to Stay, above).
Run by the acclaimed French chef, Albert Roux. The decor oozes style and chic. Just like the boutique hotel, the lunch and dinner cuisine here hits the mark – albeit at a price.

£££-££ Riva
4-6 Ness Walk, T01463-237377, www. rivainverness.co.uk. Sun-Thu 1100-1430, 1700-2130; Fri-Sat 1100-1420, 1700-2030.
A stylish and good-value riverside eatery that specializes in Italian food. Set lunch is £12.95 for 2 courses and their pizzeria upstairs offers a cheaper alternative to sit in or take away (open only Fri and Sat 1415-late).

£££-££ Rocpool Restaurant
1 Ness Walk T01463-717274, www.rocpoolrestaurant.co.uk.
Stylish interior with attentive staff and fabulous food. 2-course set lunch is £16.95, and early evening menu is £19.95. Family friendly. Book ahead.

££ Café No 1
75 Castle St, T01463-226200, www.cafe1.net. Mon-Fri 1200-1430, 1700-2130, Sat 1230-1500, 1730-2130.
Central location with reasonable selection of meat and vegetarian dishes. Early-bird offers for lunch and dinner (£15 for 2 courses).

££ The Kitchen Brasserie
15 Huntly St, T01463-259119, www.kitchenrestaurant.co.uk.
Sister restaurant of **The Mustard Seed** (see below) across the river. Thoughtfully prepared menu and lovely ambience for an evening meal. Great-value 2-course set lunch (£9.95) and early-bird (1700-1900) dinner (£13.95).

££ The Mustard Seed
16 Fraser St, T01463-220220, www.mustardseedrestaurant.co.uk. Daily 1200-1500, 1700-2200.
Cheery, stylish interior, and a lunch and dinner menu packed with local, freshly prepared produce. Also does good-value set lunch (£9.95) and early-bird (1700-1900) dinner (£13.95).

££ The Riverside Restaurant
10 Bank St, T01463-714884. Tue-Sat 1000-2130.
Perennial local favourite for lunches and delicious high tea. Now fully reopened.

£ Leakey's Bookshop
Church St, T01463-239947. Mon-Sat 1000-1730.
After browsing through over 100,000 second-hand books and old maps, where better to sup on some home-made soup, a sandwich or simply a coffee before stocking up on your book collection?

Bars and clubs

Blackfriars Highland Pub & Restaurant
93-95 Academy St.
A decent pub that runs ceilidhs and live music most nights.

Castle Tavern
1 View Place, T01463-718178. See also Restaurants, above.
CAMRA-rated establishment with great selection of real ales downstairs and a beer garden. Good views of the castle and river from upstairs.

The Den and Johnny Foxes
26 Bank St. Daily 1100-0300.
The former is a wine and cocktail bar and club while the latter features Irish folk music most nights in summer and great bar food.

The Gellions
14 Bridge St.
Claims to be the oldest pub in the Highland capital. Live sports in the back bar, or **Monty's** snug.

Hootananny
67 Church St, www.hootananninverness. co.uk. Daily 1200-0100.
A great bet for all things Scottish, has live music and ceilidhs most nights. Probably the best pub atmosphere in Inverness.

Entertainment

Cinema
The cinema attached to **Eden Court Theatre**, see below, shows a programme of art-house and newly released movies. Prices vary depending on the performance.
Vue Inverness, *Inverness Centre, Eastfield Way, T0345-308 4620.* Multi-screen complex showing all the latest releases.

Live music
The Ironworks Venue, *122b Academy St, T08/1/-894173, www.ironworksvenue.com.* Purpose-built live music venue.

Theatre
Eden Court Theatre, *Bishops Rd, over-looking the River Ness, T01463-234234, www.eden-court.co.uk.* The city is proud of its renowned theatre and cinema. Diverse theatre and art-house productions. Also has a small café-bar.

Festivals

There are numerous events held in and around Inverness throughout the year. These range from a humble pub ceilidh and a food festival to a full-blown Highland Games and the Baxters Loch Ness Marathon (Oct).
Feb/Mar Inverness Music Festival, T01463-716616.
Mar/Apr Folk festivals, T01738-623274. Local folk festivals held over Easter weekend.
Jul Inverness Highland Games, held in the 3rd week of the month.

Shopping

Inverness is a good place to buy a kilt, or practically anything else in tartan. To find your own clan tartan, head for the **Highland House of Fraser Kiltmaker Centre** (see page 163). The **Eastgate Shopping Centre** has all the usual high-street shops.

Bookshops
Leakey's Bookshop, *Church St. Mon-Sat 1000-1700.* A brilliant second-hand bookshop, with a huge wood-burning stove in the middle of the shop and a café upstairs (see above).

Highland dress and traditional gifts
Chisholm's (47-51 Castle St, T01463-234599, www.kilts.co.uk); **Highland House of Fraser** (Bridge St, T01463-222781); **James Pringle Weavers of Inverness** (21 Bridge St, T01463-236517, www.jamespringle.co.uk).

Market
Victorian Market, *accessed off Church St and Academy St.* Established in the 18th century, this market has a wide range of interesting and quirky shops.

What to do

Boat tours
Caley Cruisers, *Canal Rd, Inverness, T01463-236328, www.caleycruisers.com.* If you fancy skippering your own power boat down Loch Ness and through the Caledonian Canal, you can do it in style. From around £1000 for a for 3-4 berth up to over £2000 for 6-8.
Jacobite, *Tomnahurich Bridge, Glenurquhart Rd, T01463-233999, www. jacobite.co.uk.* Operates a variety of Loch Ness cruises, ranging from a 1-hr 'Inspiration' tour for £14 pp up to the 6½-hr 'Passion' coach and cruise for £46 pp which includes a visit to the Loch Ness Monster Exhibition Centre, Urquhart Castle and Caledonian Canal.
John O'Groats Ferries, *contact the Inverness iCentre, T01955-611353, www.jogferry.co.uk.*

For the ultimate day trip, Orkney Islands Day Tours leave from Inverness every day throughout the summer, Jun-end Aug (depart 0715, return 2100). Ancient sites include Skara Brae (older than the Egyptian pyramids) and the Ring of Brodgar. Booking essential. £74 per adult, £37 child, under 5 free.

Dolphin Discovery Inverness, *Inverness Marina, Longman Drive, T07544-800620, www.moraydolphine.co.uk*. Dolphin-spotting cruises on board the *Dolphin Spirit*, £18/12 for 1¼-hr trip along the Moray coast.

Bus tours

Citysightseeing Inverness, *leave from Bridge St outside the iCentre, T01667-459849, www. citysightseeinginverness.com*. Open-topped hop-on, hop-off bus tours around the city, mid-Jun to Sep daily 1015-1700. Tickets valid for 24 hrs from the time of travel, and can be bought online or onboard. £10, concessions £8, children £3, family £24.

Happy Tours, *T07828-154683, www.happy-tours.biz*. Run a number of exciting day tours from Inverness in 8-seater coaches, including Loch Ness, the Great Glen, Isle of Skye, Whisky Tour and the hugely popular Outlander tour which takes on all the locations on the hit TV series.

The Hebridean Explorer, *Elmbank, Lewiston, Drumnadrochit, T07943-863292, www. thehebrideanexplorer.com*. This family-run operator offers personal (for up to 5 people) and private tours to destinations including Loch Ness, Isle of Skye, Outer Hebrides and many more destinations.

Cycling

The 73-mile-long Great Glen Way can be cycled. The stretch alongside the Caledonian Canal is flat and good for families. To read about the Way, visit www. highland.gov.uk/ggw. For cycling tours and holidays along the Great Glen Way, contact **Ticket to Ride**, www.tickettoridehighlands. co.uk. Also bike hire.

Bus

Bus timetables and even operators on some routes change frequently. If in any doubt and for the latest information, call **Traveline Scotland**, T0871-200 2233, www.traveline scotland.com or bustimes.org.uk.

There are regular daily buses to **Glasgow** and **Edinburgh** (via **Aviemore**), **Pitlochry** and **Perth** with **Scottish Citylink**, www. citylink.co.uk, and Megabus, www. uk.megabus.com. Change at Perth for **Dundee**. There are regular daily **Citylink** buses to **Ullapool**, connecting with the ferry to **Stornoway**; also to **Fort William** and **Oban**. There are daily **Citylink** buses to **Kyle of Lochalsh**, **Portree** and **Uig** (connecting with ferries to **Tarbert** and **Lochmaddy**), and regular, daily **Citylink** buses to **Fort Augustus** via **Drumnadrochit** and **Urquhart Castle**, and to **Scrabster**, for the ferry to **St Margaret's Hope**, via **Wick** and **Thurso**.

Scotbus, www.scotbus.co.uk, operate 1 bus daily, Jun-Oct, between **Inverness** and **Inverewe Gardens**, via **Achnasheen**, **Kinlochewe**, **Loch Maree**, **Gairloch** and **Poolewe**. To **Tain** and **Helsmdale**, via **Dornoch** there are regular daily buses with **Citylink**. To **Lochinver** from **Ullapool** there's 1 bus, Mon-Sat, operated by **Tim Dearman**, T01349-883585, that departs Ullapool Ferry Terminal at 1055 and arrives in **Lochinver** at 1154. This bus continues to **Durness** via **Kylesku** and **Rhiconich** (for Sandwood Bay). **Dearman Coaches** carry a bike trailer on this route.

Stagecoach, www.stagecoachbus.com, run services to places around **Inverness**, including **Beauly**, **Muir of Ord** and **Dingwall**, also daily services to **Aberdeen** via **Nairn**, whilst the battle scene of Culloden and Cawdor Castle can both be reached using a **Tourist Trail Rover** ticket. To reach **Tomich** (and **Glen Affric**) via Beauly use the **Ross Minibuses** service, T01463-761250, www.ross-minibuses.

Car hire

Arnold Clark, 47 Harbour Rd and at the airport, www.arnoldclarkrental.co.uk; **Enterprise**, Harbour Rd, www.enterprise.co.uk; **Focus**, 6 Harbour Rd and at the airport, www.focusvehiclerental.co.uk. Prices vary but expect to pay from £35 per day.

Cycle hire

Ticket to Ride, see What to do, Cycling, above.

Ferry

Citylink buses run from Inverness to **John o'Groats**, **Gills Bay** or **Scrabster** for ferries to **Orkney** (see also page 381). An **Express Bus** runs from Inverness to **Kirkwall** on Orkney via **John o'Groat**s Jun-Sep, departs daily at 0715 and 1420, arriving in Kirkwall at 1200 and 1930. Operated by **John O'Groat's Ferries**, T01955-611353, www.jogferry.co.uk. £25 one-way to **Kirkwall**, £20 to **John o'Groats**.

Taxi

City Taxis Inverness, T01463-555555, www.citytaxisinverness.co.uk. Around £16 from the city centre to the airport. **Inverness Taxis**, T01463-222222.

Train

There are direct trains to **Aberdeen**, **Edinburgh** (via **Aviemore**) and **Glasgow**. There are several daily services to **London King's Cross** (via **Perth**) and **Edinburgh**, and a Caledonian Sleeper service to **London Euston** or from London Euston to **Fort William** via **Inverness**, ScotRail, www.scotrail.co.uk. There is also a regular service to **Wick** and **Thurso**, via **Tain**, **Lairg** and **Helmsdale**. The journey from Inverness to **Kyle of Lochalsh** (for Skye) is one of the most scenic in Britain. There are 2-3 trains Mon-Sat. For more times and prices www.thetrainline.com.

Around
Inverness

East of Inverness along the Moray Firth stretches a long coastline of clifftop walks, fine beaches, attractive old towns and many historic sites and castles. The Moray Firth is perhaps best known for its large resident population of dolphins. Scores of these beautiful and intelligent mammals live in the estuary, the most northerly breeding ground in Europe, and there's a very good chance of seeing them, particularly between June and August. The Moray Firth dolphins have become a major tourist attraction and several companies run dolphin-spotting boat trips. You can also see them from the shore. Two of the best places are on the southern shore of the Black Isle (see page 277) and Fort George, on the opposite shore (see page 171). The Kessock Bridge, which crosses the Moray Firth to the Black Isle, is another good dolphin-spotting location and it has a visitor centre, where you can listen in to their underwater conversations.

West of Inverness, the Moray Firth becomes the Beauly Firth, a relatively quiet little corner despite its proximity to Inverness, as most traffic heading north crosses the Kessock Bridge on the main A9. The A862 west to Beauly offers a more scenic alternative, and the chance to visit a 13th-century priory and a distillery. South of Beauly, the A831 leads to two of Scotland's most beautiful glens, Glen Strathfarrar and Glen Affric.

Culloden *Colour map 2, C2.*

T01463-796090, www.nts.org.uk. Site open daily all year, visitor centre open daily Nov-Mar 1000-1600, Apr, May, Sep and Oct 0900-1730, Jun-Jul 0900-1800, Aug 0900-1900, £11, concessions £8, family £26. Café/restaurant, educational rooms and a shop.

The eerie and windswept Culloden Moor, five miles to the east of Inverness on the B9006, was the site of the last major battle fought on the British mainland. The £8.5 million National Trust for Scotland visitor centre has a rooftop walk (10 minutes) with views over the restored battlefield, where on 16 April 1746 the Jacobite dream to place Prince Charles Edward Stuart (Bonnie Prince Charlie) on the Scottish throne was brutally crushed by Hanoverian (largely English) forces. This fateful battle was not simply Scotsmen fighting Englishmen but, tragically, saw Scottish clan pitched against clan, whilst the Jacobite side included Irish and even English soldiers. Though the battle lasted barely an hour, the Hanoverian soldiers led by the Duke of Cumberland went on to commit appalling bloodshed across the Highlands, earning Cumberland the name 'the Butcher.' Even to this day, his name is despised by many for the murderous post-battle rampage he oversaw in a bid to forever stamp out sympathy for the Jacobites.

Fashioned from natural timbers and stone, the interior of the spectacular visitor centre combines artefacts and displays (including Jacobite swords and the Prince's unfinished waistcoat) with cutting-edge interactive displays (including a 'Battle Immersion Theatre' and 'voices' from witnesses of the battle) to provide visitors with an evocative and stirring account of the build up to the battle, the fateful day and the brutal consequences of a Jacobite/Hanoverean showdown that changed the face of Scottish history. From the visitor centre, walk along the paths (35 minutes), past clan graves marked by simple headstones. Next to the visitor centre, the restored cottage of Old Leanach – which was used by the Jacobites as a headquarters, and where 30 Highlanders were burnt alive – is arranged as it would have been at the time of the battle. A memorial cairn, erected in 1881, is the scene each April of a commemorative service organized by the Gaelic Society of Inverness.

Clava Cairns

This impressive and important Bronze Age site lies only a mile southeast of Culloden and is well worth a short detour. The 5000-year-old site consists of three large burial cairns encircled by standing stones, set in a grove of trees. The less imaginative visitor may see it as merely a pile of stones but no one can fail to be affected by the spooky atmosphere of the place, especially if no one else is around. To get there, continue on the B9006 past Culloden Moor, then turn right at the **Culloden Moor Inn** and follow the signs for **Clava Lodge**. Look for the sign on the right of the road.

Fort George *Colour map 2, C2.*

T01667-460232, www.historicenvironment.scot. Apr-Sep daily 0930-1730, Oct-Mar daily 1000-1600, £9, concessions £7.20, children £5.40, wheelchair access; café open Apr-Sep daily 1000-1700, Oct-Mar Sun-Thu 1000-1500.

Standing proudly on a sandy spit that juts out into the Moray Firth is Fort George, Europe's finest surviving example of 18th-century military architecture. In today's money it's

ON THE ROAD

Battle of Culloden

The second Jacobite rebellion of 1745 was ill-fated from the start. Bonnie Prince Charlie's expedition south lacked sufficient support and was turned back at Derby. After their long and dispiriting retreat north, the half-starved, under-strength army – exhausted after an abortive night attack on Hanoverian forces at Nairn – faced overwhelmingly superior forces under the command of the ambitious Duke of Cumberland at Culloden.

The open, flat ground of Culloden Moor was hopelessly unsuitable for the Highlanders' style of fighting, which relied on steep hills and plenty of cover to provide the element of surprise for their brave but undisciplined attacks. In only 40 minutes the Prince's army was blown away by the English artillery, and the Jacobite charge, when it finally came, was ragged and ineffective. Cumberland's troops then went on to commit the worst series of atrocities ever carried out by a British Army. Some 1200 men were slain, many as they lay wounded on the battlefield. Prince Charlie, meanwhile, fled west where loyal Highlanders protected him until he made his final escape to France.

But the real savagery was to come. Cumberland resolved to make an example of the Highlands. Not only were the clans disarmed and the wearing of Highland dress forbidden, but the Government troops began an orgy of brutal reprisals across the region. Within a century the clan system had ended and the Highland way of life changed forever. For further information, see box, page 439.

estimated the mightiest artillery fortification in Britain would cost over £1 billion to build. Begun in 1748, it was the last in a chain of three such fortifications built in the Highlands – the other two being Fort Augustus and Fort William – as a base for George II's army to prevent any potential threats to Hanoverian rule. It was completed in 1769, by which time the Highlands were more or less peaceful, but it was kept in use as a military barracks. Today it remains virtually unchanged, and, as it's a functioning military base; don't be surprised to find armed sentries at the main gate. You can walk along the ramparts to get an idea of the sheer scale of the place and also enjoy the sweeping views across the Moray Firth. You may even be lucky enough to see a school of dolphins. Within the fort are the barracks, a chapel, workshops and the Regimental Museum of the Queen's Own Highlanders, which features the fascinating Seafield Collection of arms and military equipment, most of which dates from the Napoleonic Wars.

Cawdor Castle Colour map 2, C2.
T01667-404401, www.cawdorcastle.com. Castle and gardens openend Apr to early-Oct daily 1000-1700, £11.20, concessions £10.20, children £7.

Though best known for its legendary association with Shakespeare's *Macbeth*, Cawdor Castle post-dates the grisly historical events on which the great Bard based his famous tragedy. The oldest part of the castle, the central tower, dates from 1372, and the rest of it is mostly 16th or 17th century. But despite the literary disappointment, the castle is still one of the most appealing in Scotland. It has been in the hands of the Cawdor family for over six centuries and each summer they clear off, leaving their romantic home and its glorious gardens and **Big Wood** of native trees open for the enjoyment of ordinary folks like us. There's also a nine-hole golf course and self-catering accommodation on the estate at Banchor Cottage.

According to family legend, an early Thane of Cawdor, wanting a new castle, had a dream in which he was told to load a donkey with gold, let it wander around for a day and watch where it lay down, for this would be the best spot for his new castle. He duly followed these instructions and the donkey lay down under a thorn tree, the remains of which can still be seen in the middle of a vaulted chamber in the 14th-century tower.

Just to the west of Cawdor is **Kilravock Castle**. This 14th-century stately home (pronounced *Kilrawk*) is still the seat of the Rose family. Sadly, it is now closed to the public and no longer operates as a B&B and self-catering experience.

Nairn and around *Colour map 2, C2.*

With two championship golf courses, the seaside town of Nairn (population 11,900) also claims to have the driest and sunniest climate in the whole of Scotland. This alone should be reason enough visit, but there are other attractions besides the sunshine: miles of sandy beach stretching east to the Culbin Forest and two of the best castles in the country are within easy reach – Cawdor Castle, see above, and Brodie Castle, see below. Nairn is also only five miles from the airport and makes a pleasant alternative to staying in Inverness.

Nairn Museum ① *Viewfield House, Viewfield Dr, T01667-456791, www.nairnmuseum.co.uk, Apr-Oct Mon-Fri, 1000-1630, Sat 1000-1300, £3, concession £1.50, child £0.50,* gives an insight into the area's history and includes the Fishertown Room, highlighting the lives of the hardy men and women who in the 18th and 19th century made their living from the herring trade.

About two miles east of Nairn, in the little village of **Auldearn**, is a 17th-century *doocot* (dovecote). Nearby the Boath Doocot information boards record the 1645 Battle of Aldearn in which the victorious troops of Charles I, led by the Marquess of Montrose, defeated and killed almost 2000 Covenanters. For boat trips from Nairn, see page 174.

Some 10 miles south of Nairn on the A939 to Grantown is **Dulsie Bridge**, a very popular local beauty spot which is a great place for a summer picnic or to swim in the River Findhorn. On the southern shores of the Moray Firth, just east of Nairn, is **Culbin Sands**, a stretch of sand home to a variety of birdlife and managed by the RSPB. The best time to visit is from autumn to spring when bar-tailed godwits, oystercatchers, knots, dunlins, ringed plovers, redshanks, curlews, shellducks, red-breasted mergansers, greylag geese and snow buntings, to name but a few, come here in their droves.

Brodie Castle
T01309-641371, www.nts.org.uk. Castle, shop and tearoom open Mar-Oct daily 1000-1700, Nov-Feb daily 1100-1500, grounds open all year. £10.50, concessions £7.50, family £24.50.

Brodie Castle, eight miles east of Nairn, just off the main A96 to Forres, is one of Scotland's finest castles. The oldest part of the castle, the Z-plan tower house, is 16th century, with additions dating from the 17th and 19th centuries, giving it the look of a Victorian country house. The interior of the house is the epitome of good taste, with fabulous ceilings, and you can look round several rooms, including the huge Victorian kitchen. The collections of French furniture and Chinese porcelain are wonderful but most notable are the outstanding paintings, which include Edwin Landseer and Scottish Colourists. The grounds, too, are a delight, especially in spring when the daffodils are in bloom and there are specially constructed hides to observe the wildlife.

Where to stay

Nairn and around

££££ The Boath House Hotel and Spa
Aldearn T01667-454896,
www.boath-house.com.
Voted Scottish Hotel of the Year in 2013 by
Good Hotel Guide, the beautiful regency
house is the very last word in luxurious
accommodation, with 9 tastefully appointed
bedrooms, all set in 20 acres of tended lawns,
walled gardens, woodland, streams and an
ornamental lake. Their restaurant (see below)
also has a Michelin star, making it one of the
top 4 in the country.

££ Bracadale House
Albert St, T01667-452547.
3 en suite rooms in large Victorian house.
Very comfortable B&B.

££ Greenlawns
13 Seafield St, T01667-452738,
www.greenlawns.uk.com.
A friendly, 6-bedroom guesthouse where
you'll tuck into the likes of kedgeree, smoked
salmon and scrambled eggs for breakfast,
in a dining room crammed with antiques.
2-night minimum stay and only 3 rooms
available in low season. Excellent value.

Camping

Nairn Camping and Caravanning Club
Delnies Wood, Nairn, T01667-455281. Apr-Oct.
Clean with good amenities in a secluded
spot, but it's 3 miles to the pub.

Restaurants

Cawdor Castle

££ Cawdor Tavern
Close to the castle, T01667-404777,
www.cawdortavern.co.uk.
A very popular, traditional country pub serving
excellent food in a friendly atmosphere. Perfect
for lunch or dinner after visiting the castle.

Nairn and around

£££ The Boath House Hotel and Spa
See Where to stay, above.
Michelin-starred cuisine in this delightful
rural retreat. The very best of local fish,
seafood, beef, game and foraged plants
and herbs cooked with skill and
imagination and beautifully presented.

££ Classroom
Cawdor St. Lunch 1200-1635,
dinner from 1700.
Good modern Scottish menu with
classics like Cullen Skink. Good value
for lunch (**£**) or just for coffee, tasty
home-baking and sandwiches.

£ Asher's Bakery
2 Bridge St.
Award-winning bakery, recommended for a
hot snack. Run by the same folk as the one
in Inverness.

What to do

Nairn and around
Boat trips
Phoenix boat trips, *T07703-168097, www.*
dolphin-trips-nairn.co.uk. Offer enjoyable
wildlife cruises out onto the Moray Firth
to spot the seals, porpoises and possibly
dolphins. £18, £10 child for 1-hr tour.

Horse riding
Heatherfield Riding Centre, *Lochloy Rd,*
T01667-456682. Offer pony trekking.
Highland Trekking and Trail Riding,
Keepers Cottage, Cougie, Tomich by Cannich,
T01456-415323, www.highlandponytrekking.
com. Open all year. Ride in the stunning wilds
of Glen Affric.

Mountain biking
Moray Monster Trails, southeast of Nairn;
Balnain Bike Park, in Urquhart Forest east
of Cannich; and **Learnie Forest**, Black Isle,

provide miles of forest/trail cycling for
all standards on state-of-the-art tracks.
See https://forestry.gov.uk for details.
Cycle hire At **Rafford Cycles**,
Forres, T01309-672811.

Culloden
Bus
Stagecoach bus No 11 from Inverness to
Nairn runs past the battlefield site every
half hour Mon-Sat, less frequently on Sun.

Fort George
Bus
Stagecoach bus No 11 (see above) stops in
Ardersier every hour Mon-Sat.

Nairn and around
Bus
There are regular daily buses to **Inverness**
every half hour with **Stagecoach**, see above. To
Cawdor Castle there's an infrequent service,
Mon-Fri, No 252 to Nairn Academy. **Mundole
Takes and Minibuses**, T01309-673168.

Train
Nairn is on the **Aberdeen** to **Inverness** rail
line, and there are several trains daily to
Inverness, 20 mins.

Brodie Castle
Bus
Stagecoach bus No 11 runs to and from
Inverness via Forres and Nairn, 45 mins,
and stops at Brodie.

Beauly Firth *Colour map 2, C1/2.*

two of Scotland's least known and most beautiful glens

Beauly and around *Colour map 2, C1.*
The train station at Beauly has the shortest platform in the UK, so take care getting off.

The sleepy little market town of Beauly is 10 miles west of Inverness, where the Beauly river
flows into the Firth. It's a lovely wee place – hence its name. According to local legend,
when Mary Queen of Scots stayed here, at the priory, in 1564, she was so taken with the
place that she cried (in French, of course) "Ah, quel beau lieu!" (What a beautiful place!).

At the north end of the marketplace is the ruin of **Beauly Priory** ⓘ *daily Apr-Sep 0930-
1730, Oct-Mar 1000-1600, free.* It was founded in 1230 for the Valliscaulian order but, like so
much else of Scotland's ecclesiastical heritage, it was destroyed during the Reformation.
Three miles to the north of Beauly, by Muir of Ord and just off the A832, is the **Glen Ord
Distillery** ⓘ *T01463-872004, www.malts.com, Nov-Feb, Mon-Sat 1000-1600, Mar, Apr and
Oct Mon-Sat 1000-1700, May-Sep Mon-Fri 1000-1800, Sat 1000-1700, Sun 1100-1700. Tours
range in price from £8 up to £100,* which was established in 1838. The **Singleton Tour** (£18)
is recommended for connoisseurs.

The River Beauly is one of Scotland's best salmon-fishing rivers, and five miles south of
Beauly, at **Aigas**, is a **fish ladder** where you can watch salmon bypass the dam with the
aid of technology. Nearby is Aigas Field Centre, which offers wildlife courses and holidays
ⓘ *T01463-782443, www.aigas.co.uk.*

Glen Strathfarrar
Southwest of Beauly are glens Affric and Strathfarrar. Glen Strathfarrar, the lesser known
of the two, is unspoiled and considered by some to be the more beautiful. To get there,
take the A831 nine miles south from Beauly to Struy and follow the signs. Access to the
glen is restricted by the estates in the area to 25 cars at a time. As a general rule there's a
gate access from Easter to late summer but it's best to call (T01738-493942) for advice.
Once you're in, there is a tremendous feeling of peace, and there's good climbing, fishing

and walking. The little ungraded road runs for 14 miles all the way to the impressive **Monar Dam** at the head of the glen. Glen Strathfarrar can also be reached from Drumnadrochit, via Cannich (see below). Most of the walks and cycle routes here are covered by OS Landranger Nos 25 and 26.

Glen Affric *OS Landranger Nos 25 and 26. Colour map 2, C1.*

The A831 continues south from Struy through Strathglass to the village of **Cannich**, gateway to glorious Glen Affric, a dramatic and beautiful gorge, with the River Affric rushing through it, and surrounded by Caledonian pine and birch forest – in fact this is one of the few places where you can still see the native Scots pine. There are few, if any, more stunning sights in the Scottish Highlands; it's perfect for walking, or even just to drive through and stop for a picnic on a sunny day. **Ross's Minibus** has a service in summer to the beautiful and remote inner reaches of Glen Affric, see Transport, page 177, for details.

Beyond Loch Affric the serious walking starts. From **Affric Lodge**, nine miles west of Cannich, begins a 20-mile trail west to **Morvich**, near Shiel Bridge, on the west coast near Kyle of Lochalsh, see page 225. This strenuous walk is for experienced hikers only, and takes around 10 hours. You can stop off halfway at one of the most remote youth hostels in Scotland, **Glen Affric Youth Hostel** at Allt Beithe, see Where to stay, below.

There are also many shorter, easier walks around Glen Affric. There are some short, circular marked trails at the end of the road which runs west from Cannich almost to Loch Affric, and also from the car park at the impressive **Dog Falls**, 4½ miles from Cannich and a great place to stop for a picnic and swim. Cycling in the forests around Cannich is good too – you can hire bikes at the friendly **Cannich Caravan and Camping Park** (see Where to stay, below). The owner's a keen cyclist.

Glen Affric can also be reached from **Drumnadrochit** (see page 179), by heading west on the A831 through Glen Urquhart to Cannich. Just before Cannich, on the road from Drumnadrochit, a single-track road leads left (south), past the Caravan and Camping Park, to the tiny village of **Tomich**. From here, it's a three-mile hike up a woodland trail to a car park. A few hundred yards down through the trees takes you to the 70-ft plunging **Plodda Falls**. An old iron bridge affords a spectacular view of the waterfall.

Where to stay

Beauly and around

£££ The Priory Hotel
The Square, T01463-782309,
www.priory-hotel.com.
Delightful hotel in the centre of the village.
Spacious comfortable rooms and very
friendly and helpful staff. Good food in the
restaurant (**££-£**).

£££-££ Lovat Arms Hotel
Opposite end of the main street from
The Priory Hotel, T01463-782313,
www.lovatarms.com.
A reliable old 22-bedroom country house
with a relaxed air and a tartan touch. Try
the terrific Scottish game and seafood in
the **Strupag Brasserie** (**£££** with dinner) or
relax with a dram or cup of tea beside the log
fire. Terrific Sun lunch (1230-1400).

Glen Affric

£££ The Tomich Hotel
Tomich, T01456-415399, www.tomichhotel.
co.uk. Feb-Nov.
8 rooms. You'll find a friendly welcome and
good food at this former Victorian hunting
lodge that will appeal to the visitor in search
of walking, stalking and fishing alike. Good
range of local ales and malts in the bar.

£ Glen Affric Youth Hostel
T0345-293 7373.
It's a 3- to 4-hr walk on unmarked trails to this
isolated SYHA eco-hostel, a haven for walkers
and nature lovers, shared dorm and 2 private
rooms, bring your own sleeping bag.

Self-catering

Culligran Cottages
Glen Strathfarrar, T01463-761255,
www.culligrancottages.co.uk.
Enjoy your own cottage or chalet along
15 miles of private road, where you can spot
deer, fish or ride bikes. 3 rooms, sleeps 6/7.
£480 per week in high season.

Camping

Cannich Camping and Caravan Park
Cannich, T01456-415364. Mid-Mar to Oct.
Just 5 mins' walk from the Spar shop. Handy
campsite with caravans for rent. Very friendly.
Bike hire available.

Restaurants

Beauly and around

£££-££ Lovat Arms Hotel
See Where to stay, above.
Serves up terrific food in the restaurant
or relax in the bar with tasty snacks.

Transport

Beauly and around
Bus
Stagecoach buses No 28/28A to and from
Inverness to **Dingwall** via Beauly and **Muir
of Ord** every hour Mon-Sat, 3 on Sun.

Train
You can take the train to **Inverness** from
here; it stops on its way from **Thurso**.

Glen Affric
Bus
Ross's Minibus, T01463-761250,
bustimes.org.uk, departs Inverness Bus
Station at 0940 on a Mon, Wed and Fri
(Jul-Sep only) and travels via Drumnadrochit,
Balnain and Cannich to the upper car park
in Glen Affric. The return service leaves from
Glen Affric car park at 1700 and returns via
Cannich and **Drumnadrochit** to **Inverness**.

Loch Ness
& around

One of Scotland's biggest attractions is the narrow gash of Loch Ness, Britain's deepest body of fresh water, stretching 23 miles from Fort Augustus in the south almost to Inverness in the north. The loch is scenic in its own right, with rugged hills rising steeply from its wooded shores, but visitors don't come here for the views. They come every year, in their hundreds of thousands, to stare across the dark, cold waters in search of its legendary inhabitant, the Loch Ness Monster. A huge tourist trade has grown up around 'Nessie', as the monster is affectionately known, and every summer the main A82, which runs along its western shore, is jam-packed with bus-loads of eager monster-hunters, binoculars trained on the loch surface, desperate for one glimpse of the elusive beast. If you do see it, bear in mind your photograph could be worth a fortune!

Drumnadrochit

The Nessie tourist trade is centred on the village of Drumnadrochit, 15 miles south of Inverness, where the canny locals have cashed in on the enduring popularity of the monster myth. The monster hype is almost overpowering, with two rival Monster exhibitions and the inevitable souvenir shops selling all manner of awful tartan tat, including those scary-looking tartan dolls with flickering eyelids, the 'See-You-Jimmy' tartan bonnet, complete with ginger 'hair', and not forgetting the Loch Ness Monster novelty hat. Fortunately, the very friendly **iCentre** (see page 182) in the car park can offer alternative suggestions, such as exploring peaceful Glen Affric (see page 176). There are also toilets beside the iCentre (daily 0700-1800).

Following an acrimonious court case, one of the Nessie visitor centres had to change its name and is now known simply as **Nessieland** ① *T01456-450342, www.nessieland.co.uk, Apr-Oct daily 0900-1900, Nov-Mar daily 0900-1700, £6, children £3, family £15*. It features a wide-screen cinema documenting the latest 'facts' and 'sightings' of Nessie. There's also an outdoor adventure playground and a gift shop, but the most authentic experience of all is the restaurant's tasty home-baking. **Loch Ness Cruises** (*MV Nessie Hunter*) operates from here, see page 184.

The rival exhibition is the **Loch Ness Centre & Exhibition** ① *T01456-450573, www.lochness.com, Easter-Jun and Sep-Oct daily 0930-1700, Jul-Aug 0930-1800, winter 1000-1530, £7.95, concessions £6.75, children £4.95*. This Nessie exhibition also details eye-witness accounts, but more pertinently provides a more elaborate audio-visual experience.

If it all gets too much, then fear not, for Drumnadrochit gives easy access to one of the most beautiful corners of Scotland. The A831 heads west from the village through Glen Urquhart to Cannich, about 12 miles away, at the head of Glen Affric, a great place for walking or enjoying a picnic (see page 176).

Castle Urquhart *Colour map 4, A1.*

T01456-450551, www.historicenvironment. scot, Apr-Sep daily 0930-1800, Oct 0930-1700, Nov-Mar 0930-1630, £9, concessions £7.20, children £5.40. Citylink buses 919 (to/from Inverness) and 917 (to/from Invermoriston) stop at Urquhart Castle several times Mon-Sat.

Essential Loch Ness

Getting around

The best way to see the loch is on a cruise from Inverness (page 167). There are also boat trips from Drumnadrochit and Fort Augustus (see page 184). Most of the tourist traffic uses the congested A82, built in 1933, which offers few decent views of the loch. By far the best views of are from the quiet and picturesque B862/852, which runs along the eastern shore from Fort Augustus up to Inverness. It's possible to make a complete circuit of the loch, which is best done in an anti-clockwise direction heading south from Inverness on the A82, but you'll need your own transport (or take a tour), as there are no buses between Fort Augustus and Foyers. There are regular daily bus services between Inverness and Fort William, however, with additional buses between Invergarry and Fort Augustus. Fort Augustus is a convenient stopover between Fort William and Inverness. **Citylink** buses between Inverness and Kyle of Lochalsh stop at Urquhart Castle, Loch Ness Youth Hostel, Invergarry and Invermoriston. See also What to do, page 184, and Transport, page 185.

The Great Glen Way

The Great Glen Way is a waymarked walking trail that runs for 73 miles between Inverness and Fort William. Panoramic views of Loch Ness can be seen at many of the sections between Fort Augustus and Inverness. Although a relatively easy walk, there are some fairly tough sections around Loch Ness and you'll need to be properly equipped and have a good map. OS Landranger Nos 26, 34 and 41 cover the entire route. It should take four or five days to complete, depending on your level of fitness. It is probably better to walk it in 'reverse', from Fort William to Inverness, as the easiest section is then at the start. The Great Glen Way also has its own website, www.greatglenway.com.

A few miles south of Drumnadrochit are the ruins of Castle Urquhart. The castle bears the scars of centuries of fighting but its setting, perched on a rocky cliff on the loch's edge, is magnificent and, not surprisingly, one of the most photographed scenes in Scotland. Dating from the 14th century, the castle was a strategic base, guarding the Great Glen during the long Wars of Independence. It was taken by Edward I, held by Robert the Bruce against Edward II, and was then almost constantly under siege before being destroyed in 1692 to prevent it from falling into Jacobite hands. Most of the existing buildings date from the 16th century, including the five-storey tower, the best-preserved part of the complex, from where you get great views of the loch and surrounding hills. The entire complex is accessed via the stunning visitor centre, which, in addition to the obligatory café, includes an informative short-film about the history of the castle.

Invermoriston *Colour map 4, A1.*
Between Drumnadrochit and Fort Augustus is the tiny village of Invermoriston, probably the most tranquil spot on the entire Inverness to Fort Augustus stretch of the A82. It's a beautiful little piece of Highland scenery, with a photogenic old stone bridge over foaming river rapids and with marked woodland trails leading off into the hills past some lovely waterfalls. There's an interesting **Clog and Craft Shop** ① *T01320-351318*, where high-quality clogs and leather goods are made to measure. Just along the road is the **Glenmoriston Arms**, see Where to stay on page 182.

At Invermoriston the A887 heads west through **Glen Moriston** to meet the A87, which runs from Invergarry (see page 185) all the way through the rugged and dramatic Glen Shiel and under the shadow of the Five Sisters of Kintail en route to Kyle of Lochalsh and Skye (see page 225).

Fort Augustus *Colour map 4, A1.*
At the more scenic southern end of Loch Ness stands the village of Fort Augustus. The former clan village of Kilchuimen was set up as a garrison after the Jacobite rebellion of 1715 to serve as the headquarters of General Wade's campaign to pacify the Highlands. Today, Fort Augustus is a very busy little place, full of monster-hunting tourists and boats using the flight of five locks to enter or leave Loch Ness on their journey along the Caledonian Canal.

Like many visitors, you may find yourself drawn to the canal side, watching yachts and cruise boats negotiate the first of many locks to access/leave Loch Ness. Alternatively, pop into **The Clansman Centre** ① *T01320-366444, www.scottish-swords.com, Easter-Oct*

Great Monster Hunt

In a country full of myths and legends, the Loch Ness Monster is the greatest of them all. As elusive as a straight answer from a politician, Nessie has single-handedly sold more tins of tartan-wrapped shortbread to foreign visitors than Edinburgh Castle.

Tales of Nessie go way back to the sixth century, when St Columba is said to have calmed the beast after she had attacked one of his monks. But the monster craze only really took off with the completion of the A82 road along the loch's western shore in 1933. Since then there have been numerous sightings, some backed up with photographic evidence, though the most impressive of these – the famous black-and-white movie footage of Nessie's humps moving through the water, and the classic photograph of her head and neck – have been exposed as fakes.

In recent decades determined monster hunters have enlisted the help of new technology, such as sonar surveys but have failed to come up with conclusive evidence. Enter Cyber Nessie, the latest attempt to end the years of rumours, hoaxes and speculation. Nessie's very own website, www.lochness.co.uk, is a 24-hour real-time video watch of Loch Ness, and has already produced a couple of claimed sightings.

daily 1000-1800, £4.50, concessions £3.50, where young guides in traditional dress provide a lively and entertaining presentation of 17th-century Highland family life in an old turf house. If you've time, visit the **Caledonian Canal Heritage Centre** ① *T01320-366493, Apr-Oct daily 1000-1730, free*, with its history of the impressive canal system.

Fort Augustus to Dores

A very worthwhile detour from Fort Augustus is to take the B862/852 up the east shore of Loch Ness, a mostly single-track road that skirts the loch for much of its length to the village of Dores. It's a much quieter and more scenic route than the busy A82 and follows General Wade's original (and very straight) military road which linked Fort Augustus with Fort George. Though it makes a more interesting alternative to the more popular A82 route from Inverness to Fort Augustus, it's best done from south to north, if you have the time. Today, this road also attracts runners from around the world for the annual (October) Baxters Loch Ness Marathon. This route is only possible if you have your own transport. There are buses south from Inverness, but they only run as far as Foyers. If you're feeling very fit, it can be done by bike, as a tough trip from Fort Augustus or from Inverness, possibly using the one-way bike hire service offered by **Off Beat Bikes** in Fort William.

From Fort Augustus, the road winds its way up into rugged hills past Glendole where the largest hydroelectric scheme to be built in Scotland in 50 years is located. Nearby is the good real ale house of the historic **Whitebridge Hotel** and the nearby 1732 White Bridge. The road then drops back to the lochside at **Foyers**. It's worth stopping here to see the impressive waterfall where the River Foyers plunges into Loch Ness or to enjoy an overnight stay at **Foyers House** (see Where to stay, page 183). To get there, follow the steep (and slippery) track down from opposite the shops. Three miles further north, at **Inverfarigaig**, is **Boleskine House**, once home of Alastair Crowley, who is said to have practised devil worship here. In the 1970s the house was bought by Jimmy Page of Led Zeppelin, but sold some years later after the tragic death of his daughter. Those of a nervous disposition may wish to pass on quickly and continue to the little village of

Dores, at the northeastern end of the loch, where you can enjoy some fine forest walks or reasonable pub grub at the **Dores Inn.**

You can then continue to Inverness, or return via the beautiful hill road that leads up to **Loch Mhor** and back to Fort Augustus via the **Stratherrick Valley**. From **Errogie**, at the northern end of Loch Mhor, there's a dramatic section of road that winds down to the loch through a series of tight, twisting bends, reminiscent of an Alpine pass, and great for cyclists. There are also interesting marked woodland trails around Errogie.

Listings Around Loch Ness

Tourist information

Drumnadrochit

Drumnadrochit iCentre
In the car park. T01456-453165. Apr-Sep Mon-Sat 0900-1730, Sun 1000-1600, call ahead for winter hours.

Fort Augustus

Fort Augustus iCentre
In the car park next to the petrol station and cashpoint, T01320-345156. Apr-Oct.

Where to stay

Drumnadrochit

£££ Loch Ness Inn
*Lewiston, T01456-450991,
www.staylochness.co.uk.*
Fabulous and beautifully appointed accommodation and restaurant, 1½ miles south of the **iCentre** in Drumnadrochit, and with connections to the acclaimed **Applecross Inn**. In addition to 12 comfortable bedrooms (1 of which is a disabled-friendly suite), this former rustic brewery, just off the main road, has a **Brewery Bar** serving the likes of Isle of Skye real ale and a menu (**££**) of hand-dived scallops, Applecross Bay prawns and all manner of locally sourced produce.

£££-££ The Benleva Hotel
T01456-450080, www.benleva.co.uk.
A former manse, this small, atmospheric hotel prides itself on a fine range of real ales and its use of freshly prepared local produce. Each Sep, it helps host the **Loch Ness Beer**

Festival so book ahead. Now has its own on-site brewery, named after the 400 year-old chestnut tree outside the front door which was the former hanging tree. Its comfy bedrooms offer great value.

££ Bearnock Country Centre
*6 miles west of Drumnadrochit,
Glen Urquhart, T01456-476296,
www.bcclochnesshostel.co.uk.*
This backpackers' hostel oozes quality and style. Beautifully furnished, fully en suite and with great facilities, this place is within reach of both Loch Ness and Glen Affric. Ideal for mountain biking, fishing and hiking in the area. Also has luxury cottage and log cabin for rent. Highly recommended.

££ Rooms@Elmbank
Lewiston, T01456-450372, near Loch Ness Inn.
2 en suite rooms in annex, ideal for group of 4. Very comfortable and quiet location and excellent value but note that breakfast is not included and there are no cooking facilities.

££-£ Loch Ness Backpackers Lodge
*Coiltie Farmhouse, Lewiston, T01456-450807,
www.lochness-backpackers.com.*
Accommodation in 5 dorms, 1 double, 1 twin or 2 family rooms. A terrific, low-budget option run by friendly, helpful owners who can arrange boat trips and walks in the area. Provide continental breakfast for £3.50.

Invermoriston

£££ Glenmoriston Arms Hotel
*T01320-351206, www.
glenmoristonarms.co.uk.*

Formerly a 17th-century drovers inn, this comfortable, 10-bedroom hotel on the route of the Great Glen Way is proud of its freshly prepared cuisine that draws on local produce (**££**) and there are 150 malt whiskies behind the bar. Johnson and Boswell were guests during their 18th-century tour of the Highlands and it's said there's a resident ghost.

£ SYHA Loch Ness Youth Hostel
A few miles north, on the main A82, T01320-351274. Mid-Apr to end Oct.
Fantastic views across Loch Ness.

Self-catering

Lann Dearg Studios
Invermoriston, T01320-351353, www.lanndearg.com.
Right by the Great Glen Way, these 3 delightful, fully equipped self-catering studios (from £535 per week) offer a luxurious stay after a hard day's hike by the lochside. Suitable for couples, no pets or children.

Camping

Loch Ness Caravan & Camping Park
1½ miles south of Invermoriston, and 6 miles north of Fort Augustus, T01320-351207. Mar-Jan.
On the shores of the loch with great views and excellent facilities.

Fort Augustus

££££-£££ Lovat Hotel
T01456-490000, www.thelovat.com.
Acclaimed 4-star/3-Rosette family-run hotel which has been refurbished at considerable expense to ensure you enjoy a luxurious stay and delicious food (**£££-££**) in the **Station Road Restaurant** or **Brasserie**.

£££ Caledonian Hotel
T01320-366256, www. thecaledonianhotel.co.uk.
Directly opposite the **Lovat**, this is another lovely place to dine (**£££-££**) and enjoy a comfortable sleep (10 en suite rooms).

££ Bank House
Station Rd, Fort Augustus, T01320-366755. Open all year.
3 en suite rooms. Comfortable and friendly B&B. Good value.

££ Sonas
On the Inverness Rd, T01320-366291.
Run by Mr and Mrs Service who certainly live up to their name. Particularly recommended for cylists and walkers.

££-£ Morag's Lodge
Bunoich Brae, T01320-366289, www. moragslodge.com. Open all year.
Friendly and good value – another excellent option along Loch Ness. Single bunk in dorm is even cheaper (**£**). Breakfast is £3.95 extra, dinner (£8.50) and packed lunches (£3.95) are available. Also bike hire for £20/day.

Fort Augustus to Dores

£££-££ Foyers House
Foyers, T01456-486405, www.foyershouse-lochness.com.
Very comfortable accommodation in in 9 tasteful en suite double or twin rooms. Great view of Loch Ness from the decking. Best suited for couple or friends.

£££-££ Whitebridge Hotel
3 miles south of Foyers, T01456-486226, www.whitebridgehotel.co.uk.
12 en suite rooms. Old-world hotel with comfortable accommodation. Also serves good real ales and bar food.

Self catering

Hazelgrove
Inverfarigaig, T01456-486717, www.hazelgrovelochness.co.uk.
Lovely east-shore cottage available for weekly rental Apr-Oct and also short-term lets Oct-Mar. Sleeps 4. Pets welcome. £770 per week in peak season.

Camping

Fort Augustus Caravan and Camping
At the southern end of the village,
T01320-366618.
A good option for campers.

Restaurants

Drumnadrochit

The hotels all tend to serve decent bar food and some B&Bs offer evening meals.

£££-££ The Loch Ness Inn
See Where to stay, above.
Lovely setting and offering fresh seafood, locally sourced produce and a good range of real ales.

Fort Augustus

££ Lock Inn
By the canal, T01320-366302.
Cosy little pub/restaurant. A good place for a drink on a rainy evening and serves good pub food.

££ Poachers
Richmond House Hotel,
Main St, T01320-310119.
For a drink and good pub grub served nightly 1800-2100.

Festivals

Fort Augustus

Jun-Sep Highland Gatherings. Late Jun and Jul, mid-Aug and early Sep is the period when Fort Augustus hosts the Highland Gatherings, featuring traditional dancing and piping competitions, tossing the caber and sheep dog trials.

What to do

There are various monster-spotting tours of Loch Ness which leave from the tourist office in Drumnadrochit or Fort Augustus.

Drumnadrochit
Boat trips
Castle Cruises Loch Ness, *Temple Pier, T01456-450695, www.lochnesscruises.com.* Offers 60-min cruises on Loch Ness, leaving from Drumnadrochit aboard the *MV Cluaran Dubh*. £14, £12 concession, £9 child.
Jacobite, *Tomnahurich Bridge, Glenurquhart Rd, Inverness, T01463-233999, www.jacobite. co.uk.* Tours depart from the Clansman Hotel, about 5 miles north of Drumnadrochit. Offer a variety of cruises on their fleet of 4 boats, ranging from the 1-hr 'Clansman' cruise (£14) up to a 4-hr cruise on Loch Ness and Caledonian Canal with 2-hrs at Castle Urquhart. Also offer coach and cruise tours starting at £30 for 2½ hrs.
Loch Ness Cruises, *T01456-450395, www. lochness-cruises.com.* Cruises run hourly Apr-Oct 1000-1800. Trips last 1 hr, £16, children £10. Skipper George Edwards takes would-be monster-spotters out on the loch in his boat, *Nessie Hunter*, which is based near Drumnadrochit. He not only once caught a glimpse of Nessie but also discovered the deepest part of the loch (812 ft), now known as Edwards Deep.

Horse riding
Highland Riding Centre, *Borlum Farm, Drumnadrochit, T01456-450220, www. borlum.com.* Children must be over the age of 4 to ride.

Fort Augustus
Boat trips
Cruise Loch Ness, *by the canal swing bridge, Fort Augustus, T01320-366277, www. cruiselochness.com.* Apr-Oct hourly, 1000-1600, 1 hr, £14.50, children £8.50; May-Aug evening cruises at 2000. Apr-Oct also RIB rides, 90 mins £30, £18 children, 3 hrs £50/30. Sailing out of Fort Augustus by the Caledonian Canal for the past 40 years, this renowned operator has catered for Hollywood and Scottish stars alike and uses onboard 3D underwater imaging to relay 'real time' information about what is lurking in the peaty depths of Loch Ness.

Drumnadrochit

Bus

Citylink buses between **Inverness** and **Fort William** stop here several times daily in either direction. **Stagecoach** buses 17 and 117 from Inverness to **Cannich** and **Tomich**, also stop in Drumnadrochit.

Fort Augustus

Bus

Several buses daily (No 919) to **Fort William** or **Inverness**, 1-hr. The same service stops at **Invergarry** daily.

Fort Augustus to Fort William

spectacular scenery and a blood-soaked history

South of Fort Augustus, the A82 leaves behind Loch Ness and runs through Invergarry along the west shore of Loch Oich and then the east shore of Loch Lochy, until it reaches Spean Bridge. Here the A82 continues south to Fort William, while the A86 branches east through Glen Spean to join the A9 Perth to Inverness road finally at Kingussie (see page 153). All along this route are many opportunities to get off the beaten track and explore huge chunks of real wilderness, deserted since the Clearances and soaked in the blood of history.

Invergarry and around *Colour map 3, A6.*

The old village of Invergarry stands where the A82 turns west to meet the A87. There's not much to see or do in the village, but the surrounding area merits some exploring, particularly the route west through Glen Garry, and there are several places to stay.

Inside the entrance to the **Glengarry Castle Hotel**, on the shores of Loch Oich (see Where to stay, page 188) stand the ruins of **Invergarry Castle**, once the stronghold of Clan Ranald of Glengarry and later destroyed by the Duke of Cumberland as he wreaked revenge on the Highlands in the aftermath of Culloden (see box, page 172). The hotel was later built as the main house of the Ellice family, who made their fortune from the Hudson Bay Company in Canada and who were the main driving force behind the creation of the Victorian planned village.

A mile or so south of the village, at **North Laggan**, is a monument by the side of the road standing over **The Well of the Seven Heads**. This tells the grisly story of the Keppoch Murders, one of the most infamous clan murders which took place at **Roy Bridge** (see page 188) in the 17th century. It all began when the chief of the clan MacDonnell died, leaving two young sons, who were sent away to complete their education before returning to Roy Bridge to celebrate the elder brother's accession to chieftainship. Another branch of the clan present at the celebrations started a fight in which both brothers were killed. Believing they had been murdered, one of their cousins persuaded a fellow clan member to raise 50 men and march on the murderers' house at nearby Inverlair. The accused murderers – a father and his six sons – were duly slaughtered and their heads cut off, to be displayed before the local laird at Glengarry. On the way to his lodge, the heads were washed here in this well.

A few miles further south, at **Laggan**, where the A82 crosses to the east bank of Loch Lochy, is the site of the **Battle of the Shirts**.

Old as the hills

The Great Glen, which splits the Scottish mainland from Fort William in the south to Inverness in the north, is one of the world's major geological fault lines. The Glen was formed millions of years ago when the northern part of the Caledonian mountains 'slid' more than 60 miles south, leaving behind a massive glen with four freshwater lochs – Loch Linnhe, Loch Lochy, Loch Oich and Loch Ness.

The most famous of these is Loch Ness, which attracts hordes of visitors eager to catch a glimpse of its elusive monster. The renowned engineer, Thomas Telford, succeeded in connecting all these lochs when he built the impressive Caledonian Canal. The canal took 22 years to complete, and when it was opened in 1822 was the first in Britain to take ships from one coast to the other. It remains the only canal in the country capable of carrying ships of up to 500 tons.

The best way to appreciate the glen is by boat, through the 38 miles of natural lochs and rivers and the 22 miles of canal, and every summer pleasure craft of all shapes and sizes ply its length. The main A82 runs from Inverness south to Fort William. The southern section, from Fort Augustus, follows the original line of the road constructed in 1727 by General Wade to link the military garrisons at Fort William and Fort Augustus (hence their names).

Another way to travel through the Great Glen is along the excellent cycle route, which follows the canal towpaths, forest trails and quiet minor roads to avoid the busy main road. The route is outlined in the Forestry Commission leaflet, available from most iCentres.

Glen Garry to Kinloch Hourn *Colour map 3, A5/6.*

The A87 leads west from Invergarry through Glen Shiel to Shiel Bridge, on the way to Kyle of Lochalsh on the west coast, see page 225. About seven miles along the A87 is the **Glen Garry viewpoint**, from where you get one of the most stunning, and famous, of all Highland views. From this angle Loch Garry looks uncannily like a map of Scotland, so get out the camera for that classic holiday snap.

A mile or so before the viewpoint, where the A87 begins to leave the shores of Loch Garry, is the turning left for the road through Glen Garry, described as the longest and most beautiful cul-de-sac in Britain. The little single-track road turns and twists for 22 glorious miles along the shores of Loch Garry and Loch Quoich all the way to Kinloch Hourn at the head of **Loch Hourn**. Known as 'the loch of the devil' this sea loch forms the northern boundary of the wonderful wilderness area of **Knoydart** aptly dubbed the 'Rough Bounds' (see page 222).

Glen Garry is now virtually deserted but was once home to some 5000 people who were driven out during the infamous Highland Clearances in the 19th century. The road passes the tiny hamlet of **Tomdoun**, once the junction of the main road to Skye, until the massive post-Second World War hydroelectric schemes changed the landscape. Experienced hillwalkers can still follow the old route to Skye, through Glen Kingie, along Loch Hourn and then across the wild Knoydart Peninsula until they reach the tiny but welcoming settlement of **Inverie**. From here a little ferry ① *T01687-462320, www.westernislecruises. co.uk, Apr-Sep Mon-Fri, Oct-Mar Mon, Wed and Thu*, runs to Mallaig, see page 220.

Beyond Tomdoun the road passes a huge dam, built in the 1950s, which raised the waters of **Loch Quoich** by over 100 ft, flooding many of the old settlements. Also flooded was **Glen Quoich Lodge**, which can count Edward VII and Sir Edward Landseer among its notable guests. It was reputedly Glen Garry that gave Landseer the inspiration for his famous painting *The Monarch of the Glen*. The road then reaches its highest point, at 1200 ft, before descending to **Kinloch Hourn**, once a thriving crofting and fishing village.

Spean Bridge *Colour map 3, B6.*

The main A82 runs down the east shore of Loch Lochy to the village of Spean Bridge, at the head of Glen Spean, beneath the towering Lochaber Mountains. The village gets its name from Thomas Telford's bridge across the River Spean. Two miles west are the remains of the old 'Highbridge', built in 1736 by General Wade, and the site of the first clash between Government troops and the Jacobites, three days before Prince Charles raised his standard at Glenfinnan.

Spean Bridge is only eight miles north of Fort William so gets busy in the summer, but it still makes a more peaceful and attractive alternative base for exploring this astoundingly beautiful part of the Highlands. There's a small tourist information centre (see page 188) just off the main road behind the Spean Bridge Hotel. This hotel, complete with its **Shinty Bar** watering hole, also houses the excellent and free **Commando Exhibition**. The area is also the starting point for the excellent **Grey Corries ridge walk** (OS Landranger Map No 41).

Loch Arkaig and around *Colour map 3, A5/6.*

A mile north of Spean Bridge on the A82 is the striking **Commando Memorial**, which commemorates the men who trained in the area from their secret base at Achnacarry during the Second World War and the 1700 commandos who lost their lives. It's worth lingering for a few moments to appreciate the fantastic views, including (on a clear day) the summit of Ben Nevis. From here the B8004 branches west to **Gairlochy**, crossing the Caledonian Canal, then the B8005 heads north to Loch Arkaig, a long, deep and mysterious loch stretching west through the mountains. Bonnie Prince Charlie passed this way, before and after Culloden, through an area which has, for centuries, been the seat of the Camerons of Lochiel. The Camerons were fervent supporters of the Jacobite cause, so when Prince Charles landed at Loch nan Uamh, on the road from Fort William to Mallaig, he called on Cameron of Lochiel to join him at Glenfinnan.

In the tiny township of **Achnacarry**, nestled between the shores of Loch Lochy and Loch Arkaig, you can find out about the Camerons and their involvement in the Jacobite rebellion of 1745 at the **Clan Cameron Museum** ① *T01397-712090, www. clancameronmuseum.co.uk, Apr-Oct daily 1100-1630, £4 concessions £3, children free.* This interesting museum is housed in an old cottage, rebuilt after being burned by government troops in 1746.

Beyond the turn-off to Achnacarry, the single-track road runs through the Clunes Forest and The Dark Mile, a long line of beech trees which completely cuts out daylight. At the east end of Loch Arkaig, a stone bridge crosses the Caig Burn. Beside the bridge is a car park, from where a path leads up to the spectacular **Cia-Aig Falls** which tumble into a deep, dark pool known as **The Witch's Cauldron**. It was here that an old hag was accused of casting her evil eye over Lochiel's cattle, causing them to fall ill and die. But when she fell into the pool and drowned, the cattle miraculously began to recover from their illness. The road runs along the north shore of Loch Arkaig all the way to the head of the loch, from where experienced and well-equipped hillwalkers can hike through the glens to Loch Nevis, 'the loch of heaven', and Knoydart (see page 222).

Glen Roy and Loch Laggan *Colour map 4, A1/B1.*

From Spean Bridge the A86 runs east through dramatic Glen Spean to meet the A9 Perth to Inverness road which leads to Aviemore, see page 139. The road (and railway) passes through **Roy Bridge**, which is the turn-off for Glen Roy, noted for its amazing 'parallel roads'. These are not in fact roads, but three gravel ledges etched on to the mountains at different heights. The 'roads' marked the shorelines of a glacial lake formed during the last Ice Age. Roy Bridge was also the site of the infamous Keppoch Murders, see page 185.

The road continues east towards Loch Laggan. After a couple of miles it passes **Cille Choirille**, an ancient church built by a 15th-century Cameron chief as penance for a life of violence. The church fell into disrepair but was restored and reopened in 1932 and now attracts people of all creeds as it's said to inspire peace and spiritual healing. Further east, at the eastern end of Loch Laggan, is the massive **Laggan Dam**, built in 1933 to provide water for the aluminium smelter at Fort William. The water is piped through tunnels up to 15 ft in diameter carved through the core of Ben Nevis. The road runs along the north shore of the loch, past the **Creag Meagaidh National Nature Reserve**, where you can see herds of red deer right by the reserve car park. A path leads from here up to **Lochan a' Choire** (about four hours). Note that there are no bus or postbus services between Spean Bridge and Laggan.

Listings Fort Augustus to Fort William

Tourist information

Spean Bridge

Tourist information centre
Just off the main road behind the Spean Bridge Hotel, T01397-712576. Easter-Oct.

Where to stay

Invergarry and around

££££-£££ Glengarry Castle Hotel
T01809-501254, www.glengarrycastlehotel. co.uk. Mar-Nov.
26 tastefully appointed bedrooms set in 60 acres of woodland running down to Loch Oich. The hotel prides itself on its traditional Highland hospitality with the daily changing dinner menu (**£££**) serving up the best of local Scottish produce.

££ Forest Lodge
South Laggan, south of Invergarry and 24 miles north of Fort William, T01809-501219, www.forestlodgeguesthouse.co.uk.
A welcoming and comfortable B&B. Lorraine and Laura can also rustle-up a hearty evening meal whilst you enjoy the scenery.

£ Saddle Mountain Hostel
Mandally Rd, Invergarry, T01809-501412, www.saddlemountainhostel.co.uk. Open all year.
Independent hostel sleeping up to 26 in 4- to 6-bed rooms. Fully equipped kitchen and safe cycle shed.

Self-catering

Ardgarry Farm
15 mins' walk from the village, T01809-501226, www.ardgarryfarm.co.uk.
4 log cabins and 1 cottage for 4-6 people to enjoy self-catering (from £600 per week) in well-equipped lodges with spectacular views. Also 2 en suite double room in the farmhouse offering B&B (**£££-££**).

Faichemard Farm Chalets
Invergarry, T01809-501314, chalets.faichemard.scot.
Rustic, secluded, cosy and peaceful. Sleeps up to 3 at a modest price, £350 per week in peak season.

Glen Garry to Kinloch Hourn

For details of **Skiary Guesthouse** and other options on Knoydart, see page 223. You should also call the **Knoydart Foundation** rangers office at Inverie (T01687-462242).

Spean Bridge

There's no shortage of accommodation in Spean Bridge.

££££ Corriegour Lodge Hotel
9 miles north of Spean Bridge on the A82, T01397-712685, www.corriegour-lodge-hotel. com. Feb-Dec.
9 rooms. Lovely Victorian hunting lodge on the shores of Loch Lochy, with fine views and an excellent restaurant, from £49.50 for a 5-course candlelit dinner.

£££ Smiddy House
T01397-712335, www.smiddyhouse.com.
Very stylish and comfortable guesthouse with an excellent restaurant (**£££** for à la carte dinner). 4 bedrooms plus a luxurious suite (**££££**).

£££-££ Corriechoille Lodge
2 miles north of Spean Bridge, T01397-712002, www.corriechoille.com. Apr-Oct.
This secluded former fishing lodge offers a very comfortable stop for the night and a roaring open fire. Also has 2 self-catering log cabins for rent for up to 2 people in each.

Camping

Stronaba Caravan & Camping
North of the village, T01397-712259. Apr-Oct.

Loch Arkaig and around

£££ Old Pines Hotel and Restaurant
Just past the **Commando Memorial** *on the B8004, T01397-712324, www.oldpines.co.uk.*
This delightful boutique hotel is where discerning guests will experience a truly personal touch. Each of the 8 rooms is individually appointed to a very high standard. The warm scones and tea on arrival are just a hint of the treat in store at dinner

where venison, local lamb, prime beef and shellfish feature. It's not inexpensive but for a touch of class in an unpretentious manner this could be a fine choice for an overnight stay or just for dinner (**££££** including dinner).

Camping

Gairlochy Holiday Park
West towards Gairlochy, T01397-712711. Apr-Oct.
Camping and self-catering chalets.

Glen Roy and Loch Laggan

£ Aite Cruinnichidh
Achluachrach, 1½ miles from the village, T01397-712315.
Comfy bunkhouse in converted barn, even has a sauna.

£ Grey Corrie Lodge
Roy Bridge, T01397-712236.
Well equipped and friendly bunkhouse. Very handy for food and drink at the **Roy Bridge Hotel**, next door, as well as for public transport and local shop.

£ Station Lodge
6 miles east of Roy Bridge at Tulloch in the converted train station, T01397-732333.
Ideal if arriving by train or planning to hike in the hills. The friendly owners will even cook very early breakfasts to accommodate walkers and climbers. The trains stop practically at the door.

Restaurants

Invergarry and around

£££-££ The Eagle Barge Inn
Laggan Locks, northern end of Loch Lochy, T07789-858567.
The original owner has moved on but this lovingly restored Dutch barge, complete with a clean, cosy galley and fabulous wooden bar is the perfect place to enjoy a light bite or evening meal. Lunch 1200-1530, bar meals 1730-2030, dinner menu 1830-2000.

Spean Bridge

See also **Old Pines Hotel and Restaurant** (£££) under Where to stay, above.

££ Old Station Restaurant
Station Rd, T01397-712535, www.oldstation restaurant. co.uk. Sep-Jun Thu-Tue, Jul-Aug daily except Wed 1800-2100; bar 1700-0100.
As long ago as 1894, trains on the West Highland Railway Line puffed up to its door, and now the railway station has been converted it serves delicious evening meals from 1800 in a fascinating interior.

££-£ Spean Bridge Hotel
T01397-712250, www.speanbridgehotel.co.uk.
Aside from its **Commando Museum** and reasonable food, it's also worth popping into the refurbished **Shinty** bar. Here you can share a real ale or some pub grub with the locals whilst admiring the local shinty team's silverware. Also takeaway from the **Village Fryer**.

Glen Roy and Loch Laggan

£££-££ Glenspean Lodge Hotel
1½ miles east of Roy Bridge, T01397-712223, www.gleanspeanlodge.com. Mar-Oct.
For those in search of sustenance, this tastefully modernized hunting lodge rustles up a tasty bar lunch (1200-1400) and dinner.

££ Stronlossit Inn
Roy Bridge, T01397-712253, www.stronlossit.co.uk.
Food is served 1200-2100 so it's a good place to rest and have some decent pub grub. Has a fine range of real ale and malts as well as rooms (**££**).

What to do

Glen Roy and Loch Laggan
Watersports
Monster Activities, *Great Glen Water Park, east shore of Loch Oich, near South Laggan,* *T07710-540398, www.monteractivities.com.*
An outdoor activities centre, with hostel accommodation nearby, offering adventure sports including whitewater rafting (£55), canoeing and kayaking (£35), abseiling, hillwalking, clay pigeon shooting and archery.

Transport

Invergarry and around
Bus
Invergarry is on the **Fort William** to **Inverness** bus route, which stops in **Fort Augustus**. It is also on the main **Fort William** to **Kyle of Lochalsh** (and Skye) **Citylink** route (Nos 915, 916) and a couple of buses pass through daily in both directions. For times www.citylink.co.uk.

Unfortunately, there's no longer a **postbus** service that runs from **Invergarry** to **Kinloch Hourn**. Your best option is to catch the **Scottish Citylink** (No 915/917), which runs 4 times daily, and request to be dropped off at the turn-off for the long walk into the glen.

Spean Bridge
Bus
There are regular buses to **Fort William** and **Inverness**. Spean Bridge is also on the **Fort William** to **Glasgow** railway line.

Loch Arkaig and around
Bus
At least 1 **Citylink** and **Stagecoach** bus per day (Mon-Sat) travels the route to **Fort William** via **Banavie** and **Gairlochy**.

Glen Roy and Loch Laggan
Bus
There is a **Stagecoach** No 41 bus to **Fort William** from **Roy Bridge**, 3 times daily Mon-Fri, 1 on Sat. Roy Bridge is also on the **Fort William** to **Glasgow** railway line.

Fort William
& around

Fort William, the self-proclaimed 'Outdoor Capital of the UK', is also the gateway to the Western Highlands and one of the country's main tourist centres. It stands at the head of Loch Linnhe, with the snow-topped mass of Ben Nevis towering behind. Despite its magnificent setting, Fort William is not the most charming town in the Highlands. After passing a string of B&Bs on the southern outskirts, the visitor finds a dual carriageway running along the lochside past a series of uninspiring 1960s- to 1970s-era concrete boxes. Unsurprisingly, the majority of Fort William's attractions are out of town. The surrounding mountains and glens are amongst the most stunning in the Highlands and attract hikers and climbers in their droves; many come to climb or walk up Ben Nevis, Britain's highest peak at 4413 ft, or to visit the very beautiful Glen Nevis, which you may recognize from movies such as *Braveheart* and *Rob Roy*. There are also snowsports on the slopes of nearby Aonach Mor, one of Scotland's top ski areas. Here, in and above Leanachan Forest, you'll find world-class cross-country and downhill mountain biking.

Though it's short of visual appeal, Fort William is the largest town hereabouts and has all the services and facilities you'd expect. There are banks with ATMs on the pedestrianized High Street, as well as a supermarket, a good bike shop and outdoor-equipment outlets.

There's little of real interest in the town, although the **West Highland Museum** ① *Cameron Sq by the iCentre, T01397-702169, www.westhighlandmuseum.org.uk, Jan-Apr and Oct-Dec Mon-Sat 1000-1600, May-Sep Mon-Sat 1000-1700 Jul-Aug also Sun 1100-1500, free*, is a worthwhile exception. It contains excellent exhibits of Jacobite memorabilia, including a 'secret' portrait of Bonnie Prince Charlie which is revealed only when reflected in a cylindrical mirror. There are also fine displays of Highland clans and tartans, wildlife and local history. The museum also has a fine exhibition telling the story of the Commandos training in Lochaber during the Second World War.

The fort from which the town gets its name was built in 1690 by order of William III to keep the rebellious Scottish clans in order. The garrison fought off attacks by Jacobites during the rebellions of 1715 and 1745 but was then demolished to make way for the railway line. Remnants of the fort's outer walls are all that remain and can be seen by the lochshore.

Ben Nevis Distillery ① *T01397-702476, www.bennevisdistillery.com, Mon-Fri 0900-1700, Easter-Oct Mon-Sat 1000-1600, Jul-Aug Mon-Fri 0900-1800, Sat 1000-1600, Sun 1200-1600, Nov-Mar Mon-Fri 0900-1700, tours £5, children under 18 £2.50*, is at Lochy Bridge, at the junction of the A82 to Inverness and the A830 to Mallaig, about a mile north

Essential Fort William

Finding your feet

Fort William is easily reached by bus from Inverness, Glasgow and Oban, and by train direct from Glasgow via the wonderful West Highland Railway, see box, page 218. The train and bus stations are at the north end of the High Street, next to the supermarket. If you're driving, parking can be a problem. There's a big car park beside the loch at the south end of town and another behind the tourist office. You can also walk to Fort William, if you have a week to spare, from just north of Glasgow along the 95-mile-long West Highland Way, see box, page 218. See also Transport, page 197.

Getting around

The town is strung out for several miles along the banks of Loch Linnhe, though the centre is compact and easy to get around on foot. Many of the B&Bs and several backpacker hostels and camping options are within Glen Nevis or around Corpach, 1½ miles to the north. Both areas are serviced by frequent buses from the town centre. There are buses every 20-30 minutes to and from Caol and Corpach, and every hour on Sunday and in the evening. There is a daily service June-end October with **Shield Buses** (No N42) to Glen Nevis Youth Hostel (fewer on Sunday). **Stagecoach** bus No 41 runs daily to Roy Bridge via Nevis Range during the summer. During the ski season there are at least three daily buses (from 0745) to Nevis Range with the last return journey at 1630. See also Transport, page 197.

Fort William

To Ben Nevis Distillery, Banavie, Corpach, Mallaig (A830) & Inverness (A82)

River Lochy
River Nevis
Nevis Bridge
To Glen Nevis
North Rd
Nevis Bank
Croft Rd
Glen Nevis Rd
Fort William Shinty Field
Lochaber Leisure Centre
Morrisons Supermarket
Camanachd Crescent
Mary St
Nevis Terr
Belford Rd
Douglas Pl
Nevisport
Parade Rd
Bank St
Fassifern Pl
Newtown Pl
Hilra Rd
Fassifern Rd
Victoria Rd
Alma Rd
Mamore Cres
Kennedy Rd
Bruce Pl
Wallace Pl
To Camusnagul
To Camusnagul
West Highland Museum
Cameron Square
Off Beat Bikes
Cameron Rd
Argyll Rd
Glasdrum Rd
Glasdrum
Loch Linnhe
High St
Seaview Terrace
Union Rd
Heather Croft Rd
Achintore Rd
Argyll Terr
Grange Rd
Lundavra Rd
Lundy Rd
Dumfermline Rd
N
200 metres
200 yards
To 2, Glen Coe & Glasgow (A82)
To 5

Where to stay
6 Caberfeidh **1**
Ashburn House **2**
Bank Street Lodge **3**
Calluna **4**
Crolinnhe **5**
Fort William Backpackers **6**
Glenlochy Apartments **7**
Grange **8**
Lime Tree **9**

Restaurants
Crannog Seafood **1**
Grog & Gruel **2**

of the town centre. It's a bit too polished for some, though the imaginative audio-visual display that features the mythical giant Hector McDram provides light amusement. There's also a pleasant café and restaurant. Just before the distillery, on the left, are the 13th-century ruins of **Inverlochy Castle**.

Three miles from the town centre along the A830 to Mallaig, in the suburb of Banavie, is **Neptune's Staircase**, a series of eight linked locks on the Caledonian Canal. The locks lower the canal by 90 ft in less than two miles between Loch Lochy and Loch Eil and comprise the last section of the canal which links the North Sea with the Irish Sea. It's a pretty dramatic sight, with equally dramatic views of Ben Nevis and its neighbours behind Fort William. In fine weather, **The Moorings Hotel** (see page 194) by the canal is great for watching boats come and go as you enjoy a midday bite. You can also walk or cycle along the canal towpath from here. For details on the **Great Glen Way**, www.great glenway. fsnet.co.uk, which links Fort William with Inverness, see box, page 180.

Further along the A830 to Mallaig, in the village of Corpach, is **Treasures of the Earth** ⓘ *T01397-772283, www. treasuresoftheearth.co.uk, Apr-Oct daily 1000-1700, Jul-Aug daily 0930-1800, Nov-Feb 1000-1600, £5, children £3, under 5s free,* an exhibition of crystals, gemstones and fossils displayed in a huge simulated cave.

Listings Fort William

Tourist information

Fort William iCentre
Cameron Sq, just off the High St, T1397-701801. Apr-May Mon-Fri 0900-1700, Sun 1000-1700, May-Jun Mon-Sat 0900-1800, Sun 0930-1700, Jun-Sep Mon-Sat 0900-1830, Sun 0930-1830, Oct-Mar Mon-Sat 0900-1700, Sun 1000-1500.

The very busy **iCentre** stocks a good range of books, maps and leaflets covering local walks. Staff will also help arrange transport to more remote Highland parts.

Where to stay

Fort William has an abundance of accommodation, ranging from large luxury hotels to modest guesthouses and B&Bs. You'll find B&Bs and hostels on the road north towards Corpach and Banavie whilst the southern entrance to Fort William on Achintore Rd is truly packed with B&Bs and hotels. Running parallel is Grange Rd, which is also lined with B&B accommodation. Nearer to the town centre, Fassifern Rd and Alma Rd are also a hive of hostel and B&B activity. Wherever you search for a pillow, remember that as a tourist hub Fort William gets extremely busy in the high season and during key events (see Festivals, page 196). Ideally, book ahead or through the tourist office for a small fee. The **iCentre** carries copies of the *Fort William and Lochaber Accommodation Guide*.

South of Fort William, on the A82, the villages of Onich and North Ballachulish, make an attractive alternative.

££££ The Grange
Grange Rd, T01397-705516,
www.grangefortwilliam.com.
4 rooms. Superb 5-star B&B escape in a Victorian townhouse with views over Loch Linnhe. Immaculately furnished and decorated, this place simply oozes style and comfort.

££££ Inverlochy Castle Hotel
3 miles north of town on the A82
to Inverness, T01397-702177, www.
inverlochycastlehotel.com.
This is your dream castle in the Highlands. A luxurious stay is assured; unsurpassed elegance, impeccable service and a 3 AA-rosette restaurant run by Albert and Michel Roux Jr (see Restaurants, opposite), all set

in 500 acres of grounds. Awarded Scottish luxury hotel of the year in 2017.

££££-£££ Crolinnhe
Grange Rd, T01397-703795,
www.crolinnhe.co.uk. Mar-Nov.
10 mins' walk from town, this grand Victorian villa is a luxurious B&B with 3 suites that vary in price. The welcome is friendly, the food delicious and the views are exceptional.

££££-£££ The Moorings Hotel
3 miles out of town in Banavie, on road
to Corpach and Mallaig, T01397-772797,
www.moorings-fortwilliam. co.uk.
32 rooms. Overlooks Neptune's Staircase; well situated and comfortable with a reasonable restaurant (**£££-££**). Welcomes dogs.

£££ Ashburn House
Achintore Rd, T01397-706000, www.
ashburnhouse.co.uk. Apr-Oct.
Lovely guesthouse overlooking the loch, very comfortable and relaxing. No children under 12 or pets.

£££ The Lime Tree
Achintore Rd, T01397-701806,
www.limetreefortwilliam.co.uk.
Offers 9 beautifully appointed bedrooms – hardly surprising as its co-owned by a resident artist and includes an art gallery. As well as the superb breakfast on offer, the **An Eildain** restaurant serves up fabulous lunches and dinners (**£££-££**). Deserves its reputation for a quality stay. Recommended.

££ 6 Caberfeidh
Fassifern Rd, T01397-703756,
www.6caberfeidh.com.
3 rooms. A friendly B&B that will prepare packed lunches after you've slept in your 4-poster bed. Hosts Wilma and Jim know how to run a good B&B and Jim offers special taxi rates for guests.

£ Bank Street Lodge
Bank St, T01397-700070, www.
bankstreetlodge.co.uk. Open all year.

42 beds. Independent, centrally located backpackers' hostel with family/double/twin and single en suite rooms as well as dorms. Great value.

£ Farr Cottage Lodge and Activity Centre
Corpach, T01397-772315, www.farrcottage.com.
This lively set-up can accommodate individuals or groups in bunkhouse or self-catering style. Terrific facilities, including internet and laundry, and hearty breakfast and packed lunches available. Can organize everything from hillwalking and mountain-biking trips to sea fishing, kayaking, go-karting and canyoning. Also hire bikes.

£ Fort William Backpackers
Alma Rd, 500 yds from the train station, T01397-700711, www.fortwilliambackpackers.com.
Packed with information and young backpackers. Small but well-equipped with continental breakfast for an extra £2.

Self-catering

Calluna
Heathercroft, about a 15-min walk from the iCentre, T01397-700451, www.fortwilliamholiday.co.uk. Open all year.
2 modern, semi-detached apartments have been configured to suit groups of up to 8 or families, whilst the ground floor will suit a wheelchair user and carer. Also 4-bed flat and 'Alpine Loft'. Run by experienced mountain guide, Alan Kimber and wife Sue. From £390 per week for flat to £600 for apartments in high season. Minimum 3 nights.

Glenlochy Apartments
Nevis Bridge, North Rd, T01397-702909, www.glenlochyguesthouse.co.uk.
Very near Ben Nevis Woolen Mill. Substantial villa now divided into 3 comfortable apartments sleeping 2-4, available nightly (from £70) or weekly (up to £600 in high season).

Restaurants

Finally, Fort William and its environs can boast several real culinary gems ready to reward your tastebuds. Be wary, though, for there are also those still earning a crust off run-of-the-mill bar lunches and uninspiring dinners. Note that many places stop serving after 2200. A 10-mile taxi ride from Fort William is the **Lochleven Seafood Café (££)**, which serves excellent seafood. See page 210 for details.

£££ Crannog Seafood Restaurant
Town Pier, T01397-705589, www.crannog.net.
Great seafood by the pier with views across Loch Linnhe. Based in an old bait shed with distinctive red roof it has a great ambience, delicious food and there's a good wine list to help wash down delicious lobster or salmon. 2-course lunch is good value at £15.95. Book ahead.

£££ Inverlochy Castle Hotel
See Where to stay, above.
You'll experience exquisite fine dining at this 3 AA-rosette restaurant run by Albert and Michel Roux Jr. Will it be the black pudding with white truffles and scrambled eggs? Perhaps the saddle of rabbit or poached loin of venison? The food and wine list is 1st class – and so is the view out the window. Dress to impress. Built in 1863, it's regarded as one of Scotland's and indeed Europe's best country house/castle hotels.

£££-££ An Eildain at the The Lime Tree
See Where to stay, above.
In addition to its beautifully appointed bedrooms, The Lime Tree promises to serve up a flavoursome, freshly prepared dinner (including slow-cooked aromatic lamb) and a hearty lunch. Recommended.

££-£ The Grog & Gruel
66 High St, T01397-705078. Open until 2400.
There's a good atmosphere in this traditionally styled bar that serves a range of cask ales, a good selection of malt whiskies and bar meals. Choice of eating in bar or restaurant.

Festivals

Fort William annually hosts a number of high profile events.

May/Jun UCI Mountain Bike World Cup, www.fortwilliamworldcup.co.uk. Since 2002, this has been held annually at Nevis Range, 6 miles north of town. Watched by over 20,000 spectators, the downhill riders descend the 2-mile-long course at an electrifying speed.

Jul Lochaber Highland Games. Caber tossing and Highland dancing.

Sep Ben Nevis Race, www.bennevisrace. co.uk. 500 runners undertake the gruelling 10-mile run from Fort William to the summit of Ben Nevis and back. Staged for over 100 years, the record stands at 1 hr 25 mins.

Shopping

Nevisport, *High St, T01397-704921. Mon-Sat 0900-1730, Sun 1000-1630*. Also at Aonach Mor at the top of the gondola at Nevis Range ski centre, open daily 1000-1700. Has a huge selection of outdoor equipment, books, maps and guides, a bureau de change and good café-bar. Also happy to offer advice.

What to do

Adventure sports
Snowgoose Mountain Centre, *Station Rd, next to the Corpach train station, 4 miles west of Fort William on A8309 to Mallaig, T01397-772467, www.highland-mountain-guides. co.uk*. Offers lessons in mountaineering, canoeing, kayaking, skiing and mountain biking. Also hires equipment.

Vertical Descents, *Inchree, 8 miles south of Fort William*. See page 211 for details.

Boat trips
Caledonian Discovery, *The Slipway, Corpach, Fort William, T01397-772167, www. caledonian-discovery.co.uk*. Runs all-inclusive 4- and 6-day cruises in a converted Dutch 'spitz' barge that gently ploughs its way through the 60-mile waterway of the Great

Glen. In addition to sailing the length of the loch, and wildlife tours of Loch Linnhe, its Great Glen Way tour allows guests to walk up to 14-mile sections of the route each day before meeting the barge each evening at prearranged points. On board, guests can make use of mountain bikes, canoes, sailing dinghies and wind-surfers lashed to the deck. Guides and instructors are included. Cruises operate Apr-Oct and cost from £895-985 per person for the 7-day cruise. Bike & Barge and canoe tours also available.

Crannog Cruises, *Town Pier, T01397-705589, www.crannog.net*. Run trips of 1½ hrs from Mar-Oct, £15, children £7.50. Board the *Souter's Lass* in Fort William (daily 1100, 1300 and 1500) for a chance to spot local marine wildlife including seals, otters and seabirds. Also evening cruises at 1930 on Mon, Wed and Fri in Jul and Aug.

SeaXplorer, *www.seaxplorer.co.uk*. Offer thrilling RIB trips from Ballachulish, about 30 mins south of Fort William.

Canoeing
There are several good whitewater rivers around Fort William ranging in difficulty from Grade I-VI, or you can paddle the Caledonian Canal. For advice on operators and lessons, see www.canoescotland.com.

Hiking and climbing
Fort William is a mecca for hikers and climbers and boasts one of the highest concentrations of guides and instructors in the land. For information on the climb up Ben Nevis and walks around Glen Nevis, see page 198. Nevis Range offers some of the most accessible winter climbs in the country for experienced climbers. For details of the gondola ride, see page 201. If you want to hire a guide, note that the information board/staff in **Nevisport** (see Shopping, above) can provide useful advice. **Ice Factor**, the National Centre for Ice Climbing, is at Kinlochleven, see page 211.

Abacus Mountain Guides, T01397-772466, www.abacusmountainguides.com;

Alan Kimber Mountaineering, T01397-700451, www.alankimber-mountaineering.co.uk; **Alpha Mountaineering**, T07748-275825, www.alphamountaineering.co.uk; **Mountain Motion**, T01397-701731, www.mountainmotion.co.uk; **Snowgoose Mountain Centre**, see Adventure sports, above; **West Coast Mountain Guides**, T07799-863068, www.westcoast-mountainguides.co.uk.

Mountain biking

It's easy to see why Scotland is now regarded as one of the world's top mountain biking destinations. The **Leanachan Forest**, below Aonach Mhor, 3 miles north of town, covers a huge area with over 25 miles of mountain-bike trails, ranging from easy to demanding and including the (world-class) Witch's Trail. These are free cross-country routes run by the **Forestry Commission** (https://forestry.gov.uk, or www.ridefortwilliam.co.uk).

Nevis Range is also home to the 2-mile-long World Cup downhill mountain-bike course. Not for the faint-hearted or inexperienced. Bikers (over 12s) and bikes reach the top of this steep descent using the resort's gondola system (see page 201). Track open May-Sep daily 1015-1600 (subject to weather).

A more gentle alternative is the **Great Glen Cycle Route**, mainly off-road, running from Fort William to Inverness. See box, page 180. If you want to cycle this long-distance route, **Off Beat Bikes** in Fort William offer an excellent one-way bike hire service.

Offbeat Bikes, *117 High St, T01397-704008, www.offbeatbikes.com. Apr-Oct Mon-Sat 0900-1730, Sun 1000-1730; Nov-Mar Mon-Sat 0900-1730.* Bike hire, sales, repairs and advice. Adult bikes from £30 per day. Kids' and tandem bikes, helmets and armour also available. Also has outlet at the foot of the Gondola at Nevis Range, T01397-705825, May-Oct Mon-Sat 0900-1700.

Sea kayaking

Rockhopper Scotland, *2 Montrose Mansions, Corpach, T07739-837344, www.rockhopperscotland.co.uk.* Whether a beginner or expert, the friendly, fully qualified guides at Rockhopper are available for a ½-day (£45, £30 for under 16s), full-day (£80/50) or even overnight sea kayaking adventure in Ardnamurchan. Paddle down Loch Sheil, across the narrows to Ardgour or along the remote northern coastline off Glenelg with the chance to spot eagles and basking sharks. Highly recommended.

Skiing

Nevis Range Ski Centre, *see page 201.* Nevis Range hires all the snowboard and ski equipment required. You can also try **Nevisport**, High St, T01397-704921.

Swimming

Lochaber Leisure Centre, *Belford Rd, T01397-704359. Mon-Fri 0930-0900, 1230-2000 Sat-Sun 1230-1600.*

Transport

Bus

For the Fort William area check out **Stagecoach** buses, www.stagecoach.com.

Long-distance services include several daily **Citylink** buses to **Inverness**, 1 hr 50 mins; to **Oban**, 1½ hrs, via **Glencoe**, ½ hr; and to **Uig**, 3½ hrs, via **Portree** and **Kyle of Lochalsh**, 1 hr 50 mins. **Citylink** buses several times daily to **Glasgow** via **Glencoe** and **Tyndrum**, 3 hrs; and to **Edinburgh**, 4 hrs, via **Stirling**, 3 hrs. There is a bus to **Mallaig** via **Lochailort** (for **Ardnamurchan**), Mon-Sat, 1 hr 10 mins, **Shiel Buses**, T01967-431272, www.shielbuses.co.uk.

Car hire

Fort William Car Hire, at Inverlochy, T01397-701515, www.fortwilliamcarhire.com. Also campervans from £90 per day.

Ferry

There is a passenger-only ferry service to **Camusnagaul**, T07826-695160, on the opposite bank of Loch Linnhe, from the Town Pier. It sails Mon-Sat 0745-1730 and takes 10 mins, £1.80, children £0.90. The **Corran Ferry**, T01855-841243, to **Ardgour** (see page 212) is 8 miles south of Fort William, just off the A82. Throughout the year the ferry makes the 5-min crossing every 20 mins Mon-Sat 0630-2130, every 30 mins Sun from 0845. Single £8.20 per car, pedal bikes free. For further details of either ferry service look at www.lochabertransport.org.uk.

Taxi

Woody's Taxis, T01397-701066; **Lochaber Taxis**, T01397-706070.

Train

See 'Riding the rails', page 218. There are 2-3 trains daily to **Glasgow**, 3¾ hrs, via **Crianlarich**. To **Mallaig**, 1 hr 20 mins, to connect with ferries to **Armadale** on Skye. To **Oban**, daily, occasionally changing at Crianlarich. There is a sleeper service to **London Euston** (see page 466), but you'll miss the views.

Glen Nevis Colour map 3, B6.

beautiful highland glen at the foot of Britain's highest mountain

Only 10 minutes' drive from Fort William is one of Scotland's great glens, the classic Glen Nevis. If you can forget the sight of streams of campervans on the road and distant figures threading their way up the steep track towards the summit (dress appropriately) you could almost be mesmerized by the sparkling Water of Nevis as it tumbles through a wooded gorge, closed in by the steep, bracken-covered slopes of the magnificent hulk of Ben Nevis. The whole scene is both rugged and sylvan, and some may say the nearest you'll get to a Himalayan valley in the Scottish Highlands. It's not surprising, then, that this is a favourite with movie directors and has featured in films such as *Rob Roy*, *Braveheart*, *Highlander III* and *Harry Potter and the Philosopher's Stone*.

There are many walks in and around the glen, not least of which is the return trek up to the summit of Britain's highest mountain. Aside from the walks described below, there are several easy, marked forest walks which start from the car park at the **Glen Nevis Visitor Centre** ⓘ *T01397-705922, daily 0900-1700*, about half a mile up the glen. Here, you'll also find toilets and an interesting interpretive display. Pick up a leaflet here or at the **Fort William iCentre** for scenic walks around the area or check out https://forestry.gov.uk. There are buses into Glen Nevis, as far as the youth hostel, from Fort William bus station.

Ben Nevis OS Landranger No 41. Colour map 3, B6.

Every year many thousands of people make the relatively straightforward ascent of Ben Nevis, and every year a frighteningly high percentage end up injured, or lost, or dead. Don't let the infamous ascent by a Ford Model T car in 1911 fool you. It's reported an average of four people perish on the mountain every year. Whatever the figure, it's vital that anyone venturing up the Ben is appropriately dressed and equipped for the hike. It should be remembered that the weather in Scotland's mountains can change at an alarming speed. Though it may be 20°C in the Glen Nevis car park when you set off, even far from the summit you may quickly find yourself in a disorientating blizzard or hill fog. It goes without saying that you need to be well prepared. You will need a good, strong pair of boots, warm clothing, waterproofs, food and drink. You should also take a map and a compass. Allow six to eight hours for the return trip. In the winter months the top part of the mountain is covered in snow. You should not attempt the walk unless you are an experienced hill climber.

The main tourist path, built as a pony track to service the long-gone observatory on the summit, starts from the car park at Achintee Farm, on the north side of the river, reached by the road through Claggan. It climbs gradually at first across the flank of Meal an t-Suidhe, before joining the alternative path from the youth hostel. This latter route is shorter but much steeper.

The trail continues to climb steadily as it begins to follow the Red Burn, until it reaches a junction, with Lochan Meal an t-Suidhe down to the left. Here, an alternative route down from the summit heads left under the north face of the mountain (see below). This is the halfway point of the main route. The path crosses the Red Burn and then climbs by a series of long and seemingly never-ending zigzags up to a plateau. If you're tired, consider that the record for the annual 10-mile run from Fort William to the summit and back is one hour 25 minutes! The path splits in two, but both paths take you up to the summit, marked by a cairn and emergency shelter, on the ruins of the old observatory. Note that on the upper sloping plateau the path can 'disappear' in mist and snow, and some cairns and beacons have been removed by vandals masquerading as purists. If conditions deteriorate, a compass is a life-saver. There is a form of shelter on the summit but ensure you're carrying extra clothes.

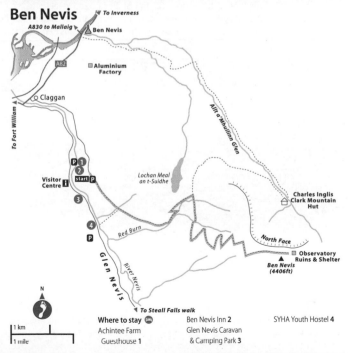

Ben Nevis

Where to stay 🛌   Ben Nevis Inn **2**   SYHA Youth Hostel **4**
Achintee Farm Guesthouse **1**   Glen Nevis Caravan & Camping Park **3**

To return, simply retrace your steps all the way. If the weather is settled enough and you have time, you can follow the alternative route below the north face. This leads right round the mountain to the Charles Inglis Clark mountain hut, then heads down into the Allt a' Mhuilinn glen, which leads all the way down to the distillery on the A82, a mile north of the town centre. Note that this route adds an extra three or four miles to the descent and should only be attempted by fit and experienced hillwalkers.

Steall Falls *OS Landranger No 41.*

A fairly easy low-level walk is to the spectacular 300-ft-high Steall Falls at the head of the glen. It's a popular walk, especially in the summer but this doesn't detract from its stunning natural beauty.

The path starts at the car park at the end of the twisty road, a few miles beyond the visitor centre. Before setting off, you might like to note the sign by the steep waterfall that cascades down to the edge of the car park. It reads 'Warning! This is not the path to Ben Nevis'. If you need to be warned against attempting to climb up Ben Nevis through a waterfall, you probably shouldn't be left alone in possession of this book, never mind let loose on the Scottish mountains. Once you've shaken your head in disbelief at the apparent mind-numbing stupidity of some of your fellow travellers, follow the track alongside the Water of Nevis. The path climbs steadily through the woods and becomes rocky, with the river thundering below through the steep gorge. It runs close to the river before emerging from the gorge and opening up into a wide, flower-filled meadow, with a high waterfall at the far end. It's a beautiful, tranquil place and ideal for a picnic. Follow the path across the valley floor until it crosses the river via a precarious bridge that consists of three ropes of thick wire in a V-shape. The path then leads to the bottom

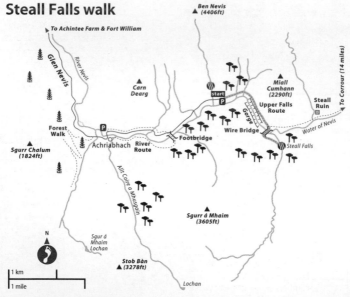

Steall Falls walk

of the falls. You can also head left at the bridge and continue up the valley to some ruins. From here the path leads to Corrour station, 14 miles away. However, it's for fit, well-prepared and experienced hillwalkers only. You can then catch a train back to Fort William. It's a very popular route, and there's even accommodation at the end of it, near the train station.

Nevis Range

T01397-705825, www.nevisrange.co.uk. Gondola open daily all year except mid-Nov to mid-Dec. Apr-Jun and Sep-Oct 1000-1700, Jul-Aug till 1800, mid-Jul to mid-Aug till 2100, winter 0900-dusk. Gondola prices: single trip return £18.50, seniors £16.50, children £10.50, under 5s free, family £50.50; day ticket £23, seniors £20.75, children £14. There is wheelchair access and guide dogs ride free.

Nevis Range, three miles north of Fort William at Torlundy, just off the A82 to Inverness, is situated on the mountain of **Aonach Mhor** (4006 ft) and is Scotland's highest skiing and snowboarding resort. The ski area is reached by Scotland's only gondola lift system and in a good season it permits skiing between Christmas and May. The 1½-mile (15-minute) ride is a popular attraction, not only with wintersport enthusiasts, but also with summer hillwalkers keen to gain easy access to the mountains. A couple of easy walks lead from the gondola station to Sgurr Finnisgaig (40 minutes) and Meal Beag (one hour), both of which offer stunning views from the top. Beside the top gondola station there's a small shop and a large self-serving **Snowgoose restaurant** (**££-£**) and **Pinemarten Café Bar** (**£**) providing fantastic vistas across Lochaber. Mountain bikers come for some truly world-class riding (see page 197).

Listings Glen Nevis *maps pages 199 and 200.*

Where to stay

Glen Nevis is excellent for camping, whilst Achintee at the start of the Ben walk has several excellent guesthouses and accommodation options.

£££-££ Achintee Farm Guesthouse
By the start of the path to Ben Nevis, T01397-702240, www.achinteefarm.com. End Apr-Oct.
Lovely setting and terrific welcome. Recommended. Also has self-catering cottage (sleeps 2) for rent all year round (£300-450 per week), and hostel (**££** in en suite apartment for 2, **£** in twin/triple).

£ Ben Nevis Inn
Above Achintee Farm; across the river and up the steep steps from the visitor centre, T01397-701227, www.ben-nevis-inn.co.uk.
An independent hostel where you'll find walkers and climbers enjoying banter, a real ale and hearty food (**££-£**) beside a roaring fire in this this 17th-century inn (see Restaurants, below). The hostel is basic and functional and a little cramped, but upstairs you'll find the best atmosphere in Fort William. Worth the walk.

£ SYHA Youth Hostel
3 miles out of town, near the start of the path up Ben Nevis, Glen Nevis, T0870-0041120, www.syha.org.uk.
Though remote, this popular hostel is an excellent choice if you plan to hike on the Ben. Book ahead.

Camping

Glen Nevis Caravan & Camping Park
2 miles up the Glen Nevis Rd, T01397-702191, www.glen-nevis.co.uk. Mid-Mar to late Oct.
Good facilities. With option to rent camping pods (sleep 2) or static caravans.

Restaurants

££ The Ben Nevis Inn
*Achintee, T01397-701227, www.ben-nevis-inn.
co.uk. Lunch served 1200-1700, evening meals
from 1700-2100.*
Yes, it's a long walk into the glen but many
of the lunch and dinner treats, including
venison, are filling and freshly prepared.
There's often live music and a generally
great atmosphere. Best in the area so be
sure to book ahead.

What to do

See under Fort William, page 196.

Glen
Coe

There are many spectacular places in the Scottish Highlands, but few, if any, can compare to the truly awesome scenery of Glen Coe. No one could fail to be moved by its haunting beauty, with imposing mountains, their tops often wreathed in cloud, rising steeply on either side from the valley floor. The brooding atmosphere of the landscape is only enhanced by the glen's tragic history. Once you've heard of the Glen Coe Massacre it sends a shiver down the spine every time you pass this way. Scotland's most famous glen is also one of its most accessible, with the A82 Glasgow to Fort William road running through it. Much of the area is owned by the National Trust for Scotland and is virtually unInhabIted, leaving huge tracts of glen and mountain which provide outstanding climbing and walking. There's also skiing at the Glencoe Mountain Resort and canoeing on the rivers Coe and Etive.

Onich and North Ballachulish *Colour map 3, B5/6.*
The A82 south from Fort William passes through tiny Onich and the Corran car ferry for Ardnamurchan before the B863 turns east at North Ballachulish and heads past the excellent **Lochleven Seafood Café** (see Restaurants, page 210) to Kinlochleven, at the head of Loch Leven.

Five miles north of the village of North Ballachulish (just south of the ferry), a turning off the A82 leads towards Inchree and **Vertical Descents** (see What to do, page 211). A moderate one-hour circular walk up to **Inchree Waterfall** begins at the car park just 100 yds past the Vertical Descents bothy following a clearly marked trail. The huge waterfall is very dramatic to the eye, particularly when it's in spate. So too are the views back towards Loch Linnhe. The path continues up past the waterfall to the forest road which leads back downhill to the car park.

Kinlochleven *Colour map 3, B6.*
Kinlochleven can also be reached on the same road from Glencoe village, seven miles west. Until the late 1990s a huge, unsightly aluminium factory dominated and was the

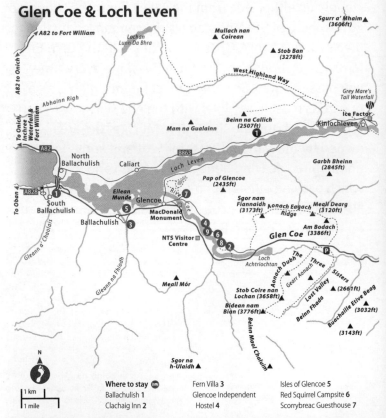

Glen Coe & Loch Leven

Where to stay 🛏
Ballachulish **1**
Clachaig Inn **2**

Fern Villa **3**
Glencoe Independent
Hostel **4**

Isles of Glencoe **5**
Red Squirrel Campsite **6**
Scorrybreac Guesthouse **7**

lifeblood of the community. Fortunately, the entrepreneurial ingenuity of a Lochaber climber has since transformed the defunct factory into **Ice Factor**, the world's largest indoor ice-climbing facility (see What to do, page 211). Industrialists can find out all about the history of aluminium-working in Kinlochleven at **The Aluminium Story** ① *Linnhe Rd, T01855-831663, Apr-Sep Mon, Wed, Fri 1000-1800, Tue, Thu 1000-2000; Oct-Mar Tue 1000-1400 and 1800-2000 Thu 1000-1400 and 1500-1700, free.*

The West Highland Way passes through the village and many walkers spend the night here before setting out on the last stretch before Fort William. There are also good walks in the surrounding hills and glens of the Mamores, a few of which are described below.

Walks around Kinlochleven *OS Landranger No 41.*
There are some relatively easy short walks from Kinlochleven up the glen of the River Leven, including the one to the impressive **Grey Mare's Tail Waterfall**. It's a short walk of under an hour, signposted from the village.

Dressed for the outdoors, a rewarding half-day walk is to follow the West Highland Way south from the village to the top of the **Devil's Staircase** (named by the 400 soldiers who had to endure severe hardship while building it in the 17th century), where it meets the A82 at the eastern end of Glen Coe. The well-signposted route begins at the wooden bridge north of **Ice Factor** and climbs gradually on a dirt jeep-track up to Penstock House, at 1000 ft. At the top, near the house, the track forks to the right and continues on a rough but well-maintained footpath to the Devil's Staircase. The path is marked with the West Highland Way thistle sign, so it's easy to follow uphill to the top of the pass (1804 ft), from where you get great views of Loch Eilde Mór and the Mamores to the north. The path then descends down the staircase to Glen Coe, with breathtaking Buachaille Etive Mór in front of you all the way. You'll have to return to Kinlochleven by the same route, or you could carry on to the **Kingshouse Hotel** (currently closed for refurbishment). The return trip from Kinlochleven should take four or five hours, or you can start out from Glencoe (see below). Before leaving, ensure you are properly equipped. This section of the West Highland Way was once part of the old military road which ran from Fort William to Stirling.

Another good hike, though more strenuous, is to **Beinn na Callich** (2507 ft). You'll need to be fairly fit as it's a steep climb; allow around six to seven hours

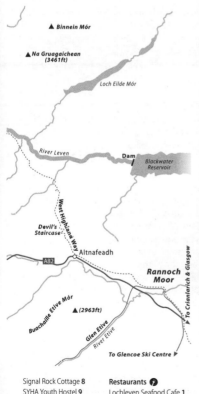

Signal Rock Cottage **8**
SYHA Youth Hostel **9**

Restaurants ⑦
Lochleven Seafood Cafe **1**

ON THE ROAD
A stab in the back

Glen Coe is probably best known as the scene of one of the most shameful and notorious incidents in Scottish history.

Following his succession to the throne, William III wanted all the clans to swear an oath of allegiance by 1 January 1692. After much hesitation, the Jacobite clans of the West Highlands agreed to do so. However, Maclain of Glencoe, chief of a small branch of the MacDonalds, was not only late in setting off on the journey, but mistakenly went to Fort William to sign, instead of Inveraray. By the time he reached Inveraray it was 6 January and the deadline had passed.

The government decided that the rebellious clan be punished in order to set an example to other clans, some of whom had not taken the oath. A company of 120 soldiers, under the command of Campbell of Glenlyon, was sent to Glen Coe and, since their leader was related by marriage to Maclain, the troops were billeted in MacDonald homes, in keeping with the long-standing Highland tradition of hospitality.

There they stayed for almost two weeks, until the cold-blooded order came through to "… put all to the sword under seventy." And so, on a cold winter's night, in the early hours of 13 February 1692, the Campbells ruthlessly slaughtered their hosts. Maclain and 37 men, women and children were slain in their beds, while many others fled into the hills, only to die of hunger and exposure. It was a bloody incident that had deep repercussions and proved to be the beginning of the end of the Highland way of life. For further information, see box, page 439.

There's a monument to the fallen MacDonalds in the village of Glencoe, where members of the clan still gather on 13 February each year. For a powerful and evocative account of the Massacre, read *Glencoe* by John Prebble (Penguin, first published 1966).

for the return trip. The route is well marked and starts from the West Highland Way footpath opposite the school, which is on the road heading northwest out of the village towards Fort William. The path climbs steeply at first, crosses the tarmac road to **Mamore Lodge**, then continues until it joins General Wade's old military road, which takes the West Highland Way on its final 11 miles to Fort William. From here, you'll see the path zigzagging up the mountain. Continue along the old military road for about 400 yds until you cross a wooden bridge. Then follow a path down to another wooden bridge, where the ground is quite boggy. Cross the bridge and the path begins to zigzag uphill until it levels out on to a plateau, before continuing relentlessly upwards through a long series of zigzags to the summit, marked by a couple of cairns and a commemorative plaque. The views from the top make the tiring climb worthwhile. You can see down on to Loch Leven, over to Glen Coe and across the magnificent Mamores.

Fit and experienced hillwalkers can access the **Mamores** from the **Mamore Lodge** road. Once you're up there you have the opportunity to bag several Munros, via a series of excellent ridge walks connecting **Am Bodach** (3386 ft) with **Stob Coire a' Chairn** (3219 ft), **Na Gruagaichean** (3461 ft), **An Gearanach** (3222 ft), **Sgor An Iubhair** (3285 ft), **Sgurr a'Mhaim** (3606 ft) and **Stob Ban** (3278 ft). These peaks and ridges can also be reached from Glen Nevis, see page 198. As well as the proper equipment, take a map and a compass.

Ballachulish *Colour map 3, B6.*

On the southern shore of Loch Leven, a mile or so west of Glencoe village on the A82, is the old slate quarrying village of Ballachulish. Aside from interpretive panels at the iCentre, there's 550 yds of wheelchair-accessible path to view the quarry and its history where for 300 years Gaelic-speaking locals toiled to excavate the slate. There are a few B&Bs and a couple of hotels close by.

Glencoe village *Colour map 3, B6.*

At the western entrance to the glen, on the shores of Loch Leven, is Glencoe village, 16 miles south of Fort William just off the A82. There are several places to stay in and around the village, as well as a post office and in stark contrast to the Spar general store next door there's also the thatched **Glencoe Folk Museum** ① *late May-Sep daily 1000-1730, £2.50*, which has collections of 17th- to 18th-century costumes, military memorabilia and, according to the owner, a chair that once belonged to none other than the Young Pretender. The most significant development in recent years has been the revamped and impressive **National Trust for Scotland Visitor Centre** ① *1 mile south of Glencoe village, T10855-811307, Mar-Oct daily 0930-1730, Nov-Feb daily 1000-11600, £6.50, concessions/children £5*. There are interesting interpretive displays, information about the area's history (including the massacre), geology, fauna and flora. During the summer, the ranger service organizes guided walks and Landrover safaris. This eco-friendly building also boasts a lovely café. There are some short, pleasant walks around **Glencoe Lochan**, an artificial loch created in the mid-19th century by Lord Strathcona for his homesick Canadian wife. From the village, cross the bridge over the River Coe, then turn left towards Scorrybreac Guesthouse. There's a choice of three walks of between 40 minutes and an hour, all detailed at the car park (or see https://forestry.gov.uk).

Climbing and hiking in Glen Coe *OS Landranger No 41.*
www.glencoemountain.com.

Glen Coe offers some of Britain's most challenging climbing and hiking, with some notoriously treacherous routes and unpredictable weather conditions that claim lives every year. The routes described below are some of the least strenuous, but you'll still need a map, good boots, warm clothing, food and water, and you should take the usual precautions, including checking on the weather forecast, see page 17.

One of the most popular walks is the relatively straightforward hike up to the **Lost Valley**, a secret glen where the ill-fated MacDonalds hid the cattle they'd stolen. Allow around four hours for the return trip. Start from the car park by the large boulder (see map), opposite the distinctive **Three Sisters**. Head down to the valley floor and follow the gravel path which leads down to a wooden bridge across the River Coe. Cross the bridge and follow the path up and over the stile. From here there's a choice of two routes. The less obvious route heads right and offers an easier climb into the valley. This eventually meets the lower, well-worn track, which involves a bit of scrambling but is more exciting as it follows the rushing waters of the **Allt Coire Gabhail**. The upper and lower paths meet a few miles further up and here you cross the river by some stepping stones. Proceed up the steep scree slope until you reach the rim of the **Lost Valley**, where many of the MacDonalds fled on the night of the infamous massacre. Once in the

Tip...
You must be equipped with good hiking boots and adequate wet-weather gear as conditions can change suddenly.

valley there are great views of Glencoe's highest peak, Bidean nam Bian ('pinnacle of the mountains') at 3776 ft, Gearr Aonach and Beinn Fhada, and you can continue for a further 50 minutes to the head of the valley. From here it's possible to climb Bidean, but you'll need to be fit, experienced and well equipped.

Glen Coe also offers one of Scotland's classic ridge walks, the **Aonach Eagach**. With potentially fatal drops, it's not for the inexperienced or faint-hearted as there are some very exposed pinnacles you must climb around. The exposed ridge runs almost the entire length of the glen, starting at **Am Bodach** and ending at **Sgor nam Fiannaidh**. Don't make the mistake of descending from the last summit straight down to the **Clachaig Inn**. Instead, take the safer marked route.

Another difficult route is to the summit of **Buachaille Etive Mór**, one of the most photographed mountains in Scotland and one you'll probably recognize immediately the first time you see it from the A82, especially on the road north up to Glencoe. The mountain is best viewed from the **Kingshouse Hotel** (currently closed for refurbishment) and the route starts from Altnafeadh, a couple of miles west of the hotel. This is also the start or finish point for the fairly easy half-day walk over the **Devil's Staircase**, which is part of the West Highland Way. For a description of the route, see page 218. **Glen Etive** runs southwest from the hotel. It's a very beautiful and little-visited place, and great for wild camping. Unfortunately, there's now no postbus so you'll need to walk in or cycle.

Glencoe Mountain Resort

T01855-851226, www.glencoemountain.com. Chairlift all year daily 0930-1700, £10, £5 children; during the winter ski season an adult day pass is £25, children £18 (£32/20 at weekends).

The **Glencoe Ski Centre** is just over a mile from the **Kingshouse Hotel**, on the other side of the A82, on **Meall a'Bhuiridh** (3636 ft). Established in 1956, it is Scotland's oldest ski centre and remains one of the best. The aptly titled Flypaper is the steepest 'black' marked piste in Scotland. In the summer months mountain bikers can enjoy all day (lift) access to its downhill course for £20.

Listings Glen Coe *map page 204.*

Where to stay

Onich and North Ballachulish

There's a wide selection of places to stay in the villages of Onich and North Ballachulish, mostly with good views of the loch. They make an attractive alternative to Fort William and you may catch sight of gannets, seals, porpoises, and even sea otters in and around Ballachulish Bay and Loch Leven.

££££ The Lodge on the Loch Hotel
Onich, T01855-821237,
www.lodgeontheloch.com.
For guests who expect that little bit extra (at a price), with some rooms (including 4-poster beds) giving views over the sea

loch. Handy for Glencoe and Fort William. Dinner served daily 1900-2130.

£££ Onich Hotel
Onich, T01855-821214,
www.onichhotel.co.uk.
Standard hotel rooms, some with loch views and a great panorama over Loch Linnhe from the conservatory. Dogs and well-behaved children welcome (or is that the other way round?).

££ Camus House
Onich, T01855-821200, www.
camushouse.co.uk. Mar-Oct.
5 rooms. Lovely Victorian guesthouse with glorious views over Loch Linnhe.

££-£ Inchree Chalets & Rooms
Inchree, on the A82 to Fort William,
T01855-821287, www.inchree.co.uk.
Buses stop 100 yds from the hostel.
Accommodation in 3 chalets for 4-6 people
(from £125 for up to 4 people)or 12 twin and
family rooms. Good facilities and on-site
pubserving lunches and evening meals
1800-2100 (££) See also Restaurants, below.
Vertical Descent (see page 211) is just up
the road.

£ The Corran Bunkhouse
6 miles south of Fort William, right by the
Corran ferry slipway off the A82, T01855-
821000, www.corranbunkhouse.co.uk.
32-bed bunkhouse with twins, family rooms
and 4- to 5-bed rooms.

Kinlochleven

£££-£ MacDonald Hotel
Fort William Rd, Kinlochleven, T01855-831539,
www.macdonaldhotel.co.uk. Year-round.
A welcoming, 10-bedroom hotel with a
Bothy bar (£) and **Purple Stag** restaurant (££)
serving reasonable food, open to residents
and campers alike. Round the back of the
hotel are 9 modern but small bunkbed-
based cabins (£) and space for 11 camping
pitches £8 per person per night. Campers
can also enjoy a full Scottish breakfast.
Dogs welcome (£5).

££ Tigh-na-Cheo Guest House
Garbhein Rd, Kinlochleven, T01855-831434,
www.tigh-na-cheo.co.uk.
9 rooms, 1 on the ground floor. Friendly,
with a superb outlook over Loch Leven
and the Mamores. Very close to **Ice
Factor** and the West Highland Way.

£ Blackwater Hostel & Campsite & West Highland Lodge
Lab Rd, Kinlochleven, T01855-831253,
www.blackwaterhostel. co.uk.
Based in a row of old stone cottages,
Blackwater is a friendly, well-run backpackers'
hostel, with 10 en suite rooms of varying
sizes. West Highland Lodge consists of 8

4-bed rooms with shared bathrooms. The
campsite has 25 pitches (£10 per night), and
there are glamping pods for 2 or 4 people
(££-£), no bedding provided but is available
for hire at £5 per person. The **Ice Factor** is
only 200 yds away and the West Highland
Way is at your feet.

Ballachulish
As well as one of the most historic hotels in
Scotland, there's a wide selection of cheaper
B&Bs and guesthouses in the village.

££££-£££ The Isles of Glencoe Hotel
T01764-651843, www.islesofglencoe.co.uk.
39 rooms. A modern hotel and leisure
complex adjacent to Lochaber. Lovely sea
views from the 'top-deck' bedrooms whilst
families will enjoy the excellent facilities,
including heated pool, sauna and outdoor
adventure play area. The restaurant (££) is
open for lunch from 1200 and dinner (£££)
from 1830-2130.

£££ Ballachulish Hotel
South Ballachulish by the bridge, T01764-
651842, www.ballachulishhotel.co.uk.
54 rooms. With a touch of tartan, the rooms
are tasteful with some affording stunning
loch views. However, it's the **Bulas Bar
& Bistro** (££) that attracts many. Try its
daily *bulas* (Gaelic pot) creations, including
venison, and seafood pie using fresh, locally
sourced produce. Price includes free use of
pool and sauna In their sister hotel, **The Isles
of Glencoe**.

££ Fern Villa
T01855-811393, www.fernvilla.org.uk.
5 en suite rooms. Very comfortable and
good-value guesthouse.

Glencoe village
There are several B&Bs and guesthouses in
the village and quite a few options around. At
the time of writing the legendary **Kingshouse
Hotel**, at the east end of the glen, almost
opposite the turn-off to the **Glencoe Ski
Centre**, is closed for refurbishment.

£££ Clachaig Inn
About 3 miles south just off the A82 on the old 'B' road that winds back to the village, T01855-811252, www.clachaig.com.
Good-value accommodation in the Ossian wing, the more modern Bidean wing or the Lodge. Popular haunt for walkers. The legendary **Boots** bar boasts real ales, including those from Kinlochleven's erstwhile **Atlas Brewery** (now brewed in Orkney), live music and hearty pub grub (**££-£**) served 1200-2100, including wild boar sandwiches. There is also the quieter **Snug** and less rough and ready **Bidean Lounge**.

££ Scorrybreac Guesthouse
1 mile from Glencoe village, T01855-811354, www.scorrybreacglencoe.co.uk.
5 rooms. Simple, unfussy and comfortable accommodation in an acre of grounds. Lovely location and good-value guesthouse.

££-£ Signal Rock Cottage
2½ miles from Glencoe village down the old road, T01855-811295, www.signalrockcottage.com.
2 rooms. This timber-clad B&B is set amidst the trees in 50 acres of land and renowned for its green credentials. Also self-catering cottage. Secluded but worth the walk. 2-night minimum stay at weekends.

£ Glencoe Independent Hostel
Near the SYHA Youth Hostel, T01855-811906, www.glencoehostel.co.uk.
This is a basic but friendly bunkhouse complete with open fire. It's a 10- to 15-min walk for food or a pint at the **Clachaig Inn**. Also has more salubrious accommodation in eco-cabins (**££**) and log cabins (**££-£**).

£ SYHA Youth Hostel
On the same road as Clachaig Inn, about 2 miles from the village, T01855-811219.
Excellent hostel very popular with cyclists and climbers. Book ahead.

Camping

Glencoe Camping and Caravanning Club Site
T01855-811397. Mar-Oct.
At the westernmost edge of Glencoe village with views down the loch towards Ballachulish.

Red Squirrel Campsite
T01855-811256. Open year-round.
If walking south from Glencoe village on the 'B' road, you'll reach this modest campsite after the hostels further along the road.

Restaurants

Onich and North Ballachulish

££ Four Seasons Pub & Restaurant
Part of Inchree Chalets and Rooms (see Where to stay, above), T01855-821393. Daily.
A friendly and informal place that produces good food and attracts a fun-loving outdoor crowd.

££ Lochleven Seafood Café
4½ miles along the B863 from North Ballachulish, T01855-821048, www.lochlevenseafood cafe.co.uk. May-Oct daily lunch 1200-1500, dinner 1800-2100 and snack menu 1430-1600.
Superb, mouth-watering and excellent. The seafood at this simple but stylish restaurant is unrivalled. Feast on oysters, scallops, langoustines, lobster, crab and razor clams fresh from live tanks, or try their gargantuan seafood platter (£40 for 1). There are non-fishy treats too but as the latest catch in the tanks highlights, affordable tasty seafood is the star attraction. Book ahead. Recommended.

Kinlochleven

££-£ Chillers Bar and Grill
Ice Factor, Kinlochleven, T01855-831100. Daily 1100-late, food till 2100.
A hip, post-climb gathering place with a good restaurant menu, including venison and Loch Leven shellfish, tasty bar snacks,

and refreshing real ales on tap. There is a wonderful wood-burning stove, the chance to watch fellow climbers on the walls and enjoy the view of Loch Leven and the Mamores.

£ Riverside Chippy
Riverside Rd, Kinlochleven, opposite the Tail Race Inn. Open all year.
Proudly proclaims to be the West Highland Way's only chip shop. Great portions.

Glencoe village
For eating options, refer to Where to stay, above.

Shopping

Glen Coe village
Crafts
Crafts and Things, *in a delightful old whitewashed croft at the northern end of Glencoe village. Daily 0900-1700.* Has expanded to offer both an array of woollens, crafts and excellent home-baking and light bites (£) in its homely café (open 0930-1700).

What to do

Glen Coe and Loch Leven
Climbing
For advice, contact the **Mountaineering Council of Scotland** (MCofS) on T01738-493942, www.mountaineering-scotland.org.uk. **Ice Factor**, *Kinlochleven, T01855-831100, www.ice-factor.co.uk. Mon, Wed, Fri-Sun 0900-1800, Tue and Thu 0900-2200.* Housed in a former aluminium smelter, the world's largest indoor ice-climbing facility is truly spectacular. A giant refrigerated toy-box for anyone in search of vertical fun, over 500 tons of snow are packed onto the 15-m-high vertical walls, which simulate as closely as possible outdoor conditions. There are also 15-m-high rock-climbing walls, a bouldering area, a well-stocked equipment shop and even a sauna and steam room, before you reflect on your day in the **Chillers Bar and Grill** upstairs (see Restaurants, above). Daily rates vary

according to the activity, with beginners only permitted to climb under instruction or expert supervision. Call for rates and times. **Ice Factor**'s professional climbing staff also run outdoor mountaineering and climbing courses. See also What to do in Fort William, page 196, for a list of recommended climbing guides.

Golf
Dragon's Tooth Golf Course, *Ballachulish, www.dragonstoothgoldclub.co.uk.* This challenging and scenic 9-hole golf course is open to the general public.

Snowsports
Glencoe Ski Centre is the oldest resort in Scotland and has pistes suitable for beginners and experts. The Flypaper is reportedly the steepest black-marked run in Scotland and is definitely for experts only. It affords stunning views southwards over Glencoe. There is also a small café (winter only) above the first chairlift.

Watersports and other activities
Vertical Descents, *Inchree Falls, Onich, T01397-747111, www.verticaldescents.com.* There are many excellent outdoor adventure operators in Scotland – this is one of them. Offers canyoning, whitewater rafting and funyakking, amongst others. Also offer a range of stag and hen packages.

Transport

Glen Coe and Loch Leven
Bus
Stagecoach runs Mon-Sat approximately every hr, Sun 3 times, between **Kinlochleven** and **Fort William**, 50 mins. En route these (No 44) buses stop at **Onich** for the Corran Ferry. They also stop at **Glencoe Junction** (the southern edge of the village). You can also catch the **Scottish Citylink** service to **Glasgow**, which leaves Fort William 4 times a day and reaches **Glencoe village** after 2½ hrs.

West of
Fort William

West of Fort William lie some of Britain's most extravagantly scenic landscapes and some of its most remote places. From southernmost Morvern, through the ruggedly handsome Ardnamurchan Peninsula, across the evocatively named 'Road to the Isles', through the haunting and tragic 'Rough Bounds' and on to the hopelessly isolated and utterly wild lands of Knoydart, this is serious wilderness, with little pockets of accessible and user-friendly Highlands thrown in for good measure.

Ardgour, Morvern and Ardnamurchan *Colour map 3, B3/4/5.*

rugged mountains, wild moorland and sparkling beaches of white sand

This lonely, southwestern corner features a dramatic landscape of rugged mountains, ancient forest, wild moorland and near-deserted glens, fringed by a coastline of sparkling white beaches and clear turquoise seas with wonderful views across to the isles of Mull, the Small Isles and Skye. This is one of the least-populated areas in Britain, mainly due to the legacy of the Highland Clearances in the mid-19th century, when whole communities were evicted by landlords in favour of more profitable sheep. Today, the issue is more finding people willing to stay year-round instead of leaving villages like Kilchoan with all too many homes run only as seasonal self-catering or second home hideaways. With so few people around, the whole peninsula is a haven for a huge variety of birds and animals, such as deer, pine martens, wildcats and eagles. If you have both the time and the energy, it's worth exploring by car, foot or even kayak (see What to do, page 217) and there are myriad (Forestry Commission Scotland) footpaths to explore. However, distances can be deceptive and, if driving, ensure you've enough fuel.

Ardgour *Colour map 3, B5.*

The name Ardgour means 'height of the goats', and you can still see feral goats in this huge, sparsely populated wilderness bordered by Loch Shiel, Loch Eil, Loch Linnhe and Loch Sunart. Access is via the A861 south from Kinlocheil, or on the Corran Ferry from Onich.

The attractive little village of **Strontian** on the shores of Loch Sunart gave its name to the element strontium, which was first discovered in the nearby lead mines in 1790.

These now-abandoned mines also produced most of the lead shot used in the Napoleonic wars. Strontian is the largest settlement in these parts and has a small grocery shop, post office and petrol pumps. One mile north of the village is the **Ariundle Nature Reserve**, which offers a pleasant two-hour nature trail through the glen and a 40-minute forest walk. It's all well signposted and there's a café/bistro.

Morvern *Colour map 3, B4.*

Just east of Strontian the A884 leads south through the dramatic, wildlife rich landscape of Morvern to the tiny remote community of **Lochaline** on the Sound of Mull, departure point for the CalMac ferry to Fishnish. About three miles before Lochaline is the turning left for the track which leads down the side of Loch Aline to the 14th-century ruins of **Ardtornish Castle**. First you'll come to **Kinlochaline Castle** (keys available at the cottage) and **Ardtornish House**. This house stands on the site of the original house, which was visited on several occasions by Florence Nightingale, who was a family member of the original owners. The author John Buchan spent many summers here in the 1930s. There's a path which leads from the estate office uphill across open moorland for an hour until it reaches **Loch Tearnait**. In the centre of the loch is a 1500-year-old crannog, an artificial island built for defensive purposes. This walk is detailed in the tourist board's leaflet, along with the Ariundle Nature Trail (see above). During the stalking season (1 July to 20 October) check at the estate office before setting out on the walk to the Loch.

Essential Ardgour, Ardnamurchan and Morvern

Getting around

Once you leave the A830 Fort William to Mallaig road, buses are few and far between, so it's not easy to get around quickly without your own transport. You'll need your own transport to reach Ardnamurchan Point and Sanna Bay as there are no buses beyond Kilchoan. If driving, note most of the roads are single-track. If you're travelling by car, access is via the A861, leaving the A830 before Glenfinnan or at Lochailort. You can also make the ferry crossing to Ardgour on the Corran Ferry, about eight miles south of Fort William on the A82, see page 198. Throughout the year the ferry makes the five-minute crossing every 20 minutes Monday-Saturday 0630-2130, every 30 minutes on Sunday 0845-2130. Single £8.20 per car, pedal bikes free. For further details look at www.lochabertransport. org.uk. See also Transport, page 217.

Tourist information

The website www.ardnamurchan.com, has lots of information on walks, as well as local events and attractions. Also worth looking at is www.moidart.com and www.walkhighlands.co.uk is good for walking route suggestions. OS Explorer Maps 383, 390 and 391 cover the entire region. See also What to do, page 217.

Ardnamurchan Peninsula and Moidart *Colour map 3, B3/4.*

The main places of interest in this area are to be found on the rugged Ardnamurchan Peninsula (from the Gaelic *Aird nam Murchan*, meaning 'Point of the High Seas'), the end of which is the most westerly point on the British mainland. The winding A861 runs west from Strontian along the north shore of Loch Sunart to **Salen**, where the single-track B8007 branches west and runs all the way out to the tip of the peninsula. The A861 meanwhile turns north and twists and turns along a spectacular single-track road to Acharacle.

The first settlement as you head west out to Ardnamurchan Point is **Glenborrodale**. Before you reach the tiny hamlet look out on the left for the castellated late-Victorian towers of **Glenborrodale Castle**, once the property of a certain Jesse Boot, who founded a chain of chemist shops which you may have heard of.

A few miles west of Glenborrodale is Scotland's greenest whisky distillery, the **Adelphi Distillery** ⓘ *T01972-500285, www.adelphidistillery.com. 45-min tours daily except Sat every hour, from £7 per person.* It only opened in 2014, so their own spirit has not yet matured but you can reserve your very own cask, if you can wait that long.

Just west of here is the excellent **Nadurra Centre** ⓘ *T01972-500209, www. nadurracentre.co.uk, Apr-Oct Mon-Sat 1030-1730, Sun 1130-1700, Nov-Mar Tue-Fri 1000-1530, Sun 1130-1530,* which should be on the list of everyone with the faintest interest in the peninsula's wildlife and nature – for which Ardnamurchan is renowned. The 'Living Building' with turf on the roof and bark on the floor ensures you will see birds and animals (including pine martens) up close, whilst the interactive displays are both fun and informative for all ages. It's a good place for kids and a life-saver when the weather is just too bad to venture outside. There's a good little Lochview **Tearoom** (£) serving home-baking and light lunches, and a decent gift shop. A mile to the east is the **RSPB Reserve** where you can see golden eagles, otters and seals. You can take a two-hour wildlife trip to the seal colonies – or further afield to Tobermory on Mull or Staffa and the Treshnish Islands (see What to do, page 217). A few miles west of the centre, the B8007 turns away from the coast. Here you'll see the beautiful bay of **Camas nan Geall** (bay of the stranger or pledge, the precise meaning is unclear). It's worth stopping at the car park to admire the fantastic views, or take the path down to the beach. Between Glenborrodale and Kilchoan, a road runs to the north coast of the peninsula and the beautiful beaches at **Fascadale**, **Kilmory** and **Ockle**.

The straggling crofting village of **Kilchoan** is the main settlement on Ardnamurchan. Shortly after passing the sign for the village, you can turn left to the scenic ruin of **Mingary Castle**, built around the 13th century. For local tourist information try the **Community Centre** ⓘ *Pier Rd, T01972-510771, Easter-Oct daily,* which provides information on local scenic walks and will help with accommodation. Beyond Kilchoan the road leads to the lighthouse at mainland Britain's most westerly point, with stunning views (on a clear day) across to the small isles of Rùm, Eigg, Muck and Canna, with the Cuillins of Skye rising behind Rùm. The former (36 m high) lighthouse was designed by Alan Stevenson, father of Robert Louis, and built in 1849. The buildings have been converted into the **Ardnamurchan Lighthouse Visitor Centre** ⓘ *T01972-510210, www.ardnamurchanlighthouse.com, tours every half-hour Apr-Oct daily 1100-1600, £6, children £4,* where you can learn about the history and workings of lighthouses and climb to the top of the tower (152 steps). There's self-catering accommodation, a café (open 1000-1700) and gift shop.

A mile northwest of Kilchoan a road branches to the right to the beautiful long, white beach at **Sanna Bay**. It's worth making the trip here just to walk on the beach, but this is also a good place to spot whales and dolphins. On the road to Sanna Bay is the tiny settlement of **Achnaha**, which is famed for its rare 'ring-dyke' system, a huge, natural rock formation which is the crater of an extinct volcano.

North of Salen on the A861 is the scattered crofting township of **Acharacle**, at the western end of Loch Shiel surrounded by rolling hills. The village has several shops, a post office, garage and plenty of places to stay. A couple of miles to the west a road leads to beautiful **Kentra Bay**. Cross the wooden bridge, follow the footpath round the side of Kentra Bay and then follow the signs for Gortenfearn, where you'll find the famous 'singing sands'. Not only is the beach music to the ears as you walk its length, but the view across to Skye and the Small Isles is a feast for the eyes.

Three miles north of Acharacle is **Loch Moidart**. Here, perched on a rocky promontory in the middle of the loch, is the 13th-century ruin of **Castle Tioram** (pronounced 'Cheerum'), one of Scotland's best-loved castle ruins. This was the seat of the MacDonalds of Clanranald, until it was destroyed by their chief in 1715 to prevent it from falling into Hanoverian hands while he was away fighting for the Jacobites. There are plans to restore the castle, but you can visit it (free) via the sandy causeway that connects it to the mainland at low tide. You can paddle the seal rich, crystal-clear waters in the **Sound of Arisaig** with **Rockhopper Seakayaking** (see Fort William What to do, page 196). The A861 follows the shores of Loch Moidart, into the region of the same name, before joining the A830 Fort William to Mallaig road at **Lochailort**.

Listings Ardgour, Morvern and Ardnamurchan

Where to stay

Ardgour

££££ Kilcamb Lodge Hotel
Strontian, T01967-402257, www. kilcamblodge.co.uk. Mid-Feb to Dec.
This luxurious Victorian country house standing in its own grounds just north of Strontian on the shores of Loch Sunart has its own private beach. The perfect bolthole, with only the occasional otter or eagle to disturb the peace, also serves superb food in its award-winning **Seafood Restaurant** and **Driftwood Brasserie** (**£££**). They also love dogs.

£££ The Inn at Ardgour
Ardgour, next to Corran Ferry, 9 miles from Fort William, T01855-841225, www.ardgour.biz.
12 en suite rooms. Small hotel dating from 1746. Cosy, lively bar with a fine selection of malts and good-value lunches and dinners. Good choice for walkers, with lovely views. Recommended.

£££-££ Strontian Hotel
Strontian, T01967-402029, www.thestrontianhotel.co.uk.
Fabulous 18th-century inn that looks right down Loch Sunart. Opportunities to spot seals and otters, fish, dine or simply relax in one of 6 comfortable bedrooms.

Breathtaking views over the sea loch from its **Dungallans** restaurant or **Bothy Bar** (**££-£**). Also has an apartment for weekly rent for up to 3 people (£110 per night).

££ Heatherbank
Upper Scotstown, Strontian, T01967-402394, www.heatherbankbb.co.uk. Easter-Oct.
6 en suite rooms. Modern house with great views to the Ardgour hills. Comfortable rooms and spacious guest lounge with log fire. Discounts for longer stays. Will provide packed lunch for £5.50 pp.

Ardnamurchan Peninsula and Moidart

££££-£££ Meall Mo Chridhe
Kilchoan, T01972-510238, www. westcoastscotland.co.uk. Year-round.
A beautiful 3-bedroom 17th-century converted manse set in over 40 acres with great sea views and fine cooking. Dinner available for non-residents (**£££**), but booking essential.

£££ Kilchoan House Hotel
Kilchoan, T01972-510200, www.kilchoanhotel.co.uk.
7 en suite rooms including a large family room. Comfortable option with views of Mull from most of the rooms. Good meals are served 1200-1400 and 1800-2030, in the bar or dining room (**££**). Excellent wine list. Very pet friendly.

£££ Loch Shiel Hotel

Acharacle, T01967-431224,
www.lochshielhotel.

8 en suite rooms, 4 of which have loch views. Comfortable hotel serving good food in the restaurant (££) or the lively bar which is open till 1200 (0100 at weekends) and often features live music.

£££ Mingarry Park Luxury Accommodation & Restaurant

Mingarry, near Acharacle, T01967-431202,
www.mingarryparkhouse.co.uk.

Top-notch accommodation in junior suites, superior rooms, standard rooms or a luxury apartment. Also has a very fine restaurant serving dinner (££) Tue-Sun 1830-2130. Recommended.

£££-££ Glenuig Inn

Glenuig, by Loch Ailort, T01687-470219,
www.glenuig.com.

18th-century inn that has undergone extensive renovation. 6 comfortable en suite rooms or bunkhouse accommodation for £30 (including breakfast) per person per night. Reasonable lunches and dinners (including lamb and fish) served in the inn's restaurant 1200-2100. Good bar and terrific views of the loch. Owner is a keen sea kayaker and has links with local operators. Great area to spot seals and basking sharks.

Self-catering

Feorag House

Glenborrodale, T01972-500248,
www.feorag.co.uk.

Great views out to sea from 2 lovely, secluded cottages set in 13 acres of grounds. Fabulous opportunities to spot wildlife and enjoy a true escape from the daily stresses of urban life.

Glenmore Holidays

Port An Aiseig, Glenborrodale, T01972-500254, www.holidayardnamurchan.co.uk.

Luxury self-catering cottages and lodges on the shores of Loch Sunart. Facilities include whirlpool baths and sauna. Choose from

Glenmore House, Glenmore Cottage, Otter Lodge, Apen Lodge or The Seashell (sleeps 2) Available all year, from £875-1325 per week in high season.

Camping

Branault Croft Caravans

Achateny by Acharacle, T01972-510284. Apr-Oct.

Offers 3 static (luxury) caravans on a working croft at the northern edge of the peninsula. A peaceful escape and ideal for young children, with acres of space to play in and explore. Lovely views across the sea towards Eigg and Skye.

Resipole Farm Holiday Park

1 mile or so east of Salen, Resipole, T01967-431235, www.resipole.co.uk.

Self-catering chalets, caravan and tent pitches, as well as caravans for rent. Also has a restaurant and bar on site. Fantastic views over the sea. Gets busy but highly recommended.

Restaurants

Ardgour

£££-££ The Inn at Ardgour

T01855-841225, www.ardgour.biz.

Family-run, atmospheric inn serving good-value bar food, full à la carte menu and takeaway snacks. Dogs and children welcome. Informal dining with fantastic sea views. Recommended.

££ Ariundle Centre

Strontian, T01967-402279. Daily 0900-1730.

Licensed tearoom/restaurant serving soups, salads and snacks. Also has bunkhouse accommodation in 2- to 4-bed rooms (£).

Morvern

£££ Whitehouse

Lochaline, T01967-421777, www. thewhitehouserestaurant.co.uk. Tue-Sat from 1100, lunch from 1200 and dinner 1800-2100.

Superb restaurant serving the very finest local organic produce. Choose 6 tapas-style dishes for the full dining experience, or 2-course lunch for £20. Excellent selection of whiskies and ales.

Ardnamurchan Peninsula and Moidart
All the hotels listed under Where to stay serve good food.

What to do

Ardnamurchan, Ardnamurchan and Morvern
Boat trips
Ardnamurchan Charters, *T01972-500208, www.west-scotland-marine.com*. Offers a 2-hr wildlife trip to the seal colonies – or further afield to Tobermory on Mull or Staffa and the Treshnish Islands. Also arranges self-catering holidays.

Sea kayaking
Rockhopper Scotland, *based in Fort William (see page 197)*. Offer sea-kayaking adventures in Ardnamurchan. Highly recommended.

Ardgour, Ardnamurchan and Morvern
Bus
Shiel Buses, T01967-431272, www.shielbuses.co.uk, run most of the bus services. There's a bus once a day on Tue, Thu and Sat to **Fort William** from **Lochaline**, 2 hrs. There's a bus twice a day, Tue-Fri (once on Mon and Sat) to **Fort William** from **Acharacle**, 1½ hrs, via Lochailort. There's a bus, if you are very patient and super organized, to **Fort William** from **Kilchoan**, Mon-Sat, 2 hrs 25 mins, via **Glenuig**, 1 hr; **Acharacle**, 1 hr 20; and **Glenborrodale**, 2 hrs. There's also a service Mon-Fri to **Fort William** from **Kilchoan**, 2½ hrs, via **Ardgour** and **Salen**.

Ferry
For details of the ferry from Lochaline to **Fishnish** on Mull and from Kilchoan to **Tobermory**, see page 86.

★ Road to the Isles
one of Scotland's most beautiful stretches of coastline

The Road to the Isles, the 46-mile stretch of the A830 from Fort William to Mallaig, runs through a series of magnificent glens before emerging on a coastline of vanilla-coloured beaches and sinuous bays backed by machair and washed by turquoise seas, with views across to Rùm, Eigg and the Cuillins of Skye. This is also the route followed by the West Highland Railway (see box, page 218), frequently hailed as one of the great railway journeys in the world. Either way – by road or rail – this is a beautiful journey, through a landscape that resonates with historical significance. For this is Bonnie Prince Charlie country, where the ill-fated Jacobite Rising began, and ended with the Prince's flight to France.

Glenfinnan *Colour map 3, B5.*
Some 17 miles west of Fort William, at the head of Loch Shiel, is Glenfinnan, a kind of single-malt distillation of Highland beauty. A grand monument marks the spot where Bonnie Prince Charlie raised the Jacobite standard in 1745 (see box, page 218). It was erected in 1815 by Alexander MacDonald of Glenaladale in memory of the clansmen who fought and died for the Prince. You can climb to the top (mind your head, though) for even better views down the loch. There's a powerful sense of history here and as you gaze across eerie Loch Shiel stretching into the distance, veiled by steep mountains, you can almost hear the wail of the bagpipes in the distance, through the mist. On the other side of the road is the **National Trust for Scotland Visitor Centre** ① *T01397-722250, Apr-Oct*

★ Riding the rails

Running from Glasgow to Mallaig via Fort William, the **West Highland Railway** is only 164 miles long but is widely acknowledged as one of the most scenic railway journeys in the world. The great thing about this journey is its variety, taking you from the distinctive red tenements of Glasgow and the former ship-building areas of the River Clyde, to the windy wilderness of Rannoch Moor and the chilly splendour of the hills. It's about an hour after leaving Glasgow that you get your first taste of Highland scenery when the train hugs the eastern bank of sinewy Loch Long. Then it's on past the 'bonnie banks' of Loch Lomond, Britain's largest body of inland water. It's impossible not to pass this serene loch without thinking of the famous ballad about two Jacobite soldiers captured after the '45 rebellion. The soldier taking 'the low road' is due to be executed, his companion taking the 'high road' is due to be released.

After Ardlui, at the top of Loch Lomond, the countryside gets more rugged. Wherever you look you see something of interest: a waterfall, a buzzard surfing on the breeze, perhaps a herd of Highland cattle wallowing in a river.

The **West Highland Way**, the long-distance footpath from Glasgow to Fort William, is close to the line now and at stations such as Crianlarich, Upper Tyndrum and Bridge of Orchy you can often spot footsore walkers with muddy boots – who get on the train looking slightly guilty and collapse on their seats with sighs of relief.

The landscape gets wilder and bleaker as the railway crosses the lonely, peaty wastes of Rannoch Moor and on to Corrour, which featured in the film version of

---

daily 1000-1700, Jul and Aug 0930-1700, £3.50, concessions £2.50, which has displays and an audio programme of the Prince's campaign, from Glenfinnan to its grim conclusion at Culloden. The Glenfinnan Games are held here in mid-August.

A mile away, in Glenfinnan village, is the **Station Museum** ① T01397-722295, May-Oct daily 0900-1700, other times by appointment, £1, which is housed in the railway station on the magnificent Fort William to Mallaig railway line. It has displays of memorabilia from the line's 100-year history as well as the Viaduct Tour which allows you to get up close and personal with the famous construction. The 1000-ft span of the **Glenfinnan Viaduct**, between the visitor centre and the village, is one of the most spectacular sections of the famous West Highland Railway, see box, above. You can also sleep and eat here (see below). A few years ago, scientific imaging proved that contrary to reports, a horse and cart were not entombed in the concrete foundations of the Glenfinnan Viaduct following an accident during its building. However, it did prove the horse and cart lie encased under the Loch nan Uamh Viaduct.

About 10 miles west of Glenfinnan the road passes through the tiny village of **Lochailort**, complete with the pleasant **Lochailort Inn** and where the A861 branches south to the remote Ardnamurchan Peninsula, see above. A couple of miles further on, is **Loch nan Uamh**, where Prince Charles first landed on the Scottish mainland (he first landed on Eriskay in the Outer Hebrides) and from where, a year later, he fled for France following the disastrous defeat at Culloden, see box, page 172. A path leads down from the car park to the Prince's Cairn, which marks the beginning and the end of the Jacobite cause.

Irvine Welsh's cult book *Trainspotting*. Then you descend to the lusher country around Tulloch, before pulling in to Fort William. Now comes the most spectacular part of the journey. Leaving Fort William, the train crosses Thomas Telford's Caledonian Canal – where you can see an impressive series of eight locks known as 'Neptune's Staircase' – hugs the shore of Loch Eil, then crosses the magnificent Glenfinnan Viaduct, a masterpiece in concrete. You soon get superb views of the evocative Glenfinnan Monument that commemorates the start of the 1745 rebellion, before pulling in to Glenfinnan Station. The train now takes you through a landscape of craggy hills and glacial lochs etched with birch and pine trees. You pass Loch nan Uamh, from where Bonnie Prince Charlie fled for France after his defeat at Culloden, then draw in to Arisaig, the birthplace of the man who inspired RL Stevenson's Long John Silver. Next is beautiful Loch Morar, Britain's deepest inland loch and home – so legend has it – to a mysterious monster. Soon you get great views across the water to the craggy islands of Eigg and Rùm, before finally pulling in to the port of Mallaig.

From April to October a steam locomotive, the *Jacobite*, makes the journey between Fort William and Mallaig, departing Fort William at 1015 Monday to Friday, arriving in Mallaig at 1225, and departing Mallaig at 1410 to arrive back in Fort William at 1600. Between mid-May and mid-September there is an additional service departing Fort William at 1430, arriving Mallaig 1630, and departing Mallaig at 1840, to arrive in Fort William at 2025. A day return costs 35, children £20, first-class return £59, children £32. For further information, contact **West Coast Railways**, T01524-737751, www.westcoastrailways.co.uk.

Arisaig and Morar *Colour map 3, A4.*

At the western end of the Morar Peninsula is the little village of Arisaig, scattered around the head of a sheltered bay with An Sgurr's knobbly peak peering above the narrow mouth. The village has sleeping and eating options, as well as a post office, general store (with ATM) and doctor's surgery and is a useful service centre for the many self-catering cottages and caravans that line this stretch of coastline. There are some nice beaches around, and the road west from the village out to the **Rhue Peninsula** is great for seal spotting. You can also take a cruise from Arisaig to the islands of Rùm, Eigg and Muck, see What to do, page 221.

Arisaig was the birthplace of Long John Silver, who worked on the construction of the nearby lighthouse at Barrahead, one of many designed by the father of Robert Louis Stevenson who met Silver and was so impressed that he immortalized him in his classic *Treasure Island*.

The main A830 bypasses Arisaig on its way to Mallaig, while a wiggly single-track road hugs the coast and heads north, past the golf course and on past beautiful Camusdarach beach (which featured in the film *Local Hero*) before joining the main road by the tiny village of Morar. A single-track road leads up behind the village of Morar to dark, mysterious **Loch Morar**, the deepest inland loch in the country and home of Morag, Scotland's other, lesser-known, but more attractive (according to the locals) monster. Two locals reported seeing her in August 1969 and a scientific investigation two years later uncovered a remarkable number of eye-witness accounts. You could always try to elicit further information from the locals over a wee dram in the bar of the **Morar Hotel**.

ON THE ROAD
Raising standards

It all started on 19 August 1745 at Glenfinnan, 19 miles west of Fort William at the head of Loch Shiel. Less than a month earlier, Prince Charles Edward Stuart had landed on the Scottish mainland for the first time, on the shores of Loch nan Uamh, between Lochailort and Arisaig. He had come to claim the British throne for his father, James, son of the exiled King James VII of Scotland and II of England.

The clan chiefs had expected French support, but when the Prince arrived with only a handful of men they were reluctant to join the cause. Undeterred, the prince raised his standard and his faith was soon rewarded when he heard the sound of the pipes and Cameron of Lochiel, along with 800 men, came marching down the valley to join them. It must have been an incredible moment.

The road runs along the north shore of the loch for three miles until it reaches the pretty little hamlets of **Bracora** and **Bracorina**. Here the road stops, but a footpath continues all the way to **Tarbet** on the south shores of Loch Nevis, from where it's possible to catch a boat back to Mallaig, see Transport, page 222. It takes about three hours to walk to Tarbet – where there's now a bothy – and you'll need to get there by 1530 for the boat.

Mallaig Colour map 3, A4.

The end of the road – and railway line – is Mallaig, a busy fishing port and main departure point for ferries to Skye. It's a no-nonsense, workmanlike place, with little in the way of worthwhile diversions, but there are decent facilities and at least the train and bus stations and CalMac ferry office are all within a few yards of each other. Also close by are banks with ATMs and the post office.

Beside the train station is the **Mallaig Heritage Centre** ⓘ *T01687-462085, Mar and Apr Mon-Thu 1200-1600, free; May, Jun and Oct Mon-Sat 1100-1600, Jul-Sep daily 1100-1800, £2.50, concession £2 under 16s free*, with interesting descriptions of the local Clearances, the railway line and the fishing industry.

Listings Road to the Isles

Where to stay

Glenfinnan

££££-£££ Glenfinnan House Hotel
Off the main road, T01397-722235, www.glenfinnan house.com. Mar-Oct.
17 en suite rooms. Charming house dating back to mid-1700s with fabulous bedrooms, lovely meals in the '45 Restaurant (£££) or the cosy hotel bar where you can enjoy a roaring fire and some local folk music. Has won more awards than you could shake a fiddle bow at, including Country House Hotel of 2017. Recommended.

££££-£££ The Prince's House
Main road, ½ mile past monument on the right, heading west, T01397-722246, www.glenfinnan.co.uk. Mar-Nov.
9 en suite rooms. Comfortable old coaching inn dating from the 17th century which offers plush rooms (their 4-poster room is **££££**) and good food in the restaurant or less formal stage **House Bistro** (£££-££).

£ Glenfinnan Sleeping Car
At the train station, T01397-722295, www.glenfinnanstationmuseum.co.uk.

Bunkhouse accommodation for up to 10 people. £5 per person extra for bedding and towels. Exclusive hire of whole car for £520 per week or £130 per night. You can eat here in the **Glenfinnan Dining Car** (**££-£**, T01397-722300).

Arisaig and Morar

£££ The Old Library Lodge
Arisaig, T01687-450651, www.oldlibrary. co.uk. Apr-Oct.
6 en suite rooms, well-furnished, 2 with sea views, 4 with patios overlooking garden. Lovely food in restaurant (**£££**). Recommended.

£££-££ Arisaig Hotel
Arisaig, I01687-450210, www.arisaighotel. co.uk. Open all year.
18th-century former coaching inn with 13 en suite rooms and good sea views. Meals served in the dining room (**££**), **Crofter's Bar** or **Lounge Bar** (**£**). Child- and dog-friendly. Also offer archery, bike hire and kayak and SUP hire.

Mallaig

£££ West Highland Hotel
T01687-462210, www.westhighlandhotel. co.uk. Apr-Oct.
Centrally located with 40 rooms of varying standard. The restaurant is proud of its seafood dishes (**££**).

££ Western Isles Guesthouse
Follow the road round the harbour to East Bay, T01687-462320. Jan-Nov.
4 rooms. Excellent-value guesthouse run by same people who operate the boat to Knoydart (see page 223). Serves locally smoked kippers for breakfast.

Restaurants

Arisaig and Morar
Very good meals can be found at the **Arisaig Hotel**, although the **Old Library Lodge** and

Restaurant definitely has the edge (see Where to stay, above).

£ Café Rhu
Arisaig, next door to the Spar store, T01687-450707, www.caferhu.com. Daily 1000-1500, Tue-Sat also 1800-2100, Sun 1700-2000.
Snacks, soups, filled rolls and burgers, also offers takeaway. Friendly and good with kids.

Mallaig
If you're heading across to Skye you could buy some delicious peat-smoked salmon from **Andy Race**, by the harbour, T01687-462626, www.andyrace.co.uk, and eat it on the ferry with some brown bread. Alternatively, grab some excellent fish and chips or freshly caught scallops at the **Cornerstone** chippy.

££ Cabin Seafood Restaurant
By the harbour, T01687-462207.
Serves decent meals and a great-value 'teatime special'.

£ Tea Garden
Below Mallaig Backpacker's Lodge, T01687-462764, www.mallaigbackpackers.co.uk.
Great-value meals, including a print of prawns and all manner of daytime hearty snacks.

What to do

Glenfinnan
Loch Shiel Cruises, *Jim Michie, Marnoch, Roshven, Lochailort, T01687-470322, www. highlandcruises.co.uk.* Runs a variety of cruises down Loch Shiel, from Glenfinnan to Acharacle, with the possibility of spotting golden eagles. Sailings most days from Apr-Oct. Parking available at the **Glenfinnan House Hotel**, see Where to stay, page 220. Cyclists can also join a cruise and disembark at the Polloch Pontoon to cycle back along the banks of the loch to Glenfinnan.

Arisaig and Morar
Arisaig Marine, *T01687-450224, www.arisaig. co.uk.* The *MV Sheerwater* sails from Arisaig pier to **Rùm**, **Eigg** and **Muck** Mon-Fri all year

and also Sat-Sun from Jun-Aug. The islands are visited on different days, though there is a boat to Eigg every day except Thu in summer. You can visit all 3 islands in a day, allowing 2-5 hrs ashore. Fares range from £18 return to Eigg, £20 to Muck and £25 return to Rùm (children 2 and under free to all islands, 3-10 years £10, 11-16 years £14). These trips cater for the island's residents as much as tourists, so don't expect a running commentary, though hot and cold drinks are served on board.

Mallaig
MV The Grimsay Isle, *Ewen Nicholson, 6 Gillies Park, T01687-462652, T07880-815158*. Available for fishing charters and ferry service.

Transport

Mallaig
Bus
Shiel Buses, T01967-431272, runs 4 buses daily Mon-Fri from Mallaig to **Fort William** (1½ hrs) and 1 on Sat in summer.

Ferry
CalMac ferries, T0800-066 5000, www.calmac.co.uk, run throughout the year to **Armadale** on Skye, to **Lochboisdale** and **Castlebay** (see page 359), and to the **Small Isles**.

Train
There are several services daily (1 on Sun) to **Fort William**, with connections to **Glasgow**. There's also a steam train which runs in the summer months (see box, page 218).

Knoydart Peninsula   *Colour map 3, A5.*

rare wildlife and remote wilderness

The Knoydart Peninsula, the most remote and unspoilt region in Britain and one of Europe's last great wildernesses, literally lies between Heaven and Hell, for it is bordered to the north by Loch Hourn (Loch of Hell) and to the south by Loch Nevis (Loch of Heaven). Knoydart is not for wimps. It can only be reached on foot, or by boat from Mallaig, and consequently attracts walkers, who can wander for days around a network of trails without seeing another soul. If you've time and love the outdoors, it's worth the trip.

Walking on the Knoydart Peninsula
A two-day hiking route starts from Kinloch Hourn, reached by bus from Invergarry, see page 190. The trail winds its way around the coast to Barrisdale and on to Inverie. Another route into Knoydart starts from the west end of Loch Arkaig, and runs through Glen Dessarry. Both are tough hikes and only for fit, experienced and well-equipped hillwalkers. An easier way in is by boat (see box, page 223, and Transport, page 224).

The peninsula's only settlement of any size is tiny **Inverie**, with just 60 inhabitants. It's one of only a few villages in Scotland which can't be reached by road, but still has a post office, a shop, a few places to stay and Britain's most remote pub, the **Old Forge**. Much of the peninsula is mountain, with four peaks over 3000 ft. Its 85 square miles are a mix of private sporting estate, conservation trust and community partnership. Almost a decade ago one chunk of the peninsula, the 17,000-acre **Knoydart Estate**, was rescued from a succession of indifferent landlords by a community buy-out, funded by public money and individual donations. The Knoydart Foundation's trustees include the conservationist Chris Brasher and impresario Cameron Mackintosh, and if you sit outside the **Old Forge** long enough, one of them might pass by, or stop for a chat. Equally possible is the sighting of otters in the Sound of Sleat or golden eagles soaring overhead.

Essential Knoydart Peninsula

Finding your feet

Western Isles Cruises (T01687-462320, www.westernislescruises.co.uk), run trips from Mallaig to the remote village of Inverie on Knoydart (45 minutes). They sail several times daily April-October and at least twice daily November-March. On weekdays April-October the 1415 boat calls in at Tarbet. If you intend to catch the boat at Tarbet you must contact them in advance to confirm numbers. The same company also runs wildlife cruises (one hour, £12, £6 children) twice daily Monday-Friday from May to October and once at weekend from June to August.

If approaching Knoydart from the Glenelg road, there's a No 712 **MacRae Kintail bus** (T01599-511384), that runs Monday to Friday from Shiel Bridge to Glenelg (see page 231), from where it's about 10 miles to Arnisdale. Note: if planning to explore the Knoydart Peninsula, it's advisable to call **Knoydart Foundation** (T01687-462242) for travel and accommodation advice, including information on deer stalking.

Listings Knoydart Peninsula

Where to stay

Knoydart Peninsula
There's a growing number of options, see www.knoydart-foundation.com. Other than those listed below, there are 3 or 4 additional great-value (**£**) backpacker options on the peninsula, including the **Kilchoan Barn** (T01687-462724); and **The Old Byre** (T01687-460099).

££££ Doune-Knoydart
3-4 miles up the peninsula's only road, standing in splendid isolation, T01687-462667, www.doune-knoydart.co.uk.
The stone lodges have 3 en suite twin/double rooms, all with bunk beds for 2 children or mattresses on the floor in the mezzanine, accessed by ladder. Minimum stay 3 nights. Price includes breakfast, packed lunch and dinner. The food is superb and cannot be praised highly enough. Guests are picked up by boat from Mallaig (£32 per person, children ½ price), where you can leave your car. The owners also run the nearby **Doune Bay Lodge**, with shared facilities, for parties of up to 14 (£408 per person for 7 nights, minimum 6 people). Can be self-catered, fully catered, or somewhere in between. Also the option to charter the *TSMV Mary Doune* boat for £545 per day for up to 12 people. Highly recommended.

££££ Skiary
T01809-511214, www.skiary.com.
The most remote guesthouse in the British Isles, this is surely the most peaceful and beautiful place to stay on the entire planet. 3 twin rooms. Reached via single-track road from Invergarry to Kinloch Hourn, where you park the car (£1 per night) and take a boat (or walk) the last mile. Hosts Tom and Claire are great chefs and serve up fantastic food, which is all included in the price. No electricity, so lighting in the evenings is by Tilley lamps. A truly unique experience.

£££ The Gathering
Knoydart, T01687-460051, www. knoydartaccommodation.co.uk. All year.
A fabulous B&B, offers stylish rooms for up to 4 people and great breakfasts. Now has a hot tub and can provide evening meals on request (**££**). Friendly host. Recommended. Also has **Gathering Lochside**, a well-equipped self-catering cottage sleeping 6 (£1250 per week in high season).

£££ Pier House

Inverie, T01687-462347, www. thepierhouseknoydart.co.uk.
4 rooms, 2 en suite, 2 with extra beds for children. Price includes dinner. Good, old-fashioned hospitality and wonderful local seafood (**££**).

£ Knoydart Foundation Backpackers

15 mins' walk from the pier and pub, Inverie, T01687-462242.
Basic but good value.

£ Torrie Shieling

Inverie, T01687-462669.
It's a bit more expensive than most other hostels, but is very comfortable, and popular with hikers. They also have their own transport for trips around the peninsula and will collect guests from Mallaig by arrangement.

Restaurants

Knoydart Peninsula

£££-££ The Old Forge

Inverie, T01687-462267, www.theoldforge.co.uk.

The most remote pub on mainland Britain, where you can enjoy some tasty local seafood and a pint of real ale in front of an open fire. The craic among the locals and visitors also produces a terrific atmosphere. There's even the occasional impromptu ceilidh. Mercifully devoid of wannabe city slickers, this isn't the place to dress to impress – think more walking boots, waterproofs and midge cream. Highly recommended.

Transport

Knoydart Peninsula

There are no roads through Knoydart so the only means of accessing and leaving the area is on foot or by boat. It's a (very) long walk north from **Inverie** via the hamlet of **Barrisdale** to the road at **Kinloch Hourn** (see page 186). Alternatively, call Peter Fletcher (T01599-235007), in Arnisdale, to arrange for a passenger-only (and bikes) pick-up from **Barrisdale**, across **Loch Hourn** to **Arnisdale** from where you can walk out to the bus at **Glenelg**.

Great Glen
to Kyle of Lochalsh

The A87 is one of the main Highland tourist routes, connecting the Great Glen with the west coast and the Isle of Skye. It runs west from Invergarry between Fort Augustus and Fort William, through Glen Moriston and Glen Shiel to Shiel Bridge, at the head of Loch Duich, and on to Kyle. At Shiel Bridge a road branches off to Glenelg, from where you can enjoy a magical and short ferry crossing to Skye. It's a beautiful journey and by far the best way to reach the island.

Glen Shiel *OS Landranger No33. Colour map 3, A5.*

The journey from Invergarry to **Shiel Bridge** is worth it for the views alone. Glen Shiel is a sight to make the heart soar as high as the 3000-ft peaks that tower overhead on either side. This is one of the most popular hiking areas in Scotland, with the magnificent and much-photographed **Five Sisters of Kintail** on the north side of the glen, and the equally beautiful South Glen Shiel Ridge on the other.

There are several excellent hiking routes in Glen Shiel, but these mountains are to be treated with great respect. They require fitness, experience and proper equipment and planning. None of the routes should be attempted without a map, compass and detailed route instructions. You should be aware of the notoriously unpredictable weather conditions and also check locally about deer stalking. The season runs from August to October, but for more details contact the local stalkers (T01599-511282).

The **Five Sisters Traverse** is a classic ridge route. It starts at the first fire break on the left as you head southeast down the glen from Shiel Bridge and finishes at Morvich, on the other side of the ridge. Allow a full day (eight to 10 hours). You can also hike from Morvich to **Glen Affric Youth Hostel** at Cannich. It's a strenuous 20-mile walk, but you can stop off midway at the remote **Allt Beithe Youth Hostel**. For details, see Glen Affric, page 176.

The magnificent **South Glen Shiel Ridge** is one of the world's great hikes. It starts from above the **Cluanie Inn**, see Where to stay, page 228. From here it heads south then meets up with a good stalking path which climbs to the summit of the first Munro, Creag a' Mhaim (3108 ft). The ridge then runs west for almost nine miles and gives you the chance to pick off no fewer than seven Munros. Allow a full day for the walk (nine to 10 hours), and you'll need to set off early.

★ Glenelg and around *Colour map 3, A5.*

One of the most beautiful journeys in Scotland and certainly overlooked by the majority of tourists is the road from Shiel Bridge to the sublime little outpost that is Glenelg; a tiny village on the shores of the Sound of Sleat, only a short distance opposite Kylerhea on Skye (for transport details see page 230). The unclassified single-track road, constructed by 17th-century Hanoverian forces to link the ruin of Bernera Barracks (see below) with Fort Augustus, turns off the A87 and climbs steeply and dramatically through a series of sharp switchbacks to the top of the **Mam Ratagan Pass** (1115 ft). From here the view back across Loch Duich to the Five Sisters of Kintail is simply amazing, and the all-time classic calendar shot.

The road then drops down through Glen More to Glenelg, the main settlement on the peninsula. Known until the 18th century as Kirkton (it's believed a church stood here as far back as the 13th century), Glenelg lies on the old drovers' route that ran from Skye to the cattle markets in the south. This little-known corner of the Western Highlands is Gavin Maxwell country and was featured in *Ring of Bright Water*, his much-loved novel about otters. He disguised the identity of this beautiful, unspoiled stretch of coastline, calling it Camusfearna, and today it remains a quiet backwater.

You can see the famous otters at **Sandaig**, on the road running south from Glenelg, where Gavin Maxwell lived. The site of his cottage is now marked with a cairn. As well as otters, you can see numerous seabirds, seals and porpoises in the Sound of Sleat, and around the peninsula you may be lucky enough to catch a glimpse of wildcats, pine martens, golden eagles and the reintroduced sea eagles. The village itself consists of a row of whitewashed cottages surrounded by trees and overlooked by the ruins of the 18th-century **Bernera Barracks**. Just before the village the road forks. The right turning leads to the **Glenelg–Kylerhea ferry**, which makes the 10-minute crossing to Skye, see page 230.

A road runs south from Glenelg to Arnisdale. About 1½ miles along this road, a branch left leads to the **Glenelg Brochs** – Dun Telve and Dun Dun Troddan – two of the best-preserved Iron Age buildings in the country. Dun Telve, excavated in 1914, stands to a height of over 30 ft and the internal passages are almost intact. The road south from Glenelg continues past Sandaig Bay and runs along the north shore of unearthly Loch Hourn, with great views across the mountains of Knoydart. The road ends at little fishing hamlet of **Arnisdale**, from where you can take a boat across the loch to Barrisdale on the Knoydart Peninsula. For details, see page 223. A bit further along the coast, the road ends at the even tinier hamlet of **Corran**.

Eilean Donan Castle *Colour map 3, A5.*

T01599-555202, www.eileandonancastle.com, end Mar-end Oct daily 1000-1800, end-Oct to end-Dec and Feb to end-Mar 1000-1600, £7.50, concessions £6.50, children £4, family £20. Citylink buses between Fort William and Inverness and Skye stop by the castle.

Some 10 miles west of Shiel Bridge on the A87 is the little village of Dornie, home to the one of Scotland's most-photographed sights, the stunningly located Eilean Donan Castle. It stands on a tiny islet at the confluence of Loch Duich and Loch Alsh, joined to the shore by a narrow stone bridge and backed by high mountains. This great calendar favourite and tourist honeypot has also featured in several movies, including *Highlander*, which starred Sean Connery.

The original castle dates from 1230 when Alexander III had it built to protect the area from marauding Vikings. It was destroyed by King George in 1719 during its occupation by Spanish Jacobite forces sent to help the 'Old Pretender', James Stuart. It then lay in ruins, until one of the Macraes had it rebuilt between 1912 and 1932. Inside, the Banqueting Hall with its Pipers' Gallery is most impressive, and there's an exhibition of military regalia and interesting displays of the castle's history. The views from the battlements are also worthwhile. However, to escape the tourist hordes, don't forget about that fantastic winding road to Glenelg across the mountains to the south.

Kyle of Lochalsh *Colour map 3, A5.*

Before the coming of the controversial Skye Bridge a mile to the north, the little town of Kyle, as it is known, was the main ferry crossing to Skye and consequently a place

Essential Kyle of Lochalsh

Finding your feet

Buses for the Isle of Skye arrive in Kyle of Lochalsh from Edinburgh, Glasgow, Inverness and Fort William via the A87 through Glen Shiel. There is also a scenic rail route to Kyle from Inverness via Stromeferry and Plockton. Getting to Glenelg without your own transport is more tricky; there is a limited minibus service from Kyle and a pre-booked taxi service from Shiel Bridge. For further details, see Transport, page 230.

which attracted a busy tourist trade. Now though, the tourist traffic bypasses Kyle, which notwithstanding tremendous views to Skye, suffers from a workaday feel. There are a couple of banks with ATMs, two small supermarkets and a post office in the village.

Plockton *Colour map 3, A5.*

If there were a poll taken of visitors' favourite Highland villages, then you can bet your sporran that Plockton would come top with most folk. If you look for a definition of picturesque in your dictionary, it'll say 'see Plockton'. Well, maybe not – but it should. Actually, the name is derived from Am Ploc that roughly translates as 'blunt promontory'.

Plockton's neat little painted cottages, built in the early 18th century by the landowner to provide fishing employment after clearing traditional crofting lands for sheep, are ranged around the curve of a wooded bay, with flowering gardens and palm trees. Yachts bob up and down in the harbour and there are views across the island-studded waters of Loch Carron to the hills beyond. Even on the telly Plockton's charms proved irresistible, and back in 1995 millions of viewers tuned in each week to watch the TV series *Hamish Macbeth*, which featured Robert Carlyle as the local bobby. Plockton's a popular place with artists who are drawn by the village's setting and the wonderful light. A good place to find some of their work, as well as other souvenirs, is The Studio (T01599-544322), on the corner of the seafront and the road leading out of town.

There are lots of good walks around the village. One of the best ways to appreciate it is to head up to **Frithard Hill**, from where there are great views of the bay. Another good walk is along the beach, starting from the High School playing fields at the top of the village. The craft shop (and newsagent) sells a booklet of local walks.

From Plockton a minor road heads east along Loch Carron before joining the main A890. This passes the turn-off for Stromeferry and continues to Strathcarron at the head of the loch (see page 232).

Where to stay

Glen Shiel

££££-£££ Grants at Craigellachie
Ratagan, T01599-511331, www.houseby theloch.co.uk. Open all year.
About 1 mile along the road to Glenelg/ Kylrerhea ferry is the turn-off to tiny Ratagan and this genuine hidden gem of a place. 4 en suite rooms, 2 in the main house and 2 in the **Butt and Ben**. Hosts Tony and Liz Taylor have created a little haven of peace, comfort and fine cuisine. It's a restaurant with rooms and the rave reviews for the former (**£££**) are matched by the style and comfort – and superb views – of the latter. The rooms in the But and Ben can be booked on a self-catering basis. Recommended.

££££-£££ Kintail Lodge Hotel
T01599-511275, www.kintaillodgehotel.co.uk. Open all year.
12 rooms. Small, cosy hotel beautifully located by the shores of Loch Duich, dinner also available in the hotel bar. **Trekkers Lodge** attached offers budget accommodation with 6 beds in 4 rooms (**£**). You can also charter their boat, *Kiki Blofeld* for up to 10 people, £400 for ½ day.

£££ Cluanie Inn
Glenmoriston, some 9 miles east of Shiel Bridge, T01320-340238, www.cluanieinn.com.
10 en suite rooms including 2 with jacuzzi and 1 with a 4-poster bed. Also offers more modest **Clubhouse** (**£££-££**) accommodation. This is one of the Highlands' classic hotels. It's a firm favourite with hikers and climbers and it's easy to see why. After a hard day's ridge walking, what could be better than jumping into the jacuzzi, then having a hot dinner and a good real ale or malt beside a log fire. Recommended.

££ Glomach House
Aullt-Na-Chruinn, T01599-511222, www.glomach.co.uk. Open all year.
3 en suite rooms. Tidy and comfortable B&B on the shores of Loch Duich at Shiel Bridge. Self-catering cottage also available for rent, comprising 2 double bedrooms. No pets.

£ Ratagan Youth Hostel
Just past Shiel Bridge, T01599-511243. Feb-Dec.
One of the great hikers' hostels.

Camping

Morvich Caravan Club Site
1½ miles past Shiel Bridge in direction of Kyle, T01599-511354. Late Mar-late Oct.
Large site with full facilities.

Shiel Bridge Caravan Park & Campsite
Shiel Bridge, T01599-511221.
Excellent facilities and location, at the heart of fantastic scenery and excellent outdoor activities. Shop with groceries on site.

Glenelg and around

£££ Glenelg Inn
Glenelg, T01599-522273, www. glenelg-inn.com. Open all year.
It's worth stopping in Glenelg, if you've got the time, to experience a night in this wonderfully cosy place. Even if you can't spend the night, at least spend an hour or 2 enjoying the atmosphere, good ale and superb food, either in the dining room (**£££**) or the bar (**££**). If you're really lucky, you may even chance upon an impromptu folk jam. Rooms are spacious and inviting. Warmly recommended.

£ Dalmhor
About a mile from the Glenelg Inn, T01599-522287. Open all year.
In a secluded spot near the beach with views across the Sound of Sleat, run by Mrs Chisholm.

Eilean Donan Castle
There are several places to stay in the nearby village of Dornie.

££ Caberfeidh House
Ardelve, by Dornie, T01599-555293, www.caberfeidh.plus.com. Open all year.
5 rooms, 4 with views of the castle. Friendly and comfortable guesthouse. Very good value.

££ Conchra House
Ardelve, T01599-555233, www.conchrahouse. com. Open all year.
5 en suite rooms. To get here, cross the bridge in Dornie and turn right for Killilan, a tiny hamlet at the head of Loch Long, the hotel is ¾ mile up this road. This historic 18th-century hunting lodge is peaceful, has lovely views and a reputation for good food.

£ Whitefalls Retreats
Near Conchra House Hotel, at Camasluinie, T01599-588205, www.holidayhighlands.co.uk.
Basic bunkhouse accommodation in 1 double and 2 twin rooms. Also has 2 self-catering cottages for weekly rent, both sleep 6 people and are pet friendly.

Kyle of Lochalsh
It's a good idea to book ahead as there's not much choice in Kyle itself.

£££-££ Tingle Creek Hotel
Erbusaig, T01599-534430, www.tinglecreek-hotel.co.uk. Open all year.
Small hotel with a big, friendly welcome. Lovely setting and great views. Good food in restaurant and guests can enjoy a drink in the **Galleon** bar before dinner.

Plockton

£££ Plockton Gallery
Innes St, T01599-544442. Open all year.
2 en suite rooms and 2 more with shared shower room. Part gallery, part guesthouse, this former manse offers something different. A bit more expensive than the

average but worth it for the quality and service. Veggie options available with a bit of notice, disabled access and parking. Also has self-catering for 10 people, £300 per night minimum 3 nights. Recommended.

£££ Plockton Hotel
Harbour St, T01599-544274, www. plocktonhotel.co.uk. Open all year.
11 en suite rooms, comfortable and tastefully furnished, above a perenially busy wee bar. All have views across the bay. There are a few places along the waterfront and this is among the best. If you eat in the excellent front restaurant (**£££-££**) you'll enjoy views out over the bay. Also has 4 rooms in the annexe a few doors along (**££**). Recommended.

£££ Plockton Inn
Innes St, T01599-544222, www.plocktoninn. co.uk. Open all year.
14 rooms. Small hotel with 7 bedrooms added in an annexe across the road. Very good seafood in restaurant or in lively bar where you can also hear live folk music twice a week (usually Tue and Thu). Open log fires and there's also a great little beer garden at the front where you can sit and enjoy a drink on a balmy summer evening.

££ An Caladh
Beside the shore T01599-544356.
3 rooms. This is a lovely option right by the shore from where the owner occasionally goes out fishing in the bay.

££ Heron's Flight
Cooper St, T01599-544220, www.heronsflight.org. Mar-Oct.
3 rooms. Friendly and welcoming B&B run by Ann Mackenzie and her dog, Ruah. Veggie and continental options for breakfast, no cards accepted. No single occupancy or single night bookings.

£ Nessun Dorma
Burnside, T01599-544235
Bunkhouse and B&B 1 mile out of Plockton at the railway station, run by Mick and Gill Coe.

B&B has 2 rooms, the bunkhouse sleeps 20 in 4 rooms. Cheapest option. Packed lunches available on request.

Restaurants

Eilean Donan Castle
There are a couple of places in Dornie serving decent food.

££ Clachan Pub
13 Francis St, Dornie, T01599-555366.
You can enjoy a good-value 3-course evening meal here.

££ Dornie Hotel
Dornie, T01599-555205,
www.dornie-hotel.co.uk.
A good option, serves very good food and has a lively bar.

Plockton
There are several good eateries in Plockton, with the **Plockton Inn**, **Haven Hotel** and **Plockton Hotel** all serving memorable seafood dishes including huge bowls of mussels. Also try:

££ Plockton Shores
Harbour St, T01599-544263, www.
plocktonshoresrestaurant.com. Open
all year, closed Mon, and Tue in winter.
Fabulous choice of scallops, locally sourced beef and vegetarian options. Recommended.

£ Harbour Fish Bar
Innes St, right by the harbour. Open all year.
Formerly known as **Grumpy's**, this is a fantastic chippy with a difference, where you'll find the local catch of the day and prawns among the bargain bites for those on a budget.

What to do

Kyle of Lochalsh
Boat trips
There are a couple of interesting boat trips from Kyle.
Seaprobe Atlantis, *T0800-9804846,*
www.seaprobeatlantis.com. The *Seaprobe*

Atlantis, is a unique sailing craft fitted with underwater windows, providing an amazing view of seals, kelp forests and even a Second World War wreck. Trips run from Easter-Oct. 1-hr trip is £14, children (4-12) £8, 2-hr trip is £25/13.

Cycle hire
Dornie bike Hire & Repair, *Bundalloch, Dornie, T01599-555294.* Bike hire £17 per adult per day for road bike, hybrid or mountain bike, £9 child's bike.

Plockton
Boat trips
Calum's Plockton Seal Trips, *32 Harbour St, T01599-544306, www.calums-sealtrips. com.* Run 1-hr seal-spotting trips from the harbour, £12, children £6. In addition to seals you may spot otters and rare birdlife. The operator even offers your money back if you don't spot any seals.

Transport

Glen Shiel
Bus
Citylink buses between **Fort William**, **Inverness** and **Skye** pass through Glen Shiel several times daily stopping in Shiel Bridge. A bus runs Mon-Fri from Kyle of Lochalsh to **Arnisdale** via **Shiel Bridge**, **Ratagan** and **Glenelg**.

Glenelg and around
Ferry
The community-owned **Glenelg**-to-**Kylerhea** ferry provides the most scenic connection to **Skye**, www.skyeferry.co.uk. 10-min crossing Easter to mid-Oct daily 1000-1800; Jun-end Aug until 1900.

Kyle of Lochalsh
Bus
Scottish Citylink buses (www.citylink. co.uk), run from Kyle to **Inverness**, 3 daily, 2 hrs; to **Glasgow** via **Fort William**, 4 daily, 5 hrs; and to **Edinburgh** via **Fort William**,

1 daily, 6½ hrs. **Scottish Citylink** also run to **Portree** 1 hr, and **Uig**, 1½ hrs, on Skye for ferries to **Tarbert** on Harris and **Lochmaddy** on North Uist. There's also a regular shuttle service across the Skye bridge to **Kyleakin**, every 30 mins.

There's no longer a postbus service between Kyle and **Glenelg**, so you'll need to call **MacRae Kintail** (No 712), T01599-511384, which runs 1 trip (Mon and Fri only) to **Glenelg** via Ratagan Youth Hostel. On demand it will continue to **Arnisdale** and **Corran**. Bus No 620 runs 3 times daily to **Plockton** from Kyle of Lochalsh.

Train

The train journey to **Inverness** from Kyle, though not as spectacular as the West Highland line, is very scenic. It runs 3-4 times Mon-Sat, 2½ hrs, and once or twice on Sun from May-Sep. There's also an observation car and dining car in the summer. The train stops at **Plockton**, **Stromeferry** and **Strathcarron**.

Wester
Ross

From Loch Carron north to Ullapool, is the region of Wester Ross, an area of dramatic mountain massifs, fjord-like sea lochs and remote coastal villages. Here lies some of Europe's most spectacular scenery, from the isolated peninsula of Applecross to Tolkien-esque peaks of Torridon, which offer some of Scotland's best climbing and hillwalking. There are also gentler attractions such as the vast, sprawling gardens at Inverewe and the beguiling pink sands of Gruinard Bay.

Loch Carron and the Applecross Peninsula   Colour map 1, C4.

a high mountain pass, stunning scenery and delicious seafood

Lochcarron village *Colour map 1, C4.*

Lochcarron village consists of little more than a main street along the shore of the loch, but it has more facilities and services than most other places in these parts. Here you should take the opportunity to withdraw cash at the Bank of Scotland ATM, fill up with petrol and buy some supplies at the small self-service store. A few miles before Lochcarron, on the road to Plockton, is the tiny village of **Strathcarron**.

Two miles south of Lochcarron village on the road to the 15th-century ruins of **Strome Castle** is Lochcarron Weavers ① *T01520-722212, open 0800-1700*, where you can see tartan being made and also buy from a vast range of woven goods.

★ Loch Kishorn to Applecross

Colour map 1, C4.

There are many scenic routes in the Highlands but the road from Kishorn, west of Lochcarron to Applecross beats them all. The **Bealach na Ba** ('Pass of the Cattle') is the highest road in Scotland and is often closed during the winter snows. It climbs

Essential Loch Carron

Finding your feet

The Inverness to Kyle of Lochalsh train service stops at Strathcarron at the head of Loch Carron. From here, **DMK Motors** (T01520-722682) run a bus service (No 702) to Lochcarron, Kishorn and Shieldaig. On Wednesdays and Saturdays **Lochcarron Garage** (T01520-722205) runs a bus (No 704) from Inverness bus station to Lochcarron, continuing to Kishorn, Shieldaig and Applecross if pre-booked in advance.

relentlessly and dramatically through a series of tortuous switchbacks – both spectacular and terrifying in equal measure. The high plateau, at 2053 ft, is cold and desolate, but from here you have the most amazing views: from Ardnamurchan Peninsula to Loch Torridon, taking in Eigg, Rùm, the Cuillins of Skye, the Old Man of Storr and the Quirang.

The narrow, single-track road then begins its gradual descent to the isolated little village of **Applecross**, site of one Scotland's first Christian monasteries, founded in AD 673. The village consists of a row of whitewashed fishermen's cottages looking across to the island of Raasay and backed by wooded slopes. It's a beautifully tranquil place where you can explore beaches and rock pools or enjoy a stroll through the garden and woodlands of Applecross House – and then of course there's the very wonderful **Applecross Inn**, see Where to stay, below. From Applecross a beautiful, winding coast road leads around the peninsula to Shieldaig on Loch Torridon, passing the bay at Sand after a couple of miles.

Listings Loch Carron and the Applecross Peninsula

Where to stay

Loch Carron and the Applecross Peninsula

£££ Applecross Inn
Applecross, T01520-744262,
www.applecross.uk.com.
7 rooms. There are, sadly, too few authentic Highland hostelries where you could quite happily while away a few hours, or even days, but if you have to be holed up somewhere to escape the rotten weather, then this place is as good as any and better than most. Owner Judith Fish ensures you receive a warm welcome, the atmosphere is friendly and the seafood is so fresh you can almost see it swimming past as you order. Bar food served 1200-2100, children welcome until 2030, ceilidhs on Fri evening. Sit outside in the beer garden on a summer's eve. The rooms upstairs have been refurbished to a high standard and downstairs now includes a bedroom adapted for guests with a disability. Excellent value and highly recommended. See also Restaurants, below.

££ The Old Manse
Lochcarron, T01520-722208,
www.theoldmanselochcarron.com.
5 rooms. Comfortable, old-world style guesthouse with views across the loch.

££ Rockvilla Guesthouse & Restaurant
Main St, Lochcarron, T01520-722379,
www.therockvilla.com. Open all year.
3 rooms. Recently refurbishged to a high standard, this small guesthouse offers very comfortable rooms and good food (**££**) in its residents-only dining room. 2 nights minimum stay Apr-Oct.

Self-catering

Callakille
8 miles north of Applecross, T01456-486358,
www.wildernesscottages. co.uk.
A beautifully converted 2-bedroom croft house that's tastefully furnished and an idyllic bolt-hole from the stresses of urban life. Unwind by the roaring fire and enjoy the panoramic views over the Inner Sound of Raasay. In addition to fantastic walking and wildlife spotting opportunities, there's also good trout and sea fishing in the area. From £475-795 per week. Highly recommended. No pets.

Camping

Applecross Campsite
At the foot of the Bealach na Ba road,
T01520-744268. Mar-Oct.
Decent facilities. Family friendly and lots to do. Also Camping Huts for rent (**£**) for up to 4 with mattresses provided.

Restaurants

Loch Carron and around

££ Applecross Inn
See Where to stay, above.
The food here is fantastic, with starters that can include seafood chowder and locally collected oysters. For mains there's the likes of locally reared venison and Applecross Bay prawns.

££ Carron Restaurant
About 5 mins' drive from Lochcarron village, across the loch on the A890, T01520-722488. Apr-Nov Mon-Sat 1000-2030, Sun 1000-1600.
An excellent option for meat lovers.

££ Potting Shed Café & Restaurant
Applecross, T01520-744440, www. applecrossgarden.co.uk. Mar-Nov.
Located in the former potting sheds and surrounded by the beautifully restored garden of Applecross House, this rustic option prides itself on locally sourced produce, including vegetables picked from the garden. It's quite an informal place to eat but the food is exquisite. Definitely worth booking ahead at weekends. Café menu available 1200-2130 (**££-£**) and evening menu from 1800.

££-£ Kishorn Seafood Bar
On the road from Lochcarron to Applecross, before the Bealach na Ba Pass, T01520-733240, www.kishornseafoodbar.co.uk. Mar to end Oct daily 1000-1700, Fri 1000-2100, mid-Jul to mid-Sep Mon-Sat 1000-2100, Sun 1000-1700.
This oasis of culinary excellence must not be missed. The seafood is very fresh and amazing value. More standard fare also on offer for those unfortunate souls who can't eat seafood. Highly recommended.

Transport

Loch Carron and the Applecross Peninsula

Updated travel information for the area can be found at www.hanszell.co.uk/timetables.shtml. There are 4 trains Mon-Sat and 2 on Sun from Strathcarron to both **Inverness** and **Kyle of Lochalsh** via **Plockton**. A bus from Strathcarron to Lochcarron, Kishorn and Shieldaig is provided by **DMK Motors**, T01520-722682. Bus service 704 travels between **Inverness** and Lochcarron Mon, Wed and Sat only, continuing to **Shieldaig** and **Applecross** if pre-booked; call **Lochcarron Garage**, T01520-722205, for times and bookings.

Torridon *Colour map 1, C4.*

towering peaks and exhilarating mountain walks

Torridon is perhaps the most striking skyline in the Scottish Highlands. The multi-peaked mountains of Beinn Alligin, Liathach (pronounced *Lee-ahakh*) and Beinn Eighe (*Ben-eay*) form a massive fortress of turrets, spires and pinnacles that provides an awesome backdrop to Loch Torridon, as well as the most exhilarating walking and climbing on the Scottish mainland. The straggly little village of Torridon makes the ideal base from which to tackle these mountains.

Torridon may offer some of the best walking on the Scottish mainland but it also presents some of the most serious challenges. You need to be fit, experienced and well prepared and also be aware of the notoriously unpredictable weather. You should have a compass and the relevant map. OS Outdoor Leisure Series No 8 covers the area. For recommended mountain guides, see page 238.

Around Loch Torridon *Colour map 1, C4.*

The coast road from Applecross meets the A896 from Lochcarron at the lovely little village of **Shieldaig** on the southern shore of Loch Torridon. There's a shop, a post office, a campsite and a couple of B&Bs. Several miles east, a side road turns off the A896 by **Torridon village** and winds its way along the northern shore of the loch, then climbs through dramatic scenery before dropping to the beautiful little village of **Diabaig** (pronounced *Jee-a-beg*), 10 miles from Torridon village. It's a worthwhile side trip, as the views across to the Applecross peninsula and Raasay are fantastic. There's also a great seven-mile coastal walk from Diabaig to Red Point (see below).

Much of the Torridon massif is in the care of the National Trust for Scotland, and just before Torridon village is the **NTS Countryside Centre**, T01445-791221, where you can get information and advice on walks in the area, as well as books and maps. About 400 yds past the centre is the **Deer Museum**, which has a small display describing the management of red deer in the Highlands as well as some live specimens outside.

Beinn Alligin *Colour map 1, C4.*

Beinn Alligin (3235 ft) is the most westerly of the Torridon peaks and probably the least demanding. The **Allt a'Bhealaich Walk** is a steep but short walk of about two hours. It starts from the car park just beyond the stone bridge that crosses the Abhainn Coire Mhic Nobuil. Follow the path that runs beside the river gorge until you reach the first bridge, cross it and follow the east bank of the Allt a' Bhealaich burn. Higher up, cross the second bridge and continue to follow the track up to the 380-m contour line, then turn back retracing your steps. This walk doesn't include the ascent of the peak, but the views are magnificent. Those who wish to climb the three **Horns of Beinn Alligin** can continue from the 380-m contour line above the second bridge. The track that follows their ridge is exposed and requires rock scrambling experience.

Liathach *Colour map 1, C5.*

Seven-peaked Liathach (3460 ft) stretches over five miles, and the magnificent ridge walk is considered by many to be the most impressive in Britain. This walk requires a high level of stamina and will take at least seven to eight hours. It also helps if you have a car waiting at the end.

A good place to start this long and strenuous challenge is about half a mile or so east of Glen Cottage, which is just over two miles east of the Countryside Centre. A steep climb takes you to a point just west of **Stuc a'Choire Dhuibh Bhig** (3000 ft). Then retrace your route to climb the twin tops of **Bidein Toll a'Mhuic** (3200 ft), linked by a narrow ridge. The path from here descends to the head of a deep ravine and keeps to the crest of the ridge around the rim of **Coireag Dubh Beag** which plunges steeply to the north. The ridge then rises across a field of huge and unstable boulders to the highest peak – **Spidean a'Choire Leith**. The view from this point is stunning, with Coire na Caime before you, surrounded by 2000-ft sheer cliffs. From here, the path follows a narrow, exposed ridge for over a mile towards **Mullach an Rathain** (3358 ft). Unless you are an experienced scrambler with a good head for heights, the best way from here is to take the path to the south, below the sharp pinnacles. Beyond the pinnacles the climb to Mullach an Rathain is straightforward. The track from here to **Sgorr a'Chadail** is a long but fairly easy walk and ends on the path in Coire Mhic Nobuil, see Beinn Alligin, above.

Coire Walk

A less difficult walk, but still requiring a fair degree of fitness and taking most of the day, is the Coire Walk. It follows the River Coire Mhic Nobuil to its watershed and down again by the **Allt a'Choire Dhuibh Mhoir** to the main road in Glen Torridon. Again, two cars will shorten the distance considerably.

The walk starts at the same point as the Beinn Alligin walk (see above). It follows the path up to the first bridge then branches east and continues on the path that runs north of the river, all the way to its source in the pass between Liathach and Beinn Dearg. Here the ground is boggy between the string of pools and lochans and the path is less distinct, but it becomes clear again in the upper reaches of the Coire Dubh Mor, a huge gully that separates Liathach from Beinn Eighe. A little further on, the track joins a stalkers' path which curves round Sail Mhor to the famous **Coire Mhic Fhearchair**, considered to be the most spectacular corrie in Scotland (see Beinn Eighe, below). The Coire path leads to a ford, which is crossed by stepping stones, then descends following the west side of the burn down to the car park on the Torridon road, from where it's about 4½ miles to Torridon village.

Diabaig to Red Point Walk *OS Landranger No 19.*

An excellent low-level coastal walk is from Diabaig to Red Point. It is far less strenuous or daunting than the others described above and there is a clear path. It starts at the wooden gate to the right of the post office in Diabaig and ends at Red Point Farm, seven miles away.

After four miles the coastal path reaches the derelict croft houses in the Craig Valley. There are two possible routes from here. You can follow the footpath above the coastline, or leave the footpath after crossing the wooden bridge over the Craig river and climb through an area of woodland. Take a reference from your OS map and you'll reach the highest point, **Meall na h-Uamha**, from where there are superb views. You can then descend to rejoin the coastal path and continue until you reach the glorious golden sands of Red Point, with wonderful views across to Skye and Raasay. Keep to the path through the farm until you reach the car park. Unless you've arranged your own transport here, you'll have to walk back the way you came, or catch the schoolbus to Gairloch, see page 238.

Beinn Eighe National Nature Reserve

While most of the Torridon massif is managed by the National Trust of Scotland, Beinn Eighe (which means 'File Peak' in Gaelic) is under the control of Scottish Natural Heritage. It is Britain's oldest National Nature Reserve, set up in 1951 to protect the ancient Caledonian pine forest west of Kinlochewe. It has since been designated an International Biosphere Reserve and extended to cover 30 square miles. The reserve is the home of a great variety of rare Highland wildlife, including pine martens, wildcats, buzzards, Scottish crossbills and golden eagles. There's also a wide range of flora which can best be appreciated on the excellent mountain trail described below which climbs from the ancient pine woods through alpine vegetation to the tundra-like upper slopes.

About half a mile northwest of Kinlochewe on the A832, is the Beinn Eighe Visitor Centre, which has excellent interactive audio visual displays about the flora and fauna in the reserve and sells pamphlets on the trails described below.

Beinn Eighe (3313 ft) has nine peaks and is the largest of the Torridon Mountains. To traverse its ridge is a mighty undertaking and can take two days. A much shorter and easier walk around the base of the mountain is described here. The mountain and woodland trails both start and end in the car park at the side of Loch Maree, about two miles beyond the visitor centre. The woodland trail heads west along the lochside then crosses the road and climbs for about a mile up to the Conservation cabin before descending back to the starting point. It should take about an hour and is easy to follow, though quite steep in parts, and you'll need a good pair of walking boots. The mountain trail is four miles long and rough and steep in parts. You should be well equipped with good walking boots, waterproofs, food and warm clothing. It should take three to four hours. The route is well marked with cairns and you should not stray from the path. The trail heads south from the car park and begins a gentle ascent through woodland to a boggy area and then begins to zigzag up a very steep and rugged section, climbing to over 1000 ft in less than half a mile. This is the steepest section of the trail, but the views back across Loch Maree to Slioch are fabulous. The summit of the mountain trail is **Conservation cairn** (1800 ft) from where you can see the tops of 31 Munros on a clear day and enjoy a close-up view of the impressive Beinn Eighe ridge a few miles to the south. The trail now begins to descend as it heads northwest towards **An t-Allt** (1000 ft), turns northwards down to a small enclosure, then heads east to the deep Allt na h-Airidhe gorge. From here the trail continues down to the treeline and runs through woodland to join up with the top of the Woodland Trail. Follow the path to the right to get back to the car park.

Kinlochewe and Loch Maree *Colour map 1, C5.*

On the northeast side of the Torridon Mountains is the sprawling village of Kinlochewe, at the southeastern end of beautiful Loch Maree. It's a good base for walking in and around Loch Maree, and has a hotel, post office within the village shop/café and one of the area's scarce **petrol stations** ⓘ *Apr-Sep Mon-Sat 0800-1800, Sun 0900-1700, Oct-Mar Mon-Fri 0800-1800, Sat 0900-1700*, which also contains a licensed grocer and coffee shop serbving hot food and snacks The loch is dotted with islands and bordered by the mass of **Slioch** (3218 ft) to the north and ancient Caledonian pine forest to the south. Running along its northern shore, from Slioch almost as far as **Poolewe**, is the remote **Letterewe Estate**, one of Scotland's great deer forests. The A832 skirts the south shore of the loch, running northwest from Kinlochewe, and passes the **Victoria Falls**, a mile or so beyond Talladale. The falls commemorate Queen Victoria's visit in 1877. To find them, look for the Hydro Power signs.

Listings Torridon

Where to stay

Torridon

££££-£££ The Old Mill Highland Lodge
On Loch Maree at Talladale, halfway between Kinlochewe and Gairloch, T01445-760271, www.theoldmillhighlandlodge.co.uk. Mar-Oct.
6 rooms. The best accommodation around here, this converted mill is set in its own gardens. It's friendly and comfortable, offers great food (price includes dinner), seclusion and views.

££££-£££ The Torridon
1 mile south of the turn-off to Torridon village, T01445-791242, www.thetorridon.com.

The hotel Is one of the very best luxury hotels In Scotland with 18 sumptuous rooms and offers everything you would expect at this price (**££££**). The 12 tastefully refurbished en suite rooms at **The Inn** (**£££-££**) form part of this fairytale Gothic pile on the lochside. There's also the **Boathouse** self-catering option with it own private jetty and beautifully appointed bedrooms (£1550 per week in high season). However, it's the dining experience for which The Torridon is renowned. Its **1887** restaurant (**£££**) offers the option to fine dine on the freshest locally sourced seafood and game. **The Inn** (**££**) serves very good food for those on tighter budgets.

£££ Kinlochewe Hotel
Kinlochewe, T01445-760253, www. kinlochewehotel.co.uk. Open all year.
9 rooms. Offers B&B as well as 12 cheaper (£17.50 per person per night) bunkhouse beds and cheap bar meals. Excellent CAMRA award-winning real ale.

£££ Tigh-an-Eilean Hotel
Shieldaig, Loch Torridon, T01520-755251, www.tighaneilean.co.uk. End Mar-Nov.
11 rooms. Great wee upmarket hotel overlooking the loch, so views are wonderful. Terrific food in the restaurant and also occasional impromptu bursts of folk music. Recommended.

££ Ferroch
Annat by Torridon, T01445-791451. Open all year.
3 en suite rooms. Superior B&B in former crofthouse. Beautiful location (£££ including dinner). Also has self-catering cottage for weekly or half-weekly rent.

£ SYHA hostel
On the easternmost fringe of Torridon village, T01445-791284.
This 44-bed hostel is ideal for exploring the surrounding Torridon hills. It's about a 20- to 25-min walk from here to the **Torridon Inn** and a well-earned pint.

Camping
There is a basic campsite at **Taangan Farm**, at the head of Loch Maree.

What to do

Torridon
Climbing and hillwalking
For those who are not experienced hillwalkers, there's a Ranger Service for visitors. Jul-Aug the ranger takes guided walks up into the mountains 3 times a week. For more details, call T01445-791221.

The **Torridon** hotel group (see Where to stay, above) offer a whole host of outdoor activities, including guided walks, gorge scrambling, coasteering, sea kayaking, mountain biking, etc.
Martin Moran, *T01520-722361, www.moran-mountain.co.uk.* A recommended local mountain guide, offers a variety of different types of climbing course.

Transport

Torridon
Bus
Westerbus, T01445-712255, run a service (No 705) on schooldays from **Shieldaig** to Gairloch via **Torridon** and **Kinlochewe** post office; for times visit https://bustimes.org.uk.

Gairloch and around *Colour map 1, C4.*
beautiful beaches, excellent walking and rare marine wildlife

Gairloch consists of a string of tiny crofting townships (Charleston, Achtercairn and Strath) scattered around the northeastern shore of the loch of the same name. It's a beautiful place, attracting a large number of visitors who come for the many sandy beaches, excellent walks, golf and fishing, and the chance of seeing seals, porpoises, dolphins and whales in the surrounding waters. There are shops and takeaways in Strath and Achtercairn and a bank near the harbour at Charleston.

Gairloch Heritage Museum
T01445-712287, Apr-Oct Mon-Fri 1000-1700, Sat 1100-1500, £4, concessions £3, children £1.

If you are interested in local history, or the weather is bad – not unknown – then this museum may entertain for an hour or so. Included are archaeological finds, a mock-up of a crofthouse room, schoolroom and shop, the interior of the local lighthouse and an archive of old photographs. It is found beside the tourist office on the A832 to Poolewe, a few yards beyond the turn-off to Strath.

Essential Gairloch

Finding your feet

There are buses to and from Inverness via Kinlochewe. See Transport, page 242.

Big Sand, Melvaig and Midtown
Colour map 1, B4/C4.

The beach by the golf course at Gairloch is nice, but the beach at Big Sand, a few miles northwest of Strath, is better, and quieter. Further north is Melvaig, from where you can walk to **Rubha Reidh Lighthouse**. Around the headland from the lighthouse is the beautiful, secluded beach at **Camas Mor**. This is a good place for spotting sea birds, and there's a great walk from here on a marked footpath to Midtown, four miles northwest of Poolewe. You'll have to walk or hitch from here or try and catch a ride with the community ring-and-ride bus.

The waters around Gairloch are home to a wide variety of marine mammals such as seals, otters, porpoises, dolphins, minke whales and even killer whales. For details of wildlife cruises, see page 242.

Road to Red Point *Colour map 1, C4.*

A lovely little side trip is to follow the narrow B8056 which runs west for nine miles to Red Point from the junction three miles south of Gairloch, at Kerrysdale; it's especially worthwhile on a clear evening to enjoy the magnificent sunsets at **Red Point beach**. The beach itself is extremely seductive, backed by steep dunes and looking across to the Trotternish Peninsula on Skye. Red Point is also the start or finish point for the excellent coastal walk to or from Diabaig, see page 236. On the road to Red Point is the picturesque little hamlet of **Badachro**, tucked away in a wooded, sheltered bay with fishing boats moored in its natural harbour. It's worth stopping off here on the way back from Red Point for a wee dram at the **Badachro Inn**.

There are many other good walks in the area, including to **Flowerdale Falls**, the **Fairy Lochs** and the **USAAF Liberator**. The iCentre has a selection of walking guides and OS maps.

Poolewe *Colour map 1, B4.*

Five miles east of Gairloch on the other side of the peninsula is the neat little village of Poolewe, straddling the mouth of the River Ewe, where it cascades into sheltered Loch Ewe. There are some good walks around Poolewe, including the one around Loch Kernsary, described below. There's also a nice little drive up the side road running along the west shore of Loch Ewe to Cove. You can walk from Midtown, midway along the road, to Rubha Reidh, north of Gairloch (see above).

Loch Kernsary *OS Landranger Map No 19.*

This straightforward but rewarding walk covers six miles and should take around 2½ to three hours. The track is very boggy underfoot in places, especially after rain, so you'll need good boots.

Start in Poolewe, from the car park by the school near the bridge over the Ewe. Head up the single-track road with the river on your right. Go through the gate, then the track heads away from the river and up into woodland. At the Letterewe Estate gate cross the stile and continue to the next fork. Turn left here to Kernsary Estate, with views of Loch Maree and Beinn Eighe to the south. Follow the track to the next gate, go through and cross the wooden bridge. Continue along the track and you'll see Loch Kernsary on your left. At the next fork, turn left over the bridge and pass Kernsary Cottage on the right. Beyond the cottage, go through the gate and immediately head left down towards the burn, where the ground may be boggy. There's no path here, but cross the wooden footbridge and continue straight on, past the piles of stones on your left. Cross the stile, and the path follows the length of Loch Kernsary. At the head of the loch, the path climbs to give you views down to Poolewe. Follow the path down until it eventually takes you to the main road. Turn left and follow the road back to the car park.

Inverewe Garden *Colour map 1, B4.*

T01445-781229, www.nts.org.uk. Garden and Visitor Centre open daily Apr 1030-1700, May-Aug 0930-1730, Sep 1000-1700, Oct 1030-1600; garden only Nov-Mar 1030-1600. £10.50, concessions £7.50, family £24.50. Osgoods Café open daily Apr 1100-1600, May-Oct 1030-1700; Bothy Café daily Apr-Oct 1100-1600, Nov-Dec Sat and Sun 1000-1500.

The reason most people come this way is to visit Inverewe Garden where you'll find an astonishing collection of exotic subtropical plants growing on the same latitude as Siberia, thanks to the mild climate created by the North Atlantic Drift. This wonderful 50-acre oasis of colour is a mecca for garden lovers, but even those who flinch at the mere sight of a lawn-mower will be bowled over by the sheer scale and diversity of plants and flowers on view. The garden was created from a treeless wilderness by Osgood Mackenzie, starting in 1862. By the time of his death in 1922 he had produced an internationally renowned walled and woodland garden. His work was continued by his daughter, who then gave the garden to the National Trust for Scotland in 1952. Since then, the plant collection has diversified even more and an intricate maze of paths leads you through ever-changing displays of Himalayan rhododendrons, Tasmanian eucalyptus, many Chilean and South African species, together with a large collection of New Zealand plants.

The garden is well worth visiting in any weather and at any time of the year, but especially from the end of April through the summer when the rhododendrons are in bloom. You should allow at least a couple of hours to do it justice. The garden is about a mile north of Poolewe on the main A832. There's a visitor centre and gift shop and a good restaurant, which serves snacks and hot meals.

Gruinard Bay *Colour map 1, B5.*

North of Poolewe the A832 passes Aultbea on its way to Laide, where it then skirts the shores of Gruinard Bay, with its lovely coves of pink sand. From Laide Post Office a side road branches north to **Mellon Udrigle** and **Opinan**, both with great beaches. It's worthwhile following the signs left to the hamlet of **Mellon Charles**. Here you'll find the fabulous **Perfume Studio** ① *T01445-731618, Apr-Oct daily 1000-1700 (closed on Mon), Nov-Dec Thu-Sat 1100-1600*, with its abundance of natural fragrances derived from wildflowers. There's also a very good café with lovely views over Loch Ewe. Between Laide and Mellon Udrigle, at **Achgarve**, a road branches left for about mile. From the end of this road you can walk all the way to **Slaggan**, a ruined village on the other side of the peninsula. It's a nice spot for a picnic but don't be tempted to swim in the sea as the tidal race makes it dangerous.

Gruinard Bay is a very beautiful part of the northwest coast but will always be synonymous with **Gruinard Island**, standing ominously in the middle of the bay. The island was used as a testing ground for biological warfare during the Second World War and was contaminated with anthrax spores. The Ministry of Defence finally agreed to decontaminate it in 1990 and it has now been declared 'safe'.

Where to stay

There are numerous B&Bs scattered throughout the area. Most of the owners will provide maps and information on local walks.

££££ Pool House Hotel
Poolewe, T01445-781272, www. pool-house.co.uk. Open all year.
7 en suite rooms, all with Royal Navy names reflecting the former use of the house as the Royal Naval headquarters for directing Second World War North Atlantic convoys. On the Cove Rd by the lochside, this former home of Osgood Mackenzie (who designed the nearby gardens) has been transformed into one of the very best hotels in the country (witness the numerous awards and accolades on their website). A stay here does not come cheap, but if you've got the money then look no further, for there is, quite simply, no better place to stay in this category. The dishes created in the hotel dining room are worthy of such luxurious surroundings (**£££**). Very highly recommended.

£££ Myrtle Bank Hotel
Gairloch, T01445-712004, www.themyrtlegairlochl.co.uk.
12 rooms. Known locally as The Myrtle, this modern hotel in the centre of Gairloch overlooking the loch has tasteful and comfortable rooms, very good food and service in the restaurant (**£££-££**) and fine ales in the hotel bar.

£££ The Old Inn
Gairloch, T01445-712068, www.theoldinn.net. Open all year.
17 rooms. This venerable old pub/restaurant with rooms is renowned for its fine ales and superb seafood (**££**). Located by the harbour, it makes an excellent base for exploring the area and staying here gives the advantage of not having to move far after enjoying the best pint of real ale for

miles around. Recommended for those who don't turn in too early.

££ Kerrysdale House
Gairloch, T01445-712292, www. kerrysdalehouse.co.uk. Open all year.
3 rooms. Charming B&B in a building that dates back to 1793, with the added benefit of a garden to enjoy in summer.

££ Old Smiddy Guest House
In Laide, near Gruinard Bay, T01445-731696, www.oldsmiddyguesthouse.co.uk. Mar-Oct.
3 rooms. Superior guesthouse in great location, with lavish breakfasts and an excellent restaurant (**£££** for 4-course dinner, BYOB). Highly recommended. Also self-catering bungalow for rent.

£ Carn Dearg Youth Hostel
3 miles beyond Gairloch, on the road to Melvaig, T01445-712219. 15 May-3 Oct.
A former hunting lodge next to the sea, with good facilities and superb views.

£ Solas
1 Big Sand, Gairloch, T01445-712753, www.solasbandb.co.uk.
2 rooms. Modern, light, airy and comfortable B&B spectacularly located by the beach at Big Sand and run by Isabel Steel.

Self-catering

Dry Island
Badachro, T01445-741263, www. dry-island.co.uk. Open all year.
3 properties for rent on a nightly or weekly basis. Here's a chance to stay on a private island, accessed from the mainland by a floating bridge or on foot at low tide. Beautiful surroundings and all the peace and tranquility you can handle. **Otter Cabin** is compact and bijoux for 2 people, from £250-465 week, the **Old Curing Station** (built 1785) is larger and more comfortable and availaible at £65 per night, and the

Bothy & Camping Barrel sleeps up to 6 in 3 bedrooms for £65-85 per night.

Camping

Badrallach Bothy & Camp Site
Near Gruinard Bay, T01445-633281, www.badrallach.com.
This campsite is situated in the tiny, remote hamlet of Badrallach. A few miles east of Dundonnell, take a side road which branches left and runs for 7 miles. The bothy (it's a lovely backpackers) has a peat fire and 12 beds.

Big Sands Holiday Centre
Big Sand, about a mile beyond Strath, T01445-712152. Easter-Oct.
Fabulous facilities and truly gobsmacking views.

Camping and Caravan Club Site
Between Poolewe Village and Inverewe Garden, T01445-781249.
An excellent site.

Gairloch Caravan & Camping Park
Strath, T01445-712373.
With full facilities and close to all amenities.

Gruinard Bay Caravan Park
In Laide near Gruinard Bay, T01445-731225. Apr-Oct.
Good facilities and great location.

Restaurants

Hotels are often the best options for eating out, see Where to stay, above. Of particular note are **The Old Inn** and the **Myrtle Bank Hotel**.

£££-££ Badachro Inn
Badachro, T01445-741255, www.badachroinn.com.

Good food in this handily placed hotel on the road to Red Point. Nice views from the dining room and beloved by the yachtie fraternity. A great place for a pint of real ale and some fresh seafood.

££-£ Osgood's Café
Inverewe Garden, Poolewe, T01445-781200. Apr daily 1100-1600, May-Oct daily 1030-1700.
Self-service licensed restaurant serving soup, sandwiches and cakes. The best place to eat cheaply around Poolewe.

What to do

Wildlife cruises
Gairloch Marine Life Centre, *by the pier (book at the Wildlife Centre), T01445-712636, www.porpoise-gairloch.co.uk.* Excellent wildlife-spotting boat trips, Mar-Oct, 2-hr cruise, 1000, 1230 and 1500 (subject to weather conditions), £20, child £15. You may spot minke whales, seals, porpoises and even killer whales (orcas) as you explore the coastline.
Hebridean Whales Cruises, *T01445-712458, www.hebridean-whale-cruises.co.uk.* Inshore wildlife cruises and offshore whale cruises with a chance of seeing humpback and minke whales, orcas and dolphins.

Transport

Bus
Westerbus, T01445-712255, service 705 runs from Gairloch (0745) to **Inverness** (1025), Mon, Wed and Sat via **Mellon Charles/ Aultbea** (0820), **Laide** (0835), **Dundonnell** (0850), **Braemore Junction** (for connections to **Ullapool**), and **Strathpeffer** (0952). The same bus company also runs a service, Tue, Thu and Fri, between **Laide** (0745) and **Inverness** (1025) with stops including **Poolewe** (0805) and **Loch Maree**.

Ullapool
& around

The attractive little fishing port of Ullapool, on the shores of Loch Broom, is the largest settlement in Wester Ross. The grid-pattern village, created in 1788 at the height of the herring boom by the British Fisheries Society, is still an important fishing centre as well as being the major tourist hub in the northwest of Scotland and one of the main ferry terminals for the Outer Hebrides. At the height of the busy summer season the town is swamped by visitors passing through on their way to or from Stornoway on Lewis, heading north into the wilds, or south to Inverness. It has excellent tourist amenities and services, and relatively good transport links, making it the ideal base for those exploring the northwest coast and a good place to be if the weather is bad.

North of Ullapool you enter a different world. The landscape becomes ever more dramatic and unreal – a huge emptiness of bleak moorland punctuated by isolated peaks and shimmering lochs. A narrow and tortuously twisting road winds its way up the coast, past deserted beaches of sparkling white sand washed by turquoise seas. There's not much tourist traffic this far north, despite the growing popularity of the North Coast 500 (see page 14), and once you get off the main A835 and on to the backroads, you can enjoy the wonderful sensation of having all this astonishingly beautiful scenery to yourself.

Ullapool's attractions are very much of the outdoor variety and include the Falls of Measach, Achiltibuie and Stac Pollaidh. However, whilst in town it's worth taking a stroll around the harbour to watch the comings and goings of the fishing fleet, and you might even see the occasional seal or otter swimming close to the shore.

The only real 'sight' as such is the **Ullapool Museum and Visitor Centre** ① *7 and 8 West Argyle St, T01854-612987, www.ullapoolmuseum.co.uk, Apr-Oct Mon-Sat 1100-1600, Nov-Mar by prior arrangement only, £4, children free,* in a converted church in West Argyle Street. It has some interesting displays on local history, including the story of those who set sail from here in 1773 on board *The Hector,* the first ship to carry emigrants from the Highlands to Nova Scotia in Canada.

Walks around Ullapool *All routes are covered by OS Maps Nos 15, 19 and 20.*
There are several good walking trails which start in Ullapool. One of these is to the top of **Ullapool Hill**, or **Meall Mhor** (886 ft). Starting from the tourist office, head to the end of Argyle Street, turn left on to North Road. Walk down the lane between Broom Court and the Hydro sub-station and then follow the path which zigzags up the hillside. There's a good cairned path up to the top of the hill. The views from the top over Glen Achall, and on a clear day, the mountains of Sutherland, are superb. You can return by traversing the hillside to the top of the Braes, or take a track leading to Loch Achall and follow the Ullapool river through the quarry road back to the village. The return trip takes one to two hours.

A relatively easy, but much longer walk, of five to six hours, is to **Rhidorroch Estate**. Take the A835 north out of Ullapool. Opposite the petrol station and before the bridge, take the road on the right signed 'Quarry'. Go through the quarry keeping to the left, and follow the Ullapool river until you see Loch Achall. Continue along the north bank of the loch for another six miles. East Rhidorroch Lodge is on the right; cross the bridge to get there, then skirt the lodge fences and cross to the track which leads up the southwestern hill. This brings you out to Leckmelm, about four miles south of Ullapool on the A835. This last section offers wonderful views across Loch Broom to An Teallach. From Leckmelm you can also climb **Beinn Eilideach** (1837 ft).

A good coastal walk is to **Rhue Lighthouse** and back. From the north end of Quay Street go down the steps to the river. Cross the bridges and head left by

Essential Ullapool

Finding your feet

Ullapool is the mainland terminal for ferries to Stornoway (Lewis). **Scottish Citylink**, www.citylink.co.uk, buses from Inverness (twice daily Monday to Saturday, one on Sunday, one hour 20 minutes) connect with the ferry to Stornoway. The local **CalMac office** (Shore Street, opposite the pier, T0800-066 5000, open Monday-Friday 0900-1730, Saturday 0900-1900, Sunday 1600-1830), also has details. Monday to Friday there's a bus to Achiltibuie at 1040 and, if requested by the passenger, it will stop in Reiff and Altandhu (1130) before continuing to Achiltibuie and Badenscallie. Also **Stagecoach** service No 61 leaves once a day Monday to Friday at 1520 from Inverness bus station to Ullapool, and from Ullapool to Lochinver at 1520. See also Transport, page 248.

the football field. Follow the path to the left by the duck pond and cross in front of the bungalow. Then follow the shoreline north for about two miles, climbing up the hillside when the tide is high. Follow the path until you reach the little white lighthouse at Rhue Point. To return, take the single-track road out of Rhue back to the main road and up over the hill to Ullapool. It's about six miles in total.

There are many more strenuous hiking routes around Ullapool. The A835 south of town gives access to **Beinn Dearg** (3556 ft) and the **Fannichs**, a range of hills on the southern side of Dirrie More. There's also **An Teallach**, a favourite with Scottish climbers, see below. North of Ullapool are the mountains within the Inverpolly National Nature Reserve (see below).

All routes require hillwalking experience and you should be well prepared for the unpredictable weather conditions. A good guidebook is *The Northern Highlands, SMC District Guide*, by Tom Strang. For details of tour operators offering trips, see What to do, page 248.

Ullapool

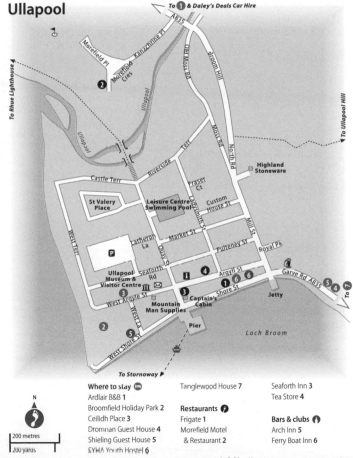

Where to stay
Ardlair B&B **1**
Broomfield Holiday Park **2**
Ceilidh Place **3**
Dromnan Guest House **4**
Shieling Guest House **5**
SYHA Youth Hostel **6**

Tanglewood House **7**

Restaurants
Frigate **1**
Morefield Motel
& Restaurant **2**

Seaforth Inn **3**
Tea Store **4**

Bars & clubs
Arch Inn **5**
Ferry Boat Inn **6**

N
200 metres
200 yards

Tourist information

iCentre
6 Argyle St, T01854-612486. Easter-Oct daily, 0900-1700, Nov-Easter Mon-Sat 0900-1400, Sun 1000-1400.
This well-run office is helpful and provides an accommodation booking service as well as information on local walks and trips. It also has a good stock of books and maps. To find out what's on, tune in to Loch Broom FM (102.2 and 96.8) or pick up a copy of the *Ullapool News* on Fri.

Where to stay

There is no shortage of places to stay in and around Ullapool, ranging from one of the very finest hotels in the UK to guesthouses and B&Bs, a couple of good youth hostels and a campsite. Garve Rd, heading south out of town, has several guesthouses, and there are lots of B&Bs along Seaforth Rd and Pulteney St.

£££ Braemore Square Country House
Braemore, T01845-655378, www. braemoresquare.com. Open all year.
11 miles south of Ullapool and set in 46 acres of grounds is the former estate house of Victorian engineer Sir John Fowler, who designed the Forth Rail Bridge. B&B, with 3 comfortable and tastefully furnished rooms, all in splendid isolation. Guests have use of the kitchen. 3 high-quality self-catering apartments for 2-4 people also available (£700-900 per week in summer). Recommended.

£££ Tanglewood House
T01854-612059, www.tanglewoodhouse. co.uk. Open all year.
3 en suite rooms. Chalet-style house in stunning location overlooking Loch Broom, set in 3 acres of headland, cliffs and rocky beach. Though it changed hands in 2017 it remains a fabulous place to relax and

unwind. All rooms have their own balcony and wonderful views across the loch. Highly recommended.

£££-££ The Shieling Guest House
Garve Rd, T01854-612947, www. theshielingullapool.co.uk.
6 rooms, 2 on ground floor. Purpose-built, charming house on the edge of Ullapool and set within an acre of its own grounds with views over the loch and mountains. Very comfortable and great breakfasts. Even has its own sauna.

£££-£ The Ceilidh Place
14 West Argyle Place, T01854-612103, www.theceilidhplace.com.
13 rooms, 10 of which are en suite, and each named after a 'famous' visitor who has recommended books to be read – and which are left in each of the different, tastefully furnished rooms. This former boatshed that grew from the inspirations of one man is not one of your run-of-the-mill hotels. It's different and refreshingly so, with a cosy lounge, bookshop, restaurant, bar and café. **The Bunkhouse** across the car park has 11 basic rooms for 1 up to 32 people. Also hosts a varied programme of arts events such as live music, plays, poetry readings, exhibitions and ceilidhs. It's a great place to relax and soak up some local culture. Highly recommended.

££ Ardlair B&B
Morefield Brae, North Rd, T01854-613417, www.ardlairullapool.co.uk.
3 rooms (1 for families or groups of 3-4). Wonderfully comfortable and friendly B&B about a mile north of the village with fabulous views over Loch Broom. A real home from home. Very good value for single travellers. No breakfast provided.

££ Dromnan Guest House
Garve Rd, T01854-612333, www. dromnan.com. Open all year.

7 rooms, 3 on ground floor. Very pleasant and friendly guesthouse with great views across Loch Broom. All rooms are tastefully furnished and decorated. 2 nights minimum stay in high season.

£ SYHA youth hostel
Shore St, T01854-612254. Mar-Dec.
A very good hostel. You can pick up some information on local walks and it also offers bike hire, internet and laundry facilities. Recommended.

Camping

Broomfield Holiday Park
Shore St, T01854-612 0020. Easter-Sep.
At the west end of the village, this campsite has great views across to the Summer Isles and a laundrette on site.

Restaurants

££ The Ceilidh Place
See Where to stay, above. Open 1100-2300.
One of those places that tourists seem to hang around for hours or even days. It exudes a laid-back, cultured ambience. The self-service coffee shop does wholefood all day during the summer, while the restaurant serves more expensive full meals, with an emphasis on vegetarian and seafood at night. There's even outdoor seating. Also hosts live music and various other events, see Bars and clubs, below. Not the cheapest in town but one of the best.

££ Morefield Motel & Restaurant
North Rd, T01854-612161, www. morefieldmotel.co.uk. May-Oct.
On the edge of town heading north, in the middle of a housing estate. The setting may be a little incongruous but the seafood is sensational, which is why people travel from miles around. Good value.

££-£ The Frigate
Shore St, T01854-612969. Daily 0900-2130.
Whether you want porridge for breakfast, a mid-morning bagel, kids' meals or steak pie,

this bright café bistro caters for all tastes. It's also a good place to stock up on picnic items. Try the ice cream.

££-£ Seaforth Inn
Quay St, T01854-612122. Breakfast served 1000-1200, lunch 1200-2000, bar open 1000-2200.
Popular pub serving delicious seafood and other staples to suit all pockets. Bar meals downstairs are good value. Their chippy next door is also very good (open 1200-2100). Gets busy at weekends.

£ Tea Store
27 Argyll St, T01845-612995. Daily 0800-2000.
No-nonsense café serving all-day breakfasts, etc, and home-baked goodies. Recommended for a hearty breakfast and to meet the local prawn fishermen. Also do takeway food.

Bars and clubs

Arch Inn
11 West Shore St, T01854-612454.
If you want reasonable bar food, a pool table and a jumping atmosphere as you down your pint, then this is the place to be.

The Ceilidh Place
See Where to stay, above.
For something a bit more sedate and civilized than the other choices, head here where you can enjoy a quiet drink in the cosy café-bar or take advantage of their varied programme of events. There's live music Mon-Sat throughout the summer, and on a Mon in winter there are also ceilidhs and poetry readings.

Ferry Boat Inn
Shore St.
Known locally as **FBI**, Ullapool's favourite pub has a Thu night live music session year-round (gets very cramped), and during the summer you can sit outside on the sea wall and watch the sun go down as you drain your pint of superb real ale.

Seaforth Inn

See Restaurants, above.
Gets busy at weekends and has a barn-like feel, but it's a great place to eat and hear live music.

Festivals

Sep Loopallu Festival, www.loopallu.co.uk. Big music festival held over a weekend in late Sep. Started in 2005 and has seized the imagination of music lovers around the country. Held in various venues around town.

Shopping

As well as **Tescos**, the town is well supplied with shops.

The Captain's Cabin, *on the corner of Quay St and Shore St*. Sells books, as well as crafts and souvenirs.
The Ceilidh Place, *see Where to stay, above.* Has a good bookshop if you don't plan to head for **Achins** by Lochinver.
Highland Stoneware, *North Rd, T01854-612980, www.highlandstoneware.com. Mon-Fri 0900-1730, Sat 1030-1700.* Look no further than here for high-quality, hand-turned and painted pottery. You can wander round the studios before browsing in their gift shop, which is pricey, but you may have luck in their bargain baskets. Their main workshop is in Lochinver (T01571-844376, Mon-Fri 0900-1730, Sat 1100-1600).
Mountain Man Supplies, *opposite the museum, West Argyle St*. A good outdoor equipment shop.
Unlimited Colour Company, *6 West Argyle St, T01854-612439. Mon-Sat 0900-1700.* An excellent option for all manner of brightly coloured, hand-dyed natural weaves, scarves, hats, cushions and throws.

What to do

Boat tours
Seascape Expeditions, *T01854-633708, www.sea-scape.co.uk.* 1¼-hr or 2-hr trips that leave from Ullapool harbour daily in summer aboard a fast-rib boat (£25/15 per person for 1¼ hrs, £30/20 for 2 hrs). It's an exhilarating 40-mile sea-trip around the Summer Isles with the chance to spot wildlife.
Shearwater Cruises, *1 Royal Park, T01854-612472, www.summerqueen.co.uk.* During the summer, the *Shearwater* runs cruises around the Summer Isles and wildlife cruises around Loch Broom, Annat Bay and Isle Martin. Call or check website for details of 2018 cruises.

Transport

Bus
Scottish Citylink buses run Mon-Sat between Ullapool and **Inverness**. There are also buses Mon-Sat to **Inverness** with **Stagecoach**, www.stagecoachbus.com, and Mon-Fri at 0910 and 1637 to **Drumbeg** via **Lochinver** from Ullapool. The bus continues to **Achmelvich Youth Hostel**. Also buses to and from Inverness with **D&E Coaches**, www.decoaches.co.uk. Cyclists can book the **Durness Bike Bus** which travels between Inverness and Durness and all points in between, www.tickettoridehighlands.co.uk. It's not a scheduled service but more like a taxi service. 2 people and bikes from Inverness to Ullapool costs £130. There's a bus Mon, Wed, Thu and Sat to **Gairloch**, operated by **Westerbus**, https//:bustimes.org.uk.

Car hire
Lochbroom Self Drive, Morefield Industrial Estate, T01854-612560.

Cycle hire
Available at hostels (see page 247).

On the southern shore of Little Loch Broom is the village of Dundonnell, from where there are spectacular views of awesome An Teallach (3484 ft), a mountain of almost mythical status amongst Scottish climbers and spoken of in hushed, reverential tones. The path to the highest of its summits is clear and begins southeast of the Dundonell Hotel. It will take a full day and you'll need to be well prepared (OS map No 19) and heed the usual advice.

The A832 coastal road meets the A835 Ullapool to Inverness main road at Braemore junction, 12 miles south of Ullapool. Before heading on to Ullapool it's worth stopping at the very impressive **Falls of Measach**, just by the junction. The falls plunge 150 ft into the spectacular **Corrieshalloch Gorge** (or 'ugly/fearsome gorge' in Gaelic) and can be crossed by a distinctly wobbly suspension bridge (not for vertigo sufferers). The falls can be reached from the A835, but the most dramatic approach is from the A832 Gairloch road.

Listings South of Ullapool

Where to stay

£££ Dundonnell Hote
In Dundonnell, south of Ullapool, T01854-633204, www.dundonnellhotel.com. Feb-Dec.
32 en suite rooms. Good-value hotel and good food, including plenty of seafood, fish and vegetarian options, in the **Broombeg**

Bar (**£££-££**). Excellent coffee in the lounge. Worth the stop.

£ Sail Mhor Croft Hostel
South of Ullapool in Camusnagaul by Dundonnell, T01854-633224, www. sailmhor.co.uk. Mid-Feb to mid-Dec.
16 beds, clean and cosy. Located at the foot of An Teallach.

North of Ullapool
breathtaking mountains and remote islands and beaches

The region immediately north of Ullapool is called Assynt, and is heaven for serious hillwalkers and climbers. Though most of its mountains are not Munros, they offer a stiff climb. The views from the summits are truly breathtaking, including across to Skye, but it's vital you dress for the mountains and prepare for harsh weather conditions that can materialize at a moment's notice from the Atlantic. Amongst the most spectacular of Assynt's distinctive 'island peaks' are Suilven (2398 ft), Ben More Assynt (3275 ft), Quinag (2650 ft) and Canisp (2778 ft). Much of this region is protected in the Inverpolly and Inchnadamph National Nature Reserves, home to an extremely rich and diverse wildlife. The whole of the northwest corner is contained within the Northwest Highlands Geopark. For more information, visit www.nwhgeopark,com. Also be sure to pay a visit to the Rock Stop, the official geopark visitor centre, just before Kylesku.

Inverpolly National Nature Reserve OS Landranger No 15. Colour map 1, B5.

About 12 miles north of Ullapool, at Knockan, on the main A835 is the exceptional SNH **Visitor Centre** ① T01854-666234, www.knockan-crag.co.uk, open all year 24 hrs a day, at Knockan Crag. It's an interactive display of the geology, flora and fauna of an area that marks some of the world's oldest geological rock formations (www.northwest-highlands-geopark.org.uk). From the visitor centre there's a marked trail which leads up to the **Crag**, and the views from the clifftop are excellent, across to Inverpolly's 'island' peaks of Cul Mór, Cul Beag and Stac Pollaidh.

Nearby, at **Elphin**, is a great tearoom offering fabulous home-baking, it's on the left as you drive towards Ullapool. Beyond Elphin is **Ledmore**, where the A837 branches east towards Lairg and Bonar Bridge. There's a good craft shop at Ledmore where you can buy hand-knitted jumpers.

Between Ullapool and Knockan Crag is the turn-off west (left) to the distinctive craggy peak of **Stac Pollaidh**. A path has been established by the John Muir Trust, which takes you on a circular walk around the peak from the car park. Take the right-hand path and go round at the same level, or climb up the rear to the top, go around the summit and descend by the same path. You'll need a head for heights to reach the summit, as much of the route is exposed, but the stunning views are worth it. Be careful not to stray from the path; it's been put there because of the damage inflicted by tens of thousands of pairs of boots each year, resulting in serious erosion on the south face. It's a fairly easy 2½-hour walk.

Achiltibuie Colour map 1, B5.

The unclassified single-track road winds its way west past Stac Pollaidh to the turn-off for Achiltibuie. This old crofting village, with whitewashed cottages set back from the sea with views across to the beautiful Summer Isles, is home to a small grocers, post office (excellent for checking out the latest community events on the go) and one of the northwest's best dining options and hotels, the **Summer Isles Hotel**. Look directly south from here and you'll clearly spot the low-lying Summer Isles over a mile offshore and a popular location for experienced sea kayakers.

An erstwhile attraction here was the **Smokehouse**, at Altandhu, five miles north of Achiltibuie. It was bought by **Summer Isles Foods** who then moved their production to Alness in Easter Ross. At the time of writing there is talk of a renewed bid for public ownership. A few miles further down the road in Polbain, is the **Coigach Craft and Gift Shop** ① T01854-622346, www.coigach.com, Mon-Sat 1000-1700, a good place for a cuppa and the chance to buy some local crafts or a fishing permit.

Lochinver and around Colour map 1, B5.

The road from Achiltibuie north to Lochinver is known locally as the 'wee mad road', and you'd be mad to miss this thrilling route which twists and winds its way through some the northwest's most magnificent scenery. A mile south of Lochinver at Inverkirkaig, is the superb **Achins Bookshop** ① T01571-844262, bookshop open all year 1000-1800, café till 1700, a friendly place packed with second-hand books. The village of Lochinver is a working fishing port and the last sizeable village before Thurso. It has a good tourist office, lots of accommodation, a bank with ATM, post office, petrol station and several good eating options. Pick up fishing permits at the post office or **Assynt Visitor Centre** ① T01854-844654, www.discoverassynt.co.uk, Apr-Oct Mon-Fri 1000-1700, Sun 1000-1600, which houses the iCentre. It has displays on the local geology, history and wildlife and there's also a ranger service with guided walks throughout the summer. Those looking for high-quality hand-crafted, earthenware gifts should head for **Highland Stoneware**, see page 248.

A few miles south of Lochinver, beyond Inverkirkaig, is the trail along the river to the **Kirkaig Falls**. The path starts near the Achins Bookshop. Follow the path for about two miles until it branches right to the falls in the gorge below. Continue along the main path for about another ¾ mile until you reach Fionn Loch, with superb views of mighty Suilven. The walk up to the falls and back should take around 1½ hours. This is one of the main approaches to the foot of the mountain.

Loch Assynt and Inchnadamph *Colour map 1, B5/6.*

The area east of Lochinver is a remote wilderness of mountains and moorland dotted with lochs and lochans. As well as being a favourite haunt of hardy climbers and walkers (ask at the **Lochinver iCentre** for the leaflet about local walks), Assynt is a paradise for anglers. Most of the lochs are teeming with brown trout, and fishing permits are readily available throughout the area from the **iCentre** in Lochinver or at local hotels, guesthouses and B&Bs. There's also salmon fishing on the River Kirkaig, available through the **Inver Lodge Hotel** and on Loch Assynt through the **Inchnadamph Lodge**, see Where to stay, page 254.

The A837 Lochinver to Lairg road meets the A894 to Durness 10 miles east of Lochinver at Skiag Bridge by Loch Assynt. Half a mile south of here, by the loch, are the ruins of **Ardvreck Castle**. The castle dates from 1597 and was the stronghold of the Macleods of Assynt until a siege in 1691, when it was taken by the Seaforth Mackenzies. Before that, the Marquess of Montrose had been imprisoned here following his defeat at Carbisdale in 1650. Access to the castle is free, but the ruins are in a dangerous state and should be approached with care.

To the east of the road lies the **Inchnadamph National Nature Reserve**, dominated by the massive peaks of Ben More Assynt and Conival, which should only be attempted by experienced hillwalkers. A few miles south of the village of Inchnadamph, at the fish farm, is a steep, but well-marked footpath up to the **Bone Caves**. This is one of Scotland's oldest historical sites, where the bones of humans and animals such as lynx and bear were found together with sawn-off deer antlers dating from over 8000 years ago.

Lochinver to Kylesku *Colour map 1, B5.*

The quickest way north from Lochinver is the A837 east to the junction with the A894 which heads to Kylesku. But by far the most scenic route is the B869 coast road that passes moorland, lochs and beautiful sandy bays. It's best travelled from north to south, giving you the most fantastic views of the whale-backed hump of **Suilven**, rocky talisman of the great poet, Norman MacCaig. Untypically, most of the land in this part of Assynt is owned by local crofters who, under the aegis of the Assynt Crofters' Trust, bought 21,000 acres of the North Assynt Estate, thus setting a precedent for change in the history of land ownership in the Highlands.

The trust now owns the fishing rights to the area and sells permits through local post offices and the tourist office in Lochinver. It has also undertaken a number of conservation projects, including one at **Achmelvich**, a few miles north of Lochinver, at the end of a side road which branches off the coast road. It's worth a detour to see one of the loveliest beaches on the west coast, with sparkling white sand and clear turquoise waters straight out of a Caribbean tourist brochure. It's a terrific place for a family picnic. There's a great youth hostel here, though the caravan site jars with the beauty of the surrounding landscape.

From the beach car park below the hostel a path leads northwest along the coast. Bear left off the sandy path shortly after the white cottage on the hill ahead comes into view, and follow the footpath until the road is reached at Alltan na Bradhan, where there are the remains of an old meal mill. Continue north from here along the coast for about a mile until you reach a small bay just before Clachtoll and its **campsite** (see Where to stay, page 254). Close by are the remains of an Iron Age broch, but don't cause further damage by clambering over the ruins. Return to the beach by the same path. The walk there and back should take about 1½ hours.

Old Man of Stoer *Colour map 1, B5.*
Check access locally during the deer-stalking season which runs from mid-Aug to mid-Oct.

A side road turns left off the B869 north of Stoer and runs out to **Stoer Lighthouse**. From here you can walk across the Stoer Peninsula to the Old Man of Stoer, a dramatic rock pillar standing offshore, surrounded by sheer cliffs. Allow about three hours for the circular walk which starts and ends in the lighthouse car park. There is no public transport to the lighthouse, but the Lochinver to Drumbeg postbus runs to Raffin, one mile away. A clear path runs from the car park to the cliffs then follows the line of the cliffs northwards. The path heads inland for a short distance as it bypasses a deep gully then meets the clifftop again, and after a mile or so you can see the Old Man tucked away in a shallow bay, battered by huge waves. Beyond the Old Man the path continues to the headland, the **Point of Stoer**, from where it turns back on itself and climbs **Sidhean Mór** (532 ft). The views from here are fantastic, across to Harris and Lewis and south to the mountains of Assynt. From here, follow the faint path south, back towards the lighthouse, passing a small loch below Sidhean Beag on your left and an obvious cairn on your right. Then you pass a radio mast and follow the clear track back to the lighthouse car park. OS Landranger Map No 15 covers the route. Nine miles further on, in beautiful **Eddrachillis Bay**, is **Drumbeg**, a popular place for anglers who come to fish in the many lochs of North Assynt.

Kylesku *Colour map 1, B5.*
The road runs east from Drumbeg, under the shadow of towering **Quinag** (2650 ft), to meet the A894 heading north to Kylesku, site of the sweeping modern road bridge over Loch a'Cháirn Bháin. From Kylesku you can visit Britain's highest waterfall, the 650-ft high **Eas a'Chùal Aluinn**, near the head of Loch Glencoul. Cruises leave from the old ferry jetty below the **Kylesku Hotel** to the falls, see What to do, page 256.

There's also a trail to the top of the falls. It starts at the south end of Loch na Gainmhich, about three miles north of Skiag Bridge. Skirting the loch, follow the track in a southeasterly direction up to the head of the Bealach a Bhuirich (the Roaring Pass). Continue until you meet a stream, with several small lochans on your right. Follow this stream until it plunges over the Cliffs of Dubh (the Dark Cliffs). You can get a better view of the falls by walking to the right about 100 yds and descending a heather slope for a short distance. Allow about three to four hours for the round trip.

Scourie and Handa Island *Colour map 1, A5.*
Some 10 miles north of Kylesku is the little crofting community of Scourie, sitting above a sandy bay. Anyone remotely interested in wildlife is strongly advised to make a stop here to visit Handa Island, a sea bird reserve run by the Scottish Wildlife Trust, and one of the best places in the country for bird life. The island is now deserted, except for the warden, but once supported a thriving community of crofters, until the potato famine of 1846 forced them to leave, most emigrating to Canada's Cape Breton. Now it's home to huge colonies of shags, fulmars, razorbills, guillemots and puffins, in season. The best time to visit is during the summer breeding season, from late May to August. There's a footpath right round the island, which is detailed in the free SWT leaflet available at the

warden's office when you arrive. You should allow three to four hours. There's a **ferry service** ① *T07780-967800 (Roger), Mon-Sat at 0900 and 1400, last return at 1700, £12.50 return, children £5*, to the island from Tarbet Beach, three miles northwest off the A894, about two miles north of Scourie. It sails continuously, depending on demand, from April to September, and the crossing takes 15 minutes. To get from Scourie to the jetty for Handa Island you'll need to walk, cycle, drive or take a taxi. It's worth it though. There is also an excellent wildlife boat trip that leaves from Fanagmore, a mile from Tarbet on the other side of the peninsula. See What to do, page 256.

Kinlochbervie and around *Colour map 1, A5.*
The road north from Scourie passes Laxford Bridge, where it meets the A838 running southeast to Lairg, see page 273. The A838 also runs north to Durness, on the north coast, see page 257. At **Rhiconich**, the B801 branches northwest to Kinlochbervie, a small village with a very big fish market. This is one of the west coast's major fishing ports, and huge container lorries thunder along the narrow single-track roads carrying frozen fish and seafood to all corners of Europe.

A few miles beyond Kinlochbervie is **Oldshoremore**, a tiny crofters' village scattered around a stunning white beach, and a great place to swim. The less hardy can instead explore the hidden rocky coves nearby.

At the end of the road is **Blairmore**, from where a footpath leads to ★ **Sandwood Bay**, one of the west coast's most wonderful beaches and on protected land managed by the John Muir Trust conservation charity. It's a four-mile walk in each direction but because of its isolation you'll probably have this glorious mile-long stretch of white sand all to yourself. At one end is a spectacular rock pinnacle and it is said to be haunted by the ghost of an ancient shipwrecked mariner. Allow three hours for the walk there and back, plus time at the beach. Romantic souls may wish to take a tent and watch the sunset with a loved one and a bottle of their favourite single malt. Sandwood Bay can also be reached from Cape Wrath, a hard, long day's hike to the north, see page 258.

Listings North of Ullapool

Where to stay

Achiltibuie

££££-£££ Summer Isles Hotel
T01854-622282, www.summerisleshotel.com. Apr-end Oct.
10 en suite rooms (3 of which are log cabins with turf-covered roofs, 1 is disabled-friendly), 2 suites and 1 cottage. Easter to mid-Oct. This relaxing, civilized hotel is under the ownership of the Mackays, who also own a hotel on Barra. The hotel enjoys magnificent views across to the Summer Isles and boasts a fabulous restaurant, see Restaurants, below.

£ SYHA Youth Hostel
A few miles south at Achininver, T01854-622254. Mid-May to early Oct.
Basic and very cheap.

Lochinver and around

££££ The Albannach Hotel
Baddidaroch, T01571-844407, www.thealbannach.co.uk. Mar-Nov.
5 en suite rooms (2 doubles and 3 suites). This wonderful 18th-century house overlooking Loch Inver is one of the very best places to stay in the northwest and everything a romantic Highland hotel should be. Rooms are tall, dark and handsome and the food in the Michelin-starred restaurant

is sublime and well worth going out of your way for, featuring only the freshest of local fish, fowl and game. The price includes dinner, but B&B is also available (**££££-£££**) and B&B-only guests can have a table booked at the **Caberfeidh** pub in the village (see Restaurants, below) which is now owned by the same people. Highly recommended.

££££ Inver Lodge Hotel
Iolaire Rd, T01571-844496, www.inverlodge.com. Apr-Nov.
The spacious, luxuriously appointed rooms, each named after a local mountain or loch, look out over the hills and sea and their **Chez Roux** restaurant (**£££**) makes the best use of the finest local ingredients. Bar lunches (**££**) are available 1200-1800. This is a fabulous retreat and one of the very best hotels in the northwest of Scotland. Recommended.

££ Polcraig
T01571-844429, www.polcraig.com. Open all year.
6 en suite rooms. Large modern house offering a friendly welcome and good-value B&B. The new hosts Steve and Amanda have maintained the high standards.

Loch Assynt and Inchnadamph

£££ Inchnadamph Hotel
Assynt, T01571-822202, www. inchnadamphhotel.com. Mar-Oct.
An old-fashioned Highland hotel on the shores of Loch Assynt, catering for the hunting and fishing fraternity. Welcomes pets. Offers B&B or dinner B&B (£20 extra per person)

££-£ Inchnadamph Lodge
Assynt Field Centre, T01571-822218, www.inch-lodge.co.uk. Mar-Oct.
Great hostel accommodation in bunk rooms, as well as twin, double and family rooms. Continental breakfast is included. It's ideally situated for climbing Ben More Assynt and guides are available. Wheelchair-accessible room. 2 self-catering cottages (£560 per week).

Lochinver to Kylesku
There's not much accommodation around here other than self-catering cottages.

Camping

Clachtoll Beach Campsite
6 miles north of Lochinver, T01571-855377, www.clachtollbeachcampsite.co.uk. May-Sep.
Good facilities, friendly owners and a superb location. Recommended.

Kylesku

£££ Kylesku Hotel
T01971-502231, www.kyleskuhotel.co.uk.
11 en suite rooms, 1 on the ground floor, all tastefully furnished; 7 of the rooms have views across the sea lochs and neighbouring mountains. This is a great place simply to relax, enjoy a malt and dine on great-value pub meals and restaurant fare that draws on the best of the region's lamb, beef and seafood (**££**). Dogs welcome.

Self-catering

Kylesku Lodges
T01971-502003, www.kyleskulodges.co.uk.
9 beautifully appointed Scandinavian-style lodges sleeping 2-4 people, with a patio and delightful wood finishings that overlook sea lochs. A great option for couples and families who wish to escape, fish (wild brown trout), spot wildlife or simply relax. Dogs welcome. £810-860 per week in high season, 3-night minimum stay.

Scourie and Handa Island
There are lots of options in this area, including the following:

£££ Eddrachilles Hotel
Badcall Bay, T01971-502080, www.eddrachilles.com. Mar-Oct.
10 en suite rooms, 6 with sea views. This charming 200-year-old building stands in 300 acres of grounds overlooking the bay. The food on offer is superb (**£££**) and there's

an excellent range of malt whiskies behind the bar.

£££ Scourie Hotel
Scourie, T01971-502396, www.scourie-hotel.co.uk. Apr-Oct.
21 rooms. A 17th-century former coaching inn popular with anglers, which is also an excellent place to eat (£30 for 4-course set meal). **££££** for dinner B&B. Dogs welcome.

£££ Scourie Lodge
Scourie, T01971-502248, www.scourielodge.com.
4 rooms. There are several B&Bs in the village, but none better than this welcoming lodge in a stunning location.

Camping
There's a campsite on Harbour Rd, T01971-502060.

Kinlochbervie and around

£££ Rhiconich Hotel
Rhiconich, T01971-521224, www.rhiconichhotel.co.uk. Open all year.
10 en suite rooms. Modern functional hotel with good facilities and surrounded by superb scenery. Good-value lunch and dinner (1800-2100), whilst you enjoy fine views over Loch Inchard and try to spot the otters, seals and the myriad wildlife in the area. Good-value family rooms and single room only £60.

£££-££ Old School B&B
Inshegra, halfway between Kinlochbervie and the A838 at Rhiconich, T01971-521383, www.oldschoolklb.co.uk. Apr-Oct.
6 rooms, 4 are en suite. This is the best place to stay in the area, with great food served in an intimate former classroom that dates back to the 1800s. Bedrooms are in a modern annexe. Recommended.

Camping
There's a small campsite at Oldshoremore, T01971-521281.

Restaurants

Achiltibuie

£££ Summer Isles Hotel
See Where to stay, above.
This hotel boasts a great restaurant serving some of the best seafood on the planet, all landed with a few yards of the front door. The sublime 5-course set dinner is pricey (£49 per head) but unforgettable, or you can enjoy delicious bar lunches for a fraction of the price. Even if you're not staying or eating here, it's worth stopping to have a drink on the terrace and watch the sun set over the islands. Recommended.

££ Am Fuaran Bar
Altandhu, 101854-622339. Open 1100-2345, lunch 1200-1430, evening means 1800-2030.
Decent pub grub and seafood or just a pint and game of pool.

Lochinver and around

££ The Caberfeidh
Main St, T01571-844321, www.thecaberfeidh.co.uk.
Now run by the owners of **The Albannach Hotel** (see Where to stay, page 253). If the weather is clement, then come here and enjoy a meal and a drink in the beer garden overlooking the River Inver. Very good food and even better views, especially at sunset.

££ Lochinver Larder
Main St, on the way into town on the A837, T01571-844356.
You have to try their famous pies which use the best in local venison, beef, poultry and seafood, and there are also vegetarian and sweet options available. Eat in, takeaway or you can even have them mailed to you when you get back home (www.piesbypost.co.uk). Not cheap but tasty, with views over the sea.

Scourie and Handa Island

££ Old School Hotel & Restaurant
See Where to stay, above. Daily 1200-1400, 1800-2000.

Serves really good, home-cooked food to grateful souls who have ventured this far north. The best for miles around.

££ The Shorehouse Seafood Restaurant *Tarbet, just above the tiny jetty, T01971-502251, www. shorehousetarbet.co.uk.* Run by Julian Pearce, son of Essie who opened it in 1971, and his family If you're up this way, don't miss a visit to this restaurant which serves the latest catch from their own boat, the *MV Fulmar*. It's a wonderful, if unexpected, place to find, with views across the sea inlets. Recommended.

What to do

North of Ullapool
Boat tours
Laxford Cruises, *Seafood Restaurant, Tarbet, T01971-502251.* Sail around beautiful Loch Laxford, where you can see lots of birds from nearby Handa Island, as well as seals, porpoises and otters. Trips leave Easter-Sep Sun-Fri 1000, 1200 and 1400 (and at 1600 in Jul-Aug). The trips last 1¾ hrs and cost £16. For bookings contact Julian Pearce at the restaurant just above the jetty.
Summer Isles Sea Tours, *call Ian Macleod on T07927-920592, www.summerisles-seatours. co.uk.* For cruises around the Summer Isles from Achiltibuie pier on board the *Isabella*. Cruises leave Mon-Sat in morning, afternoon and evening May-Sep and cost £30 per person (£15 for children). Family tickets available.
Kylesku Boat Tours, *T01971-502231, www. kyleskuboattours.co.uk.* Cruises go from Kylesku to Eas a'Chùal Aluinn waterfall leaving from the old ferry jetty below the Kylesku Hotel. You can also see porpoises, seals and minke whales en route. The 1¾-hr

round trip runs Apr-Sep daily at 1200 and 1400. Costs £25, children £18.

Fishing
With over 150 lochs filled with wild trout and salmon, Assynt is also excellent for fishing. **Assynt Angling Group** (www.assyntangling. co.uk); **Assynt Crofters Trust** (T01571-855298, www.assyntcrofters.co.uk).

Tour operators
Ridgway Adventure, *Ardmore, Rhiconich, T01971-521006, www.ridgway-adventure.co.uk.* For multi-adventures, including walking weeks and weekends, and sea kayaking, contact this excellent outdoor operator.

Transport

Achiltibuie
Bus
Scotbus run twice daily (1040 and 1630) Mon-Fri between **Ullapool** and Achiltibuie, www.scotbus.co.uk.

Lochinver and around
Bus
Stagecoach No 67 runs to Lochinver from **Ullapool** along the main road via **Elphin** and continues to **Drumbeg** via **Clashnessie** and **Stoer**.

Scourie and Handa Island
Bus
See above for bike bus service from **Inverness bus station**.

Kinlochbervie and around
Bus
See above for bike bus service from **Inverness bus station**.

North
coast

Scotland's rugged north coast is not for the faint-hearted: over 100 miles of storm-lashed cliffs, sheer rocky headlands and deserted sandy coves backed by a desolate and eerily silent wilderness of mountain, bog and hill loch. It's the only place on mainland Britain where arctic flora and fauna come down to sea level. This is Britain's most spectacular and undisturbed coastline, a great place for birdwatching, with vast colonies of seabirds, and there's also a good chance of seeing seals, porpoises and minke whales in the more sheltered estuaries.

Durness and around   *Colour map 2, A1.*

spectacular sea cliffs, secret coves and a legendary pop star

Durness is not only the most northwesterly village on the British mainland, but also one of the most attractively located, surrounded by sheltered coves of sparkling white sand and machair-covered limestone cliffs. It's worth stopping here for a few days to explore the surrounding area. One of the village's most famous visitors was John Lennon, who used to spend childhood summers here with his Aunt Elizabeth, a local resident. This unlikely relationship was marked in 2002 with the creation of the **John Lennon Memorial Garden**. Beatles fans can now visit this lovely spot which features sculptures by local artist Lotte Glob, as well as standing stones bearing the lyrics to the fab four's classic *In My Life*.

Smoo Cave

A mile east of the village is the vast 200-ft-long Smoo Cave. A path from near the youth hostel leads down to the cave entrance which is hidden away at the end of a steep, narrow inlet. Plunging through the roof of the cathedral-like cavern is an 80-ft waterfall which can be seen from the entrance, but the more adventurous can take a boat trip into the floodlit interior.

A few miles east of the Smoo Cave are a couple of excellent beaches, at **Sangobeg** and **Rispond**, where the road leaves the coast and heads south along the west shore of stunning **Loch Eriboll**. Eriboll is Britain's steepest sea loch and was used by the Royal Navy during the Second World War as a base for protecting Russian convoys.

Essential North coast

There is an airport at Wick (see page 269), with good onward connections throughout Caithness. Getting around the far north without your own transport can be a slow process. Getting to Thurso, the main town, by bus or train is easy, but beyond that things get more difficult. **Stagecoach North Scotland** (No 80) run a regular service between Thurso train station and John o'Groats from Monday to Saturday, with at least three daily stopping en route at Gill's Bay. They also run a daily service from Thurso train station to Scrabster (at least three times daily) but it's strongly advised to call ahead (T01463-239292) to confirm times in order not to miss your ferry connection. See also Transport, page 265.

Balnakeil

About a mile northwest of Durness is the tiny hamlet of Balnakeil, overlooked by a ruined 17th-century church. In the south wall is a grave slab with carved skull-and-crossbones marking the grave of the notorious highwayman Donald MacMurchow. If you're looking for souvenirs, or an escape from the rat race, then head for the **Balnakeil Craft Village** ① *Apr-Oct daily 1000-1800*, an alternative artists' community set up in the 1960s in a former RAF radar station. Here you can buy weavings, pottery, paintings, leatherwork and woodwork in the little prefab huts. The Chocolatier and 'Chocolate Bar' café, **Cocoa Mountain**, is a must visit, specializing in fresh handmade truffles, hot chocolates, coffees and organic teas. You can watch the chocolates being made on the premises. Balnakeil has also become well known in golfing circles as this is the location of the Durness Golf Club's nine-hole **golf course** ① *T01971-511364*, the most northerly on mainland Britain. Its famous ninth hole involves a drive over the Atlantic Ocean. The beach here is glorious, especially in fine weather when the sea turns a brilliant shade of turquoise. Even better, walk north along the bay to **Faraid Head**, where you can see puffin colonies in early summer. The views across to Cape Wrath in the west and Loch Eriboll in the east, are stupendous.

Cape Wrath *Colour map 2, A1.*

There are several excellent trips around Durness, but the most spectacular is to Cape Wrath, Britain's most northwesterly point. It's a wild place and the name seems entirely appropriate, though it actually derives from the Norse word *hwarf*, meaning 'turning place'. Viking ships used it as a navigation point during their raids on the Scottish west coast. Now a lighthouse stands on the cape, above the 1000-ft-high Clo Mor Cliffs, the highest on the mainland, and breeding ground for huge colonies of seabirds.

You can walk south from here to ★ **Sandwood Bay**, see pages 24 and 253. It's an exhilarating but long coastal walk, and will take around eight hours. It's safer doing this walk from north to south as the area around the headland is a military firing range and access may be restricted, which could leave you stranded.

To get to Cape Wrath, first take the passenger **ferry** ① *T01971-511246, May at 1100 and 1330, Jun-Sep daily from 0930 (weather permitting), £7 return, child £5, bikes £8.50*, across the Kyle of Durness from Keoldale, two miles south of Durness. The ferry connects with a **minibus** ① *T01971-511284, £12, child £7*, for the 11-mile journey to the cape (50 minutes). Passengers then spend about an hour at the cape before heading back on the bus to the ferry.

Tongue to Thurso *Colour map 2, A1/2/3.*
The road east from Durness runs around **Loch Eriboll** on its way to the lovely little village of **Tongue**. A causeway crosses the beautiful Kyle of Tongue, but a much more scenic route is the single-track road around its southern side, with great views of **Ben Hope** (3041 ft) looming to the southwest. The village of Tongue is overlooked by the 14th-century ruins of **Varick Castle**, and there's a great beach at **Coldbackie**, two miles northeast.

The A836 runs south from Tongue through Altnaharra to Lairg, see page 273. It also continues east to the crofting community of **Bettyhill**, named after the Countess of Sutherland who ruthlessly evicted her tenants from their homes in Strathnaver to make way for more profitable sheep. The whole sorry saga is told in the interesting **Strathnaver Museum** ⓘ *T01641-521418, Apr-Oct Mon-Sat 1000-1700, £3, concessions £2, children, £1,* housed in an old church in the village and tells the story of crofting life at the time of the Strathnaver Clearances. There are also Pictish stones in the churchyard behind the museum.

The museum sells a leaflet detailing the many prehistoric sites in the Strathnaver Valley which runs due south from Bettyhill. There are a couple of great beaches around Bettyhill, at **Farr Bay** and at **Torrisdale Bay,** which is the more impressive of the two and forms part of the **Invernaver Nature Reserve**. East from Bettyhill the hills of Sutherland begin to give way to the fields of Caithness. The road passes the turn-off to **Strathy Point** before reaching **Melvich**, another small crofting settlement overlooking a lovely sandy bay.

South from Melvich the A897 heads to Helmsdale, see page 267, through the **Flow Country**, a vast expanse of bleak bog of major ecological importance. About 15 miles south of Melvich at Forsinard is an **RSPB Visitor Centre** ⓘ *T01641-571225, ww2.rspb.org.uk, Easter-Oct daily 0900-1730*; the guided walks through the nature reserve leave from here. These peatlands are a breeding ground for black- and red-throated divers, golden plovers and merlins as well as other species. Otters and roe deer can also be spotted.

Listings Durness and around

Tourist information

Durness Visitor Centre
T01971-511368, Apr-Oct Mon-Sat, Jun-Aug daily.
Arranges guided walks and has a small visitor centre with displays on local history, flora and fauna and geology.

Where to stay

£££ Borgie Lodge Hotel
Skerray, by Tongue, T01641-521332, www. borgielodgehotel. co.uk. Open all year.
8 rooms (7 en suite). Fine, small, country hotel with appeal for gun sports and fishing types but also very fine food.

£££ Mackay's
Durness, T01971-511202, www. visitdurness.com. May-Oct.

7 en suite rooms in the boutique B&B. The modern, uninspiring exterior hides one of the best hotel experiences in the north of Scotland. Rooms are spacious and tastefully furnished with not a hint of tartan cheesiness on display. Staff are efficient and the breakfasts are superb. Excellent value. There is also cheaper accommodation in the **Lazy Crofter Bunkhouse** (**£**) as well as a luxury self-catering **Cottage** (£1100 per week for up to 6), a **Cabin** (£895 per week for 2 or more) and the amazing, luxury eco-friendly self-catering **Croft 103** (prices on application). Highly recommended.

£££ Smoo Lodge
Durness, T01971-511423, www.smoolodge.co.uk.
Luxury B&B situated in a beautiful former 18th-century hunting and fishing lodge.

Set in nearly 2 acres close to Smoo Cave, the lodge enjoys stunning sea views. The paddock facing the sea is set aside as a mini nature reserve. Highly recommended.

£££ Tongue Hotel
Tongue, T01847-611206, www.tonguehotel.com. Feb-Christmas.
19 en suite rooms. This former hunting lodge of the Duke of Sutherland has great views across the Kyle of Tongue and the staff are extremely accommodating. Catering mostly for anglers it can arrange impromptu fishing trips and the restaurant does good food.

£££-££ Ben Loyal Hotel
Tongue, T01847-611216, www.benloyal.co.uk. Open all year.
11 en suite rooms. Friendly, hospitable, small hotel and a good choice for the area. The food is recommended and the bar is a good place to while away an evening or 2.

£££-££ Farr Bay Inn
Bettyhill, T01641-521230, www.farrbayinn.co.uk.
Recently refurbished to a good standard, this cosy wee hotel offers 4 en suite rooms and good bar food. A popular choice for those travelling the NC500 route.

££ Glengolly B&B
Durness, T01971-511255, www.glengolly.com. Open all year.
3 rooms, all with en suite or private facilities. Good-value B&B in a working croft. Very friendly and comfortable stay guaranteed and you can get to know Martin's 5 border collies.

££-£ Cloisters
Talmine, T01847-601286, www.cloistertal.demon.co.uk. Open all year.
3 en suite twin rooms, 1 with disabled facilities. Friendly and welcoming B&B in 19th-century converted church.

£ Durness SYHA Youth Hostel
Smoo, to the east of the village, T01971-511264, www.syha.org.uk. Mid-Mar to early Oct.
Basic but comfortable, and handy for the beach and Smoo cave.

£ SYHA Youth Hostel
Tongue, T01847-611789, T08701-553255. Mid-Mar to late Oct.
Beautifully situated at the east end of the causeway, with views towards Ben Loyal and the sea lochs. Great value.

Camping

Talmine
T01847-601225, 5 miles north of Tongue.
By the beach.

£ Cocoa Mountain
Balnakeil Craft Village, Durness, T01971 511233, www.cocoamountain.co.uk. Easter-Sep 0900-1800, Oct-Easter 1000-1700.
Very popular, high-quality chocolatier and café.

Bus
Durness Bus runs a service from Durness to **Thurso** on Sat only, T01971-511223, and to **Lairg** via **Altnaharra**, Mon-Sat, departing at 0805. Mon-Sat (Sun Jul-Aug only) there's a daily bus from Durness to **Inverness** via **Rhiconich**, **Scourie**, **Kyleskuand**, **Lochinver**, **Ullapool** with **Tim Dearman coaches**, and which carries a bike trailer too. See Inverness Transport, page 168, for details.

Thurso is the most northerly town on the British mainland and by far the largest settlement on the north coast. In medieval times it was Scotland's chief port for trade with Scandinavia, though most of the town dates from the late 18th century when Sir John Sinclair built the 'new' extension to the old fishing port. The town increased in size to accommodate the workforce of the new nuclear power plant at nearby Dounreay, but the plant's demise has threatened the local economy. Today Thurso is a fairly nondescript place, mostly visited by people catching the ferry to Stromness in Orkney, or the occasional hardcore surfer.

Sights

There's little of real interest in the town centre, but the train station is at the south end of Princes St. Near the harbour are the 17th-century ruins of **Old St Peter's Church**, which stand on the site of the original 13th-century church founded by the Bishop of Caithness. The excellent **Caithness Horizons** ⓘ *www.caithnesshorizonsmuseum.co.uk, T01847-896508, Apr-Oct Mon-Fri 1000-1800, Sat 1000-1700, Sun 1200-1700 (May-Sep only), Nov-Mar Mon-Sat 1000-1700, £4, £2 children*, is in the old town hall on the High Street and includes exhibitions on local history, geology and archaeology and features some Pictish carved stones. It also houses the **Dounreay Visitor Centre**, which offers the opportunity to learn more about nuclear power. **Dounreay Nuclear Power Station** lies 10 miles west of Thurso. Though its fast breeder reactors were decommissioned in 1994, the plant is still a major local employer and now reprocesses spent nuclear fuel. The museum's **Gallery Café** serves snacks, drinks and light lunches.

Strathmore to Braemore *OS sheet No 11 covers the route.*

This walk gives a flavour of the bleak but beautiful landscape of the Caithness hinterland. The 16-mile linear route starts from **Strathmore Lodge**. To get there, head south from Thurso on the B874. After a short distance turn on to the B870 and follow it for 10 miles to the little hamlet of Westerdale, which stands on the River Thurso. Turn right here on to an unnumbered road and follow this road for about five miles. Just past the white Strathmore Lodge the road splits. Follow the right-hand track which runs through commercial forestry, before emerging on to open moor with Loch More on the left.

Where the forestry begins again on the right, the track swings left across an arm of the loch and heads southwards. At the southern end of the loch a track runs left to **Dalnaha**, but keep going straight ahead, along the valley of the River Thurso. You then reach a cluster of buildings at **Dalnawillan Lodge**. Ignore the track which heads off to the right and carry straight on, past the house at **Dalganachan**, over Rumsdale Water and on to the junction before **The Glutt**, which is a series of buildings. Turn left here and follow the track for a further four miles until you reach the junction beside Lochan nan Bò Riabach. Continue down the valley of Berriedale Water to Braemore. There is no public transport from here, so you'll have to arrange your own transport if you don't want to retrace your steps.

Dunnet Head *Colour map 2, A3.*

About 10 miles northeast of Thurso is the most northerly point on the British mainland. No, not John o'Groats, but Dunnet Head. It's reached by turning off the Thurso to John o'Groats road at Dunnet, at the east end of Dunnet Bay, a three-mile long sandy beach that's popular with surfers who come to tackle the gigantic waves of the **Pentland Firth**, the wild and treacherous strait between the mainland and Orkney. Dunnet Bay has an excellent reef break and there's another good reef break at Brims Ness to the west. Further west still, at Strathy Bay, you'll find rollers that can match anything in Hawaii (though the water's obviously a lot colder). Dunnet Head is a much nicer place than John o'Groats, with marvellous views across to Orkney and along the entire north coast (on a clear day). There's a Victorian lighthouse out at the point, and the dramatic seacliffs are teeming with seabirds. There's also a great little café.

Some 15 miles east of Thurso are the **Castle and Gardens of Mey** ① *T01847-851473, www.castleofmey.org.uk, May-Sep daily 1030-1600, £11.50, concessions £9.75, children £6.50, under 5s free, family £30, gardens and grounds only £6.50/3, visitor centre, tearoom and shop open daily 1000-1700.* Built by the 4th Earl of Caithness, the castle's future was under threat until the intervention of the late Queen Mother who bought it in 1952 and who holidayed here every year. The castle still welcomes royal visitors in the shape of Prince Charles who holidays here each summer.

Thurso

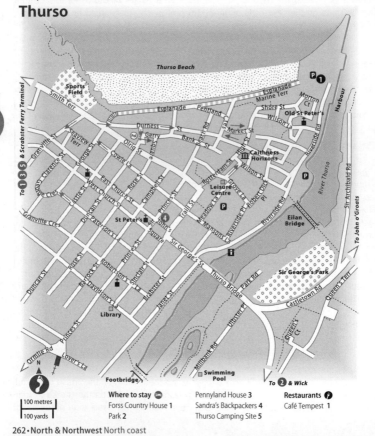

Where to stay
Forss Country House 1
Park 2
Pennyland House 3
Sandra's Backpackers 4
Thurso Camping Site 5

Restaurants
Café Tempest 1

ON THE ROAD
The light fantastic

Due to the absence of light pollution, Scotland offers some of the best areas of inky dark sky in Europe. Visit www.darkskyscotland.org.uk. A feature of visiting the far north of Scotland in winter is the chance of seeing the Aurora Borealis, or Northern Lights, which decorate the night skies like a gigantic laser show. The best time to see them is between October and March – especially during December and January. Try to get as far north as you can, though there are no guarantees of a sighting as cloud cover can obscure visibility. Any of the north-facing coastal villages are a good bet.

John o'Groats *Colour map 2, A4.*

John o'Groats used to be a rather forlorn place, beloved by tourists who think they've reached the northernmost point of the UK mainland (it's actually Dunnet Head) and charity walkers, runners and cyclists who've made the admirable long haul from Land's End, some 876 miles to the south. The area, however, has received a much-needed boost with the multi-million pound development by **Natural Retreats** (see Where to stay, below). It gets its name from the Dutchman Jan de Groot, who was commissioned by King James IV to run a ferry service to Orkney in 1496. Ferries still operate from here to Burwick in Orkney, see Transport, page 265. There are a few craft shops and the **Puffin Croft Petting Farm and Farm Shop** ① *www.puffincroft.com, daily 1000-1800, £2*, where you can get up close and personal with cuddly farm animals and also enjoy some home-baked goodies.

Two miles east of John o'Groats is **Duncansby Head**, which is far more rewarding. South of the headland a path leads to the spectacular **Duncansby Stacks**, a series of dramatic rock formations. The 200-ft cliffs are home to countless seabirds and you can see the narrow, sheer-sided inlets known locally as *geos*.

Archaeological sites around Caithness

Caithness may lack the impressive henges of other parts of the UK but it does boast a number of stone rows: areas covered by large numbers of small stones arranged in geometric patterns. These are thought to date from circa 2000 BC. The best and most easily accessible is the **Hill o' Many Stanes**. To get there, drive nine miles south of Wick. On the A9 and turn right onto a minor road where you see the signpost. A short way up this road is a signposted gate into the field, on the left-hand side. A path leads to the curious fan-shaped configuration of Bronze Age standing stones; 200 of them in 22 rows. No one yet knows their precise purpose but studies have shown that there were once 600 stones here.

There are also a couple of Pictish Brochs in Caithness. These were almost entirely unique to the north and northwest of Scotland and were windowless, dry-stone towers, between 10 and 45 ft in height, with a circular ground plan. The walls were hollow in places to allow staircases and small chambers. These were built between 2000 BC and AD 200, though they continued in use after that time, and were used for both domestic and defensive purposes. There are remains of a broch at **Nybster**, seven miles south of John o'Groats on the A9. Look out for the sign for the harbour and broch on the right heading north. Turn onto the minor road which leads down to a small car park. Follow the path along the clifftop to the broch, which stands on a headland surrounded by steep cliffs on three sides. Just to the south of here, at Keiss, are the remains of another broch.

One of the most interesting archaeological sites in the north are the well-preserved **Grey Cairns of Camster**. These chambered cairns, dating from the third and fourth millenia BC, are burial mounds of stone raised around carefully structured circular chambers with narrow entrance passages. To get there, head a mile east of Lybster on the A9, then turn left on to the minor road leading north to Watten. The cairns are five miles along this road, on the left-hand side. They comprise two enormous prehistoric burial chambers dating from 2500 BC. They are amazingly complete, with corbelled ceilings, and can be entered on hands and knees through narrow passageways.

Listings Thurso and around *map page 262.*

Tourist information

Thurso iCentre
High St, in the Caithness Horizons Museum (see page 261), T01847-893155. Open all year.

Where to stay

Thurso has a wide variety of accommodation, most of it fairly average.

££££ Forss Country House Hotel
4 miles out of Thurso at Bridge of Forss, T01847-861201, www.forsshousehotel.co.uk.
The nicest place to stay by far around Thurso, if not the entire north coast. This family-run hotel is set in 20 acres of lovely woodland and has an excellent restaurant (**£££**), open to non-residents (but pre-book). Rooms are spacious (the en suite bathrooms are bigger than many other hotel rooms), the attention to detail is impressive and the service is spot on. Nothing is too much trouble for the staff here. Highly recommended. Also offers self-catering in a traditional mill house.

£££-££ Park Hotel
Oldfield, at the south end of town, 10 mins' walk from the train station, T01847-893251, www.parkhotelthurso. co.uk. Open all year.
21 en suite rooms. Modern and rather functional building but clean, comfortable and extremely hospitable with good food at reasonable prices. Rooms at the front have the best views. There's a pet-friendly room and also a fully disabled-friendly room.

££ Pennyland House B&B
On the A9 heading west out of town, T01847-891194.
6 en suite rooms, all named after Scottish golf courses. Excellent B&B in 18th-century house that was the birthplace of Sir William Alexander Smith, founder of the Boys Brigade. Very friendly and welcoming and offer a good variety of vegetarian and gluten-free choices for breakfast. Recommended.

££ Sharvedda
Strathy Point, north of Strathy on the road between Thurso and Durness, T01641-541311, www.sharvedda.co.uk.
3 rooms. Excellent B&B in a beautiful location overlooking the Pentland Firth. By far the best place to stay around here at this price. Provides everything you'd want from a B&B and can even cook a light supper for £12 pp between 1830 and 1930. Highly recommended.

£ Sandra's Backpackers
24-26 Princes St, T01847-894575, www.sandras-backpackers.co.uk.
Probably the best option at the very cheapest end of the scale and right beside a good chip shop. Also rents bikes.

Self-catering

Inn at John o'Groats
T01625-416430, https://naturalretreats.co.uk.
Natural Retreats have refurbished this 19th-century hotel and added a colourful Scandinavian-style extension. Superior accommodation in 20 lodges or 17 1- to 4-bed apartments, not all with kitchens.

Camping

There are a couple of campsites at John o'Groats and further west by the beach at Huna. Ask at the **Thurso iCentre**.

Thurso Camping Site
North of town on the road to Scrabster, T01847-892244.
The nearest campsite to Thurso.

Restaurants

The **Forss Country House Hotel** (see Where to stay, above), is the best place to eat in the area; the other hotels listed are good options in town for a decent meal.

£££ The Captain's Galley
Scrabster, T01847-894999, www.captains galley.co.uk. Dinner Tue-Sat 1900-2100.
Small restaurant so booking is a must. Multi award-winning seafood restaurant in unpretentious surroundings, just the freshest of food brought to you within minutes of being landed (or so it seems). Best choice hereabouts and worth the trip here alone.

£ Café Tempest
By the harbour next to the surf shop of the same name (see What to do, below), T01847-892500, www.tempestsurf.co.uk. Apr-Dec Mon-Sat 1000-1930, Sun 1000-1700, Jan-Mar open till 1600.
Good, chilled vibe. Menu features typical surfer-type fare (ie loads of carbs).

Entertainment

Check details of cinema listings at T01847-894152, www.merlincinemas.co.uk.

What to do

Boat trips
John O'Groats Ferries, *Ferry Office, John o'Groats, T01955-611353, www.jogferry. co.uk.* Operate **Orkney Islands Maxi Day Tours**, which leave May-Sep daily at 0845 and return at 1945 (£66, children £33, under 5s free). A shorter day tour (missing out Stromness) goes daily from Jun-Sep at 1030, returns at 1800

(£62, children £31, under 5s free). There's also a wildlife cruise Jun-Aug, which departs at 1430 (£18, children £9, under 5s free, family £45).

Surfing
The best break in the region, indeed, one of the best breaks in the world, is Thurso East. A good surf shop is **Tempest Surf**, by the harbour in Thurso, T01847-892500, www.tempestsurf.co.uk.

Transport

Bus
Citylink buses, www.citylink.co.uk, run to **Inverness** 4 times daily, 3½ hrs. Those from Inverness continue to **Scrabster** to connect with ferries to **Stromness** in **Orkney**. **Citylink** buses to **Inverness** connect with buses to **Edinburgh**.

   Stagecoach run local services to **Bettyhill**, 3 times daily Mon-Fri, 1 hr 10 mins, on a route that includes **Reay**. There are regular daily buses to **Wick** via **Halkirk** or **Castletown**.

Car hire
William Dunnet & Co, T01847-894164, www.dunnets.co.uk.

Cycle hire
The Bike Shop, 35 High St, T01847-895385. Bike rental and repairs and sales of parts and equipment.

Ferry
Northlink Ferries, www.northlinkferries. co.uk, to **Stromness** in (Orkney) leave from **Scrabster**, 2 miles north of Thurso. **John O'Groats Ferries** sail to **Burwick** (Orkney) twice daily from May-Sep, 40 mins. A connecting bus takes passengers on to **Kirkwall**, 40 mins, price included in ferry ticket.

Train
3 trains leave daily from **Inverness** (3½ hrs), 2 of them connecting with the ferries from **Scrabster** to **Stromness** (Orkney). Trains continue to **Wick** (30 mins) and trains to **Inverness** leave from here.

Northeast
coast

The northeast coast, from the northeastern tip of Caithness down to Inverness, doesn't have the same draw as the west coast and attracts fewer visitors, but it has its own gentler appeal and there are many lovely little seaside towns to explore, such as the former sea port of Cromarty. The main attraction in these parts is undoubtedly the resident pod of bottlenose dolphins, which can be seen along the Moray coast between May and September.

Far northeast coast

proud fishing heritage and a fairytale castle

From John o'Groats the A99 runs due south to the village of Freswick before following the coast around Sinclair's Bay, past a series of straggling fishing villages till it reaches Wick, the chief town in these parts and once the busiest herring port in Europe.

Wick and around *Colour map 2, A4.*
A century ago Wick was Europe's busiest herring port, its harbour jam-packed with fishing boats and larger ships exporting tons of salted fish to Russia, Scandinavia and the West Indian slave plantations. The fishing industry has long since gone and the demise of the nearby nuclear power station at Douneray only added to the sense of neglect. Wick, however, has been given a new lease of life with the growing popularity of the North

Essential Far northeast coast

Finding your feet

A few miles north of Wick is Wick John o'Groats Airport. There are direct flights here from Kirkwall (Orkney), Sumburgh (Shetland) and Aberdeen, Stornoway, Durham, Bristol, Newcastle, Edinburgh and Southampton. For the most up-to-date information on the taxi, car hire and bus service options available to you on arrival at Wick John o'Groats Airport, contact airport information, T01955-602215. The train and bus stations are next to each other behind the hospital. If you don't fancy flying, there are regular trains from all points south to Inverness and from there to Thurso and Wick. Visit www.scotrail.co.uk.

Coast 500 tourist route (see page 14) and makes a useful base for exploring the unique delights of the far northeast.

Wick is actually two towns. On one side of the river is Wick proper and on the other is **Pulteneytown**, the model town planned by Thomas Telford for the British Fisheries Society in 1806 to house evicted crofters who came to work here. Now it's one great living museum of fishermen's cottages and derelict sheds and stores around the near-deserted quays. It gives a good idea of the scale of the herring trade during its heyday in the mid-19th century, when over 1000 boats set sail to catch the 'silver darlings'. Here, on Bank Row, is the superb **Wick Heritage Centre** ① *T01955-605393, www.wickheritage.org, Easter-end Oct Mon-Sat 1000-1700, £4, children 50p*. The highlight of the centre is its massive photographic collection dating from the late 19th century.

Three miles north of Wick are the impressive 15th-century clifftop ruins of **Sinclair and Girnigoe Castle**. There is a good walk along the rocky shore east of town to **The Trinkie**, a natural rock pool fed by the sea, and about a mile further on to the **Brig o' Trams**. Before Wick, at Ulbster, is another archaeological site, the **Cairn o' Get**. Opposite the sign are the precipitous **Whaligoe Steps**, which lead to a picturesque harbour.

Dunbeath *Colour map 2, B3.*

The A99 coast road runs southwest from Wick to meet the A9 at Latherton, before dropping down into Dunbeath, a pleasant little village at the mouth of a small *strath* (or glen). This was the birthplace of one of Scotland's foremost writers, Neil Gunn (1891-1973). His finest works, such as *The Silver Darlings* and *Highland River*, reflect his experiences of growing up in the northeast and are fascinating accounts of life here during the days of the herring boom, though the sleepy harbour of today is barely recognizable as the erstwhile bustling fishing port. The villages of Dunbeath, and Latherton to the north, are included on the **Neil Gunn Trail**, as is the beautiful walk up the glen, described in the leaflet available at the **Dunbeath Heritage Centre** ① *T01593-731233, www.dunbeath-heritage.org.uk, Apr-end Oct Mon, Thu, Fri 1000-1630, Nov-Mar same days 1000-1600 (best to check nearer the time), £3, children free*. Here, in Neil Gunn's former school, you can learn all about the life and works of the famous novelist as well as the history of Caithness. Just outside the village is the **Laidhay Croft Museum** ① *T01593-731244, Easter-Sep daily 1000-1700, £3, children £1*, a restored traditional longhouse with stable, house and byre all under the same roof. It also has a tearoom.

Helmsdale *Colour map 2, B3.*

The A9 continues the line of the coast southwest. At **Berriedale**, a farm track leads west to the Wag, from where you can climb **Morven** (2316 ft), the highest hill in Caithness, with amazing views across the desolate, treeless landscape. This area was devastated during the Clearances and to get some idea of the hardships people had to endure, stop at the ruined crofting village of **Badbea**, just beyond Ousdale. The A9 then drops dramatically to the former herring port of Helmsdale, which gets busy in the summer. The village is most notable for its excellent **Timespan Heritage Centre** ① *T01431-821327, www.timespan. org.uk, Mar-Oct daily 1000-1700, Nov-Mar Sat-Sun 1000-1500, Tue 1400-1600, £4, concessions £3, children £2, family £10*, which brings the history of the Highlands to life through a series of high-tech displays, sound effects and an audio-visual programme. There's also a café and shop on site.

Brora *Colour map 2, B2.*

The next town, Brora (population 1860), sits at the mouth of the River Brora which, as everywhere on this coast, is the site of a once-lucrative salmon netting industry. At the

After the goldrush

A short drive from Helmsdale, up the Strath of Kildonan (or Strath Ullie), is Baile an Or (Gaelic for 'goldfield'), site of the great Sutherland Gold Rush of 1869. It all started after local man Robert Gilchrist returned home from the Australian gold fields only to discover gold here, on his doorstep. His success brought others rushing to Kildonan, and soon a shanty town had sprung up to accommodate them.

Within a year the gold rush was over, but small amounts are still found today. Anyone who fancies their luck can try a bit of gold panning in the Kildonan Burn at Baile an Or, about a mile from Kildonan train station.

harbour, the ice house is a relic of the herring boom. Coal mines, opened in the 16th century, salt pans and a brickworks are all defunct. Still very much alive, however, is **Hunter's**, the local weavers of heavyweight traditional tweeds, and a good place to invest in some natty headwear. A mile or so north of town is the interesting **Clynelish Distillery** ① *T01408-623000, www.malts.com, Mar-Oct Mon-Sat 1000-1700, Nov-Feb Mon-Sat 1000-1500, tours all day, basic tour £6 (includes £3 off a bottle of malt), special tasting tours from £12 up to £70.* Something of a cult amongst whisky lovers, this malt is distinctive for its briny flavour.

Castle Cole in lovely Strath Brora, eight miles northwest, is one of several ruined brochs. Another, **Carn Liath** (signposted), is by the main road, three miles south of Brora.

Golspie *Colour map 2, B2.*

The picturesque little village of Golspie (around 1800 inhabitants) offers more than just a couple of banks and a supermarket. For half a mile from here are the **Highland Wildcat Trails** ① *www.highlandwildcat.com*, Scotland's most northerly purpose-built mountain bike tracks with over 20 miles of trail to suit every level of rider. What's more, after you've hired a bike at **Square Wheels** in Strathpeffer (see page 276) the forested trails are free to explore.

In Golspie there's also an 18-hole golf course, and the **Orcadian Stone Company** has a large display of fossils and geological specimens from the Highlands and beyond. The town lies in the dark shadow of the Sutherlands: on **Beinn a'Bhraggaidh** (1293 ft), to the southwest, is a huge, 100-ft-high monument to the Duke of Sutherland. Those who make it up to the monument and who know something of the duke's many despicable acts may find the inscription risible, as it describes him as "a judicious, kind and liberal landlord". There's no reference to the fact that he forcibly evicted 15,000 tenants from his estate. A mile north of the village is **Dunrobin Castle** ① *T01408-633177, www.dunrobincastle. co.uk, Apr, May and Oct daily 1030-1630, Jun-Sep daily 1000-1700, £11, concessions £9, children £6.50.* This is the ancient seat of the Dukes of Sutherland, who once owned more land than anyone else in the British Empire. Much enlarged and aggrandized in the 19th century, with fairytale turrets, the enormous 189-room castle, the largest house in the Highlands, is stuffed full of fine furniture, paintings, tapestries and objets d'art. The extravagant confection overlooks beautiful gardens laid out with box hedges, ornamental trees and fountains. The museum is an animal-lover's nightmare, with a spectacular Victorian taxidermy collection. There are also local antiquities, some from ancient brochs, and Pictish stone carvings.

Where to stay

Wick and around

££ The Clachan
13 Randolph Place, South Rd, T01955-605384, www.theclachan.co.uk. Open all year.
3 en suite rooms. Best B&B in town in our opinion.

££ Seaview Guest House
14 Scalesburn, T01955-602735.
3 rooms. Another excellent choice. Friendly and welcoming with views of the harbour.

Helmsdale

£££-££ Navidale House Hotel
Navidale, T01431-821258, www.navidalehousehotel.co.uk. Feb-Nov.
10 rooms. This former hunting lodge for the Dukes of Sutherland is now a charming country house hotel and is the most upmarket choice hereabouts. Hostess Florence Is a wonderful cook and will also provide dinner for non-residents if booked in advance (**££**).

££ Culgower House
At Loth between Helmsdale and Brora, T01431-821268, www.culgowerhouse.com. Mar-Oct.
2 rooms. Victorian farmhouse set in its own grounds providing tasteful, stylish and very comfortable accommodation. Perfect stop for those travelling the NC500. Will provide supper for £15 a head with prior notice.

Brora

£££-££ Royal Marine Hotel
Golf Rd, T01408-621252, www.royalmarinebrora.com. Open all year.
Early 20th-century country house designed by Robert Lorimer, this fine golf hotel boasts an indoor pool, spa and gym. Has an excellent reputation for its food (**££**).

££ Inverbrora
On the A9 south of Brora, T01408-621208.
4 rooms, 2 en suite. Friendly, comfortable B&B in Georgian farmhouse set in 3 acres of grounds on a working farm. Good value.

Restaurants

The best places to eat are usually the hotel restaurants and bars listed above under Where to stay. Additional good options are listed below.

Wick and around

££ Bord de L'Eau
Market St, T01955-604400.
Tue-Sat for lunch and dinner.
French bistro-style cooking. Very popular with locals.

££ Norseman Hotel
Riverside St, T01955-603344.
Probably the next best place in town. Good, filling meals, friendly service, good for Sun lunches.

Helmsdale

££ La Mirage
Dunrobin St, T0143-821 615, www.lamirage.org. Daily 1100-2100.
Famous tearoom whose erstwhile proprietress, the inimitable Nancy Sinclair, modelled herself, and her tearoom, on her friend Barbara Cartland, queen of romantic novels. The whole effect is pure kitsch. Good food though, especially their fish and chip teas and scrummy meringues. Also do takeaway.

Transport

Wick and around
Air
Direct flights to/from **Aberdeen** with **Eastern Airways**, T01652-680600, www.easternairways.com, and to/from **Edinburgh**

and **Southampton** with **Flybe/Loganair**,
T0871-700 0535, www.flybe.com.

Bus

Scottish Citylink, www.citylink.co.uk, buses
between **Inverness** and **Thurso** stop en route
in **Wick** (3 daily). There are also regular local
buses to **Thurso**, via **Halkirk** or **Castletown**,
and buses to **Helmsdale**, daily, and **John
o'Groats**, Mon-Sat. There's no established
bus station in Wick; the main pick-up point
is outside the Norseman Hotel, on the other
side of the river from the train station.

Train

Trains leave for **Inverness**, daily, 4 hrs, via
Helmsdale, **Golspie**, **Lairg** and **Dingwall**.
Also in the other direction to **Thurso**.

Helmsdale

Bus and train

Buses and trains are the same as for Wick
(see above). Helmsdale is on the **Inverness**
to **Wick/Thurso** rail line.

---

ancient history and a world-famous golf course

South of Golspie, on the north shore of the Dornoch Firth, the town of Dornoch
is an architectural delight, with its deep, golden sandstone houses and leafy
cathedral square. Bishop Gilbert of Moravia (Moray) built the cathedral circa
1245. His family's success in gaining a foothold in northeast Scotland against the
Norsemen was rewarded with the Earldom of Sutherland. It was trouble with
the Jarls which prompted Gilbert to move his power base here from Caithness,
mindful that his predecessor had been boiled in butter by the locals (proof that
too much of the stuff can kill you).

The **Dornoch Visitor Centre** ① *T08452-255121, Oct-May Mon-Fri 0900-1700, Jun and Sep
Sat 1000-1600, Jul-Aug Mon-Fri 0900-1700, Sat 1000-1600, Sun 1000-1600,* is in the Carnegie
Court House on Castle Street.

The 13th-century **cathedral** ① *Mon-Fri 0730-2000, volunteers welcome visitors
mid-May to mid-Sep 1000-1600,* was badly damaged in 1570, then subjected to an ill-
conceived 'restoration' by the Countess of Sutherland in 1835. Among the few surviving
features is a series of gargoyles, including a green man, and the effigy of an unknown
knight. Opposite the cathedral is the 16th-century **Bishop's Palace**, now a hotel, see
Where to stay, page 271.

Nowadays Dornoch is famous for its links **golf course**, one of the world's finest and
relatively easy to get on. It overlooks miles of dunes and a pristine sandy beach. A stone
near the links marks the spot where the last witch in Scotland was burned, in 1722. Folklore
recounts a bloody battle against raiding Vikings in 1259 on the beach at Embo, just to the
north, in which Sir Richard Murray was killed. The battle is commemorated at the **Earl's
Cross**. Trout fishing is available on Dornoch Lochans; enquire locally. North of Embo is
Loch Fleet, a river estuary with a ferocious tidal race at its mouth and an SNH reserve
protecting rare birds and plants. The rotting skeletons of the fishing fleet abandoned in
the First World War lie in the sand on the south shore west of the car park.

West of Dornoch, at Clashmore, the Dornoch Bridge carries the A9 across the
Dornoch Firth to Tain. Near Clashmore is **Skibo Castle**, the former home of 19th-
century industrialist and philanthropist Andrew Carnegie, once the world's richest

man. It is now home to the very exclusive **Carnegie Club** ① *www.carnegieclub.co.uk*, for envious voyeurs or those with too much money. There are several walks in the forestry plantations in the area.

Listings Dornoch and around

Where to stay

There are lots of good B&Bs.

££££-£££ Dornoch Castle Hotel
Castle St, T01862-810216, www. dornochcastlehotel.com. Apr-Oct.
22 rooms. Formerly the Bishop's Palace, this 16th-century building is full of character and boasts excellent food (**£££-££**). Good special offers.

£££ 2 Quail Restaurant and Rooms
Castle St, T01862-811811, www.2quail.com. Apr-Oct Tue-Sat for dinner, Nov-Mar Fri and Sat only.
3 rooms above 1 of the very best (and smallest) restaurants in the region, run by Michael and Kerensa Carr. Rooms are not huge but the magnificent set 3-course menu using Scottish produce (**£££**) more than compensates. Highly recommended.

££ Auchlea Guest House
Auchlea, T01862-811524, www.auchlea.co.uk. Open all year.
3 en suite rooms. Superior B&B in a modern bungalow run by John and Fiona. Serves a full, traditional Scottish breakfast with porridge.

Camping

Dornoch Caravan Park
T01862-810423.
By the golf course and the beach.

Restaurants

The best places to eat are usually the hotel restaurants and bars listed above under Where to stay.

Shopping

The Dornoch Bookshop, *High St, T01862-810165. Mon-Sat 0930-1730.* The only bookshop in the area and it stocks local books.

Transport

Bus
Hourly buses run daily between **Inverness** and **Lairg** stop in **Ardgay** and **Bonar Bridge**. Citylink buses between **Inverness** and **Thurso** also stop in Dornoch up to 8 times daily.

Train
Services between **Inverness** and **Thurso** stop at **Ardgay** and **Culrain**.

Tain and around *Colour map 2, B2.*

castles, whisky and the tragic history of the Clearances

Squeezed between the Cromarty Firth to the south and the Dornoch Firth to the north is the Tain Peninsula, whose largest town is Tain, a place with a 1950s time-warp feel. It has an impressive historical portfolio: its backstreets are an intriguing jigsaw of imposing merchants' houses, steep vennels, secret gardens and dormer windows.

The town serves a vast hinterland. Among the hills are little-visited backwoods and farm towns, narrow valleys lined with crofts where cattle graze in boggy haughs and, to the west, glens and moorland. Along the seaboard are the windswept fields of the Tarbat Peninsula.

Good sea angling is to be had from the harbours of the otherwise dull coastal villages such as Balintore, and at Shandwick is a massive Pictish stone. It is said that unbaptized children were buried near the stone, which is now in the Museum of Scotland in Edinburgh.

Sights

The **Collegiate church** is on Castle Brae, just off the High Street, and inside is a 17th-century panel painted with the badges of the trade guilds, a reminder of the town's busy international trade. Another reminder is the imposing 16th-century **Tolbooth** in the High Street. Next to the church and housed in the Pilgrimage is **Tain through Time** ① *T01862-894089, www.tainmuseum.org.uk, Apr-Oct Mon-Fri 1000-1700, Jun-Aug Mon-Sat 1000-1700, entry to Pilgrimage, church and museum £3.50, children over 6 and concessions £2.50, family (up to 2 adults and 4 children) £10, entry to museum only £1.50/£0.50*, a museum, charts the town's medieval history. One of Tain's main attractions, just off the A9 to the north of town, is the very fine **Glenmorangie whisky distillery** ① *T01862-892477, www.glenmorangie.com, Mon-Fri 0900-1700, Jun-Aug Sat 1000-1600, Sun 1200-1600, tours (45 mins) from 1030-1530, £5*, where you can see how the world-famous whisky is made and try a sample. Famous for its various wood finishes, Glenmorangie remains Scotland's best-selling single malt whisky. You can now stay here, in some considerable style and comfort, at **Glenmorangie House** (see Where to stay, page 273).

Just to the south of town, off the A9, is the **Aldie Water Mill**, a restored 16th-century mill in working order, with various high-quality craft shops attached. Nearby is the **Tain Pottery** ① *T01862-894112, www.tainpottery.co.uk, Apr-Oct Mon-Sat Sun 1000-1700, Nov-Mar Mon-Fri 0900-1730, Sat 0930-1700*, which you can also visit.

West of Tain *Colour map 2, B2.*

A pleasant and interesting route is to follow the A836 northwest from Tain along the south shore of the Dornoch Firth. From The Struie, reached by the B9176 which branches south at Easter Fearn, there's a panoramic view over the Dornoch Firth and the Sutherland hills. In the churches of **Edderton** and Kincardine are Pictish stones. Another stands in a field northwest of Edderton (but don't disturb the crops or livestock). A quartz boulder at **Ardgay**, the 'Clach Eiteag', commemorates the cattle tryst and fair which once took place locally.

Some 10 miles from Ardgay, at the end of lovely Strathcarron, is the isolated **Croick church**, one of the most poignant reminders of the infamous Clearances. Here, in 1845, 90 local folk took refuge in the churchyard after they had been evicted from their homes in Glencalvie by the Duke of Sutherland to make way for his sheep flocks. A reporter from *The Times* was there to describe this "wretched spectacle", as men, women and children were carted off, many never to return. His report is there to read, but far more evocative and harrowing are the names and messages the people scratched in spidery copperplate in the window panes.

North of Ardgay is the **Kyle of Sutherland**, where several rivers converge to flood into the sea through lush water meadows. Montrose was defeated here, at Carbisdale, in 1651. Overlooking the Kyle, at **Culrain**, is the 19th-century **Carbisdale Castle**, once home of the exiled King of Norway. After the Dornoch Ferry disaster of 1809, a bridge was built over the Kyle at **Bonar Bridge**, from where the A949 runs eastwards to join the main A9 just before Dornoch, while the A836 continues north to Lairg (see below). A few miles north of Invershin are the **Falls of Shin**, an excellent place to watch salmon battling upstream on their way to their spawning grounds (best seen June to September). There are several easy walks in the immediate area; all are under an hour long. A new visitor centre was opened in May 2017 with a very good restaurant (see page 274), gift shop and adventure playground, and there is now easier access to the falls themselves.

Lairg *Colour map 2, B1.*

Some 11 miles north of Bonar Bridge is the uninspiring village of Lairg, the region's main transport hub. Lairg is best known for its annual lamb sale, when young sheep from all over the north of Scotland are bought and sold. It is said that all roads meet at Lairg, and it's certainly a hard place to avoid. From here, the A839 heads east to meet the A9 between Dornoch and Golspie and west to meet the A837 which runs out to Lochinver. The A836 heads north to Tongue, and south to Bonar Bridge. The A838 meanwhile heads northwest to Laxford Bridge and on to Durness, near Cape Wrath.

There are several interesting walks around the village, some of which lead to prehistoric sites, such as the Neolithic hut circles at nearby **Ord Hill**. These walks, and many others in the region, are described with maps in the Forestry Commission's leaflet *Forests of the Far North*, which is available at the **Ferrycroft Visitor Centre** ① *T01549-402160, Apr-Oct daily*, which also has a café, shop and toilets.

East of Tain *Colour map 2, B2.*

Some 5 miles southeast from Tain is **Hill of Fearn**. Fearn Abbey was moved here around 1250 from its original site near Edderton, where it was too vulnerable to sea raiders. It later became the parish church, but one Sunday in 1742 lightning struck and the roof fell in, killing 38 worshippers. This tragedy was preceded by a fairy harbinger sighted at nearby Loch Eye. In Hill of Fearn is the excellent **Anta Factory Shop** ① *T01862-832477, www.anta. co.uk, Mon-Sat 0930-1730, Sun 1000-1700*, one of the very best places in the country for classy tartan furnishing fabrics, as well as tartan rugs and throws, and pottery.

Portmahomack *Colour map 2, B2.*

The seaside village of Portmahomack, or 'port of Colman', is named after the missionary who was keen as mustard to found a religious settlement here. Archaeological work is revealing the importance of this area in Pictish times. The **Tarbat Discovery Centre** ① *T01862-871351, www.tarbat-discovery.co.uk, Apr Mon-Sat 1400-1700, May Mon-Sat 1000-1700, Jun-Sep Mon-Sat 1000-1700, Sun 1400-1700, Oct daily 1400-1700, £3.50, child £1.50 (under 12s free), concession £2*, in Tarbat Old Church, displays recently discovered Pictish stone carving. From the harbour, with its 18th-century girnals (grain warehouses) and sheltered sandy beach, you can see a huge stretch of the Sutherland coast, and the great sandbanks – the 'gizzen brigs' – at the mouth of the Dornoch Firth. Boat trips are available from the harbour for sea angling. A worthwhile trip is out to Tarbat Ness lighthouse, about three miles north.

Listings Tain and around

Where to stay

Tain

££££ Glenmorangie House at Cadboll
Fearn, by Tain, T01862-871671,
www.theglenmorangiehouse.com.
6 en suite rooms. Owned by the
whisky people, this place oozes style.

Accommodation in the main house is supplemented by 3 cottages which sleep a total of 6. Price includes a lavish 5-course dinner and afternoon tea as well as breakfast. Recommended.

££££-£££ Mansfield Castle Hotel
Scotsburn Rd, T01862-892052. Mar-Nov.

19th-century baronial splendour and superb cuisine. Restaurant also open to non-residents (**£££**).

£££ Morangie House Hotel
Morangie Rd, T01862-892281,
www.morangiehotel.com.
26 rooms. This Victorian hotel serves excellent food in its restaurant. Very good value.

£££-££ Golf View House
13 Knockbreck Rd, T01862-892856,
www.golf-view.co.uk. Feb-Nov.
3 double and 2 twin rooms. Substantial house offering very fine B&B.

Lairg
There are a couple of hotels and B&Bs which are fairly average.

£ Sleeperzzz.com
Rogart Station, Rogart, T01408-641343,
www.sleeperzzz.com.
The most interesting place to stay, where you can get cheap hostel accommodation in the 3 old rail carriages that have been converted to sleep 20 people. There's a 10% discount for bike or train users and children under 12 receive a 25% discount. Also has a studio apartment for up to 3 people (**££**).

Restaurants

Lairg

££-£ Falls of Shin Restaurant
Achany Glen, by Lairg, T01549-402888. May-Sep 1000-1600, seasonal hours in winter.
A gastronomic oasis housed in the most unlikely of places. Simple food cooked to perfection, probably better than your mum makes. Good value.

Shopping

Tain
Bannerman Seafoods, *The Burgage,*
T01862-892322, www.bannerman-seafoods.
co.uk. A fish and seafood wholesalers, sells local mussels.
Brown's Gallery, *Castle Brae, T01862-893884,*
www.browns art.com. Mon-Sat 1000-1730.
Showcases work by Highland artists.

Transport

Tain
Bus
Citylink buses between **Inverness** and **Thurso** pass through Tain Mon-Fri. There are also 4 buses a day to from Tain **Lairg** via **Bonar Bridge**, Mon-Sat, with **DE Coaches**, www.decoaches.co.uk.

Train
Tain is on the **Inverness** to **Thurso** rail line. There are 3 trains daily in each direction.

Lairg
Bus
Far North Bus, T07782-110007, www.thedurnessbus.com, service No 804 runs from here to **Ullapool**, with connections to **Lochinver** and **Durness**, during school summer holidays in Jul and Aug, Mon-Sat. Carries bikes if booked in advance. Also services to/from Inverness.

Train
Trains between **Inverness** and **Thurso** stop at Lairg and Rogart stations 3 times daily.

Dingwall and around *Colour map 2, C1.*

Dingwall, at the head of the Cromarty Firth, has two major claims to fame. Not only is it believed to be the birthplace of Macbeth, it was also the home for many years of Neil Gunn (1891-1973), perhaps the Highlands' greatest literary figure, see also page 267. It's a fairly dull, though functional town, with good shops and banks lining its long main street. **Dingwall Museum** ① *T01349-865366, mid-May to end Sep Mon-Sat 1000-1630, nominal entry fee payable*, tells the history of this Royal Burgh.

East of Dingwall, before Evanton, is **Storehouse of Foulis** ① *T01349-830038, www. storehouseoffoulis.co.uk, Mon-Sat 0900-1800, Sun 1000-1700, free*, which has history and wildlife exhibitions, and offers the chance to see the local seal population. Standing on a hill above **Evanton** is the **Fyrish Monument**, a replica of the Gate of Negapatam in India, built by local men and funded by local military hero, Sir Hector Munro, to commemorate his capture of the Indian town, in 1781. To get there, turn off the B9176 towards Boath. It's a stiff two-hour climb up to the top.

The Cromarty Firth is a centre for repairing North Sea oil rigs, and many of the villages along its north shore have benefited from the oil industry. One of these is **Invergordon**, just west of Nigg Bay, which has suffered in recent years due to the closure of the local aluminium factory. Beyond Invergordon, a road branches south to Nigg Ferry. The ferry from Cromarty to **Nigg** was once a major thoroughfare, and now a tiny two-car ferry makes the 20-minute crossing in the summer months (every 30 minutes from 0800-1815). From the ferry you get a good view of **Nigg Bay**, a vast natural harbour used in both world wars by the Royal Navy. Its entry is guarded by the dramatic headlands of the Sutors, identified in folklore as friendly giants. The oil rigs ranged along the firth and the oil terminal at Nigg, are a dramatic and not unpleasant contrast with Lilliputian Cromarty.

Strathpeffer and around *Colour map 2, C1.*

Just along from the Cromarty Firth is Strathpeffer, which gets busy in the summer with coach parties, but it's a pleasant place and there are some excellent walks in the surrounding hills. The little village gained recognition in 1819 when Doctor Morrison, a physician from Aberdeen, bathed in its sulphur springs and cured himself of rheumatoid arthritis. He quickly spread the word and Strathpeffer became a fashionable spa resort attracting thousands of visitors. Two world wars intervened and the town's popularity declined. Today the only reminder of its past is the **Water Sampling Pavilion** in the square where you can test the waters.

Just outside Strathpeffer on the road to Dingwall is the **Highland Museum of Childhood** ① *T01997-421031, Apr, May, Sep and Oct Mon-Sat 1000-1700, Jun-Aug Mon-Sat 1000-1700, Sun 1200-1600, £3, concessions £2.50, children £1.75, family £7*, which has historical displays on childhood in the Highlands, as well as collections of dolls, toys and games.

A fine walk is to **Knock Farrel** and the **Touchstone Maze**, site of an Iron Age vitrified fort which lies at the north end of a ridge known locally as the **Cat's Back**. A marked trail starts from Blackmuir Wood car park. Head up the hill from town, turn left up a road immediately before the youth hostel, and the car park is on the left. The walk is six miles in total and takes about three hours. Aside from OS Landranger sheet 26, the route is also described in a Forestry Commission leaflet *Forests of Easter Ross*, available from tourist offices.

Another excellent side trip is to **Rogie Falls**, near **Contin**, which is three miles southwest of Strathpeffer on the main A835 Inverness to Ullapool road. The short walk up to the falls starts from the car park three miles north of Contin on the A835. There are also some pleasant woodland walks around here. Experienced hikers can tackle magnificent **Ben Wyvis** (3432 ft). The route to the summit starts four miles north of Garve, seven miles northwest of Contin.

Listings Cromarty Firth

Where to stay

Dingwall and around

£££ The Dower House
2 miles north of Muir of Ord on A862 to Dingwall, T01463-870090, www. thedowerhouse.co.uk. Open all year.
3 en suite double rooms and 1 suite (**££££**). Very comfortable small hotel set in 5 acres of woodland and gardens, excellent food (dinner **££**). Well worth the money. Recommended.

£££ Kinkell House Hotel
Easter Kinkell, Conan Bridge, by Dingwall, T01349-861270, www.kinkellhousehotel.com.
9 en suite rooms. Lovely country hotel in farmland. Style, comfort and attention to detail, as well as superb cooking.

£££ Tulloch Castle Hotel
Tulloch Castle Drive, T01349-861325, www.tullochcastle.co.uk. Open all year.
20 en suite rooms. This 12th-century castle is the smartest place around and retains many period features such as the 250-year-old panelled Great Hall, 4-poster bed costs a bit more. Pets welcome.

Strathpeffer and around

££££-£££ Coul House Hotel
Contin, 3 miles southwest of Strathpeffer, T01997-421487, www.coulhousehotel.com. Open all year.
20 rooms. Top of the list is this elegant 19th-century country house offering a range of rooms at various rates and also fine food available at any time of the day. Also doggie-friendly. An excellent choice.

£££ Craigvar
The Square, Strathpeffer, T01997-421622, www.craigvar.com. Open all year.
3 en suite rooms. Elegant Georgian house offering considerable style and comfort at this price, one of the best B&Bs in the region. Recommended.

££ White Lodge
The Square, T01997-421730, www. the-white-lodge.co.uk. Open all year.
2 en suite rooms. Very good B&B, cosy, comfortable and welcoming. Self-catering cottage available.

Transport

Dingwall and around
Bus

There are hourly buses between **Inverness** and **Invergordon**, via Dingwall. There are also hourly buses between **Inverness** and Dingwall via **Muir of Ord**. There are buses between Dingwall and **Rosemarkie**, Mon and Fri, and between Dingwall and **Cromarty**, Mon and Fri.

Train

Dingwall is on the rail line between **Inverness** and **Kyle of Lochalsh** and **Thurso**. There are several trains daily in each direction, 30 mins to Inverness.

Strathpeffer and around
Bus

There are regular buses between Strathpeffer and **Dingwall**.

Cycle hire
Square Wheels, The Square, T01997-421000. The place to buy or hire your mountain bike kit for a fantastic day in the hills.

Across the Kessock Bridge from Inverness is the Black Isle, which is neither an island nor black. It enjoys long hours of sunshine and low rainfall, and is an attractive landscape of rolling acres of barley and stately woods of oak and beech dropping down to the Moray coast. It also has a compelling atmosphere – a combination perhaps of its soft microclimate, lush vegetation and attractive architecture. Its main attractions are the picturesque town of Cromarty and Chanonry Point, on the southern side near Rosemarkie, which is one of the best dolphin-spotting sites in Europe.

Cromarty *Colour map 2, C2.*
On the northeastern tip of the Black Isle Peninsula, at the mouth of the Cromarty Firth, is the gorgeous wee town of Cromarty, one of the east coast's major attractions. Its neat white-harled houses interspersed with gracious merchants' residences are almost unchanged since the 18th century when it was a sea port thriving on trade as far afield as Russia and the Baltic. Many emigrants bound for the New World embarked here. The town's prosperity, based on textiles and fishing, turned to decline and dereliction. Although restored and fully populated, Cromarty now has the atmosphere of a backwater, though a very attractive one at that, where you feel as if you're stepping back in time, in stark contrast to the numerous oil rigs moored on the opposite shore in Nigg Bay.

For an insight into the history of the area, visit the 18th-century **Cromarty Courthouse** ① *Church St, T01381-600418, www.cromarty-courthouse.org.uk, Apr-Sep daily 1000-1700, Adults £2, includes loan of headset for recorded tour of the town's other historic buildings*, which houses the town's museum. Next to the courthouse is the thatch-roofed **Hugh Miller's Cottage** ① *T08444-932158, www.nts.org.uk, Mar-Sep daily 1300-1700, £6.50, concessions £5, family £16.50*, birthplace of the eminent local geologist and author. Also worth seeing is the elegant 17th-century **East Church**.

There's a good walk along a coastal path from the east end of the village through woodland to the top of the **South Sutor** headland, one of the two steep headlands guarding the narrow entrance to the Cromarty Firth. There are excellent views from here across the Moray Firth. Leaflets describing this and other local walks are available at the Cromarty Courthouse.

One of Cromarty's main attractions is its dolphins. They can be seen from the shore, or with a boat trip (see What to do, page 278). To the west, the mudflats of **Udale Bay** are an RSPB reserve and a haven for wading birds and wintering duck and geese, which can be viewed from a hide. **Poyntzfield Herb Garden** is an organic plant nursery specializing in rare and native medicinal herbs. Worth visiting if only for a glimpse of the house, and the view from the car park over the Cromarty Firth through massive beech trees.

Rosemarkie
About 9 miles south from Cromarty on the north side of Chanonry Point is the tiny village of Rosemarkie. Celtic saints Curitan and Boniface selected this sheltered spot on the southern shore for their Christian mission in the seventh century. St Boniface is remembered at nearby St Bennet's Well. **Groam House Museum** ① *T01381-620961, www.groamhouse.org.uk, Apr-Oct Mon-Sat 1000-1700, Sun 1400-1630, Nov-Mar Fri-Sun 1400-1600, free*, houses a huge collection of Pictish sculptured stones found locally, imaginatively

displayed alongside contemporary artwork inspired by them. A year-round programme of events and lectures is devoted to the study of Pictish culture. A lovely marked trail leads into **Fairy Glen**, now a nature reserve, from the top end of the High Street, through a wooded gorge where you may spot woodpeckers and treecreepers. The name obviously derives from the fairies that live here, though the last sighting was in the 1970s.

Fortrose and Chanonry Point

A mile west is the village of Fortrose. The magnificent cathedral at Fortrose is now largely a ruin; rainwashed carved faces of rose-coloured sandstone peer down from roof bosses, and snapped-off stumps of window tracery are a reminder of Reformation vandalism. On the golf course at **Chanonry Point**, overlooking the Moray Firth, a plaque marks the spot where the Brahan Seer was boiled in a barrel of tar. Chanonry Point is also a great place for seeing dolphins. They come close to shore at high tide and there's a good chance of seeing them leaping above the waves.

Listings The Black Isle

Where to stay

Cromarty

For such an appealing place, there's precious little accommodation, so it's advisable to book ahead during the summer months.

£££ Factor's House
Denny Rd, T01381-600394.
5-star luxury B&B offering stylish and elegant accommodation, a wram and friendly welcome and fantastic food. 3 double rooms. Dinner is available for non-residents if booked in advance. Recommended.

£££-££ Royal Hotel
Marine Terrace, T01381-600217, www. royalcromartyhotel.co.uk. Open all year.
8 rooms. The best place to stay, with a good restaurant (**£££-££**), and cheaper meals available in the bar. Pet friendly and also good value for families.

Restaurants

Cromarty
££ Cromarty Arms
Opposite Cromarty Courthouse, T01381-600230.
Cheap home-made bar food served daily 1200-2100. Also has live music some nights and 2 rooms for B&B.

££ Sutor Creek
21 Bank St, T01381-600855, www. sutorcreek.co.uk. Thu-Sun 1200-2100.
Cooperative café/restaurant that's famous for its superb wood-fired pizzas, but also other dishes using local ingredients in season. Also takeaway. Recommended.

What to do

Cromarty
Boat trips
Dolphin-spotting boat trips leave from Cromarty; be sure to go with an accredited operator.
EcoVentures, *Harbour Workshop, Victoria Place, T01381-600323, www.ecoventures. co.uk.* Leave from the harbour Apr-Oct to see porpoises, seals, dolphins, and perhaps even killer whales further out. The 2-hr 'Wildlife Watch' trip costs £30, £23 for children. Also charters. Accredited operator.

Mountain biking
The challenging tracks of **Learnie Red Rock Trails** are just 3 miles from Rosemarkie village. See also www.HiMBA.org.uk and https://forestry.gov.uk/mtbscotland.

Transport

Cromarty
Bus
Stagecoach run services to/from Inverness via **Fortrose** and other places on the Black Isle several times daily Mon-Sat, once on Sun. There is also a daily service on Mon and Fri from **Dingwall**. Also buses with to **Inverness** with **DE Coaches**, www.decoaches.co.uk.

Skye & the Small Isles

remote islands and rugged mountain scenery

Skye's spectacular combination of mountains and sea creates some of Britain's most breathtaking scenery. There are the surreal rock formations of the Trotternish Peninsula, the hummocky strangeness of Fairy Glen and the gentler pleasures of Sleat in the south.

And then there are the Cuillins. Standing in the centre of the island, these implacable mountains are the greatest concentration of peaks in Britain and among the most challenging. Certainly, Skye is one of the best places in Scotland for outdoor types: it offers air, sea, land and light in their purest form and any visitor will return home physically refreshed and spiritually uplifted.

The Small Isles is the collective name given to the four islands of Eigg, Muck, Rùm and Canna, lying south of Skye. Seen from the mainland, they look a very tempting prospect. Visiting the islands isn't the logistical nightmare of yesteryear, though sailings are less frequent than on many routes and accommodation and facilities remain limited. However, the determined traveller with time on their hands will be well rewarded, particularly on Eigg and mountainous Rùm, with its superb walking and abundant wildlife.

Best for
Mountain scenery ▪ Walking ▪ Wildlife

Isle of Skye 283
The Small Isles 307

Footprint picks

★ Old Man of Storr, page 291

One of Skye's most famous walks takes you up into a world of weird and wonderful rock formations and stunning views.

★ Dunvegan Castle, page 293

Home of the chiefs of the Clan Macleod and the oldest inhabited castle in Britain features some fascinating ancient relics.

★ Neist Point, page 295

One of the most photographed places in the Highlands and Islands; the walk out to the point is well worth the effort.

★ Loch Coruisk, page 298

This dramatic sea loch can be reached from Elgol via a demanding 9-mile walk, or by the famous boat trip, with seals and porpoises for company.

★ Isle of Raasay, page 302

The peaceful little island is a nature conservancy, where you can see seals, eagles and otters and enjoy superb walking opportunities.

★ Rùm, page 311

Wild, beautiful and mountainous Rùm is a haven for wildlife, most notably the white-tailed sea eagle.

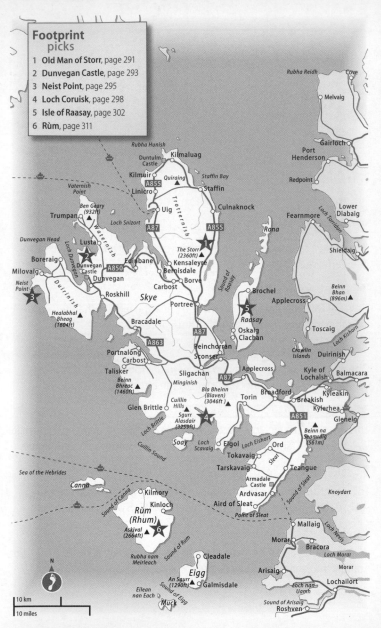

Footprint picks

1 Old Man of Storr, page 291
2 Dunvegan Castle, page 293
3 Neist Point, page 295
4 Loch Coruisk, page 298
5 Isle of Raasay, page 302
6 Rùm, page 311

Rubha Reidh
Cove
Melvaig

Rubha Hunish
Kilmaluag
Duntulm Castle
Kilmuir
Quiraing
Staffin Bay
Linicro
Staffin
Uig
Culnaknock
Vaternish Point
Ben Geary (932ft)
Loch Snizort
Trumpan
Waternish
Rona
Gairloch
Port Henderson
Redpoint
Lower Diabaig
Fearnmore
Loch Torridon
Shieldaig
Lusta
Borreraig
Loch Dunvegan
Dunvegan Castle
Edinbane
The Storr (2360ft)
Kensaleyre
Dunvegan Head
Milovaig
Neist Point
Dunvegan
Roskhill
Bernisdale
Borve
Brochel
Beinn Bhan (896ft)
Applecross
Duirinish
Healabhal Bheag (1604ft)
Skye
Carbost
Portree
Raasay
Applecross
Toscaig
Loch Kishorn
Bracadale
Oskaig
Clachan
Portnalong
Carbost
Peinchorran
Sconser
Crowlin Islands
Duirinish
Talisker
Beinn Breac (1460ft)
Sligachan
Applecross
Kyle of Lochalsh
Balmacara
Minginish
Bla Bheinn (Blaven) (3046ft)
Broadford
Kyleakin
Glen Brittle
Cuillin Hills
Torin
Breakish
Kylerhea
Glenelg
Loch Brittle
Sgurr Alasdair (3259ft)
Beinn na Seamraig (561m)
Soay
Loch Scavaig
Elgol
Loch Eishort
Ord
Cuillin Sound
Tokavaig
Sleat
Sea of the Hebrides
Tarskavaig
Teangue
Armadale Castle
Knoydart
Canna
Kilmory
Ardvasar
Aird of Sleat
Sound of Canna
Kinloch
Point of Sleat
Sound of Sleat
Mallaig
Loch Nevis
Rùm (Rhum)
Askival (2664ft)
Morar
Bracora
Loch Morar
Sound of Rum
Rubha nam Meirleach
Cleadale
Arisaig
Morar
Eigg
An Sgurr (1290ft)
Galmisdale
Lochailort
Eilean nan Each
Sound of Eigg
Loch nan Uamh
Muck
Sound of Arisaig
Roshven

N

10 km
10 miles

Isle of
Skye

The Isle of Skye (An t-Eilean Sgitheanach), the best known of all the Scottish islands, gets its name from the Norse word for cloud (skuy) and is commonly known as Eilean a' Cheò (the Misty Isle), so it obviously rains a lot here. But when the rain stops and the mist clears, the views make the heart soar.

Aside from swooning at the island's natural beauty, the most popular destination on the Isle of Skye is Dunvegan Castle, stronghold of the Macleod clan; their old enemies, the MacDonalds, hail from the Sleat Peninsula in the south of the island. The most famous MacDonald, Flora, who helped Bonnie Prince Charles flee to France, was born at Milton on South Uist but latterly moved to Skye and was buried at Kilmuir in 1790.

Essential Isle of Skye

Finding your feet

The quickest route to Skye is across the **Skye Bridge** (no toll) from Kyle of Lochalsh to Kyleakin. Coach services run to Skye from Edinburgh and Glasgow (via Fort William) and Inverness with **Scottish Citylink** and **Stagecoach**. The Citylink bus service from Inverness runs three times daily and the journey takes three to four hours. The Glasgow service runs to Kyleakin, Portree and Uig, three to four times daily and it takes three hours to reach Portree from Fort William. Winter services are less frequent with only a few buses in each direction each day. For the train service from Inverness to Kyle of Lochalsh, see page 169.

Eyed from the south, the high arch of Skye Bridge is certainly dramatic. However, a still more scenic approach to the island is by **ferry** from Mallaig to Armadale, on the southern Sleat Peninsula. The car and passenger ferry makes this 30-minute crossing eight times each way Monday to Saturday, and six times on Sunday (reduced sailings in winter). Booking is recommended, call T08000-665000 or visit www.calmac.co.uk for current fares and discount passes. Trains from Fort William and Glasgow Queen Street to Mallaig connect with some of the ferries, see www. scotrail.co.uk, T0344-811 0141.

The best and least frequented route to Skye is from Glenelg to Kylerhea, south of Kyleakin. The tiny community-owned car ferry, the last manually operated turntable ferry in Scotland, makes the 10-minute crossing every 20 minutes, daily from Easter to October between 1000 and 1800. Between June and the end of August it sails until 1900. The cost per car is £15 or £25 return (with up to four passengers), see page 230 for details. Information and ticket bookings can be found at www.skyeferry. co.uk. For further details, see Transport, page 289.

Getting around

Skye is the second largest Hebridean island (after Harris and Lewis), at almost 50 miles long and between seven and 25 miles wide. It is possible to run up a hefty mileage as the extensive road system reaches all but the most remote corners of its many peninsulas. It is possible to get around by public transport midweek but, as everywhere in the Highlands and Islands, buses are few and far between at weekends, especially Sunday, and during the winter. Buses run between Portree, Broadford, Uig (for ferries to the Western Isles), Kyleakin, Armadale (for ferries to Mallaig), Dunvegan and Carbost, and a more limited service runs from Broadford to Elgol and Portree to Glen Brittle. Getting around by public transport is more time consuming in winter (October to March) as bus services are less frequent on some routes. **Stagecoach**, www.stagecoachbus. com, runs services to all the main points on the island, including from Portree to Sligachan, Dunvegan (for the castle), Uig and around the north end of the island, Broadford, Armadale and around the south of the island. An open-top service is also available. For further details, see What to do, page 288, and Transport, page 289.

When to go

The Cuillins attract stormy weather off the Atlantic. You'll maximize your chance of enjoying fine weather between April and October. From October to March the weather is less settled. Most accommodation and tourist sights are likely to be closed between November and Easter.

attractive fishing port and island hub

Portree is Skye's capital and, as such, is a functional kind of place with all the attendant facilities and services you'd expect to find in the island's main settlement. That said, it's a fairly attractive, busy fishing port built around a natural harbour, with a row of brightly painted houses along the shorefront and the rest of the town rising steeply up to the centre which is now dominated by a public car park (pay and display).

Sights

Aros ① *Viewfield Rd, ½ a mile from town centre on the road to Broadford, T01478-613649, box office 613750, www.aros.co.uk, year-round daily 0900-1700, free,* is a community arts and cultural centre. It houses the island's only theatre and features a varied programme of events, including drama, traditional music, comedy and films (see Entertainment, page 288). There's also a restaurant with lunches and snacks and a shop selling souvenirs, children's play areas and a series of changing exhibitions, which have to be booked separately.

A nice, gentle introduction to walking in the area, and an opportunity to stretch your legs before tackling more strenuous routes such as the Old Man of Storr or the Quiraing, starts out from Bosville Terrace. Follow the street as it curves round, then take the right fork at the first junction, down towards the shore. Just after the car park to the right the road splits: follow the path to the right along the northern shore of the bay. The path follows the shore and passes a viewpoint and flagpole. It then becomes rougher as it swings round the headland and reaches a gate in a dyke. Go through the gate and cross the muddy field, then follow the fence up to the left until you reach another gate. Climb over the gate and continue along the edge of the next field, then cross a stile at the top. Walk up the slope to the clear track and follow this left as it heads uphill. You'll then see some houses; take the track beyond the house on the left and follow it down between two large farm buildings. The path heads down across rough moorland towards Portree. Cross the stile and continue downhill through some woods; then you'll see a hotel on your left before rejoining the original road near the car park. It's about 2½ miles and takes about 1½ hours at an easy pace. The path can get very muddy in places. Details of several local walks can be found in the **iCentre**.

Essential Portree

Finding your feet

Portree is ideally placed for trips to all but the most southwesterly parts of the island. Buses leave from the bus station in Somerled Square to Dunvegan, Uig, Broadford, Kyleakin, Armadale, the Talisker Distillery and Glenbrittle. There are also services to the mainland. The town is compact enough to get around easily on foot, though there is a regular town bus service for those needing to get into the centre from the outskirts.

Tip...

Skye is well served by all types of accommodation: B&Bs, guesthouses, hostels, bunk-houses, campsites and some very fine hotels. During the peak summer months advance bookings are recommended. These can be made directly or through the island's main tourist information centre in Portree. See www.visitscotland.com, and www.theskyeguide.com. For local tourist information centres see individual sections.

Tourist information

Portree iCentre
Bayfield Rd, T01478-612992. Year-round Mon-Sat.
The centre has bus timetables, a good selection of books and maps, internet access and several (20p) leaflets outlining local walking routes including the 2-mile-long Portree Forest walk.

Where to stay

Skye does not lack quality accommodation to suit every budget, though in the busy summer season it's strongly advised to book ahead. **Portree iCentre** has lists of

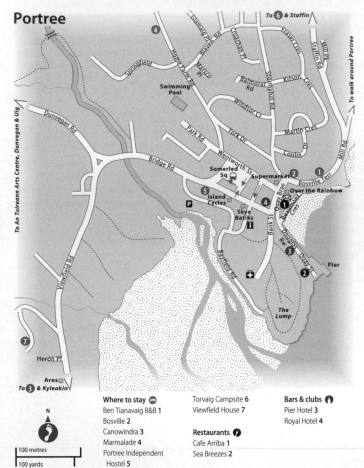

Portree

Where to stay 🛏	Torvaig Campsite 6	Bars & clubs 🍸
Ben Tianavaig B&B 1	Viewfield House 7	Pier Hotel 3
Bosville 2		Royal Hotel 4
Canowindra 3	Restaurants 🍴	
Marmalade 4	Cafe Arriba 1	
Portree Independent	Sea Breezes 2	
Hostel 5		

available accommodation and for a small fee will book it for you.

There are several guesthouses on Bosville Terrace and many B&Bs on Stormyhill Rd and the streets running off it. Prices tend to be slightly higher in Portree than the rest of the island, though B&Bs on the outskirts of town are usually cheaper. There's also an excellent campsite and 2 good backpackers.

££££ Bosville Hotel
Bosville Terrace, T01478-612846, www.bosvillehotel.co.uk.
18 rooms. Comfortable, contemporary and stylish accommodation in central, upmarket boutique hotel with views across the harbour. Enjoy a single malt or one of the many Scottish craft gins in the **Merchant Bar** – once the village bank – and the **Dulse & Brose Restaurant** is one of the best on Skye (see Restaurants).

££££ Canowindra
Peinifiler, T01478-613640, www.canowindraskye.com.
Luxury B&B on the outskirts of Portree offering style, comfort and great attention to detail that is often lacking in more expensive places to stay. Hosts Rick and Georgie go out of their way to make guests feel welcome and also provide a fanstastic breakfast to set you up for the day. Recommended.

££££ Marmalade
Home Farm Rd, T01478-611711, www.marmaladehotel.com. Open all year.
This Georgian period building with views across the harbour boasts 15 en suite chic, contemporary-styled rooms (including family) and excellent food – especially their steaks – in the restaurant. Lovely gardens and family friendly.

£££ Viewfield House Hotel
On the road into Portree from the south, T01478-612217, www.viewfieldhouse.com. Mid-Apr to mid-Oct.
11 bedrooms. A 200-year-old country house full of antiques, set in 20 acres of woodland

garden. Good food (**£££-££**) with old-world hospitality, and the log fire adds to the welcoming atmosphere. Also has a charming 5-bedroom cottage suitable for rent.

£££-££ Ben Tianavaig
5 Bosville Terrace, T01478-612152, www.ben-tianavaig.co.uk.
4 en suite rooms. Very friendly and comfortable B&B, handily placed for all amenities in town. Good choice. 2-night minimum stay.

£ Portree Independent Hostel
Old Post Office, The Green, T01478-613737, www.hostelskye.co.uk.
60 beds. Right in the centre of town, 100 yds from the town square. Laundrette, internet access in the lounge and kitchen.

Camping
There's a well-maintained, friendly campsite with great showers at Torvaig, 2 miles north of Portree centre, T01478-611849, Apr-Oct.

Restaurants

There are notable exceptions, but some of the best food on Skye is to be found in hotel dining rooms, so also check the Where to stay section for places to eat. Many B&Bs also provide evening meals on request.

£££ Dulse & Brose
Bosville Hotel, see Where to stay.
Dulse is a Scots word for seaweed and Brose is an uncooked form of porridge, but fear not for, this restaurant serves exquisite fine food, drawing on the local larder of fresh meats and fish. Oozes style and ambience. The best place in town.

£££-££ Sea Breezes Restaurant
2 Marine Buildings, right by the pier, T01478-612016, www.seabreezes-skye.co.uk. Daily 1200-1400, 1700-2130.
This snug, bright restaurant will delight the seafood lover and steak aficionado alike. It's not the cheapest in town but you're assured of quality and ambience. Early-bird, 2-course

Shopping on the Isle of Skye

There's a Co-op supermarket, diagonally opposite the Bosville Hotel, and a large Tesco supermarket on the road to Uig. **Cioch Outdoor Clothing**, *4 Ullinish, Struan, T01470-572707, www.cioch-direct. co.uk.* For mountain gear.
Isle of Skye Baking Co Ltd, *in Old Skye Woolllen Mill building, Dunvegan Rd, T01478-612669, ww.isleofskyebakingco.co. uk.* Delicious baked goodies for sale in their shop, also gallery and café where you can enjoy the goodies on offer.
Isle of Skye Crafts@Over the Rainbow, *at the top of Quay Brae, T01478-612555, www.isleofskyecrafts.com.* Open 0900-2200 in the high season. A good place to buy woollens and other locally made crafts.
Ragamuffin, *T01470 844217, at Armadale's ferry pier in Sleat.* Filled with vibrant knitwear and interesting gifts.
Skye Batiks, *The Green, Portree, near the iCentre, T01478-613331, www.skyebaticks. com.* Sells handmade 'batiks' (colourful cotton fabrics), which are pricey but unique souvenirs from Skye, see also box, page 295.

dinner from 1700-1800. Recommended, but always book ahead in summer.

££-£ Café Arriba
Quay Brae, T01478-611830. Daily 0700-1700, 1800-late.
A cosy, bright place with a slightly bohemian air, serving mouth-watering breakfasts, lunches and dinners to suit vegetarians and meat-eaters alike. A starter can include the eastern dukkah aromatic spice mix or try a main of venison and apricot, or butterbean and apricot korma. Always busy so be prepared to wait for a table, or squeeze in and make friends.

Bars and pubs

The town's nightlife is mainly confined to eating and drinking.

The **Pier Hotel** (Quay St, T01478-612094), by the harbour, is a real fishermen's drinking den; the refurbished **Royal Hotel** (Bank St, T01478-612525), is also popular and serves reasonable bar food (**££**) until 1000.

Entertainment

Aros, *see page 285.* Call the box office for details of their monthly programme, T01478-
613750. Has a theatre which shows drama, movies and live music.

Festivals

Early Aug Highland Games, www.skye-highland-games.co.uk. A 1-day event held in Portree. These games, first held in 1877, include traditional highland dancing and piping competitions.

What to do

If the weather's good, Portree offers a wide variety of outdoor activities.

Boat trips
MV Stardust boat trips, *Portree Harbour, T07798-743858, www.skyeboat-trips.co.uk.* Sail daily from the pier, and offer a range of cruises, fishing forays and wildlife trips (£20-25/10-15), including the chance to spot the rare white-tailed sea eagle, as well as to see the seals at Griana Sgeir and the birdlife at Holm Island. Trips can also be made to Rona, north of Raasay.

Cycle hire
Island Cycles, *The Green, T01478-613121, www. islandcycles-skye.co.uk. Mon-Sat 1000-1700.*

Bike hire, sales and repairs. Also good for game and sea-fishing rod hire.

Transport

Bus
There are buses (No 57A) Mar-Oct Mon-Sat around the Trotternish Peninsula, in each direction, via **Uig**. Daily buses to **Kyleakin**, and to **Armadale** via **Broadford**. There are buses Mon-Sat to **Carbost** (for the **Talisker Distillery**). Also use this service to access **Glenbrittle**, alighting at Carbost and walking 8 miles. There are buses daily Mon-Sat to **Glendale** via **Dunvegan**, and buses Mon-Sat to **Waternish** via **Dunvegan**.

For more information, see Essential Portree, page 285.

Car hire
S Morrison Ltd, Broom Place, Portree, T01478-612688, www.morrisoncarrental.com.

Taxi
Gus's Taxis, T01478-613000, www.skye-taxis.co.uk. Airport/ferry/train transfers and also island tours.

Trotternish Peninsula Colour map 1, C3.

bizarre rock formations and a fairy glen

North from Portree is the 30-mile-long Trotternish Peninsula, sticking out like a giant thumb hitching a lift from a passing ferry. The interior of the peninsula is a basaltic lava wilderness full of bizarre rock formations. A 20-mile-long escarpment of sheer cliffs and towering pinnacles dominates the landscape. The best known of these strange formations, the Quiraing and Old Man of Storr, can be explored on foot (see page 290). The A855 and A87 roads follow the coast around the peninsula, and a spectacular minor road bisects the ridge from Staffin Bay to Uig. Trotternish is best explored with your own transport, but there are a few daily buses covering the circular route from Portree.

Uig Colour map 1, C3.
The A87 runs northwest from Portree to the tiny ferry port of Uig, dramatically set in a horseshoe bay and the departure point for ferries to **Tarbert** (Harris) and **Lochmaddy** (North Uist). The island's busy and helpful Caledonian MacBrayne ⓘ *T0800-665000, www.calmac. co.uk*, ferry booking office is here whilst just 20 yards past CalMac's door you'll also find the production nerve centre (and shop) of the acclaimed Isle of **Skye Brewing Co** ⓘ *T01470-542477, www.skyeale.co.uk, shop open Mon-Fri 1000-1800, Sat 1000-1600, Sun 1200-1600*, which has gone from strength to strength and now exports its renowned ales around the world. Alternatively, also by the CalMac office, kids will enjoy painting their own earthenware pot at the **Uig Pottery** ⓘ *T01470-542421, www.uigpottery.co.uk, May-Sep Mon-Sat.*

Just outside the village is the magical **Fairy Glen**. Turn right just before the Uig Hotel coming down the hill from the Portree direction. About a mile up the single-track road you enter an eerie, mysterious world of perfect conical hills, some up to 60 ft high. It's almost inconceivable that these are natural formations, and the inevitable mist only adds to the spooky strangeness of the place.

Uig to Duntulm Colour map 1, C3.
At **Kilmuir** is the **Skye Museum of Island Life** ⓘ *T01470-552206, www.skyemuseum. co.uk, Easter to end Sep Mon-Sat 0930-1700, £2.50, children £0.50.* The group of thatched houses give a fascinating insight into a crofting community's way of life of at the end of

ON THE ROAD

Take no prisoners

Violent conflict between neighbouring clan chiefs was so commonplace on Skye and in the rest of the Western Highlands that it was almost accepted as part of the very fabric of society. One particularly gruesome example took place on Eigg in 1577. The Macleods had taken refuge in a cave but their presence was discovered by the MacDonalds, who piled brushwood at the entrance and set fire to it, burning alive the 395 people sheltering inside, almost the entire population of the island. Revenge came the following year, at Trumpan church in Ardmore Bay on Skye. The Macleods landed under cover of the early morning fog and set light to the church, burning the congregation inside.

the 19th century, and is the most authentic of several such museums on Skye. Behind the museum, at the end of the road, is **Flora MacDonald's Monument**, which marks the grave of Skye's most famous daughter, with her husband buried alongside. The rather austere memorial is inscribed with Dr Johnson's poignant tribute, see box, page 291. Indeed, so highly regarded was 'Flory' that it's said her funeral was the largest ever seen in the Highlands. Apparently, her cortege stretched for 1½ miles whilst over 300 gallons of whisky were drunk at her wake!

At the northwest tip of the peninsula, 15 minutes' drive from Uig, is **Duntulm Castle**, a dramatic ruin perched atop a steep cliff, haunted by keening winds and the ghosts of its tragic past: according to local legend, the castle was abandoned around 1732 when a nursemaid accidentally let the baby heir fall from a window onto the cliffs below. The 15th-century structure, built on the site of an ancient Norse stronghold, became the chief Skye residence of the powerful MacDonalds and was the most imposing castle in the Hebrides.

The Quiraing walk *Colour map 1, C3.*

Beyond Duntulm, the A855 heads across the tip of the peninsula to the east coast, where the famous bizarre rock scenery is found. At the north end of **Staffin Bay**, a minor road cuts across the peninsula to Uig. This road is the access point for the Quiraing, the famous jumble of strangely shaped hills and rocks that is one of the island's classic walks. This four-mile walk is quite demanding, but the dramatic scenery more than compensates. To get to the starting point, drive 19 miles north from Portree on the A855. At Brogaig, just north of Staffin, take the single-track road to Uig. Follow it and, just after the road has zigzagged its way up the face of the ridge, park in the car park to the left. Cross the road and follow the well-defined path along the base of the cliffs, with a steep grassy slope down to the right. After about one mile you'll start to see some of the well-known rocky features on the far side of a rough valley. The most imposing of these is **The Prison**, a huge, tilted square block. On the left, among the towering cliffs, is **The Needle**, a shaft of rock about 120-ft high. Scramble up the narrow gully to the left of The Needle to reach **The Table**, an area of flat grassland surrounded by high cliffs (local shinty teams used to play here). From The Table continue along the path at the foot of the cliffs, past a small lochan on the right and through a stone dyke, until you reach the lowest point of the ridge on your left. Scramble up on to the ridge and make your way back along the tops of the cliffs (take care at this point). There's a hard climb up the slopes of Meall na Suirmamach, but the views from the top are spectacular. Continue along the top of the cliffs for just

Faithful Flora

In Kilmuir graveyard is the memorial which marks the grave of Flora MacDonald, one of the most famous characters in Skye's long history. The memorial bears Dr Johnson's fitting epitaph: *A name that will be mentioned in history, and if courage and fidelity be virtues, mentioned with honour.*

It was Flora MacDonald who helped Bonnie Prince Charlie to escape capture following the Jacobite defeat at Culloden in 1746. Pursued by government troops, the prince fled from South Uist "over the sea to Skye" aboard Flora's boat, disguised as an Irish servant girl by the name of Betty Burke. He then made his way to Portree, where he bade farewell to the young woman who had risked her own life to protect his.

When Flora's part in the prince's escape became known, she was immediately arrested and sent to the Tower of London. She was released a year later, married a Skye man and then emigrated to North Carolina where she spent the next 12 years of her life. They returned to her husband's house in Kingsburgh in 1786. Flora died on Skye in 1790, and it is said that her funeral was the largest ever witnessed in the Highlands.

over a mile and you'll see the car park. Even if you don't attempt the walk, the road over the back of the Trotternish ridge from Uig makes a worthwhile detour.

Kilt Rock *Colour map 1, C3.*

A few miles south of Staffin Bay is Kilt Rock, an impressive 60-m sea cliff which gets its name from the vertical columnar basalt strata overlying horizontal ones beneath. A rather tenuous comparison perhaps, but the cliffs south of Staffin are particularly spectacular, as are the **Lealt Falls**, a torrent of mountain water at the head of a gorge, a few miles south of Kilt Rock. The falls are signposted by the road, so all you have to do is park the car and peer over. Just before the turn for Kilt Rock at Ellishadder is the wee **Staffin Museum** ① *T01470-562321, May-Oct*, sporting such finds as a dinosaur bone and Bronze Age artefacts. Close by, at **Glenview B&B** at Culnacnoc, you can buy high-quality handspun Scottish merino wool and cashmere at **Shilasdair Yarn** ① *T01470-562248, glenviewskye.co.uk, year-round Mon-Fri 1130-1700.*

★ Old Man of Storr walk *Colour map 1, C3.*

A few miles further south, and seven miles north of Portree, is a car park which is the starting point for another of Skye's famous walks: up to the Old Man of Storr, the distinctive pinnacle which has detached itself from the cliffs of the Storr behind. This basalt finger of rock, 165-ft high, stands beneath the steep cliffs of **The Storr** (2360 ft) and is visible from the A855. The starting point for the 3½-mile walk up and back (1½ hours) is the car park on the left, just over six miles north of Portree, near the northern end of Loch Leathan, which can be reached by bus from Portree. Cross the stile over the wall by the Forestry Commission sign and follow the clear track up through the conifer plantation. The track is a gradual uphill climb until you come out into open grassland. Go through the gate in the fence and then it's a steep climb up the grassy slope with the massive pinnacle towering overhead. Once at the top you enter an area of weird and impressive rock formations. You can follow any of the dozens of paths that lead between the rocks, or just enjoy the fantastic views across to Raasay and the mainland beyond. You can follow the same path back down to the car park.

Where to stay

££££ Flodigarry Country House Hotel
A few miles north of Staffin, T01470-552203,
www.hotelintheskye.co.uk.
Beautifully located at the foot of the
mighty Quiraing and with stunning views
across Staffin Bay, this is one of the great
country house hotels, with a relaxing old-
world atmosphere and restaurant. Flora
MacDonald's cottage is in the grounds and
has been tastefully refurbished, giving the
chance to stay in a place steeped in the
island's history. The **Skye** restaurant (**£££**)
serves sumptuous food, especially fish and
seafood, which can be enjoyed to the full
with their 4-course seafood taster menu at
£64 a head. The lively bar is a good place to
enjoy a laugh and a jig.

£££ Cuil Lodge Guest House
Cuill, Uig, T01470-542474, www.blue-skye-
thinking.org. Open all year.
3 en suite rooms. Cosy and friendly B&B with
excellent facilities set on shore of Uig Bay, all
rooms with sea views.

£££ Uig Hotel
On the right of the road into Uig from Portree,
beside a white church, opposite Frazer's Folly,
T01470-542205, www.uig-hotel-skye.com.
Open all year.
11 en suite rooms. Comfortable
accommodation in a traditional country
house with great views across the bay,
good food and a friendly island welcome,
especially for those with dogs. Restaurant
open Mon-Sat for lunch 1200-1500 and
dinner 1800-2030, also on Sun for a their
huge and amazingly good-value lunches at
£14.99. Cheaper rooms are available behind
the hotel in the **£££-££ Uig Lodge**.

£££ Woodbine House
Woodbine House, Uig, T01470-542243,
www.woodbineskye.co.uk. Easter-Oct.

5 rooms. Whitewashed stone cottage
renowned for flexible room options (ideal
for families) and a warm welcome. Excellent
value. Recommended. Also check out their
boat trips (www.puffinsandwhales.co.uk).
The whole house (sleeps 11) is available for
self-catering Oct-Mar.

£ Dun Flodigarry Backpackers Hostel
100 yds from the bar of the Flodigarry
Country House Hotel, T01470-552212,
www.flodigarryhostel.scot. Mar-Oct.
40 beds. Clifftop seaviews and adequate
facilities including laundry, drying room
and kitchen. Camping also available.

£ SYHA Youth Hostel
1 mile from the Uig ferry terminal,
T01470-542746. Mid-Mar to Oct.
High above the port on the south side of the
village. Offers spectacular views over the bay.
Basic but comfortable, with a few family and
private rooms. The warden can help arrange
bike and canoe hire.

Camping
There's camping at **Flodigarry Backpackers
Hostel** (above) and south of Staffin Bay,
T01470-562213. Mid-Apr to end Sep.

What to do

Skye Activities, *Woodbine Guest House, Uig,*
T01470-542243. Boat trips on a nippy 6-m
RIB, wildlife watching, fishing and charters.
Mountain biking, archery and waterskiing
too. See also Where to stay, above.
Whitewave, *a few miles north of Uig, on*
the A855 at Linicro, T01471-542414, www.
white-wave.co.uk. Outdoor centre where you
can try windsurfing, rock climbing, archery,
walking and sea kayaking. There's also a café
specializing in vegetarian, seafood and Celtic
music, and a B&B.

Transport

Ferry
From **Uig** to **Lochmaddy** on **North Uist**

(1 hr 45 mins) and to **Tarbert** on **Harris** (1 hr 45 mins). For details see page 284, or contact **Uig**, T01470-542219.

Waternish, Dunvegan and Duirinish *Colour map 1, C2/3.*
an ancient clan seat, a giant's museum and the best food on the island

In the northwest of Skye the peninsulas of Waternish (or Vaternish) and Duirinish point out into the Minch towards the Western Isles. The larger Duirinish Peninsula holds more interest for the visitor, featuring the beautiful green valley of Glendale, an area brimming with history, the dramatic walk to Neist Point and Dunvegan Castle, Skye's most famous landmark.

Edinbane *Colour map 1, C3.*
The turn-off to this much-visited part of the island is four miles northwest of Portree. The A850 swings west towards Dunvegan but eight miles before the castle and at the head of Loch Greshornish is the tiny village of Edinbane, where there's a campsite, two hotels, several B&Bs, a petrol station and the renowned **Edinbane Pottery** ① *T01470-582234, www. edinbane-pottery.co.uk, 0900-1800 Nov-Easter weekdays and Easter-Oct daily, workshop and showroom*, which is a must for hunters of imaginative hand-crafted souvenirs.

Waternish Peninsula *Colour map 1, C2/3.*
The A850 continues west. Those with their own transport and time on their hands might wish to make an interesting little detour at the **Fairy Bridge**, where the B886 runs north to **Trumpan**, near the tip of the Waternish Peninsula. If the weather's good (and it is, occasionally), this is the best place to watch the sun set in a blaze of red over the Outer Hebrides. If there's no sunset, then you could always visit **Skyeskyns** ① *T01470-592237, www.skyeskyns.co.uk, daily Apr-Oct 0900-1800, Nov-Mar 0930-1730, café Apr-Oct daily 1100-1700*, in Loch Bay, the country's only traditional exhibition tannery. While here, you could also pop into the island's oldest pub, the **Stein Inn** (see Bars and pubs, page 297).

The ruined church at Trumpan, at the end of the road, has some grisly skeletons in its cupboard (see box, page 290). In the graveyard is the 'trial stone'. A hole in the stone was used to test whether or not an accused person was telling the truth. If they could quickly find the hole and stick their arm through it while blindfolded, they were found innocent, but if not, they were guilty. The church is also the starting point for the strenuous eight-mile walk out to **Waternish Point** and back.

★ Dunvegan *Colour map 1, C2.*
A few miles further on from the turn-off to Waternish is the little village of Dunvegan. Just to the north of the village is proud **Dunvegan Castle** ① *T01470-521206, www.dunvegan castle.com, Apr-mid Oct daily 1000-1730; castle and gardens £14, concessions £11, children £9, family £34, gardens only £12, concessions £9, children £7*, the island's most important tourist attraction. The No 56 **Stagecoach** bus serves the castle, running from Portree to Glendale via Dunvegan, and back.

The castle is the home of the chiefs of the Clan Macleod who have lived here for over seven centuries, making it the oldest continuously inhabited castle in Britain. The present structure dates from the 15th and 16th centuries and, though the Victorian restoration has left it looking more like a baronial house, a look inside reveals its true age. Among the few genuinely interesting relics on display is Rory Mor's horn, a huge drinking vessel which the chief's heir must drain 'without setting down or falling down', when filled with claret (about 1½ bottles). There's also a lock of Bonnie Prince Charlie's hair, clipped from his head by Flora MacDonald as a keepsake, but pride of place goes to the Fairy Flag. The flag has been dated to between the fourth and seventh centuries and is made of Middle Eastern silk. It is said to have been given to the clan chief by a fairy, and has the power to ensure victory in battle for the clan on three occasions. It has been used twice so far. The lovely castle gardens lead down to the lochside jetty, from where you can take a **seal-spotting cruise** ① *T01470-521500, Apr-end Sep daily, £7.50, concessions £6.50, children £5.50, there are also 1-hr loch cruises, £18, children £11.* These shores are reportedly inhabited by 35% of Skye's seal population. Nevertheless, you'll get a refund if you fail to spot one. There's also a busy restaurant and gift shop by the castle gates.

In the village of Dunvegan is **Giant Angus MacAskill Museum** ① *T01470-521296, Easter-Oct daily 0930-1800, £2, concessions £1, children free,* housed in a thatched, whitewashed cottage, which relates the life story of the tallest ever Scotsman, Angus MacAskill, born on the Outer Hebridean island of Berneray and who grew to 7 ft 9 ins tall. He emigrated to Novia Scotïa and toured the United States with the midget General Tom Thumb, who is said to have danced on his outstretched hand. More interesting than the museum, though, are the stories of its owner, Peter MacAskill, in particular the one about the replica coffin, which is worth the admission fee alone. Peter is a descendent of Angus and also runs the museum at Colbost (see below); he is also the father of the legendary street trials biker, Danny, and will happily tell you all about his son's remarkable career.

Duirinish Peninsula *Colour map 1, C2.*

West of Dunvegan is the Duirinish Peninsula. The northern half is populated along the western shores of **Loch Dunvegan** and in the beautiful and green **Glendale**, an area brimming with history but with hardly an island family left. Glendale is now dubbed 'Little England', owing to the large number of incoming settlers from the south. The area is famed throughout the Highlands and Islands, for it was here in 1882 that local crofters, spurred on by the **Battle of the Braes**, see box, page 299, resisted the cruel and petty tyranny of their estate manager. The authorities sent a gunboat to deal with the uprising and arrested the ringleaders, some of whom were imprisoned in Edinburgh and became known as the 'Glendale Martyrs'. This episode sparked a radical movement throughout the Highlands and led to the Crofter's Holdings Act of 1886, which gave the crofters a more secure tenure and fair rent. The uninhabited southern half of the peninsula is dominated by Healabhal Bheag (1604 ft) and Healabhal Mhor (1545 ft), a pair of decapitated hills known as **Macleod's Tables**. They are so named because legend has it that the clan chief held a huge open-air feast for King James V on one of the hilltops.

The **Glendale Visitor Route** is signposted from just before Dunvegan village and leads westwards along the shores of the loch and across the peninsula. There are several interesting little sights along the way. Those interested in finding out more about the region's history, and crofting on the island, should head for the **Colbost Folk Museum** ① *T01470-521296, Easter-Oct daily 0930-1800, £1.50, concessions £1, children free,* housed in a restored blackhouse, with a peat fire burning and an illicit still out the back. The museum is adjacent to the renowned **Three Chimneys** restaurant (see Restaurants, below) and four miles from Dunvegan on the B884 to Glendale. A little further on is **Skye Silver** ① *T01470-511263, www.skyesilver.com, Mar-Oct daily 1000-1800,* where you can buy silver jewellery

ON THE ROAD
Things to do on Skye when it's raining

Just in case you didn't know, it can rain quite often on Skye and, unless you're one of those hardy souls who's prepared to brave the elements, you'll need to know about the island's main indoor attractions. There are numerous opportunities to shelter from the rain, but most of them cost money and many will leave you regretting it, so here's our list of the top 10 things to do. Details of opening times and admission prices are given under each relevant destination.

Beginning in Portree, there's **Aros** (page 285), which gives a good introduction to the island's history. North of Uig, at Kilmuir on the Trotternish Peninsula, is the **Skye Museum of Island Life** (page 289), which pretty much does what it says on the sign. Northwest from Portree is **Dunvegan Castle** (see below), home of the Clan Macleod and top of most visitors' itineraries. On the road to Dunvegan is **Edinbane Pottery** (page 293), where you can buy pots of every shape and size and watch them being made.

Travelling south from Dunvegan, you'll reach the turn-off to the **Talisker Distillery** (page 298), the island's only whisky distillery, where you can sample the distinctive peaty taste. If you're in need of some refreshment after all that culture and shopping, you could do a lot worse than the bar at the **Sligachan Hotel** (page 299), which boasts an impressive array of whiskies and climbers' beards. In the southern peninsula of Sleat, near the Armadale ferry terminal, is **Armadale Castle** (page 305), with a visitor centre that is worth visiting. Nearby is one of the branches of **Skye Batiks** (page 288), with a huge selection of these 'new age' style fabrics in a range of original Celtic designs (the other branch is in Portree). And for that final drink before boarding the ferry to Mallaig, pop into the cosy bar of the **Hotel Eilean Iarmain** (page 306), which serves wonderful food.

in traditional Celtic designs. Further north, at Borreraig Park, is the studio of **Diana Mackie** ① *T01470 511795 (phone for appointment), www.diana-mackie.co.uk*, who designed the interior of the Three Chimneys as well as No 10 (see Where to stay) and whose landscape artwork is inspired by the dramatic coastal scenery just beyond her door.

Borreraig was home to the famous MacCrimmons, hereditary pipers to the Macleod chiefs and the first composers, players and teachers of *piobaireachd* (pibroch), which can be heard at an annual recital at Dunvegan Castle in early August. The ruins of the ancient piping college can still be seen.

The B884 continues west, then a road turns off left for Waterstein. At the end of this road (just over two miles) is a car park which is the starting point for the walk out to the lighthouse at ★ **Neist Point**, the most westerly point on Skye and one of the most pleasant walks on the island. It's about 1½ miles there and back and well worth the effort. The path is easy to follow and the views of the sea cliffs are wonderful. There are lots of nesting seabirds around and you might even spot whales offshore. The **lighthouse**, built in 1909, is now unmanned.

Where to stay

There are many places to stay in and around Dunvegan, and the **iCentre** in Portree will arrange accommodation for you.

££££ Greshornish House Hotel
Edinbane, T01470-582388, www. greshornishhouse.com. Open all year.
9 rooms. Set in 10 acres of land at the end of a single-track road by the shores of the eponymous loch. If you're after peace and tranquillity then look no further than this classy manor house. Superb food in the dining room, and there's also a billiard room, tennis court and croquet lawn for those clement days.

££££ The House Over-By
Colbost, Dunvegan, T01470-511258, www.threechimneys.co.uk.
A few yards away from the very wonderful **Three Chimneys** (see Restaurants, below) on Duirnish Peninsula and run by the same folk. 6 sumptuous rooms, all with sea views, and all the luxurious touches you would expect at these prices (£345 for B&B). This is pampering at a whole new level. A table at the legendary restaurant is automatically booked for all guests.

££££ Skeabost Country House Hotel
Skeabost Bridge, 6 miles north of Portree on A850 to Dunvegan, T01470-532202, www.skeabosthotel.com. Open all year.
18 rooms. This former Victorian hunting lodge on the shores of Loch Snizort, has been given a long-overdue refurbishment and is now a truly great hotel with all the awards to prove it. Old-fashioned decadence is now married to modern style and flair and the effect is stunning, with snooker room, guest lounges, its own 9-hole golf course and trout and salmon fishing on the River Snizort that flows through its grounds. As part of the Sonas Hospitality group (along with Duisdale and Toravaig in the south of the island) it has

its own luxury yacht, the 50-ft *Solus a Chuain*, and guests can enjoy a fabulous day's sailing around the island with a champagne lunch thrown in for good measure.

£££ Shorefield House
Edinbane, T01470-582444, www. bedandbreakfast-skye.com. Open all year.
3 rooms. Superb B&B in modern home with flexible room options for families and groups, as well as separate self-catering accommodation for 2 or 4 people. Much praised breakfasts served in bright conservatory room.

££ Hillside
34 Lochbay, T01470-592263, www.bed-and-breakfast-on-skye.co.uk.
3 rooms. Traditional-looking house built in 2007 with clever eco-friendly facilities such as geothermal heating via a 90-m borehole, light-filled rooms and jaw-dropping lochside views. Great value.

Self-catering

The Spoons
75 Aird Bernisdale, T01470-532217, www. thespoonsonskye.com. Open all year.
Luxury self-catering cottage for 2 people. 3-night weekend £550, 4-night weekdays £650 or full week for £975.

Camping

£ Kinloch Campsite
Dunvegan, T01470-521531, www. kinloch-campsite.co.uk. Apr-Oct.
Pleasant, small campsite with sea views and bakery, fuel, Wi-Fi and shop nearby.

Restaurants

£££ The Three Chimneys
Duirnish Peninsula, Calbost, T01470-511258, www.threechimneys.co.uk. Mon-Sat 1230-1400, 1830-2130.

Savour the creative dishes produced by head chef Scott Davies and his team and you'll appreciate why this remote dining experience is considered by many (including the Good Food Guide) to be the best in the country. Their **Skye Land & Sea** tasting menu is unforgettable. Also accommodation (see Where to stay, above).

£££ Loch Bay Restaurant
Waternish Peninsula, T01470-592235, www.lochbay-restaurant.co.uk. Mar-late Oct Tue-Sun.
You should finish off the day with a meal at this wonderful restaurant where you can almost see your dinner being landed. One of the very finest seafood restaurants in the region and chef Michael Smith is rightly proud of their new Michelin star. Recommended. Book ahead.

£££-££ Stein Inn
Waternish, T01470-592362, www.stein-inn. co.uk. Bar meals Mon-Sat 1200-1600, 1800-2130, Sun 1230-1600, 1800-2100, closed Mon in winter.
Reputedly the oldest inn on Skye, book a table here and enjoy a real ale or malt before feasting on local venison or shellfish. If you over indulge, there's accommodation (**££**).

Bars and pubs

Stein Inn
See Restaurants, above.
There are few pleasures in life equal to sitting outside this venerable old pub with a pint of ale from the local Isle of Skye brewery and tucking into an excellent pub supper while watching a Hebridean sunset. On less clement evenings the old peat-burning fire inside provides an alternative feel-good factor.

What to do

Edinbane
Horse riding
Isle of Skye Trekking and Riding Centre, *near Suladale and about 10 miles west of Portree towards Dunvegan, T01470-582419, www.theisleofskyetrekkingcentre.co.uk.* Friendly and fully trained staff. Trekking and horse riding for all ages and abilities.

The Cuillins and Minginish   *OS Landranger No 32 & OS Outdoor Leisure No 8.*
the most spectacular and challenging mountain range in Britain

---

The district of Minginish is the wildest and least populated part of the island, but for many it is the greatest attraction, for this is where the Cuillins are to be found. This hugely impressive mountain range, often shrouded in rain or cloud, is the spiritual heartland of the island and, when it's clear, their heart-aching grandeur can be appreciated from every other peninsula on Skye. Though officially called the Cuillin 'Hills', these present some of the toughest climbing in Britain. Indeed, the magnificent scenery and vast range of (high and low level) walks and scrambles have attracted climbers and walkers for centuries, but have also claimed many lives.

Walks into the Cuillins *Colour map 3, A3.*
There are three routes into the Cuillins: from the Sligachan Hotel, from Glen Brittle, and from Elgol. The eastern part of the range is known as the **Red Cuillins**. Their smoother, conical granite peaks contrast sharply with the older, darker gabbro of the jagged-edged **Black Cuillins** to the west. The latter are particularly suitable for rock climbing and best approached from Glen Brittle, while the former are accessed from the Sligachan Hotel. There are 20 'Munros' (mountains over 3000 ft in height) in the Cuillins, with the highest

being **Sgurr Alasdair**, at 3251 ft. Though the sheer majesty of the mountains can only be appreciated at close quarters by the climber, there are impressive views from Elgol, from the road into Glen Brittle and, more distantly, from the west coast of Sleat. **Glen Sligachan** is one of the most popular routes into the Cuillin range and the main access point for the more forgiving Red Cuillins, the walk to **Loch Coruisk**, or the ascent of **Marsco**.

Tip...
It cannot be stressed too strongly that the Cuillin ridge, whilst famous and spectacular is also an exposed and demanding route that should only be attempted by experienced climbers and/or with a qualified guide. For further information, see page 21.

Glen Brittle *Colour map 3, A3.*

Six miles along the A863 to Dunvegan from Sligachan is a turning left to Portnalong, Carbost and the Talisker Distillery (see below), which soon leads to the entrance to Glen Brittle. To reach Glen Brittle, take the Portree–Carbost–Fiscavaig bus (**Stagecoach** No 53/54). Get off at the turn-off and then walk the remaining eight miles.

The road down Glen Brittle affords great views of the western side of the imposing Black Cuillins, until it ends at the campsite and shore at the foot of the glen. From Glen Brittle there are numerous paths leading up to the corries of the Black Cuillins. There are many alternative options for those wishing to continue up to the upper corries or to the main ridge. One of the finest of the Cuillin corries is **Coire Lagan**. This walk starts from the beach at Glen Brittle village and takes you up to the lochan in the upper coire, with Sgurr Alasdair, the most difficult of the Munros, towering overhead. A fine Cuillin sampler is the short walk to the spectacular **Eas Mor** waterfall.

Talisker *Colour map 3, A3.*

A recommended trip for whisky drinkers, or if it's raining, is to the excellent **Talisker Distillery** ⓘ *T01478-614308, www.malts.com, Jan-Mar Mon-Fri 1000-1630, Apr and Oct Mon-Sat 0930-1700, Sun 1000-1700, May Mon-Fri 0900-1730, Sat 0900-1700, Sun 1000-1700, Jun and Sep Mon-Fri 0900-1800, Sat 0900-1700, Sun 1000-1700, Jul-Aug Mon-Fri 0930-1830, Sat 0900-1700, Sun 1000-1700, tours throughout the day, book ahead to avoid a long wait, £10 for 45-min tour, £25 for 1½-hr tour, £25 for 2-hr tour,* at **Carbost** on the shores of Loch Harport, on the B8009 (not in the village of Talisker itself, which is on the west coast). This is Skye's only whisky distillery and produces a very smoky, peaty single malt, with a distinctive hot, peppery palate, particularly the 20- and 25-year-old expressions. The tour fee includes a discount voucher on any 70cl bottle of malt whisky sold in the shop.

Elgol *Colour map 3, A4.*

One of the most rewarding drives on Skye is the 14-mile single-track road from Broadford to Elgol (Ealaghol), a tiny settlement near the tip of the Strathaird Peninsula, from where you can enjoy the classic view of the Cuillins from across Loch Scavaig and also see the islands of Soay, Rùm and Canna. It was from here, on 4 July 1746, that the Young Pretender finally left the Hebrides. Before leaving, he was given a farewell banquet by the MacKinnons in what is now called **Prince Charlie's Cave**. There's also the added attraction of a dramatic boat trip, to the mouth of ★ **Loch Coruisk**, in the heart of the Black Cuillin. The glacial sea loch, romanticized by Walter Scott and painted by Turner, is over two miles long but only a few hundred yards wide, closed in by the sheer cliffs on either side and overshadowed by the towering mountains of black basalt and gabbro. The road to Elgol

Law of the land

One of the most significant incidents in the island's history took place in April 1882, when a group of around 100 local crofters and their families fought a pitched battle against a force of 60 police sent by the government from Glasgow. The 'Battle of the Braes', as it became known, was caused, like many other such uprisings throughout the Highlands and Islands, by threatened evictions. The local crofters were so incensed by the injustice of the eviction notices served on them that they destroyed the offending documents, leading the government to dispatch its police force. The defeat of the government forces of law and order by a bunch of men, women and children with sticks and stones is often described as the last battle fought on British soil, and led eventually to the establishment of a Royal Commission to look into the crofters' grievances.

also gives great views of **Bla Bheinn** (pronounced Blaven), best seen from Torrin, at the head of Loch Slapin.

Elgol to Camasunary Bay

Elgol is the starting point for the walk to Camasunary Bay. This nine-mile coastal walk is quite demanding, but on a clear day the views of the Cuillins make it well worth the effort. It starts from the car park in Elgol. From here, walk back up the road for a short distance, then turn left along a track behind some houses, signposted for 'Garsbheinn'. Beside the last of these houses is a sign for the path to Coruisk. Follow this path along a steep grassy slope. The views across Loch Scavaig to the island of Soay and the Cuillins behind are marvellous. The slope gets even steeper beneath Ben Cleat, and you'll need a good head for heights to continue across the foot of Glen Scaladal, crossing a burn in the process (which can be tricky if it's in spate). Then it's on along the path beyond Beinn Leacach to Camasunary Bay, with its backdrop of mighty Sgurr na Stri and Bla Bheinn. The shortest way back is to retrace your steps but, as an alternative, follow the clear track from Camasunary up the right side of Abhainn nan Lean over the hills to the east until it joins the B8083 from Broadford. From here it's about 3½ miles back along the road to Elgol.

Listings The Cuillins and Minginish

Where to stay

££££-£££ Coruisk House
On the right-hand side just after the Elgol village sign on the road from Broadford, T01471-866330, www.coruiskhouse.com. *Mar-Oct.*
Restaurant with 2 stylish en suite rooms. Worth coming here for the freshest of seafood (lunch **££**, dinner **£££**), which can be enjoyed al fresco (they have a

Midge Master). Also has a self-catering cottage and traditional crofthouse for rent. Recommended for the superb food.

££ Sligachan Hotel
7 miles south of Portree, where the A87 Kyleakin–Portree road meets the A863 to Dunvegan, T01471-865 0204, www.sligachan.co.uk.
With the Cuillins almost at its back door, this is the legendary rallying point for climbers (though it also has its fair share

of more sedentary guests). 21 refurbished bedrooms, a genteel **MacKenzies** bar and a rather barnlike though lively **Seumas'** bar, which stocks a selection of over 400 malts and also serves real ales from the adjacent Cuillin Brewery as well as hearty bar (**££**) meals. Or you can eat in the more formal **Harta** restaurant. There's also a 20-bed bunkhouse (Mar-Oct), luxury self-catering cottages (sleep up to 8) and a campsite, although there's superb and free wild camping just upriver.

£ Croft Bunkhouse
Wigwams & Bothies, north of Carbost, near Portnalong, T01471-640254, www.skyehostels.com. Open all year. Sleeps 40 and there's also room for camping. Transport from Sligachan or Portree, rents mountain bikes, there's a pub and shop nearby.

£ Skyewalker Hostel
Beyond Portnalong on the road to Fiscavaig, T01471-640250, www.skyewalkerhostel.com. This pleasant hostel is in a converted school. Basic and clean 36 bunk accommodation with adjoining lounge area. On-site café and shop, live folk music and a giant al fresco chessboard.

Camping
The well-run campsite opposite **Sligachan Hotel** is possibly the most popular budget place to stay in the area, clean, central and with hot showers. There's also a campsite by the shore in Glen Brittle, T01471-640404.

What to do

Boat trips
Bella Jane (Elgol, T01471-866244, www.bellajane.co.uk), and **Misty Isle Boat Trips** (Sealladh na Mara, Elgol, T01471-866288, www.mistyisleboattrips.co.uk). Both make the spectacular trip from Elgol into the gaping maw of Loch Coruisk, one of the highlights of any trip to Skye. Trips vary in length from 3 hrs, including 1½ hrs ashore, up to a full day, several departures. You should be able to see seals and porpoises en route. There's also a 1-way trip for experienced walkers/climbers who wish to make the return journey on foot or to explore the Cuillins. Both also run whale- and wildlife-watching trips around the Small Isles. **Bella Jane** also offer exhilarating RIB trips around Loch Coruisk and around the Small Isles aboard the **AquaXplore** (£20 for 1 hr, £30 for 1½ hrs).

Climbing
Guiding on Skye, *George Yeomans, T01478-650380, www.guidingonskye.co.uk.* Also offers bushcraft and survival instruction, £100 per day for 2 people.
Richard 'Paddy' MacGuire, *4 Matheson Place, Portree, T01478-613180, www.blavenguiding.co.uk.* Operating since 1995.
Skye Guides, *Mike Lates, 3 Luib, Broadford, T01471-822116, www.skyeguides.co.uk.*

Transport

Bus
To **Portree** via **Sligachan** from **Portnalong**, take the No 54 Stagecoach bus that runs Mon-Fri. The same service stops at the **Talisker Distillery**, Carbost.
  If you've walked into the remote areas of Glenbrittle and Eynort, the only option is to walk out for 8 miles until you meet the B8009, where you can pick up the No 54 at Carbost to return to Drynoch junction on the A863. Here you can either stay on the No 54 to **Sligachan** and **Portree** or wait for the No 56B **Portree** to **Dunvegan** service that stops (schooldays only) at **Drynoch** and heads north to **Struan** and Dunvegan Hotel. **Murdo Macleod** bus 608 also travels this route Mon-Fri, T01470-572216.

Broadford (An t-Ath Leathann), Skye's second-largest village, basically consists of a mile-long main street strung out along a wide bay. The village may be low on charm but it's high on tourist facilities and makes a good base for exploring the south and east of the island. The road north from Broadford to Portree passes through Sconser, departure point for the short ferry ride to the little-visited island of Raasay.

Broadford has plenty of accommodation and places to eat. Next to the Esso station is a Co-op, there's a laundrette in the petrol station shop (open 24 hours) and a bank with ATM. Broadford is also the home of the International Otter Survival Fund (IOSF) ① T01471-822487, www.otter.org. Contact them for information on their various projects worlwide and more locally.

Kyleakin Colour map 3, A5.

The opening of the Skye Bridge, linking the island with the Kyle of Lochalsh (see page 227), has turned the former ferry terminal of Kyleakin (Caol Acain) into a quiet backwater, though the absence of road traffic and coastal views north and across to Lochalsh make it a pleasant place to stay. It's particularly popular with backpackers. The bridge is supported in the middle on the small islet of **Eilean Ban**, erstwhile home of author and naturalist, Gavin Maxwell, and now home to an otter sanctuary. It can be visited as part of tour from the **Bright Water Visitor Centre** ① Kyleakin, T01599-530040, www.eileanban.org, Apr-end Sep Mon-Fri 1000-1600 (opening times vary so call ahead), free (donations welcome). The interactive centre is worth a visit, especially if you have kids, and the author's former cottage can be rented (sleeps up to four), which is ideal for wildlife enthusiasts (visit www.scottish-cottages.co.uk). In Kyleakin, by the pier, history buffs can read up about the ruin of **Castle Maol** on the headland and how in 1263 King Haakon once sailed into the area with 120 ships in preparation for doing battle with King Alexander III of Scotland. The village pub, **King Haakon**, serves good bar meals.

Kylerhea Colour map 3, A5.

About four miles out of Kyleakin a road turns left off the A87 and heads southeast to Kylerhea (pronounced Kile-ray). The bridge may be the most convenient route to Skye, but the best way to cross is on the small car and passenger ferry that makes the 10-minute crossing to Kylerhea from Glenelg. For full details of times and prices, see page 284. About half a mile from the ferry slipway is the Forestry Commission **Otter Haven** ① T01320-366322, daily 0900 till 1 hr before dusk, free. An hour-long nature trail takes you to an observation hide where you can look out for these elusive creatures. There is also an RSPB guide on hand to tell you about the island's wildlife, including Britain's largest bird of prey, the magnificent white-tailed eagle.

Broadford to Portree Colour map 3, A5-1, C3.

The road north to Portree runs between the fringes of the Red Cuillins and the coast, giving good views across to the **Isle of Scalpay**.

Continuing north, the road then turns west past Luib and along the shores of brooding Loch Ainort until it reaches **Sconser**, the departure point for the ferry to Raasay, and then climbs around Loch Sligachan before descending into Portree. On the opposite side of the

Gaelic spread

Outside the Outer Hebrides, Skye is the most important centre of Gaelic culture, with a large proportion of the island's population speaking Gaelic in everyday life. This in itself is remarkable given the significant drop in population during the Clearances and the continued undermining of Gaelic culture ever since, especially through the State education system.

Today, as in other parts of the Hebrides, the native culture is again under threat, this time from the huge influx of 'white settlers' from the south, but there is also a new-found pride and interest in the Gaelic language. This has been helped by the existence of the Gaelic college on Sleat, through Gaelic writers such as the late Sorley Maclean, a radical local newspaper (*The West Highland Free Press*), economic support from Highlands and Islands Enterprise, and spiritual under-pinning from the Sabbatarian Free Church. Gaelic is being taught again in schools and can be heard on television. The ancient heritage of the Highlands and Islands is fighting back and reasserting itself as an important European culture.

loch from Sconser are the crofting communities known as **The Braes**, who successfully opposed their landlords' eviction notices and brought the crofters' cause to the public's attention (see box, page 299).

★ **Isle of Raasay** *OS Landranger No 24. Colour map 1, C3/4.*

The lush and beautiful island of Raasay lies only a few miles off the east coast of Skye, yet despite its attractions it is all too often ignored by the tourist hordes. The island is a nature conservancy, where you may see seals, eagles and otters. Its hilly terrain and superb cliff scenery also offer numerous walking opportunities, the best of which is to the distinctive flat-topped summit of **Dun Caan**, the island's highest point at 1456 ft. The views from the top are amongst the finest in Scotland. Raasay falls away to the sea, with the Cuillins on one side and the peaks of Torridon and Kintail on the other, shouldering past one another, their great blunt heads bumping the clouds. The walk to the top of the extinct volcano, via an old iron mine, is relatively straightforward and one of the most rewarding anywhere in the islands. So much so, in fact, that Boswell was inspired to dance a Highland jig on reaching the top in 1773, during his grand tour with Dr Johnson. Another excellent walk starts from North Fearns, at the end of a road running east from **Inverarish**, to the deserted township of **Hallaig**, down the side of Beinn na Leac and back to North Fearns. The circular route is five miles long.

Raasay was for much of its history the property of the Macleods of Lewis, whose chief residence was the ruined **Brochel Castle**, before moving to **Clachan**, where **Raasay House** is now located. The original Raasay House was torched by government troops after Culloden, along with all the island's houses and its boats, as punishment for the Macleods giving refuge to Bonnie Prince Charlie. After the Macleods sold the island in 1843, the Clearances began in earnest and Raasay suffered a long period of emigration, depopulation and poverty. It is not surprising, then, that the island's most famous son, the great poet **Sorley Maclean**, wrote so passionately about this lost society. Born in Oskaig in 1911, he wrote in his native Gaelic as well as in English, and is highly regarded internationally. He died in 1996. Raasay's population now numbers around 150 and the island is a bastion of the Free Church, whose strict Sabbatarian beliefs should be respected by visitors.

Those who make it to the north of the island may wish to note that the two miles of road linking **Brochel** to **Arnish** were the work of one man, Calum Macleod. He decided to build the road himself after the council turned down his requests for proper access to his home. He spent between 10 and 15 years building it with the aid of a pick, a shovel, a wheelbarrow and a road-making manual which cost him three shillings. He died in 1988, soon after its completion, and it continues to be known as 'Calum's Road'. For an account of Calum's Road, read the book of that name penned by the journalist and author, Roger Hutchinson.

Listings Broadford and the east coast

Where to stay

£££-££ Tir Alainn
8 Upper Breakish, T01471-822366, www.visitskye.com. Open all year.
3 rooms, 2 doubles 1 single, all en suite. Just outside Broadford on road to Kyleakin. Pam and Ron are extremely welcoming and run a cosy B&B, offering exceptional food, good views, comfy guest lounge and expert mountain-guide advice. 4-course dinner for £30. 2 nights minimum stay.

Self-catering

Fossil Cottage
A mile or so south of Broadford, at Lower Breakish off the A87 to Kyleakin, T01471-822297, www.fossil-cottage-skye.co.uk.
Has been beautifully converted from a 15-year-old croft (and recently a bothy) to a 1-bedroom, TV-free zone right by the water. Sleeps 2. £599 per week in high season.

Kyleakin

£££-££ White Heather Hotel
T01599-534577, www.whiteheatherhotel. co.uk. Mar-Oct.
9 en suite rooms. Friendly and welcoming small hotel overooking the harbour. Hosts, Gilllian and Craig, are very helpful and breakfasts are excellent, with views of the harbour thrown in for good measure. Good selection of family rooms. Also guests' study and kitchenette.

£ Skye Backpackers Hostel
T01599-534510, www.skyebackpckers.com.
A good budget option with the pub and ruin of Castle Maol close at hand. Completely refurbished in 2017.

Isle of Raasay

£££-££ Raasay House
T01478-660300, www.raasay-house.co.uk.
The main settlement on the island is Inverarish, a 15-min walk from the ferry dock. Half a mile further is this hotel/ hostel/outdoor centre housed in the huge, 260-year-old Georgian mansion that was Raasay House. Offers everything from 'hotel-style' accommodation in double, twin, family rooms or dorms as well as cheaper 'hostel-style' accommodation for backpackers, families and educational groups. After a day's exertions on sea and land, refuel with the home-baking, hearty fare and real ales served in the good-value **café-bar** (**££-£**) (0900-2300, evening meals 1830-2100) or the more formal **restaurant** (**£££-££**). The best value are their packages that include all accommodation, meals and activities for 1 night or more.

Restaurants

£££-££ Creelers Restaurant
*Just off the main road behind the old
Serpentarium, T01471-822281, www.skye-
seafood-restaurant.co.uk. Easter to end Oct
Tue-Sat (also some Mons), 1200-1000.*
Tiny shack from the outside but inside
attentive, friendly staff serve simple,
appetizing seafood, memorable desserts
and a tapas option, Recommended.

££ Red Skye Restaurant
*Breakish, T01471-822180, www.
redskyerestaurant.co.uk. Daily
1200-2100 (last orders).*
Housed in the handsome old village
schoolhouse, this relative newcomer to
the Skye dining scene is proving popular
with punters from near and far. The new
husband-and-wife team of Alastair and
Nicola Kelly offer high-end cuisine in a
relaxed atmosphere. Expect local classics like
Loch Eishort mussels and Black Isle beef.

What to do

Isle of Raasay
Raasay House, *see Where to stay, above,
T01478-660300, www.raasay-house.co.uk.*
This reputable operator runs various
adventure courses, from climbing
to sailing. Also offers a variety of
accommodation options and packages.

Transport

Bus
Daily **Citylink** buses run from **Broadford**
to **Portree**, **Inverness** and **Fort William**.
Buses run daily to **Kyleakin**, **Portree** and
Armadale/Ardvasar. There are buses
from **Kyleakin** to **Portree** via **Broadford**,
to **Armadale** and **Ardvasar** via Broadford
(Mon-Sat) and every 30 mins to **Kyle of
Lochalsh**, see page 227, via the Skye Bridge.

Ferry
CalMac car and passenger ferry from
Sconser to **Raasay** several times Apr-end
Oct, daily Mon-Sat, twice on Sun, 25 mins.
For times and fares, see www.calmac.co.uk.

Sleat Peninsula *Colour map 3, A4.*

historic stronghold of the Clan Donald

East of Broadford is the turn-off to the peninsula of Sleat (pronouned 'slate'), a part
of the island so uncharacteristically green and fertile that it's known as 'The Garden
of Skye'. Sleat is another entry point to the island. Ferries cross from Mallaig on
the mainland to Armadale on the southeastern shore of the peninsula. While the
rest of the island is the preserve of the Macleods, Sleat is MacDonald country. The
MacDonalds of Sleat are one of the major surviving branches of Clan Donald and
have the right to use the title Lord MacDonald (but not Lord of the Isles, which is
now used by the heir to the throne).

Isle Ornsay
South of Duisdale is the signed turning for Isle Ornsay, or Eilean Iarmain (pronounced
eelan yarman) in Gaelic, a very beautiful place in a small rocky bay overlooking the tidal
Isle of Ornsay with the mountains of Knoydart in the background. This was once Skye's
main fishing port, and the neat whitewashed cottages and tiny harbour are still there. It is
also largely Gaelic-speaking, thanks mainly to the efforts of its landlord, Sir Iain Noble, who
owns the hotel (see Where to stay, page 306) and his own local Gaelic whisky company
as well as the northern half of the peninsula, which is known as Fearan Eilean Iarmain.

A few miles further on is a turn-off to the left which leads to the villages of **Ord**, **Tokavaig** and **Tarskavaig**, on the west coast of the peninsula, from where, on a clear day, there are views across to the Cuillins. Near Tokavaig is the ruin of **Dunsgaith Castle**, home of the MacDonalds of Sleat until the 17th century. Tarskavaig is a typical crofting township. In the early 19th century the MacDonalds claimed the more fertile glens inland for their sheep farms and evicted the people to coastal townships like Tarskavaig. Just beyond the turn-off to Ord are the remains of **Knock Castle**, yet another MacDonald stronghold.

Ostaig

At Ostaig is the Gaelic College, **Sabhal Mor Ostaig** ① *T01471-888000*, founded by Sir Iain Noble. All subjects are taught in Gaelic, including full-time courses in business studies and media, as well as short courses in Gaelic music and culture during the summer months. The bookshop has a good selection of books and tapes for those wishing to learn the language. Ostaig is also the beginning or end (depending on which direction you're heading) of the detour to Tarskavaig, Tokavaig and Ord.

Armadale to the Point of Sleat *Colour map 3, A4.*

Just before the ferry pier at Armadale is **Armadale Castle** ① *T01471-844305, www. clandonald.com, Apr to mid-Oct gardens daily 0930-1730, museum 1000-1730, mid-Oct to end Oct museum and gardens 1000-1630, £8.50, concessions/children 5-15 £6.95, closed Nov-Mar*, which was built in 1815 as the main residence of the MacDonalds of Sleat. Most of the castle is now a roofless ruin but the servants' quarters contain an excellent exhibition and accompanying video explaining the history of the Lordship of the Isles. The Clan Donald Lords of the Isles took over from their Norse predecessors in ruling the Hebrides until their power was broken in 1493. The former stables at the entrance comprise offices, a restaurant and bookshop, while the estate manager's house has been converted to accommodate an extensive library and archives. The castle is surrounded by 40 acres of handsome gardens and woodland, and there are ranger-led walks along nature trails with fine views across to the mainland.

Just beyond Armadale Castle is the tiny village of **Armadale**, which is strung out along the wooded shoreline and merges into the neighbouring village of **Ardvasar** (pronounced Ard-vaa-sar), which has a post office and general store. Armadale's raison d'être is the ferry pier and there's not a huge amount to keep you occupied except for **Ragamuffin**, T01471-844217, a friendly shop famed for its colourful knitwear and quirky gifts. Also on the ferry pier is the excellent **Seafari Adventures** boat trip operator (see What to do, page 58). About four or five miles past the ferry port, at the end of the road, is **Aird of Sleat**, a crofting township, from where you walk out to the lighthouse at the **Point of Sleat**. It's a five-mile walk on a clear path across moorland with fine coastal scenery.

Listings Sleat Peninsula

Where to stay

££££ Duisdale Hotel
Duisdale, T01471-833202, www.duisdale.com.
Extensively refurbished, this former Hunting Lodge boasts 18 individually styled rooms (2 with 4-poster beds), tasty lunches,

afternoon tea and superb dinner fare that draws on the local seafood. There's a fabulous Chart Room in which to savour a malt, an outdoor hot tub, and also the chance to enjoy a day's sailing around the offshore islands aboard its private 50-ft yacht.

££££ Hotel Eilean Iarmain
Isle Ornsay, T01471-833332,
www.eilean-iarmain.co.uk.
12 rooms, 6 in main house, 6 in garden
house. Award-winning Victorian hotel full
of charm and old-world character, with
wonderful views. It is lovely and romantic,
and an absolute must if you're in the
area and can afford it. Its award-winning
restaurant features local shellfish landed
only yards away (open to non-residents).
A cheaper option is to eat in the cosy bar
next door, which serves pub grub of an
impossibly high standard in a more informal
atmosphere. The hotel also offers winter
shooting on the local estate plus a variety
of tours and activities, and you can enjoy
a tasting of the local whisky.

££££ Kinloch Lodge
At the head of Loch na Dal, T01471-833333,
www.kinloch-lodge.co.uk.
The track that leads to the 19th-century
Sporting Lodge turns off the A851 about
8 miles south of Broadford. Lord and Lady
MacDonald's former family home oozes
comfort and refined style with its antiques,
prints and classy touches such as Egyptian
cotton sheets. Now run by their daughter
Isabella and renowned chef, Marcello Tully,
who worked at the legendary **La Gavroche**
in London. This is a place to enjoy one of
Scotland's finest culinary experiences in
the grandest of settings. The 5-course fixed
menu is a whopping £85 a head, but well
worth it.

££££ Toravaig House Hotel
Knock Bay, Teangue, T01471-820200,
www.toravaig.com. Open all year.
9 plush and contemporary en suite rooms.
Multi-award-winning hotel and restaurant.

Perfect for those seeking peace and quiet and
a romantic break. It's isolated for those who
like a pub within walking distance, but why
go elsewhere when you're surrounded by
such luxury. Part of the **Sonas Group**, which
also owns the Duisdale and Skeabost Country
House hotels (see pages 296 and 305).

£££ Ardvasar Hotel
In Ardvasar, near ferry terminal, T01471-
844223, www.ardvasarhotel.com.
Traditional whitewashed coaching inn with
10 very comfortable rooms, an excellent
restaurant and the liveliest pub in the
vicinity. (**££££** including dinner).

Restaurants

£££ Kinloch Lodge
See also Where to stay. Daily in high season.
Lady Claire Macdonald's renowned
restaurant may be pricey but head chef
Marcello Tully's inventive, changing menus
based on seasonal and local produce are
perfect for that special dining occasion in
the Garden of Skye. Reservations essential.
They boasted a Michelin star for 7 years
until 2017 but this will not detract from a
spectacular dining experience.

Transport

Bus
No 52/55 Mon-Sat from **Ardvasar** and
nearby **Armadale Pier** to **Portree** (1 hr
20 mins) and **Kyleakin** (1 hr) via **Broadford**
(40 mins). 1st bus leaves at 0940.

Ferry
For crossings to Mallaig, see page 284.

The Small Isles

These four tenacious little siblings are a world away from the Scottish mainland and not for the faint or fickle traveller. It almost takes longer to reach them from London than it does to fly to Australia, so you have to be pretty determined. Those who do make it this far are rewarded with perfect peace and an almost primeval silence and solitude. This is nature in the glorious, unabashed raw: a slow-moving, sepia-tinged counterpoint to the frenetic pace and special effects of 21st-century life.

Essential The Small Isles

Finding your feet

Ferry

On a Monday and Thursday from late March to late October, the **CalMac** passenger-only ferry departs **Mallaig** at 1015 to arrive at **Eigg** at 1130. The Monday sailing continues to **Rùm** (1245) and **Canna** (1355), before returning to Mallaig (1750) via **Rùm** and **Eigg**. The Thursday morning boat leaves **Eigg** to reach **Muck** at 1220, returns to **Eigg** for 1310 and disembarks at Mallaig at 1435. On a Tuesday and Friday morning, the boat sails for **Muck** and **Eigg**, whilst the Friday afternoon sailing calls in at **Rùm** and **Canna** only. On a Wednesday, the boat from Mallaig calls in at **Rùm** (1135), **Canna** (1245) and **Rùm** again (1555) before returning to **Mallaig** at 1725. For more details of latest seasonal timetable, contact the **CalMac** office in Mallaig, T01687-462403. The **Fort William** train is timetabled to await the Small Isles boats.

From April to September the CalMac ferries from Mallaig are supplemented by daily cruises from Arisaig with **Arisaig Marine** (T01687-450224, www.airsaig. co.uk), aboard *MV Shearwater*. There's a good chance of seeing dolphins, seals, porpoises and even whales during the bumpy ride. Refer to their website for a comprehensive sailings timetable and full list of fares.

Getting around

On Eigg, Muck and Rùm, walking is the primary means of transport, but you should also be able to hire a bike from the locals.

> **Tip...**
> Make sure that you come well armed to fight off the islands' ferocious midges.

ON THE ROAD

The end of an era

George Bullough and his wife, Lady Monica, brought a slice of Belgravia to the tiny Hebridean island of Rùm. Every autumn the family showed up to stalk deer and throw lavish parties for the glitterati and aristocracy of the day. Guests would be met at the pier by chauffeur-driven Albion cars while those arriving by ferry would step into a horse-drawn carriage, or be given a piggy-back by the castle staff when the tide was out. The outrageously wealthy Bulloughs guarded their privacy with a level of ruthlessness that would make even today's pop and film stars blush. Guns were routinely fired at passing boats to warn off any unwanted commoners and discourage the curious.

All this frivolous excess ended suddenly with the outbreak of war in 1914. George Bullough was appointed to a military post, the island's able-bodied staff were sent to the trenches to die for their country and the family's 220-ft steam-yacht, *Rhouma*, became a minesweeper. After the war, the Bulloughs visited less and less often and the castle began to show signs of neglect. Even the poor hummingbirds died when the heating failed. Sir George himself died in 1939 and Lady Monica abandoned the place in 1954 – literally – leaving musical instruments on the stands in the ballroom and wine in the cellar. In 1957 the Bullough family sold Rùm to the Nature Conservancy for £23,000.

Eigg *Colour map 3, A/B3.*

a cracking little island

Little Eigg (pronounced *egg*), only five miles long by three miles wide, has had something of a chequered past. In 1577 it was the scene of one of the bloodiest episodes in the history of clan warfare (see box, page 290). More recently it was at the heart of a bitter land ownership debate. Having endured a succession of absentee landlords, ranging from the merely eccentric to the criminally negligent, the 70 remaining islanders seized the moment in 1997 and bought the island themselves, in conjunction with the Scottish Wildlife Trust. In February 2008, Eigg's own solar, wind and hydro-powered electricity supply was switched on.

The island's wildlife includes otters, seals, eagles and many other birds, such as the Manx shearwater, guillemots and black-throated divers. It's worth tagging along on one of the regular walks organized by the Scottish Wildlife Trust warden. For details, email isleofeiggranger@scottishwildlifetrust.co.uk.

The island is dominated by **An Sgurr**, a distinctive 1289-ft flat-topped basalt peak with three vertical sides. It can be climbed fairly easily by its western ridge, though the last few hundred feet are precipitous, and there are superb views of the Inner Hebrides and mountains of Knoydart from the summit. Sitting in the shadow of the Sgurr, at the southeastern corner, is the main settlement, **Galmisdale**. This is where the ferries drop anchor (passengers are transferred to a smaller boat), and there's a post office, shop, craft shop, tearoom and bike hire all by the pier. At the northern end is the small township of **Cleadale**, on the Bay of Laig. Just to the north are the '**Singing Sands**', a beach that makes a strange sound as you walk across it. At the end of the island's only road you'll find its most famous property, **Howlin' House**, which apparently once belonged to JRR Tolkien. More details on the island are available at www.isleofeigg.org.

Listings Eigg *map below.*

Where to stay

In addition to the options below, self-catering cottages and camping are also available. For details, visit www.isleof eigg.org. Places listed here will transport guests and luggage from the ferry.

£££ Lageorna
T01687-460081, www.lageorna.com.
Green Tourism Scheme B&B offering 2 comfortable, unfussy rooms. Also has a self-catering cottage at £650 per week; shorter stays available on request. Serves excellent food in its restaurant (**£££** for non-residents, **££** for residents). Restaurant open Easter-Sep for dinner most nights,

Mon-Wed and Fri for lunch; in winter for residents only).

£££-££ Kildonan House
T01687-482446, www. kildonanhouseeigg.co.uk.
3 rooms, 1 en suite. Very friendly and hospitable B&B offering great home cooking (dinner included) and a cosy guest sitting room with log-burning stove and huge selection of books to read.

£ The Glebe Barn
T01687-315099, www.glebebarn.co.uk. Apr-Oct (all year for groups).
An independent hostel and outdoor centre. Comfortable accommodation in twin, family and bunk rooms. Residential courses and retreats, self-catering or fully catered options for groups. There's a self-contained 2- to 3-person apartment (from £50 per night for 6+ nights). Groceries can be pre-ordered from the local shop (T01687-482432) and delivered.

Restaurants

See Where to stay, above.

£ Galmisdale Bay Café
An Laimhrig. Mon-Sat from 1000 and Sun from 1130.
Standard bar fare and evening meals served 1800-2000 Mon, Wed, Thu and Sat. They serve the island's own Laig Bay beer. Housed in the island's community building, **An Laimhrig**, which is by the pier and also home to the well-stocked grocery store, post office and gift shop, T01687-482432, Mon and Wed-Sat.

Eigg

Eilean Thuilm
Singing Sands
Beinn Bhuidhe
Cleadale
Bay of Laig — St Donnan's
Cuagach
Loch Beinn Tighe
Loch Nam Ban Mora
Standing Stone
School
Church of Scotland — Ruined Chapel
An Sgurr (1289ft)
Galmisdale
Shop & ⊠
Kildonan
Poll Nan Partan
Pier
Eigg Adventures
Castle Island

1 km
1 mile

Where to stay 🛏
Glebe Barn **1**
Kildonan House **2**
Lageorna **3**

Restaurants 🍴
Galmisdale Bay
Café & An Laihmrig **1**

What to do

The islands are rich in wildlife, with plenty of opportunities to spot seals and possibly basking sharks, porpoise and even orca whilst inter-island hopping aboard the *MV Sheerwater*, www.arisaig.co.uk. See also Finding your feet, page 307.

Eigg Adventures, *next to An Laimhrig at the pier, T01687-347007, www.eiggadventures.com*. They run a variety of outdoor activities including mountain biking, walking, kayaking and sailing and also hire bikes and kayaks.

Transport

Bus/taxi
If you can't walk or cycle around Eigg, call Charlie on T01687-482404 for a taxi.

Ferry
See Finding your feet, page 307.

Muck *Colour map 3, B3.*

peace, perfect peace on this tiny island

Tiny Muck, just two miles long by one mile wide, is the smallest of the four islands and is flat and fertile, with a beautiful shell beach. It has been owned by the MacEwan family since 1879. The island gets its unfortunate name (*muc* is Gaelic for pig) from the porpoises, or 'sea pigs', that swim round its shores.

The ferry berths at **Port Mór** close to which there's a range of accommodation, including a bunkhouse and hotel. There's also a tearoom and craftshop. The 38 islanders use wind power to generate their own electricity. Visit the island's website, www.isleofmuck.com, for more information.

Listings Muck

Where to stay

Places listed here will transport guests and luggage from the ferry. For more details visit www.isleofmuck.com.

££££ Gallanach Lodge
T01687-462305.
New, purpose-built accommodation with 8 en suite rooms all finished to a very high standard with handmade beds and underfloor heating in the bathrooms. Price includes 3-course dinner, breakfasts feature their home-made sausages and Stornoway black pudding.

Self-catering

Port Mór House
T01678-462218.

The former hotel is now available as self-catering for 14+. Rooms also available as hostel accommodation when not full.

Restaurants

The few places to stay on the islands serve food, and there's a tearoom and a shop on Muck.

What to do

See Eigg, above.

Transport

See Essential Small Isles, page 307.

wild, beautiful mountains and rare birdlife

Diamond-shaped Rùm, known as the Forbidden Island, is the largest of the group and the most wild, beautiful and mountainous. The island is owned and run by Scottish Natural Heritage as an enormous outdoor laboratory and research station, and most of the 30 or so inhabitants are employed by them. Studies of the red deer population are among the most important areas of their work, and access to parts of the island is restricted. This is not prohibitive, though, and there are many marked nature trails, walks and birdwatching spots. The island is a haven for wildlife and perhaps its most notable resident is the magnificent white-tailed sea eagle, successfully re-introduced on to Rùm in the 1980s and now spreading beyond the island. Rùm is also home to golden eagles, Manx shearwaters and, less appealingly, millions of midges. The island is the wettest of the Small Isles and a haven for the little buggers. For more information, visit www.isleofrum.com.

Kinloch

Ferries are anchored at the new pier, at the mouth of Loch Scresort, from where it's a 15-minute walk to Kinloch Castle. The castle stands at the head of narrow Loch Scresort by the little hamlet of Kinloch, where you'll find the one-and-only shop, and the community hall which also operates a tearoom. Visit the old boat shed by the pier, where there's a (very) small exhibition of wildlife and marine life, a reminder that Rùm is a National Nature Reserve with its colony of Manx shearwater, golden- and white tailed sea eagles and red deer. The **SNH Reserve Office** ① *T01687-462026, Mon-Fri 0900-1230,* is located in the White House, 10 minutes' walk from the pier.

Kinloch Castle

By daily guided tour only (45 mins) Mon-Sat, and timed to coincide with the arrival of the ferry, £9, concessions £8, children £4.50, call the SNH Reserve Office (above) for details.

Though it looks like a wilderness, Rùm once supported a population of 300. Most of them were shipped off to Canada in the mid-19th century, leaving behind an uninhabited deer forest for sporting millionaires. One of these, John Bullough, a cotton millionaire from Accrington, bought it in 1888 and passed it on to his son, Sir George Bullough, who built the extravagant and extraordinary Kinloch Castle. No expense was spared on this massive late-Victorian mansion, built in 1900 at a cost of £250,000 (which equates to £15 million today). It took 300 men nearly three years to build Bullough's dream, using red Annan sandstone from Dumfrieshire shipped by puffer from the mainland. For the gardens, 250,000 tons of soil were shipped from Ayrshire and used for planting exotic specimens collected from around the world. A nine-hole golf course and bowling green were laid out, along with a Japanese-style garden and huge walled garden. Hothouses were built to grow tropical fruits, and palm houses were home to hummingbirds, turtles and even alligators. One of these creatures escaped, only to be shot by Bullough to prevent them 'interfering with the comfort of the guests'. As well as the elaborate carvings, wood panelling, furniture and flooring, the castle also incorporated many state-of-the-art features such as an electricity generator, central heating, air conditioning and an internal telephone system (the first private residence in Scotland to do so). Pride of place, however, went to the magnificent Orchestrion, a fantastical mechanical contraption that simulated a 40-piece orchestra and belted out military marches, polkas, operatic excerpts and popular tunes of the day from its position under the main staircase. It is still in working order and visitors today will be treated to a surreal rendition of *The Liberty Bell March* (the Monty Python theme tune to you and me).

Note that visitors must take off their shoes as they are escorted round the lavish rooms, many of them fading, peeling or leaking. The castle is testament to Edwardian wealth and extravagance and the tour is worth the boat trip alone. You can stay close by, in a purpose-built hostel (see Where to stay, below). The future of the castle remains in doubt as plans to continue its costly restoration are currently stalled. £1.5 million has been spent in the last five years on roof repairs alone.

Island walks

Rùm's other great attraction is its mountain range, which offers some of the best island mountain treks outside the Cuillins of Skye. The highest point is **Askival** (2664 ft), which can be reached by the main ridge from **Halliva**, though the route involves some rock scrambling and is only advised for fit and experienced walkers. Before setting out, ask permission from the SNH Reserve Office (see above).

The Bullough family mausoleum, built in the style of a Greek Doric temple, stands incongruously on the west coast at **Harris Bay**. It's an interesting 7½-mile walk across

Rùm

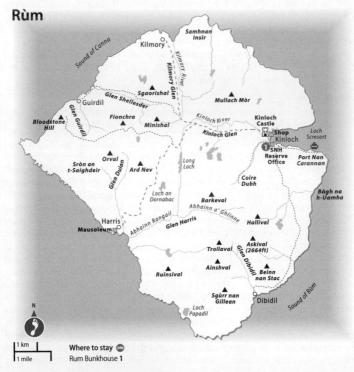

to the mausoleum from Kinloch. A less strenuous alternative is the **Kinloch Glen Trail**, which is signposted by the stone bridge as you head from the castle to the farmstead. The circular route is 2½ miles and takes a leisurely one to two hours.

Listings Rùm *map page 312.*

Where to stay

For more options and general information check www.isleofrum.com.

££-£ Rum Bunkhouse
T01687-460318, www.rumbunkhouse.com.
This modern and comfy bunkhouse (opened in 2014) sleeps up to 20 in mixed dorms or twin room. All rooms and facilities are on ground level. Also has campsite (no booking required) and 2 camping cabins for up to 4 (£). Great value for small or larger groups.

Camping
If camping on Rùm be aware that the local midges are voracious and repellent and hoods are essential. These are available at the island shop. Wild camping is also permitted (no fires) near the pier where a stand pipe provides water. You must inform the reserve manager at the **White House** if camping, T01687-462026.

Restaurants

The café/tearoom is housed in the village hall (always open as an escape from the rain or midges), and serves hot drinks, cakes, soup and other home-made food. It's open several afternoons a week during summer.

The shop/post office opens on ferry arrival days from 1000 till 1200 and is usually open 1700-2000, T01687-460328.

What to do

See Eigg, page 310.

Transport

See Essential Small Isles, page 307.

Canna *Colour map 3, A3.*

great walking in splendid isolation

Canna is the most westerly of the Small Isles and is owned by the National Trust for Scotland (NTS). It's a small island, five miles long by one mile wide, bounded by cliffs and with a rugged interior, fringed by fertile patches. It's attached to its smaller neighbour, Sanday, by a narrow isthmus which is covered, except at low tide. There's now also a bridge linking them. The main attraction for visitors is some fine walking. It's about a mile from the ferry jetty up to the top of Compass Hill (458 ft), so called because its high metallic content distorts compasses. The highest point on the island is Carn a' Ghaill (690 ft). During the summer, a day trip from Mallaig allows you over nine hours in which to explore Canna and enjoy the fantastic views across to Rùm and Skye.

The population of 20 mostly work on the island's farm. Canna was gifted to the National Trust by its benevolent owner, the late Dr John Lorne Campbell, a notable Gaelic scholar. The island continues to be run as a single working farm and, since it was sold in 1938, has been an unofficial bird sanctuary with 157 recorded bird species, including Manx shearwater and puffins. In 2008, after a £500,000, two-year eradication project to protect the seabird population, the NTS officially declared the entire island rat-free.

Where to stay

There is a new campsite on Canna, as well as B&B/self-catering. For details visit www.theisleofcanna.com.

Restaurants

There's now a community shop on the island selling provisions and souvenirs.

££ Café Canna
T01687-482488, www.cafecanna.co.uk. Apr-Sep daily except Tue, May-Aug 1000-2200, dinner served 1800-2030.

Tasty food on offer at this remote culinary outpost.

What to do

See Eigg, page 310.

Transport

See Essential Small Isles, page 307.

Canna & Sanday

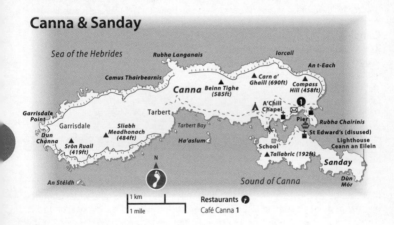

Outer Hebrides

remote wilderness and stunning beaches

The Outer Hebrides are a narrow, 130-mile-long chain of more than 200 islands lying 40 miles off the northwest coast of the Scottish mainland. Only 10 of these are populated, giving a total population of just under 30,000.

Despite the frequency of transport connections with the mainland, the Outer Hebrides remain remote in every sense. Unlike Skye and the Inner Hebrides, tourism is of far less importance to the local economy. In many ways, the islands are the last bastion of the old Highland life. Though newer industries such as fish farming have been introduced, the traditional occupations of crofting, fishing and weaving still dominate and, outside Stornoway, life is very much a traditional one, revolving around the seasons and the tides.

Relentlessly battered by fierce Atlantic winds, the islands can seem a hostile environment and an unappealing proposition. Much of the interior is bleak peat bog, rocks and endless tiny lochs, and the long, straggling crofting communities only add to the feeling of desolation. But anyone who has stood on a clifftop and felt a thrill at the power and potential of all that water should come here. Nowhere else in Britain is there such a sense of emptiness and of the sheer forces of nature. These are islands at the very edge of our imagination.

Best for
Beaches ▪ Cycling ▪ Walking ▪ Wildlife

Leodhas (Lewis) 319
Na Hearadh (Harris) 337
The Uists, Benbecula & Barra . . . 347
St Kilda 364

Footprint
picks

★ The Hebridean Way, page 324

The best way to appreciate the Outer Hebrides in all their glory is to walk
or cycle the length of The Hebridean Way, a spectacular route that
stretches from Vatersay in the south to the Butt of Lewis in the north.

★ Calanais, page 332

The imposing 5000-year-old standing stones can be appreciated up close
and at certain times of the day you can have the whole place to yourself.

★ Luskentyre Beach, page 343

Regularly voted one of the best beaches in the world, this vast expanse
of flawless white sand is washed by gin-clear water.

★ Fishing on South Uist, page 357

South Uist is one of the best places in the country, if not the world, to
catch wild brown trout. There are some 800 lochs and lochans between
South Uist and Benbecula and most of them contain wild brown trout.

★ Barra, page 358

The best of the islands in miniature: beaches, machair, peat-covered hills,
tiny crofting communities and Neolithic remains.

★ St Kilda, page 364

Spectacular, isolated and home to the largest colony of seabirds in Europe.

Footprint
picks
1 **The Hebridean Way**, page 324
2 **Calanais**, page 332
3 **Luskentyre Beach**, page 343
4 **Fishing on South Uist**, page 357
5 **Barra**, page 358
6 **St Kilda**, page 364

Port Nis
Tabost
Dail Bho Dheas
A857
Siadar
Baile an Truiseil
Arnol
Barabhas
Tolastadh
Ur
Siabost
A858
Griais
Cárlabhagh
Leodhais
(Lewis)
A858
Miabhig
Newmarket
Timsgearraidh
Calanais
Stornoway
(Steòrnabhagh)
Tunga
Crulabhig
A866
Breanais
Achadh
Mór
Crosbost
Mealasta
Island
Uig
Baile Ailein
Cearsiadar
Scarp
Ceann a Tuath na
Hearadh
(North Harris)
Airidh
a'Bhruaich
Grabhair
Huisinis
Gasker
A859
Leumrabhagh
Abhainnsuidhe
Bun Abhainn Eadarra
Tarasaigh
Reinigeadal
An Tairbeart (Tarbert)
Caolas Scalpaigh
Eilean Scalpaigh
(Scalpay)
Shillay
Taobh
Tuath
An t-Ob
Ceann a Deas
na Hearadh
(South Harris)
Pabbay
Bearnaraigh
Boreray
Òtternish
Ròghadal
To St Kilda
6
Baile
Mhartainn
Solas
Loch nam Madadh
(Lochamaddy)
Kilmuir
Kilmaluag
Linicro
Staffin
Culnaknock
Uibhist a'Tuath
(North Uist)
A867
Saighdinis
Trumpan
Uig
Trotternish
A855
Claghan
na Luib
Lusta
Heisker or
Monach
Islands
Uachdar
A865
Beinn na Faoghla
(Benbecula)
Boreraig
Milovaig
Colbost
Dunvegan
Waternish
Durinish
Kensaleyre
Carbost
Creag Ghoraidh
Wiay
Roskhill
Bracadale
Portree
Skye
Stadhlaigearraidh
Loch Sgioport
Uibhist a Deas
(South Uist)
Portnalong
Peinchorran
Oskaig
4
Gearraidh
Bhailteas
Loch Baghasdail
(Lochboisdale)
Talisker
Sligachan
Dalabrog
Cille Bhrighde
Ludag
Soay
Elgol
Èiriosgaigh
Eriskay
Sea of the Hebrides
Canna
Eilean Barraigh
(Barra)
5
Bagh a'Chaisteil
(Castlebay)
A888
Earsáiridh
Kilmory
Rùm
(Rhum)
Kinloch
Bhatarsaigh
(Vatersay)
1
Sanndraigh
Mingulay
(Miughalaigh)
Atlantic Ocean
Cleadale
Bearnaraigh
Wiay
Eigg
Eilean
nan Each
Galmisdale
Muck

Little Minch

Sound of Barra

N

10 km
10 miles

Leodhas
(Lewis)

Lewis constitutes the northern two-thirds of the most northerly island in the Outer Hebrides. It is by far the most populous of the Outer Hebridean islands and, with over 20,000 inhabitants, makes up two thirds of the total population. Just over 8000 people live in and around Stornoway, the largest town in the Hebrides and the administrative capital of the Western Isles. The majority of the rest of the population live in over 280 crofting townships strung out along the west coast between Port Nis (Ness) and Càrlabhagh (Carloway). The west coast is also where you'll find the island's most interesting sights: the prehistoric remains of Dùn Chàrlabhaigh (Carloway) Broch, the impressive Calanais (Callanish) Standing Stones, the restored blackhouse village of Garenin and the Arnol Blackhouse. These can all be visited as a day trip from Stornoway, either on an organized tour or on the 'West Side Circular' bus service. The interior of the northern half is flat peat bog, hence the island's name which means 'marshy' in Gaelic. Further south, where Lewis becomes Harris, the scenery is more dramatic as the relentlessly flat landscape gives way to rocky hills, providing the backdrop to the sea lochs that cut deep into the coast and the beautiful beaches around Uig.

Essential Outer Hebrides

Finding your feet

Air Loganair (www.loganair.co.uk) flies daily (limited service on Sundays) from Glasgow to Stornoway on Lewis, Barra and Benbecula. **Flybe** (www.flybe.com) also flies from Glasgow to Stornoway. There are also flights from Edinburgh, Manchester and Inverness to Stornoway, and from Benbecula to Stornoway. **Eastern Airways** flies from Aberdeen to Stornoway (www.easternairways.com), Monday to Friday. Weather conditions are so changeable that flights are prone to delay and can be very bumpy. Flights to Barra have an added complication: they land on the beach meaning that the runway disappears twice a day under the incoming tide.

Bus For details of bus connections on Skye and on the mainland, contact **Scottish Citylink** (www.citylink.co.uk) or **Stagecoach** (www.stagecoachbus.com). For further details, see Transport, pages 326 and 342.

Ferry CalMac car and passenger ferries sail to Stornoway (Lewis), Tarbert (Harris), Lochmaddy (North Uist), Lochboisdale (South Uist), Eriskay and Castlebay (Barra). Ferry details are given under each destination, but note that times change according to the day of the week and time of the year. For full details of ferry timetables contact **CalMac** (T0800-0665000, www.calmac.co.uk). A 'CalMac Status' App can be downloaded free of charge for iPhones and Android. Alternatively, look on the website to see how to receive updates by text (but remember a signal is not always possible in some parts of the islands). Some routes, including the Stornoway to Ullapool crossing, are very busy and, if travelling with a car, it's strongly advised to book your ticket in advance. A cost-effective and super-flexible way to get around the islands with a car is to purchase a **CalMac Island Rover** ticket.

Available for eight or 15 consecutive days of travel, these allow you to travel on as many routes as you like without paying any additional fares. Children under go free, aged five to 15 pay half price. Bicycles are carried free with a Rover ticket. Another option is to purchase the **CalMac Island Hopscotch** ticket, available for use on 26 routes and valid for 30 days unlimited travel on each route. See the CalMac guide or call the numbers above for full details.

Getting around

There's an ever-improving public bus service and regular sailings to the main islands. You'll need a car, bike or hiking boots to explore the more remote areas. You will need to allow for the lack of public transport on Sundays on most islands (taxi is the only way around), and for the fact that weather conditions (including the tide at Barra airport) can occasionally affect ferry and flight timetables.

Air Loganair (www.loganair.co.uk, T0344-800 2855), flies daily between Barra, Benbecula and Stornoway; limited service on Sundays.

Bus Bus services run regularly to most main towns and villages on the islands (see www.cne-siar.gov.uk).

Car Most of the islands' roads are single track but in good condition and, unlike other parts of the Highlands and Islands, not too busy, though you may encounter a road blocked by cattle and wandering sheep! On Sunday you'll barely meet another soul. The normal rules for single track roads apply and, as elsewhere in the Highlands, you need to look out for sheep. Distances are greater than most people imagine. For example, the distance from Nis (Ness) at the northern tip of Lewis to Leverburgh in the south of Harris is 85 miles. From Stornoway to Tarbert is 37 miles. And the distance from Otternish in the north of North Uist to Lochboisdale, the main ferry port on South Uist, is 50 miles. Several local car hire agencies offer reasonable rental deals. Expect to pay around £30 per day, depending on the size of engine and age of the car. You cannot take a rented car off the islands.

Cycle Cycling is a great way to explore the islands. You can fully appreciate the amazing scenery around, and it only costs a few pounds to transport a bike by ferry. There is, of course, the major problem of strong winds, which can leave you frustrated and exhausted, especially if cycling into a prevailing southwesterly. For further details, see Transport, pages 327 and 342.

Ferry A ferry sails to Berneray from Leverburgh (Harris) at least three times daily. Several ferries sail daily from Barra to the island of Eriskay. There's also a regular passenger ferry from Ludag in South Uist to Eoligarry on Barra.

What to do

Those intent on walking in the islands should visit the excellent websites www.walkhighlands.co.uk and www.walkhebrides.co.uk which have details of dozens of walks in the Hebrides. Several operators offer guided walking holidays, see Essentials A-Z, page 481, for further details. See also the box on the Hebridean Way, page 324.

A great way to experience the islands is to get out onto the water and, in addition to excellent wildlife cruises, don't forget that the Outer Hebridean chain is now regarded as one of Europe's best locations for sea kayaking (see **Clearwater Paddling**, www.clearwaterpaddling.com, page 362). If surfing's your thing then you're also in the right place. The northwest coast of Lewis, especially the stretch between Dalmore Bay and the beach at Barabhas, has some of the best surfing in Britain. Windsurfing is also gaining in popularity, as well as kite surfing and wind karting.

When to go

From April to September the weather can be surprisingly warm and settled. In winter, be prepared for storms. From October to March some hotels, restaurants and tourist attractions may be closed.

Time required

You should allow plenty of time to explore the islands fully. With your own transport and travelling from top to bottom, a week would be enough time for a whistle-stop tour but not enough to explore in any depth or scratch beneath the surface.

Tourist information

There are tourist information centres (**iCentres**) in Stornoway and Tarbert, which are open all year. Full details are given under each destination. The islands' official tourist information website, www.visitouterhebrides.co.uk, lists places to stay, eat and drink as well as what to do and how to get around. The iCentres in Stornoway and Tarbert also stock the free and handy *Explore the Outer Hebrides Guide with Maps*, which details key routes and places of interest. Accommodation on the islands is generally not difficult to find, except perhaps at the height of the summer when you should book in advance, either directly or through the local tourist office. The Outer Hebrides are renowned for the quality of their seafood, meat and real ale. Check the **Eat Drink Hebrides Trail** at www.visitouterhebrides.co.uk. There are many excellent self-catering options on the islands and this is a most cost-effective way to get to know one particular island. Community-run shops are a lifeline on the islands and are a great way to find out what's going on or get recommendations from local people. Be sure to pick up a copy of the islands' community shops leaflet, which gives details of where they all are, opening times, etc; you can also download a pdf from www.visitouterhebrides.co.uk.

The fishing port of Stornoway, the only town in the Outer Hebrides, is the islands' commercial capital and, as such, boasts more services and facilities than you might expect in any town of comparable size. It's not a pretty place, dominated as it is by the oil industry, but has the full range of banks, shops, hotels, guesthouses, pubs and restaurants, garages, car hire firms, sports facilities, an airport and ferry terminal, and, for the visiting tourist, it presents a rare opportunity to stock up on supplies.

Stornoway is also the administrative capital and home to the Comhairle nan Eilean (Western Isles Council), which has done much to broaden the local economy and to promote and protect Gaelic language and culture. The BBC is rapidly developing programmes and a digital network dedicated to the Gaelic language. Indeed, every July, Stornoway and the Hebridean islands host the **Hebridean Celtic Festival** ① *www.hebceltfest.com*, an ever expanding and popular celebration of Celtic music and the arts that also attracts international acts.

Sights

Stornoway is short on conventional tourist sights and once you've been to the tourist office and bought the necessities from the local supermarkets, there's not much else to do. The focal point of the town has always been its sheltered deep-water **harbour** and, though the fishing industry has declined since its peak at the end of the last century, there's still a fair amount of activity in the early morning as the latest fresh catch is loaded onto trucks for far-flung European destinations. On a Saturday morning you can buy the latest fresh batch of fish from a market stall on Point Street by the town hall. The harbour is usually full of seals, giving the town its nickname of Portrona (port of seals). There's a

Essential Stornoway

Finding your feet

Stornoway is the island's transport hub. The airport is four miles east of the town centre. For a list of taxi services check www.hial.co.uk. **Loganair** flies from Glasgow, Edinburgh and Inverness to Stornoway several times a day from Monday to Friday, twice a day on Saturday and once a day on Sunday. There are two flights a day to/from Benbecula Tuesday to Thursday only. Flybe also flies from Glasgow. The **CalMac** ferry terminal is just beyond the bus station, which is on South Beach, a short walk from the town centre. CalMac runs a ferry service from Ullapool to Stornoway, two or three times a day in the summer and twice daily

in the winter, Monday to Saturday. Contact the **CalMac offices**, T0800-0665000, for further details. Buses leave from Stornoway to all parts of the island, see page 327 for further details. Note that buses do not run on Sunday. It is advisable to pick up a free copy of the comprehensive Lewis and Harris bus timetables at the **iCentre**, or visit www.cne-siar.gov.uk.

The town is compact and most of what you need is within easy walking distance of the tourist office. Some of the B&Bs in the residential areas are quite a distance from the centre, but there's an hourly town bus service, or hire a taxi. For further details, see Transport, page 326.

good view across the harbour to **Lews Castle**, a 19th-century edifice built by Sir James Matheson with money earned from opium and tea. The castle underwent a massive £14 million restoration and conversion programme and now houses the **Museum nan Eilean** ① *T01851-822746, www.lews-castle.co.uk, open Apr-Sep Mon-Wed and Fri-Sat 1000-1700 (closed Thu and Sun), Oct-Mar 1300-1600.* This new museum features exhibitions on the history of the Outer Hebrides, an audio-visual presentation and various activities for children, but its main draw is a collection of six of the famous Lewis Chessmen (see

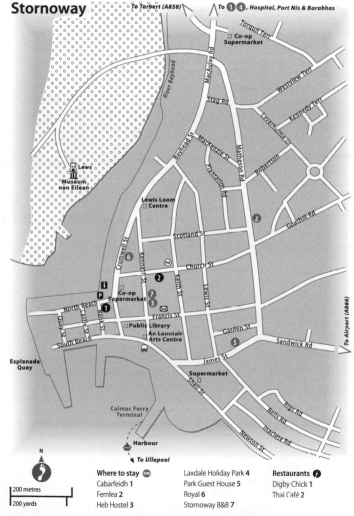

Stornoway

Where to stay 🛏
Cabarfeidh **1**
Fernlea **2**
Heb Hostel **3**
Laxdale Holiday Park **4**
Park Guest House **5**
Royal **6**
Stornoway B&B **7**

Restaurants 🍴
Digby Chick **1**
Thai Café **2**

★ The Hebridean Way

The best way to appreciate the islands in all their glory is to walk or cycle the length of The Hebridean Way, a spectacular route that takes you through some of the best scenery in the whole of Scotland. The 185-mile cycling route follows the National Cycle Network (NCN) Route 780 on main and quiet roads while the 156-mile walking route has a combination of purpose-built sections, existing footpaths, peat tracks and quiet back roads. Both routes are steeped in history and stretch from Vatersay in the south to the Butt of Lewis in the north, passing through 10 islands linked by causeways and ferries, over hills and along the dazzling Atlantic coastline. Those cycling the route can call on **Heb Shuttle** (T01851-706911, www.hebshuttle.co.uk; office open April-October daily 0800-1800, November-March Monday-Friday 0900-1700), a transfer service that will meet you at the Butt of Lewis at the end of the journey and transfer you, your bike and bags to Stornoway, Tarbert, Lochboisdale or Castlebay ferry terminals for the return ferry to Oban. They also offer a six-day all-inclusive trip with support and guide.

page 335). The castle also houses luxury accommodation by **Natural Retreats**, the Storehouse Café and Whisky Bar and the Outfitters retail store.

Anyone remotely interested in Harris Tweed should visit the **Lewis Loom Centre** ⓘ *T01851-704500, Mon-Sat 1000-1700, £2.50*, housed in the Old Grainstore at the northern end of Cromwell Street, just off Bayhead. The 40-minute guided tour includes demonstrations of traditional methods of warping, dyeing and spinning, and offers a detailed history of Harris Tweed. There's also a craft shop.

The **An Lanntair Arts Centre** ⓘ *Kenneth St, T01851-708480, www.lanntair.com, Mon-Sat 1000-late, free*, is the main venue for social and cultural events on the islands. The light and airy building has exhibition spaces for local, national and international artists, a cinema, and stages for various musical and theatrical events. There's also a very good café (see Restaurants, page 326).

Listings Stornoway *map page 323.*

Tourist information

iCentre
26 Cromwell St, T01851-703088. Easter-Sep Mon-Sat 0900-1800, Oct-Easter 0900-1700 (though opening hours vary) and for the arrival of the evening ferry.
This helpful centre stocks maps, bus timetables and various books and brochures. It also sells tickets for minibus tours to Calanais, and wildlife trips around Lewis and Harris.

Where to stay

As the largest settlement on the islands, Stornoway has a good selection of accommodation from which to choose, though you should book in advance in the peak summer season. The **iCentre** will do this for you, for a small fee. There are many B&Bs in and around the town centre, some of which offer a 'room only' rate, including on Matheson Rd close to the town centre and ferry terminal.

£££ Cabarfeidh Hotel
Perceval Rd South, T01851-702604,
www.cabarfeidh-hotel.co.uk.
46 rooms. On the outskirts of town and not as convenient as the **Royal** (see below). Free broadband and all modern trappings.

£££ Park Guest House
30 James St, T01851-702485,
www.the-parkguesthouse.co.uk.
6 rooms, including a suite for up to 3. This Victorian townhouse is comfortable, only 500 yds from the ferry terminal, and is the best of the guesthouses. It also has an excellent restaurant, **Café No 30** (see Restaurants, below).

£££ Royal Hotel
Cromwell St, T01851-702109,
www.royalstornoway.co.uk.
26 rooms. Billed as Stornoway's most historic hotel, good value, central and with views across the marina. Reasonable food in its contemporary, all wood **HS-1 café-bar**, but for atmosphere and a tremendous meal book a table in its **Boatshed** restaurant (see Restaurants, below).

£££ Stornoway Bed & Breakfast
29 and 32 Kenneth St, T07917-035295,
www.stornowaybeadandbreakfast.co.uk.
9 rooms in 2 properties. No 29 is an old building with original featues and stone walls on the ground floor. Very friendly and welcoming, comfortable rooms and close to ferry and everything else in town. On-street parking. Best of the B&Bs.

££ Fernlea
9 Matheson Rd, T01851-702125, www.
fernlea-guesthouse.co.uk. Open all year.
Upgraded Victorian listed building with 4 en suite rooms. Dinner also available

Tip...
It's a good idea to book ahead if you're staying on a Sunday, and if you're staying in the countryside you should check if there's a convenient pub or hotel to eat in.

(**££** for 2 courses). Off-street parking. Very good value.

££-£ Laxdale Holiday Park
Laxdale Lane, about a mile out of town on the road to Barabhas, T01851-703234, www.
laxdaleholidaypark.com. Open all year.
Bunkhouse has 16 beds and good facilities, including showers and toilets suitable for the disabled. Also caravans at £500 per week in high season, self-catering lodge £700 per week and wigwams (sleep 2) for £40-45 per night. The park also has space for 37 tents.

£ Heb Hostel
25 Kenneth St, T01851-709889,
www.hebhostel.com.
Centrally located hostel with 26 beds. Clean and friendly. 4-bed family dorm costs £75 per night.

Restaurants

The pubs and hotels serve the usual range of bar meals. Note that pubs are closed on Sun and some hotels cater only for residents.

£££ The Boatshed
In the Royal Hotel, see Where to stay, above.
Mon-Sat 0730-0930, Fri and Sat lunch 1200-1430, dinner 1700-2100, Apr-Sep also Sun.
Fabulous maritime-themed setting with the addition of a roaring open fire, wooden table and stone finishings. Local langoustines and scallops are a speciality; also worth sampling is the Lewis lamb, local venison or Leurbost mussels. Recommended. Their HS1 café-bar is less upmarket and offers a reasonably priced menu in a contemporary styled setting. Steaks, pasta, salads, wraps, burgers, curries and good veggie options.

£££-££ Digby Chick
5 Bank St, T01851-700026, www.digbychick.
co.uk. Mon-Sat for lunch and dinner (closes 2100).
This contemporary family-run restaurant is a popular local choice and one of the best places in town for seafood. Their 2-course lunch menu is good value at £14.95 or early-bird (served 1730-1830) at £23.50.

££-£ Thai Café
27 Church St, T01851-307181.
Mon-Sat until 2300.
Few would expect such authentically good Thai cuisine so far north, but it's true. Come and be amazed. The BYO policy also helps keep prices down. Also takeaway.

£ An Lanntair Arts Centre
Kenneth St, Stornoway, T01851-703307.
Good for snacks and light lunches in airy surroundings.

Shopping

There's a **Tesco** supermarket beside the ferry terminal (closed Sun), and a **Co-op** by the 1st roundabout on the road out to Barabhas.

Engebret Ltd, *Sandwick Rd, T01851-702303, www.engbret.co.uk. Mon-Sat 0600-2300, Sun 1000-1600.* A petrol station and much more. Sells fishing and hunting supplies, groceries and is also tearoom/café serving hot drinks and snacks. They also run a variety of boat trips which leave from the pontoon next to the lifeboat station and take you to the bird colonies of the Shiant Islands.

For a taste of the Hebrides, pop into some of the following outlets in and around Stornoway:
Hebridean Brewing Company, *18a Bells Rd, T01851-700123, www.hebridean-brewery.co.uk. Mon-Fri 0900-1700.* A real ale taste of the Hebrides.
MacLeod & MacLeod, *17 Church St.* A butcher making the renowned Stornoway black pudding.
Sportsworld, *1-3 Francis St, T01851-705464.* Sells bait and fishing gear all year round if you want to catch your own supper.

What to do

Surfing
Surf Lewis, *T07920-427194, www.surflewis. co.uk.* Lewis is excellent for surfing. £40 for a half-day session (minimum 2 people),

£30 for children. Also hire boards and offer SUP lessons.

Tour operators
Engebret Boat Trips, *see Shopping, above.*
Maclennan's Coaches, *at the ferry terminal, T01851-702114.* Day-trips to Calanais, Carloway and the Arnol Blackhouse.
The RSPB, *T01851-703296 www.rspb.org. uk.* Lead a number of guided walks around breeding grounds and migration stop-offs.

Transport

Air
See Essential Stornoway, page 322.

Bus
From Stornoway to **Port Nis (Ness)** via **Barabhas (Barvas)**, 4-6 times daily; to **Arnol, Siabost (Shawbost), Càrlabhagh (Carloway), Calanais (Callanish)**, and back to Stornoway, 'West Side Circular', 4-6 times daily; to **Bear-naraigh (Great Bernera)** via **Gearraidh na h-Aibhne (Garynahine)**, 4 daily; to **Uig District**, 3-4 daily; to **Ranais (Ranish)**, 6-8 times daily.
   There are also buses from Stornoway to **Tarbert** and **Leverburgh** on Harris (for the ferry to North Uist), Mon-Sat 4-5 times daily. Bus timetables are available from the iCentre in Stornoway, T01851-703088, or call the bus station, T01851-704327, or visit the website of Comhaire nan Eilean Siar, www.cne-siar.gov.uk.

Car hire
Carhire Hebrides, T01851-706500, www. carhire-hebrides.co.uk. Operates from Stornoway airport and ferry terminal, also Tarbert, Benbecula and Barra airports.

> **Tip...**
> Petrol stations are few and far between, expensive and closed on Sundays so if low on petrol think carefully before passing a fuel sign.

Other options are **Lewis Car Rentals**, 52 Bayhead St, T01851-703760; **Stornoway Car Hire**, 18 Inaclete Rd, T01851-702984.

Cycle hire
Alex Dan's Cycle Centre, 67 Kenneth St, T01851-704025. Mon-Sat 0900-1800. Rents bikes for £20 per day and £60 per week. **Bike Hebrides**, T07775-943355, www. bikehebrides.com. Hires bikes and kayaks.

Ferry
CalMac runs a ferry service to **Ullapool**, 2 times Mon-Sat (Mar to mid-Jun) 3 times on Wed (Mid-Jun to Aug) and 1 daily Nov-Feb. It also now runs once on a Sun all year round (2 hrs 40 mins). Contact **CalMac** offices in Stornoway, T01851-307470, for further details.

Taxi
Stornoway Taxis, T01851-701234; **Island Taxis**, T01851-705533.

North to Nis (Ness)   *Colour map 1, A3.*

crofts, crafts and coastal walks

The A857 leaves Stornoway and runs northwest through barren, treeless and relentlessly bleak moorland to Barabhas (Barvas). The landscape is scarred by deep gashes caused by peat digging, and the unfamiliar smell you detect in your nostrils is peat burning – a strange mixture of burning grass, whisky and coffee. Peat is the main source of domestic fuel used on the islands, and outside most houses you'll see large stacks of peat, or *cruachs*.

The road from Barabhas northeast to Nis runs through a series of forlorn-looking, scrawny settlements that all seem identical and merge into one. They consist of modern, characterless grey pebble-dash cottages with the ubiquitous piles of peat in the gardens; the abandoned cars and vans scattered around everywhere only add to the ugly and depressing scene.

Just beyond Barabhas a sign points left to the **Morvern Art Gallery** ① *T01851-840247, www.morverngallery.com, open Apr-Sep Tue-Sat 1030-1700*, which exhibits contemporary local artworks and has a café, making it a welcome refuge in bad weather. A few miles further on is a turning right to **Baile an Trùiseil (Ballantrushel)**, site of the huge **Clach an Trùiseil**, a 20-ft monolith (the largest in Europe), which was the scene of the last major battle on the island, fought between the Morrisons of Nis and the MacAuleys of Uig in the 16th century. This is the first of a number of prehistoric sights between here and **Siadar (Shader)**, which may be of interest to the keen archaeologist. Otherwise there's little of note on the road north to Nis as it passes through the typical crofting townships of **Coig Peighinnean Buirgh (Five Penny Borve)**, **Gàbhsann bho Dheas (South Galson)**, **Dail (Dell)**, **Suaineabost (Swainbost)**, **Tàbost (Habost)** and **Lìonal (Lionel)**. In saying that, those who are keen to buy souvenirs should look in at the **Borgh Pottery** ① *T01856-850345, www.borghpottery.com, Apr-Oct Tue-Sat 1030-1730,* by the bridge at Coig Peighinnean. Here you'll find a wide range of beautiful and original domestic and decorative ware.

The road continues north, passing through a number of villages that collectively make up **Nis (Ness)**, until it ends at the fishing village of **Port Nis (Port of Ness)**. It's a lovely spot, with a picturesque little harbour, and a golden sweep of beach enclosed by steep cliffs. Each September the locals head out to the island of **Sula Sgeir**, 30 miles to the north, for the annual cull of young gannets (*gugas*), which are considered something of a delicacy by the people of Lewis (but be warned: they're an acquired taste). In Nis, the kids will love the community established play park set amidst the machair and dunes.

ON THE ROAD

Never on a Sunday

The islands are the Gaidhealtachd, the land of the Gael. Gaelic culture has remained more prominent here than in any other part of Scotland, and the way of life and philosophy of the islanders will seem totally alien and fascinating to many visitors. Gaelic is the first language for the majority of the islanders – and the only one for the older generation – but the all-pervading influence of the English media has taken its toll and the language is under threat. Though Gaelic is still taught in schools, the younger generation tends to speak to each other in English. Visitors will not have any language problems, as the Gaelic-speaking inhabitants are so polite they will always change to English when visitors are present (though place names and signposts are in Gaelic).

The church is also an important factor in preserving the language, and services are usually held in Gaelic. In fact, religion is one of the most pervasive influences on Hebridean life, and the islanders' faith is as strong as the winds that pound their shores. The islands are split between the Presbyterian Lewis, Harris and North Uist, and the predominantly Roman Catholic South Uist and Barra. Benbecula, meanwhile, has a foot in both camps. On Lewis and Harris the Free Church is immensely powerful and the Sabbath is strictly observed. Don't expect to travel anywhere by public transport; shops and petrol stations will be closed, and you'll be hard pressed to find a place to eat. Even the swings in the playgrounds are padlocked! Things have changed in recent years, however, and October 2002 saw the revolutionary move to allow Loganair to fly to Stornoway on a Sunday. Despite a tsunami-like wave of protest from the church, who described the idea as "a breach of God's moral law", Loganair's tourist-friendly flights took to the air.

Just before Port Nis is Lìonal, where the B8015 turns off right and leads to the start of the 10-mile coastal trail to **Tòlstadh** (**Tolsta North**) and the beautiful beaches of Traigh Mhor and Garry. Numerous shielings (basic stone huts where farming communities lived during summer grazings in high pasture) pepper the landscape from an earlier era when local crofters drove their cattle to the summer pastures in the island's interior. The beaches can be reached much more easily by road north from Stornoway. For details of the coastal walk, ask at the tourist information centre in Stornoway.

Another minor road heads northwest to the tiny hamlet of **Eòropaidh** (**Eoropie**) (pronounced 'Yor-erpee'). By the road junction that leads to Rubha Robhanais is the ancient **Teampull Mholuaidh** (**St Moluag's Church**), thought to date from the 12th century and restored to its present state in 1912. It is now used on certain Sundays by Stornoway's Episcopal Church. From Eòropaidh a narrow road runs to the lighthouse at **Rubha Robhanais** (**Butt of Lewis**), the most northerly tip of the island. It's a great place for spotting seabirds or whales and dolphins, but also very wild and windy. Half a mile back down the road a path leads to the tiny beach of **Port Sto**, which is more sheltered.

Croft conversion

The word 'croft' is derived from the Gaelic *croit*, meaning a small area of land. Crofting has been the traditional way of life in the Scottish Highlands for many centuries. Its emotive hold on the psyche of the Highlander comes from the long, hard struggle for security of tenure, see box, page 439.

A croft is aptly described as a parcel of land entirely surrounded by regulations. Most crofts consist of a few acres of arable land with a proportion of grazing land shared with other crofts. Each crofter is, in effect, a kind of small tenant-farmer, the distinction being that he has almost absolute security of tenure and has the right to assign the croft to a member of his family whether the landlord agrees or not. In fact, over the years, the crofter has managed to acquire most of the rights of ownership with few of the disadvantages.

The croft is the area of land involved and not the house which is called the 'croft house'. Crofts can vary in size, from a quarter of an acre upwards. Those on Lewis are small and relatively unproductive, with an average size of only about 5 acres, while on the Uists, where the land is more fertile, crofts are up to 50 acres or more.

As well as having the sole tenancy of the croft, the crofter usually has a share in a huge area of 'common grazing' along with the other members of the crofting community – commonly called a township. They also work together in such activities as fencing, sheep dipping or cutting peat.

In reality, crofting does not provide a viable means of living. Very few crofters rely solely on their smallholding for an income and most need to have several occupations (including running a B&B) to make ends meet. But without the family croft, whole communities would just pack up and leave, so crofting functions as a means of preventing the depopulation of remote rural areas.

The crofter's lot may change for the better, however, thanks to the Scottish Parliament's Land Reform Bill, which includes a special right to buy for the crofting communities.

Listings North to Nis

Where to stay

££££ Broad Bay House
Back, Lewis, T01851-820990,
wwwbroadbayhouse.co.uk.
About 9 miles north of Stornoway. Modern, luxurious 4-bedroom guesthouse overlooking the sea. Beautifully appointed rooms, each with its own decking area. 1 of the rooms is category-1 accessible. Also offer 'light supper platters' for 2 to share, from £25-40. Superb breakfast. Recommended but no children under 14.

£££ Galson Farm Guest House and Hostel
Gàbhsann bho Deas (South Galson),
halfway between Barabhas and Port Nis,
T01851-850492, www.galsonfarm.co.uk.
Open all year.
Friendly and beautifully restored 18th-century house with sea views. 2-course dinner available £20 per person. Owners also have **Galson Farm Hostel (£)**, with 6 beds and basic facilities.

Restaurants

££ The Cross Inn
*Cross, Nis (Ness), T01851-810151,
www.crossinn.com.*

The islands' most northerly restaurant serving locally grazed beef and the catch of the day. Was up for sale at the time of writing so check in advance.

West coast of Lewis

ancient standing stones and traditional blackhouses

The west coast of Lewis contains most of what you'll want to see and can be covered in a day trip from Stornoway, either with your own transport, by public bus or as part of a tour.

Arnol *Colour map 1, A3.*

At the end of the village of Arnol is the **Blackhouse Museum** ⓘ *T01851-710395 (HES), Apr-Sep Mon-Sat 0930-1730, Oct-Mar Mon, Tue and Thu-Sat 1000-1630, £5, concessions £4, children 5-15 £3*, one of the best surviving examples of an original blackhouse in Scotland and well worth visiting. These traditional thatched houses were once common throughout the Highlands and Islands, and were inhabited until the 1960s. They were built in the tradition of 'longhouses', which can be traced back 1000 years to the time of the Viking invaders. The name 'blackhouse' dates back to the 1850s when modern buildings were introduced. These were known as 'white houses' so the older-style houses were called 'blackhouses'. The blackhouses were well adapted to the harsh local climate. They had no windows or chimney and were built with local materials – stone, turf and thatch of oat, barley or marram grass – with a peat fire burning continually in the central hearth. Attached to the living quarters was the cattle byre. This particular blackhouse was built in 1885 and inhabited until 1964.

Siabost and around *Colour map 1, A2.*

Two miles south of the Arnol turn-off, at **Bragar,** look out for an archway, formed from the jawbone of a blue whale that was washed up on the coast nearby in 1920. A few miles further on is the township of Siabost (Shawbost), where the charmingly ramshackle **folk museum** ⓘ *Apr-Sep Mon-Sat 0900-1800, free*, which was started as a project by local school children, now contains an interesting collection of Hebridean artefacts.

Just south of Siabost, beside a small loch, is the sign for the restored **Norse Mill and Kiln**, which is a half-mile walk over the hill from the car park but worth a look. A little further on is the popular surfing beach at Dalmore before you reach the turning for **Dail Beag (Dalbeg)**, another lovely secluded beach.

Gearrannan (Garenin) *Colour map 1, A2.*

The landscape gradually becomes more undulating and scenically interesting as the road then passes through the village of **Càrlabhagh (Carloway)**, Lord Leverhume's proposed fishing port. Here, a branch road leads to the ruined and deserted blackhouse village of Gearrannan (Garenin). Since 1989, the old village has been extensively renovated, with the aid of EU funding, and several derelict crofts have been painstakingly restored to their original style of stone walls and thatched roofs. One of these is now a living **museum** ⓘ *T01851-643416, www.gearrannan.com Apr-Sep Mon-Sat 0930-1730*. There's also a Gatliff Trust hostel (see Where to stay, page 339), called **Garenin Hostel**, a café serving snacks and light lunches, and four self-catering cottages. An old cart track leads down to the bay, from where the sight of the sun setting out at sea really is something to behold. Above the village, a four-mile coastal footpath can be followed through the 'lazy beds' (see page 344) and above the sea cliffs to reveal a stunning view of beautiful **Dalmore Bay**. The Atlantic waves seem to break relentlessly on golden sands and the beach is, not surprisingly, a favourite haunt of surfers from Stornoway and further afield. Swimmers and bathers should be careful, however, because, as with many of the west coast beaches, there can be a fierce rip-current carrying the unwary into deeper water out at sea. Ask at the Gearrannan village, where you can also stay in unique blackhouse accommodation (see Where to stay, page 333), for a map of this coastal walking route that ends in Dalbeg.

Dùn Chàrlabhaigh (Doune Carloway) Broch *Colour map 1, A2.*

A little further on, standing a few hundred yards from the main road, is the Dùn Chàrlabhaigh Broch (Dun Carloway), the best-preserved building of its type in the Outer Hebrides. The impressive 2000-year-old drystone habitation is beautifully situated on a rocky outcrop, commanding great views across Loch Carloway to the sea beyond. The remaining outer wall is 30-ft high and slopes inwards, with an inner wall which rises vertically, leaving chambers between the walls. Parts of the inner wall have collapsed, revealing the interior stairs and galleries. The **Doune Broch Visitor Centre** ① *T01851-621422, Apr-Sep Mon-Sat*

ON THE ROAD

Music to your ears

As the heartland of Gaelic culture, the Outer Hebrides are host to many music events throughout the year ranging from a spontaneous ceilidh to one of the three local mods. Mods usually consist of three days of competition in piping, singing, instrumental music, drama and poetry, and are an opportunity to see the best of the local talent. More information can be obtained from An Comunn Gaidhealach, www.acgmod.org.

Also listed below are the various Highland Games and agricultural shows, where you can also see piping competitions and Highland dancing.

Late March Feis nan Coisir, Stornoway, Lewis.

First Friday in April Donald Macleod Memorial Piping Competition, Stornoway, Lewis.

May to June Highland Festival, held in various locations.

Early June Harris Mod, Tarbert, on Harris.

Second week in June Lewis Mod, Stornoway, Lewis.

Mid-June Uist Mod, Iochdar, on South Uist.

May to June Lochmaddy Boat Festival, Lochmaddy, North Uist.

Mid-July Berneray Week, Bearnaraigh (Berneray), North Uist.

July Ceolas Music School, South Uist.

Early July Barra Festival for two weeks.

Early/mid-July Feis Tir an Eorna, Paibeil, North Uist; Barra Highland Games, Borgh (Borve), Barra, lasting for a week.

11-14 July Hebridean Celtic Music Festival, Stornoway, Lewis.

Mid-July North Uist Highland Games, Hosta, North Uist.

Mid/late July Harris Gala; South Uist Highland Games, Aisgeirnis (Askernish), South Uist; Lewis Highland Games, Tong, Lewis.

Mid-July Barra Highland Games.

Third week of July Harris Festival.

Late July Barra Live, Barra; West Side Agricultural Show, Barabhas (Barvas), Lewis; South Uist Agricultural Show, Iochdar, South Uist; South Harris Agricultural Show, Leverburgh.

July Feis Eilean an Fhraoich, Stornoway, Lewis.

Late July/early August North Uist Agricultural Show, Hosta, North Uist.

Early August Carloway Agricultural Show, Càrlabhagh (Carloway), Lewis; Fies Tir a Mhurain, Lionacleit, Benbecula; Lewis Carnival, Stornoway; Fish Festival, Stornoway; Twin Peaks Hill Race, North Uist.

Second week August Harris Arts Festival, Tarbert.

1000-1700, free, which can be found here, tastefully complements the architectural style of the site and gives a good audio-visual description of how life must have been in one of these structures around 50 BC. There's also a small shop and public toilets.

★ **Calanais (Callanish)** *Colour map 1, B2.*
T01851-621422 (HES), www.calanaisvisitorcentre.co.uk, site and visitor centre open all year Mon-Sat 1000-1800, free.

Five miles south of Dun Chàrlabhaigh is the jewel in the islands' prehistoric crown and one of the most atmospheric and evocative places in Scotland, if not the UK. The **Calanais Standing Stones** are the equal of Stonehenge in historical value but what sets them apart is their imposing physical presence, which can be appreciated at close quarters, and their spectacularly beautiful setting. The stones are aligned in the form of a Celtic cross and, in the centre, is a main circle of 13 stones, with a central monolith over 12-ft tall, and a chambered burial cairn. The oldest part of this great ceremonial site – probably the stone circle – dates from around 3000 BC (older than Stonehenge) and continued in use until about 800 BC. The full significance of the site is not yet known, though it is thought to be a lunar calendar, built to track the path of the lunar cycle. Every 18.6 years the moon returns to the same point and the stones at Calanais plot its slow progress over the intervening years until the moon 'sets' inside the stone circle. This astounding event – known as a lunar standstill – last occurred in 2006. There are also a number of smaller and more isolated stone circles a few miles south of Calanais on the road to Gearraidh na h-Aibhne (Garynahine). Next to the stones is the **Calanais Visitor Centre**, which features 'The Story of the Stones' exhibition, a very good restaurant (see Restaurants, page 333) and a shop. Margaret Curtis, who has been studying and excavating the site for over 30 years, offers a guided archaeological tour (see What to do, page 333).

Listings West coast of Lewis

Where to stay

If you want to stay near the stones and visit them at dusk or sunrise, there are several inexpensive B&Bs in and around the village of Calanais.

£££-££ Loch Roag Guest House
22a Breasclete, T01851-621771, www.lochroag.com.
6 rooms. A few miles from the stones. Offers high-quality accommodation and 3-course dinner for £25 a head.

££ Leumadair Guest House
7a Callanish, T01851-621706, www.leumadair.co.uk.
Good-value guesthouse with views of the stones which are just 2 mins away. It offers a 3-course dinner (£25 per person) or 1-pot supper for £15.

££-£ Garenin Hostel
Garenin, near Carloway, T01851-643416, www.gearrannan.com.
Sleeps 10 plus family room for 3 (**££**). A renovated blackhouse (Taigh Dhonnchaidh, or Donald's house), situated by a gorgeous beach and with the added benefit of a ground-source heat pump, making it awfully cosy in cold weather. No telephone or TV and no arrivals on Sun. Recommended.

Self-catering

Gearrannan Blackhouse Village
Carloway, T01851-643416, www. gearrannan.com. Open all year.
4 blackhouses have been restored and refurbished as self-catering thatched cottages in a fantastic location, all named after the people who used to live in them. 1 cottage sleeps 2 (£88 per night in high season), 2 of the cottages sleep 5 (£115) and 1 of the cottages sleeps up to 16 (£200 per night).

Restaurants

£ Calanais Visitor Centre Café
See page 333.
The best place to eat near the stones, offering diners reasonably priced, freshly made soups, salads and home-baking.

What to do

Tour operators
Margaret Curtis, *Olcote, New Park, Callanish, T01851-621277, http://www.geo.org.* The 1-hr tour of the Calanais site gives an insight into the history and purpose of the stones.

From Gearraidh na h-Aibhne the main A858 runs back to Stornoway, while the B8011 forks west to the remote Uig Peninsula in the southwest of the island. Here are some of the Outer Hebrides' finest beaches and most dramatic coastal scenery, and you'll barely see another soul.

Bearnaraigh (Great Bernera) to Cnip

Four miles down this road is a turning to the right onto the B8059, which leads to the island of Bearnaraigh, now connected to the mainland of Lewis by a single-track road bridge. The main settlement on the island is **Breacleit** (**Breaclete**), where you can find out about the island's history and the Iron Age village at Bostadh from the **Bernera Museum** ⓘ *T01851-612331, Jun-Sep Mon-Sat 1100-1800, Oct-May Tue and Thu 1300-1500, £1.50, children free.* The rest of the island is fairly interesting with tiny fishing villages, one or two brochs and some standing stones. The nicest part, though, is on the north coast, near the tiny hamlet of **Bostadh** (**Bosta**), where a lovely little sandy bay looks out to the nearby island of **Bearnaraigh Beag** (**Little Bernera**).

The B8011 continues across bleak moorland, then cuts north to **West Loch Roag**, which is fringed by some fine sandy beaches and backed by a much hillier landscape. Just beyond **Miabhag** (**Miavaig**) is the turn-off right to **Cliobh** (**Cliff**), with its picturesque beach which is unsafe for swimming. A mile further on is the little village of **Cnip** (**Kneep**), to the east of which is the beautiful **Traigh na Berie**, a long sandy beach backed by flat machair which is ideal for camping.

Gallan Head

Beyond Miabhag, the eerie peninsula of Gallan Head provides a setting befitting a science fiction drama or Cold War Orwellian novel, with empty, decaying Ministry of Defence buildings battered by the Atlantic storms. Wandering around the abandoned site, it is easy to form ideas of bizarre, top-secret government experiments and early-warning missile tracking in this seemingly edge-of-the-world place, far removed from the unwanted, prying eyes of everyday society.

Mangersta and the Flannan Islands

Beyond Ardroil the road continues to Mangersta where, at **Aird Fenish**, is some of the most spectacular coastal scenery in the Outer Hebrides. The cliffs plunge dramatically beyond the road to the inaccessible beach below, with a series of crumbling sea stacks battered by the fearsome waves, and seabirds riding the updraughts adding to the sense of natural beauty, energy and sheer power. Further south at **Brenish**, about a 10-minute walk from the road, is a menacing blowhole connected to the sea by an underground passage.

Far out into the Atlantic are the haunting **Flannan Islands**, scene of the mysterious disappearance in 1900 of three lighthouse keepers. Various explanations have been put forward over the years, ranging from a freak wave in stormy weather to a monster sea serpent or even a dispute and fight between the men; whatever the real reason, the legend continues. See page 336 for boat trips.

Timsgearraidh (Timsgarry)

At Timsgearraidh (Timsgarry) are the **Traigh Chapadail** (**Uig sands**) at the village of **Eadar Dha Fhadhail** (**Adroil**). This is the loveliest of all the beaches on Lewis, with miles of sand

BACKGROUND
Lewis

Lewis was controlled by the Vikings and the Norse influence can be seen in many of the place names, such as Uig (which is Norse for 'a bay'). After the end of Norwegian sovereignty in 1266, the island was ruled by the Macleods, said to be descendants of early settlers from Iceland. Control of the island was wrested from them by the Mackenzies, who then proceeded to sell it, in 1844, to Sir James Matheson. The new owner built Lews Castle in Stornoway and began to develop the infrastructure of the island, as well as investing in new industries. Though many crofts were cleared and families sent to Canada, the people of Lewis fared well and certainly much better than their counterparts in the Southern Isles.

The next proprietor was Lord Leverhulme, founder of Lever Brothers, who bought the island (along with Harris) in 1918. He planned to turn Lewis into a major fishing centre and ploughed money into developing the infrastructure. He was forced to abandon his plans, however, partly because of the decline of the fishing industry, and partly owing to the growing conflict between him and the islanders returning from the war who wanted land of their own to farm. As a final benevolent gesture, Lord Leverhulme offered Lewis to the islanders, but only Stornoway Council accepted. The island was then divided into estates and sold, and hundreds of people emigrated.

Today the economy of Lewis is still based on the traditional industries of crofting, fishing and weaving, though there are other economic activities such as fish farming, which is now a major employer, service industries, construction, tourism and, hopefully in the not-too-distant future, renewable energy from the island's wind turbines.

dunes and machair, but it is famous for an entirely different reason. It was here in 1831 that a crofter dug up the 'Lewis Chessmen', 78 pieces carved from walrus ivory and belonging to at least eight incomplete chess sets from 12th-century Scandinavia. Some are now in the Museum of Scotland in Edinburgh, but most can be found outside their country of origin, in the British Museum in London. In recent years six of the pieces have been returned to the island and are on display in the Museum nan Eilean in Stornoway (see page 323).

Listings Uig Peninsula

Where to stay

Great Bernera to Cnip

£££ Auberge Carnish
5 Carnish, Uig, T01851-672459,
www.aubergecarnish.co.uk.
4 en suite rooms, 1 on ground floor. 5-star accommodation and food in a stunning setting overlooking the beach, run by Richard and Jo, who formerly owned the acclaimed **Bonaventure** (now **Gallan Head**

Hotel). Stylish luxury and superb 'Franco-Hebridean' cuisine (**£££**). Residents' lounge with wood-burning stove and decking area for guests to sit and enjoy the views. Book in advance. Highly recommended.

£££ Baile Na Cille Guest House
Timsgarry, T01851-672242, www.
bailenacille.co.uk. Easter-Oct.
6 en suite rooms. One of the best places to stay around Uig bay, this restored 18th-century manse is beautifully located

overlooking a 2-mile stretch of sand. Superb home cooking 4-course dinner for £35) and one of the warmest welcomes in the islands. Children half price and dogs welcome (except very large and badly behaved ones!). Recommended.

For those who want to visit the South Lochs on the east of Lewis, there are a couple of accommodation options: **Tigh Na Bruaich** (**££**), 8 Balallan, off the A859 and 14 miles from Stornoway, T01851-830742, a traditional croft house; and **Kershader Hostel** (**£**), on the south shore of Loch Erisort off the A859 near North Harris, T01851-880236, www.ravenspoint.co.uk, open Mar-Oct, cosy community-run 14-bed hostel with great facilities including a café and knitwear shop, ideal for accessing local birdwatching, fishing and walking.

Restaurants

The best options are the **Auberge Carnish** and **Gallan Head Hotel**, see Where to stay, above.

Shopping

Uig Lodge Smoked Salmon, *T01851-672396, www.uiglodge.co.uk*. The place to buy smoked salmon.

What to do

Island Cruising, *1 Erista, Uig, T01851-672381, www.island-cruising.com*. For wildlife, diving, birdwatching and live-aboard boat trips as far afield as the Flannan Islands and St Kilda. **Seatrek**, *Murray MacLeod, 16 Uigean, Uig, T01851-672469, www.seatrek.co.uk. Apr-Sep*. Aboard a high-speed RIB, this operator offers a host of trips, including a 2-hr (1000-1200) easy cruise off Uig during which you'll also check on the seals and lobster pots; a Sea Stack trip off Little Bernera (1300-1500); an island trip with ruins and sea caves, and a full-blown day that includes the chance to see the isle of Scarp, famous for the film *The Rocket Post* (see Scarp, page 339).

Na Hearadh
(Harris)

Harris is not an island but, together with Lewis, forms the largest of the Outer Hebrides, with Harris taking up the southern third. The two parts are divided by the long sea lochs of Loch Seaforth in the east and Loch Resort in the west, though this division is rarely shown on maps. Though joined, the two are very different in terms of geography. Harris is largely mountain and rock, whereas Lewis is flat moorland. The largest town and site of the ferry terminal is An Tairbeart (Tarbert). To the north are the highest peaks in the Outer Hebrides, surrounded by some of the finest unspoilt wilderness in the whole country. To the south are miles of wonderful beaches, sands and stunning seascapes that will convince you it's the Caribbean, for it's not just the flawless white sand but the gin-clear water that breaks over it. When the sun comes out, it's as if someone had been fiddling with the colour control: cool greens mutate to psychedelic shades of turquoise and blue. The east coast is not so much a contrast as a shock to the system, a preternaturally strange lunar landscape straight out of a science fiction film. With your own transport you could 'do' Harris in a day quite comfortably, but why just spend a day? Whatever the weather, you'll want to spend more time here and appreciate its precious natural beauty.

North Harris is the most mountainous part of the Outer Hebrides and its wild, rugged peaks are ideal for hillwalking. In 2003, 135,900 acres of the wildlife-rich former North Harris Estate (including its deer) were purchased for the community for around £8 million to be managed by the North Harris Community Trust.

The A859 south from Lewis gets progressively more scenic as it skirts **Loch Siophort** (**Seaforth**), and the mountains rise before you like a giant barrier. The road then climbs past **Bogha Glas** (**Bowglass**) and **Aird a Mhulaidh** (**Ardvourlie**) with **Clisham** (2621 ft), the highest peak in the Outer Hebrides, and **Sgaoth Aird** (1829 ft) towering overhead on either side. Clisham in particular, though not a Munro, is a very satisfying peak to bag: steep, spectacularly craggy and the views from the top will make your heart sing.

The A859 winds its way south until you reach the turn-off to **Reinigeadal** (**Rhenigidale**), which was the most remote community on Harris and accessible only by sea or by a rough hill track until the access road was built. Here you'll find a **Gatliff Trust Youth Hostel**, see Where to stay, page 339. From Reinigeadal an ascent of shapely **Toddun** (528 m) provides exhilarating exercise rewarded with fine views east across the Minch to the mainland and, in the other direction, to the mountain wilderness of North Harris.

The A859 continues southwest across the crest of the craggy hills then drops down to the turn-off for the single-track B887, which winds its way all the way out to **Huisinis** (**Hushinish**) between the impressive mountains of the Forest of Harris on one side and the northern shore of West Loch Tarbert on the other, with views across to the Sound of Taransay and the beaches of South Harris. Immediately beyond the turn-off, you pass through **Bun Abhainn Eadarra** (**Bunavoneadar**), which was a thriving whaling station until 1930 and one of Lord Leverhulme's many schemes for the island. The old whaling station is worth a visit even though the site has not been developed as a tourist attraction.

Just before the village of **Miabhag** (**Meavaig**), a defined footpath heads north into the hills up Glen Meavaig to Loch Voshimid. Further on, though, is a better opportunity for walking. Just before the gates of **Amhuinnsuidhe Castle** (pronounced 'Avan-soo-ee') is a signpost for Chliostair Power Station. From here you can walk two miles up to the dam, then follow the right-hand track round the reservoir and the left-hand track round the upper loch, before you arrive in a wild and remote glen.

Just beyond the castle gates you'll see a beautiful waterfall spilling straight into the sea. The road then runs right past the front door of the castle, built in 1868 by the Earl of Dunmore, and still a private residence, before passing through an archway and continuing to the tiny crofting township of **Huisinis** (**Hushinish**), beautifully situated in a sandy bay. This is where the road ends; next stop the USA. Follow the track to the right across the machair, where a footpath above the jetty and rocky beach can be followed to the old fishing lodge at **Cravadale** and Loch Cravadale beyond. Make a detour to the golden sands and turquoise waters of **Traigh Mheilein**, overlooking Scarp. From

Essential Na Hearadh (Harris)

Finding your feet

There's a regular bus service between Stornoway and Tarbert (four to five times a day) Monday to Saturday, which continues to Leverburgh, via the west coast of South Harris. Ferries sail from Uig (Skye) to Tarbert (one hour 35 minutes), once or twice a day, Monday to Saturday.

BACKGROUND
Harris

The separation of Harris and Lewis dates back to Norse times, when the island was divided between the two sons of Leod, progenitor of the Macleods. Harris remained in Macleod hands until 1834. The recent history of Harris is closely bound up with that of Lewis. Both were bought by the soap magnate, Lord Leverhulme, see page 344, whose grandiose schemes for Lewis came to nothing. Leverhulme then turned his attentions to Harris, where the peaceful little village of An t-Ob (Obbe) was renamed Leverburgh and transformed into a bustling port with all manner of public works programmes under development. His death in 1925 brought an end to all his plans for Harris and, instead of becoming a town with a projected population of 10,000, Leverburgh reverted to being a sleepy village, with only the harbour, the roads and the change of name to show for it all.

Since the Leverhulme era there has been no main source of employment for the population of 2400 on Harris, though a successful fishing industry continues on Scalpaigh (Scalpay). There is still some crofting, supplemented by the acclaimed but financially precarious Harris Tweed industry (www.harristweed.org), though most of the estimated 130-plus Hebridean weavers reside on Lewis. In addition to public services and crafts, tourism is increasingly important to the island. Indeed, with its wealth of Caribbean-like beaches, diversity of wildlife, excellent walking terrain and fabulous accommodation and eating options, this compact Hebridean 'island' is now establishing itself as a year-round destination.

the coast, strong walkers can follow Glen Cravadale inland, eventually rejoining the main road near Amhuinnsuidhe Castle.

The rocky island of **Scarp** supported a population of more than 100 as late as the 1940s but was abandoned in 1971, and now the crofters' cottages are used as holiday homes. The island was the scene of a bizarre experiment in 1934, when a German rocket scientist, Gerhard Zucher, tried to prove that rockets could be used to transport mail and medical supplies to remote communities. His theory went up in smoke, however, when the rocket exploded before it even got off the ground, with 30,000 letters on board.

Listings North Harris

Where to stay

£££ Ardhasaig House
Aird Asaig, 4 miles northwest of Tarbert off A859, T01859-502500, www.ardhasaig.co.uk. Open all year.
5 en suite rooms. Small hotel with a big reputation, especially for its wonderful cooking (4-course set dinner is around £60 a head). Lovely location, good

disabled facilities and also offers romantics accommodation in a cosy, self-contained barn (**££££**). Self-catering available for up to 4 in **Clisham Cottage** from £550 per week.

£ Gatliff Trust Youth Hostel
Rhenigidale, www.gatliff.org.uk.
Spectacular location at the head of remote Loch Seaforth. Here you'll find a converted croft house (no phone), which sleeps 13 and is open all year. If properly equipped, you can

walk the 5 miles from Tarbert using the path once used by the local schoolchildren.

What to do

See under Tarbert, page 342.

Transport

See under Tarbert, page 342.

An Tairbeart (Tarbert) and around *Colour map 1, B2.*

tiny island capital and main ferry port

Tarbert, the largest settlement on Harris, lies in a sheltered bay on the narrow isthmus that joins North and South Harris. It's a tiny 'capital' but still the main ferry port for the CalMac ferry from Harris to Uig on Skye. Tarbert is also where to find groceries, Harris Tweed, www.harristweedandknitwear.co.uk, a post office, petrol, and a range of eating and accommodation options.

The iCentre (see page 340) is close to the ferry terminal. Also nearby is the recently opened **Isle of Harris Distillery** ① *T01859-502212, www.harrisdistillery.com, open Mon-Sat 1000-1700*. This is a newcomer to the Hebridean whisky distillery (opened in 2015) so their own malt is still a work in progress but visitors can find out all about the process and also sample their other product, Isle of Harris gin.

An interesting little excursion from Tarbert is the 10-mile return route that runs east through the tiny villages of **Urgha** and **Caolas Scalpaigh** to **Carnach** at the end of the road. Just beyond Urgha, on the north side of the road, is a path which leads across the hills, part of the land managed by the North Harris Community Land Trust, to the remote settlement of **Reinigeadal**. The twisting path was originally used by the community in Reinigeadal; hardy children would make the daily journey across the hills to Tarbert before the village was connected to the A859 by the new road. The zigzagging, exposed path, on which several people are known to have perished, passes through enchanting scenery above **Loch Trollamarig** in a setting more reminiscent of Scandinavia's fjordland. A visit can easily be made to the deserted village of **Molinginish**, nestled snugly in a small glen above the loch and reputedly where the royal family once anchored for a picnic. Ensure you are properly equipped with boots and rainwear for the six-mile walk.

The island of **Scalpaigh (Scalpay)**, now connected to Harris by a road bridge opened by Tony Blair in 1998, is a thriving fishing community with a population of over 400. It's a pleasant three-mile walk across the island to **Eilean Glas Lighthouse**, built by the Stevensons and the first ever on the Outer Hebrides.

Listings Tarbert and around

Tourist information

iCentre
By the ferry terminal, T01859-502011. Apr-Oct Mon-Sat 0900-1700 and for the arrival of the evening ferry, in winter check times.

Where to stay

Harris isn't lacking in places to stay, most notably there are luxurious self-catering accommodation and comfortable hotels or guesthouses.

The Forest of Harris is a vast mountain wilderness extending north from West Loch Tarbert to Loch Resort and forming the de facto boundary with Lewis. It is one of the most isolated and unspoilt upland landscapes in Scotland and, because of its remoteness, receives very few visitors. For experienced hillwalkers, however, it is a paradise, offering rugged mountains, dramatic escarpments, airy ridges and desolate glens. There are endless walking possibilities, including a horse-shoe walk around Clisham and a long walk through Glen Ulladale to Kinloch-resort, a former crofting community now abandoned, but once described as the most remote habitation in Britain. Known as the North Harris Estate, this 22,000-acre tract of land was owned and managed by the family of the Bulmer cider empire – until 2003. In a move that had Scottish lairds incandescent with rage, the 800 residents of the estate were granted the right to take over the land on which they live, for more than £2 million, and finally throw off the shackles of feudal rule. Now that they have become masters of their own destiny, the community can relish the thought of a prosperous future, with energy development plans, sporting rights and tourism top of the agenda.

Some hotels may offer a room-only rate if you are catching the 0730 ferry back to Skye on Mon, Wed and Fri.

££££-£££ Hotel Hebrides
Beside the ferry pier, Tarbert, T01859-502364, www.hotel-hebrides.com.
This boutique-style 21-room hotel includes luxurious family and double rooms and also 4 luxury serviced apartments. From their wonderful **Pierhouse Restaurant** you can enjoy views over the sea whilst tucking into breakfast or a dinner of fresh seafood (**£££-££**). Has the **Mote Bar** for more informal bar meals (**££**) and a children's menu for £6 or pizzas for around £10 each. Check out the nearby **Machair Kitchen** (see Restaurants, below).

£££ Ceol na Mara
At Direcleit, just mins' drive from Tarbert, T01859-502464, www.ceolnamara.com.
Stands above a sea loch and offers a guest lounge and 4 comfortable rooms on each floor. The Gaelic name translates as 'Music of the Sea'.

£££ Harris Hotel
On the main road from Stornoway, on the left, before the turning for the ferry, Tarbert, T01859-502154, www.harrishotel.com.

Built in 1865 and sporting the initials of the acclaimed 19th-century novelist J M Barrie in its window, this welcoming hotel has 22 comfortable bedrooms to retire to after enjoying a fine meal (**££** for lunch, **£££** for dinner) or malt in the bar.

££ Avalon Guesthouse
12 West Side, just under a mile before Tarbert on left-hand side of road coming from Stornoway, T01859-502 334, www.avalonguesthouse.org. Open all year.
3 rooms. Comfortable B&B on family croft, wonderful views over Loch West Tarbert.

££ Hirta House
Scalpay, T01859-540394, www.hirtahouse.com. Open all year.
3 lovely en suite rooms. Great sea views and a guest lounge and library. Very friendly and comfortable. Good value.

Self-catering

Croft Cottage
5 mins' walk from Tarbert T01859-502338, www.croftcottageharris.co.uk.
A wonderfully luxurious self-catering option. Ingeniously converted from a former byre

and with stunning views over East Loch Tarbert towards the Minch. 3-bedroom, family-friendly hideaway packed with stylish finishes, including solid oak floors and an irresistible sauna and jacuzzi. From £1220 per week. Recommended.

Restaurants

£££-££ Harris Hotel
See Where to stay, above.
Serves tasty food every day till around 2100. They do a 3-course fixed menu and reasonably priced bar meals.

££ Machair Kitchen
Housed in the Talla na Mara Community Enterprise Centre by the pier, T01859-550333. Open 1200-1600 for lunch and Fri and Sat also 1800-2000 for dinner, closed Sun and Mon.
Part of the **Hotel Hebrides**, this new venture offers the best of local produce in a bright, friendly setting. Also organizes live folk music, art exibitions and film nights.

£ Croft 36
36 Northton, just off the A859 Tarvert–Leverburgh road, 3½ miles from Leverburgh ferry, T01859-520779.
This is an absolute gem of a place and truly unique. It's little more than an unmanned shed where you can take away baked goodies, soup, etc and pay into the honesty box, or call in at the house next door and order a delicious meal to be delivered to your self-catering cottage, campsite or wherever you happen to be staying. The French-influenced menu includes crab ravioli, fish curry and beef bourgignon and is a bargain at £14 for starter and mains. Not to be missed.

£ First Fruits Tearoom
Tarbert, T01859-502439. Easter-end Aug Mon-Sat 1030-1700.
Cosy traditional Hebridean tearoom serving delicious home-baking.

What to do

Fishing
Obbe Fishings, *Leverburgh T01859-520466, www.obbefishings.com*. Will help you hook the freshest supper.

Tour operators
Kilda Cruises, *T01859-502060, www.kilda cruises.co.uk*. Fantastic day trip to St Kilda on board the *Hirta* or *Orca III*, £210, £190 for under 16s. They also sail to the Shiant Islands, Flanna Islands, Rona or Monarch Islands on request.
Mike Briggs, *T01859-502376, www. mikeandpeggybriggs.co.uk*. Offer informative walking trips to spot wildlife.
Sea Harris, *T01859-502007, www.seaharris. co.uk*. Skipper Seumas Morrison offers full-day boat trips to St Kilda, 3 days a week Apr-Sep, £185pp, depart Leverburgh harbour at 0800 and return at 1900. Also offers wildlife and sea trips to the Shiants, Taransay and Scarp and a cruise of the entire Harris coastline on their new RIB.

Transport

Bus
There's a regular bus service between **Tarbert** and **Stornoway**, Mon-Sat, 1 hr 15 mins.
There's also a bus service from **Tarbert** to **Leverburgh** via the east coast (for the ferry to North Uist), 3-4 times daily, 1 hr 5 mins, along the so-called 'Golden Road' and 'Bays' route. This bus service (W13) includes stops at **Drinishader**, **Geocrab** and **Rodel**. To **Huisinis**, 2-4 daily on school days, 45 mins; to **Reinigeadal**, 2 daily on school days; to **Scalpaigh**, 2-5 daily, 10 mins. Bus timetables are available at the Tarbert **iCentre** or see www.cne-siar.gov.uk.

Cycle hire
Bikes for hire from **Sorrel Cottage**, see Where to stay. Prices start from about £15 per day. Also rents children's bikes.

Ferry

A ferry sails from **Leverburgh** to **Berneray**, 3-4 times daily. The trip takes 1 hr. For times and prices, see www.calmac.co.uk. Note that, although this is a short crossing, the service can easily be disrupted by high winds so try and be flexible with your travel plans.

Ceann a Deas na Hearadh (South Harris) *Colour map 1, B2.*
glorious white beaches and a strange lunar landscape

An absolute must while you're in the Outer Hebrides is the 45-mile circular route around South Harris. If you only do one thing while you're here, then make sure this is it, for the change in scenery from the west coast to the east is utterly astounding. One thing you're sure to puzzle over as you travel round is the fact that most people live on the harsh and inhospitable east coast, known as Na Baigh (Bays), while the beautiful west coast with its miles of glorious golden sands is scarcely populated. This is not through choice. The fertile west coast housed most of the population until the end of the 18th century when they were cleared to make way for sheep farms. Some emigrated to Cape Breton, while others were 'resettled' by landowners, forced to farm the infertile, rocky soil of the east side.

West coast

The main road from Tarbert runs south, skirting East Loch Tarbert, then cuts inland and heads west through a dramatic lunar landscape of rocks dotted with tiny lochans. It then begins to descend towards the sea revealing to your right the vast golden expanse of ★ **Losgaintir (Luskentyre)** beach. A single-track road turns off to the right and runs out to the tiny settlement where, in his tiny workshop overlooking the machair and azure sea, weaver Donald John Mackay, MBE, is among the dozen or so Hearrachs (indigenous inhabitants of Harris) who produce the world famous hand-crafted Harris Tweed using his loom. The weaver, who once famously supplied cloth to Nike for a range of training shoes, sells hats and hand-woven tweed jackets from his workshop at 6 Luskentyre (T01851-550261). The road cuts through the rich machair as it follows the magnificent stretch of bleached white sand that fills the entire bay, washed by turquoise sea and backed by steep dunes, all this set against the backdrop of the mountains to the north. If you do make it this far, then you won't be surprised to know that Luskentyre is included in most lists of the top 10 beaches in the world.

A short distance offshore is the island of **Tarasaigh (Taransay)**, which was well populated at the beginning of the 1900s but was subsequently abandoned. The island gained national prominence in 2000 as the setting for the popular BBC television series *Castaway*, in which an assortment of supposedly normal people from a variety of backgrounds were challenged to pit their wits against the elements and each other for a period of a full year. You can enjoy a day trip to the island (see What to do, page 342).

The road follows the coast, passing through the tiny settlements of **Seilebost**, **Horgabost** and **Burgh (Borve)**, Norse names highlighting the fact that the Vikings once plundered these lands. At **Horgabost** it's worth making the brief 10-minute stroll above the white sands to marvel at the roughly hewn MacLeod's Stone that overlooks the sea and which dates back to the Bronze Age. There's B&B accommodation at Seilebost and Horgabost, while, a few miles further on, is another beautiful stretch of white sands at

Sgarasta Bheag (Scaristabeg), perfect for surfing, golf and with a couple of stunning places to stay (see Where to stay, page 345).

Beyond Sgarasta Bheag, the village of **An Taobh Tuath (Northton)** provides access to the scenic promontory of **Toe Head**, almost cut off from the rest of Harris by the huge expanse of the golden sands at Sgarasta. At the excellent **Sigallam!** ① *T01859-520258, www.seallam.com, summer Mon-Fri 1000-1700, winter Wed-Fri 1000-1700, £2.50, £2 concession*, you can learn all about the history and natural environment of Harris and take the chance to determine if you have ancestral links to the Hebrides. There's also a lovely café here. Nearby, a ruined chapel of 16th-century origin is situated on the machair below **Chaipaval** (365 m), whose heathery slopes can be climbed for one of the best views out to sea towards St Kilda, some 40 miles distant.

South coast

The road then runs along the south shore until it reaches **An t-Ob** (formerly Obbe, now **Leverburgh**), site of Lord Leverhulme's ambitious plan to turn a sleepy crofting township into a major fishing port, see page 339. A tiny, unremarkable village where some of the original buildings can still be seen, this is also the base of the excellent **Am Bothan Bunkhouse** (see Where to stay, page 345) and the departure point for CalMac's car ferry to Berneray.

Three miles east of Leverburgh, at the southeastern tip of Harris, is **Ròghadal** (Rodel), dominated by the beautiful 12th-century **St Clement's Church**, something of an unusual sight in such a remote spot and one of the most impressive religious building in the Hebrides. (Only the Benedictine abbey on Iona is larger.) The church stands on a site that dates back 1500 years and was built by Alastair Crotach (Hunchback) Macleod of Harris in the 1520s. Though impressive from the outside, particularly the huge tower, the real interest lies in the silent, chilly atmosphere of the interior, where you'll find a collection of remarkable carved wall tombs, some blackened by fire that once ravaged these walls. There are three tombs, the most notable of which is that of the founder, Alastair Crotach. The one in the south wall of the choir is also worth a close look.

Na Baigh (Bays)

Running north from Ròghadal up the east coast of South Harris is the **Golden Road**, so named by the locals because of the huge cost of building it. This twisting, tortuous single-track road runs through a bizarre and striking moonscape, and driving through it is a unique experience (but keep your eyes on the road or you'll end up in one of the many narrow sea lochs). It seems inconceivable that anyone could survive in such an environment, but the road passes through a string of townships, including picturesque **Geocrab**, all created in the 19th century by the people evicted from the west coast. People here have spent years eking a meagre living from the thin soil by building 'lazy beds' (thin strips of piled-up earth between the rocks) for planting potatoes. Weaving and fishing also provide much-needed income.

At **Lingreabhagh (Lingarabay)** the road skirts the foot of **Roinebhal**, which was, until recently, the proposed site of one of the largest super-quarries in Europe. This would have demolished virtually the entire mountain over many decades. Local people and environmentalists fought a successful campaign to prevent the proposal going ahead, thus protecting a precious natural asset. The road passes through a succession of tiny settlements before joining the A859 just south of Tarbert.

Where to stay

££££ Scarista House
Scaristabeg, T01859-550238, www. scaristahouse.com. Open all year.
5 tastefully furnished rooms and 2 comfortable self-catering cottages at the rear of this 19th century former manse. The bedrooms are well equipped in a residence that truly oozes old-world character. Antiques and books greet guests, who can then relax by the roaring open fire with a malt or bottle of fine wine (there's an extensive collection). Forget the TV, this is where to enjoy great company, fantastic food (£48 for 3 courses and £55 for 4) and even impromptu live ceilidh music. Recommended. Also have a well-appointed self-catering cottage that sleeps up to 7 for £780 per week in high season.

£££-££ Beul Na Mara
Seilebost, T01859-550205, www.buelnamara.co.uk.
A 3-bedroom guesthouse on the west coast between Tarbert and Leverburgh. It enjoys one of the most stunning backdrops anywhere on the islands with the golden beaches of Luskentyre, the hills of North Harris and Taransay off-shore. Also has 2 self-catering cottages for weekly rent; 1 sleeps 5 and the other sleeps 7, £660-850.

£££-££ Carminish House
1a Strond, 10 mins' walk from the Leverburgh ferry, T01859-520400, www.carminish.com.
3 rooms. Faultless guesthouse accommodation in a beautiful location overlooking the Sound of Harris with views of the Carminish Islands, Berneray and North Uist, this place is perfect for those who crave peace and quiet. Val and Peter cannot do enough for their guests and offer a delicious supper if requested (**££**).

££ Sorrel Cottage
2 Glen, Leverburgh, T01859-520319, www.accommodationisleofharris.co.uk. Open all year.
3 rooms. This converted old croft house is a very comfortable and relaxing place to stay, with meals available, including vegetarian (**£££** with dinner), and cycle hire.

££-£ No 5 Drinishader
Drinishader, 3 miles south of Tarbert, T01859-511255, www.number5.biz. Open all year.
Hostel with a difference on a converted traditional croft by the sea. A variety of accommodation with 2 twin rooms and 1 4-bed dorm in the **Croft Hostel** (**£**) and 5 rooms in the **Croft House** (family rooms, twin rooms, 4-bed dorm and studio apartment). Also arranges a variety of activities including fishing, kayaking, canoeing and walking. Easily accessed by bus from Tarbert, and there's a shop close by but the nearest pub is 4 miles away.

£ Am Bothan Bunkhouse
Leverburgh, T01859-520251, www.ambothan.com. Open all year.
A fabulous, well equipped and friendly bunkhouse packed with character and situated close to the pier. Has 3 rooms with 4 beds and 1 room with 6 beds. Space for tents.

Self-catering

Blue Reef Cottages
Overlooking Scarista beach, T01859-550370, www.stay-hebrides.com.
Couples who seek the ultimate in luxurious self-catering need look no further than here. Fashioned from local stone and timbers, these identical 2 croft cottages built into the hillside enjoy breathtaking views over the machair (and golf course) to the Atlantic and offshore Isle of Taransay. There's champagne

and home-baking on arrival, bikes and golf clubs to use, a fabulous kitchen, comfy sofas, a wood burning stove and after a day hillwalking or at sea, a jacuzzi and sauna to enjoy before retiring into the tastefully furnished bedroom with its hints of Harris Tweed and queen-sized bed. You'll never want to leave. From £935 per week in low season. Recommended.

Camping
In **Luskentyre**, you can camp on the machair, but ask for permission at the 1st house.

Restaurants

£££ Scarista House
Scaristabeg, T01859-550238,
www.scaristahouse.com.
For a mouth-watering 4-course dinner that may include local lamb, freshly caught shellfish and heavenly desserts, followed by a malt or glass of wine by the fire, you'll not beat the culinary experience at this homely former Georgian manse with views towards the sea. Book ahead. Fabulous and highly recommended.

£££-££ The Anchorage
By the pier, Leverburgh, T01859-520225.
Mar-Sep.
Café/restaurant near the bunkhouse, offering reasonable lunches and dinners

Tip...
Harris may be small and remote but the enterprising islanders can guarantee that even in the depths of winter you can enjoy a snack, lunch or full-blown candlelit dinner in style. However, it's advisable to book ahead just to ensure the restaurant/café is open.

including the freshest if local seafood. Great location by the pier for a romantic sunset dinner (if the weather's fine).

££ Skoon Art Café
Geocrab, T01859-530268, www.skoon.com.
Easter-end Sep Tue-Sat 1000-1630.
Overlooking the rocky Bays area on the east coast, this cosy, bright traditional croft house is adorned with the artworks of the resident artist-cum-chef, Andy. His wife, Emma, serves up the delicious soups, sandwiches and home-baking. Recommended.

What to do

See under Tarbert, page 342.

Transport

See under Tarbert, page 342.

The Uists,
Benbecula & Barra

South from Harris lies the southern 'half' of the Outer Herbides. The Uists, north and south, and Benbecula are all connected by a series of causeways; you can drive their length, past a never-ending series of fish-filled lochs, windswept beaches backing onto wildflower rich machair and tiny, straggling crofting communities. The quality of the seafood, livestock (and baking) on the Uists also sees these islands make a notable contribution to the acclaimed Eat Drink Hebrides Trail (www.visitouter hebrides.co.uk). At South Uist's southernmost tip, you cross a half-mile-long causeway to the tiny and beautiful Isle of Eriskay where Bonnie Prince Charlie first stepped ashore on Scotland in his bid to seize the Scottish Crown for the Stuarts. The road runs out at the CalMac ferry slipway for Barra. Alternatively, you can fly from Glasgow to Barra and land on its famous cockle strand – at low tide, of course!

Essential The Uists, Benbecula and Barra

Finding your feet

In recent years, the network of public transport on the islands has improved. Nonetheless, if relying on a bus to get around, don't expect one every five minutes – or even every hour. Buses on most routes run Monday-Saturday but it is highly recommended to get hold of a free copy of *Uist and Barra Bus and Ferry services* from **iCentres** in Tarbert (Harris), Lochmaddy (North Uist) and Castlebay (Barra) or view the timetables online at www.cne-siar.gov. uk. There are six to seven buses per day (except Sunday) from Bearnaraigh (Berneray) just off the north coast in the sound of Harris to Lochmaddy. Some of these buses continue to Baile a Mhanaich (Balivanich) on Benbecula, where there is an airport, see page 353, and Lochboisdale and Ludag on

South Uist, see page 354. There are three buses per day from Lochmaddy to Clachan na Luib (Clachan-a-Luib) which run in an anti-clockwise direction around the north and west coasts. Two buses per day connect Clachan-a-Luib with Baile Sear (Baleshare) and also with Saighdinis (Sidinish).

A mile-long causeway connects South Uist to Benbecula by road and regular buses (four per day Monday to Saturday) run between Lochboisdale and Lochmaddy on North Uist, stopping en route at Dalabrog (Daliburgh), Tobha Mòr (Howmore) and Lionacleit and Balinavich on Benbecula. There is also a regular bus service between Lochboisdale and Ludag (for ferries to Barra). A causeway links Eriskay to South Uist. **CalMac** operates a ferry to Eriskay from Barra, see page 359.

Uibhist a Tuath (North Uist) Colour map 1, C1.

rare birdlife, great fishing and prehistoric sites

North Uist is the largest island in the southern chain of the Outer Hebrides, about 13 miles from north to south and 18 miles east to west at its widest point. At first sight it comes as something of a disappointment after the dramatic landscapes of Harris. In fact, it's barely a landscape at all, as over a third of the island's surface is covered by water. The east coast around Lochmaddy, the main settlement, is so peppered with lochs it resembles a giant sieve. But, heading west from Lochmaddy, the island's attractions become apparent, particularly the magnificent beaches on the north and west coasts. Also on the west coast, is the Balranald Nature Reserve, the ideal place for birdwatching. You're also likely to see otters. There are numerous prehistoric sites scattered across the island and, with all that water around, there's obviously plenty of good fishing to be had.

Loch nam Madadh (Lochmaddy)

Lochmaddy, the island's main village and ferry port, is a tiny place, so small you're almost through it before you realize. Though it's on the east coast and not close to the beaches, it's a good start point and base for exploring the island as it boasts most facilities. It has a bank, a hotel and pub, a tourist office, a few shops, post office, hospital and petrol station.

If you have time, the **Taigh Chearsabhagh Museum and Arts Centre** ① *T01876-500293, www.taigh-chearsabhagh.org, Mon-Sat 1000-1700, £3, £1.50 concession*, is worth visiting and has a small café (open Monday to Saturday 1000-1600) and a post office (open Monday to Friday 1000-1600). You can also purchase home-made preserves, crafts and even Harris Tweed handbags. The seasonal **iCentre** (see page 350) will provide transport timetables and sells a number of useful walking maps if you plan to hike the beaches and hills.

Around the island

There are a number of interesting archaeological sites of different periods dotted around the island. The most notable is **Barpa Langass**, seven miles southwest of Lochmaddy on the slope of Ben Langass, just off the A867, which cuts across the bleak peaty hinterland of North Uist. This is a huge chambered burial cairn dating from around 3000 BC. Unfortunately, it is now too dangerous to enter. About a mile away, on the southern side of Ben Langass, is the small stone circle known as **Pobull Fhinn**, standing on the edge of Loch Langass. Three miles northwest of Lochmaddy on the A865 are three Bronze Age standing stones called **Na Fir Bhreige** (The False Men), said to be the graves of three spies who were buried alive.

The real charms of North Uist, though, are the fabulous beaches on its north and west coasts. Heading anti-clockwise from Lochmaddy, the A865 runs northwest, passing the turning for Otternish and the wild and beautiful lands of Bearnaraigh (see below), which is now connected to North Uist by a causeway. It continues west through the township of **Sollas** (Solas), where there are a couple of B&Bs, and then passes the beautiful sands of **Bhalaigh** (Vallay) **Strand**. Near the northwestern tip of the island, standing on an islet in Loch Scolpaig, is **Scolpaig Tower**, a 'folly' built to provide employment and income for local men in the 19th century.

Three miles south of here is the turning to **Balranald RSPB Reserve**, an area of rocky coast, sandy beaches and dunes, machair and lochs. The reserve is ideal for watching birds, especially waders. A two-hour guided walk along the headland allows you to see Manx shearwaters, gannets, skuas and storm petrels, and, during the summer, you can listen out for the distinctive rasping call of the corncrake, one of the rarest birds in Britain. There's a basic visitor centre which is open from April to September.

As the road continues south, pop into the sparse but tasty **Claddach Kirkibost Centre and Café** ① *T01876-580390, café open Wed-Fri 1100-1500*, a community enterprise that sells peat-smoked salmon, jams and an amazing selection of home-baking, including their famous tablet. A mile further south the A865 meets the A867, which heads east back to Lochmaddy. Staying on the A865, after another mile you can turn off for the tidal and sparsely inhabited island of **Baile Sear** (Baleshare), now connected by a causeway to North Uist and with a three-mile-long beach from where you can just see the low lying **Monach Isles** (also known by their old Norse name of *Heisker*) lying five miles off the west coast. They were once connected to North Uist at low tide until the 16th century, when a huge tidal wave swept away the

Essential Uibhist a Tuath

Finding your feet

There are two car ferry services to North Uist. One is from Leverburgh on South Harris to the Isle of Berneray, which is joined to Uist by a causeway at Otternish; the other is to Lochmaddy from Uig on Skye (one or two daily, the journey takes one hour and 40 minutes). Contact **CalMac** for further information. North Uist is joined to the islands of Benbecula and South Uist to the south by a causeway and bridge. There are several buses daily (Monday to Saturday) from Otternish to Lochmaddy and on to Lochboisdale on South Uist.

sand bridge, thus isolating them. Even so, the islands were inhabited until as recently as the 1930s. Now they are populated by the largest breeding colony of grey seals in Europe.

In Clachan a viewing gallery provides an insight into the fish smoking process of the acclaimed **Hebridean Smokehouse** ① *T01876-580209, www.hebrideansmokehouse.com, Mon-Fri 0800-1730, Sat (in summer) 0900-1700,* and you can also purchase some of their wonderful peat-smoked salmon or scallops South of here the road runs past **Cairinis (Carinish)** and the Carinish Inn over a series of causeways to the little-visited lobster-fishing island of **Griomasaigh (Grimsay)**, before heading across another causeway to Benbecula. Near Cairinis is **Feith na Fala (Field of Blood)**, site of the last battle fought in Scotland solely with swords and bows and arrows, in 1601, between the MacDonalds of Sleat and Macleods of Harris. The bloodshed was provoked by one of the MacDonalds divorcing his Macleod wife. When 60 Skye Macleods set off to North Uist to wreak revenge, they were met by 16 MacDonalds who literally chopped them to pieces, proving that divorce was a messy business even back then.

Listings Uibhist a Tuath (North Uist)

Tourist information

Lochmaddy

iCentre
Near the ferry pier, T01876-500321. Apr-Oct Mon-Sat 0900-1700, and for the arrival of the evening ferry.

Where to stay

£££ Bagh Alluin
21 Baleshare, T01876-580370, www.jacvolbeda.co.uk.
This aptly named B&B (it means 'beautiful bay' in Gaelic) has 2 bright, airy and very spacious, modern bedrooms. The ground-floor room has underfloor heating, its own entrance and south-facing French windows.

£££ Langass Lodge
Near Pobhull Fhinn, T01876-580285, www.langasslodge.co.uk.
12 en suite rooms. Stylish and comfortable accommodation in this secluded hotel overlooking a sea loch. Some rooms are in the main lodge while others (more expensive) are in the new hillside extension with fabulous views of the loch. Friendly, and welcomes children. The restaurant has a menu rich in local seafood and game (dinner £££) or you can enjoy the wonderful

food in the more informal bar setting. Recommended.

The same couple also run **£££ Hamersay House**, T01876-500700, www.hamersay house.co.uk, a small and stylish guesthouse with 10 rooms offering the same levels of comfort and also serving great food in their brasserie (**££**).

£££ Lochmaddy Hotel
Right by the ferry terminal, Lochmaddy, T01876-500332, www.lochmaddyhotel.co.uk. Open all year.
15 en suite rooms (8 with sea view), the family rooms are great value. The restaurant and bar serve good-value food (**££**) in a pleasant setting (restaurant open for dinner 1730-2100, bar open 0900-2100). Also offers takeaway (**£**) burgers, fish, etc, daily 1730-2030. This is the place to ask about fishing, as they rent out boats and sell permits for trout and salmon fishing. Proud of its walker- and cycle-friendly status, and this is reflected in its drying rooms and lockable bike storage facilities for guests.

£££ Temple View Hotel
On the main road, Carinish, T01876-580676, www.templeviewhotel.co.uk.
10 rooms, 4 singles, 6 double/twin, 1 of which has disabled facilities. This is a lovely,

modest family-run hotel which has recently been extended, with views towards the 13th-century ruin of Trinity Temple. Hearty meals served in the dining room daily 1200-1400 and 1800-2100 (**££**).

££ Ardnastruban House
Just off the A865, Grimsay, T01870-602452, www.ardnastrubanhouse.co.uk. Open all year.
2 rooms. This friendly guesthouse is surrounded by wildlife and rugged scenery. Excellent value.

££ The Old Shop House
Bayhead, T01876-510395, www.theoldshophouse.co.uk.
Has 2 en suite rooms on ground floor, 1 is a twin/family room and 1 a double. Friendly and comfortable B&B run by Mrs Morag Nicholson. Great value.

Self-catering

Tigh na Boireach
4 Clachan Sands, T07884-277236, www.tichnaboireach or book through www.uistcottages.co.uk.

Sleep in a 4-poster bed in this modernized yet traditional thatched blackhouse surrounded by wildlife and rugged scenery. Sleeps 2.

Restaurants

A number of eating options can be found under Where to stay, above.

What to do

Birdwatching
Western Isles Wildlife, *7 Carinish, T01876-580619, www.western-isles-wildlife.co.uk.* The only bird and wildlife tour company based on the islands. Steve Duffield runs day tours at £55 pp.

Transport

For information on local bus journeys, see Finding your feet, page 349.

Bearnaraigh (Berneray) *Colour map 1, B1.*

fantastic beaches and delicious seafood

Ferries from Leverburgh on Harris arrive at the low-lying island of Bearnaraigh (believed to be Old Norse for Bear Island) connected by a causeway to North Uist. The island, rich in birdlife, is famous as the place where Prince Charles spent a holiday helping out on a croft. It's also the birthplace of Angus 'Giant' MacAskill, see page 294. Its real attraction, though, apart from the splendid isolation and its cosy Lobster Pot Tearoom (see Restaurants, page 352) at Ardmaree is the long sandy beach along its western shoreline. On the east coast, there are more stunning white sands, behind which stands the fabulously earthy bunkhouse of the Gatliff Trust with views over the skerries and to the brooding rounded hills of Harris.

A half-mile east of the Lobster Pot is the **Berneray Historical Society and Visitor Centre** ① *Mon-Fri 1100-1500, internet access £1 for 20 mins, admission by donation*, with photographs and exhibits highlighting the hardy life islanders once endured.

A booklet for Bearnaraigh, *Visit Berneray* is available from **Lochmaddy iCentre** (see page 350). It describes all of the key places of interest, including the 16th-century gunnery at **Baile**, the beaches and machair of the north and west coasts, and archaeological sites dating from the Viking period near **Borgh**. It also highlights a lovely 7½-mile-long circular walk. **Berneray Week** (late July) is a busy week with several ceilidhs held in the community hall and attracting visitors from far afield – including Gaelic-speaking Germans!

Where to stay

£ Gatliff Trust Hostel
1 mile up the east coast from the old ferry pier, www.gatliff.co.uk, T0870-1553255. Open all year.
No advance bookings just turn up and hope there's a bed, though you won't be turned away even if they're full. Relax in 2 restored and truly rustic blackhouses overlooking a lovely sandy beach and old Viking pier. 12 beds, shower, no phone. It's far from luxurious but it's true old-world, earthy hostelling and the views are priceless. £16 for a hostel bed, £8 for under 18s and £11 to camp. Recommended.

Self-catering

The Smiddy
Burnside Croft, near 3-mile west beach, T01876-540235, www.burnsidecroft.com.
Superior self-catering experience for 2 with all mod cons. Excellent walking, birdlife and beaches in the area. £780 per week in Jul-Aug. Sleeps 2.

Restaurants

££-£ Ardmaree Stores & Lobster Pot Tearoom
T01876-540288. Mon-Sat 0900-1800 in summer, 0900-1730 in winter.
Aside from a packed grocery shop (they'll deliver to the **Gatliff Trust Hostel**), there is a friendly café (the only on the island) where you can tuck into toasties, crayfish salads, Hebridean smokehouse's famous peat-smoked salmon and home-baking. They also provide lots of good tourist information on the island and sell permits for trout fishing on nearby Loch Bhrusda.

Transport

Ferry
From **Berneray** to **Harris**, 3-4 times daily, 1 hr.

Beinn na Faoghla (Benbecula) *Colour map 1, C1.*

miles of glorious white sand

Tiny Benbecula (population 1803) may be suffering from delusions of stature. Its Gaelic name means 'mountain of the fords', but the highest point is a mere 407 ft, with the rest of the island as flat as a pancake. It lies between Protestant North Uist and Catholic South Uist, and most visitors use it solely as a means of getting from one to the other via the A865, which cuts straight through the middle.

Sights

Like North Uist, the east of the island is so pitted with lochs that most people live on the west coast. Until recently, a large percentage of the population were Royal Artillery personnel stationed at **Baile a Mhanaich (Balivanich)**, a sprawling army base of utilitarian buildings in the northwest of the island. There's little to hold your interest in this village dominated by the (albeit diminishing presence) of the military and civilian airport. There is a **Bank of Scotland** (ATM), a post office, **MacLennans Supermarket** (T01870-602308) and you can browse for high-quality tweeds, hand-knitted jumpers, confectionery, prints and jewellery at **MacGillivrays** (T01870-602525), or visit the notable **Stepping Stone** restaurant.

South of Balivanich, the B892 runs around the west coast offering the opportunity to stroll down miles of white sands before joining the main A865 at the southern end of the island. It runs past **Culla Bay**, overlooked by **Baille nan Cailleach (Nunton)**. It was from here in 1746 that Bonnie Prince Charlie, disguised as a maid, set off with Flora MacDonald over the sea to Skye, see box, page 291. To the south is **Poll-na-Crann**, better known as 'stinky bay' because of the piles of seaweed deposited there by fierce Atlantic storms. From the mid-18th century this kelp was used to provide soda ash for making glass and provided a source of income for many communities. By 1820 the so-called kelp boom was over, but it is still gathered today and used as fertilizer.

The B892 ends at **Lionacleit (Liniclate)**, where the community school serves the Uists and Benbecula. It has extensive facilities, including a swimming pool, library, theatre and the small **Museum nan Eilean** ① *T01870-602864, Mon, Tue and Thu 0900-1600, Wed 0900-1230, 1330-1600, Fri 0900-2000, Sat 1100-1300, 1400-1600, free*, all housed in the community school building. Close by, there's a very large Co-op supermarket at Creagorry and a petrol station, the only one for miles around.

Essential Beinn na Faoghla

Finding your feet

Benbecula's airport is at Balivanich (T01870-602310) and there are direct flights from Glasgow, Barra and Stornoway. For flight details visit www.hial.co.uk. The island is connected by causeways to North and South Uist, and buses travelling from Lochmaddy and Lochboisdale pass through the villages of Balivanich, Lionacleit (Liniclate) and Creag Ghoraidh (Creagorry). There are also regular island buses which run between these settlements. For further details, see Transport, page 354.

Listings Beinn na Faoghla (Benbecula)

Where to stay

£££ Dark Island Hotel
Lionacleit, T01870-603030, www. isleshotelgroup.co.uk. Open all year.
38 en suite rooms. Comfortable and perfectly serviceable accommodation, family rooms are good value at £150 for up to 4 (kids in bunk beds). Meals available in the restaurant or bar (**££-£**). The same group also run the **£££ Isle of Benbecula Hotel**, T01870-603046, which has similar standard of comfort and cuisine.

££ Hebrides House
Inniscarra, Lionacleit, T01870-603813.
6 en suite rooms. Very welcoming and comfy B&B and great value. Family room sleeps up to 4 and 1 room has a sauna-steam shower room for added indulgence. Recommended.

Camping

Shellbay Caravan and Camping Park
Lionacleit, T01870-602447. Apr-Oct.

Restaurants

££-£ The Stepping Stone Restaurant
Balivanich, T01870-603377. Mon-Fri 0900-2100, Sat 1100-2100, Sun 1200-2100.
The best place to eat on Benbecula, with family links to the acclaimed **MacLeans Bakery** (of Hebridean Oatcake fame), half a mile up the road. Lunchtime specials may include cockles in oatmeal while dinner includes the likes of local lamb and dessert of traditional crowdie and cream. 3-course set Sun lunch (£15).

Transport

Air
Loganair, www.loganir.co.uk, flies to/ from **Glasgow**, **Edinburgh**, **Inverness** and **Stornoway**, Mon-Sat, twice daily.

Car hire
Ask Car Hire, Linicleit, T01870-602818 www.askcarhire.com; **Maclennan Bros Ltd**, Balivanich, T01870-602191; **Car Hire Hebrides**, T01870-603228, in the airport terminal.

Uibhist a Deas (South Uist)   Colour maps 1, C1 and 3, A1.

great fishing and more beautiful beaches

South Uist (population 2285) is the largest of the southern chain of Outer Hebridean islands and, like North Uist and Berneray, isn't lacking in wildlife, fishing and dramatic scenery. However, like its southern neighbour, Barra, South Uist is Roman Catholic and generally more relaxed about Sunday openings. Its 20-mile-long west coast is one sandy beach, backed by dunes, with a mile or two of beautiful, flowering machair behind. To the east of the main A865, which runs the length of the island, rises a central mountainous spine of rock and peat dotted with numerous lochs. Its two highest peaks, Beinn Mhor (2034 ft) and Hecla (1988 ft), tower over the rocky cliffs of an inaccessible eastern coastline indented by sea lochs.

Loch Baghasdail (Lochboisdale)
South Uists's largest settlement is set on a rocky promontory in a beautiful island-dotted sea loch. The imposing entrance is guarded by Calvay Island with its 13th-century castle ruin. Lochboisdale is a tiny place, with little in the way of tourist sights, though it does have a few hotels, a bank with ATM and a post office.

There is also a Co-op with cash machine and a post office at **Daliburgh**, a few miles west of Lochboisdale, and a Lovats supermarket, cash machine and a post office at **Carnan**, at the north end of the island.

Essential Uibhist a Deas

Finding your feet

The island's main ferry port is Lochboisdale, which is reached from Oban four times a week (arriving at night) and twice a week from Castlebay on Barra. There's one direct sailing from Oban on Tuesday, Thursday and Saturday (five hours and 20 minutes), and one via Castlebay (Barra) on Sunday (six hours and 30 minutes). There are also early morning departures (0700) from Castlebay on Wednesday and Friday, and at 2010 on Sundays. There are limited bus services on Sundays. For further details, see Transport, page 357.

Around the island
At the north of the island a causeway leads across **Loch Bi** (pronounced 'Bee') to the distinctive modern statue of Our Lady of the Isles, standing by the main road on the lower slopes of **Rueval Hill**. Further up the hill is the Royal Artillery control centre, known by the locals as 'Space City', due to its forest of aerials and 'golf balls', which tracks the missiles fired from a range on the northwestern corner of the island out into the Atlantic. However, to home in on delicious food and a comfortable stay, it's worthwhile following the signs for the **Orasay Inn** by Lochcarnan (see Where to stay, page 356). Just 1½ miles further down the road, you can further tickle your tastebuds by popping into the shop of the

BACKGROUND
South Uist

The dominant family in South Uist was Clanranald, who also owned Benbecula. They were descendants of the first Lord of the Isles, who was a MacDonald. The island's connections with Clanranald came to a sorry end, however, in 1837, when it was sold, along with Benbecula, to pay off bad debts, and became the property of the infamous Lieutenant-Colonel John Gordon of Cluny. Though all the southern isles suffered during the brutal Clearances of the 19th century, the experiences of people on South Uist were particularly cruel and inhumane. Between 1849 and 1851 over 2000 were forcibly shipped to Quebec in Canada. Those who refused to board the transport ships were hunted down by dogs and bound, before being thrown on board and shipped to Canada, where they were left to starve. Today, owned by the community, the destiny of South Uist fortunately lies in the islanders' hands.

acclaimed **Salar Smokehouse** ① *T01870-610324, www.salarsmokehouse.co.uk*, for some of their famous flaky smoked salmon.

Just to the south of here is **Loch Druidibeag Nature Reserve**, on the site of the large freshwater loch, one of the largest breeding grounds in the British Isles for greylag geese and also a favourite haunt of mute swans (there's a warden nearby at Groigearraidh Lodge). From here the main road runs down the spine of the island; all along the way little tracks branch off to the west, leading down to lovely beaches.

Not far south of Loch Druidibeag is the turning to the tiny village of **Tobha Mòr** (**Howmore**), where you can see a collection of old traditional thatched blackhouses beside the seemingly endless stretch of golden sand. One of the houses has been converted into a **Gatliff Trust Youth Hostel**, see Where to stay, page 356. From the hostel, it's a five-minute walk across the machair to the sandy beach which stretches almost the entire length of South Uist.

Periodically, down the A865 you'll spot signs for accessing paths across the machair. In addition, from Tobha Mòr, there are superb walks through the lonely hills of **Beinn Mhor** (620 m), **Beinn Corodale** (527 m) and **Hecla** (606 m) to the picturesque and dramatic valleys of Glen Hellisdale, Glen Corodale and Glen Usinish on the east coast. In 1746 that ubiquitous troglodyte, Bonnie Prince Charlie is reputed to have taken refuge in a cave above **Corodale Bay** for three weeks after his defeat and escape from Culloden.

Near **Bornais** (**Bornish**) another minor road can be followed east of the A865 to **Loch Eynort**, which penetrates far inland from the Minch. An old stalkers' path can be followed along the north shore of the loch towards the sea, with views of numerous seals, the occasional otter and the steep upper slopes of Beinn Mhor towering above to the north.

A few miles south, at **Gearraidh Bhailteas** (**Milton**), a memorial cairn sits amidst the ruins of the cottage that was Flora (Flory) MacDonald's birthplace, that famous Hebridean lass who helped save the skin of Bonnie Prince Charlie, see box, page 291. Nearby is the **Kildonan Centre** ① *Apr-Oct daily 1000-1700*, which houses a museum with exhibits of the area's history, craft work and archaeology, a craft shop, a Gaelic culture performance room and also Barbara's café. A few miles further on, the A865 cuts east to the island's main ferry port of **Lochboisdale**. For those in search of great food and tremendous views towards Eriskay and Barra, leave the A865 for the B888 and enjoy the hospitality of the 17th-century **Polochar Inn** (see Where to stay, page 356) on the southwestern tip of South Uist.

Where to stay

£££ Lochboisdale Hotel
*Close to the ferry terminal, Lochboisdale,
T01878-700332, www.lochboisdalehotel.com.
Open all year.*
16 en suite rooms. Family-owned hotel with
music sessions every fortnight and frequent,
spontaneous outbreaks of fiddling by the
open fire. They cater for fishing tourists and
will arrange trips for £130 for 2 people, also
have a rod room for guests' equipment
and the chef will freeze your catch or
even prepare it for taking home.

£££-££ Orasay Inn
*Lochcarnan, T01878-610298, www.
orasayinn.com. Open all year.*
9 en suite rooms. Small, friendly, family-run
hotel. A variety of rooms at different prices
but the restaurant (1200-2100) is the star
attraction, serving up delicious lunches
(£) and dinners (££). Don't miss their
scallops with bacon or freshly caught crab.
Recommended.

£££-££ Polochar Inn
*A few miles to the west of Ludag, Pollachar,
T01878-700215, www.polocharinn.com.
Open all year.*
11 comfortable en suite rooms. Terrific
food (see Restaurants, below), stunning
views towards Barra. A small, refurbished
hotel steeped in history, with its 1750 built
walls and Neolithic standing stone by
the shore. Live music till the wee small
hours in the summer months. Great value.
Recommended.

££ Anglers Retreat
*Ardmore, T01870-610325, www.
anglersretreat.net. Mar-Dec.*
3 en suite rooms and a 4-berth EcoPod
(£75 per night). Comfortable, modern
guesthouse that's perfect for the keen angler
and birdwatcher as the owners have a ton of
information and can even provide a ghillie

service for £65 per day. Dog friendly with
specially built kennels for 4-legged visitors.
Will provide packed lunch for £6 a head and
3-course dinner for £20.

££ Borrodale Hotel
*At the junction where the road splits south to
Eriskay and east to Lochboisdale, Dalabrog,
T01878-700444, www.isleshotelgroup.co.uk.*
12 rooms. Run by the same group that have
the **Dark Island** and **Isle of Benbecula** hotels
(see above), same standards and good food
but a bit cheaper. Family room is £100 for up
to 4. Hearty lunch (£) from 1200 and dinner
(££) from 1800-2100.

£ Gatliff Trust Youth Hostel
Howmore, www.gatliff.co.uk. Open all year.
Converted blackhouse which overlooks the
ruins of an ancient church and graveyard,
beside the seemingly endless stretch of
golden sand. 16 beds in 3 shared rooms, no
phone. £16 for a hostel bed, £8 for under 18s
and £11 to camp. The warden of the hostel also
runs **Rothan Cycles**, see What to do, opposite.

Restaurants

£££-££ Orasay Inn
*See Where to stay, above, in
the northeast, Lochcarnan.*
Isobel, the owner/chef, is a 'Natural Cooking
of Scotland' trainer. Expect fresh and locally
sourced game, lamb, beef, shellfish and
vegetables, as well as freshly baked breads,
scones and home-made desserts. The dining
is relaxed, the service attentive and expect a
warm welcome. Recommended.

£££-££ Polochar Inn
See Where to stay, above.
Good range of lunch and dinner options,
with an emphasis on locally sourced
produce. Try the hearty cullen skink (seafood)
soup, the flakey smoked salmon with
mussels or the leg of Uist lamb. Rustic interior
with attentive service. Terrific food.

What to do

Birdwatching

Gannets, golden eagles and the elusive corncrake can all be seen on South Uist. **Loch Druidibeg Nature Reserve**, in the north of the island, www.isle-of-south-uist.co.uk, is a great place to spot wildlife, including redshank and otters. Or book a tour with Western Isles Wildlife, see page 351.

Cycling

Cycle hire Rothan Cycles, *on the A856 by the turn-off for the Gatliff Trust Hostel, 9 Howmore, T01870-620283, www.rothan.com.* Hires basic bikes for £10 and tourers for £12. It's £18 and £20 respectively for 2 days. Will also repair your bike and deliver to/pick-up at Eriksay (£20), Lochboisdale (£15), the airport (£18) and Berneray (£28).

★ Fishing

South Uist is one of the best places in the country, if not the world, to catch wild brown trout. There are some 800 lochs and lochans between South Uist and Benbecula and most of them contain wild brown trout. You can fish the lochs of South Uist through **Storas Uibhuist**, T01878-700101, or email fishing@ storasuibhist,com, or the **South Uist Angling Club**, www.southuistfishing.com. Permits can be obtained through the Lochboisdale Hotel (see Where to stay, above). The brown trout season runs from 1 Apr to 30 Sep, the sea trout/salmon season run from early- to mid-Jul to end of Oct.

Golf

Askernish Golf Club, *Lochboisdale, South Uist, T01878-700083, www.askernishgolfclub. com.* 'Rediscovered' amidst the machair, this is now regarded by the golfing cognoscenti as one of the world's classic links courses, having been laid out in 1891 by the legendary Scottish golfer and course designer, 'Old Tom Morris.'

Transport

Car hire

Laing Motors, Lochboisdale, T01870-700267, www.laingmotors.co.uk.

Ferry

No boats leave South Uist on Sun. **Lochboisdale** to **Oban**, 1 daily, Tue, Thu and Sat, 5 hrs 20 mins and via **Castlebay** (Barra) on Sun, 6 hrs 30 mins.

Eirisgeidh (Eriskay) *Colour map 3, A1.*

starting point for the Jacobite Rebellion and site of a famous shipwreck

The tiny island of Eriskay, with a population of less than 200, gives its name to the native breed of pony said to have been ridden by King Robert the Bruce at the Battle of Bannockburn in 1314. In the late 1970s the ponies nearly became extinct, but one surviving stallion saved the breed and numbers are growing. A series of paths take you around the island in about three hours. For more details, see www.walkhighlands.co.uk.

Most people come to Eriskay to pay a visit to **Coilleag a' Phrionnsa** (**Prince's beach**), the sandy beach on the west coast where Bonnie Prince Charlie first stepped on to Scottish soil on 23 July 1745, at the start of the ill-fated Jacobite Rebellion. The rare pink convolvulus (field bindweed) which grows there today is said to have been planted by the Prince himself from seeds brought from France. A small memorial cairn in the dunes behind the beach was erected by the local school to commemorate the occasion. Just 200 yds away is the CalMac jetty that will take you to neighbouring Barra.

Tight little island

Between Eriskay and South Uist is the wreck of the famous *SS Politician*, the island's other claim to fame. In 1941 the 12,000 ton ship went aground just off the island of Calvey and sank with its cargo, which included 20,000 cases of whisky. This not only provided many islanders with a supply of whisky for many years, but also provided the plot for Compton Mackenzie's book *Whisky Galore!*, which was later made into the famous Ealing comedy of the same name (called *Tight Little Island* in the US) and filmed on Barra. It's very difficult to spot the wreck, even at low tide, but if you pop into the friendly Am Politician pub in the village on Eriksay, Baile (Balla), you'll find more information and some memorabilia.

It's now almost impossible to see the wreck of the *SS Politician* (see box, above) when crossing the causeway from South Uist (look left), but at the **Am Politician** pub you can (carefully) hold an original whisky bottle taken from its hold and look at other artefacts from the wreck. Another sight worth seeing is **St Michael's**, the Roman Catholic church built in 1903 and funded by the local fishing fleet.

Listings Eirisgeidh (Eriskay)

Where to stay

Self-catering

Aird na Haun
T0141-321 1326, www.eriskayselfcatering.com.
2 self-catering apartments, 1 on ground floor sleeps 8 and 1 on upper floor sleeps 4. Well-equipped and very comfortable and great location by the beach. £300-700 per week depending on season.

Camping

You can wild camp on the machair at Howbeg near the Gatliff Trust hostel at Howmore, or in the grounds of the hostel, and you can use the facilities if you pay the camping fee.

Restaurants

££-£ Am Politician
Baile, see box, above.
This pub serves food (1200-2100), and occasionally hosts live bands. Its small conservatory offers lovely views over the sea.

Bharraigh (Barra), Bhatarsaigh (Vatersay) and Mingulay   *Colour map 3, A1.*

the best of the Outer Hebrides in miniature

★ Bharraigh

It may be tempting to overlook the little island of Barra, only about eight miles long by five miles wide, but that would be a mistake, as it's one of the most beautiful of all the islands in the Outer Hebrides – 'Barradise' indeed. Here, despite an appalling lack of public toilets (there are only three: at the Ardmhor Ferry Terminal, Eoligarry and Castlebay Hall) and other facilities for campers (wild camping is tolerated) you'll find the best of the islands in miniature – beaches, machair, peat-covered hills, tiny crofting communities and Neolithic remains. A couple of days spent on Barra, including excursions to the wild and beautiful lands of Vatersay and the outlying (deserted) Isle of Mingulay, gives a real taste of Hebridean life. Gaelic and the traditional fishing culture is also strong here but, with its Catholicism, Barra is arguably more laid-back than its northern neighbours which strictly observe the Sabbath.

Bàgh a' Chaisteil (Castlebay) The main settlement is Castlebay, on the southern side of the island, situated in a wide sheltered bay and overlooked by **Sheabhal** (383 m), on top of which is a marble statue of the Blessed Virgin and Child. It's a short but steep walk up to the top from the town, and the views are well worth it. The once-thriving herring port is also overlooked by the large Roman Catholic church, **Our Lady, Star of the Sea**.

As the main ferry port, rather drab Castlebay provides the full range of services: hotels, B&Bs, shops, petrol, a bank (with ATM) and post office. There's a Co-op supermarket and AC MacLean which is a shop/petrol station. The helpful little tourist information centre has sadly closed, like many such information centres in the Highlands and Islands.

Castlebay's most notable feature is the impressive 15th-century **Kisimul Castle** ⓘ *T01871-810313, Apr-Sep daily 0930-1730, £6, concessions £4.80, children £3.60, including boat trip*, reached by boat from Castlebay pier (five minutes), weather permitting, built on an island in the middle of the harbour. This was the ancient home of the Chief of the MacNeils, one of the oldest Scottish clans, who owned the island from 1427 until 1838. It was then sold to the notorious Colonel Gordon of Cluny, along with neighbouring South Uist and Benbecula (see pages 354 and 352), and the poor people of Barra suffered the same cruel fate, 600 of them being shipped to Canada to starve. One hundred years later the castle and much of the island was bought back for the MacNeils by an

Essential Bharraigh

Finding your feet

The best way to arrive is by air at Tràigh Mhòr ('Cockle Strand'), the famous airstrip on the beach at the north end of the island. This is the only airport in the UK where flight schedules are shown as 'subject to tides' and wild campers are warned to keep off the beach on hearing the drone of an aircraft. For airport information, T01871-890283, www.hial.co.uk. **Loganair**, T0344-800 28550, www.loganair.co.uk, flies from Glasgow to Barra, Monday to Saturday once or twice a day. The journey takes one hour and five minutes.

Barra can also be reached by car ferry from Oban on the mainland, by car ferry from Lochboisdale on South Uist (Monday at 0730, Tuesday at 1900 and Thursday at 2100, one hour 40 minutes) and from Eriskay, five times daily, journey time is 40 minutes. Ferries run once daily direct from Oban taking four hours and 50 minutes except on Tuesdays and Thursdays when they go via Lochboisdale (see above) taking seven hours and 20 minutes.

Getting around

There is a regular bus service (Monday to Saturday) that runs from Castlebay to the ferry port of Eòlaigearraidh, via the airport. There are also buses (Monday to Saturday) from Castlebay to Bhatarsaigh (Vatersay) and a service that runs from Castlebay east or west around the island to/from Airdmhor and Eòlaigearraidh. You can hire a car or a bicycle to tour the island at your leisure. It's 14 miles round the main road. For further details, see Transport, page 363.

American architect, Robert Lister MacNeil, who became the 45th Clan Chief and restored the castle to its present state before his death in 1970. His son, Ian Roderick MacNeil, used it as his residence when visiting the island, before handing it over to Historic Scotland in 2000 on a 1000-year lease, in exchange for a rent of £1 and a bottle of whisky.

If you're interested in finding out about the island's history, you should visit the Barra Heritage Cultural Centre, known as **Dualchas** ⓘ *T01871-810413, www.barraheritage.com, Apr-Oct Mon-Sat 1030-1630, £3, concessions £2, children £1.*

Around the island The A888 follows a circular route of 14 miles around the island, making an ideal day's bike tour from Castlebay. Heading west, it passes the turning for the causeway to **Vatersay** (see below), then runs north past stunning beaches including **Halaman Bay**, near the village of Tangasdal (**Tangasdale**) and overlooked by the Isle of Barra Beach Hotel (see Where to stay, opposite), before climbing between two hills (Sheabhal to the east and Beinn Tangabhal to the west). Before reaching the north coast, at the turning for **Borgh** (**Borve**) there are standing stones followed by the small settlement of **Baile Na Creige** (**Craigston**), where you'll find the **An Dubharaidh Thatched Cottage Museum** ⓘ *Easter-Oct Mon-Fri 1100-1700, £2*, an original white house, and the chambered burial cairn of **Dun Bharpa**. From Dun Bharpa there are pleasant walks into the surrounding hills, with the summit of **Sheabhal** offering tremendous views from the highest point on the island.

Near **Allathsdal** (**Allasdale**) is another lovely beach and, just beyond, are the remains of **Dun Cuier**, an Iron Age fort. Make a short detour at Greian, and follow the headland to the rugged cliffs at **Greian Head**.

The A888 then descends eastwards to **Bagh a Tuath** (**Northbay**), where a branch left leads to the village of **Eòlaigearraidh** (**Eoligarry**), near the northern tip, surrounded by sandy bays washed by Atlantic rollers. A private passenger ferry leaves from here to Ludag on South Uist.

The road to Eoligarry passes the island's airport at **Tràigh Mhòr**, the 'Cockle Strand', which once provided 100 to 200 cartloads of delicious cockles each day. Now the cockle-shells are gathered and used for harling, the roughcast wall covering used on many Scottish houses. By the beach is the house that was once the home of Compton MacKenzie, author of *Whisky Galore!*, see box, page 358. He lies buried at picturesque **Cille Bhara**, to the west of the village of Eòlaigearraidh, along with members of the MacNeil clan. This was one of the most important religious complexes in the Outer Hebrides, built in the 12th century, and consists of a tiny church and two chapels. One of these, St Mary's, has been re-roofed and houses several carved medieval tombstones and a copy of a runic stone. Much to the chagrin of locals, the original stone is in the Museum of Scotland in Edinburgh.

Bhatarsaigh (Vatersay) and Mingulay

A worthwhile trip from Castlebay is to the island of Vatersay, linked since 1990 to Barra by a causeway built in an effort to stabilize the tiny community (around 70) on what is the most southerly inhabited Outer Hebridean island. Home to the acclaimed folk singing group The Vatersay Boys, it boasts several idyllic sands including two shell-sand beaches backed by machair, only a few hundred yards apart on either side of the narrow isthmus that leads to the main settlement of Vatersay. On the west beach, Bagh Siar, is the **Annie Jane Monument**, commemorating the terrible tragedy in 1853, when the emigrant ship *Annie Jane* was wrecked off the coast of Vatersay, with the loss of 333 lives, many of them islanders. There's a scenic four-mile circular walk from the monument. You can buy coffee and sandwiches at the café in the **Vatersay Community Hall** ① *Apr-Oct 1000-1700* (also, note, the only public toilets on the island), and wild camp or park your campervan nearby (£4 donation to the Vatersay Township).

On a clear day from Vatersay you can enjoy the view of the smaller islands to the south – Sandray, Pabbay and Mingulay. The latter was inhabited until 1912 and can still be visited from Barra. It was acquired by the National Trust for Scotland in 2000. For details of tours, see Barra Fishing Charters, page 362.

Listings Bharraigh (Barra), Bhatarsaigh (Vatersay) and Mingulay

Where to stay

Barra
It's a good idea to book in advance if arriving on the evening ferry from Oban. There are neither independent hostels nor a Gatliff Trust Hostel on Barra.

££££-£££ Castlebay Hotel
Overlooking the ferry terminal and Kisimul Castle, Castlebay, T01871-810223, www. castlebayhotel.com. Open all year.
10 en suite rooms, most are in the **£££** range though the MacNeil room is a bit more expensive. Dinner B&B is £15 extra, 2-night minimum stay. Arguably, the best place to stay on the island, combining comfort with tasty, good-value food (**£££-££**) and a lively, adjoining public bar.

£££ Heathbank Hotel
Castlebay, T01871-890266, www.barrahotel.co.uk.
5 spotless en suite rooms of varying sizes with a bar/restaurant downstairs serving good food Apr-Sep daily 1300-2000. Bar open daily 1300-2300 in summer and Wed-Sun 1600-2300 in winter.

£££ Isle of Barra Beach Hotel
2 miles west of Castlebay, T01871-810383, www.isleofbarrahotel.co.uk. May-Sep only.
38 en suite rooms and a good restaurant (**£££-££**) and selection of bar food (**£**). Fabulous views of the white sands below, though the 1970s exterior isn't exactly in keeping with the landscape. 2-night minimum stay. Adjacent to the hotel is the

self-contained 'Bolt Hole' with 6 beds. The hotel also hires out cars or electric bikes.

£££-££ Craigard Hotel
Castlebay, T01871-810200, www. craigardhotel.co.uk. Open all year.
7 en suite rooms. Great views from the conservatory over the bay, reasonable food and walls adorned with photos from the filming of *Whisky Galore!*

££ Tigh-Na-Mara
Castlebay, T01871-810304, www. tighnamara-barra.co.uk. Apr-Oct.
5 rooms. Comfortable and welcoming guesthouse only a few mins' walk from the ferry terminal.

£ Dunard Hostel & Lodge
Just along from the Co-op and Heritage Museum, Castlebay, T01871-810443, www.dunardhostel.co.uk.
This bright, well-equipped hostel offers 2 twin rooms (£45), a family room (£65) and 2 4-bed bunk rooms(£20 pp) as well as a sitting room and fully equipped kitchen. The **Garden Lodge** has 3 twin rooms, a double room and guests' sitting room. There are also 2 garden town cabins (£40) with use of the hostel facilities. This is also the place to come to arrange sea kayaking with **Clearwater Paddling** (see What to do, below).

Self-catering
There are many options on Barra. As well as the www.visitouterhebrides.co.uk, check out www.isleofbarra.com.

Camping

The island's main campsite is at Borve Point (west Barra), T01871-810878, www.barracamping.co.uk, with all facilities. 18 pitches. £16 for 2-person tent, £19 for campervan and hook-up. For provisions, there are 2 well-stocked mini-supermarkets in Castlebay, as well as hotels and cafés.

Vatersay
Self-catering

Those who find Barra too busy can escape to the silence and golden sands of neighbouring Vatersay. For other self-catering options on Vatersay, check out www.visitouterhebrides.co.uk or barra-accommodation.co.uk.

Vatersay School
Mrs Patricia Barron, T01871-810283, www.vatersayschool.co.uk.
A converted schoolhouse overlooking a glorious south-facing beach. It sleeps 6 and gets booked up well in advance.

Restaurants

Barra

The best places for an evening meal are the **Castlebay Hotel** in Castlebay or the **Isle of Barra Beach Hotel** at Tangasdale Beach (both **£££-££**). See Where to stay, above.

££ Café Kisimul
On the main street, Castlebay, T01871-810645, www.cafekisimul.co.uk.
The place to feast on tasty Italian and Indian fare with a seafood twist.

££-£ The Deck at the Hebridean Toffee Shop
On the main street, Castlebay, T01871-810898. Mar, Apr and May Mon-Sat 1000-1700, Jun-Aug Mon-Sat 1000-1800, Sun 1200-1700, Sep-Feb Thu 1000-1700, Fri 7 Sat 1000-1900.
Produces 1st-class toffee (tablet) and will serve you tea, sandwiches and great home-baking on its deck overlooking the castle.

£ Airport Café
Tràigh Mhòr.

A great place to enjoy tea and cakes or fish and chips and watch the twin Otters take off and land on the legendary beach runway.

£ The Otter Café
Clearly signposted, by the Ardmhar ferry terminal, T01871-890269. Daily.
A great tearoom and you can catch the ferry to Eriskay nearby.

What to do

Barra
Boat trips
Barra Fishing Charters, *Northbay, T01871-890384, www.barrafishingcharters.com.* Run by local fisherman Francis Gillies, who offers a range of trips aboard his 10-m-long cruiser, *Boy James.* Fishing enthusiasts (free tackle and rods) pay £40 for a 4-hr offshore trip. Those who wish to take to the high seas without fishing kit can instead explore the remote but spectacular Hebridean isle of Mingulay from £50pp (£25 per child). This 6-hr trip includes a 2-hr sail from Barra past the neighbouring islands of Sandray and Pabbay, a circumnavigation of Mingulay to view the spectacularly high western sea cliffs, and a landing on the east coast for a 3-hr exploration of the beautiful beach of Mingulay Bay, the deserted village and surrounding hills and coast. There are also fine views to the lighthouse on Barra Head, the most southerly outpost of the Outer Hebrides island chain where, weather permitting, the *Boy James* will also sail. It's also possible to charter the boat for private hire or wildlife excursions. Call for prices.

Cycling
Barra Bike Hire, *T07876-402842, www.barrabikehire.co.uk.* Hires bikes, £16 for full day, £8 for children, booking recommended.

Kayaking
Clearwater Paddling, *just along from the Co-op and Heritage Museum, Dunard, Castlebay, T01871-810443, www.clearwaterpaddling.com.*

Experienced operator that offers a huge range of kayaking and wild camping or lodge-based trips around Barra and the rest of the Hebrides, lasting from 3 nights up to a week. Prices start from £395 for a kayak-only week-long trip up to £785 for all-inclusive.

They also run Isle of **Barra Surf & Coastal Adventures**, www.barrasurfadventures.co.uk, who organize surfing, coasteering, stand-up paddleboard (SUP) and snorkeling trips.

Transport

Barra
Air
Loganair flies to **Glasgow** from Barra, 1 daily, Mon-Sat, 1 hr 5 mins.

Car hire
Barra Car Hire, Hugh MacNeil, Northbay, T01871-890313.

Ferry
Castlebay to **Oban**, Mon, Wed, Fri, Sat, Sun, 4 hrs 50 mins. Also sailings via **Lochboisdale** on Tue and Thu, 7 hrs 20 mins; and a sailing via **Coll** and **Tiree**, Thu, 6 hrs 45 mins. Early morning departures are available to **Lochboisdale**, Wed and Fri 0700, Sun 2050. Ferries sail from Barra to **Eriskay** at least 3 times daily. Bikes are free. For times and fares visit www.calmac.co.uk.

Taxi
Barra Taxis, T01871-810012; **Campbell Taxis**, T01871-810216.

St Kilda

★ Some 41 miles west of the Outer Hebrides lie the spectacular and isolated islands of St Kilda, Scotland's first UNESCO World Heritage Site and home to the largest colony of seabirds in northern Europe. St Kilda consists of several islands, remnants of an ancient volcano, and manages to capture the imagination of most visitors to the Outer Hebrides, whether they actually get there or just dream about romantic voyages to mysterious lands across perilous seas. Inhabited for almost 4000 years until evacuated by its remaining 36 islanders on 29 August 1930, the isles, which are also a National Nature Reserve, were bequeathed to the National Trust for Scotland in 1957. Each year, during the brief summer months, teams of volunteers work on Hirta, maintaining what remains of the abandoned houses, studying the wildlife and glorying in the peace and isolation of a dramatic island group inhabited by a million seabirds and where the Soay sheep has bred for thousands of years.

How St Kilda was killed off

Friday 29 August 1930 was the end of life as it had been for centuries on St Kilda. For a least 1000 years the inhabitants of this remote group of islands had been tenants of the Macleods of Dunvegan on Skye. In earlier days the trip from Skye, undertaken in longboats, would require 16 hours of rigorous rowing and sailing. Even now, the trip to St Kilda is no easy matter.

Until 1930 the islanders had been supported from the mainland by the provision of a nurse and a post office. But the Scottish Office decided that their subsidy of the islands was no longer economic. This meant that life for the residents without those facilities would be untenable.

In 1930, to the younger of the 36 residents, including a man with nine children, evacuation was an attractive prospect. There would be better schooling for the children, and better health care. Although many had never seen a tree, a new life in forestry appealed. The more elderly residents, most of whom had never left the island and who could not speak English, must have viewed the drastic change with alarm but the younger majority view prevailed and evacuation was planned.

There were 500 Soay sheep to be moved first. Their coats of fine wool were not sheared but plucked by the inhabitants using only a penknife. The resultant locally woven tweed, either shipped ashore or sold to rare visitors, had provided the inhabitants' only contact with actual money. No taxes on income or on anything else were paid. Their internal economy took the form of barter. The plentiful supply of gannets, when dried, provided winter food. No inhabitant had ever fought in any war. Their distance and isolation earned them no consideration by the rest of Scotland.

Despite protestations by the Canine Defence League, all dogs were destroyed. Just two were put down by injections of hydrocyanic acid. The rest, at the islanders' insistence, had stones tied around their necks and were hurled from the jetty. Small boats were used to ferry only a dozen or so sheep out to the SS Dunara Castle. Ten cows with four calves were also evacuated. Then HMS Harebell, of the Fishery Protection Service, came on the final day to take the islanders to the mainland. The Under Secretary of State for Scotland imposed a ban on photography, thus ensuring the people of St Kilda privacy during the evacuation. It was not possible to house all of the inhabitants in Argyll, as had been hoped, so the community was split, their communal lives coming to an end.

The history of the island has been documented in a number of scholarly works, including The Life and Death of St Kilda by Tom Steel, and Island on the Edge of the World by Charles Maclean.

Visiting St Kilda

A 14-hour boat journey from Oban and eight hours from the Outer Hebrides, St Kilda is a long way out in the North Atlantic. The cost and the sea conditions are the two factors that will make or break your plans to reach St Kilda, but from expert sea kayakers on an expedition, to yachts and cruise boats, it is possible … at a price. **Island Cruising** ⓘ 1 Erista, Uig, Lewis, T01851-672381, www.island-cruising.com, arranges boat trips to

BACKGROUND
St Kilda

In 1957 the islands become the property of the National Trust for Scotland and, in 1986, they became a UNESCO World Heritage Site. St Kilda is the most important seabird breeding station in northwest Europe. The islands are home to a quarter of the world's population of northern gannets, the largest colony of fulmars in Britain and one of the largest colonies of puffins in Scotland. These huge numbers of seabirds were vital to the islanders' survival. Their eggs provided food in the summer, and gannets and fulmers were caught each season to be plucked, dried and stored for the winter. Their feathers and oil were kept for export, whilst their bones were shaped into useful tools and their skins into shoes.

The largest of the islands, Hirta, was the most remote community in Britain, if not Europe, until 1930, when the remaining 36 Gaelic-speaking inhabitants were evacuated at their own request, in one of the most poignant episodes of Scottish history (see box, page 365).

St Kilda from April to October. The tour comprises the journey to and from St Kilda and a landing on Hirta with a visit to the **museum**, the **old village** and a wider exploration of the island, including a climb up to the highest sea cliffs in the British Isles at **Conachair** (430 m). They also run a six-day cruise allowing an extra day or two on St Kilda and will often try to visit the isolated, wildlife-rich **Monach Islands** and **North Rona** en route.

Other companies that sail to St Kilda are **Kilda Cruises**, who sail from the Isle of Harris (for details, see page 342) and **Sea Harris**, who also depart from Harris (see page 342). **Go to St Kilda** ⓘ *T07789-914144, www.gotostkilda.co.uk*, run fast-boat trips from Waternish on Skye.

For trips to St Kilda, see www.visitouterhebrides.co.uk, and the 'Visiting St Kilda' portal at www.nts.org.uk.

National Trust for Scotland ⓘ *T0844-493 2237, www.nts.org.uk*, also organizes fortnight-long voluntary work parties in the summer months every year to undertake restoration, maintenance and archaeology projects around the old village on Hirta. The trips are very popular and each volunteer must complete an application form, so apply early. Note that the sea journey can be arduous.

St Kilda today

Today, **Hirta** is partly occupied by the army as a radar-tracking station for the rocket range on South Uist and managed by Scottish Natural Heritage. Across a narrow channel lies **Dun**. Nearby **Boreray** is home to the world's largest colony of gannets, and **Soay** on which the rare Soay sheep breed, completes the group. There are several dramatic 'stacs' rising sheer from the Atlantic Ocean. At 430 m, the sea cliffs at **Conachair** are the highest in the British Isles.

Orkney & Shetland

Viking ships meet Stone Age settlements in these archipelagos

To some, these two archipelagos will never be anything other than distant and overlooked specks of land peppering the wild North Atlantic, above an already distant north coast of mainland Scotland.

They certainly are remote and they have maintained a social and political, as well as geographical, distance from the rest of Scotland. Both were under Norse rule until the mid-15th century and, somehow, seeing them as a part of Scotland can be very misleading.

Shetland's northern islands, on the same latitude as Alaska, are as strange and different as Britain gets, while beguiling Orkney just smiles serenely as the rest of world races headlong into the future at alarming speed. It is these qualities that make the islands worth visiting. Both Orkney and Shetland are littered with outstanding archaeological evidence, not just of six centuries of Norse occupation, such as at Jarlshof at the very southern tip of Shetland, but also of life back in 3000 BC at Skara Brae and the Knap of Howar in the Orkneys. They are also among the best places in Britain to see wildlife as yet untamed by the 21st century. Here you can sail alongside porpoises and seals, potentially spot killer whales (orca) and watch a million migratory seabirds nest and raise their young during the summer months. And, thanks to fast and frequent transport links, it doesn't take an Arctic expedition to get here.

Best for
Coastal scenery ▪ Prehistoric sites ▪ Remote islands ▪ Wildlife

Orkney 371
Shetland 405

Footprint
picks

★ **Stromness**, page 381

A classic Scottish fishing town with a fascinating trading history, Stromness makes the prefect introduction to Orkney.

★ **Skara Brae**, page 382

The best-preserved Stone Age village in northern Europe set amongst the dazzling white sands of the Bay of Skaill.

★ **The Italian Chapel**, page 390

A remarkable church built by Italian POWs during the Second World War from two Nissen huts.

★ **Papa Westray**, page 402

Reached by the shortest scheduled flight in the world, tiny Papay is home to Europe's oldest house and many thousands of breeding seabirds.

★ **Isle of Mousa**, page 417

Site of the best-preserved broch in Scotland, best visited at dusk in the summer when it is swarmed by thousands of storm petrels.

★ **Hermaness National Nature Reserve**, page 426

Over 100,000 nesting seabirds in a place that feels like the very edge of the world.

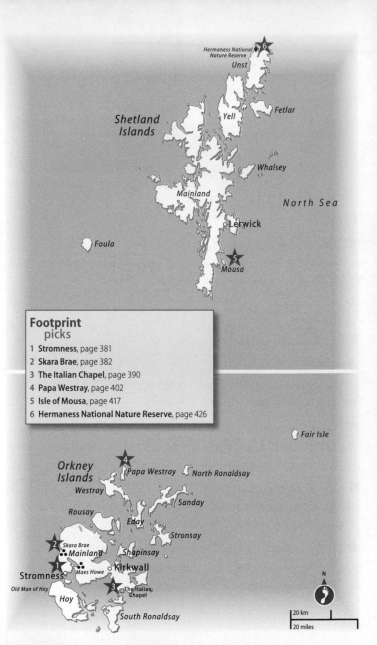

Hermaness National
Nature Reserve

Unst

Shetland
Islands

Yell

Fetlar

Whalsey

Mainland

North Sea

Lerwick

Foula

Mousa

Footprint
picks

1 **Stromness**, page 381
2 **Skara Brae**, page 382
3 **The Italian Chapel**, page 390
4 **Papa Westray**, page 402
5 **Isle of Mousa**, page 417
6 **Hermaness National Nature Reserve**, page 426

Fair Isle

Orkney
Islands

Papa Westray

North Ronaldsay

Westray

Sanday

Rousay

Eday

Stronsay

Skara Brae

Mainland

Shapinsay

Kirkwall

Stromness

Maes Howe

The Italian Chapel

Old Man of Hoy

Hoy

South Ronaldsay

N

20 km

20 miles

Orkney

Orkney may be separated from the north coast of Scotland by a mere six miles of the notoriously changeable waters of the Pentland Firth, but to the fiercely independent Orcadians 'Mainland' means the largest of the Orkney islands and not the Scottish mainland. Mainland is also the site of the two main towns and ferry terminals: the capital Kirkwall and the beautiful old fishing port of Stromness. Orkney has the densest concentration of prehistoric monuments in Britain and Mainland is where you'll find many of these archaeological relics: the Stones of Stenness, Maes Howe, the Broch of Gurness and the remarkable Neolithic village of Skara Brae, all of which give Orkney a rare continuity of past and present. Aside from Mainland, there are a dozen smaller islands to explore, including Hoy, with its wild, spectacular coastal scenery. The even more remote northerly islands offer miles of deserted beaches and nothing but the calls of birds to shatter the peace and quiet. Quiet also describes the taciturn locals. They aren't unfriendly – quite the opposite, in fact – but it's said that Orcadians will rarely use one word where none will do.

Essential Orkney

Finding your feet

Air

There are direct flights to Kirkwall airport Monday to Saturday from Aberdeen, Edinburgh, Glasgow, Inverness, Sumburgh (Shetland), Manchester and Bergen in Norway (summer only). These are operated by **Loganair** (T0344-800 2855, www. loganair.co.uk). **Flybe** (T0371-700 2000, www. flybe.com) also fly to Kirkwall from Aberdeen.

The **airport** (T01856-886210, www.hial. co.uk), is three miles southeast of Kirkwall on the A960. **Stagecoach** (T01856-886210, www.stagecoachbus.com) runs a shuttle bus service to and from town. Or book a taxi with **Craigies Taxis** (T01856-878787), around £8.

Ferry

Northlink Ferries (T08456-000449; T01856-885500 from UK and international mobiles, www.northlinkferries.co.uk) sail from Aberdeen to Kirkwall (six hours) on Tuesday, Thursday, Saturday and Sunday at 1700, and from Scrabster to Stromness (1½ hours) three times a day Monday to Friday and twice a day on Saturday and Sunday. Between mid-June and mid-August, they sail three times a day Monday to Saturday.

Rapsons Coaches (www.rapsons.com) and **Citylink** (www.citylink.co.uk) operate bus services between Thurso and Scrabster. Citylink buses also run to John o'Groats and Gill's Bay. **Stagecoach** operates a daily service from Inverness to Scrabster. There is also a regular train service to Thurso from Inverness.

Northlink Ferries also sail from Lerwick (Shetland) to Kirkwall on Monday, Wednesday and Friday at 1730, the journey takes seven hours and 45 minutes. Cars should be booked in advance and all passengers must check in at least 30 minutes before departure.

John O'Groats Ferries (T01955-611353, www.jogferry.co.uk) run a service from John o'Groats to Burwick, with a bus connection to Kirkwall (45 minutes). The ferries leave twice a day and four times a day between June and August. The journey takes 40 minutes. John o'Groats Ferries also operate the **Orkney Bus**, a daily direct bus/ferry/bus service between Inverness and Kirkwall, via John o'Groats. It leaves Inverness at 0715 and 1420 from 1 June to 31 August. Advance booking is essential.

Pentland Ferries (T01856-831226, bookings T0800-688 8998, www. pentlandferries.co.uk) sail from Gill's Bay (between John o'Groats and Thurso) to St Margaret's Hope, three times a day. For further details, see Transport, page 472.

Getting around

Air

There are flights from Kirkwall to and from Eday, Stronsay, Sanday, Westray, Papa Westray and North Ronaldsay which are operated by **Loganair**. For inter-island reservations and queries, T01856-872494. They are very reasonable, costing £17 one way Economy (see **Loganair** website for terms and conditions). There are also inter-island saver flights costing £21 return (only applicable between Kirkwall and the North Isles), and excursion flights (requiring a minimum of one night's stay at the destination), which cost £15 return. There are also sightseeing flights in July and August costing £39, which can only be booked on the day of departure for round-trip flights originating in Kirkwall with no stopover.

Boat

Orkney Ferries (T01856-872044, www. orkneyferries.co.uk) operates daily car and passenger ferries to Rousay, Egilsay and Wyre from Tingwall, to Shapinsay, Eday, Stronsay, Sanday, Westray and Papa Westray from Kirkwall and to Graemsay and Hoy from Stromness and to Hoy and Flotta from Houton. See their website for all current fares and timetables. If travelling by car, book ferry journeys in advance. All these prices are return with single fares 50% of the return price. A seven-day Island **Explorer Ticket** can be purchased for the North and Inner Isles (summer timetable only), costing £42, concessions and children £21. Bikes travel free of charge.

Bus, car and bike

Only the main population centres on Mainland are served by public transport. **Stagecoach** (T01856-878014) operate the bus service and have stations in Kirkwall and Stromness. Having a car is highly recommended to visit many of the most interesting sights. Bringing a car to Orkney is expensive, but there are several car hire firms on the Mainland and on the other islands. An alternative could be taking a bike. Orkney is relatively flat and most of its roads are quiet, which makes it ideal for touring on two wheels, though the wind can make it difficult if it's blowing in the wrong direction. Bicycles can be hired in Kirkwall, Stromness and on many of the other islands. Those with limited time may prefer to book a tour of the islands. For further details, see What to do, page 380, and Transport, page 381.

Tourist information

The islands' tourist information service, **Visit Orkney**, has an office in Kirkwall, see page 378.

Many of Orkney's monuments are managed by **Historic Environment Scotland** (www.historicenvirnoment.scot). They include the Bishop and Earl's Palaces, Broch of Gurness, Maes Howe, Skara Brae and Skaill House, Brough of Birsay and Hackness Martello Tower. If you plan to visit all or most of these sights, it is cheaper to buy an **Orkney Explorer Pass** which costs £19 for adults, £15.20 concessions, £11.40 child and £38 for a family. It allows access to seven sites on the islands and is valid for 30 consecutive days.

Orkney

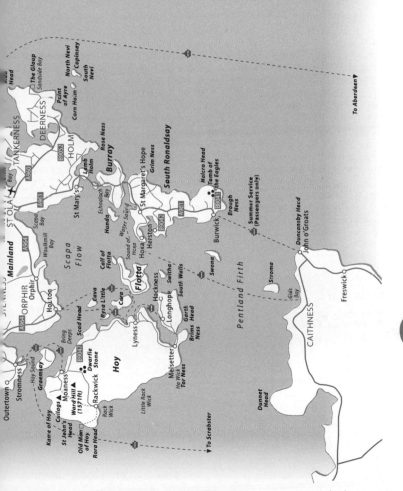

Orkney's rugged, Nordic-feeling capital (population 7000) is built around a wide sheltered bay and is the main departure point for ferries to the northern islands. First impressions are a little misleading, as the harbour area has been blighted by modern development. More appealing, however, are the narrow winding streets and lanes of the old town, which has not changed much over the centuries. There are many houses dating from the 16th, 17th and 18th centuries, as well as Kirkwall's greatest attraction, its magnificent cathedral, the finest medieval building in northern Scotland.

Sights

The town's outstanding sight is the huge and impressive red sandstone **St Magnus Cathedral** ⓘ *T01856-874894, Apr-Sep Mon-Sat 0900-1800, Sun 1300-1800, Oct-Mar Mon-Sat 0900-1300, 1400-1700, free*, built by masons who had worked on Durham Cathedral in the north of England. It was founded in 1137 by Rognvald Kolson, Earl of Orkney, in memory of his uncle, Magnus Erlendson, who was slain by his cousin, Haakon Paulson, on Egilsay in 1115. Magnus was buried at Birsay and it is said that heavenly light was seen over his grave. It soon became a shrine, attracting pilgrims from as far afield as Norway. Magnus was canonized in 1133, and four years later his nephew commissioned construction of the cathedral. The building wasn't completed until the 14th century. Major additions have been made over the centuries, the most recent of which was a new west window for the nave, to celebrate the cathedral's 850th anniversary in 1987. The bones of St Magnus now lie in the north choir pillar, while those of St Rognvald lie in the south one. There's also a memorial to John Rae, the 19th-century Arctic explorer who is buried in the graveyard, as well as a monument to the 833 men of the *HMS Royal Oak* who died when it was torpedoed in Scapa Flow in 1939.

Looming impressively nearby are the ruins of the **Bishop's Palace** ⓘ *T01856-871918, Apr-Sep daily 0930-1730, Oct 1000-1600, entry by combined ticket with Earl's Palace*, built in the 12th century as the first Kirkwall residence of the Bishop of Orkney. Here King Haakon of Norway died in 1263 after his defeat at the Battle of Largs. The palace was repaired and extended in the mid-16th century by Bishop Reid, and most of what you see dates from that period. There's a good view of the town from the top of the 'Moosie Too'r'.

The adjacent **Earl's Palace** ⓘ *T01856-871918, Apr-Sep daily 0930-1730, Oct 1000-1600, £5, concessions £4, children £3*, was built around 1600 by the notorious Patrick Stewart, Earl of Orkney, using forced labour. Still very much intact, it is one of Scotland's most elegant Renaissance buildings and was occupied by the tyrannical Stewart

Essential Kirkwall

Finding your feet

The town is compact and it's easy to get around on foot. The main street changes its name from Bridge Street to Albert Street, then to Broad Street and Victoria Street as it twists its way south from the busy harbour. The cathedral is on Broad Street, and most of the shops and banks are on Broad Street and Albert Street. The bus station is five minutes' walk west of the town centre. For further details, see Transport, page 380.

only for a very short time, until he was imprisoned and later executed. Wandering around both these impressive and solid palaces is a very good way to get a feel for this period of Orkney's history.

Opposite St Magnus Cathedral is **Tankerness House and Gardens**, a 16th-century former manse which has been restored and now houses the **Orkney Museum** ① *T01856-873535, www.orkney.gov.uk, May-Sep 1030-1700, Oct-Apr Mon-Sat 1030-1230, 1330-1700, free*, which highlights 5500 years of human presence on Orkney, including archaeological

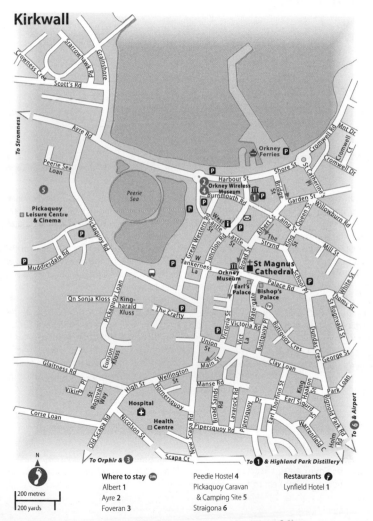

Kirkwall

Where to stay	Peedie Hostel **4**	Restaurants ❼
Albert **1**	Pickaquoy Caravan	Lynfield Hotel **1**
Ayre **2**	& Camping Site **5**	
Foveran **3**	Straigona **6**	

Learning the lingo

Despite the disappearance of the Norse language, many of the Viking place names have survived. Here are some of the most common Old Norse elements which will help explain the meaning of many place names:

a(y)	island	*holm*	small island
a, o	stream	*howe*	mound
aith	isthmus	*kirk*	church
ayre	beach	*lax*	salmon
bard	headland	*ler*	mud, clay
bister	farm	*lyng*	heather
brae, brei	broad	*minn*	mouth
fell, field	hill	*mool, noup*	headland
fors	waterfall	*setter*	farm
garth	farm	*thing*	parliament
geo	creek	*toft*	house site
grind	gate	*voe*	sea inlet
ham(n)	anchorage	*wick, vik*	bay

artefacts from Neolithic times to the Vikings. If you are spending any time in Kirkwall at the beginning of your stay, then this is an exceedingly worthwhile exhibition. It is a great way to whet your appetite for the archaeological treats that are lying in wait for you all over the islands, and it also puts them into a useful chronological context.

Old radio buffs should not miss the **Orkney Wireless Museum** ① *Kiln Corner, at the harbour end of Junction Rd, T01856-871400, www.orkneywirelessmuseum.org.uk, Apr-Oct Mon-Sat 1000-1630, Sun 1430-1630, small entry fee*, which houses a jumble of domestic and wartime communications equipment from the 1930s onwards.

A mile south of the town centre on the road to South Ronaldsay is the 200-year-old **Highland Park Distillery** ① *T01856-874619, www.highlandparkwhisky.co.uk, tours on the hour every hour May-Sep Mon-Sat 1000-1600, Sun 1200-1600, Apr Mon-Fri 1000-1600, Oct-Mar Mon-Fri 1400 and 1500 only; the Viking Soul tour costs £10, Viking Heroes is £20 and Viking Legends £100*. This is one of the few distilleries that still has its own floor maltings – as well as its own mouser cat – and there's a dram of this particularly fine single malt at the end. Don't leave without buying a bottle, for this is one of the great all-round whiskies, with a distinctive smoky flavour. It rivals those from more fashionable Islay.

Listings Kirkwall *maps pages 374 and 377.*

Tourist information

Historic Environment Scotland
www.historicenvirnoment.scot.
Manage many of Orkney's monuments
(see page 373).

Visit Orkney
1st floor, the Travel Centre, West Castle St, T01856-230300, www.visitorkney.com. Mon-Sat.
Very helpful. They will book accommodation for you, or provide a list of what's available, though many B&Bs are not included in the

tourist board scheme. They can also provide information on various sights, walks and the islands' wildlife. They can change money and stock a wide range of guidebooks and maps and have details of forthcoming events. Their website is packed with information and you can also download digital guides. Another good source is the weekly newspaper *The Orcadian* (www.orcadian.co.uk).

Where to stay

There are plenty of good-value B&Bs, though don't always expect en suite.

£££ Albert Hotel
Mounthoolie Lane, T01856-876000, www.alberthotel.co.uk.
This old Kirkwall hotel has been revamped mixing modern (stylish rooms) with traditional (the cosy **Bothy Bar**). The restaurant serves a range of hearty standard pub-type dishes and is good value (**££**). Very friendly and helpful staff.

£££ Ayre Hotel
Ayre Rd, T01856-873001, www.ayrehotel. co.uk. Open all year.
33 en suite rooms. Kirkwall's most upmarket hotel sits right on the harbour front. Very comfortable with a good restaurant and a bar. Also has a new annex across the road with 6 1-bed and 3 2-bed fully equipped apartments for rent (**££££-£££**).

£££ Foveran Restaurant with Rooms
2 miles from town on the A964 Orphir road at St Ola, T01856-872389, www.foveranhotel. co.uk. Open all year.
8 en suite rooms. Modern, chalet-style hotel overlooking Scapa Flow. Friendly, stylish and very comfortable rooms but it is the food that is the real draw here (see Restaurants, below).

£££-££ Straigona
Tankerness, T01856-861328, www.straigona.co.uk.
3 rooms. Excellent B&B, rural location east of town but only a few mins from the airport.

Very friendly and welcoming, comfortable and great breakfasts. Hosts Julie and Mike will also provide packed lunch or evening meal on request. Recommended.

£ Peedie Hostel
Ayres Houses, T01856-877177, www.stayinorkney.co.uk.
A smaller (Peedie is an an Orcadian word meaning small) and more intimate hostel overlooking the harbour with 3 single rooms, 3 twin rooms and 2 4-bed rooms. This is a better option than the SYHA youth hostel (60 beds) about 15 mins' walk from the town centre.

Camping

Pickaquoy Caravan & Camping Site
On the western outskirts of Kirkwall, off the A965, T01856-879900. Apr-Sep.

Restaurants

£££ Foveran Restaurant with Rooms
2 miles from town on the A964 Orphir road at St Ola, T01856-872389, www. foveranhotel.co.uk.
This modern, chalet-style hotel overlooking Scapa Flow is famed for its food, especially the local scallops, langoustines, partans (large crabs) and lobster, or their beef cooked in the local Highland Park whisky.

£££-££ Lynnfield Hotel
Holm Rd, T01856-872505, www.lynnfieldhotel.com.
Next to the Highland Park distillery, this hotel is renowned for its fanastic food, including North Ronaldsay mutton and cooked-to-perfection lobster and scallops.

££ Albert Hotel
Mounthoolie Lane, T01856-876000, www. alberthotel.co.uk. See Where to stay, above.
Serves good pub grub made with home-grown produce in its traditional 'bothy' bar, which is a favourite with locals and visitors.

Bars and clubs

Nightlife revolves around its lively pubs. Check in *The Orcadian* for folk nights, etc.

Ayre Hotel
See Where to stay, page 379.
Quiet and relaxed but also stages folk music nights.

Bothy Bar
Albert Hotel, Mounthoolie Lane, T01856-876000, www.alberthotel.co.uk.
A good place for a drink, and sometimes has live folk music.

Entertainment

For details of what's going on visit www.visitorkney.com, which has up-to-date listings, or buy *The Orcadian*, www.orcadian.co.uk, which comes out on Thu, or pick up a free copy of the Tourist Board's guide.

Kirkwall
The town's **cinema** is in the Pickaquoy Centre (Pickaquoy Rd, T01856-879900, www.pickaquoy.co.uk). Also has sports and fitness facilities, a café and bar.

Festivals

There are numerous events which take place throughout the year.

May Orkney Folk Festival, www.orkneyfolkfestival.com. An excellent event, which takes place for 3 days at the end of May at various locations throughout the islands. It is always well attended and can be rather boisterous.
Jun St Magnus Festival, www.stmagnusfestival.com. This high-brow event is one of the UK's most prestigious and popular festivals. Held in Kirkwall during midsummer, it consists of 6 days of music, drama, literature and the visual arts, with many internationally renowned performers.
Jul Regattas, during this month there are several regattas held on most of the islands. Visit the **iCentre** or read *The Orcadian* for more information.

Sep Orkney International Science Festival, T01343-540844, www.oisf.or. 1st week in Sep. Offers visitors the chance to participate in a range of talks and exhibitions about astronomy, zoology and even renewable energy. The week also includes a ceilidh and concerts.
Dec The Ba' (**ball**), in Kirkwall, www.bagame.com. Amongst the best-known annual events. It takes place on Christmas Eve and New Year's Eve and is a bit like rugby, basketball and a full-scale riot all rolled into one, and is contested between 2 sides – the Uppies and the Doonies – representing different districts of the town. As many as 200 'players' may be involved, and a game can last up to 7 hrs as both sides attempt to jostle the ball along the streets until one reaches their 'goal' to win the prized ba'.

Shopping

The Odin Stone, *14 Junction Rd, T01856-877785, www.odinstone-orkney.co.uk.* You can browse and buy the work of over 50 local crafts-folk at this delightful store.
Orkney Handcrafted Furniture, *Dellovo, New Scapa Rd, T01856-872998.* Authentic and award-winning range of traditional Orkney chairs made by Fraser Anderson.
Ortak, *Hatston, T01856-873201, www.ortak.co.uk.* Popular jewellery with designs that are influenced by Viking, runic carvings.

What to do

Tour operators
Tour Orkney, *Ardconnel Rd, Kirkwall, T01856-873885, www.tourorkney.co,uk.* Run by John and Margaret Graham. Day tours around Mainland for £45.

Transport

Check the **Loganair** website (www.loganair.co.uk) for all inter-island flights. A good website for Orkney transport details is www.orkney.com.

Air

Loganair, T01856-872494, flies Mon-Sat from Kirkwall to **Eday**, **Stronsay**, **Sanday** and **Westray** and to **North Ronaldsay** and **Papa Westray**. See also Finding your feet, page 376.

Bus

There's a limited bus service around the Mainland, the timetables of which can be found at the **Travel Centre** or on the transport pages of www.orkney.gov.uk. **Stagecoach**, T01856-878014, runs buses Mon-Sat from Kirkwall bus station to **Stromness**, 30 mins. It also runs 3-5 buses a day, Mon-Sat, to **Houton**, 35 mins, which connect with ferries to **Hoy**; and a daily bus, Mon-Sat, to **East Holm**, 25 mins, and **Stromness** via **Dounby**, 45 mins. There are buses daily to **St Margaret's Hope**, 30 mins and there are also buses to **Tingwall** and **Evie**. Note that there is a very restricted Sun bus service on Orkney.

Car hire

Orkney Car Hire, Junction Rd, T01856 872666; **John G Shearer & Sons**, T01856-872950. Also **Europcar** at Kirkwall airport, T01856-872262.

Cycle hire

Cycle Orkney, Tankerness Lane, T01856-875777 www.cycleorkney.com. Mountain bikes from £20 per day.

Ferry

Northlink Ferries, T0845-6000449, www.northlinkferries.co.uk, sails from Kirkwall to **Aberdeen**, Mon, Wed and Fri, 2345, 6 hrs. They also sail from Kirkwall to **Lerwick** (Shetland) on Tue, Thu, Sat and Sun, 2345, 7 hrs 45 mins. Return fares are double the cost of single fares and children under 16 travel for 50% less. Cars should be booked in advance and all passengers must check in at least 30 mins before departure. 2-berth and 4-berth cabins are available on all journeys.

There are buses between Kirkwall and **Burwick**, 45 mins, to connect with all ferry sailings to John o'Groats (see below). **John O'Groats Ferries** also operate the Orkney Bus, a daily direct bus/ferry/bus service between Kirkwall and **Inverness**, via **John o'Groats**.

Stromness and West Mainland *Colour map 7.*
beautiful fishing town and the best-preserved Stone Age village in northern Europe

Ferries from Scrabster arrive in Stromness, and newcomers are greeted by rows of stone-built houses hugging the shore, each with its own jetty. Stromness is a much more attractive town than Kirkwall, and its narrow, winding main street, its *wynds* and *closes*, its fascinating shops and its unique atmosphere make it the ideal base for exploring the West Mainland, the name given to everything west of Kirkwall.

It's an area of rich farmland, rolling hills and moorland, fringed by spectacular cliffs along the Atlantic coastline and with the greatest concentration of prehistoric monuments in Britain. Here you'll find, amongst many others, the well-preserved Neolithic village of **Skara Brae**, silent monuments to human endeavour in the form of the **Standing Stones of Stenness** and the **Ring of Brodgar**, and the chambered tomb of **Maes Howe**, with its many still-unresolved mysteries.

★ Stromness

Stromness is a classic Scottish fishing town and a perfect introduction to Orkney. Though referred to in the Viking Saga as *Hamnavoe*, the town dates from the 17th century. Its importance as a trading port grew in the 18th century when wars and privateers made the

Essential Stromness and the West Mainland

Finding your feet

There are several buses between Kirkwall and Stromness, Monday to Friday, and two buses daily between Kirkwall and Birsay Palace. To get to Skara Brae you'll need your own transport, or you can visit as part of a guided tour (see Visit Orkney, page 378), or walk north along the coast from Stromness, via Yesnaby. For further information, see Essential Orkney, page 372, and Transport, page 388.

English Channel too dangerous and ships used the northern route across the Atlantic, calling in at Stromness for food and water and to hire a crew. Until the late 19th century, ships of the Hudson Bay Company made Stromness their main base for supplies. Whaling ships bound for Greenland also hired local labour. By the late 19th century the herring boom had reached Stromness and there were 400 boats using its harbour, but within two decades the boom had ended due to over-fishing. Today Stromness remains a fishing port, as well as Orkney's main ferry terminal and the headquarters of the Northern Lighthouse Board.

Stromness consists largely of one narrow, winding main street, paved with flagstones, which hugs the shoreline. Running off the street are numerous little lanes and alleyways, many with names such as **Khyber Pass**, that are full of interesting buildings that reflect the town's proud maritime heritage. The houses on the seaward side of the street are gable end to the waterfront and each has its own jetty. The town is not designed for the car, so you'll have to park by the harbour and explore its delights on foot. The main street changes its name from Victoria Street to Graham Place, Dundas Street, Alfred Street and South End as it runs south from the harbour.

Stromness Museum ① *52 Albert St, T01856-850025, www.stromnessmuseum.co.uk, Apr-Oct daily 1000-1700, Nov-Mar Mon-Sat 1100-1530, £5, concessions £4, children £1, family £10*, run by a community trust, is packed to the gunnels with exhibitions on Stromness' social and maritime history, including the story of Arctic whaling and artefacts from Scapa Flow and the days of the Hudson Bay Company. Upstairs the beautiful Victorian glass cases house a complete collection of Orkney birds and butterflies. Recommended. Opposite the museum is the house where George Mackay Brown (1921-1996), Orkney's most famous poet and story writer, spent the last two decades of his life, see also page 448. On a jetty to the south of the new harbour is the excellent **Pier Arts Centre** ① *T01856-850209, www.pierartscentre.com, Tue-Sat 1030-1700, free*, housing a permanent collection of works of the St Ives school, including Barbara Hepworth, Ben Nicholson and Patrick Heron, amongst others, in a lovely contemporary gallery.

★ Skara Brae and Skaill House
T01956-841815, Apr-Sep daily 0930-1730, Oct-Mar (Skara Brae only) 1000-1600, entry as part of HES Orkney Explorer ticket or a joint ticket for both sites (Apr-Sep only) £7.50, concessions £6, children £4.50; Oct-Mar (Skara Brae only) £6.50, concessions £5.20, children £3.90. Café open daily Apr-Oct.

Eight miles north of Stromness, in the magnificent setting of the dazzling white sands of the Bay of Skaill, is Skara Brae, the best-preserved Stone Age village in northern Europe. Explore here and you may feel you have just joined the cartoon world of The Flintstones. First revealed in 1850 after a violent storm blew away the dunes, this amazing site dates from around 5000 years ago and was occupied for about 600 years.

Scandinavian settlements

The history of Orkney and Shetland is bound up with the history of the Vikings, who first came to the islands in the latter half of the ninth century and stayed for about 650 years. This was part of a great Viking expansion westwards, and in less than a century emigrants from Norway and Denmark settled in Orkney, Shetland, Iceland, Greenland, Caithness, the Western Isles, Isle of Man and parts of Ireland and the northern half of England.

In 872 the King of Norway set up a Norse earldom in Orkney, from which the Vikings ruled Orkney, Shetland and the Western Isles and took part in raids around Britain and Europe, creating the popular image of Vikings as aggressive, bloodthirsty invaders. At home, however, they lived a peaceful life, adhering to the laws of their parliament, the 'thing', and many converted to Christianity.

In the late 14th century Norway, Denmark and Sweden were united under a Danish king. In 1469 the Royal estates and prerogatives in Orkney and Shetland were pledged to Scotland as part of the marriage dowry of Margaret, daughter of the King of Denmark, on her marriage to Prince James of Scotland, later to become King James III. Orkney and Shetland were to revert to rule by the kings of Norway when the debt was paid, but the pledge was never redeemed and the islands remained under Scottish control.

Soon after assuming control, the Scots began to change the old Norse laws, which they had agreed to maintain, and Scottish influence grew. In 1564 Mary, Queen of Scots granted the control and revenues from Orkney and Shetland to her half-brother, Robert Stewart. His prime motivation, however, was to extract as much money as possible through taxes. He was succeeded by his son, the infamous Patrick Stewart, who demanded even more rents, dues and fines. Earl Patrick eventually got his come-uppance when he was executed in Edinburgh for treason, but the changes he had made continued and Scots and English gradually began to usurp Old Norse as the native language of the islands.

The houses contain stone furniture, fireplaces, drains, beds, dressers and even have damp-proof coursing in the foundations. The whole complex presents a unique picture of the lifestyle of its inhabitants, and there's also a replica 'house' that you can wander around in the gloom, empathizing with that 3000 BC lifestyle.

The swish, modern visitor centre has a useful introductory video and exhibition which is definitely worth seeing before you look round the site (and it's also worth buying their guidebook), and there's also a café. After leaving the visitor centre, you walk down a 'path of time', which takes you back through landmark achievements of the last seven millennia, gradually building up the suspense and putting the achievements of Skara Brae in perspective – they may only be rudimentary buildings that once had turf for their rooves, but they were built 2000 years before the pyramids of Egypt, and in one of the world's most northerly outposts.

During the summer a ticket to Skara Brae includes admission to nearby **Skaill House** ① *T01856-841501, www.skaillhouse.com*, an early 17th-century mansion which contains a few old artefacts, including Captain Cook's dinner service from the *Resolution* and the trappings and frippery of the Lairds of Brackness over 400 years. Seeing these Orcadian dwellings, thousands of years apart, is remarkable.

Sandwick and Yesnaby

A short distance inland from here, at **Sandwick**, is the **Orkney Brewery** ① *T01856-841777, www.orkneybrewery.co.uk, 40-min tours daily 1200-1500 Mar-Dec, £6.50, concessions £5.50, children £3.50*, housed in the old Quoyloo School. It brews the island's **Raven Ale** and various bottled beers, including **Skull-splitter**, named after the Viking earl, Thorfinn Skull-splitter. There's a visitor centre with gift shop and **Tasting Hall Café (££-£)** serving snacks and hot meals.

South of the Bay of Skaill is **Yesnaby**, one of the most spectacular places on the islands, where the cliffs have been eroded into a series of stacks and geos by the fierce Atlantic seas. An exhilarating and precarious half-mile walk south from the car park and old Second World War lookout post brings you to **Yesnaby Castle**, a huge sea stack similar to the Old Man of Hoy. It's a dramatic sight, especially in a full force gale.

Markwick Head

North of Skara Brae at the southern end of Birsay Bay are the wild and spectacular 300-ft-high cliffs of Marwick Head, topped by the distinctive **Kitchener Memorial**, erected after the First World War to commemorate Lord Kitchener and the crew of the *HMS Hampshire*, which was sunk by a German mine off the coast in 1916 with the loss of all but 12 of her crew. Marwick Head is also an **RSPB Reserve**, and during the nesting season in early summer is home to many thousands of guillemots, razorbills, kittiwakes and fulmars, as well as a few puffins.

A mile inland, by the Loch of Isbister, is another RSPB reserve, **The Loons**, an area of marshland where you can see breeding and migrating wildfowl and waders. Further east, between Boardhouse Loch and Hundland Loch, is the **Kirbuster Farm Museum** ① *T01856-771268, Mar-Oct Mon-Sat 1030-1300, 1400-1700, Sun 1200-1700, free*, the last surviving Orkney blackhouse which was inhabited till the 1960s and gives an insight into 19th-century rural life on the islands.

Birsay

At the far northwestern corner of the Mainland is the parish of Birsay, which was a favourite residence of the Earls of Orkney in Viking times as well as the first seat of the Bishop, before the building of St Magnus Cathedral in Kirkwall. Earl Thorfinn the Mighty lived here (1014-1064) and built Orkney's first cathedral, **Christchurch**, for the new Bishop.

In the centre of the village are the ruins of the **Earl's Palace** ① *open at all times, free*, built by the infamous Earl Robert Stewart in the late 16th century, and once described as "a sumptuous and stately dwelling". Not much remains today, but enough to give some idea of the sheer scale of the place. Close by is **St Magnus Church**, built in 1760 on the site of an earlier church, which in turn was built on the foundations of what is believed to be the original Christchurch. Also in Birsay, just south of the A966 and A967 junction, is **Barony Mills** ① *T01856-721439, www.birsay.org.uk, May-end Sep daily 1100-1700, free*, the last working water-powered mill in Orkney.

Lying half a mile off the coast near the village is the **Brough of Birsay** ① *phone the Earl's Palace (see above) or T01856-841815 for crossing times, open (when tides permit) mid-Jun to end Sep daily 0930-1730, £5, concessions £4, children £3*. The tidal island, managed by Historic Scotland, juts out into the north Atlantic and is visible from several other points all the way down the west coast of the Mainland. It is only accessible for a couple of hours at low tide (times available from Kirkwall and Stromness tourist offices) but, if possible, it is best seen at the end of the day, as the sun sets – you'll probably have the whole island to yourself. Pick your way over the causeway and wander at your leisure (but don't forget the tide) amongst the remnants of a Pictish, and then Viking, community. The island was an important Pictish settlement from around the sixth century, and many artefacts have been found here. Some of these can be seen at the small ticket office at the entrance to the island. The Brough was also the site of an important Viking settlement, and there are extensive remains, including the 12th-century **St Peter's church** where St Magnus was buried after his murder on Egilsay. You can also walk out to the island's lighthouse along the top of the cliffs and see puffins – amongst other migrating seabirds – and possibly minke whales, pilot whales and killer whales.

Evie and the Broch of Gurness
Nine miles northwest of Kirkwall, or 14 miles east of Birsay, is the tiny village of Evie. A track leads from the village towards the coast, past a sandy beach, to the **Broch of Gurness** ⓘ *T01856-751414, Apr-end Sep daily 0930-1730, Oct 1000-1600, £6, concessions £4.80, children £3.60*. Standing on a lonely, exposed headland on the north coast, with gentle views across towards the island of Rousay, this is the best-preserved broch on Orkney, thought to date from around 100 BC. It is surrounded by an Iron Age village whose houses are also remarkably well preserved, with the original hearths, beds, cupboards and even a toilet still in evidence. The broch and village were occupied by the Picts up until Viking times, around AD 900. Many Pictish artefacts have been found on the site, and the grave of a ninth-century Norse woman was also discovered.

To the southwest of Evie is the **Birsay Moors RSPB Reserve**, and at **Lowrie's Water** on Burgar Hill there's a bird-hide from where you can watch breeding red-throated divers. Also on Burgar Hill you'll see several huge aerogenerators built to take advantage of Orkney's fierce winds.

Standing Stones of Stenness and Ring of Brodgar
Northeast of Stromness on the road to Kirkwall is the tiny village of **Stenness**, near some of Orkney's most interesting prehistoric sites. The Standing Stones of Stenness comprise the four remaining stones from an original circle of 12 stones, dating from 3000 BC. The largest of the stones stands over 15 ft high. A path leads from the stones to the nearby **Barnhouse Settlement**, a recently excavated Neolithic village.

About a mile northwest of Stenness is another stone circle, the **Ring of Brodgar**. This is a particularly impressive henge monument. It is over 100 yds in diameter and 27 of the original 60 stones are still standing, some of them up to 15 ft high. Given the importance of these sites, it is particularly refreshing to realize when you get there that you can walk amongst the stones in the calm of a summer evening, with only a few oystercatchers for company, but both get busy with coach parties during the day.

On the other side of **Loch of Harray**, in the tiny settlement of Harray, is the **Corrigal Farm Museum** ⓘ *T01856-771411, Apr-Oct Mon-Sat 1030-1300, 1400-1700, Sun 1200-1700, free*, a typical Victorian-era Orkney farmhouse and steading with a working barn and grain kiln and various items of farm machinery.

Maes Howe
T01856-851266, www.historicenvironment.scot. Tours daily every hour 1000-1600, £6, concessions £4.80, children £3.60. Tickets must be bought from the Maese Howe Visitor Centre at Stenness and visitors should arrive here 15 mins before tour starts, best to book online in advance.

Less than a mile northeast of the Stones of Stenness is Maes Howe, the finest Neolithic burial chamber in Europe. It was built around 2750 BC, making it contemporary with the

Standing Stones and Skara Brae, and is amazingly well preserved. A huge mound covers a stone-built entrance passage which leads into a central chamber – over 12 ft square and the same in height – with three smaller cells built into the walls of the tomb.

When it was opened in 1861, no human remains or artefacts were found, giving no clues as to its usage. However, in the 12th century Vikings returning from the Crusades broke into the tomb searching for treasure. They found nothing, but left behind one of the largest collections of runic graffiti anywhere in the world, as well as carvings of a dragon, serpent and walrus. Many of the inscriptions are pretty basic, along the lines of 'Thorfinn wrote these runes', but some are more intriguing, such as "Many a woman has come stooping in here no matter how pompous a person she was".

A guide gives you an excellent overview of the chamber's mysterious architectural attributes, but the fact remains that the history of this extraordinary place is still largely unsolved – something that obviously adds to the site's attraction. Unfortunately, you do not get to spend much time in the chamber, so you are unlikely to uncover any great secrets.

Orphir

On the southern shores of West Mainland, southeast of Stenness and overlooking Scapa Flow, is the scattered community of Orphir, which has a few sights worth visiting, especially if you're heading across to Hoy from the ferry terminal at **Houton**, a little further west. The main point of interest in Orphir is the **Orkneyinga Saga Centre** ① *T01856-811319, open all year daily 0900-1700, free*, where a small exhibition and video introduces the saga of the Viking Earls of Orkney from around AD 900 to 1200, when the islands became a part of Scotland rather than Norway. It was written circa 1200, possibly by an Icelander. As you would expect, there's plenty of gore and Machiavellian goings-on, including an assassination attempt that went disastrously wrong, when a poisoned shirt meant for Earl Harold was unwittingly and fatally worn by his brother Paul instead.

Behind the centre is **The Earl's Bu**, looking out across Orphir Bay south to Cava Island. These are the 12th-century foundations of the home of the Norse Earls of Orkney written about in the saga. Inside the cemetery gates is a section of the circular church built by Haakon and modelled on the rotunda of the Church of the Holy Sepulchre in Jerusalem.

Listings Stromness and West Mainland *map page 374.*

Tourist information

There is now no tourist information office in Stromness. The websites www.stromnessorkney.com and www.visitorkney.com both have lots of good information.

Where to stay

£££-££ Merkister Hotel
On the shores of Loch Harray, Stenness, between Stromness and Kirkwall, T01856-771366, www.merkister.com.
16 rooms, including 3 terraced garden suites. A favourite with anglers, but also handy for

archaeological sites, this place has a great location, an excellent restaurant (**£££**) and a popular bar. **£££** for dinner B&B and standard double rooms are in **££** category. Good deals out of season. One of the best in Orkney. Recommended.

£££-££ Mill of Eyreland
Stenness, 3 miles from Stromness, T01856-850136, www.millofeyreland.co.uk.
4 rooms and 1 suite (for up to 5 guests) in a beautiful and lovingly converted 19th-century mill with many of the original workings on display. There can be fewer more idyllic settings, with great views across

to Scapa Flow and Hoy. Fantastic value given the quality of accommodation.

££ Burnside Farm
10 mins walk from Stromness town centre, T01856-850723, www.burnside-farm.com.
3 rooms. Superb B&B on a working dairy farm. Comfortable, relaxing and hosts Joy and Robbie can't do enough for their guests. 4-star tourist board rating. Recommended.

££ Netherstove
Sandwick, T01856-841625, www.netherstove.com. May-Oct.
2 rooms on ground floor. Neat B&B near Skara Brae, overlooking the Bay of Skaill, run by the delightful Mrs Poke who will make guests feel very welcome with her delicious home-baked goodies. Also has 2 self-catering chalets and a cottage (available all year). It's a 15-min walk to Skara Brae from here.

££-£ Brown's Hostel
45-47 Victoria St, Stromness, T01856-850661, www.brownsorkney.co.uk. Open all year.
14 beds in single, twin, triple and family rooms. Popular family-run hostel only 5 mins from ferry terminal and bus stop, has no curfew. Also has self-catering house 10 mins' walk away with 4 rooms, can be rented per night or weekly, £200 per night for whole house or £50 per double room.

££-£ Orca Hotel
Victoria St, near the harbour and ferry terminal, Stromness, T01856-850447, www.orcahotel.com. Open all year.
6 en suite rooms. Clean and tidy rooms in this small hotel/guesthouse. Nothing fancy but very good value. Good self-catering deals available Nov-Mar. **£** for room only.

£ Hamnavoe Hostel
10a North End Rd, Stromness, T01856-851202, www.hamnavoehostel.co.uk.
6 rooms with 13 beds in single, twin and family rooms. Clean and comfy and great value.

Self-catering

Eviedale Cottages
Beside the junction of the road to Dounby, T01856-751714, www.eviedale-cottages.co.uk. Apr-Oct.
Has accommodation in 2 cosy and well-equipped cottages, 1 sleeps 4 (£525 per week in high season) and the other sleeps 2-3 (£465 per week). Also has a campsite, £20-25 per tent) and a lovely bistro where you can enjoy home-baked goodies, soup or lunch in front of a roaring fire.

Woodwick House
Evie, T01856-751330, www.woodwickhouse.co.uk.
8 rooms, 4 en suite. Lovely, old country house in beautiful surroundings. Perfect peace, walks through woods and views across to the islands. From £1000 per week for whole house. 4 en suite rooms are available for B&B out of season (**£££-££**).

Camping

Ness Point
1 mile south of the ferry terminal, T01856-873535. May to mid-Sep.
A well-equipped campsite with incomparable views, but it is very exposed.

Restaurants

£££-££ Hamnavoe Restaurant
35 Graham Place, Stromness, T01856-850606. Apr-Oct Tue-Sun from 1900, Fri-Sat Nov-Mar 1200-1400, Sat-Sun from 1900.
The best place to eat in town, this cosy wee restaurant specializes in local seafood but also offers good vegetarian dishes.

££ Julia's Café and Bistro
Opposite the ferry terminal, Stromness, T01856-850904. Mon-Sat 0900-1700, Sun 1000-1700. Open some evenings in summer.
Very good home-cooked food and huge cakes right on the harbour.

Orkney offers some of the best scuba-diving in the world, thanks to the part played by Scapa Flow in both world wars, see box, page 390. The wreckage on the sea bed, combined with the wildlife that teems around it – sea anemones, seals, whales and porpoises – make for great diving. Visibility is sharp and the water is not as cold as you expect, thanks to the Gulf Stream. Several companies offer diving courses for beginners and wreck diving for more experienced divers. This can be as a dive package, including accommodation, meals and boat charter, or simply as a boat charter. Most companies are based in Stromness, see below. For a list of dive operators, check out www.scapaflowwrecks.com.

£ Ferry Inn
Near the ferry terminal, John St, Stromness,
T01856-850280, www.ferryinn.com.
Decent bar food and lively bar.
Children welcome.

Bars and clubs

The best places for a drink in Stromness are the **Stromness Hotel** (see Where to stay); the **Ferry Inn** (10 John St, T01865-850280); and the bar of the **Royal Hotel** (Victoria St, T01856-850342).

Shopping

Stromness Books and Prints, *1 Graham Place, Stromness, T01856-850565*. A wee gem. No '3 for 2' offers, no sofas, no internet, no skinny lattes with cinnamon, just books – ones that you might want to read – and an owner, Tam McPhail, who knows what he's talking about. A real bookshop for real book lovers.

What to do

Diving
Orkney & Shetland Charters, *Northfield, Holm, T01856-781769, www.mv-valkyrie. co.uk*. Top-class liveaboard dive trips on the *MV Valkyrie* or *Valhalla* to explore Scapa Flow wrecks, also other Orkney sites and further afield to Shetland and Norway. Recommended.

Scapa Flow Diving Holidays, *Lerquoy, Outertown, Stromness, T01856-851110, www. scapa-flow.co.uk*. Offers liveaboard packages or day trips on the *MV Invincible*.
Scapa Scuba, *Lifeboat House, Stromness, T01856-851218, www.scapascuba.co.uk*. Orkney's only dive centre offers a range of guided dives and PADI courses.

Tour operators
Wildabout Orkney, *Glenacres, Quoyloo, Sandwick, T01856-877737, www.wildabout orkney.com*. Offers highly rated wildlife, historical, folklore and environmental tours.

Transport

Bus
There are several buses Mon-Sat between Stromness and **Kirkwall**, 30 mins, via Hatston Ferry Terminal.

Car hire
Brass's Car Hire, Blue Star Garage, North End Rd, Stromness, T01856-850850, www.stromnesscarhire.co.uk.

Cycle hire
Orkney Cycle Hire, 54 Dundas St, Stromness, T01856-850255, www.orkneycyclehire.co.uk.

Ferry
Northlink Ferries from Stromness to **Scrabster**, 1½ hrs.

The East Mainland is mainly agricultural land and though it contains little of the amazing archaeological wealth of its western counterpart, there are some attractive fishing villages, fine coastal walks and many poignant reminders of Orkney's important wartime role. Linked to East Mainland by a series of causeways, South Ronaldsay is the southernmost of the Orkney islands, only six miles from the Scottish mainland across the stormy Pentland Firth, the most dangerous stretch of water in the British Isles.

Deerness

There is not much to see inland on the road running southeast from Kirkwall past the airport, but head on towards the Deerness Peninsula and you will be richly rewarded by a truly serene, gentle beauty. There are sandy bays, which make for very pleasant short walks and picnics (if you can find a sheltered spot), jutting cliffs and a great variety of birdlife. The peninsula makes the West Mainland seem positively crowded by comparison, and is one of the best places on the Mainland to 'get away from it all'.

When the weather's good, the view southwest from Sandside Bay to the Isle of **Copinsay** (an RSPB reserve) is glorious, and is a perfect example of the whale-like properties that have been attributed to the Orkneys by the islands' most famous poet George Mackay Brown. There is a footpath following the coast from Sandside Bay to Mull Head (a nature reserve) and round the tip of the peninsula to the **Covenanters Memorial** (1679), a five-mile circular walk.

If you continue along the B9050, the road ends at The Gloup car park at Skaill Bay, from where it's a 200-yd walk to **The Gloup**, a dramatic collapsed sea cave, separated from the sea by a land bridge about 80 yds wide. The word comes from the Old Norse 'gluppa', meaning chasm, the local name for a blow-hole. A network of signposted footpaths covers the northeastern part of the peninsula and there are circular walks of between two to five miles which start from The Gloup car park. At the northeastern tip is **Mull Head**, a clifftop nature reserve which is home to guillemots, shags, fulmars, razorbills, terns and skuas.

On the south coast of East Mainland, near the northern end of the Churchill Barriers, is the old fishing village of **St Mary's**, once a busy little place but largely forgotten since the building of the causeways.

The Churchill Barriers

East Mainland is linked to a string of islands to the south by four causeways, known as the Churchill Barriers, built on the orders of Prime Minister Winston Churchill during the Second World War as anti-submarine barriers to protect the British Navy which was based in Scapa Flow at the time. Churchill's decision was prompted by the sinking of the battleship *HMS Royal Oak* in October 1939 by a German U-boat which

Essential East Mainland and South Ronaldsay

Finding your feet

John O'Groats Ferries (T01955-611353, www.jogferry.co.uk) run a small passenger ferry from John o'Groats to Burwick on the southern tip of South Ronaldsay and **Pentland Ferries** (www.pentlandferries. co.uk) sail from Gill's Bay to St Margaret's Hope. For details, see page 372. There are daily buses from Kirkwall to St Margaret's Hope and Burwick on South Ronaldsay.

ON THE ROAD
The graveyard of Scapa Flow

The huge natural harbour of Scapa Flow has been used since Viking times, and in the years leading up to the First World War the Royal Navy held exercises there, sometimes involving up to 100 ships. But Scapa was vulnerable to attack, and over the course of the war defences were improved with 21 blockships sunk at the eastern approaches. Scapa Flow continued to be used as the main naval base in the Second World War, but the blockships were not enough to prevent a German U-boat from torpedoing *HMS Royal Oak*, and the huge task of building the Churchill Barriers began, see page 389.

Scapa Flow's most famous incident happened at the end of the First World War, when, under the terms of the Armistice, Germany agreed to surrender most of her navy. Seventy-four German ships were interred in Scapa Flow, awaiting the final decision, but as the deadline approached the German commander, Admiral Von Reuter, gave the order for all the ships to be scuttled, and every ship was beached or sunk.

The scuttled German fleet, however, proved a hazard for fishing and a massive salvage operation began. Today seven German ships remain at the bottom of Scapa Flow – three battleships and four light cruisers – along with four destroyers and a U-boat and the Royal Navy battleships *HMS Royal Oak* and *HMS Vanguard*, which blew up in 1917.

had slipped between the old blockships, deliberately sunk during the First World War to protect Scapa Flow, and the shore. After the war, a road was built on top of the causeways, linking the islands of Lamb Holm, Glimps Holm, Burray and South Ronaldsay to Mainland.

On the island of **Lamb Holm** camps were built to accommodate the men working on the construction of the barriers, many of whom were Italian prisoners of war. The camps have long since gone, but the Italians left behind the remarkable ★ **Italian Chapel** ⓘ *T01856-781580 (for Mass times), open daily Jun-Aug 0900-1830, Apr and Oct 1000-1600, May and Sep 0900-1700, Nov-Feb 1000-1300, £3, under 12s free*, fittingly known as 'The Miracle of Camp 60'. It is difficult to believe that such a beautiful building could have been made using two Nissen huts, concrete and bits of scrap metal, and the chapel's enduring popularity with visitors is a tribute to the artistic skill of the men involved. One of them, Domenico Chiochetti, returned in 1960 to restore the interior paintwork.

Burray
On the island of Burray the road passes the **Orkney Fossil and Heritage Centre** ⓘ *T01856-731255, www.orkneyfossilcentre.co.uk, mid-Apr to end-Sep daily 1000-1700, £4.50, child/concession £3.50,* which houses an eclectic collection of old furniture, various relics and 350 million-year-old fish fossils found locally. There's also an archive room where you can browse old books and photographs. Also has a good tearoom (£) for soup, snacks and hot meals.

South Ronaldsay
The main settlement is the picturesque little village of **St Margaret's Hope** on the north coast. It is said to be named after Margaret, Maid of Norway, who died near here in 1290 at the age of seven while on her way to marry Prince Edward, later Edward II of England. She had already been proclaimed Queen of Scotland, and her premature death was a major

factor in the long Wars of Independence with England. The word 'hope' comes from the Old Norse word *hjop* meaning bay.

The village smithy has been turned into the **Smiddy Museum** ① *T01856-831567, mid-Apr to mid-Oct daily 1400-1630, free*, with lots of old blacksmith's tools to try out. The museum also features a small exhibition on the annual **Boys' Ploughing Match**, a hugely popular event first held circa 1860. Each year in August, boys from the village (and now girls as well) dress up as horses and parade in the village square (prizes are given for the best costume). Afterwards the boys and their fathers, or grandfathers, head for the **Sand of Wright**, a few miles west, and have a ploughing match with miniature ploughs, which are usually family heirlooms. The categories are: best ploughed ring, best feering or guiding furrow, neatest ends and best-kept plough. This sheltered beach is well worth a visit anyway, ploughing or no ploughing. The views stretch in a spectacular 180° panorama, south across the Pentland Firth to Caithness on mainland Scotland, west to South Walls and Cantick Head on Hoy, and northwest to Flotta and the west Mainland. It is yet another good place to spot snipe, lapwing, curlew and redshank. Arctic terns nest nearby and you can spot them diving dramatically as they fish in the bay.

To the north of the beach is the **Howe of Hoxa**, a ruined broch where Earl Thorfinn Skull-Splitter was buried in AD 963, according to the Orkneyinga saga. South Ronaldsay is a good place to buy local arts and crafts, and there are several workshops dotted around the island. One of these is the **Hoxa Tapestry Gallery** ① *T01856-831395, www. hoxatapestrygallery.co.uk,* three miles west of the village on the way to Hoxa Head. Local artist Leila Thompson's huge tapestries are well worth a visit; you cannot help but marvel at the extraordinary amount of work and dedication involved in their creation; many of them take years to finish. Due to the success of the gallery, Leila Thompson now works mostly to commission with lengthy waiting times. Her daughter, Jo, helps to run the gallery and is also an artist in her own right.

At the southeastern corner of South Ronaldsay is the **Tomb of the Eagles** ① *T01856-831339, www.tomboftheeagles.co.uk, Mar daily 1000-1200, Apr-Sep daily 0930-1730, Oct 0930-1230, last tour an hour before closing, £7.50, concessions £6.50, children 13+ £3.50, children 5-12 £2.50,* one of the most interesting archaeological sights on Orkney. The 5000-year-old chambered cairn was discovered by local farmer and amateur archaeologist, Ronnie Simison, whose family now runs the privately owned site and museum. The contents of the tomb were practically intact and there were up to 30 people buried here, along with carcasses and talons of sea eagles, hence the name. Various objects were also found outside the tomb, including stone tools and axes.

Before visiting the tomb you can handle the skulls and other artefacts at the visitor centre, which also features various activities for children, toilets and picnic areas, as well as a gift shop. It's about a mile walk to the tomb along a farm track and across fields. Halfway there is a **burnt mound**, a kind of Bronze Age kitchen, which is included in the tour. Next you walk out along the cliff edge to the spectacularly sited tomb which you must enter by lying on a trolley and pulling yourself in using an overhead rope. It is particularly eerie being here because there is generally no-one else around, and as you haul yourself into the tomb, with the sound of the North Sea crashing into the cliffs nearby, you wonder to yourself how those buried here met their fate. There is also a lovely, but generally wild and windy, walk back along the cliffs, via a different route, to the car park.

Where to stay

There's a good selection of accommodation in St Margaret's Hope.

£££ Creel B&B
Front Rd, St Margaret's Hope, T01856-831311, www.thecreel.co.uk.
3 en suite rooms, 2 of which can sleep up to 3. Offers stylish, spacious and comfortable rooms with sea views. 2 nights minimum stay. Also have self-catering apartment for rent for 3 nights or more (£875 per week in high season).

£££ Eastward Guest House
St Margaret's Hope, T01856-831551, www.eastwardhouse.com.
3 rooms. The accommodation in this converted kirk is effortlessly smart with lovely touches such as underfloor heating and silent mini fridges, but it's the food in the **Missing Bell** restaurant made by owner Keiko that's the draw. Her Japanese buffet makes the most of Orkney's seafood (**££££-£££** with dinner). The 3-course gourmet breakfasts aren't bad either. Highly recommended.

££ Commodore Chalets
St Mary's, Holm, T01856-781319, www.commodorechalets.co.uk.
This place looks like an army barracks but offers good-value accommodation in 9 self-catering chalets and 6 overnight lodges. Good location, with views of Churchill Barriers and within walking distance of Italian Chapel. Price is for room only, a continental breakfast is available on request for £5pp. For self-catering, large chalet (sleeps 4-6) is £490-665 per week and small chalet (sleeps 2-4) is £385-490 per week.

££ St Margaret's Cottage B&B
South Ronaldsay, T01856-831637, www.stmargaretscottage.com.
3 rooms, 2 en suite. Comfortable B&B offering early breakfast option for guests using the Pentland Ferries. Dogs welcome. Good value.

££-£ Wheems Organic Farm
Wheems, Eastside, a few miles southeast of St Margaret's Hope, T01856-831556, www.wheemsorganic.co.uk. Apr-Oct.
Organic farm offering wooden camping pods which sleep 2 adults (£40 per night), bell tents (sleep 3, £30 per night), a yurt (£50 per night sleeps up to 4), a cottage (£60 per night sleeps up to 3) and campsite. 3-night minimum stay and dogs welcome but not in tents or yurt.

Restaurants

£££-££ Skerries Bistro
T01856-831605, www.skerriesbistro.co.uk.
Great food served in a purpose-built glass building by the cliffs with stunning views across the Pentland Firth. Seafood is a speciality and if you want to push the boat out try their seafood tasting menu at £55 a head served in a self-contained 'dining pod'.

Festivals

Aug Festival of the Horse and Boys' Ploughing Match, South Ronaldsay, www.orkneyjar.com. There are numerous agricultural shows in Aug which culminate in this festival, see page 391.

What to do

Dawn Star Boat Trips, *T01856-876743, www. orkneyboattrips.co.uk.* Departing from the pier at St Mary's, Holm, these tours take you all round Scapa Flow with an emphasis on both history and wildlife. The boat holds 6 passengers so prices depend on how many are in your party (a 2- to 3-hr trip for 2 costs £120, for 6 it costs £200).
Orkney Aspects, *Daisybank Farm, Deerness, T01856-741433, www.orkneyaspects.co.uk.* Green Badge guide Pat Stone offers a variety of tours of the islands, including day tours which can be tailored to suit requirements.

Ferry
John O'Groats Ferries, T01955-611353,
www.jogferry.co.uk. Operates a passenger

and bike-only ferry service from **Burwick** to
John o'Groats.

Hoy Colour map 7.

great walking and a famous old man

To the southwest of the Mainland is Hoy, the second largest of the Orkney islands. The name is derived from the Norse *Ha-ey*, meaning High Island, which is appropriate as much of the island is more reminiscent of the Scottish Highlands than Orkney, with only the southern end being typically low and fertile.

Orkney's highest point, **Ward Hill** (1571 ft) is in the north of the island, and the north and west coasts are bounded by spectacular cliffs. At **St John's Head**, the sheer cliffs rise out of the sea to a height of 1150 ft, the highest vertical cliffs in Britain. The island is most famous for its **Old Man of Hoy**, a great rock stack rising to 450 ft. This northern part of Hoy forms the **North Hoy RSPB Reserve** which has a variety of habitats ranging from woodland to tundra-like hilltops and sea cliffs. The reserve is home to a huge variety of birds including great skuas and Arctic skuas, Manx shearwaters and puffins. On the hills there are red grouse, curlews, golden plovers and dunlins, peregrine falcons, merlins, kestrels and even golden eagles. Mountain hares are quite common and, if you are lucky, you can also see otters along the Scapa Flow coastline.

On the southeast coast of the island is **Lyness**, site of a large naval base during both world wars when the British fleet was based in Scapa Flow. Many of the old dilapidated buildings have gone, but the harbour area is still scarred with the scattered remains of concrete structures, and there's also the unattractive sight of the huge oil terminal on **Flotta**. Lyness has a large **Naval Cemetery**, last resting place of those who died at Jutland,

Essential Hoy

Finding your feet

There are two ferry services to Hoy, both run by **Orkney Ferries** (T01856-872044, www. orkneyferries.co.uk). A passenger ferry sails between Stromness and Moaness Pier in the north (30 minutes) three times a day from Monday to Friday, twice on Friday evenings, and twice a day on Saturday and Sunday. There's a reduced winter service from mid-September to mid-May. There's also a car and passenger service (T01856-811397) between Houton and Lyness and Longhope (45 minutes) up to six times daily, Monday to Saturday. There's a limited Sunday service from mid-May to mid-September.

Transport on Hoy is very limited. There is a **Community Bus** hail-and-ride service (T01856-701356) between Longhope and Lyness Monday-Friday and between Longhope and Moaness Pier on Sundays only. This latter route goes past the turn-off to Rackwick for Old Man of Hoy and the driver will stop on request. From May to September the **Hoy Hopper** (T01856-872044) departs from Kirkwall at 0840 and stops at all the sites for just long enough to see them before returning you to Kirkwall (for 1820), £17, child/concession £8.50. There are shops and petrol stations in Lyness and Longhope. For further details, see Transport, page 395.

of Germans killed during the scuttle and of the crew of *HMS Royal Oak*. The **Scapa Flow Visitor Centre** is closed for refurbishment until spring 2019. In the meantime a small exhibition is on display at Lyness and there's a guided trail around the buildings (leaflet from **Visit Orkney** office in Kirkwall, see page 378). At South Walls, overlooking Longhope Bay, is **Hackness Martello Tower and Battery** ① *T01856-701727 (HES), Apr-Sep daily 0930-1730, Oct 1000-1600, £5, concessions £4, children £3*, which, along with another tower on the north side at Crockness, was built in 1815 to protect British ships in Longhope Bay against attack by American and French privateers while they waited for a Royal Navy escort on their journey to Baltic ports.

Walking on Hoy

Hoy's great attraction is its many excellent walking opportunities. Transport is very patchy (see above), but it's a lovely two-hour walk by road through beautiful **Rackwick Glen**, once populated by crofters and fishermen, but now quiet and isolated. On the way you'll pass the **Dwarfie Stone**, a huge, lonely block of sandstone which is the only rock-cut tomb in Britain, dating from around 3000 BC. Be careful, though, because, according to Sir Walter Scott, this is the residence of the Trolld, a dwarf from Norse legend. On your return you can take a different route through a narrow valley between the **Cuilags** (1421 ft) and **Ward Hill** and **Berriedale Wood**, the most northerly woodland in Britain. The most popular walk on Hoy is the spectacular three-hour hike from Rackwick to the cliffs facing the **Old Man of Hoy**. The path climbs steeply westwards from the old crofting township, then turns northwards before gradually descending to the cliff edge.

Listings Hoy *map page 374.*

Where to stay

There's not much accommodation in the north of the island, except for the 2 SYHA hostels. There are a few very good B&Bs in the south.

£££-££ Stromabank Hotel
Longhope, T01856-701494,
www.stromabank.co.uk.
4 rooms. Great views across to Orkney and the Scottish mainland. Also serves evening meals to residents and the public during the summer months in the **Conservatory Restaurant** or public bar (see Restaurants, below). Meals served Sat-Sun only in winter.

££ Quoydale
1 mile from ferry, T01856-791315,
www.orkneyaccommodation.co.uk.
B&B in self-contained en suite room on working farm. Also 2-bed self-catering cottage for £250-300 per week. Taxis, tours and evening meals available.

£ Hoy Centre
About 1 mile from Moaness Pier, T01856-876327, 873535, www.hostel-scotland.co.uk. May-Sep.
Refurbished hostel sleeping 32 in 8 rooms. Family room also available and groups catered for. Book ahead.

£ Rackwick Outdoor Centre
Rackwick Glen, north Hoy, T01856-873535, www.hostelsorkney.co.uk. Mid-Mar to mid-Sep.
2 rooms with 4 beds each, also campsite. Book ahead.

Restaurants

££ Stromabank Hotel
Longhope, South Walls, T01856-701494, www.stromabank.co.uk. Open to non-residents but book May-Sep.
A bar and restaurant which serves local produce, including beef and lamb.

£ Beneth'ill Café
5 mins' walk from the Moaness ferry.
Daily 1000-1630.
Great little place for drinks and snack,
soup and sandwich or some delicious
Orkney ice cream.

Taxi
Steve and Debbie provide a taxi service
in their 9-seater MPV, T01856-701632,
www.islandtourshoy.co.uk. Steve is a
qualified guide and will also arrange
tours of the island.

Transport

Ferry
A passenger ferry sails between **Moaness
Pier** and **Stromness**, daily, 30 mins. There's a
reduced winter service (mid-Sep to mid-May).

Rousay, Egilsay and Wyre *Colour map 7.*

rare birdlife and ancient tombs

These three islands lie a short distance off the northeast coast of Mainland and,
together with Shapinsay to the southeast, are the closest of Orkney's North Isles
to Kirkwall.

Rousay
Rousay is a hilly island about five miles in diameter and is known as the 'Egypt of the
North' due to the large number of archaeological sites. It also has the important **Trumland
RSPB Reserve**, home to merlins, hen harriers, peregrine falcons, short-eared owls and
red-throated divers, and its three lochs offer good trout fishing.

A road runs right around the island, and makes a pleasant 13-mile bike run, but most
of the sights are within walking distance of the ferry pier on the southeast side of the
island, where most of the 200 inhabitants live. A short distance west of the pier by the
road is **Tavershoe Tuick**, an unusual two-storey burial cairn, which was discovered in the
late 19th century by Mrs Burroughs, wife of General Traill Burroughs who lived at nearby
Trumland House. A mile further west, to the
north of the road, is **Blackhammer**, a stalled
Neolithic burial cairn. Further west still, and
a steep climb up from the road, is **Knowe
of Yarso**, another stalled cairn, which
contained the remains of at least 21 people.
The tomb dates from around 2900 BC.

Most of the island's archaeological sights
are to be found along the **Westness Walk**, a
mile-long walk which starts from Westness
Farm, about four miles west of the ferry
pier, and ends at the remarkable Midhowe
Cairn. The walk is described in detail in a
leaflet available from the tourist offices on
Mainland. **Midhowe Cairn** is the largest
and longest cairn – over 100 ft long and
40 ft wide – excavated on Orkney thus far

Essential Rousay, Egilsay
and Wyre

Finding your feet

A small car ferry operated by **Orkney
Ferries** sails from Tingwall to Rousay up
to six times a day Monday to Saturday,
and five times a day on Sunday. Most of
the ferries call in at Egilsay and Wyre, but
some are on demand only and should be
booked in advance at the Tingwall office,
T01856-751360. For further information,
see Transport, page 397.

and, like the others, dates from around 3000 BC. Housed in a large building to protect it, the 'Great Ship of Death', as it is known, contained the remains of 25 people in crouched position on or under the eastern shelves of the chamber, which is divided into 12 sections. Standing nearby, with fine views across to Eynehallow island, is **Midhowe Broch**, one of the best-preserved brochs on Orkney, occupied from around 200 BC to AD 200. The outer walls are about 60 ft in diameter and up to 14 ft high in places.

Another fine walk on the island is around the **RSPB Reserve**. A footpath leads from beside Trumland House and heads up towards the island's highest point, **Blotchnie Fiold** (821 ft). A leaflet describing the walk is available from the tourist offices on Mainland or the **Trumland Orientation Centre** by the pier.

Egilsay and Wyre

These two small islands lie to the east of Rousay and have a couple of interesting sights of their own. Egilsay's claim to fame is the murder here of St Magnus in 1115, and a **cenotaph** marks the spot where he was slain. The island is dominated by the 12th-century **St Magnus church**, built on the site of an earlier church, possibly as a shrine to St Magnus. It is the only surviving example on Orkney of a round-towered Viking church. Much of Egilsay has been bought by the RSPB as a reserve to preserve the habitat of the very rare **corncrake**, whose distinctive rasping call may be heard.

Tiny Wyre features strongly in the Viking saga as the domain of Kolbein Hruga, and the remains of his 12th-century stronghold, **Cubbie Roo's Castle**, and nearby **St Mary's chapel** can be still be seen. Kolbein's home was on the site of Bu Farm, where the poet Edwin Muir (1887-1959) spent part of his childhood. The far westerly point of the island, known as **The Taing**, is a favourite haunt of seals, and a great place to enjoy a sunset.

Listings Rousay, Egilsay and Wyre *map page 374.*

Where to stay

Accommodation is very limited on Rousay, and non-existent on Egilsay and Wyre.

Rousay

£££-££ Taversoe Hotel
Near Knowe of Yarso, about 2 miles west of the pier, T01857-821325, www.taversoehotel. co.uk. Restaurant closed Mon to non-residents.
4 rooms with lovely views over Eynhallow Sound. Offers excellent-value meals (**££-£**), the seafood is particularly recommended. Bar stocks local ales. Transport available to/from the pier.

£ Rousay Hostel
Half a mile from the ferry, Trumland Organic Farm, T01856-821252, www.hostel-scotland. co.uk. Open all year.

Accommodation for 13. Laundry facilities and camping available. Bikes for hire.

Restaurants

££-£ Taversoe Hotel
Near Knowe of Yarso, about 2 miles west of the pier, T01857-821325, www.taversoehotel. co.uk. Restaurant closed Mon to non-residents.
Offers excellent-value meals, the seafood is particularly recommended. Bar stocks local ales.

What to do

Rousay Tours, *T01856-821234.* Run very informative minibus tours from Jun to early Sep Tue-Fri, meeting the 1040 ferry from Tingwall.

Transport

Ferry
A small car ferry operated by **Orkney Ferries** sails from Rousay to **Tingwall**, daily, 20 mins, with onward buses to **Kirkwall**.

Less than 30 minutes by ferry from Kirkwall is the fertile, low-lying island of Shapinsay. The small car ferry makes up to six sailings daily (including Sunday in summer) to Shapinsay from Kirkwall (25 minutes).

Shapinsay is home to **Balfour Castle**, an imposing baronial pile which is in fact a Victorian extension to a much older house called 'Cliffdale'. The house, and the rest of the island, was bought by successive generations of the Balfour family who had made their fortune in India.

In the village, built by the Balfours to house their estate workers, is the **Shapinsay Heritage Centre** ① *T01856-711258, open daily May-Sep, free*, in the old Smithy. It has displays on the island's history and downstairs is the **Smithy Café**. There's a **pub** in the village, in the old gatehouse, a couple of shops and a post office.

A mile north of the village is the **Mill Dam RSPB Reserve**, where there's a hide overlooking a loch from which you can see many species of wildfowl and wader. Four miles from the pier, at the far northeast corner of the island, is the well-preserved **Burroughston Broch**, with good views of seals sunning themselves on the nearby rocks. West of here, at **Quholme**, is the original birthplace of the father of Washington Irving, author of *Rip Van Winkle*.

Listings Shapinsay *map page 374.*

Where to stay

££ Hilton Farm House
T01857-711239, www.hilton orkneyfarmhouse.co.uk.
3 rooms. Very comfortable B&B, which offers evening meals as well as transport and fishing tours. No credit or debit cards accepted.

Transport

Ferry
Small car ferry makes up to 6 sailings daily (including Sun in summer) to **Kirkwall** (25 mins).

Eday

great walking and ancient burial tombs

The long, thin and sparsely populated island of Eday lies at the centre of the North Isles group. It is less fertile than the other islands, but its heather-covered hills in the centre have provided peat for the other peatless Orkney islands. Eday's sandstone has also been quarried, and was used in the building of St Magnus Cathedral in Kirkwall.

Essential Eday

There are flights from Kirkwall to Eday airport, called London Airport, on Wednesdays with **Loganair** (see page 372). There are ferries also from Kirkwall twice daily via Sanday or Stronsay. Note that the pier is at Backaland, on the southeast of the island, a long way from the main sights. For further details, see Transport, below.

The island has numerous chambered cairns and these, along with the other attractions, are concentrated in the northern part. They are all covered in the signposted five-mile **Eday Heritage Walk**, which starts from the Community Centre and leads up to the cliffs of Red Head at the northern tip. The walk takes about four hours to complete, and it's worth picking up the *Eday Heritage Walk* leaflet.

The walk heads past **Mill Loch**, where an RSPB hide allows you to watch rare red-throated divers breeding in spring and summer. Further north is the huge, 15-ft tall **Stone of Setter**, the largest standing stone in Orkney and visible from most of the chambered cairns. Close by are the **Fold of Setter**, a circular enclosure dating back to 2000 BC, and the **Braeside** and **Huntersquoy** chambered cairns. Further north along the path is **Vinquoy Chambered Cairn**, one of the finest in Orkney and similar to the better-known tomb at Maes Howe, dating from around the same time. An acrylic dome provides light to the main chamber, which can be entered by a narrow underground passage.

The path continues to the summit of **Vinquoy Hill**, which commands excellent views of the surrounding islands of Westray and Sanday. From here you can continue north to the spectacular red sandstone cliffs at **Red Head**, home to nesting guillemots, razorbills and puffins in summer, or head southeast along the coast to **Carrick House** ① *T01857-622260, guided tour mid-Jun to mid-Sep, Sun from 1400, other times by appointment, £2.50, £1 children*. Built for Lord Kinclaven, Earl of Carrick, in 1633, the house is best known for its associations with the pirate, John Gow, whose ship ran aground during a failed attack on the house. He was captured and taken to London for trial and hanged. Sir Walter Scott's novel, *The Pirate*, is based on this story.

Listings Eday *map page 374.*

Where to stay

£££ Sui Generis
Redbanks, 2 mins' walk from ferry, T01857-622219, www.suigenerisfurniture.co.uk.
Beautiful guesthouse/furniture maker. The 2 en suite rooms are truly imaginative and unlike anything else in this part of the world. 3-course dinner, £20. Recommended.

££ Blett, Carrick Bay
Opposite the Calf of Eday, T01857-622248.
2 rooms. Very friendly. Evening meal and packed lunch provided if you wish. Mrs Poppelwell also has a self-catering cottage for up to 3 nearby.

£ Youth Hostel
London Bay, T07447-460169. Open all year.
Run by Eday Community Enterprises, just north of the airport. Basic lodging but recently refurbished.

Transport

Air
There are flights from Eday to **Kirkwall** with **Loganair**, T01856-872494, Wed only.

Ferry
Orkney Ferries sail to **Kirkwall** (1 hr 15 mins to 2 hrs) twice daily.

beautiful beaches and Stone Age houses

Sanday is the largest of the North Isles, 12 miles long and flat as a pancake except for the cliffs at Spurness. It is well-named, as its most notable feature is its sweeping bays of sparkling white sand backed by machair and fronted by turquoise seas. There are Loganair flights to Sanday from Kirkwall twice daily from Monday to Friday and once a day on Saturday. Ferries run twice daily from Kirkwall (1½ hours) and arrive at Loth, at the southern tip of the island, where they're met by a minibus.

There are numerous burial mounds all over the island, the most impressive being **Quoyness Chambered Cairn**, a 5000 year-old tomb similar to Maes Howe. The 13 ft-high structure contains a large main chamber with six smaller cells opening through low entrances. Most of the burial tombs remain unexcavated, such as those at **Tofts Ness** at the far northeastern tip, where there are over 500 cairns, making it potentially one of the most important prehistoric sites in Britain. At **Scar**, in Burness, a spectacular Viking find was made, and at **Pool** a major excavation has uncovered the remains of at least 14 Stone Age houses.

Sanday is known for its knitwear, though the factory unfortunately closed down. You can still visit the **Orkney Angora craft shop**, in Upper Breckan, near the northern tip of the island.

Listings Sanday *map page 374.*

Where to stay

££ Backaskaill B&B
Backaskaill, T01857-600305, www. backaskaill.co.uk. Open all year.
Friendly B&B with a wood-burning stove in the lounge. Geoff and Jane are great hosts who do all the cooking, preparing inventive dinners (**£££-££**) using the finest local ingredients.

££ The Belsair
Kettletoft, T01857-600206, www.belsairsanday.co.uk.
3 rooms. Large house overlooking the old harbour. Meals served in the bar and dining room, packed lunches available on request. New owners have completely renovated the hotel. Very good value.

££ Kettletoft Hotel
Kettletoft, T01857-600217, www.kettletofthotel.com.
Most rooms are en suite and are clean, though simply furnished. Serves meals using local produce and has a lively bar. Fish and chip takeaways available on Wed and Sat.

£ Ayre's Rock Hostel
Ayre, T01857-600410, www.ayres-rock-hostel-orkney.co.uk.
Good facilities, 8 beds in 4 rooms. En suite family room sleeps 4. Also a campsite and 'pods' sleeping 2 for £35 per night. Also now has self-contained double room in cottage annex. Cooked breakfast for £7.50 and 2-course evening meal for £12.50. Great value.

What to do

Emma Webb, *Sanday Ranger, T01857-600252, www.sandayranger.org.* Guided walks and tours of the island.

Transport

Air
There are **Loganair** flights to **Kirkwall** twice daily Mon-Fri and once on Sat.

Ferry
There's a ferry service twice daily to **Kirkwall**, 1½ hrs.

The peaceful, low-lying island of Stronsay has some fine sandy beaches and cliffs, which attract large colonies of grey seals and nesting seabirds. There are few real sights on this largely agricultural island, but the coastline has some pleasant walks.

Essential Stronsay

Finding your feet

There are **Loganair** flights from Kirkwall twice daily from Monday to Friday. A ferry service runs from Kirkwall twice daily Monday to Saturday and once on Sunday (1½ hours), and the ferry from Eday runs once a day from Monday to Saturday (35 minutes).

One of the best walks is to the **Vat of Kirbister** in the southeast, a spectacular 'gloup' or blow-hole spanned by the finest natural arch in Orkney. To the south of here, at **Burgh Head**, you'll find nesting puffins and the remains of a ruined broch, and at the southeastern tip, at **Lamb Head**, is a large colony of grey seals, lots of seabirds and several archaeological sites.

The main settlement is the quiet village of **Whitehall**, on the northeast coast where the ferry arrives. It's hard to believe it now, but this was one of the largest herring ports in Europe. During the boom years of the early 20th century, 300 steam drifters were working out of Whitehall and nearly 4000 fishing crew and shore workers were employed. In the peak year of 1924 over 12,000 tons of herring were landed here, to be cured (salted) and exported to Russia and Eastern Europe. Whitehall developed considerably and the **Stronsay Hotel** was said to have the longest bar in Scotland. On Sundays during July and August there were so many boats tied up that it was possible to walk across them to the little island of Papa Stronsay. By the 1930s, however, herring stocks were severely depleted and the industry was in decline. The old Fish Mart by the pier houses a **Heritage Centre** ⓘ *T017856-616386, May-Sep daily 1100-1700, free*, with photos and artefacts from the herring boom days. It also has a café and hostel (see Where to stay, below).

The **Stronsay Bird Reserve** ⓘ *Mill Bay, south of Whitehall, www.stronsaybirdreserve. co.uk*, is one of the best sites in Europe for spotting rare migrants.

Listings Stronsay *map page 374.*

Where to stay

££ Stronsay Hotel
Near the ferry terminal, T01857-616213, www.stronsayhotelorkney.co.uk.
Offers 3 doubles and 1 family room, all en suite and 1 with full disabled facilities. Cheap bar food available. Room only price is £25pp. Operates as the island's hotel, restaurant and pub.

£ Stronsay Fish Mart Hostel
Next to ferry terminal, T01857-616401, www.stronsayfishmart.co.uk. Open all year.
Well equipped and comfortable and only a min's walk from the ferry. 4 bedrooms with double bunk beds. Their café does cheap meals 1100-1500 every day except Thu.

Transport

Air
There are **Loganair** flights to **Kirkwall** twice daily Mon-Fri.

Car hire and taxis
DS Peace, Samson's Lane, T01857-616335.

Ferry
A ferry service runs to **Kirkwall** daily, 1½ hrs, and once daily Mon-Sat to **Eday**, 35 mins.

coastal walks and one of the largest sea bird reserves in the islands

Westray is the second largest of the North Isles, with a varied landscape of farmland, hilly moorland, sandy beaches and dramatic cliffs. It is also the most prosperous of the North Isles, producing beef, fish and seafood, and supports a population of 700.

Around Westray
The main settlement is **Pierowall**, in the north of the island, but, though it has one of the best harbours in Orkney, the main ferry terminal is at Rapness, on the south coast. Pierowall is a relatively large village for the North Isles and there are shops, a post office, a hotel and the **Westray Heritage Centre** ⓘ *T01857-677414, www.westrayheritage.co.uk, early May-late Sep Mon 1130-1700, Tue-Sat 1000-1200, 1400-1700, Sun 1330-1700, £3, concessions £2.50, children 50p*, with displays on local and natural history, and a tearoom. Also in the village is the ruined 17th-century St Mary's church. About a mile west of the village is Westray's most notable ruin, **Noltland Castle**, a fine example of a 16th-century fortified Z-plan tower-house. To explore inside, pick up the key from the back door of the nearby farm.

Walks on Westray
There are some great coastal walks on the island, particularly to the spectacular sea cliffs at **Noup Head**, at the far northwestern tip, which are an **RSPB Reserve** and second only to St Kilda in terms of breeding seabirds, with huge colonies of guillemots, razorbills, kittiwakes and fulmars, as well as puffins. The cliffs on the west coast of Westray are five miles long and there's an excellent walk down the coast from Noup Head, past **Gentleman's Cave**, used as a hiding place by four Jacobite lairds in 1746. Near the southern end of the walk is **Fitty Hill** (554 ft), the highest point on the island, which you can climb for great views, and the walk ends at **Inga Ness**, where you can also see puffins. The best place to see them is at **Castle o'Burrian**, a sea stack on **Stanger Head**, on the southeastern coast near the Rapness ferry terminal.

Essential Westray

Finding your feet

Flights to Westray with **Loganair** depart Kirkwall twice daily from Monday to Friday and once a day at weekends and there's a car ferry service to Rapness, on the south coast of the island (1½ hours). It sails twice daily in summer (mid-May to mid-September) and once daily in winter.

Listings *Westray map page 374.*

Where to stay

£££ Pierowall Hotel
Pierowall, T01857-677472,
www.pierowallhotel.co.uk.
4 en suite rooms. Comfortable and friendly small family hotel. Also serves good-value bar meals (**££-£**), try their monkfish and chips.

££ No 1 Broughton
Pierowall, T01857-677726,
www.no1broughton.co.uk.
Renovated house overlooking the bay, with 3 nicely furnished rooms (2 doubles and a twin). Packed lunch and light supper on request and also use of their sauna.

££-£ Chalmersquoy

About ½ mile south from village along the coast, T01857-677214, www. chalmersquoywestray.co.uk.
Varied accommodation in Westray comprising a B&B with 3 comfortable en suite rooms (twin, double and large suite), Ben End, a self-catering cottage that sleeps 5/6 (£350 per week), a self-catering apartment (sleeps 3/4, £300 per week), high-quality hostel accommodation with great views and also a campsite. Owners Michael and Teehie also organize live music events Jun-Aug on a Tue night.

Self-catering

Bis Geos

T01857-677420, www.bisgeos.co.uk.
3 well-equipped self-catering cottages with great views. Minibus available from the pier. 1 cottage sleeps 2 and the others sleep 4 and 8.

Transport

Air
Loganair flights to **Kirkwall** depart twice daily Mon-Sat.

Bus
M&J Harcus, Pierowall, T07789-034289. Run the bus service round the island.

Ferry
There's a car ferry service to **Kirkwall** from **Rapness**, 1½ hrs. It sails twice daily in summer (mid-May to mid-Sep) and once daily in winter. There's also a passenger ferry from **Pierowall** to **Papa Westray**.

Taxi
Graham Maben, T07766-073088. Also runs **Westraak Tours**.

★ Papa Westray   *Colour map 7.*

home to the oldest house in Europe

Tiny Papa Westray, known locally as 'Papay', is best known as being the destination for the world's shortest scheduled flight, from Westray; it takes all of two minutes, or less with a good following wind, and there's no shortage of that.

But there are other reasons to visit this little island, one of the most remote of the Orkney group. Papay is home to Europe's oldest house, the **Knap of Howar** ⓘ *open at all times, free*, which was built around 5500 years ago and is still standing (they knew how to build 'em in those days). It's on the west coast, just south of the airport. Half a mile north is **St Boniface Kirk**, one of the oldest Christian sites in the north of Scotland, founded in the eighth century, though most of the recently restored building dates from the 12th century. Inland from the Knap of Howar is **Holland Farm**, former home of the lairds of the island, where you can rummage around the farm buildings and museum.

Essential Papa Westray

Finding your feet

The famous two-minute flight leaves Westray twice daily Monday to Saturday and once on Sunday. There is also a direct flight to Papay from Kirkwall, daily Monday to Saturday. There's a passenger ferry from Pierowall on Westray three to six times a day, and the car ferry from Kirkwall to Westray continues to Papa Westray on Tuesdays and Fridays (two hours and 15 minutes).

Papay is famous for its birds, and **North Hill**, on the north of the island, is an important RSPB Reserve. The cliffs are home to many thousands of breeding seabirds, and at **Fowl Craig** on the east coast you can see nesting puffins. The interior is home to the largest arctic tern colony in Europe, as well as many arctic skuas. A guided tour is possible with the **RSPB warden** ① *T01857-850176, May-Aug Wed and Sat only*. For details of full-day ranger-led tours of Papa Westray or for details of bike hire on the island, see What to do, below.

It's worth taking a boat trip to the even tinier, deserted **Holm of Papay**, off the east coast. This is the site of several Neolithic burial cairns, including one of the largest chambered cairns on Orkney. You enter the tomb down a ladder into the main chamber which is nearly 70 ft long, with a dozen side-cells. For boat trips between May and September, call T0776-4569790.

Listings Papa Westray *map page 374.*

Where to stay

£ Papa Westray Hostel
Beltane House, T01857-644321,
www.papawestray.co.uk.
A row of converted farm workers' cottages to the east of Holland Houserun by the island community co-operative. Cosy and comfortable accommodation in shared dorms and single, twin, double and family rooms, also camping bothies for 2 people (like upturned wooden boats) and a campsite. The community co-operative also runs the well-stocked grocer shop and hot drinks and home-bakes are available in the hostel dining room. The shop is open Mon-Thu and Sat 1000-1200, also Mon, Wed-Fri 1500-1700 and Sat 1800-1900. They have a minibus which takes ferry passengers from the pier to anywhere on the island.

What to do

Papay Peedie Tour, *run by the Papa Westray ranger, T07931-235213, papayranger@gmail. com.* Tours on Wed, Thu and Sat between May and Aug, £50 for a full day, £25 for children. The ranger can also arrange boat trips to the Holm of Papay and bike hire on the island, £10 per day, £5 child.

Transport

Air
The 2-min flight to **Westray** leaves twice daily Mon-Sat. There is also a direct flight to **Kirkwall**, daily Mon-Sat.

Ferry
There's a passenger ferry to **Pierowall** on Westray, 3-6 times daily, 25 mins.

North Ronaldsay *Colour map 7.*

a bastion of ancient traditions

Remote and storm-battered, North Ronaldsay is the most northerly of the Orkney islands and a place where old Orcadian traditions remain. It seems remarkable that anyone should live here at all in these extreme conditions, but 'North Ron' – as it is known locally – has been inhabited for many centuries and continues to be heavily farmed. The island's sheep are a hardy lot and live exclusively off the seaweed on a narrow strip of beach, outside a 13-mile stone dyke which surrounds the island. This gives their meat a unique, 'gamey' flavour.

This small, flat island, only three miles long, has few real attractions, except to keen ornithologists who flock here to catch a glimpse of its rare migrants. From late March to early June, and mid-August to early November there are huge numbers of migratory birds. The **Bird Observatory**, in the southwest corner of the island by the ferry pier, gives information on which species have been sighted, as well as providing accommodation. There are also colonies of grey seals and cormorants at **Seal Skerry**, on the northeast tip of the island. There are **Loganair** flights from Kirkwall, twice daily from Monday to Saturday and there's a car and passenger ferry which sails from Kirkwall twice a week (usually Tuesday and Friday). Contact **Orkney Ferries** for details.

Listings North Ronaldsay *map page 374.*

Where to stay

You can rent the old lighthouse keeper's cottages which sleep 4 people, www.nts.org.uk for full details.

££ Observatory Guest House
T01857-633200, www.nrbo.co.uk.
4 doubles and 2 twins. Offers wind- and solar-powered accommodation that's popular with birdwatchers and serves a great-value hearty dinner (**£££** for half board). It also has a small hostel next door (**£**).

Restaurants

££-£ Burrian Inn and Restaurant
T01857-633221.
Orkney's most northerly pub, also serves food.

Transport

Air
There are **Loganair** flights to **Kirkwall** twice daily Mon-Sat.

Ferry
There's a car and passenger ferry which sails to **Kirkwall** twice a week (usually Tue and Fri), 2 hrs 40 mins.

Shetland

Shetland is so far removed from the rest of Scotland it can only be shown as an inset on maps. It is closer to the Arctic Circle than it is to London, and it's easier and quicker to get there from Norway than it is from the UK's capital. This seems entirely appropriate, for Shetland is historically and culturally closer to Scandinavia than Britain. Indeed, whilst the Scottish debate on independence waxes and wanes, so some Shetlanders argue that the islands should go it alone. Many of its place names are of Norse origin, and people here still celebrate the Vikings in the annual Up-Helly-Aa festivals. Modern-day visitors tend to come by plane rather than longboat, and usually bring binoculars, for Shetland is a birdwatcher's paradise. It is home to countless species, many of them seeking refuge from the madding crowds. And there's no better place than here to get away from it all. Moreover, due to its latitude, in high summer there's daylight for more than 20 hours so if you want to pack as much as possible into your visit this is the place where you can enjoy a coastal walk or round of golf at midnight.

Essential Shetland

Finding your feet

Air

Getting to Shetland by air can be expensive but booking well in advance can help keep the costs down. Shetland has good air connections with the rest of Scotland and there are regular flights from several mainland airports which are operated by **Loganair** (T0344-800 2855, www. loganair.co.uk). There are direct daily flights from Aberdeen (one hour, up to five a day), Glasgow (1½ hours, up to two a day), Edinburgh (1½ hours, up to three a day)), Inverness (1¾ hours with brief stop in Orkney, up to two a day), Kirkwall (40 minutes, up to two a day) and Manchester (one hour 35 minutes, one on Saturday in summer). There are also regular international flights from Bergen (Norway) in summer. **Loganair** have a code-share agreement with **BA** and **BMI Regional** allowing seamless connections with other main UK airports. There are also direct flights to Sumburgh from Aberdeen, Edinburgh, Glasgow and Inverness with **Flybe** (www.flybe.com).

Shetland's main **airport** (T01950-460905, www.hial.co.uk), is at Sumburgh, 25 miles south of Lerwick and there are regular daily buses (No 6), which connect with flights. These buses also stop at several main sights, including Jarlshof and Sandwick (for Mousa Broch).

Sea

Ferry links with the UK are provided mostly by **Northlink Ferries** (T0845-600 0449, www.northlinkferries.co.uk). It operates daily car ferry sailings to Lerwick from Aberdeen (some are via Kirkwall, Orkney), the journey takes 12 hours (14 hours if it goes via Kirkwall). There are also ferries from Norway, Iceland and the Faroe Isles.

Getting around

A regular scheduled inter-island service is operated by **Air Task** on behalf of **Shetland Isles Council** (T01595-840246 for reservations, for timetables and fares visit www.airtask.com) from Tingwall airport near Lerwick to Foula, Fair Isle, Papa Stour and Out Skerries. An extensive public bus service links Lerwick with all towns, villages and tourist sights (there are several operators). Bus No 4 runs to Scalloway (Monday to Saturday) and there are also buses (Monday to Saturday) to Walls (No 9), Sandness, Aith (No 9 and 12), North Roe (No 21), Hillswick (No 21), Vidlin (No19), Toft (No 23) and Mossbank (No 23). Buses leave from the **Viking bus station** on Commercial Road in Lerwick to destinations all over the Mainland. The council sold the surrounding buildings to some local cafés and restaurants a few years back and getting on and off buses can be quite chaotic due to customers parking their cars in bus lanes.

Frequent ferry services also link many of the islands with the Shetland mainland. These services are operated by **Shetland Islands Council** (T01595-693535, www.shetland. gov.uk). Fares vary according the route and booking in advance is essential. Times and fares can be found on the **Shetland Council** website or are available from the **iCentre** in Lerwick. A *Shetland Transport Timetable*, published by the Shetland Council, contains details of all air, sea and bus services throughout the islands. It is available from the tourist office in Lerwick. Shetland has around 500 miles of good roads, and the best way to explore the islands is by car, but note that it is cheaper to hire a car in Lerwick rather than at the airport. Hitching is a feasible way to get around and is relatively safe, and cycling is a good way to experience the islands, though most places are very exposed and the winds can be relentless and punishing. For further details, see Transport page 412.

Shetland

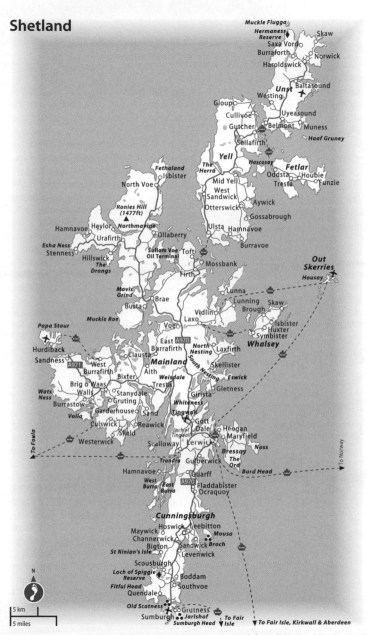

home to a Viking fire festival

Lerwick (population 7600) is the capital and administrative centre of Shetland and the only sizeable town, containing over 7000 of the islands' 22,000 strong population. Though the islands have been inhabited for many centuries, Lerwick only dates from the 17th century, when it began to grow as a trading port for Dutch herring fishermen, thanks to its superb natural sheltered harbour, the Bressay Sound. The town spread along the waterfront, where merchants built their lodberries, which were houses and warehouses with their own piers so that they could trade directly with visiting ships. By the late 19th century Lerwick had become the main herring port in northern Europe. Lerwick has continued to grow: the discovery of oil in the North Sea in the early 1970s led to the building of the Sullom Voe Oil Terminal, and the effect on the town has been dramatic. It is now the main transit point to the North Sea oil rigs and there have been major extensions to the harbour area, bringing increased shipping and prosperity to the town.

Sights

The town's heart is the attractive **Commercial Street**, which runs parallel to the Esplanade. At the southern end are many old houses and lodberries, and you can continue south along the cliffs to the **Knab** or to lovely **Bain's beach**. Lerwick Walks is a leaflet detailing many interesting walks in and around town.

Overlooking the north end of Commercial Street is **Fort Charlotte** ① *Jun-Sep daily 0900-2200, Oct-May daily 0900-1600, free,* built in 1665 and later rebuilt in 1780 and named after Queen Charlotte, George III's consort. It has since been used as a prison and Royal Naval Reserve base and, though there's little to see in the fort, there are fine views of the harbour from the battlements. (As an aside, if you're hungry, the Fort chip shop below the fort by the war memorial serves up cheap and tasty fish suppers.) One

of Lerwick's most impressive buildings is the Victorian **town hall** ① *Mon-Fri 0900-1700, free,* on Hillhead. The stained-glass windows of the main hall depict episodes from Shetland's history. Built on the historic site of Hay's Dock, is the fabulous **Shetland Museum and Archives** ① *T01595-695057, www.shetlandmuseumandarchives.org.uk; museum open Mon-Sat 1000-1600, Sun 1200-1700; archives open Mon-Fri 1000-1600, free,* which uses interactive technology to give an introduction to the islands' history. Amongst the artefacts on display are Viking runes, whale bones carved by fishermen and all manner of things knitted in the Fair Isle style. On the first floor is **Hay's Dock Café Restaurant** (see Restaurants, page 411). Next to the museum, housed in an impressive new building, is **Mareel**

Essential Lerwick

Finding your feet

Ferries from Aberdeen arrive at the main Holmsgarth terminal, about a mile north of the old harbour. There's a regular bus service between Lerwick and Sumburgh airport (50 minutes) run by **John Leask & Son** (T01595-693162, www.leaskstravel.co.uk). Taxis (around £40-45) and car hire are also available. All island bus services start and end at the Viking bus station, which is on Commercial Road, a short distance north of the town centre. The town is small and everything is within easy walking distance.

① *T01595-745500, www.mareel.org, Sun-Thu 1000-2300, Fri-Sat 1000-0100*, a live music, cinema and creative arts centre managed by Shetland Arts Development Agency. The café is a great place for a quick lunch or a drink and a snack in the evening.

Also in town, in the Galley Shed off St Sunniva Street, is the **Up-Helly-Aa Exhibition** ① *www.uphellyaa.org, mid-May to early Sep Tue 1400-1600, 1900-2100, Fri 1900-2100, Sat 1400-1600, £3, concessions and children £1*. This gives a taste of the famous fire festivals, the biggest of which is held annually in Lerwick on the last Tuesday in January, when there's a torch-lit procession through the town with hundreds of people dressed in Viking costumes (*guizers*). The procession is followed by a replica Viking longship built especially for the event. At the end of the procession the ship is set ablaze when the guizers throw their flaming torches on to it.

A mile west of town are the substantial remains of **Clickimin Broch**, a fortified site occupied from 700 BC to around the fifth or sixth century AD. A path leads to the site from opposite the supermarket on the A970. About a mile north of the ferry terminal is the **Böd of Gremista and Shetland Textile Working Museum** ① *T01595-694386,*

Lerwick

N

200 metres
200 yards

Where to stay 🛏	Rockvilla Guest House **5**	Hay's Dock **2**
Brentham House **1**	Westhall B&B **6**	Peerie Shop Café **3**
Glen Orchy House **2**		
Islesburgh House Hostel **3**	**Restaurants 🍴**	**Bars & clubs 🍸**
Kveldsro House **4**	Bay Brasserie **1**	Lounge Bar **4**

www.shetlandheritageassociation.com, end Apr to early Oct Tue-Sat 1000-1700, Thu till 1900, £3, a restored 18th-century fishing *böd* (booth) which was the birthplace of Arthur Anderson (1791-1868), co-founder of the Peninsular and Oriental Steam Navigation Company, now P&O. One of the rooms features an exhibition on Anderson's life and involvement with P&O. The textile museum houses a collection of Shetland textiles from the 1800s to present day and you can often see practitioners weaving, spinning and lace knitting.

Bressay

Lying to the east of Lerwick across the Bressay Sound is the island of Bressay (pronounced 'bressah'), which creates a sheltered harbour for the capital and led to its establishment as a major trading port. Seven miles long by three miles wide, it makes an ideal day trip for cyclists. Another good way to get around is on foot, and there's a fine walk to the top of **Ward Hill** (742 ft), the highest point, from where you get great views of the island and as far afield as Foula and Out Skerries. There are also good coastal walks, particularly along the cliffs from Noss Sound south to **Bard Head**, **The Ord** and **Bressay Lighthouse**, where you can see large colonies of seabirds. For wildlife cruises to Bressay and Noss, see page 412.

Noss

Serious birdwatchers should head for Noss, a tiny, uninhabited island off the east coast of Bressay, which is a **National Nature Reserve** with over 100,000 pairs of breeding seabirds. A walk around the perimeter of the island takes at least three hours but is highly recommended. At the east side is the **Noup of Noss**, where the 600-ft cliffs are packed full of nesting gannets. The reserve is managed by Scottish Natural Heritage who have a small visitor centre at **Gungstie**.

Listings Lerwick and around *maps pages 407 and 409.*

Tourist information

Lerwick iCentre
Market Cross, Commercial St, T01595-693434.
May-Sep Mon-Fri 0800-1800, Sat 0800-1600,
Sun 1000-1300, Oct-Apr Mon-Fri 0900-1700.
Shetland's main tourist office is an excellent source of information, books, maps and leaflets. They will also change foreign currency and book accommodation. It's also worth looking at www.shetland.org, which has links to events, transport, accommodation and local operators.

Where to stay

Most of Shetland's best accommodation is outside Lerwick, where hotels are mostly geared towards the oil industry.

During the peak months of Jul-Aug and the **Folk Festival** in Apr, it's a good idea to book in

advance. There are several decent guesthouses and B&Bs in town, which are all much of a muchness. The tourist office can supply details.

£££ Glen Orchy House
20 Knab Rd, T01595-692031,
www.guesthouselerwick.com.
Excellent guesthouse with 23 en suite rooms and its own Thai restaurant.

£££ Kveldsro House Hotel
Greenfield Place, T01595-692195,
www.shetlandhotels.com.
17 rooms. The most luxurious hotel in town. Pronounced 'kel-ro', it overlooks the harbour and has an upmarket restaurant (**£££**) as well as cheaper bar food.

£££-££ Brentham House
7 Harbour St, T01950-460201,
www.brenthamhouse.com.
3 en suite rooms (**££**) plus 2 self-catering apartments for 1 or 2 people (**£££**) and 1 self-

catering suite for up to 4 (**£££**). Luxurious rooms featuring Victorian bathtubs and with a continental breakfast waiting in the fridge.

£££-££ Rockvilla Guest House
88 St Olaf St, T01595-695804.
3 spacious rooms providing single, double, twin and family accommodation. Friendly and welcoming, 5 mins' walk from centre and with ample parking outside.

£££-££ Westhall B&B and Cottage
Lower Sound, T01595-690364,
www.bedandbreakfastlerwick.co.uk.
3 rooms. A big old house, just 20 mins' walk from the town centre along the bay. Excellent B&B in a great location by the beach. They also offer a very comfortable and well-equipped cottage from £100 per night for 2, or £130 for 4, minimum 3 nights. Recommended.

£ Islesburgh House Hostel
King Harald St, T01595-745100,
islesburgh@shetland.govuk. Apr-Sep.
Clean and well-run SYHA hostel with 62 beds and an excellent café.

Restaurants

Despite a ready supply of fresh local produce, with a few notable exceptions (and of course during its excellent 'Flavour of Shetland' food festival in Jun), the archipelago can feel like a gastronomic desert.

£££-££ Hay's Dock
Shetland Museum, www.haysdock.co.uk, see page 408. Mon-Thu 1000-1430, Fri 1700-2100, Sat 1000-2100.
This café/restaurant is worth a try for some tasty local seafood, salmon, beef and lamb. Lunch menu is also good and they cater for kids with their special 'Mootie Moose Menu'.

££ Bay Brasserie
Lerwick Hotel, 15 South Rd, T01595-692166, www.shetlandhotels.com. Open daily for dinner or bar lunch.
Extensive menu is big on local beef, lamb and fish. Their lunch menu (**£**) is good value.

££ Gallery Restaurant
Kveldsro Hotel, see Where to stay, above.
Same hotel group as the **Lerwick Hotel** and similar menus.

£ Peerie Shop Café
Esplanade, T01595-692816.
Mon-Sat 0900-1800.
The best cappuccino in Shetland and muffins the size of Bressay. Also does cheering soups.

Bars and clubs

Lounge Bar
Mounthooly St, near the iCentre.
The locals mingle downstairs, whilst upstairs the bar is quite touristy but definitely one of the best places for a drink. Moreover, this remains a magnet for enjoying planned and impromptu sessions of Shetland's wonderful fiddle and folk music. Whenever you arrive, there's usually someone playing.

Festivals

The *Shetland Times*, www.shetlandtimes. co.uk, has details what is going on. Also check www.shetland.org.

Jan Up-Helly-Aa, www.uphellyaa.org. Lerwick's annual fire festival is celebrated on the last Tue in Jan with torch-lit processions, Viking costumes and the burning of a Viking longboat. If you miss this one, there are a number across the islands over the next 2 months. See also page 409.
May Shetland Folk Festival, www.shetland folkfestival.com. Folk music has a strong following in Shetland and this is one of Scotland's top folk events. Over 3 days in early May musicians from around the globe come to play.
Oct Taste of Shetland Food Festival, www. tasteofshetland.com. The 4-day food festival is a gastronome's dream with the best of Shetland lamb and shellfish among the treats to be found by the harbour in Lerwick.
Mid-Oct Shetland Accordion and Fiddle Festival, for details contact the Folk Festival

office, 5 Burns Lane, Lerwick, T01595-693162 or www.shetandaccordionandfiddle.com.

Shopping

Ninian, *110 Commercial St, T01595-696655, www.ninianshetland.co.uk.* For new takes on traditional Fair Isle knitting.
Peerie Shop, *Esplanade T01595-692816.* Colourful homeware, postcards and knits.
Shetland Times, *Commerical St, T01595-695531.* For books about Shetland.
The Spiders Web, *51 Commercial St, T01595-695246. Mon-Sat 0900-1700.* The place to buy authentic Shetland knit-wear sourced directly from the local knitters. Hand-spun yarn and hand-knitted Fair Isle jumpers, waistcoats, cardigans, scarves and shawls.

What to do

Boat trips
A boat trip to the seabird colonies on Noss and Bressay is unmissable, so don't even think about coming here and not doing it.
Seabirds-and-seals, *Bressay, T07831-217042 or T07876-550224, www.seabirds-and-seals.com.* Award-winning wildlife cruises run by Jonathan Wills. If you go at the right time of year, you are almost certain to see seals, porpoises and the astounding gannetry on the spectacular cliffs of Noss' east coast. Trips leave at 0515 (2 hrs), 1015 and 1415 (both 3 hrs) mid-Apr to end-Sep, weather permitting, £45 for 3-hr trip, £40 for 2-hr trip, under 16s £25/20.

The **Mousa Boat** also runs wildlife trips to Noss (see page 417).

If you want to learn about the islands' stunning geology and how man and nature has made these islands their own, Allen Fraser of **Geo-Tours** (Burra Isle, T01595-859218, www.shetlandgeology.com), has a fine grasp of the last 500 million years.

Cycling
Cycle hire Eric Browns Cycles at Grantfield Garage, *North Rd, T01595-692709, www.grantfieldgarage.co.uk. Mon-Sat 0800-*

2300, Sun 1100-2300. Hires bikes for £12.50 per day or £50 per week.

Sea kayaking
Sea Kayak Shetland, *T01592-840272, www.seakayakshetland.co.uk.* Tours with Angus Nichol. Full-day trip £80pp, introductory session £27pp.

Tour operators
John Leask & Son, *the Esplanade, Lerwick, T01595-693162, www.leaskstravel.co.uk.* Travel agent and tour operator. Can arrange fly-drive packages to Shetland with car hire and accommodation. Also offer a variety of bus tours, prices depending on the destination.

Transport

For more information, see Finding your feet, page 408.

Lerwick
Bus
Bus No 4 runs to **Scalloway** (Mon-Sat) and there are also buses to **Walls** (No 9); **Sandness, Aith** (No 9 and 12); **North Roe** (No 21); **Hillswick** (No 21); **Vidlin** (No19); **Toft** (No 23), 1 hr; **Mossbank** (No 23). All buses leave from Lerwick's **Viking** bus station/shelter. There are several buses daily between **Lerwick**, **Sandwick** and **Sumburgh Airport**. 2 buses daily Mon-Sat to **Quendale**, with a change at **Channerwick junction**. Regular daily buses from **Lerwick** stop at the Sumburgh Hotel, **Scatness** and **Grutness Pier** (for Fair Isle) en route to the airport.

Regular buses Mon-Sat to **Brae** and **Hillswick** to the northwest, and **Toft** and **Mossbank** to the north, pass through **Voe**. To **Hillswick** and **Toft/Mossbank** stop in **Brae**. There is a daily bus service from here to **Hillswick**, Mon-Sat, 1710. From there, a feeder service (No 21) continues to **Eshaness**, 20 mins. Contact **Johnson Transport**, T01806-522443, www.johnsontransport.co.uk. There are daily buses between **Bixter** and **Clousta** via Twatt, run by **Whites Coaches**, T01595-809443.

For detailed information on all bus services on Shetland, T01595-744868, or see www.zettrans.org.uk.

Car hire
Bolts Car Hire, Toll Clock Shopping Centre, 26 North Rd, T01950-460777, www.boltscar hire.co.uk; **John Leask & Son**, the Esplanade, T01595-693162, www.leaskstravel.co.uk; **Star Rent-a-Car**, 22 Commercial Rd, T01595-692075, www.starrentacar.co.uk, which also has an office at Sumburgh Airport.

Ferry
See Essential Shetland, page 406.

Taxi
There are several taxi companies in Lerwick; **Allied Taxis**, I01595-690069; **Sinclair's Taxis**, T01595-696060.

Bressay
Ferry
Regular ferries sail from **Lerwick** to Bressay (7 mins), T01595-743974. **Noss** can only be visited from late Apr-late Aug Tue, Wed and Fri-Sun, 1000-1700. From the 'Wait here' sign overlooking Noss sound on the east side of Bressay an inflatable dinghy shuttles back and forth to Noss during the island's opening hours. In bad weather, call T0800 101 7818, to check if it's sailing. A **postcar** service runs once a day Mon, Wed and Fri from Maryfield ferry terminal to Noss Sound, www.bressay.org.

Bus
There are buses Mon-Sat between **Scalloway** and **Lerwick**, John Leask & Son, see What to do, opposite.

Central Mainland *Colour map 7.*

headquarters of the famous Shetland Bus

The Central Mainland is Shetland's slim waist, where only a few miles of land separate the east and west coast. There's not a huge amount of tourist interest here but the area's history is fascinating and the Scalloway Museum is certainly worth a visit.

Scalloway and around
Six miles from Lerwick on the west coast is Scalloway, once the capital of Shetland and now a fishing port and fish-processing centre. In 1942, during the Second World War, Scalloway became the headquarters of the Shetland Bus operations. This was the name given to the Norwegian fishing boats which sailed to Shetland during the night from German-occupied Norway, bringing refugees to safety and returning with ammunition and resistance fighters. An interesting and poignant exhibition on the Shetland Bus can be seen at **Scalloway Museum** ① *Main St, T01595-880734, www.scallowaymuseum.org, mid-Apr to end Sep Mon-Sat 1100-1600, Sun 1400-1600, £3, child/concession £1.*

The harbour is dominated by the ruins of **Scalloway Castle** ① *T01595-841815, free to visit, the key is available from the Scalloway Musuem,* built in 1600 by the notorious Earl Patrick Stewart using local slave labour (see box, page 383). After his execution the castle fell into disrepair, though the four-storey main block and one wing remain. Inside, an interpretative display explains its history.

South of Scalloway lie the islands of **Trondra** and **Burra**, now connected to the Mainland by bridges. At the south of the promontory at Houss, East Burra is the workshop of **Burra Bears** (call to arrange a visit T01595-859374, www.burrabears.co.uk), where you can buy these unique and cuddly teddy bears made from recycled Fair Isle jumpers. On the road back, over towards West Burra is the attractive little fishing village of **Hamnavoe**,

Tingwall

North of Scalloway, the B9074 runs through the fertile Tingwall Valley, past a nine-hole **golf course** at Asta and the **Loch of Tingwall**, which is good for brown trout fishing and also home to swans and otters. At the northern end of the loch is a promontory called **Law Ting Holm**, which was the site of the Althing, or parliament, during the period of Norse rule. Overlooking the loch is **Tingwall Kirk**, built in the late 18th century on the site of the earlier church of St Magnus which dated back to the early period of Norse Christianity. In the graveyard is the old burial vault with several interesting old grave slabs.

Weisdale

The A971 continues northwest towards Weisdale, a district with some worthwhile attractions. At the head of **Weisdale Voe** the B9075 branches north to **Weisdale Mill** ⓘ *T01595-745750, www.shetlandarts.org, Wed-Fri 1100-1500, Sat-Sun 1100-1600, free*, which houses the **Bonhoga Gallery**, a purpose-built art gallery featuring varied exhibitions of local, national and international works. There's also a nice café serving snacks. Weisdale Mill was part of the Kergord Estate, known until 1945 as Flemington, and was built from the stones of evacuated crofthouses. Over 300 crofters were forcibly evicted in the mid-19th century during the Clearances, when lairds expanded their more profitable sheep-farming activities. In 1940 the mill was requisitioned as the intelligence and administrative HQ for the **Shetland Bus** operations (see Scalloway, above). The Kergord estate today is the largest area of woodland in Shetland and attracts migratory birds.

On the west shore of Weisdale Voe, south of the mill, are the ruins of the house where John Clunies Ross (1786-1854) was born. He settled in the Cocos Islands in the Indian Ocean in 1827; the islands were owned by the Estate of the Clunies Ross family until purchased by the Australian government in 1978. In 1984 the islanders voted to become part of Australia.

Listings Central Mainland *map page 407.*

Where to stay

£££ Herrislea House Hotel
Tingwall, near the airport, by the crossroads, T01595-840208, www.herrisleahouse.co.uk.
9 en suite rooms (4 singles, 2 doubles and 3 sleeping 3-4). Country house in lovely setting with well-furnished rooms. Their restaurant (**£££**) specializes in local meat and fish (Mon-Sat 1830-2045) but also does home-made pizzas. Dogs welcome.

£££ Scalloway Hotel
Main St, Scalloway, a few miles west of Lerwick, T01595-880444, www.scallowayhotel.com.
23 rooms. A very comfortable family-run hotel with a fine restaurant (**£££**, Mon-Sat 1700-2100, Sun 1200-2000), the 1st on Shetland to be awarded 2 AA Rosettes. Their

fish, shellfish and local lamb is a speciality. Bar meals also available (**££**) Mon-Sat 1200-1500 and 1700-2100, Sun 1200-2000. Recommended.

Restaurants

££-£ Cornerstone Café
On the main road in Scalloway, near the castle, T01595-880346. Mon-Thu 0930-1700, Fri-Sat also 1800-2100, Sun 1200-1700.
No-nonsense staples such as burgers, steak pie, etc. Good-value lunches and takeaways.

£ Da Haaf Restaurant
NAFC Marine Centre, Porth Arthur, Scalloway, T01595-772480, www.nafc.ac.uk. Mon-Thu 0830-1600, Fri and Sat 1730-2100.
A canteen-style restaurant in the North Atlantic Fisheries college specializing in

seafood. Does a good fish supper, as well as a more upmarket menu for the evenings.

Transport

Air
Tingwall airport, T01595-840246, has flights to most of the smaller islands, including the **Skerries**. Getting to the airport is straightforward as the regular buses between Lerwick and Westside stop in Tingwall.

The Westside *OS Landranger Nos 3 and 4. Colour map 7.*

spectacular sea cliffs and rare wildlife

The western Mainland of Shetland, stretching west from Weisdale to Sandness, is known as The Westside. This part of Shetland is notable for its varied landscape of spectacular sea cliffs, rolling green hills, bleak moorland, peaty freshwater lochs and numerous long sea lochs, or voes. This is excellent walking country, with many fine coastal routes, especially around Culswick and Dale of Walls. It is also great for birdwatching and trout fishing, and there are many opportunities for spotting whales, dolphins and otters.

Stanydale, Walls and Sandness
There are a few interesting archaeological sites here, too. At Stanydale, signposted from the road between the villages of **Bixter** and **Walls**, is the site of a Neolothic settlement with the remains of houses, field boundaries and clearance cairns. Near the **Brig o' Waas**, just north of Walls, is the **Scord of Brouster**, a prehistoric farm which has been excavated.

The pretty little village of **Walls** (pronounced *waas*) is set around a sheltered natural harbour and is a popular spot with visiting yachts. It also attracts many visitors during its Agricultural Show in August, the biggest such event on Shetland. Walls is the departure point for ferries to the remote island of Foula, see below.

Northwest of Walls, the A971 crosses bleak moorland before descending to the crofting township of **Sandness** (pronounced *saa-ness*), surrounded by fertile land and facing little Papa Stour, about a mile offshore. There's a good beach here and also a **woollen spinning mill** where you can watch how they spin the famously fine wool into yarn.

Foula
Lying 15 miles west of the Shetland Mainland, tiny Foula – whose name derives from the Norse *fugl ey*, meaning 'bird island' – is the second most remote inhabited island after Fair Isle. It supports a population of around 40 people, who are greatly outnumbered by the many thousands of seabirds, including a small colony of gannets and the rare Leach's petrel. There are also about 2500 pairs of great skuas, the largest colony in the UK. The island is dominated by its sheer cliffs, which reach their peak at **The Kame** (1220 ft), the second-highest sea cliffs in Britain after St Kilda.

An interesting feature of the island's people is that they still observe the old Julian calendar replaced in 1752 in Britain by the present Gregorian system which deleted 11 days from the year. Remote areas of the country kept to the old calendar, adding an extra day in 1800, which was a leap year, and some parts of Shetland continued to observe festivals 12 days after the dates in the new calendar. The most remote areas kept to the

ON THE ROAD

A böd for the night

There is only one youth hostel in Shetland, but budget travellers shouldn't panic. Shetland Camping Böd project has developed a network of camping *böds* (pronounced 'burd') which provide basic and cheap digs throughout the islands.

A *böd* was a building used to house fishermen and their gear during the fishing season and the name has been used to describe these types of accommodation which are similar to English 'camping barns'. They are all located in scenic places and each has its own fascinating history. They are very basic and the more remote ones have no electricity. You'll need to bring a stove, cooking and eating utensils, a sleeping bag and a torch (flashlight). All *böds* must be booked in advance through Shetland Amenity Trust in Lerwick and cost between £10 and £12 per person per night. They are open from April till the end of September. There are at present nine camping *böds* on Shetland (listed in the relevant places). See also www.camping-bods.com.

old calendar longest, and the people of Foula still celebrate Christmas on 6 January and New Year's Day on 13 January.

Papa Stour

A ferry sails from West Burrafirth on the Westside, near Sandness, to the little island of Papa Stour, only a mile offshore. The island, which has a population of around 30, is mostly made up of volcanic rock which has been eroded to form an amazing coastline of stacks, arches and caves, most spectacular of which is **Kirstan's Hole**. The island is home to large colonies of auks, terns and skuas, and also has an interesting history of its own. Pick up the island trails leaflet from the **iCentre** in Lerwick (see page 410).

Listings The Westside *map page 407.*

Where to stay

Stanydale, Walls and Sandness

£££ Burrastow House
2 miles southwest of Walls, T01595-809307 www.burrastowhouse.co.uk.
6 well-furnished and spacious rooms. A restored 18th-century house overlooking Vaila Sound, it's full of character. The owner cooks magnificent local lamb and seafood, see Restaurants, below. **££££** including dinner. Children half price, under 3s free. Also have a lovely self-catering cottage by the sea, sleeps up to 5 (available Apr-Oct). Recommended.

Camping

Voe House
Walls, www.camping-bods.com. Mar-Sep.
This is a camping *böd* – a restored 18th-century house overlooking the village. 16 beds in 5 sleeping areas with separate kitchen and dining area. Can also be booked through Lerwick tourist office.

Foula
Self-catering

Burns Self Catering
T01595-753273, www.selfcateringfoula.co.uk.
Old crofter's cottage in the middle of the island in splendid isolation. Sleeps 6.

Papa Stour

£ Hurdiback Hostel
T01595-873227, www.hurdibackhostel.co.uk.
Small, secluded hostel with 2 rooms of
4 bunks. You can order bread and eggs
before you arrive.

Restaurants

Stanydale, Walls and Sandness

£££ Burrastow House
*See Where to stay, above. Open to non-
residents Sat-Sun.*
The Belgian owner of this restored 18th-
century house cooks magnificent seafood.
This is the best place to eat on the islands, so
you'll need to book ahead. Recommended.

Shopping

Shetland Jewellery, *Soundside, Weisdale,
T01595-830275, www.shetlandjewellery.com.*

*Mon-Fri 0900-1700, Jun-Aug also Sat 1000-
1700 and Sun 1400-1700.* This small workshop
and studio is set right beside a sea loch.
Great place to buy authentic gold and silver
Shetland rings and brooches, etc. Guided
tours available over a cup of tea.

Transport

Bus
A minibus (No 10 and No 11) runs to
Sandness from **Walls** once a day Mon-Sat.
Contact **A&K Transport**, T01595-809337.

Ferry
There's a passenger/cargo ferry service
between **West Mainland** and **Papa Stour**,
Mon, Wed, Fri, Sat and Sun, 40 mins. Ferries
should be booked through **Shetland
Council**, T01595-745804. There are ferries
from Walls to **Foula** with **BK Marine** on Tue
and Thu year-round and also Sat in summer,
T01595-840208, www.bkmarine.co.uk.

South Mainland *Colour map 7.*

a 4000-year-old settlement and a close encounter with nature

From Lerwick a long, narrow finger of land points south. The main road runs down
the east coast for 25 miles till it ends at Sumburgh Head, near Shetland's main
airport. This southern part of the Shetland Mainland holds the islands' two most
important archaeological sites and main tourist attractions.

★ Isle of Mousa

The **Mousa Boat** ① *Sandwick, T07901-872339, www.mousa.co.uk,* runs daily trips from
April to mid-September to Mousa from Sandsayre. Departs daily except Saturday at 1130
and returns at 1430, allowing three hours on the island. The 15-minute crossing provides
the chance to spot seals and seabirds before exploring well-preserved Pictish brochs on
Mousa. The trip costs £16, children £7, no booking required, cash only. This trip is also
suitable for wheelchairs. The Storm Petrel Dusk Trip is available from late May to mid-July,
departing at 2230 and costs £25/10.

Some 15 miles south of Lerwick, the scattered crofting communities of Sandwick look
across to the Isle of Mousa, site of the best-preserved broch in Scotland. This fortified tower
was built around 2000 years ago and still stands close to its original height of 45 ft. It's a very
impressive structure when you see it from the inside and has chambers, galleries, an internal
staircase and a parapet. The broch features in a Viking saga of the 12th century when the
mother of Harald, Earl of Orkney, took refuge there with her lover. The Earl, who did not
approve of the liaison, laid siege to the broch, but it proved impregnable and he gave up.

Close encounters of the bird kind

Shetland is famous for its birds. As well its huge seabird colonies, the islands attract Arctic species and are an important crossroads for migrating birds. Over 340 species have been recorded on Fair Isle, including rare and exotic birds from Asia and America. Twenty-one out of the 24 seabirds common to Britain breed in Shetland. These can be found around the coastline, but the largest colonies are at the Hermaness and Noss reserves.

Amongst the many species which can be seen are the puffin. About one fifth of Scotland's puffins breed in Shetland. Its cousins in the auk family, guillemots, and razorbills, are also here in abundance during the summer months, along with kittiwakes, shags and that most common of seabirds, the fulmar. Britain's largest seabird, the gannet, can be seen diving spectacularly for fish at Hermaness, Noss, Fair Isle and Foula, while its smallest seabird, the storm petrel, is best seen around dusk on the tiny island of Mousa.

Summer heralds the return of the Arctic tern which breeds along low coastlines, as do the eider, oystercatcher, ringed plover and black guillemot, or tystie, which stays here all year round. The best place to see waders and shelduck are the nutrient-rich tidal mudflats at the Pool of Virkie in the South Mainland.

Many birds breed on agricultural land, and these include the lapwing, skylark, meadow pipit and wheater. The hills and moorland provide breeding grounds for many summer visitors such as that pirate of the skies, the great skua, or bonxie, and the Arctic skua. Another Arctic species, the whimbrel, also nests here, mainly in Unst, Yell and Fetlar. Moorland habitats are also favoured by the curlew, golden plover and merlin, Shetland's only bird of prey, while the lochs are home to large numbers of red-throated divers. Fetlar is home to 90% of the population of one of Britain's rarest birds, the red-necked phalarope.

Many of Shetland's bird habitats are protected as RSPB Reserves and National Nature Reserves, and it is an offence to disturb the birds and their young at or near their nests. You also risk being dive-bombed by some of the more aggressively protective species. For a full list of all species recorded on the islands and more practical birdwatching information, get a copy of the *Shetland Bird Chart*, by Joyce Gammack, available from the tourist office in Lerwick.

Mousa island is also home to many seabirds and waders, most notably the storm petrel – or *alamootie*, as the locals call it – which is best seen at dusk as it returns to its nest amongst the beach rocks. The **Mousa Boat Storm Petrel Dusk Trip** (see above) allows the chance to see storm petrels swarm the broch: a sight, sound and indeed a vibration you will never forget. You can also see seals on the white sand beach at West Voe. If you have time, it's a good idea to walk right around the coast, starting from the landing stage at West Ham and first heading south to the broch. Watch out for dive-bombing bonxies (arctic terns).

South of Sandwick

Further south on the east coast, at Boddam, is the **Shetland Crofthouse Museum** ① *T01595-695057, May-Sep daily 1000-1300, 1400-1600, donations welcome*, a restored thatched crofthouse built in the early 19th century. This was inhabited by a crofting family until the 1960s, with the women working the land whilst the men went fishing or whaling. The two rooms – the but and the ben – hold all the original furnishings and utensils and there is a typical kale yard and upturned boat shed outside.

St Ninian's Isle to Quendale

On the west coast, near Bigton village, a signposted track leads to the spectacular sandy causeway (known as an ayre or tombolo) which leads to St Ninian's Isle. The tombolo is the best example of its kind in Britain, and you can walk across to the island which is best known for the hoard of Pictish treasure which was discovered in 1958 in the ruins of the 12th-century church. The 28 silver objects included bowls, a spoon and brooches, probably dating from around AD 800, and are now on display in the Royal Scottish Museum in Edinburgh, though you can see replicas in the Shetland Museum in Lerwick.

The west coast south of Bigton is beautiful with long, sandy beaches interspersed with dramatic cliff scenery. On the other side of the road from the long, sheltered beach at **Scousburgh Sands** is the **Loch of Spiggie RSPB Reserve**. The loch is an important winter wildfowl refuge, particularly for wooper swans, and during the summer you can see various ducks, waders, gulls, terns and skuas. There's a hide on the northern shore with an information board. A few miles south of the loch is the village of **Quendale**, overlooking a wide, sandy bay. Here you'll find the beautifully restored and fully working 19th-century **Quendale Mill** ① *T01950-460969, www.quendalemill. co.uk, mid-Apr to mid-Oct daily 1000-1700, £4, concession £3, children 12-16 £1, under 12 free,* the last of Shetland's watermills, has a craft shop and tourist information point. You might not see it, but you will hear the groan of the wreck of the Braer oil tanker that lies between Garth's Ness and Fitful Head. It ran on to the rocks in 1993. A disaster of epic proportions was averted by the hurricane-force gales which dispersed the huge oil spillage.

Sumburgh and Jarlshof

At the southern tip of Mainland is the village of Sumburgh, site of Shetland's main airport for external passenger flights and for helicopters and planes servicing the North Sea oil industry. South of the airport is Shetland's prime archaeological site, **Jarlshof** ① *T01950-460112, Apr-Sep daily 0930-1730, phone for opening times Oct-Mar, £6.50, concessions £4.80, children £3.60,* a hugely impressive place which spans 4000 years of occupation from Neolithic times through Norse settlement to the 16th century. The original Stone Age dwellings are topped by a broch, Pictish wheelhouses, Viking longhouses and, towering over the whole complex, the ruins of a 16th-century mansion. This remarkable site was only discovered at the end of the 19th century when a violent storm ripped off the top layer of turf. Jarlshof is, in fact, not a genuine name, but the exotic invention of Sir Walter Scott in his novel *The Pirate*. A useful guidebook available from the visitor centre helps bring the place to life.

Another fascinating excavation has been going on nearby, at **Old Scatness** ① *T01595-694688, www.shetlandamenity.org, guided tours and reconstructions every Fri from mid-May to end Aug between 1015 and 1630, adults £5, concessions £4, group visits at other times by arrangement (£125 for up to 25 people).* Since 1995, a team from Bradford University alongside local volunteers from Shetland Amenity Trust have been excavating the site and plans are in the pipeline, including roofing the site with a dome to protect it from the elements and building walkways to access the more fragile areas.

South of Jarlshof, the Mainland ends abruptly at **Sumburgh Head**, an RSPB Reserve. The **lighthouse** on top of the cliff was built by Robert Stevenson in 1821, and the keepers' cottages are now rented out as self-catering accommodation. The lighthouse isn't open to the public, but from its grounds you can see many nesting seabirds such as puffins, kittiwakes, fulmars, guillemots and razorbills. To the east of the airport is **Pool of Virkie**, a good birdwatching area.

Listings South Mainland *map page 407.*

Where to stay

There's accommodation in Bigton, Scousburgh and around Sumburgh, but it is limited.

£££ The Spiggie Guest House
Scousburgh, Dunrossness, T01950-460409, www.spiggie.co.uk.
Less than 30 mins' drive from Lerwick and close to Sumburgh airport. A small, friendly guesthouse with 6 comfy rooms overlooking Spiggie Loch. Hosts will provide evening meals featuring the best of seafood. Also open to non-residents if booked in advance.

£££ Sumburgh Hotel
Next to Jarlshof, Sumburgh, T01950-460201, www.sumburghhotel.com.
32 en suite rooms. 19th-century former home of Laird of Sumburgh, with great views across to Fair Isle. The good restaurant serves meat and fish dishes (**££**) daily at lunch and dinner, children's menu (**£**), limited choice for vegetarians.

££ Hayhoull
Bigton T01950-422206, www.bedandbreakfastshetland.com.
This spick and span B&B has 3 rooms with beautiful views of St Ninian's Isle and towards Foula. Evening meals are available. Good value. Recommended.

Camping

Betty Mouat's Cottage
Next to the excavations at Old Scatness and the airport, www.camping-bods.com. Mar-Sep.
This camping *böd* sleeps up to 8 and can also be booked through Lerwick tourist office.

What to do

Guided tours
Island Trails, *Bigton, T07880-950228, www.island-trails.co.uk.* A variety of guided walks and small group tours run by local guide and crofter, James Tait. Prices vary, eg guided half-day walk of St Ninian's Isle £25pp.

Transport

Air
Flybe, www.flybe.com, and Loganair, www.loganair.co.uk, fly directly from Sumburgh to **Aberdeen**, **Kirkwall**, **Inverness**, **Glasgow** and **Edinburgh**. **Loganair** also operates a regular service from Sumburgh to **Fair Isle**.

Ferry
Regular daily car ferries from **Scalloway** to **Foula**, alternate Thu, 3 hrs; and **South Mainland** to **Fair Isle**, Tue, Sat and alternate Thu, 2½ hrs.

Fair Isle *Colour map 7.*

Britain's most isolated inhabited island

Fair Isle, 24 miles southwest of Sumburgh and 27 miles northeast of North Ronaldsay in Orkney, is the most isolated of Britain's inhabited islands. Only three miles long by 1½ miles wide, the island has a population of around 70 and is best known for its intricately patterned knitwear, which is still produced by a co-operative, Fair Isle Crafts. Co-operative could be said to sum up the friendly islanders, whose lifestyle is based on mutual help and community effort.

Around Fair Isle

Fair Isle is a paradise for birdwatchers, and keen ornithologists form the majority of the island's visitors. Celebrity birdwatcher and former Goodie, Bill Oddie, has dubbed it the 'Hilton of the bird world'. It stands in the flight path of many thousands of migrating birds, and over 340 species have been recorded here at the **Fair Isle Bird Observatory** ① *T01595-760258, www. fairislebirdobs.co.uk, Apr-Oct*, which also offers accommodation and where visitors are welcome to take part. As well as the almost obscenely rich birdlife, there are around 240 species of flowering plant, making the island an especially beautiful haven for naturalists. Fair Isle's coastline, especially in the north and west, also boasts some outstanding cliff scenery.

The bird observatory was the brainchild of George Waterston, an ornithologist who first visited in 1935 and then bought the island in 1948 to begin his task of building the observatory. The island was given to the National Trust for Scotland in 1954 and declared a National Scenic Area. It was also designated a place of outstanding natural beauty and cultural heritage by the Council of Europe. The **George Waterston Memorial Museum** ① *T01595-760244, May to mid-Sep Mon-Fri 1400-1600, Wed 1000-1200, donations welcome*, has exhibits and photographs detailing the island's natural history, as well as the history of crofting, fishing, archaeology and knitwear. **The Fair Isle Textile Workshop** ① *T01595-760248, www.kathycoull.com, open year round by prior arrangement*, offers demonstrations in textile techniques. Individuals and small groups can be accommodated for short courses.

Essential Fair Isle

Finding your feet

Getting to Fair Isle requires patience, persistence and a strong stomach to survive the white-knuckle 2½-hour ferry journey, booked through **Good Shepherd IV** (T01595-760363), sails to/from Gutness at the southern end of Shetland on Tuesday, Thursday and Saturday in summer, Tuesday only in winter, and once a fortnight to/from Lerwick. There are also flights from Tingwall airport, Monday to Saturday in summer (Monday to Friday in winter), and from Sumburgh airport every Saturday in summer. For bookings, T01595-840246. You can also fly from Kirkwall on Orkney, which allows 2½ hours on the island. Check out the **Loganair** website (www.loganair.co.uk) for details. A subsidized taxi service runs to Tingwall airport; book at least a day in advance, T01595-745745. For more information on Fair Isle, and on boat and flight times, visit www.fairisle.org.uk. For further details, see Transport, page 412.

Listings Fair Isle *map page 407.*

Where to stay

There are a few places to stay on the island, but accommodation must be booked in advance and includes meals. There are no hotels, pubs or restaurants. Note that only O2 and Vodaphone mobile networks work on the island.

£££ Fair Isle Guest House
Upper Leogh, T01595-760248, www.kathycoull.com.
Situated beside a working crofthouse, with sea views. Offers full board and is run by Kathy Coull who also runs textile workshops on Unst.

£££ Fair Isle Lodge and Bird Observatory
T01595-760258, www.fairislebirdobs.co.uk.
The price is for full-board accommodation
in private rooms. No B&B available. Children
aged 6-12 pay ½ price, under 6s free. Meals
available for non-residents (**££-£**) if booked
in advance.

£££ South Lighthouse
T01595-760355, www.southlightfairisle.co.uk.
B&B in one of the most dramatic locations
anywhere in the UK. The price includes
dinner and a packed lunch. No electricity
between 2330 and 0730.

North Mainland   *Colour map 7.*

dramatic and rugged coastline and Britain's most northerly fish and chip shop

The main road north from Lerwick branches at Voe, a peaceful and colourful little
village nestling in a bay at the head of the Olna Firth. One branch leads to the Yell
car and passenger ferry terminal at Toft, past the turn-off to the massive Sullom
Voe Oil Terminal, the largest oil and liquefied gas terminal in Europe. The other
road heads northwest to Brae (see below).

Brae and Muckle Roe

Brae is not a very pretty place and was built to accommodate workers at the nearby Sullom
Voe oil terminal. However, it does boast a good selection of accommodation and decent
facilities – such as Frankie's, Britain's most northerly fish and chip shop – and makes a good
base from which to explore the wild and wonderful coastal scenery around the Northmavine
peninsula to the north. There's also good walking and spectacularly good westerly views
around the island of **Muckle Roe** to the southwest, and up the island's small hill, **South Ward**
(554 ft). But be careful of the overly protective bonxies, which will attack if you get too close
to their nests in the grass. The island is attached to the mainland by a bridge.

Northmavine

The charmingly named **Mavis Grind**, the narrow isthmus where it's claimed you can
throw a stone from the Atlantic to the North Sea, leads into Northmavine, the northwest
peninsula of North Mainland. It is one of Shetland's most dramatic and beautiful areas,
with rugged scenery, spectacular coastline and wide empty spaces. This is wonderful
walking country, and it's a good idea to abandon the car and explore it on foot. **Hillswick
Ness**, to the south of **Hillswick** village, is a nice walk, but further west, around the coastline
of **Eshaness**, is the most spectacular cliff scenery and amazing natural features, all with
unusual and evocative names.

North of the lighthouse are the **Holes of Scraada**, **Grind o' da Navir** and the **Villians
of Hamnavoe**, which are not the local gangs but eroded lava cliffs with blowholes,
arches and caves. East of Eshaness are the **Heads of Grocken** and **The Drongs**, a series of
exposed sea stacks, which offer superb diving. Further north, overlooking the deep sea
inlet of **Ronies Voe**, is the dramatic red-granite bulk of **Ronies Hill** (1477 ft), with a well-
preserved burial cairn at the summit. The coastal scenery to the north and west of here
is even more breathtaking, but very remote and exposed. You should be well equipped
before setting out.

Between Eshaness and Hillswick, a side road leads south to the **Tangwick Haa Museum**
ⓘ *T01806-503389, Apr-Sep daily 1100-1700, free*, which features displays and photographs
on the history of fishing and whaling and the hardships of life in these parts.

Where to stay

£££ Busta House Hotel, Brae
T01806-522506, www.bustahouse.com.
Open all year.
22 rooms. The best place to stay around Brae and probably one of the best on Shetland is this luxurious and wonderfully atmospheric 16th-century country house overlooking Busta Voe about 1½ miles from Brae village. The superb **Pitcairn** restaurant (**£££**) is one of the finest on Shetland, with a selection of malts to match, and there are also meals in the homely **Busta Bar** (**££**). Highly recommended.

££ Almara
Upper Urafirth, T01806-503261,
www.almara.shetland.co.uk.
This friendly and comfortable B&B is the pick of the bunch and excellent value. Also have a self-catering chalet in the grounds.

££ Westayre
Westayre, Muckle Roe, Brae, T01806-522368,
www.westayre.shetland.co.uk.
Friendly and welcoming B&B in 2 rooms on a working croft. Great value.

Camping

Johnny Notion's Camping Böd
Hamnavoe, Northmavine, www.camping-bods.com, reached by a side road which branches north from the road between Hillswick and Eshaness. Mar to end Sep.
This is the birthplace of John Williamson, an 18th-century craftsman who developed an effective inoculation against smallpox. Has no electricity or hot water. Book through Lerwick tourist office.

Sail Loft
In Voe by the pier. Mar to end-Sep.
16 beds in 2 rooms, 1 with 12 beds the other with 4, separate kitchen and dining room. This former fishing store is now Shetland's largest camping *böd*.

Restaurants

£££ Busta House Hotel
Brae, see Where to stay, above.
The best option hereabouts, serving Shetland hill lamb, free-range pork from Unst and Yell Sound scallops. Has a good malt whisky selection. Recommended.

££ Frankies Fish and Chips
Brae, T01806-522700.
Serves all sort of fried seafood (squid, skate wings, prawns) as well as the old classics. They also steam the fattest, juiciest local mussels for those watching their waistlines.

Transport

Ferry
There are frequent car and passenger ferries from **Toft** on North Mainland to **Ulsta** on the south coast of **Yell**. It's not essential, but it's a good idea to book in advance, T01595-743972, 20 mins.

Whalsay and Out Skerries *Colour map 7.*

former home of one of Scotland's greatest poets

South of Voe, the B9071 branches east to Laxo, the ferry terminal for the island of Whalsay. There are regular daily car ferries (for times and fares go to www.shetland.gov.uk). The journey takes 30 minutes. Whalsay is one of Shetland's most prosperous small islands owing to its thriving paelagic fishing industry, which helps support a population of around 1000. There are rumoured to be more millionaires here per head of population that anywhere else in Scotland. Certainly its golf course above the cliffs is rich with sea views.

In the seas around Whalsay you can see porpoises, dolphins, minke whales and orcas, hence its viking name which means 'island of whales'. The fishing fleet is based at Symbister, the island's main settlement. Beside the harbour at Symbister is the Pier House, a restored *böd* (see box, page 416) which was used by the Hanseatic League, a commercial association of German merchants who traded in Shetland from the Middle Ages to the early 18th century. Inside is an exhibition explaining the history of the Hanseatic trade, and general information on the island. One of Scotland's great poets, Hugh McDiarmid (Christopher Grieve), spent most of the 1930s in Whalsay, where he wrote much of his finest poetry, until he was called for war work in 1942, never to return. His former home, at Sodom near Symbister, is now a camping *böd*, see Where to stay, page 424.

The Out Skerries is a small group of rocky islands about five miles from Whalsay and 10 miles east of Shetland Mainland. It's made up of three main islands: the larger islands of **Housay** and **Bruray**, which are connected by a road bridge; and the uninhabited island of **Grunay**. The Skerries boast some spectacular and rugged sea cliffs which are home to many rare migrant seabirds in spring and autumn.

Listings Whalsay and Out Skerries *map page 407.*

Where to stay

Camping

Hugh McDiarmid's Camping Böd (The Grieve House)
Near Symbister, www.camping-bods.com. Mar to end-Sep.
The former home of this great poet, see above. Sleeps 5 in 1 room. No electricity.

Transport

Ferry
There are regular daily car and passenger ferries between **Laxo** and **Symbister**. There are also ferries to the Skerries from **Vidlin**, about 3 miles northeast of Laxo. For bookings, call **Shetland Council**, T01595-743975. There's a less-frequent car ferry service between **East Mainland** and **Skerries**, Mon, Fri, Sat and Sun, 1½ hrs.

Yell, Fetlar and Unst Colour map 7.

dramatic clifftop walks at Britain's most northerly point

Yell
Yell, the second largest of the Shetland Islands, was described rather damningly by the Orkney-favouring writer Eric Linklater, as 'dull and dark'. And it's true that the interior is consistently desolate peat moorland. But the coastline is greener and more pleasant and provides an ideal habitat for the island's large otter population. Yell is also home to a rich variety of birds, and offers some good coastal and hill walks, especially around the rugged coastline of **The Herra**, a peninsula about halfway up the west coast.

At **Burravoe**, about five miles east of the ferry terminal at **Ulsta**, is the **Old Haa Museum** ⓘ *T01957-702431, Apr-Sep Mon-Thu and Sat 1000-1600, Sun 1400-1700, free, donations appreciated, garden open every day*, housed in Yell's oldest building which dates from 1672. It contains an interesting display on local flora and fauna and history. Also has tearoom (see page 427).

The island's largest village, **Mid Yell**, has a couple of shops, a pub and a leisure centre with a good swimming pool. About a mile northwest, on the hillside above the main road, are the reputedly haunted ruins of **Windhouse**, dating from 1707. To the north is the **RSPB Lumbister Reserve**, where red-throated divers, merlins, great and Arctic skuas and many other bird species come to breed. The reserve is also home to a large population of otters. A pleasant walk leads along the nearby steep and narrow gorge, known as the **Daal of Lumbister**, filled with many colourful flowers. The area to the north of the reserve provides good walking over remote moorland and coastline.

The road continues north past the reserve and around **Basta Voe**, where you can see otters. North of **Gutcher**, the ferry port for Unst, is the village of **Cullivoe**, with some good walks along the attractive coastline.

Fetlar

Fetlar is the smallest of the North Isles but the most fertile and is known as 'the garden of Shetland'. Indeed, the name derives from Norse meaning 'fat land', as there is good grazing and croftland and a wide variety of plant and bird life. The whole island is good for birdwatching, but the prime place is the 1700 acres of **North Fetlar RSPB Reserve** around Vord Hill (522 ft) in the north of the island. This area has restricted access during the summer months, and visitors should contact the warden at Bealance (T01957-733246). The warden will also let you know if and when you can see the one or two female snowy owls which sometime visit.

The north cliffs of the reserve are home to large colonies of breeding seabirds, including auks, gulls and shags, and you can also see common and grey seals on the beaches in late autumn. Fetlar is home to one of Britain's rarest birds, the red-necked phalarope, which breeds in the loch near **Funzie** (pronounced 'finnie') in the east of the island. You can watch them from the RSPB hide in the nearby marshes. Red-throated divers and whimbrel also breed here. The island is also good for walking, and a leaflet describing some of the walks is available from the tourist office in Lerwick.

The main settlement on the island is **Houbie** on the south coast. Here you'll see a house called Leagarth, which was built by the island's most famous son, Sir William Watson Cheyne, who, with Lord Lister, pioneered antiseptic surgery. Nearby is the excellent **Fetlar Interpretive Centre** ① *T01957-733206, www.fetlar.com, May-Sep Mon-Sat 1100-1600, Sun 1230-1600, £2, concessions £1, under 16s free*, which presents the island's history and gives information on its bounteous birdlife.

Unst

Unst is the most northerly inhabited island in Britain and some believe it is where the Vikings first landed on Shetland, but there is more to the island than its many 'most northerly' credentials. Aside from being where the local bakery makes 'oceanic' oatcakes from sea water, it is scenically one of the most varied of the Shetland Islands, with spectacular cliffs, sea stacks, sheltered inlets, sandy beaches, heather-clad hills, fertile farmland, freshwater lochs and even a sub-arctic desert. Such a variety of habitats supports over 400 plant species and a rich variety of wildlife. Unst is a major breeding site for gannets, puffins, guillemots, razorbills, kittiwakes, shags, Arctic and great skuas and whimbrels, amongst others, and in the surrounding waters you can see seals, porpoises, otters and even killer whales.

In the east of the island, north of **Baltasound**, is the **Keen of Hamar National Nature Reserve**, 74 acres of serpentine rock which breaks into tiny fragments known as 'debris', giving the landscape a strange, lunar-like appearance. This bleak 'desert' is actually home to some of the rarest plants in Britain. Baltasound is the island's main settlement, with an airport, hotel, pub, post office and leisure centre with pool. To the north of here is the village of **Haroldswick**, home of Britain's most northerly post office, where your postcards are sent with a special stamp to inform everyone of this fact. Here you'll also find **Unst Boat Haven** ⓘ *T01957-755282, May-Sep Mon-Sat 1100-1600, Sun 1400-1600, £3, £2 concession, under 16s free*, where you can see a beautifully presented collection of traditional boats and fishing artefacts. A little way further north is the **Unst Heritage Centre** ⓘ *T01957-755244, May-Sep Mon-Sat 1100-1600, Sun 1400-1600, £3, £2 concession, under 16s free*, which has a museum of local history and island life. Nearby is an RAF radar-tracking station at Saxa Vord. The road ends at Skaw, where there's a lovely beach and Britain's most northerly house. The road northwest from Haroldswick leads to the head of **Burra Firth**, a sea inlet flanked by high cliffs, and site of Britain's most northerly golf course.

To the west of Burra Firth is the remote ★ **Hermaness National Nature Reserve**, 2422 acres of dramatic coastal scenery and wild moorland that is home to over 100,000 nesting seabirds, including gannets and the largest number of puffins and great skuas (or 'bonxies') in Shetland. There's an excellent **visitor centre** ⓘ *T01975-693345, mid-Apr to mid-Sep daily 0800-1700*, in the former lighthouse keeper's shore station, where you can pick up a leaflet which shows the marked route into the reserve, and see the artistic efforts of many of Unst's children. Whilst in the reserve, make sure you keep to the marked paths to avoid being attacked by bonxies; they are highly protective and they will attack if they think that their territory is being threatened. For a detailed description of the three-hour walk from the car park to Hermaness, see www.shetland.org.

The views from Hermaness are wonderful, out to the offshore stacks and skerries including **Muckle Flugga**, and then to the wide open North Atlantic Ocean. Muckle Flugga is the site of the most northerly lighthouse in Britain, built in 1857-1858 by Thomas Stevenson, father of Robert Louis Stevenson. The writer visited the island in 1869, and the illustrated map in his novel *Treasure Island* bears a striking similarity to the outline of Unst. Beyond the lighthouse is **Out Stack**, which marks the most northerly point on the British Isles. With nothing between you and the North Pole but water, this is the place to sit and contemplate what it feels like to be at the end of the world.

Listings Yell, Fetlar and Unst *map page 407.*

Where to stay

Yell

££ Old Post Office
Gutcher, T01957-744293, www.oldpostoffice-gutcher.com.
1 en suite double and 2 singles. Friendly and welcoming B&B, welcomes dogs. Evening meals and packed lunch on request.

Camping

Windhouse Lodge
www.camping-bods.com. Mar to end Sep.
Sleeps 8 in 3 rooms. A well-equipped camping *böd* below the ruins of haunted Windhouse.

Fetlar

££ The Gord
Houbie, T01975-733226, www.fetlar.org.
B&B attached to the shop in Houbie. 3 en suite rooms, offers dinner and is easy to find.

Camping

Fetlar has no dedicated camping facilities but wild camping is freely available.

Unst

There's a decent selection of accommodation on Unst.

£££ Baltasound Hotel
T01957-711334, www.baltasoundhotel.co.uk.
24 rooms. Accommodation in the main hotel buildings or in log cabins in the garden. Food served in the restaurant (1745-2015) is very good and features local fish and meat.

£££ Buness House
Baltasound, T01975-711315.
Top choice has to be the faded grandeur of this 17th-century Haa in Baltasound which has fine views. Staying here is a bizarre and rather surreal experience, given that you are on the most northerly island in Britain. The house is crammed full of Indian Raj relics, and the stuffed eagle, tiger and leopard skins hanging in the hallway are a wildlife close up almost as impressive, though considerably more unsettling and un-'PC', as the Hermaness Nature Reserve in the north of the island that the family own. The food is excellent (£££) and accommodation comfortable. Full board is ££££.

££ Gerratoun
Haroldswick, T01975-711323.
Claims to be Britain's most northerly B&B. Located within walking distance of Hermaness and with excellent views, this restored crofthouse offers 1 twin bedroom. Caters for special diets.

£ Gardiesfauld Hostel
Baltasound, T01975-755259, www. gardiesfauld.shetland.co.uk. Apr-Sep.
A well-equipped independent hostel, which also has hook-ups for 5 caravans/ motorhomes and a small campsite.

Restaurants

Yell

£ Old Haa Museum Tea Room
Burravoe, southeast Yell. Apr-Sep Mon-Thu and Sat 1000-1600, Sun 1400-1700.

A small tearoom on the ground floor of the museum. Serves teas, coffees, great home-baking and sandwiches.

£ Gutcher Goose Café
Opposite the Post Office, Gutcher, T01957-744321. Mon-Fri 0900-1700, Sat-Sun 1000-1700.
Cosy surroundings, where you can enjoy home-baking, coffee, soup of the day or a burger. Welcoming and recommended. Run by owners of nearby **Baltasound Hotel (£££-££**, T01975-711334), which serves meals and drinks to non-residents.

Transport

Yell
Bus
A service runs to/from **Lerwick** to **Cullivoe** once a day with **RG Jamieson**.

Ferry
There are regular daily car ferries to **Belmont** on **Unst**, 10 mins, and Hamars Ness on **Fetlar**, 25 mins, from **Gutcher**. Booking is advised, T01595-745804.

Fetlar
Bus
There's a dial-a-ride service run by **RG Jamieson** which runs around Fetlar from the ferry once a day. For bookings T01595-745745.

Ferry
There are regular car and passenger ferries between Hamars Ness on Fetlar, **Gutcher** (Yell) and **Belmont** (Unst).

Unst
Bus
There's an island bus service (No 28), which runs a few times a day, Mon-Sat between **Baltasound**, **Belmont** and **Haroldswick**. For times see www.zettrans. org.uk, T01595-744868.

Background

History 429
Culture 443
Religion 456
Land & environment 457
Books 462

History

Prehistory

Scotland's earliest known inhabitants are the hunter-gatherers of around 6000-5000 BC. By 2000-1500 BC these Mesolithic people had been joined by Beaker folk, so named from their distinctive pottery, and grain-cultivating Megalithic people, arriving by sea via Spain and Portugal, who were tempted to settle by a then prevailing near-Mediterranean climate. Several climate changes for the worse triggered much population movement and also, along with extensive deforestation, caused the formation of peaty soil, now characteristic of much of Scotland, by around 1000 BC.

The pottery and other artefacts of the Beaker people have been found in burial mounds or cairns, such as Maes Howe on the Orkney Mainland (see page 385). They suggest a complex social structure and perhaps, more importantly, a belief in the afterlife, as do the prehistoric settlements and monuments in Caithness, Orkney, Shetland and the Outer Hebrides, notably at Skara Brae (see page 382), Stenness, and the Ring of Brodgar on Orkney Mainland, and Callanish on Lewis (see page 332). But throughout Scotland there are hundreds of standing stones and circles, a legacy of the megalithic peoples. In Aberdeenshire surveys reveal precise orientations indicating their use as observatories charting lunar cycles and eclipses. The layout of Clava Cairns, near Inverness (see page 171), bears similarities to the great temple at Newgrange in Ireland. And at Kilmartin in Argyll (see page 63), cup and ring marks, stone alignments and burial cairns, formed in a complete 'landscape temple', suggest a geomantic sophistication that has now been forgotten.

At the beginning of the first millennium BC, Bronze Age traders from far afield were busy around the coasts. Celts arrived from Germany, bringing with them new agricultural technology and weaponry such as swords and shields, which in turn necessitated impressive earthwork defences in the form of hillforts and *crannogs* (see page 443) as competition for land increased. In about 200-100 BC more Celts arrived with superior iron-working skills, and consequently, more fortifications were also built. The brochs, or towers, the remains of many of which can still be seen dotted along the west coast and in the islands, date from this time (see also page 443).

The Picts and the Romans

Indigenous Iron Age tribes inhabited most of the country and were identified by the Romans as 'Picts' – possibly meaning 'painted, or tattooed, people'. They thwarted Roman imperial ambition in Alba, the land north of the Forth and Clyde, in around AD 80, and a string of Roman military outposts along the Highland line remain from this abandoned campaign. At Fortingall near Aberfeldy, the ancient yew tree is said to mark the birthplace of Pontius Pilate, possibly the son of a Roman soldier who later found preferment in Rome. To add credence to this theory, a gravestone marked 'PP' was found.

Defensive walls built by Emperors Hadrian (circa AD 123 from the Solway Firth to the Tyne) and Antoninus (from the Clyde to the Forth circa AD 143) against the Picts inadvertently set a precedent for the eventual polarization of Scotland and England, beginning around the ninth century, out of the mass of tribal kingdoms. An endlessly disputed border led to centuries of retaliatory raids and devastation on either side.

Picts south of the Antonine wall became semi-Romanized and were known as Britons, kin to the Welsh. Their kingdom of Strathclyde, with a stronghold on Dumbarton Rock near Glasgow, once extended into Lancashire and retained a separate identity into the 11th century. The Lothians, territory of the British Gododdin, was overrun by Anglians from Northumbria. In the seventh century the Anglians challenged the Picts in Alba and were finally defeated at Dunnichen.

Meanwhile an Irish tribe, the Scots, who claimed descent from an Egyptian Pharaoh's daughter, had been settling in Pictish territory in Argyll from around the fourth century. Once in Argyll, the sons of the Scots' leader, Erc, established a kingdom called Dalriada, sharing it between themselves under a high king at Dunadd (see page 63). When their fellow countryman, Columba, arrived in the sixth century on Iona, they were aided in their cause by his diplomatic skills at the hostile Pictish court of King Brude, in Inverness. In the ninth century the Scots under Kenneth MacAlpin took over the Picts. Although their written records were destroyed, or falsified by the conquering Scots, they left a rich legacy of unique sculptured stones denoting a civilized and artistic culture. When Kenneth set up at Scone, and Alba became Scotland, the seven kingdoms of Pictland in the north and east survived as great earldoms.

The early church

Some claim Joseph of Arimathea brought Christianity to Whithorn in Galloway, which had been a religious centre since the first century. Around AD 397 Ninian founded a Christian Mission in Whithorn, along eastern Mediterranean monastic lines vastly different from the Roman model. From here he and countless missionaries such as Kentigern, Moluag and Comgan went north to convert the Picts, as far as St Ninian's Isle in Shetland. Their communities, oak churches and cells are remembered in innumerable place names, wells and simple cross-marked stones, often established on pre-Christian sacred sites.

In AD 563 Columba arrived on Iona (see box, page 89), where he went on to found the Celtic Church, or the Church of the Culdees, with centres throughout Scotland, which differed in many ways from the Church of Rome. Iona became known as the 'Cradle of Christianity in Scotland', but the arrival of the Vikings inhibited sea travel and the monks were driven from Iona. About this time, the Scots took over the Pictish nation and the Columban church moved to Dunkeld, with Columba's relics transported in the breacbannoch, or Monymusk reliquary. This was carried at Bannockburn and is now in the Museum of Scotland in Edinburgh.

St Andrews later became the principal seat of the church, although Iona retained special status. Communities of Culdees (one of which was at St Andrews) survived into the 13th century, outwith the Columban and later Roman church. These were thought to be adherents of Ninian's church, preserving elements of pre-Christian druid religion.

A common origin for the cross symbol found on both the Pictish cross slabs and the free standing crosses of Iona and Islay is the *chi-ro*, or wheeled cross, as found at Whithorn. However, the enigmatic symbols, vivid hunting scenes and mythical beasts of the Pictish stones found throughout Pictland are unique, and their function remains a mystery. Another mystery is the brief flourishing in the early 13th century of an accomplished school of sculptors around Loch Awe, in Argyll. In ancient burial grounds throughout Knapdale are found grave slabs depicting swords, warriors and foreign ships, thought to mark the graves of the Knights Templar who fled here from France.

The Vikings

Pagan Norsemen in dragonships are first heard of in Argyll in AD 795, the first of many such coastal raids of unimaginable savagery, which included ritual killings. Colonies of monks were not spared; 68 suffered the 'red martyrdom' on Iona in 807, and its library, 'a shop window crammed with the loot of centuries' was a magnet for raiders. By the late ninth century Norsemen had colonized Orkney (see box, page 383), and from Birsay Palace Earl Sigurd wielded power as far south as Moray. A renegade bunch of mixed Norse and Gaelic ancestry, the Gall-Gaels, appeared in the Hebrides and Galloway. Some of these, like chieftain Ketil Flatnose's family, became early settlers of Iceland.

Once surrounded by aggressive Norse colonies, now also in Dublin and York, the newly formed 'Scotland' survived through a combination of fighting spirit and a network of shifting alliances with the various Norse powers. Some of these alliances were enduring. In the ninth century 'Torf' Einar, credited with introducing peat cutting, founded a dynasty from which sprang the Earls of Angus.

After the Dublin colony collapsed in 1014, a Viking kingdom of 'Man and the Sudreys' (Hebrides) filled the vacuum, and the isles continued to be ravaged by warring Norsemen. By around 1100 Norwegian king Magnus Barelegs' empire included the entire northern and western seaboard. Against this backdrop, pursuing his own interests, appears Somerled, Hebridean hero of Norse-Gaelic blood, progenitor of Clan Donald and the powerful Lordship of the Isles. In 1153 he supported a rebellion against the Scottish crown. Later, in the early 13th century, he built a series of castles around the coast, such as Sween, Tioram, Mingary and Dunstaffnage, which foiled the intermittent attempts made by the Scottish crown to assert control.

The last of the great Norse kings, Hakon, was defeated by the Scots in 1263 at Largs, with the aid of bad winter weather. Orkney and Shetland were only returned to Scotland in the 15th century. A Norse dialect was spoken there into the 18th century, and vestiges of Norwegian law still survive, as does the Viking St Magnus Cathedral in Kirkwall.

Macbeth and the battle for kingship

Macbeth, the earl-king of the vast land of Moray, rose to high kingship with popular support, reigning for a relatively long (1040-1057) and peaceful time with his queen Gruoch, grand-daughter of Kenneth III of Scots. The popular image of Macbeth as portrayed by Shakespeare is, in fact, a false one. The great bard vilified Macbeth in order to please his James VI, who claimed descent from Duncan, Macbeth's rival. But it was Duncan who was the nasty piece of work, and he was slain not at Glamis, as in the play, but on the battlefield, while invading Macbeth's territory. Duncan features in the *Orkneyinga saga*, a Viking history, as Karl Hundason, 'low-born son of the hound'.

Competition for the throne was a part of Pictish custom. A suitable 'tanist' or candidate was elected from anyone whose great-grandfather had been king, and the candidates would then fight it out: in practice, survival of the fittest. This competition for the right to be king was complicated by the ancient dynastic rivalry among the Dalriadic Scots and perpetuated when they merged with the Picts under Kenneth MacAlpin. This later precipitated the Wars of Independence.

One part of Shakespeare's Macbeth which is historical fact is the Birnam Wood incident, when Malcolm, Duncan's son, and his Northumbrian allies used tree branches as camouflage to advance on Macbeth in his Dunsinnan stronghold near Perth. He was later hunted down and slain at Lumphanan by Malcolm's ally, MacDuff, Earl of Fife, and is buried on Iona.

Macbeth, the last truly Celtic king, was also one of the most able early kings. He was the first to establish and implement a fair legal system and, a firm supporter of the Celtic church, he went on pilgrimage to Rome where an Irish monk observed him liberally scattering money to the poor; further evidence of the great disservice done to his memory by Shakespeare.

The Canmores and the Norman Conquest

Macbeth's usurper, the uncouth Malcolm III, Canmore (meaning 'big head'), was an illegitimate son of Duncan and a miller's daughter. In 1067 Malcolm married Margaret, a Saxon princess born in Hungary and sister of Edgar Atheling, the English heir to the throne, who had fled north with his family to escape William the Conqueror and the Norman Conquest. Margaret was a devout Catholic and was largely responsible for introducing the religious ideas of the Roman Catholic Church into Scotland, for which she was canonized in 1251. In 1072 she founded Dunfermline Abbey and introduced southern manners to the Scottish court.

Malcolm's belligerent instincts were not curbed by the influence of the saintly Margaret, however, and one of his many raids into Northumberland provoked a visit from William the Conqueror. The result was that Malcolm was forced to swear allegiance to William, an oath he didn't take too seriously, as he continued to raid England at whim, but one which would lead to a greater degree of southern interference in Scottish constitutional matters.

The Normans began to exert their influence over Scotland in many other ways. They were granted land as far as the Highland fringes, establishing a feudal system based on loyalty to the crown. The traditional patriarchal tribal culture was eroded, causing constant rebellions in the North and Galloway. The Norman successor to the Scottish throne, David I, like many of his Norman friends, had English estates, acquired through his wife. This wealth built the great Border abbeys and established the Roman church more fully. New parishes and dioceses revolutionized administration, and burghs were founded to develop international trade, attracting Flemish settlers. Society in medieval Scotland became more typically European than England or even France.

One of the depressingly familiar themes running through Scottish history has been the unwillingness of the Scots nobility to resist English ambitions towards Scotland. This has always been their Achilles heel and, in 1290, it provoked a crisis of succession, when the new child queen, Margaret, Maid of Norway, died en route from Norway. Margaret had been recognized as heiress of Scotland, the Hebrides and the Isle of Man, and the planned child marriage to the prince who would become Edward II, son of Edward I, was not to be. Following her death, no fewer than 13 rival contestants materialized. Two main factions emerged: the Balliols and Comyns against the Bruces. But instead of reverting to the traditional method of tanistry, or 'natural selection', the pusillanimous Scots nobles appealed to Edward I of England to adjudicate.

Wallace and Bruce: the Wars of Succession

Edward eventually chose John Balliol, and he was crowned king at Scone in June 1292. Balliol was anxious to prove to his fellow Scots that he was not as weak as they claimed him to be. He negotiated a defensive agreement with the French, the beginning of the Auld Alliance. He then invaded Cumberland in 1296, but in retaliation Edward attacked Berwick and slaughtered its inhabitants. The Scottish army was then defeated at Dunbar, and thereafter the castles of Edinburgh, Roxburgh, Perth and Stirling were captured.

In the same year, Balliol abdicated at Stracathro and went into exile. Edward then destroyed the great Seal of Scotland and, worse still, moved the Stone of Destiny, the traditional crowning throne for all Scottish kings, to Westminster Abbey, where it lay under the Coronation Chair for 700 years. Scotland, as a result, was left in disarray.

However, resistance found a leader in William Wallace, son of a Renfrew laird. He began a revolt against the English in 1297 and built up a substantial army. By September of that year he he had secured a small but strategic victory against English forces at Stirling Bridge. This galvanized support, and he was quickly declared 'Guardian of the Realm'. Following his defeat at Falkirk he was betrayed to Edward by one of the Scots noblemen, captured and taken south to be executed (disembowelled, then hung, drawn and quartered) in Smithfield, London, in 1305.

This stirred Robert the Bruce to take up the cause of independence. Encountering his treacherous rival, 'Red' Comyn, in a Dumfries church, he seized the initiative, stabbing him at the altar. With Comyn dead, and the support of patriotic church leaders, as well as Sir James, 'The Black Douglas', Bruce was able to consolidate his gains, and he was crowned king with full ceremony at Scone before the inevitable blow of Papal excommunication fell. But it was not only that Rome refused to recognize Bruce as king. Edward I, the self-proclaimed 'Hammer of the Scots', was not best pleased, and for the next seven years Bruce was a virtual outlaw fighting a guerrilla campaign against Edward from hiding in the west.

During this time the indomitable Edward died, and Bruce felt bold and confident enough to raid the northern counties of England as far south as Appleby and Richmond. Of his castles captured by the English, only Stirling remained to be wrested from Edward's successor, Edward II. So the scene was set for the most significant battle in Scottish history: in 1314 at Bannockburn, near Stirling, Bruce confronted Edward II's vastly superior army. His incredible victory, aided by Angus Og of the Isles, and a number of Knights Templar recently arrived seeking sanctuary from persecution in France, has ensured him a place in the heart of every patriotic Scot.

Bannockburn brought the Scots a rare victory over their southern enemy, and led to the 'signing' of the Declaration of Arbroath, manifesto of Scotland's independence, in 1320. There followed a temporary peace with England, and Bruce was finally recognized as king by the Pope, before he died in 1329. His friend Douglas, as requested, took Bruce's heart on pilgrimage to the Holy Land, but when Douglas died en route it was returned to Melrose Abbey.

The Stewart dynasty

From Robert the Bruce's title of 'High Steward' sprang the dynasty of Stewart kings. The early Jameses (of whom there were seven in all) all followed a tragic pattern: succeeding as infant kings, imprisoned throughout childhood, and suffering untimely deaths. James I and III were both murdered, and James II blew himself up accidentally with a cannon. Unscrupulous regents frequently took charge, and hugely powerful nobles like the house of Douglas competed both amongst themselves and against the king. James II hot-bloodedly murdered the Earl of Douglas over dinner at Stirling Castle by throwing him out of the window. The Lords of the Isles were put down by the Earl of Mar and his followers in one of the bloodiest battles of all, 'Red Harlaw' near Inverurie. Like the Douglases, they too were finally forfeited, in 1543.

However, the early Stewarts made progress towards rescuing the country from anarchy by laying the foundations for a modern state through a series of constitutional reforms. Mostly cultured and progressive, they found time to write poetry (James I wrote the *King's Quair*), to build Renaissance palaces, and to father sufficient illegitimate 'James Stewarts' to fill numerous ecclesiastical sinecures (James IV and V). James IV was a true Renaissance prince with a glittering court, but a self-destructive streak led to his early death – along with most of the nobility – at Flodden, in 1513, sacrificed for the long-standing 'Auld Alliance' with France.

Mary, Queen of Scots

There is no more tragic and romantic figure in Scottish history than Mary, Queen of Scots. Raised in France for safekeeping as a Catholic, her brief reign was dogged by bad luck, bad judgement and bad timing. She arrived back in Scotland in 1561, a young widow, at the height of Reformation turmoil in which both France and Catholicism were inimical. Something of a loose cannon, she was embroiled in a power struggle not helped by her disastrous choice of husbands. Implicated in the celebrated murder of the first husband, her cousin, Henry Lord Darnley, she then swiftly married one of the chief suspects, the Earl of Bothwell, incurring the fury of everyone else. Imprisoned after the Battle of Carberry on the island fortress of Loch Leven, she escaped only to throw herself on the mercy of her cousin Queen Elizabeth I, who, mindful that in Catholic eyes Mary had the better claim to the English throne, locked her up at Fotheringhay for 19 years before deciding to do away with her altogether.

Reformation and the roots of Scottish education

The Reformation, converting the Catholic church to Protestant, came relatively late to Scotland and the motives were as much political as religious, though, of course, in 16th-century terms the two were inextricably linked. A pro-English Protestant faction had grown over decades, opposing the French Catholic Regent, Mary of Guise, and in 1560 a rebel parliament banned Catholic Mass, thus shattering for good the Auld Alliance with France, first formalized in 1295.

The casualties of the Reformation were countless, and included religious buildings, works of art and even whole libraries. It amounted to a complete obliteration of the past over which even today amnesia prevails, though, unlike in England, there were very few martyrs. So began 100 years of bitter struggle to establish the reformed church. Cue the Protestant exile, John Knox, a Calvinist rabble-rouser of dubious character and little diplomacy who was prone to blasting his trumpet off against the 'monstrous regiment of women,' namely Mary, Queen of Scots. Knox's skills as a colourful orator, and his self-appointed role as official historian of the Reformation, have allowed him to eclipse the real hero, Andrew Melville, who sacrificed his career of reforming university education to devote himself to the nuts and bolts of church reform.

Schooling for all as a passport to intellectual freedom and moral probity was a dream of the reformers. While grammar and song schools already existed, by the end of the 17th century most parishes had schools using the bible as textbook. The 'Dominie' (schoolmaster) was, until recently, a hugely influential community figure. Prior to the Reformation the Universities of St Andrews (1412), Glasgow (1451) and Aberdeen (1495) had been established, and Edinburgh University was added to the list in the 1580s.

James VI and the Union of Crowns

After Elizabeth's death, Mary's son became James VI of Scotland. Jacobean Scotland was vibrant and vigorously European. Religious extremists were checked by James VI, the 'Wisest fool in Christendom,' and unprecedented peace allowed Renaissance culture to blossom. But trouble was brewing. In 1603 James VI ascended to the English throne as James I, with the Union of Crowns. At this time the Scottish Parliament had so little power that James VI/I was able to write from his palace in London: "Here I sit and govern Scotland with my pen. I write and it is done." In contrast, the English parliament had begun to assume some genuine power.

What's in a name?

Before Culloden and the Clearances, Highland tradition decreed that a person's loyalty lay first and foremost with their own particular clan, or family group. There were two classes of clan: clansmen of the clan who were related by blood and shared the same family name, and individuals and groups who sought and obtained the protection of the clan. This resulted in a clan having septs, or sub-groups, of different surnames. The first Scots to be organized into clans or kindreds were known in early Scots Gaelic as cenela, and there is documentation of three such clans in the seventh-century kingdom of Dalriada, present-day Argyll. Certain features persisted from those early days until the demise of the clan system in the 18th century, in that chiefs could be elected or deposed, but there was no need for kilts or tartans. What held the clan together was a shared knowledge of history and genealogy, reinforced through the oral tradition of the bards and story-tellers. The great majority of 'clan' tartans are, in fact, a 19th-century invention, inspired by the creative genious of Sir Walter Scott.

Charles I and the Covenanters

James believed in the Divine Right of Kings – the God-given right of monarchs to rule their subjects. It was a belief that he passed on to his son Charles I, who succeeded in 1625 and quickly proved that he had little desire to consult parliament in either Scotland or England. Although he was born in Dunfermline, he showed little interest in Scotland and was essentially an absentee monarch. He did not even bother to come to Scotland to be crowned until 1633, calling a parliament at the same time – and then overseeing proceedings, making sure that the voting went his way.

Charles also showed little tact and diplomacy in matters ecclesiastical, and by reasserting the powers of the bishops he rode roughshod over the authority of the General Assembly of the Church of Scotland. Not surprisingly, the rumblings of revolution could soon be heard.

The struggle of the kirk (church) against the king erupted into full-scale civil war, with hostility towards bishops the recurrent theme. A riot in St Giles in Edinburgh expressed public feeling and resulted in The National Covenant, signed in Edinburgh in 1638, pledging faith to 'the true religion' and affirming the authority of the powerful General Assembly of the Church of Scotland in all matters spiritual. Covenanters and king came to blows, followed by an extremist group of Presbyterians allying with the English parliament against the king, in the Solemn League and Covenant. Battle-hardened Scots flooded back from European campaigns to take up arms.

A supporter of the original Covenant, Montrose, led a spirited but doomed campaign for the king against the extremists. At Ardvreck in Assynt he was betrayed to his arch-enemy 'King Campbell', Duke of Argyll, who gave him a traitor's death in Edinburgh. After the Restoration Argyll found himself on the wrong side and met the same end on the same spot.

Civil War

Throughout the 17th century the dark side of religious idealism – fanaticism and paranoia – were epitomized by the 'kirk sessions': courts in which the church conducted an orgy of scapegoating and witch-hunts. Fundamental differences of ideology, constitution and culture between two countries only recently 'twinned', opened cracks in the alliance with the Parliamentarians. The following year Civil War broke out in England, with parliamentarians led by Oliver Cromwell fighting to wrest power from the king. In 1649 Charles was executed and England became a republic. The Scots, however, wanted to keep the monarchy and proclaimed his son, Charles II as their king, despite falling under Cromwell's military 'Protectorate'. Cromwell acted swiftly to bring the country under his control. In 1651 he forbade the Scots from holding their own parliament – forcing them to send representatives to Westminster instead.

Charles II and Restoration

The Commonwealth under Cromwell lasted until 1660, when Charles II was restored to the English throne. The Scottish Parliament was revived and met again in 1661. This time the Presbyterian Covenanters, who had gained such control of Parliament prior to the Commonwealth, were tamed. The Scottish Parliament was again largely run by nobles loyal to the king.

Although Charles II was greeted with wild rejoicing, the reinstatement of the bishops once again proved problematic. Some unconsenting ministers of the church were outlawed and, finding a loyal following, especially in the southwest, they held illegal services, 'Conventicles', in the open air. Crippling fines and brutal persecution from officers of the crown, including Graham of Claverhouse, merely increased their resistance, and many died in the 'Killing Times' as martyrs to high principle.

Religion and the monarchy

Scotland and England continued to disagree, both about the succession and about religion. Charles II's brother and successor, James VII/II, was a Roman Catholic, and in 1687 he tried to introduce more tolerant policies towards Catholics. His actions were seen as a threat to the privileged position held by the Church of England, which since the time of Henry VIII had been the official church in England, and also displeased Presbyterians in Scotland. At first the feeling was that this state of affairs wouldn't last: James was ageing, and as both his daughters were Protestants, the Protestant succession seemed safe. However, when his heir James Francis Edward was born and brought up as a Catholic, a crisis was precipitated, James was ousted from the throne, and fled ignominiously in 1689. His Protestant daughter, Mary, and her husband William of Orange, were invited to take the throne of England, and were later reluctantly accepted by the Scots under the terms of the Revolution Settlement.

The Darién Scheme

Although both countries shared a monarch, England was growing significantly wealthier than Scotland. Like other European countries, it was thriving economically through trade generated by its colonies. Scotland, however, had no colonies of its own. To remedy this, a monopoly company was founded with the approval of the king, modelled on the English East India Company. Wealthy Scots helped to fund it, but much of the capital was raised in England. However, the English East India Company exercised its considerable power to protect its monopoly. Strings were pulled and the House of Commons soon threatened to prosecute the Scottish company's English directors. The king, who had agreed to its establishment, now came under pressure to oppose it. Not surprisingly, most of the English backers withdrew and Scotland saw it as a matter of national pride to raise the starting capital itself – a sum of £400,000, roughly half the nation's capital.

The intention of the scheme was to establish a permanent colony at Darién, on the Panama Isthmus in Central America. Darién was a strategically important site, and the plan was that goods sent to and from Europe would sail to Panama, be carried overland across the isthmus, then reshipped – the new Scottish company carrying out this lucrative work.

However, the project had not been thoroughly researched. For one thing, the land was owned by Spain, a major world power who King William could not afford to offend. Consequently, he ordered English colonists in the area not to help the Scottish settlers defend their new home against the Spanish. In addition the terrain was hostile (which was why the Spanish had not set up a similar scheme already), and diseases like malaria and yellow fever were rife. Within months large numbers of colonists had died. Another attempt was made and was also unsuccessful, and by 1700 the colony had been abandoned.

The consequences were far reaching. Scotland lost a vast proportion of her wealth; national pride and confidence were dented; and the country lost faith in the dual monarchy. The king had sided with his wealthiest subjects – and Scotland felt betrayed.

Union of Parliaments

While Darién produced much anti-English feeling, a number of Scots began to feel that greater co-operation with England could be economically advantageous. At around the same time a further constitutional crisis was brewing. William of Orange had no children and was to be succeeded by James VII/II's daughter, Anne, who was Protestant. However, Anne had no surviving children and English politicians began to search for an heir – who had to be both Protestant and have Stuart blood. They decided on the Hanoverians, who were descended from the daughter of James VI/I. In 1701 the English parliament passed the Act of Settlement, ruling that on Anne's death the throne should pass to the House of Hanover. In 1702 William died and the throne passed to Anne.

The assumption was that the Scots would follow England's lead and accept the Hanoverian succession. But the nation was still smarting over Darién and, as Anne turned out to have little interest in Scotland, relations were strained. The difficulties over having two separate governments under one monarch would not go away. In 1703 the Scottish parliament passed the Act of Security which declared that on Anne's death Scotland would take a different successor to England, unless some settlement could be agreed upon that restored "the honour and sovereignty of this Crown and Kingdom". They wanted to guarantee the power of the Scottish parliament; the freedom of Scottish religion; and freedom of trade. In addition Parliament ordered people to arm themselves and prepare to fight. It was sabre rattling that the English could hardly ignore.

Although Anne signed the Act of Security, Scotland's triumph was shortlived. England passed the Alien Act, which declared that all Scots except those resident in England should be treated as aliens, and Scottish trade with England was to be blocked. The act was to remain in force until Scotland agreed to make moves towards parliamentary union, or accepted Hanoverian succession.

There were obvious economic advantages to closer ties with England, and Scotland was in a vulnerable position. Not only had the Darién venture weakened the economy, the country was also suffering from several years of harvest failure which had led to famine. Although public opinion was against Union with England, it counted for little. It certainly appealed to many in parliament. Financial inducements were offered – and accepted – causing Robert Burns to comment later that Scotland had been "bought and sold for English gold". The Church of Scotland, initially suspicious of Union, withdrew its objections when it was assured that Presbyterianism would be safeguarded. A propaganda campaign was carried out on both sides of the border, many of the pamphlets being written by the author Daniel Defoe. The English were assured that Union would end the threat of invasion from Scotland; the Scots assured of great economic benefits.

The people were not swayed. There were violent demonstrations in the streets, and riots in Glasgow, Dumfries and Edinburgh. Opponents even went as far as claiming that Union would be sinful. The riots in Edinburgh were particularly violent, causing Defoe, who was acting as a spy for the English government, to say: "A Scots rabble is the worst of its kind." The Scots – he said – were a "hardened and terrible people". Pro-Union MPs were attacked, and plans were made in Lanarkshire to raise an army to march on Edinburgh. But public opinion was not of consequence. The Duke of Argyll, for instance, stated that anti-Union petitions were only fit to make paper kites out of. Although some members, notably Andrew Fletcher of Saltoun, were opposed to Union, the treaty was comfortably passed by the Scottish Parliament on 16 January 1707. It had to be signed in secret in Edinburgh to protect politicians from the mob.

In April the act was passed in the English Parliament, and on 1 May 1707 the Union came into effect. The Kingdoms of Scotland and England were united into Great Britain, though Scotland preserved its separate legal system, educational system and church. Despite the vigorous opposition, threats and bribery assured that a bankrupt and exhausted Scotland was, in popular mythology, sold to England for £398,085 – part compensation for Darién, part wages for the Commissioners who closed the deal.

Jacobite rebellion

Rebellion against the imposition of William of Orange began in 1689, when William's government redcoats clashed with supporters of James II (the Jacobites) at Killiecrankie (see page 118). They were led by Graham of Claverhouse, 'Bonnie Dundee', who was killed in the battle. In 1692 an expedition to weed out the Jacobites in the Highlands resulted in the Glencoe massacre, which provoked unprecedented public outcry (see box, page 206).

The Act of Settlement was not forgotten, and dwindling trade and increased taxation fuelled dissatisfaction with the Union. A lively underground resistance, aided by long-standing French connections, revolved around the Jacobite court in exile at St Germain. Sympathy also came from English quarters.

Four attempts ensued to reinstate a Stewart monarchy, supported erratically by France, and culminating at Culloden in 1746 (see box, page 172). Much support came from north of the Tay, which was Catholic and Episcopalian country. The term 'Jacobite' popularly denoted anti-establishment and Episcopalian. There was also a linguistic, social and cultural divide between Lowlander and Highlander which had grown since the 15th century.

Highland culture and independence was not diminished after the demise of the Lords of the Isles, hence the rise of the Campbells to enormous power as government agents, dealing for instance with the troublesome MacGregors. Claiming descent from Kenneth MacAlpin, the MacGregors were almost annihilated in 1603, and outlawed until 1774. They played a significant part in the Jacobite rebellions.

Although traditionally indifferent to the monarchy, many clans came out in support of Prince Charles (of 'Bonnie Prince Charlie' fame) in 1745. After defeat at Culloden, savage reprisals were led by the 'Butcher' Cumberland. Rebels were beheaded or hanged, estates confiscated, and the pipes and Highland dress proscribed until 1782. Clansmen were enlisted into Highland regiments and 1150 were exiled, swelling the ranks of emigrants to the colonies. Gaelic culture was effectively expunged and Scotland as a whole suffered disgrace. See also box, page 439.

BACKGROUND
Death of the clans

Though events such as Culloden played a part in the demise of traditional clan society as central government sought to 'civilize' the lawless fringes of society, the repression of clanship had already been effected largely by the changing role of the clan elites.

By the time of Bonnie Prince Charlie's defeat at Culloden in 1746, the clan chief had virtually become a commercial landlord, no longer trustee of his people's territory but sole owner of the land, thanks to the new legalistic definition of clanship agreed between the clan chiefs and central government.

Tensions between the state and the leading clans over authority and control of the Highlands and Islands of Scotland had grown in the wake of the Union of Crowns in 1603 and the government introduced a series of measures, known as the Statutes of Iona, in 1609 (revised 1615-1516) to curb the most disruptive aspects of clanship and to educate the clan chiefs about their responsibilites as members of the Scottish landed classes.

These new laws defined the clan elite's superior position at the expense of their clansmen. Traditionally, all clansfolk considered themselves noble, due to their relationship with previous chiefs, but the Statutes limited the wearing and use of arms, lowered expectations of hospitality, restricted the deployment of military retinues and made the clan elite accountable to the Scottish legal establishment. This had particular impact in the Hebrides where further measures such as the promotion of English schooling and establishment of a Protestant Church ministry were designed to force the pace of change and assimilation.

During the course of the 17th century central government control was further extended. The notion of heritable trusteeship exercised by the clan chiefs over their clan territories gave way to the more legalistic alternative of heritable title, ending the notion of collective land rights and replacing it with sole ownership of the land by the clan elite.

The spread of agrarian capitalism further changed the nature of the clan system, as the clan elites took a more propietorial role in their dealings with their kinsfolk. Civil War, occupation by Oliver Cromwell's forces and the massive ideological and financial pressures generated by the Covenanting movement all had a devastating effect on the Scottish Gaeldom, leading to social dislocation and a polarization of the clans.

The policies of the restored regime of Charles II only made things worse. The increased burden of high taxation and accountability for his clansmen consolidated the tendency of the clan chiefs to act in their own interests rather than as patrons and protectors. So clansmen became alienated from their elite and the role of the chief changed as head of the kindred was sub-ordinated to his role as head of the elite.

The Jacobite Rebellions of 1715 and 1745 not only gave the British government the excuse to wipe out all traces of the clan system, and, in the process, the Gaelic language, in favour of commerce and 'civility', but also provided clan leaders with an excuse to end their traditional responsibilities.

Rise and fall of Bonnie Prince Charlie

Charles Edward Stuart, the 'Young Pretender', grandson of James II, was born in Italy. First setting foot on Scottish soil aged 23 with seven companions (the Seven Men of Moidart), his forceful personality persuaded reluctant clan chiefs to join him in raising the Standard for his father at Glenfinnan in 1745. Inadequately prepared government troops under 'Johnny Cope' enabled his swift progress to Edinburgh, where he held court at Holyrood, dazzling the populace with a grand ball. Edinburgh was charmed but embarrassed.

With sights set on the English throne, he reached Derby. Encouraging reports about panic in London were offset by news of advancing government troops which prompted retreat. The pursuing redcoats were outwitted as far as Inverness, and the ensuing bloodbath at Culloden, though Charles' only defeat, was decisive. Fleeing to the Hebrides, he was given shelter by Flora MacDonald (see box, page 291) and then spent a summer as a lone fugitive. Despite a £30,000 reward for his capture, he managed to escape on a French frigate in 1746. Too late by just a fortnight, 40,000 Louis d'ors then arrived from France, enough to have revived the whole campaign.

This failure has been ascribed to a fatal weakness of character and a collapse of resolve at Derby. He ended his days a degenerate and broken man, ensuring the complete collapse of the Jacobite cause. But Bonnie Prince Charlie is remembered in numerous nostalgic songs, a toast to 'the King over the Water', and a host of memorabilia.

The Enlightenment

Intellectual life flourished in late 18th-century Scotland. Embracing all the arts, its roots lay in the philosophical nature, shaped by European thought, underlying Scots law, education and the church. The sceptic David Hume (1711-1776) was the foremost of a school of philosophers, best known for his *Treatise on Human Nature and Essays, Moral and Political*. Kirkcaldy-born Adam Smith pioneered political economy in his *Wealth of Nations* (1776), a powerful impetus to later political reform.

An emphasis on research and practicality in the sciences fostered inventiveness in applied science, contributing much to industry and agriculture. James Watt developed the steam engine which powered the machinery of the Industrial Revolution, medicine flourished at Edinburgh University, and further generations spawned engineers and inventors like Alexander Graham Bell and John Logie Baird, inventors of the telephone and television.

Classicism was espoused in architecture and by painters like Allan Ramsay, Raeburn and Naysmth, and gave way in literature to the Romanticism of Robert Burns whose work profoundly influenced popular culture and notions of democracy.

Sir Walter Scott's best selling historical novels worked miracles for Scotland's public image. It was he who stage-managed the visit of George IV, who sportingly donned a kilt and, for modesty's sake, pink tights for the occasion. Later on, Queen Victoria was inspired to adopt a Highland home and, with the craze for 'Balmorality', the Highlands assumed a romantic glamour, becoming a fashionable resort for southern sportsmen.

Industrial revolution and the Clearances

Until around 1750 a large percentage of Scotland's population lived north of the Clyde and Tay. Emigration to the Lowlands or North America was already a problem, as a money economy threatened traditional ways of life. The decision of landlords to resettle their tenants on the coasts, replacing black cattle with sheep, was a disastrous economic and social experiment, with brutal evictions in some areas – although popular myth forgets that famine, disease and overpopulation were rife and many went willingly. Eventually, in 1886, crofters' rights were to some extent recognized (see also box, page 329).

The gap between Highland and Lowland life continued to widen as overgrazing, deforestation for industry, and deer 'forests', led to desolation in the Highlands, while improvements and drainage transformed Lowland agriculture.

At the same time industrialization was soon to bring a massive population shift. Wool, cloth and linen, long established as cottage industries, were undergoing mechanization. By 1820 mills were established in the coalfields of Lanark, Renfrew and Ayr. Linen declined in favour of cotton, spun and woven in Paisley and New Lanark, while tweed was first woven in Galashiels in 1830. Dundee substituted jute for linen and Kirkcaldy developed linoleum. Thriving on trade with America, Glasgow's population mushroomed, absorbing many from the Highlands, as well as thousands of Irish refugees from the potato famine of the 1840s. Poor housing, overcrowding and disease became chronic.

20th-century Scotland

By 1900 iron and later steel, mainly in the west, had become manufacturing mainstays, serviced by new canals, railways and roads. As well as emigrants, Scotland supplied goods to North America: locomotives, girders, bridges, textile machinery and tools. Shipyards flourished on the Clyde. The first iron steam ships were launched around 1800, although fast wooden clippers like the *Cutty Sark* were still competitive in the mid-19th century, when major shipping companies such as Cunard came to the fore. From 1880 skilled labour built steel ships for world markets as well as for the Royal Navy. Business boomed during the First World War, when political activity among skilled workers, inspired by the Bolshevik revolution and led by Marxist and Scottish Nationalist John Maclean, gave rise to the myth of 'Red Clydeside'.

Post-war slump hit all industries in the 1920s, from which they never really recovered. A dangerous dependency on mining, metalworking and heavy engineering was a crucial factor in industrial decline, and the innovative spirit of the 19th century is only now re-emerging among pioneering computer software development companies in the central belt.

In a long Liberal tradition dedicated to political reform, the issue of Home Rule reared its head repeatedly after the 1880s. The first stirrings of nationalism were heard after the First World War and voiced by writers in the 1920s, such as Lewis Spence, Hugh MacDiarmid and Neil Gunn. These sentiments took political shape as the Scottish National Party (SNP) in 1934. Support grew through the 1950s and 1960s, and in 1967 the SNP was revealed as a potent political force when Winifred Ewing won the Hamilton by-election.

Nationalist fervour reached its height in the 1970s, roused by expectations that revenue from the oil and gas recently discovered in the North Sea would reverse economic decline. These hopes were dashed by oil revenues disappearing into the British Treasury at Westminster. In 1974, 11 SNP MPs were elected to Westminster – and, although many felt that this was a protest vote, Labour was concerned. In 1979 it held a referendum on the establishment of a Scottish Assembly. Turnout was low and support was luke warm, so no assembly was established.

Labour were soon ousted from office and the Thatcher government swept to power in 1979, bringing with it a disdain for Scotland that was to have far-reaching consequences. The new Conservative government also introduced policies that did not sit easily with most Scots. When the unpopular Poll Tax, which notoriously taxed 'dukes the same as dustmen', was introduced in Scotland a year earlier than in the rest of Britain, the country felt that it was increasingly being governed by politicians who cared little for its people. Years of Tory rule served only to widen the gap between Scotland and Westminster, and it was almost inevitable that some form of devolution would follow.

Scotland in the 21st century

Twenty years on, the Scots voted emphatically in favour of devolution, and the Scottish Parliament reconvened after 292 years on 12 May, 1999. The new Parliament has 129 MSPs (Members of the Scottish Parliament) who are elected by proportional representation. It has the power to pass legislation and to alter the rate of taxation. Defence and foreign affairs are still handled by Westminster.

Five years after devolution, the bold, stunning new parliamentary building finally opened to a barrage of criticism. It was subject to a public inquiry into why its costs increased tenfold (from an estimated £40 million to over £400 million), and why it opened three years later than planned. Blame was laid at the door of bureaucrats.

Many at the time saw devolution as a step on the road to full independence, and so it may yet come to pass. In 2007 the SNP became the largest party in the country at the Scottish elections. They won 47 seats to Labour's 46 and formed a minority government with the backing of the Greens. The SNP manifesto pledged to hold a referendum on Scottish independence by 2010 but later announced this would not happen before the 2011 elections for the Scottish Parliament, in which the SNP swept to power with 69 seats, forming a majority government for the first time. This was Labour's worst result in Scotland since 1931; they lost 22 seats to the SNP, many in their traditional heartlands in and around Glasgow.

In May 2012, SNP leader Alex Salmond launched the campaign for Scottish Independence and on Thursday 18 September 2014, the Scottish electorate voted in a referendum on whether or not to become and independent country. After several months of rancorous and often bruising campaigning the people of Scotland voted by 55.3% to 44.7% to remain a part of the United Kingdom. The defeat of the independence campaign led to the resignation of First Minister Alex Salmond. The SNP rebounded from the loss of the referendum at the UK General Election in 2015, led by Salmod's successor, Nicola Sturgeon. The party went from holding six seats in the House of Commons to 56, mostly at the expense of the Labour Party, meaning that all but three of the 59 constituencies in Scotland elected an SNP candidate. At the 2016 Scottish Parliamentary elections the SNP lost its overall majority but returned for a third consecutive term as a minority government. Following the UK referendum on EU membership in 2016, which the Leave side won by a narrow majority of 51.89% to 48.11%, Prime Minister Theresa May called a surprise snap general election in 2017. Given that Scotland had voted overwhelmingly in favour of remaining a part of the EU, the SNP called for a second independence referendum but this backfired when they performed badly, losing 21 seats, bringing their total number of Westminster MPs down to 35 and seeing a swing to the Unionist parties, with SNP seats being won by the Conservatives, Labour and the Liberal Democrats, and a reduction in SNP majorities in the other seats.

What happens next is anybody's guess, especially as the Scottish people are more pro-European than their English counterparts, and Scottish independence is sure to remain a hot political issue.

Culture

Architecture

Early structures: from brochs to towers

A thousand years before Stonehenge, a Neolithic architect was supervising the construction of Maes Howe (see page 385) in Orkney. Dramatically accompanied by two stone circles, its massive precision-cut stonework houses a tomb. Religious architecture evolved into the Bronze Age, and over 22 centuries of chambered tombs survive, notably at Camster and Kilmartin. Henges and stone circles, as at Cairnpapple, also abound. At Skara Brae (see page 382) is a 5000-year-old village, a Neolithic Pompeii where stone furniture and utensils survive in rooms straight out of the *Flintstones*.

Brochs, fortresses not dissimilar to diminutive industrial cooling towers such as at Mousa on Shetland (see page 417), appeared around 75 BC. A staircase ascended within double walls and a well often provided water for the besieged within. On duns and hilltops, timber-laced forts, built from 700 BC into the Middle Ages, are sometimes found to have been fired to such an extent that stonework fused solid or vitrified. Whether this was intentional, or the result of attack, remains a mystery.

Ninth-century wheelhouses, with stone piers radiating from a central hearth, are visible at Jarlshof on Shetland, and appeared later in the Hebrides. Timber began to be used for Pictish hall houses, *crannogs* (lake dwellings on wooden rafts) and early churches.

In the 11th century round towers, such as those at Brechin and Abernethy, were used for defence and as belfries by Culdee communities. Around this time the first cathedrals were built. The one at Birsay on Orkney, founded in 1050 by Earl Thorfinn, was soon replaced by another in Kirkwall commemorating the Norse St Magnus (see page 376). This was built by masons from Durham Cathedral after working at Dunfermline Abbey, also Romanesque, built for St Margaret. She also commissioned St Rule's in St Andrews, whose tall square tower suggests Northumbrian influence, echoed in those at Muthill, Dunning (in Strathearn) and Dunblane.

Abbeys and cathedrals

David I (1124-1153) granted land to Roman monastic orders and two centuries of abbey and cathedral building ensued, though mostly in the Lowlands. Years of neglect and depredations by English troops and iconoclastic reformers left many as picturesque ruins, stripped of magnificent wood and stone carving, stained glass and wallpainting. The wallpaintings at Fowlis Easter, 15th-century collegiate churches, are a rare survivor. The ruins of Oronsay Priory and the Valerian-clad cloisters of Iona's nunnery (see page 87) are the legacy of the Augustinians.

Medieval castles

Symbols of feudalism built by Norman settlers appear in the form of timber motte and bailey fortresses – timber towers with defensive earthworks – though they are found mostly south of the Forth and Clyde.

Square or oblong tower houses, with a defensive entry at first floor level, barrel vaulting and great hall, were to be an enduring form of dwelling, evolving from the 14th century into the 17th. More elaborate are L-plan and Z-plan versions, with one or two towers added at the corners to defend the entry.

Renaissance palaces

While ordinary folk lived in thatched turf and stone hovels (some into the 20th century), the cosmopolitan and cultured Stewart kings set about building new palaces and improving existing residences. The old castle at Linlithgow had emerged by 1540, a wholly residential Renaissance palace ranged around a quadrangle, which even impressed the French Mary of Guise. While the Great Hall at Stirling is a triumph of late Gothic, the later Palace block (1540-1542) reveals many Renaissance features, such as the recessed bays along the exterior with sculpted figures, and the famous carved wooden ceiling medallions, the 'Stirling Heads'.

The tower house

A minor building boom in the late 16th century was a result of church land being transferred over a long period into private hands. The old tower house formula found favour, preferred over earlier royal examples of Renaissance innovation. Everyone from nobility to minor gentry was afforded both defence against troublesome neighbours as well as gracious living. Claypotts in Dundee is a good example of 'the castle with a country house built on top', while at Craigievar, finished as late as 1626, idiosyncratic inventiveness reaches its apogee where the roofline explodes in a flurry of fairytale turrets. Families of masons developed individual styles detectable in Aberdeenshire where many tower houses, great and small, are still inhabited or have been recently revived. Defensive features like gun loops (apertures for guns) survived less out of necessity than as status symbols, and interiors, especially timber ceilings, were vividly painted, with exuberant imagery, as at Crathes.

16th- to 18th-century townhouses

'New towns' to promote trade were established by David I and settled with English and Flemish merchants, with a strict hierarchy of trading rights and privileges. Stone houses first replaced wood in the east coast burghs in the 16th century, setting a precedent for future urban design. Every burgh had its symbols of commerce and government at its centre: the Mercat (market) cross and the Tolbooth (town hall).

Two centuries later, the spirit of vernacular architecture had not changed dramatically. Nor had urban layout, many houses still being built gable end on to the street. The multi-storey tenement became a distinctive feature of urban living, pioneered in Edinburgh's Canongate, where buildings such as Gladstone's Land are still intact. Culross Palace and Argyll's Ludgings in Stirling are outstanding examples of grand town houses.

William Bruce and the 17th-century mansion

The country mansion was a concept pioneered by Alexander Seton, paragon of a new kind of architectural patron, at Pinkie House in Musselburgh, a daring essay in elegance and erudition. Post Restoration, William Bruce exemplifies a new concept: the architect. Introducing classical symmetry to existing buildings such as Holyrood and Thirlestane, he also designed Hopetoun in 1699-1703. The innovative oblong shape and hipped roof of Kinross are characteristic of his many other country house designs with their Anglo-Dutch interiors and plasterwork. He also revolutionized garden and landscape design. Bruce's protégé, James Smith, was a pioneer of British Palladianism. Rising from master mason to King's Master of Works and private architect, his own house, Newhailes (circa 1690), was the inspiration for countless lairds' houses, both grand and humble, built throughout Scotland in the 18th century.

Victorian Baronial

Not content with Classicism, architects raided the Gothic, Tudor, Jacobean and Scottish past, even Asia and Europe, for ideas. Late 18th-century country houses by Gillespie Graham were asymmetrical and castellated. Inspired by the picturesque movement, they are the harbingers of the High Victorian revival of Scottish baronial which reached its peak in the 1860s. New and unprecedented wealth found industrial tycoons and landowners beating a path to the doors of fashionable architects like Burn and Bryce, to build colossal and fantastic country seats with room for entertaining on a huge scale, and the latest in comforts – like plumbing. Some followed Queen Victoria's example at Balmoral, building extravagant Highland shooting lodges. Most eclectic of all is Mount Stuart on Bute (1870s) a neo-Gothic/Renaissance palace whose sumptuous interior even includes details from Charlemagne's tomb (see page 74). Flamboyant design extended to monumental industrial buildings like textile mills and foundries, also railway stations, viaducts and bridges.

Literature

Any overview, no matter how brief, of Scotland's literary tradition must begin with a poet who has become inextricably linked with the image of Scotland and all things Scottish across the globe. **Robert Burns** was born on 25 January 1759 in Alloway, Ayrshire, in very humble surroundings, later referring to himself as "a very poor man's son". Burns wrote in the dialect of plain country people and about the lives they led, but the emotions he described were so genuine that they appealed to all classes.

His poetry mainly concerned itself with life as he was living it. He was also keen to point out what he saw as a kinship between all living things, such as in his famous *To A Mouse*. The most frequently quoted lines of this poem; "The best laid schemes o' mice an' men – Gang aft a-gley," has entered the language, as have many sayings originated by Burns, and is a perfect summing up of his point of view. His most celebrated work, *Auld Lang Syne* expresses the joys of human companionship and is practically an anthem when friends gather to celebrate New Year around the world. His love of the companionship of friends is also a focus of *Tam O'Shanter*, which also serves as a cautionary warning against overindulgence and is a ghost story in the tradition of the mythic, while his irritation against the assumed superiority of some was put into words in *A Man's A Man For A' That*, which also returns to his theme of kinship.

The 'heav'n-taught' Ayrshire ploughman died on 21 July 1796, and was buried in St Michael's Churchyard, Dumfries. Such is his standing that his memory is celebrated every year on 25 January, his date of birth, now referred to as Burns Night.

Another writer forever associated with the Borders is **Sir Walter Scott**, who not only ruled the roost in his native Scotland but the world of literature in general. Born in 1771, the son of a wealthy Edinburgh lawyer, Scott spent much of his childhood in the Borders during which time he immersed himself in tales and ballads of Jacobites and Border heroes, giving him a passion for history which would infuse his later work. It was this material which would eventually become poems in his three volumes of *Minstrelsy of the Scottish Border* which established his name as a literary figure. Other romantic poetic works followed, such as *The Lady of the Lake*.

In 1811 Scott purchased Abbotsford, a farmhouse near Melrose, and during the following years developed the style which would remain his best-remembered contribution to literature, the historical novel. Collectively known as the Waverley novels,

Not surprisingly, given the relatively low numbers of people who can speak the language (around 80,000), Gaelic writers have never enjoyed anything like the same success of their English-language counterparts. Two writers who have managed to transcend the linguistic barrier are Sorley Maclean (1911-1996) and Iain Crichton Smith (1928-1998).

Sorley Maclean in particular is something of a cult figure, and it has been argued that he did for the Gaelic language what Hugh MacDiarmid did for Scots. The fact that Maclean translated much of his work into English made him accessible to a much wider audience and this sparked a Renaissance in Gaelic literature. He was also influencial in the preservation and promotion of the teaching of Gaelic in schools.

It was the publication of Gordon Wright's *Four Points of a Saltire* – poems from Goerge Campbell Hay, Stuart MacGregor, William Neill and Sorley Maclean – that brought his work to the outside world in the 1970s, and the bilingual *Selected Poems* of 1977 brought him a whole new generation of readers. He won the Queen's Gold Medal for Poetry in 1990 and died in 1996, at the age of 85.

Another important Gaelic writer of the 20th century was Lewis – raised Iain Crichton Smith. Like Sorley Maclean, Crichton Smith was bilingual, allowing him to reach a wider audience, as well as translate other Gaelic works – including the 'Gaelic Homer', Duncan Ban McIntyre. Smith was awarded an OBE in 1980 and won numerous literary prizes, travelling frequently to read his work around the world. His heart, though, remained in the Highlands of Scotland, and he lived in the village of Taynuilt, near Oban, until his death in 1998.

these included *Old Mortality*, *Rob Roy* and *The Heart Of Midlothian*. The original Waverley was a romantic tale of the Jacobite Rebellion of 1745 and the Highland society of the time. By 1819 Scott had moved beyond purely Scottish history and wrote *Ivanhoe*, set in 12th-century England. It remains his most enduring work, and he followed it with *Kenilworth*, *Redgauntlet* and *The Talisman*.

Scott died on 21 September 1832. His huge popularity was believed to have kept the spirit of Scotland alive and he is commemorated by the Scott Monument in Princes Street, Edinburgh.

A contemporary of Scott's, though far less well known, was **James Hogg**, the Ettrick Shepherd, born at Ettrickhall Farm in Selkirkshire in 1770. Like Burns before him, Hogg was of humble origins and did not receive a proper education he but inherited a vast store of balladry from his mother, Margaret, some of which Scott published in his *Minstrelsy Of The Scottish Border*. Like Burns, Hogg was lionized by the Edinburgh elite as another heaven-taught rustic with a flair for poetry, but that is to severely undermine his importance to the world of philosophy and psychology as well as literature. His writings dealt with the notion of a divided nature within a single individual, reflecting Hogg's own double life as rough Border shepherd and sophisticated urban intellectual. Hogg's thinking and writing reached their apotheosis is his extraordinary *The Private Memoirs and Confessions of a Justified Sinner*, published in 1824 and one of the true masterpieces of Scottish literature. There is nothing else like it and, prior to the Freudian era, nothing to match its insight into fractures of human nature.

This exploration of the dual nature of man received its quintessential expression in **Robert Louis Stevenson**'s *The Strange Case of Doctor Jekyll and Mister Hyde*, published some 50 years after Hogg's death and one of the classics of horror literature. The tale was inspired by Edinburgh's notorious Deacon Brodie, a seemingly respectable pillar of the community by day and a criminal, gambler and womanizer by night.

Stevenson's fondness of the macabre is also apparent in stories like *The Bottle Imp* and *The Bodysnatcher*, but it is for his romantic historical adventures that he is best known. Born at 8 Howard Place, Edinburgh, on 13 November 1850, Stevenson was fond of travel which led to his employment as a writer of travel articles and essays. While staying in Braemar in 1881, Stevenson drew pirate maps of an island, and these became the basis of his tale, *Treasure Island*, published two years later. For Stevenson it was just the first of the many adventure tales, including *Kidnapped*, its sequel, *Catriona* and *The Master of Ballantrae*, he wrote before his death in Samoa on 3 December 1894. The tradition of the adventure story has continued throughout the 20th century in the works of Perth-born **John Buchan**, author of *The Thirty-Nine Steps*.

One of Stevenson's contemporaries at Edinburgh University was **Sir Arthur Conan Doyle**. Born at Picardy Place, Edinburgh, on 22 May 1859, Conan Doyle was schooled in Lancashire before returning to study medicine at Edinburgh University in 1876. It was while serving as an out-patient clerk at Edinburgh Royal Infirmary that Doyle met Doctor Joseph Bell, the man who was to influence most the creation of his famous character. "His strong point", Doyle later noted, "was diagnosis, not only of disease, but of occupation and character".

Doyle was living in London and had published several short stories and essays when memories of his former mentor, combined with a love of the detective fiction of Edgar Allan Poe, inspired him to write *A Study In Scarlet*, which first appeared in the 1887 edition of *Beeton's Christmas Annual*. Doctor Watson recounted Sherlock Holmes' unique detective skills in this, followed by a further three novels and 56 short stories, with all but *The Sign Of Four* making their initial appearance in *The Strand Magazine*.

Holmes became a phenomenon that not even Doyle could control. In fact, by 1893 he was so annoyed that his more serious literary endeavours were being neglected that he achieved what many criminals had failed to do. He killed Holmes. Following publication of *The Final Problem*, in which Holmes and his mortal foe, Professor Moriarty plunged over the Reichenbach Falls, there were public displays of grief and mourning. It was clear that the public were not going to let Holmes rest in peace, and eventually Doyle was forced to find an ingenious way of reviving the character. He penned his last Holmes story in 1927, a mere three years before his own death. Doyle's other famous character was Professor Challenger, who famously discovered the Lost World, which later inspired Steven Spielberg's *Jurassic Park*.

Another classic of literature was written by Doyle's older literary friend, **JM Barrie**. Born in Kirriemuir in 1860, James Matthew Barrie was the son of a weaver. Educated at Glasgow Academy and Edinburgh University, Barrie spent some years in Nottingham as a journalist before returning to Kirriemuir to write. He moved to London in 1885, and it was there that he wrote his first novel, *Better Dead*. More novels and plays followed, best known of which is *Peter Pan* and *The Lost Boys*. First published in 1904, it was written for the children of a friend, Llewelyn Davis. Before his death in 1937, he bequeathed the copyright for Peter Pan to Great Ormond Street Hospital in London.

20th century

A common criticism of 19th- and early 20th-century Scottish literature was the relative absence of novels dealing with the whole issue of industrialization, growing social division and immigration. Rather than explore the vexed issues of poverty, class division and the growing Celtic influence, most writers belonged to the 'Kailyard School', which presented a romantic, sentimental and completely unrealistic image of Scotland, perhaps reflecting the overwhelmingly middle-class background of novelists at that time.

The Kailyard came to be detested by a growing band of writers in the 20th century, and a new phase of realistic literature – known as the Scottish Renaissance – began in the 1920s, inspired by one of the greatest novels to emerge from Scotland, **George Douglas Brown**'s ground-breaking *House of the Green Shutters*. Published in 1901, the novel brings Greek tragedy to 19th-century rural Ayrshire and, more than any other, destroyed the bucolic escapism of the Kailyard School.

In the same year **James Leslie Mitchell** was born in rural Aberdeenshire. Better known by his pseudonym **Lewis Grassic Gibbon**, his novel, *Sunset song*, published in 1932 (only three years before his untimely death), has become one of the mainstays of modern Scottish literature, and taught as part of the national curriculum. It was written as the first book in the trilogy, *A Scots Quair*, which charts the life of Chris Guthrie, from late 19th century through to the 1920s. Written from the girl's perspective, it is remarkable not only for its strong evocation of this part of Scotland, but also for its uncanny emotional resonance.

Another renowned northeast writer is **Neil Gunn**, born in Dunbeath, Caithness, in 1891. His writings, which deal with the disintegration of the old Highland way of life in the wake of the Clearances and the struggle to adapt to new conditions, also convey a strong sense of place and are as important to Scottish literature and identity as Faulkner and Dostoevsky are to the USA and Russia. Amongst his best-known works is *Silver Darlings* (1939), the title of which refers to the booming herring industry. Gunn died in 1973.

For its size, Orkney has produced a disproportionate number of well-loved and much-read authors. The poet, novelist and playwright, **George Mackay Brown**, gained even more popularity after the posthumous publication of his autobiography, following his death in 1996. Like Gunn and Grassic Gibbon before him, Brown is inextricably linked to his homeland and evokes the spirit and landscapes of his beloved Orkney with a deft sensitivity, bringing a strong poetic impulse to bear on the social realism of his novels. Amongst his best is *Greenvoe*, published in 1972. **Eric Linklater** (1899-1974) is another Orcadian whose copious output of books and poems gained him international recognition. *The Dark of Summer* best represents his compelling style.

One of the most important 20th-century Scottish writers, perhaps *the* most important, is **Hugh MacDiarmid** (1892-1978). Born Christopher Murray Grieve, in the Scottish border town of Langholm, MacDiarmid, as with many Scottish writers of the 20th century, was fiercely political, becoming a founding member of the Scottish National Party (SNP) in 1928. During the 1930s, MacDiarmid moved to the remote Shetland island of Whalsay. He continued writing ground-breaking poetry, becoming increasingly convinced that the essential Scottish human condition could not be fully expressed through the English language alone but rather through a plurality of voices, including Lowland Scots dialect and the Gaelic language. Though recognized as the major force behind the Sottish Literary Renaissance, MacDiarmid's life was a frugal one and he died a man of modest means, near Biggar, in 1978. His best-known work, *A Drunk Man Looks at the Thistle*, was published in 1926.

Another 20th-century giant is **Robin Jenkins**, referred to as 'the Scottish Thomas Hardy'. It was Jenkins who put his native city of Glasgow firmly on the literary map. His most Glaswegian of novels, *A Very Scotch Affair* (Gollancz, 1968), is still regarded as a high point in pre-1970s Glasgow fiction. Jenkins is also recognized as the founder of new Scottish fiction and a precursor to Kelman and Welsh as portraying an unsentimental view of Scottish life. Among his other novels are *The Cone Gatherers* (MacDonald 1955), *Fergus Lamont* (Edinburgh Canongate 1979) and *Childish Things* (Canongate 2001).

Another Glasgow literary talent of this time is **William McIlvanney**. Though he had already published two Glasgow novels in the 1960s, it was the following decade which saw him emerge as one of the city's greats. In *Laidlaw* (Hodder and Stoughton, 1977), McIlvanney explored Glasgow's seedy, criminal underbelly through the eyes of the eponymous police Detective-Inspector, who became as much a part of the city as Ian Rankin's *Rebus* has become a part of Edinburgh. Two subsequent crime thrillers featuring Laidlaw, *The Papers of Tony Veitch* (Hodder and Stoughton, 1983) and *Strange Loyalties* (Hodder and Stoughton, 1991) helped McIlvanney transcend the crime novel genre, in the same way that Ian Rankin has done today.

Writers, of course, are interested in people and as Ian Rankin says: "Edinburgh's dualism makes it perfect for tales of people who are not what they seem. It's a very secretive place, its residents reticent". It was this characteristic that **Muriel Spark** captured in her classic novel *The Prime of Miss Jean Brodie* (1965). In 1981 **Alasdair Gray**'s totally original debut novel, *Lanark: A Life in Four Books* (Canongate, 1981), changed everything. It single-handedly raised the profile of Scottish fiction. Suddenly, the outside world stood up and took notice. Since then, Scottish writers have gone from strength to strength, most notably with **James Kelman**, a giant on the literary scene, whose brilliant fourth novel, *How Late It Was, How Late* (Secker and Warburg, 1994), won the Booker Prize. A one-time bus conductor, Kelman is a committed and uncompromising writer whose use of dialect has attracted as much criticism from the literary establishment as it has praise from fellow writers at home. When some reviewers accused him of insulting literature, he retorted that "a fine line can exist between elitism and racism. On matters concerning language and culture the distinction can sometimes cease altogether."

Kelman has revolutionized Scottish fiction by writing not just dialogue but his entire novels in his own accent, and the debt owed to him by young contemporaries is immense. Writers such as **Duncan Mclean**, **Alan Warner** and **Irvine Welsh** all cite Kelman as a major influence on their writing. Cairns Craig, who has written widely on the modern Scottish novel, states that Kelman's real importance lies in his original use of the English language. "He can be seen as a post-colonial writer who has displaced and reformed English in a regional mode". Among Kelman's finest is his first novel, *The Busconductor Hines* (Polygon Books, 1984) and *A Disaffection* (Secker and Warburg, 1989). Kelman's *Translated Accounts* (Secker and Warburg, 2001) is believed to be his most 'difficult' to date. One literary critic claimed that, while it took Kelman three years to write, it might take the reader three years to understand it.

There are many other notable Glasgow novelists who began to make their name from the 1980s onwards. **Jeff Torrington**, the Linwood car-plant shop steward who was discovered by Kelman, won the Whitbread Prize for his debut novel *Swing Hammer Swing* (Secker and Warburg, 1992), which is set in the Gorbals of the late 1960s. **Janice Galloway** received much praise for her first novel, *The Trick is to Keep Breathing* (Vintage, 1990), which was on the short-list for Whitbread First Novel, and followed it up with an excellent collection of short stories, *Blood* (Secker and Warburg, 1991). Another brilliant collection of mostly Glasgow short stories is **AL Kennedy**'s *Night Geometry and the Garscadden Trains* (Edinburgh: Polygon, 1991), while *So I am Glad* (Jonathan Cape, 1995) is a Glaswegian take on Magic Realism.

Scottish literature has long been known for its dark hue. Crime, poverty and social dysfunction have provided rich copy for writers in a world where detectives are never less than hardened and profanity is as prevalent as punctuation. **Irvine Welsh** whose 1994 cult novel, *Trainspotting*, shone a spotlight on the city's drug-ridden underbelly, spawned an entire generation of gritty, realist writing. After a succession of hit and miss follow-ups, Welsh is back to rude health with his latest, *Porno* (2002), a sequel to *Trainspotting*, which sees the return of Renton, Sick Boy, Spud and Begbie.

From the same stable is **Alan Warner**, whose bleakly humorous *Morvern Callar* not only put Oban on the literary map but also signalled the arrival of a major and serious new talent, and **Laura Hird**, whose debut novel, *Born Free* (Rebel Inc 1999), tells the tale of a dysfunctional family trying to cope with life in one of West Edinburgh's most notorious housing schemes.

One of the most successful and best-known Scottish authors is **Iain Banks**, whose shocking debut, *The Wasp Factory* (1984), heralded a new Scottish writer of considerable imagination and wit. Banks went on to become one of the most prolific writers around, penning his best-seller, *The Crow Road*, and many others, as well as science fiction novels written under the name **Iain M Banks**. Sadly, this much-admired and universally loved writer died from cancer in 2013, aged just 59.

Perhaps the most successful current Scottish writer is Fife-born **Ian Rankin**, currently the finest exponent of so-called 'Tartan Noir'. Rankin's Inspector Rebus novels give a striking depiction of contemporary Edinburgh. Rankin lives in Edinburgh and walks around the city a lot while researching new titles. He uses real locations and gruesome historical events in his books. Rebus drinks in a real city pub, the Oxford Bar, and in one book *Set in Darkness*, Rankin uses the story of an act of cannibalism which took place in the 18th century Scottish Parliament. Like the rest of Rankin's Inspector Rebus novels, this paints a stark, honest picture of contemporary Edinburgh through the eyes of a cynical detective straight out of the Philip Marlowe school of hard cops. His other Rebus novels include *The Falls* (2001), *Black and Blue* (1998), *A Question of Blood* (2003), and *The Naming of the Dead* (2006). Rumour has it that, like Conan Doyle with Sherlock Holmes, Rankin is planning to get rid of Rebus. Another successful crime writer is Peter May, whose Lewis Trilogy – *The Blackhouse* (2011), *The Lewis Man* (2012), *The Chess Men* (2013) – evokes life (and death) on the wild and windswept Hebridean island.

Music

It could easily be argued that, in its music, Scotland produces the finest and clearest expression of its culture. All tastes are currently catered for within its music scene, reflecting the cosmopolitan nature of a country standing at the threshold of a new era with its own parliament and a deep sense of love of its history and traditions, while keeping a weather eye on the future. Although the words 'Scottish music' often conjure up images of a tartan-clad piper on a mist-covered moor, that same piper is just as likely to be found supplying stirring melodies to the decidedly 1990s edge of 'drums and bass' styles heard in clubs around the country. And that's not all – the sheer number of options available to those seeking any style of music, ranging from folk to funk, from 'Tattoo' to 'T In The Park', is truly remarkable.

Yet, despite the fact a new millennium has come and gone, bringing with it so many changes in music and technology, Scotland as a nation still responds, virtually as one, to the skirl of a full set of **Highland bagpipes**. Little wonder the pipes have been a dominant instrument for centuries – in celebration, in battle, in mourning – and are never far from the traveller's notion of all things Scottish. The pipes' unique sound is enjoyed the world over, not just in Scotland – witness the large numbers of pipe bands in the USA, Canada, across Europe, Australia and New Zealand. However, perhaps the best way to enjoy the pipes is to visit the country in summer when, accompanied by a full complement of drummers, many pipe bands can be seen taking part in competitions or playing at Highland Games in the open air. It would also be totally remiss not to mention the **Edinburgh Military Tattoo**, which takes place annually during August at the world-renowned Edinburgh Festival on the esplanade of Edinburgh Castle.

Traditional Scottish music can be passionate or jocular, mournful or joyous. In the hands of a good player, few instruments compare to the violin, or '**fiddle**'. For confirmation, simply seek out the work of **Ally Bain**. With The Boys Of The Lough, Phil Cunningham or solo, his handling of all traditional Scottish styles is superb. The folk circuit is alive and well and, crucially, features many contemporary songwriters as well as tradionalists. Apart from those already listed above, the players worth checking out include Dougie Maclean, Eric Bogle, Hamish Imlach, the Battlefield Band, Dick Gaughan and the Tannahill Weavers, all of whom have a worldwide following.

Delving a little deeper into traditional Scotland's music, you may come across Strathspey and Reel societies. These are groups of fiddlers, large or small, which are well attended across the length and breadth of Scotland. Most welcome visitors to their meetings to enjoy the music and, as most of these take place in pubs and hotels, to enjoy the local brew. On a more informal level, there are ceilidhs which often employ the help of a 'caller' to call out the moves to beginners and experienced dancers alike. The emphasis here is on enjoyment rather than precision and it is well worth seeking out some of the finest ceilidh dance bands, such as Tayside's Benachally Ceilidh Band, featuring former members of Silly Wizard and Capercaillie, The Craigenroan Ceilidh Band, The Occasionals and Alisdair MacCuish and the Black Rose Ceilidh Band. Two rapidly emerging contemporary Scottish folk bands are the **Vatersay Boys** from Vatersay and Barra on the Outer Hebrides and **Skipinnish** from the Isle of Tiree.

There are also numerous Scottish music festivals, which range from the massive **Celtic Connections** and the well-respected **Shetland Folk Festival**, to smaller events which feature ceilidhs and more informal jam sessions.

Folk fusion

Scottish folk music struggled hard to shake off its couthy image, no doubt fuelled by too many dreadful hogmanay TV shows and shameless shysters in kilts. Things then took a turn for the better in the 1970s with the emergence of bands such as North Uist's **Runrig**, who married Gaelic lyrics to rock stylings and even reached the UK Top 10, and **Capercaillie**, whose reworkings of traditional West Highland songs with Karen Mattheson's haunting vocals have brought them significant commercial success. These two in particular have managed to promote Gaelic language and culture as well as promoting the image of traditional music as an exciting, innovative and relevant medium. Another innovative folk fusion band is **Afrocelts**, formerly the Afro Celt Sound System, which has been at the cutting edge of Celtic/World Music for several years and strongly identified with the new age/rave scene. Others worth checking out include **Silly Wizard** (featuring Phil Cunningham), **Salsa Celtica**, **The Easy Club**, **Mouth Music**, **Deaf Shepherd** and **Shooglenifty**, whose radical mixing of folk music with trance – 'acid croft' as they call it – has made a huge impact internationally. Also worth listening to are **The Peatbog Faeries**, from Skye, with their high-octane fusion of Celtic folk with reggae, dub and soca, and newcomers **Pipedown**, from Edinburgh, who successfully marry the pipes with guitar, mandolin and percussion. Their debut album, *The First Measure*, has won many plaudits.

Scottish rock, pop and dance

The Scots may be stereotyped as a bunch of kilt-wearing, haggis-munching bagpipe players, but there's so much more to the country's musical heritage. This is the country that gave the world **Lonnie Donegan**, **Lulu**, **Donovan** and **The Incredible String Band**. Ex-Faces lead singer and sun-tanned bad-hair boy, **Rod Stewart**, though born in England, still remembers his roots and wraps himself in tartan every time Scotland (used to) qualify for a World Cup. And speaking of tartan, there's the **Bay City Rollers**, who blazed a trail in the 1970s as the forefathers of the teeny-bop market. The 1970s were also notable for the peerless white funk of **Average White Band**, whose singles *Pick up the Pieces* and *Let's Go round Again*, dented the charts. Glasgow-born **Sheena Easton** made it big stateside in the 1980s, while that decade was dominated by the **Eurythmics**, led by Aberdeen-born singer, **Annie Lennox** and **Dave Stewart**. Also big in the 1980s were **Simple Minds**, whose early post-punk sound and look gave no hint of their later stadium rock credentials.

One of the most influential bands of the 1980s were the **Jesus and Mary Chain**, whose distinctive feedback-drenched sound and notoriously shambolic live gigs brought them a huge cult following. Their drummer, **Bobby Gillespie** went on to form the equally influential **Primal Scream**, whose prodigious alcohol and drug consumption was only matched by the size of their egos.

The 1980s also saw the emergence of the innovative Postcard label, which launched the careers of **Orange Juice**, whose frontman **Edwyn Collins** went on to huge international solo success with A Girl Like You, Josef K, the Bluebells (featuring Lonnie Donegan's son) and the 16-year old **Roddy Frame** and his band, **Aztec Camera**. Also big in the 1980s was the Celtic-influenced guitar sound of **Big Country**, fronted by former Skids man, **Stuart Adamson**, **Wet Wet Wet**, who still hold the record for the number of weeks at number one (15) with *Love is all around*, and who could forget **The Proclaimers** who released the unashamedly sentimental *Letter from America*. Other notable Scots names from that decade include **The Cocteau Twins**, **Love & Money**, **Altered Images**, **Texas**, **Del Amitri**, **Blue Nile**, **Billy Mackenzie** and **The Associates**, **Waterboys**, **Danny Wilson**, **Goodbye Mr Mackenzie** (who featured Shirley Manson on vocals, later of Garbage). As dance began to take hold in the latter half of the decade, another Scottish band provided one of the key albums of the period, namely **Primal Scream**'s epic *Screamadelica*.

The 1990s were no less productive with **Bronski Beat**, **The Shamen**, **Soup Dragons**, the hugely important **Teenage Fanclub**, and the bizarre and enigmatic **KLF**, who produced one of the soundtracks of the time with their 1990 ambient classic, 'Chill Out'. The 1990s also saw the arrival of **Travis**, whose 1999, *The Man Who*, brought them massive commercial success.

Behind the scenes, too, Scots have been influential, and none more so than **Alan McGee**, whose Creation label signed up the cream of talent north of the border in The Jesus and Mary Chain, Primal Scream and Teenage Fanclub (as well as a bunch of Mancunian upstarts by the name of Oasis). And Glasgow's fecund indie scene continues to produce a stream of contenders. There are established favourites like **Belle and Sebastian**, **Idlewild**, **Mogwai**, **Arab Strap**, **The Delgados**, **The Cosmic Roughrider** and **Uresei Yatsura**, and the fabulous avant garde funk of **Franz Ferdinand**. Not to be outdone, Edinburgh, too, has produced some fine pop bands, including the very melodic **Aberfeldy**, named after the Perthshire town. One of the most interesting performers of recent years is **Kenny Anderson**, whose Anstruther-based Fence Collective spawned the massively successful **KT Tunstall**. His own band, **King Creosote**, feature regularly in Highland music festivals with their own folk-inspired music.

Language

Though the vast majority of Scots speak English, one ancient Scottish language which survives is Scottish Gaelic (*Gaidhlig*, pronounced 'Gallic'). Preceded by the speech of the Celts, it is now Scotland's oldest surviving language. Often referred to as the national language, it has been spoken the longest. Introduced to the country by Irish immigrants in the third and fourth centuries, its use soon spread and became well established. The language is spoken by about 60,000 people in Scotland (just over 1% of the population). This is in the **Gaidhealtachd**, the Gaelic-speaking areas of the Outer Hebrides, parts of Skye and a few of the smaller Hebridean islands. Gaelic is one of the Celtic languages, which has included Irish Gaelic, Manx, Welsh, Cornish and Breton. Today only Scottish and Irish Gaelic, Welsh and Breton survive.

Argyll (which means 'coastland of the Gael') was the prime Gaelic-speaking area from the time Columba landed there in 563. Scottish Gaelic expanded greatly from the fifth century to around the 12th century and became the national language, spoken throughout most of the country with the exception of the Norse-speaking Orkney and Shetland isles. Galloway had a Gaelic community which was separated from the Highlands, but the language died out there about the 17th century

From that point, Gaelic began a steady decline over the following centuries and, even before Union with England, was being usurped by English as more and more wealth and power passed into non-Gaelic hands. This transfer of power was given a major boost by the Reformation in the mid-16th century, as strong anti-Gaelic feeling was to the fore in the Church of Scotland.

Gaelic culture still flourished in the Highlands, but the failure of two successive Jacobite rebellions in the 18th century helped to seal its fate. In the wake of Culloden, all features of traditional Gaelic culture were proscribed and the clean sweep by government and landlords culminated in the Highland Clearances of the 19th century. The final nail in the coffin came in 1872, with the Education Act that gave no official recognition to Gaelic.

After two centuries of decline, Gaelic is now staging a comeback, thanks to financial help from government agencies and the EU which has enabled the introduction of bilingual primary and nursery schools and a massive increase in broadcasting time given to 'Alba' – Gaelic-language digital broadcast programmes. This renaissance can also be seen, and heard, in the fields of music and literature, and the return of the Scottish Parliament and with the Scottish National Party (SNP) in power can surely only help to strengthen the position of Gaelic in Scottish society.

Arts and crafts

Many of the handicrafts you'll see during your visit to the Highlands and Islands, such as pottery and jewellery, though undeniably beautiful, are produced by non-indigenous residents. Two traditional craft skills which have survived are weaving and knitting. Two areas where these skills reach their apotheosis are Harris and Orkney and Shetland and Fair Isle.

Knitting

Scottish sheep, particularly Orkney and Shetland, are characterized by their fine wool. The sheep of the original breed of Orkney and Shetlands, small bodied with low carcass weights, were probably a cross with Scandinavian animals. These Moorit sheep still thrive on North Ronaldsay, protected by the Rare Breeds Survival Trust. For most of the year they feed on seaweed but are moved on to grass in the lambing season. All the males and 20% of the females are horned.

Gossamer fine shawls made from Shetland wool are soft but hardwearing. Shetland wool is very loosely spun, which adds to the lightness of the finished garment. Knitted on fine needles the famed characteristic of the shawls is that they can be pulled effortlessly through a wedding ring.

Intricate patterns in bright colours characterize Fair Isle knitting. When not being worked into the design, the wool in the spare colour is taken across the back of the work, caught at regular intervals in the stitches so that there are no long loops. It is important for the tension to be correct as too tight carrying of the spare wool would distort the finished garment. This double use of wool also means that Fair Isle garments as well as being extremely colourful, are very warm, consisting as they do of two or more layers of wool.

Before the advent of mass-produced fleece clothing and other warm store-bought wear, a Scottish fisherman wore a sea jersey, sometimes known as a Guernsey or a Gansey. Tradition says that each village had its own peculiar design. Thus, if a man were lost at sea, his jersey pattern might be the only means of identification if he were not found very quickly. But in reality, every family and knitter in that family would have their own pattern.

Cable stitch represented rope; hearts, anchors and waves could also be part of a design. The jerseys were made from five-ply Yorkshire 'wheeling', still available from Richard Poppleton of Wakefield, Yorkshire. This is a pure wool worsted yarn, tightly spun which makes it warm and hardwearing. When unwashed, the wool would contain lanoline, the natural oil, which would make garments practically waterproof too. Wool with the natural oils would be widely used for the knitting of seaboot stockings.

The jerseys are knitted in the round on four or five needles. There is no sewing together of the garment, all is done by knitting. Some jerseys have three little pearl buttons to close the neck. The sleeves are knitted from the armholes downwards and are never too long as they get wet as the seamen work with the nets. Also, when the wrist edges eventually become frayed, the knitter unravels the cuff and knits it up afresh.

The needles are long as more than 500 stitches are cast on. In order to make the work easier to handle, the right-hand needle would be anchored at the waist by a 'shield', a pouch of straw or a bunch of feathers. Quite an intricate design might be woven into the shields and they fetch a good price in auctions today. Alternatively, a knitting stick or knitting goose would anchor a needle under the right arm.

It is said that Kaffe Fasset, who is now one the world's leading knitwear designers, began his career thanks to Scottish wools. He was in the north and saw for sale wools of every delicious colour. Knowing little about knitting at that point, he nevertheless bought wool of every shade and also two needles. Boarding the train from Inverness back to London, he was in a carriage with several women. Soon after they began the journey he said 'I'm sure that some of you ladies can knit?' Indeed they could. By the time that they reached London, they had shown Kaffe Fasset how to cast on and off and how to increase and decrease. This was all that was needed to start his amazingly successful career. To this day, his designs use no complicated stitches, their unique beauty derived from inspired use of vibrant or subtle colours.

Religion

The Highlands and Islands of Scotland are largely Protestant, and religion, as in the rest of the country, plays a relatively small part in the lives of most people. This does not apply, however, in the Outer Hebrides, where religion plays a vitally important role in the islanders' lives, and priests and ministers still wield considerable power in the community. This particularly applies in the Calvinist Protestant islands of North Uist, Harris and Lewis, which still strictly adhere to the creed of Sabbatariansim. Here, Sunday is the Lord's Day and the whole community stops work. But despite the fact that the Outer Hebrides are sharply divided between the Protestant northern islands and the Roman Catholic southern islands of Benbecula, Barra and South Uist, there has been little confrontation.

The only conflict has arisen within the Presbyterian Church of Scotland (or Kirk) itself, which has split into various factions over the years. The main split had its roots in the 1712 Patronage Act, which allowed a landlord the right to choose the parish minister, thus breaking the fundamental rule of the church ministers and elders. In 1843, in protest at the state's refusal to change the Patronage act, a third of Scottish ministers walked out of the established Church of Scotland to form the Free Church of Scotland – the so-called 1843 Disruption. In 1893 a second disruption occurred, this time within the Free Church of Scotland itself when a minority seceded and formed the Free Presbyterian Church. Now it becomes really confusing. In 1900 most congregations in the Free Church of Scotland and the United Presbyterian Church joined together to form the United Free Church of Scotland. However, a large proportion of people in Lewis were opposed to this union and the largest congregations decided to continue as the Free Church of Scotland, or 'Wee Frees' as they are popularly known. Later, in 1929, the United Free Church joined with the Established Church of Scotland. And it doesn't end there. As recently as 1988, the Wee Frees split over the threatened expulsion of a minister who attended a requiem mass during the Catholic funeral of a friend. He and his supporters have since formed the breakaway Associated Presbyterian Churches.

Now all this may seem pedantic to many outsiders, but to the people of Lewis, Harris and North Uist (and also much of Skye and Raasay), the Free Church is of enormous social and cultural, as well as spiritual, importance. Not only did it organize resistance to the Highland Clearances but it has also done the most to preserve the Gaelic language.

Land &
environment

Geographically, Scotland can be divided into three areas: Southern Uplands, Central Lowlands and Highlands. The Southern Uplands is the area south from Edinburgh and Glasgow to the English border, and consists of a series of hill ranges sandwiched between fertile coastal plains. The Central Lowlands, the triangle formed by Edinburgh, Glasgow and Dundee to the north, contains most of the population, and is the country's industrial heartland. The Highland Boundary Fault is the geographical division running northeast from Helensburgh (west of Glasgow) to Stonehaven (south of Aberdeen). To the north of this line lie the Highlands and Islands, which comprise roughly two-thirds of the country.

Much of Scotland was long ago covered by the Caledonian forest, which consisted mainly of the Scots pine, along with oak, birch and other hardwoods. Over the centuries, the trees were felled for timber and to accommodate livestock, and now only around 1% of this ancient forest still remains. Small pockets of native Scots pine can be found scattered around the Highlands, at Rothiemurchus, near Aviemore, at Glen Tanar, near Ballater in Deeside, around Braemar, at Strathytre near Callander and Achray Forest near Aberfoyle, at Rowardennan on Loch Lomond, in Glen Affric and on the shores of Loch Maree.

Several decades ago the Forestry Commission, a government body, set about fencing off large areas of moorland for reforestation. Now much of the landscape is dominated by regimented rows of fast-growing sitka spruce, which are not particularly attractive. There are also serious concerns over the damage coniferization causes to the unique habitats in many areas, in particular to large areas of bogland in the 'Flow Country' of Caithness and Sutherland, a unique natural environment as precious as any tropical rainforest. This and other endangered habitats are registered as an SSSI – a Site of Special Scientific Interest – but this has proved less than adequate. The only real guarantee of protection is for such areas to be owned or managed by environmental organizations such as Scottish Natural Heritage, the Scottish Wildlife Trust, the Royal Society for the Protection of Birds, the Woodland Trust and John Muir Trust.

In recognition of this, the Scottish Parliament produced a draft bill to establish a series of national parks, based on advice from Scottish National Heritage. This is aimed to reduce the conflict between social and economic development and long-term protection of the natural and cultural environment. In April 2002 Loch Lomond and The Trossachs National Park opened, and in early 2003 Cairngorms National Park.

Wildlife

The Scottish countryside plays host to some of Europe's rarest and most celebrated wildlife, though much of it has disappeared over the centuries. The ancient Caledonian forests were once home to wildlife that we now identify with other far-flung countries: including the brown bear, lynx, wolf, reindeer and beaver to name but a few. Small numbers of beaver and reindeer have been reintroduced in recent years and there is the ongoing controversial debate regarding the reintroduction of the wolf in the far northeast of Scotland. Meanwhile, wildlife enthusiasts and nature conservation body's

Munros, Corbetts and Grahams

There are 284 mountains over 3000 ft (914 m) in Scotland, known as 'Munros', after Sir Hugh Munro, first president of the Scottish Mountaineering Club (SMC), who published the first comprehensive list of these mountains in 1891. In the 1920s a further list was published, of the 221 summits between 2500 and 3000 ft, by J Rooke Corbett, and these became known as 'Corbetts'. A third list, of summits between 2000 and 2500 ft was compiled by Fiona Graham and published in 1992. This list was subsequently revised and corrected and now all peaks that are between 2000-2500 ft are called 'Grahams'.

This is where the term 'Munro-bagging' comes from – one of Scotland's favourite pastimes – climbing as many peaks over 3000 ft as possible.

continue to press for tighter legislation and resources to tackle illegal hunting and baiting of Scotland's birds of prey.

Coastal wildlife

Scotland boasts over 13,000 km of the British coastline. As a result seabirds and some sea mammals abound and both the resident and visitor list is impressive. Some of the more notable avian 'stars' include the eider duck, most famous for its feather down which the birds use to keep their eggs warm and we use in quilts to keep us cosy. Both sexes are about the size of a small goose yet are quite different in appearance. The male, for courting purposes, looks very regal, being predominantly black and white with lime green cheeks and a pastel pink breast, while the female, for the purposes of camouflage, is a dull brown colour. During the breeding season on the coast fringes and off-shore islands it is not unusual to encounter the females at very close quarters while sitting on the nest. They are very confident about their camouflage and will stay perfectly still even when you are within a few feet.

During the winter the firths (large coastal inlets) and estuaries play host to large numbers of predominantly arctic seaduck including the beautiful jet black common and velvet scoter, the scaup (very similar to the common tufted duck) and the spectacular and rare king eider. Waders too are present in large numbers around the coast and again, especially in winter. Knot, dunlin and turnstones are also common along the beaches and mudflats. During the summer perhaps the most commonly seen coastal wader is the oystercatcher which is black and white with a conspicuous orange beak. While around estuaries keep your ears open for the high-pitched call of the curlew.

These estuaries, along with many of the offshore islands also play host to Scotland's two resident seal species, the common seal and the grey seal. Although the two are at long range quite hard to distinguish, the common is generally lighter in colour and smaller with more delicate dog-like facial features. The common seal breeds in summer and generally tend to be independent of one another, while the grey breeds in mid-winter in rookeries predominantly on offshore islands. Both species can be seen throughout the year with the most common on the west coast and the grey on the east.

Dolphins, porpoises, basking sharks and some species of whale can also been seen regularly around the Scottish coastline. The resident pod of bottlenose dolphins in the Moray Firth is best viewed between May and September, while minke whales, basking sharks and even orca (killer whales) are spotted off the west coast and Western Isles far more frequently than you may imagine.

Island wildlife

The many offshore islands scattered around the Scottish coast provide sanctuary to a wide variety of seabirds, often in huge numbers. These islands are important both nationally and internationally for many breeding species and as such are designated National Nature Reserves (NNRs) and Sites of Special Scientific Interest (SSSIs). The most noted are the islands around Orkney and Shetland and on the west coast Handa Island near Cape Wrath.

To visit these islands and the massive seabird colonies that inhabit their towering cliffs in the breeding season (April to September) is an unforgettable experience. Classic residents include members of the auk family, including the guillemot, razorbill and the puffin, without doubt the most colourful and charming seabird in Britain. Unlike the hardy guillemots and razorbills that nest precariously on the cliff ledges, the puffin nests in burrows, which they excavate with razor-sharp claws. After the eggs are incubated and the eggs hatch the chicks are raised in the burrow and this is the best time to view the birds.

The best places to see puffin and the seabird colonies are in Orkney and Shetland, or Handa Island in the far north west of the country, near Cape Wrath. Several other species inhabit other neighbourhoods within these seabird cities including the Manx shearwater and fulmar, which are both specialist pelagic petrels. The fulmar is worth special mention because it has the admirable habit of vomiting all over you should you stray too close. One of the most famous seabirds around Scotland is the large and very stern looking gannet which is black and white in colour with a 6-ft wing span and an ochre coloured head. Its most famous international breeding site is the Bass Rock in the Firth of Forth where over 50,000 pairs breed annually. So famous is the Bass that it lends its name to the Northern or Atlantic gannet's official scientific name, *Morus bassanus*.

Other more unusual rare and resident species you might be very lucky to see on the coast is the white-tailed sea eagle around the Western Isles or the beautiful snowy owl on Fetlar in Shetland. The sea eagle used to be fairly common but was wiped out in Scotland by early last century. Now, after a successful reintroduction on the Isle of Rùm on the west coast, several pairs breed. The specific nesting locations are understandably kept secret but you may still see one on a fishing foray over its huge territorial range. Like the golden eagle its sheer size is an instant give away while the tail distinguishes it from its more common relative. The snowy owl is rarely seen outside Shetland and is instantly recognizable.

Some islands around the coast of Scotland are also well known internationally as migratory stopovers for vagrant species. Fair Isle, between Shetland and Orkney, is particularly important and well known often providing life-saving shelter in spring and autumn storms for such exotically named species as the jack snipe or black redstart.

Rivers, lochs and wetlands

Otter are more commonly found along riverbanks in Europe but in Scotland are best observed on the tidal fringes searching for seafood. The Isle of Skye and Shetland are the best venues. The otter was for decades almost hunted to extinction in Britain but is now fully protected. It is often confused with the feral mink or ferret, which is far more commonly seen in the countryside throughout Britain.

Loch Garten in Speyside near Aviemore is the home to the osprey and the venue of one of Scotland's most successful avian conservation stories. After being absent for many years the Loch Garten breeding site became a catalyst for what is now the successful national comeback of the species. You can view the birds nesting in summer at Loch Garten but if you are really lucky you will see one catching fish in a spectacular display of aerial acrobatics on the lochs and rivers of the region. The rivers Tay and Spey are world famous for their salmon. Some of the hydroelectric dams in Scotland have fish ladders where you can observe this archetype of inherent motivation as the fish struggle relentlessly upstream to breed. Pitlochry is one such venue.

Although not endemic to Scotland one of the most beautiful bird species you may encounter on the more remote lochs are divers (or loons as they are called in North America) – most commonly the red-throated diver, the rarer black-throated diver and occasionally the largest, the great northern diver. All three can be seen on the coast in winter. The best time to see these birds is in their superb summer breeding attire but it is perhaps their call that is most memorable. The haunting cry of the great northern or black throat that carries for miles across the moors and wide-open spaces is quite simply unforgettable. Red-throated divers breed on lochs throughout the Highlands while black-throated divers can be found in the far north, especially round Lochinver and in Caithness. Also both rare and beautiful is the delicate black-neck grebe which supports a headpiece in the breeding season to beat any human fashion label at the annual Royal Ascot horse races. Loch Ruthven near Inverness is an excellent place to observe this particular avian fashion parade.

For any Scot who is in tune with the countryside the first calls of greylag and pink-footed geese are a sure sign that summer has ended. Huge numbers winter in Scotland especially in the central lowlands and parts of the west coast. Similarly, barnacle geese invade the Solway Firth in the south in their thousands. The V-shaped flying formations and constant honking of course make the type of bird if not the actual species instantly identifiable. Of course no mention of Scotland's waterways and wildlife would be complete without mention of Scotland's most famous aquatic creature – the Loch Ness Monster. Nessie does of course exist but like the wild haggis is very very shy and elusive.

Forests and lowlands

As opposed to its introduced North American cousin the native red squirrel is a delicate and shy creature. Their beautiful rustic colours can often herald their occasional public appearance in the forests of the Central Highlands, especially Speyside. If it were not for the grey squirrel pushing them out of former habitats and man destroying the habitat itself they could once again be classed as common. Even rarer is the elusive and rarely seen wildcat and pine marten. The wildcat is larger than the domestic 'moggy' and has a much courser, thicker fur coat, piercing, wild eyes and untamed attitude. Over the years the feral cat and wild variety have interbred and now it is very unusual to see the species in its rawest form. The pine marten is about the size of a mink and is occasionally seen in forested areas of more remote and unpopulated areas of the country.

The forests and lowlands are also home to some familiar bird species. The quite bizarre and wonderfully named capercaille (pronounced 'capper-kay-lee') is a member of the grouse family and the largest of the three species found in Scotland. It is the handsome black male that is most often seen deep in the forests, most commonly crossing forest paths and fire breaks while guarding his extensive territory. This is necessary not so much as protection from predators, but invasion by other highly sexed males intent on one thing and one thing only. An encounter and subsequent dispute results in audible threats and much puffing up of the plumage. Even more spectacular are the fights between the capercaillie's smaller relative the black grouse. Their version of a 'boxing ring' is called a 'lek' and can be the sight of spectacular displays of male hormonal overload.

Other unusual birds of the forest includes the crossbill, which is about the size of a overweight canary and has a beak that intersects, which it uses to expertly extract pine seeds from the cone. Crossbills can regularly be seen in the Central Highlands with National Nature Reserves like Loch Garten being a good bet. While in the Loch Garten area you may also see the delicate little crested tit, which although not endemic, only breeds in this part of Scotland. In much of western Scotland the hooded crow, or 'hoodie' replaces the common crow found throughout Britain. The hooded crow can be distinguished by the diagnostic grey patches on its plumage.

Britain's only venomous snake, the adder, is relatively common throughout Scotland and is mainly found on open ground covered in bracken or heather. It is rarely seen and generally keeps well out of your way, though you may be lucky enough to encounter one sunning itself on rocks early in the day. In 2007, a man required emergency medical help after he picked up an adder on the Isle of Arran. The lesson – don't touch!

Highlands

The red deer are as much an environmental problem as a feature of the Scottish landscape. They now number over 300,000 and in the absence of natural predators are essentially out of control in the Central Highlands. However, steps are increasingly being taken to sustainably manage wild deer numbers, including through targeted culling. Indeed, in November 2008, a new approach to deer management was launched by the Minister for the Environment. In summer, deer remain in herds on high ground and, despite their size, they are actually very hard to spot. In winter however you can often see them in large numbers on lower ground in the glens and beside the main roads. During the 'rut' in autumn the males (stags) become highly aggressive and use their impressive antlers in fierce combat to win the females (hinds). This fighting is often accompanied by a loud roar that carries for miles. Other deer species seen commonly in Scotland in the Highlands, Central Lowlands and Borders are the roe, sitka and fallow deer.

Another famous Highlands inhabitant is the golden eagle. After periods of decline they are now present in relatively healthy numbers especially in the Central and Western Highlands but are not exactly widespread or commonly seen. To the uninitiated the eagle is very often confused with the common buzzard, though the latter is actually much smaller. The golden eagle also dwarfs the large and menacing raven that is also a regular sight in central and western Scotland – usually accompanied by a raucous, 'throaty' call. Another regal and masterful lord of the highland skies is the peregrine falcon. In both flight and appearance they are the epitome of power. To watch a peregrine hunting other birds in flight is to witness one of the most spectacular acts in nature.

Two quite common masters of camouflage on the mountain slopes are the mountain hare and the ptarmigan, a bird similar in size and appearance to a red grouse. Both go through an incredible phase of moult from dark browns in summer to pure white in winter. They do this of course in order to blend in with their surroundings and avoid predators like the peregrine. Any time spent around the ski-fields in summer or winter should reveal one or both species.

Other rarer birds found breeding on the inhospitable high tops, especially in the Cairngorms, are the dotterel, a small attractive wading bird and the sparrow sized snow bunting. The snow bunting, like the mountain hare and ptarmigan, assumes a predominantly white plumage in summer. Few breed in Scotland as it is mainly a winter visitor to the coast. On the lower slopes the red grouse is a common sight. Vast tracks of land are maintained to provide the ideal breeding habitat for this 'game bird', which is then hunted for sport.

Books *See also page 445.*

History, politics and culture

Herman A *The Scottish Enlightenment (Fourth Estate, 2001).* A brilliant account of Scotland's contribution to the world.
Kennedy, L *In Bed with an Elephant* (Corgi, 1996). An entertaining account of Scotland's often turbulent relationship with England.
Lawson, B *Harris in History and Legend* (Birlinn, 2006). Essential read for all interested in the land of the Hearrachs.
Lynch, M *Scotland A New History* (Pimlico 1999). A worthy contender.
Macdonald, M *Scottish Art* (Thames & Hudson, 2000). Good overview.
Magnusson, M *Scotland the Story of a Nation* (Harper Collins, 2000). A mighty tome.
McIntosh, A *Soil and Soul: People Versus Coporate Power* (Aurum Press, 2004). Ecology, spirituality and politics woven into a spell-binding tale of the power of the community.
Nairn, T *The Break-up of Britain* (Common Groundb, 2003). Radical perspective of independence. *Scotland's Story* (Fontana).
Prebble, J *1000 years of Scotland's History, The Lion in the North, Glen Coe, Culloden* and *The Highland Clearances* (Penguin). Emotive and subjective view of highland history.
Smout, T C *A History of the Scottish People (1560-1830)* (Fontana, 1998); *A Century of the Scottish People (1830-1950)* (Fontana, 1997).

Biographies and travelogues

Banks, I *Raw Spirit: In Search of the Perfect Dram* (Arrow, 2004). Slightly uneven but enjoyable romp around Scotland's distilleries.
Bathurst, B *The Lighthouse Stevensons* (Harper Collins, 1999). Well-documented account of Robert Louis Stevenson's family.
Boswell and Johnson, S *A Journey to the Western Islands of Scotland* (UK Penguin). If you only read one travelogue, make it this.

Crumley, J *A High and Lonely Place and Gulfs of Blue Air – A Highland Journey* (Mainstream).
Duff, D (ed) *Queen Victoria's Highland Journal* (UK Hamlyn). Another interesting read.
Fraser, A *Mary, Queen of Scots* (UK Mandarin).
Grant of Rothiemurchus, Elizabeth *Memoirs of a Highland Lady* (Canongate).
Liptrot, Amy *The Outrun* (Canongate Books Ltd, 2016). Captivating account of the author's escape from the excesses of London and return to the Orkney sheep farm where she grew up.
Maclean, F *Bonnie Prince Charlie* (Canongate).
Maxwell, G *The Ring of Bright Water* (Penguin). One of the best known Highland memoirs, a tale of otters and other wildlife set in Glenelg.
Miller, K *Electric Shepherd: A Likeness of James Hogg* (Faber & Faber, 2003). A study of the life and works of one of Scotland's most enigmatic literary figures.
Morton, H V *In Search of Scotland* (Methuen).
Nicolson, A *Sea Room* (Harper Collins, 2002). Beautiful and lyrical 'love letter' to the Shiant Islands, written by the man who owns them.
Skinner Sawyers, J (ed) *The Road North – 300 years of Classic Scottish Travel Writing* (The Inn Pinn, 2000). A selection of the best, including **Daniel Defoe, Edwin Muir** and **Jan Morris**.
Tomkies, M *A Last Wild Place*, An account of life in a remote West Highland croft.

Outdoor activities

Walking

There are numerous walking guides available, 2 of the best are *Great Walks Scotland* by **Hamish Brown**, and *100 Best Routes on Scottish Mountains* by **Ralph Storer**.

Helpful hillwalking guides published by the **Scottish Mountaineering Trust** are *The Munros* by **Donald Bennett** and

The Corbetts by **Scott Johnstone et al**. The SMT also publishes a range of district guides listing mainly high level walks. Also useful are *The Munro Almanac* and *The Corbett Almanac* by **Cameron McNeish**.

Those wishing to attempt one of the long-distance walks should read *The West Highland Way* or *The Southern Upland Way*, both highly informative guides by **Roger Smith** (HM Stationery Office).

An excellent guide for both walkers and mountain bikers is **Ralph Storer**'s *Exploring Scottish Hill Tracks*.

Ian Mitchell's *Scotland's Mountains before the Mountaineers* (Luath press, 1999), offers insights about those who may have beaten you to the summit.

Cycling

With 40 illustrated routes **Fergal MacErlean**'s *Bike Scotland* pocket guide is a must read for anyone planning on putting pedal to the metal (Pocket Mountains). Other recommended cycling guides include: *The Scottish Cycling Guide* by **Brendan Walsh**; *101 Bike Routes in Scotland* by **Henry Henniker** (Mainstream); *Cycling in Scotland* by **John Hancox** (Collins Pocket Reference, Harper Collins); and *Cycling in Great Britain: Bicycle Touring Adventures in England, Scotland and Wales* by **Tim Hughes & Jo Cleary** (Bicycle Books, US).

Birdwatching

A good birdwatching guide is *Where to Watch Birds in Scotland* by **Michael Madders and Julia Welstead** (UK Christopher Helm).

Miscellaneous

Black, G *The Surnames of Scotland: their origin, meaning and history* (New York, 1940). Available in most public libraries.

HM Stationery Office *Exploring Scotland's Heritage*. A beautifully illustrated series of books on historic buildings and archaeological sites in different regions of Scotland.

Jackson, M *The Malt Whisky Companion* (UK Dorling Kindersley). Those wishing to bone up on their malt whiskies should refer to this.

MacDonald, Lady C *The Claire MacDonald Cookbook* (UK Bantam). An excellent Scottish recipe book, Lady Claire, runs a hotel on Skye.

Prior, C *Scotland The Wild Places* (Constable). Colin Prior's stunning photographs of the nation's landscape and wildlife.

Sinclair, C *Tracing your Ancestors* (HM Stationery Office). For more detailed genealogical study.

Smith Haswell, H *The Scottish Islands* (2004, Canongate).A wonderful reference book to the history, wildlife and ownership of Scotland's myriad of islands.

Stuart, M and Balfour Paul, J *Scottish Family History* (Edinburgh, 1930). For a comprehensive history of Scottish clans and families. In most public libraries.

Poetry

Crawford, R and Imlah, M (eds) *The New Penguin Book of Scottish Verse* (2000). An excellent overview.

Crichton-Smith, I *Collected Poems*. Bilingual (English and Gaelic) poet writing passionately about life in the Outer Hebrides.

McCaig, N *Selected Poems*. Challenging poet whose work is deeply rooted in the landscapes of the Highlands.

McDiarmid, H *Selected Poems*. A huge figure on the Scottish literary landscape. His nationalist views and use of Scots have been as influential as they have been provocative.

Morgan, E *New Selected Poems*. Scotland's poet laureate is one of the country's foremost living writers and both entertaining and experimental.

Muir, E *Collected Poems*. One of the most distinguished poets of the last century.

Paterson, D *Landing Light*. The latest work of an innovative voice in Scottish poetry.

Practicalities

Getting there 465
Getting around 469
Essentials A-Z 473

Getting there

Air

Generally speaking, the cheapest and quickest way to travel to Scotland from outside the UK is by air. There are good links to **Edinburgh** and **Glasgow**, with direct flights from many European cities, and direct flights from North America to Glasgow. There are also flights from a few European cities to **Aberdeen** and **Inverness**. There are no direct flights from North America to Edinburgh; these are usually routed via London or Dublin. There are also daily flights from Ireland and regular flights to most Scottish airports from other parts of the UK. There are no direct flights to Scotland from Australia, New Zealand, South Africa or Japan; you will have to get a connection from London.

From the UK and Ireland

There are direct flights to Scotland's four main airports – Glasgow, Edinburgh, Aberdeen and Inverness – almost hourly from London Heathrow, Gatwick, Stansted and Luton airports. There are also daily flights from provincial UK airports and from Dublin. To fly on to the smaller airports, you'll need to change planes, see page 469, for domestic flights. The cheapest flights leave from London Luton or Stansted, plus a few provincial airports, with **Ryanair** and **easyJet**. If you book online, fares can be as little as £15 one-way during low season (excluding taxes), and you can expect to fly for around £70-100 return if you can be flexible with dates and times. These tickets are often subject to rigid restrictions, but the savings can make the extra effort worthwhile. Cheaper tickets usually have to be bought at least a month in advance (or much further in advance around school holidays) and apply to only a few midweek flights. They are also non-refundable, or only partly refundable, and non-transferable. A standard flexible and refundable fare from London to Glasgow or Edinburgh will cost at least £150-200 return. The flight from London to Glasgow and Edinburgh is roughly one hour.

There are flights to Inverness from London and from many regional UK airports, as well as flights from Glasgow to Islay, Tiree, Barra, Benbecula, Stornoway, Kirkwall (Orkney) and Sumburgh (Shetland), from Edinburgh to Wick, Stornoway, Kirkwall and Sumburgh and from Inverness to Benbecula, Stornoway, Kirkwall and Sumburgh with **Loganair** ⓘ *www.loganair.co.uk*. There are also flights from Manchester to Stornoway, Kirkwall and Sumburgh. **Flybe** (www.flybe.com) has a more limited service to some of the Scottish islands. For full details of all flights to Highlands and Islands airports from the rest of the UK, visit the **Highlands and Islands Airports Ltd** website, www.hial.co.uk.

From the rest of Europe

There are direct flights to **Glasgow International** from many European capitals, including Copenhagen, Amsterdam, Paris (Beauvais), Dublin, Frankfurt, Stockholm, Brussels, Milan, Oslo and Barcelona. There are flights to **Edinburgh** from Paris (CDG), Zurich, Amsterdam, Brussels, Copenhagen and Frankfurt; direct flights to **Aberdeen** from Amsterdam, Copenhagen and Stavanger; and to **Inverness** from Amsterdam and Zurich. There are now flights from Bergen (Norway) to **Orkney**, **Shetland** and **Stornoway**.

From North America

Because of the much larger number of flights to London, it is generally cheaper to fly there first and get an onward flight, see above for the best deals. East Coast USA to Glasgow

TRAVEL TIP
Packing for the Highlands and Islands

You'll be able to find everything you could possibly need for your trip in Scottish cities, so if you wish you can pack light and buy supplies as you go along. Given the variable climate, whatever the time of year it's advisable to include warm and waterproof clothing in your suitcase. Also bring light clothes in the summer, preferably long-sleeved to protect you from the midges, see box, page 475. If you're planning on doing some hillwalking you should come properly prepared, as the weather can change rapidly in the mountains (see page 17 for details). It's worth treating your boots with a waterproofing agent as some of the trails cross boggy ground.

If you are backpacking, a sleeping bag is useful in hostels, and a sleeping sheet with a pillow cover is needed if staying in Scottish Youth Hostel Association (SYHA) hostels (or you can hire one there). A padlock can also be handy for locking your bag if it has to be stored in a hostel for any length of time. Other useful items include an alarm clock (for those early ferry departures), an adaptor plug for electrical appliances, an elastic clothes line and, if you're hillwalking or camping, a map, Swiss Army knife, torch (flashlight) and compass are essential. If planning to undertake watersports, it's a good idea to bring a waterproof pouch for your wallet/purse and other small essential items.

takes around six to seven hours direct. To London it takes seven hours. From the West Coast it takes an additional four hours.

To Glasgow International Continental Airlines and KLM fly from New York, Aer Lingus and KLM fly from Chicago and Air Canada from Toronto.

Airport information
Glasgow International ⓘ T0344-481 5555, www.glasgowairport.com, is eight miles west of the city, at junction 28 on the M8. It handles domestic and international flights. Terminal facilities include car hire, bank ATMs, currency exchange, left luggage, tourist information, and shops, restaurants and bars. **Edinburgh airport** ⓘ T0844-448 8833, www.edinburghairport.com, has all facilities, including a tourist information desk, currency exchange, ATMs, restaurants and bars (first floor), shops (ground floor and first floor) and car hire desks in the terminal in the main UK arrivals area. For details of facilities and amenties at all Highlands and Islands airports, visit www.hial.co.uk. For Inverness airport, see also page 161.

Rail

There are fast and frequent rail services from London and other main towns and cities in England to Glasgow, Edinburgh, Aberdeen and Inverness. Journey time from London is about 4½ hours to Edinburgh, five hours to Glasgow, seven hours to Aberdeen and eight hours to Inverness. Two companies operate direct services from London to Scotland: **National Express** ⓘ www.east coast.co.uk, trains leave from King's Cross and run up the east coast to Edinburgh, Aberdeen and Inverness, and **Virgin** trains leave from Euston and run up the west coast to Glasgow. One of the best ways to travel from London to Scotland is on board the *Caledonian Sleeper*, which is an overnight service from London Euston Edinburgh, Glasgow, Aberdeen, Inverness and Fort William. This runs nightly from Sunday to Friday. There are numerous fare options. For more information, see www.sleeper.scot.

Eurostar ⓘ *T0343-218 6186 (bookings T0123-361 7575), www.eurostar.com*, operates high-speed trains through the Channel Tunnel to London St Pancras International from Paris (2½ hours), Brussels (two hours) and Lille (1½ hours). You then have to change trains, and stations, for the onward journey north to Scotland. If you're driving from continental Europe you could take *Le Shuttle*, which runs 24 hours a day, 365 days a year, and takes you and your car from Calais to Folkestone in 35 to 45 minutes. Depending on how far in advance you book, or when you travel, cheaper fares are available.

Enquiries and booking

National Rail Enquiries ⓘ *T03457-484950, www.nationalrail.co.uk*, are quick and courteous with information on rail services and fares but not always accurate, so double check. They can't book tickets but will provide you with the relevant telephone number. The website, www.qjump.co.uk, is a bit hit-and-miss but generally fast and efficient, and shows you all the various options on any selected journey, while www.thetrainline.co.uk, also has its idiosyncrasies but shows prices clearly and is best for advance card bookings. Also try **ScotRail** ⓘ *www.scotrail.co.uk* and **Virgin** ⓘ *www.virgintrains.co.uk*.

Fares

To describe the system of rail ticket pricing as complicated is a huge understatement and impossible to explain here. There are many and various discounted fares, but restrictions are often prohibitive, which explains the long queues and delays at ticket counters in railway stations. The cheapest ticket is an Advance ticket or Value Advance (**Virgin**), which must be booked in advance (obviously), though this is not available on all journeys. All discount tickets should be booked as quickly as possible as they are often sold out weeks, or even months, in advance. A Caledonian Sleeper return ticket from London to Inverness costs from around £70-90 and a sleeping berth costs around £200-250; to book visit www.sleeper.scot.

Railcards

There are a variety of railcards which give discounts on fares for certain groups. Cards are valid for one year and most are available from main stations. You need two passport photos and proof of age or status. For up-to-date prices and details, T0345-3000 250, www.railcard.co.uk.

Road

Bus/coach

Road links to Scotland are excellent, and a number of companies offer express coach services day and night. This is the cheapest form of travel to Scotland. The main operator between England and Scotland is **National Express** ⓘ *T08717-818181, www.nationalexpress.com*. There are direct buses from most British cities to Edinburgh, Glasgow, Aberdeen and Inverness. Tickets can be bought at bus stations or from a huge number of agents throughout the country. Fares from London to Inverness with **National Express** start at around £15-20 return (online discount fare). The London to Glasgow/Edinburgh journey takes around eight hours, while it takes around 11 to 12 hours for the trip to Inverness. Also worth checking is **Megabus** ⓘ *www.megabus.co.uk*.

On the buses

Those who wish to venture off the beaten track may bemoan the fact that fewer buses ply the remote rural roads.

Consequently, a great cheap way to quickly experience the more famous sites around Scotland is on one of the backpacker bus tours. These leave from Edinburgh daily, except Sunday, and stop off at independent hostels in Perth, Pitlochry, Inverness, Loch Ness, the Isle of Skye, Fort William, Glen Coe, Oban and Glasgow. There's tremendous rivalry between the various operators so you benefit from keen prices for what are excellent value tours of the Highlands and Islands.

Tours vary from a one-day tour of Loch Ness (£46pp) to a 10-day jaunt around the Highlands and Islands (£539pp). However, prices with these 'backpacker' operators don't tend to include accommodation (from £15 per night) in, for the most part, clean and comfortable hostels. See page 481 for a list of tour operators.

Car

There are two main routes to Scotland from the south. In the east the M1/A1 runs to Edinburgh and in the west the M6 and A74(M) runs to Glasgow. The journey north from London to either city takes around seven to 7½ hours. From London to Inverness takes around 10 hours via the M6, A74 and A9. The A74(M) route to Glasgow is dual carriageway all the way.

Sea

P&O Irish Sea ① *www.poferries.com*, has several crossings daily from Larne to Cairnryan (one hour), and from Larne to Troon (two hours). Fares are from around £120 each way for car and driver. **Stena Line** ① *T0844-770 7070, www.stenaline.co.uk*, runs numerous ferries (three hours) and high-speed catamarans (1½ hours) from Belfast to Stranraer, fares from £89 single for car and driver.

Getting around

It is easy to visit the main towns and tourist sights by bus or train, but getting to more remote destinations without your own transport requires careful planning and an intimate knowledge of rural bus timetables. Public transport can also be expensive, though there's a whole raft of discount passes and tickets which can save you a lot of money. Hiring a car can work out as a more economical, and certainly more flexible, option, especially for more than two people travelling together. It will also enable you to get off the beaten track and see more of the country. Even if you're driving, however, getting around the remote Highlands and Islands can be a time-consuming business as much of the region is accessed only by a sparse network of tortuous, twisting single-track roads. Be sure to refuel regularly, allow plenty of time for getting around and book ferries in advance during the busy summer season. For details of all public transport services in Scotland, visit **Traveline Scotland** ① *T0871-200 2233, www.travelinescotland.com*.

Air

As well as the main airports of Glasgow, Edinburgh, Aberdeen and Inverness, there are also numerous small airports, many of them on islands (one of them, on Barra, uses the beach as an airstrip). There are discounted tickets available, which must be booked at least 14 days in advance, and special offers on some services. There is no departure tax on flights from Highlands and Islands airports.

The majority of flights to the Outer Hebrides are operated by **Loganair** ① *www.loganair.co.uk*). **Flybe** also operate flights to and from Stornway and **Eastern Airways** fly from Aberdeen to Stonorway. For inter-island flights in Orkney, you should book direct through **Loganair** ① *T01856-872494*. For information on flight schedules, call the airports listed on page 466, or check the **Loganair** website. Inter-island flights on Shetland are operated by **Air Task** ① *www.airtask.com*, on behalf on **Shetland Isles Council** ① *www.shetland.gov.uk*, from Tingwall airport near Lerwick (T01595-840246).

Rail

The rail network in Scotland is limited and train travel is comparatively expensive, but trains are a fast and effective way to get around and also provide some beautifully scenic journeys. The West Highland line to Fort William and Mallaig and the journey from Inverness to Kyle of Lochalsh are amongst the most beautiful rail journeys in the world and well worth doing. Services between Glasgow, Edinburgh, Stirling, Perth, Dundee and Aberdeen are fast and frequent, and there are frequent trains to and from Inverness.

ScotRail operates most train services within Scotland. You can buy train tickets at the stations, from major travel agents, or over the phone with a credit or debit card. For information and advance credit or debit card bookings visit www.scotrail.co.uk. Details of services are given throughout the guide. For busy long-distance routes it's best to reserve a seat. Seat reservations to Edinburgh, Glasgow, Aberdeen or Inverness are included in the price of the ticket when you book in advance. If the ticket office is closed, there's usually a machine on the platform. If this isn't working, you can buy a ticket on the train. Cyclists should note that though train companies have a more relaxed attitude to taking bikes on trains, reservations at a small fee for bikes are still required on some services. Cycles are carried free of charge on ScotRail services, although reservations are required on longer distance routes.

Eurorail passes are not recognized in Britain, but ScotRail offers a couple of worthwhile travel passes. The most flexible is the Freedom of Scotland Travelpass, which gives unlimited rail travel within Scotland. It is also valid on all CalMac ferries on the west coast, many Citylink bus services in the Highlands, some regional buses and offers discounts on some city centre bus tours. It also gives 20% discount on Northlink Ferries between Scrabster–Stromness, Aberdeen–Lerwick and Aberdeen–Kirkwall–Lerwick. The Highland Rover ticket allows unlimited rail travel in the Highlands region, plus the West Highland line from Glasgow, and travel between Aberdeen and Aviemore. It also allows free travel on Citylink buses between Oban, Fort William and Inverness. Ferry travel between Oban–Mull and Mallaig–Skye is also included on this ticket. Book any of these tickets at www.scotrail.co.uk.

Road

Bus and coach

Travelling around Scotland by bus takes longer than the train but is much cheaper. There are numerous local bus companies, but the main operators are Scottish Citylink (www.citylink.co.uk) and Stagecoach North Scotland (www.stagecoachbus.com). Bus services between towns and cities are good, but far less frequent in more remote rural areas. There are a number of discount and flexible tickets available and details of these are given on the Citylink and Stagecoach websites. Citylink runs a daily bus service between Scotland's six cities and strategic ports including Oban, Uig (Skye) and Ullapool. It offers a diverse range of discount and saver cards including an Explorer Pass that offers unlimited travel on its routes for a specified number of days. Stagecoach offer a Megarider pass which offers discounts across various regions.

Available to overseas passport holders, the Brit Xplorer Pass offers unlimited travel on all National Express buses. They can be bought from major airports and bus terminals.

Many parts of the Highlands and Islands can only be reached by Highland Council's Dial-a-Bus service. These buses operate on demand and don't follow a fixed timetable, see www.highland.gov.uk. There's a restricted service on Saturdays and none on Sundays. A good website for all rural bus timetables is https://bustimes.org.

Car and campervan

Travelling with your own private transport is the ideal way to explore the country, particularly the Highlands. This allows you to cover a lot of ground in a short space of time and to reach remote places. The main disadvantage is the relatively high fuel costs (around £1.30+ per litre for unleaded and up to £1.35-1.40 for diesel. Roads in the Highlands and Islands are a lot less busy than those in England, and driving is relatively stress-free, especially on the B-roads and minor roads. In more remote parts of the country, on the islands in particular, many roads are single track, with passing places indicated by a diamond-shaped signpost. These should also be used to allow traffic behind you to overtake. Remember that you may want to take your time to enjoy the stupendous views all around you, but the driver behind may be a local doctor in a hurry. Don't park in passing places. A major driving hazard on single-track roads is the huge number of sheep wandering around, blissfully unaware of your presence. When confronted by a flock of sheep, slow down and gently edge your way past. Be particularly careful at night, as many of them sleep by the side of the road (counting cars perhaps). Also keep a sharp lookout for deer, particularly at night.

To drive in Scotland you must have a current **driving licence**. Foreign nationals also need an **international driving permit**, available from state and national motoring organizations for a small fee. Those importing their own vehicle should also have their vehicle registration or ownership document. Make sure you're adequately **insured**. In all of the UK you drive on the left. **Speed limits** are 30 miles per hour (mph) in built-up areas, 70 mph on motorways and dual carriageways, and 60 mph on most other roads.

It's advisable to join one of the main UK motoring organizations during your visit for their 24-hour breakdown assistance. The two main ones in Britain are the **Automobile Association (AA)** ① *T0344-209 0754 (emergency T0800-887766), www.theaa.com*, and the **Royal Automobile Club (RAC)** ① *T0800-015 6000 (emergency T0800-828282), www.rac. co.uk*. They also provide many other services, including a reciprocal agreement for free assistance with many overseas motoring organizations. Check to see if your organization is included. Both companies can also extend their cover to include Europe. You can call these numbers even if you're not a member, but you'll have to a pay a large fee. In remote areas you may have to wait a long time for assistance. Also note that in the Highlands and Islands you may be stranded for ages waiting for spare parts to arrive.

Car hire need not be expensive in Scotland if you shop around for the best deals. Major international companies such as **Hertz** and **Avis** offer good deals, though whichever operator you choose be wary of high charges for additional mileage. Even without deals you should be able to hire a small car for a week from £150. Local hire companies often offer better deals than the larger multi-nationals, though **easyCar** offer very good rates if you book in advance and don't push up the charges with high mileage. They are based at Aberdeen, Glasgow, Edinburgh and Inverness airport. Many companies such as **Europcar** offer the flexibility of picking up in Glasgow and leaving in Edinburgh, and vice versa. Most companies prefer payment with a credit card, otherwise you'll have to leave a large deposit (£200 or more). You'll need a full driver's licence (one or two years) and be aged over 21 (23 in some cases).

Alternatively, why not hire your own transport and accommodation at the same time by renting a campervan. Campervans can be rented from a number of companies and it's best to arrange this before arriving as everything gets booked up in the high season (June-August). Inverness-based **Highland Camper Vans** ① *www.highlandcampervans.com*, is a good bet with a range of vans starting at £925 per week in high season for its two-person touring van.

Hitching

As in the rest of the UK, hitching is never entirely safe, and is certainly not advised for anyone travelling alone, particularly women travellers. Those prepared to take the risk should not find it too difficult to get a lift in the Highlands and Islands, where people are far more willing to stop for you. Bear in mind, though, that you will probably have to wait a while even to see a vehicle in some parts.

Sea

There are around 60 or so inhabited islands off the coast of Scotland, and nearly 50 of them can be reached by a scheduled ferry service. Most ferries carry vehicles and can be booked in advance. If you're travelling to the islands by car, it's a good idea to book ferries in advance whatever the time of year, particularly to the more popular islands.

The majority of ferry services on the west coast are operated by **Caledonian MacBrayne** ① *T0800-066 5000, www.calmac.co.uk*, or **CalMac** as they're more commonly known. They sail from Oban, Mallaig and Ullapool to over 20 islands in the Inner and Outer Hebrides. They also run services on the Firth of Clyde. Fares are expensive, especially with a car, but if you're planning on using ferries a lot, you can save much hassle with an **Island Hopscotch** ticket, which allows you to plan your trip more easily on 25 set routes. The ticket is valid for one month and you need to follow your set itinerary, though this can be changed en route without too much fuss. **CalMac** summer and winter timetables are listed in full on their website. **Western Ferries** ① *T0136-970 4452, www.western-ferries.co.uk*, runs services between Gourock and Dunoon, and Islay and Jura.

Northlink Ferries ① *T0845-6000 449, www.northlinkferries.co.uk*, run car ferries to Orkney and Shetland. Ferries to Orkney depart from Aberdeen or from Scrabster, near Thurso. There are also car and passenger ferries to Orkney with **Pentland Ferries** ① *www.pentlandferries.co.uk*, and a passenger-only ferry (summer only) with **John O'Groats Ferries** ① *www.jogferry.co.uk*. Ferries to Shetland sail from Aberdeen.

The Orkney Islands are linked by services run by **Orkney Ferries** ① *www.orkneyferries.co.uk*, while Shetland's heavily subsidized inter-island ferries are run by **Shetland Islands Council** ① *www.shetland.gov.uk*. There are also numerous small operators offering daytrips to various islands. Details of these are given in the relevant chapters.

Maps

You'll find a good selection of maps of Scotland in many bookshops and at the main tourist offices. Road atlases can be bought at most service stations. The best of these are the large-format ones produced by the **AA**, **Collins** and **Ordnance Survey**, which cover all of Britain at a scale of around three miles to one inch and include plans of the major towns and cities. The **Michelin** and **Bartholomew** fold-out maps are also excellent, as are the official regional tourist maps published by **Estate Publications**, which are ideal for driving and are available from most tourist offices.

The best detailed maps for walking are the Ordnance Survey (OS) maps, which are unsurpassed for accuracy and clarity. These are available at different scales. The Landranger series at 1:50,000 (1¼ inches to a mile) covers the whole of Britain and is good for most walkers. The new Explorer and Outdoor Leisure series are 1:25,000 and offer better value for walkers and cyclists. An excellent source of maps is **Stanfords** ① *12-14 Longacre, London, T020-7836 1321, www.stanfords.co.uk*. There are branches of Stanfords in Bristol and Manchester too.

Essentials A-Z

Accident and emergency

For police, fire brigade, ambulance and, in certain areas, mountain rescue or coastguard, T999 or T112.

Bank holidays

There are also local public holidays in spring and autumn. Dates vary from place to place. Banks are closed during these holidays, and sights and shops may be affected. Contact the relevant Area Tourist Board for more details.

1 Jan New Year's Day
2 Jan Also a holiday in Scotland.
Mar-Apr Good Fri and **Easter Mon**
1 May May Day
May Victoria Day (the last Mon in May).
25 Dec Christmas Day
26 Dec Boxing Day

Children

Visiting the Scottish Highlands with kids is no different from other parts of the UK, though you may find that the locals are just that little bit more tolerant and helpful. If you're near a beach, toddlers will be in rock pool heaven, rooting around to their little hearts' content as you sit nearby, shivering in the rain. Even teenagers should have no reason to moan as there are all manner of thrill-a-minute adventure sports to try and, crucially, internet access is generally not an issue.

If you're travelling with babies and/or toddlers you may find eating out a frustrating experience in some establishments, though the days of families being banished to some grubby room at the back, well out of the way of other diners, are, thankfully, a thing of the past in most places. The attitude to breastfeeding, while some way behind the likes of Scandinavia, is more relaxed than the US and becoming ever more civilized and progressive. In major towns and cities, Italian restaurants are generally more child-friendly. The child may not be quite be king, but they are allowed to be seen and heard.

If you are flying, inform the airline in advance that you're travelling with a baby or toddler, and check out the facilities when booking as these vary with each aircraft. British Airways operates a Skyflyers programme specifically to help passengers travelling with young children. Facilities include special seats for under 2s, allowing foldable pushchairs to be taken on-board or stored in the hold and the provision of skycots for long-haul flights. With 24 hrs' advance notice, children's meals can also be provided on-board. However, take snacks and toys for in-flight entertainment, and remember that swallowing food or drinks during take-off and landing will help prevent ear problems.

A recommended website is www.baby goes2.com, while www.mumsnet.com is useful for parents with older kids.

Customs and duty free

Visitors from EU countries do not have to make a declaration to customs on entry into the UK. The limits for duty-paid goods from within the EU are 3200 cigarettes and 200 cigars, 10 litres of spirits, 20 litres of fortified wine, 90 litres of wine and 110 litres of beer. There is no longer any duty-free shopping. Visitors from non-EU countries are allowed to import 200 cigarettes, or 250 g of tobacco, 2 litres of wine, and 2 litres of fortified wine or 1 litre of spirits. There are various import restrictions, most of which should not affect the average tourist. There are tight quarantine restrictions which apply to animals brought from overseas (except for Ireland). For more information on British import regulations, contact **HM Revenue and Customs** www.gov.uk.

Many goods in Britain are subject to a Value Added Tax (VAT) of 20%, with the major exception of books and food. Visitors from non-EU countries can save money through the Retail Export Scheme, which allows a refund of VAT on goods to be taken out of the country. Note that not all shops are participants in the scheme and that VAT cannot be reclaimed on hotel bills or other services.

Disabled travellers

For travellers with disabilities, visiting Scotland independently can be a difficult business. While most theatres, cinemas, libraries and modern tourist attractions are accessible to wheelchairs, tours of many historic buildings may be tricky and finding accommodation remains problematic. Many large, new hotels do have disabled suites, but far too many B&Bs, guesthouses and smaller hotels remain ill-equipped to accept bookings from people with disabilities. However, through the work of organizations like **Disability Scotland** the Government is being pressed to further improve the Disability Discrimination Act and access to public amenities and transport. As a result, many buses and ScotRail's train services now accommodate wheelchair-users whilst city taxis should carry wheelchair ramps.

Wheelchair users, and blind or partially sighted people are automatically given

30-50% discount on train fares, and those with other disabilities are eligible for the Disabled Person's Railcard, which costs £20 per year and gives a third off most tickets. If you will need assistance at a railway station, call ScotRail before travelling on T0800-912 2901. There are no discounts on buses.

If you are disabled you should contact the travel officer of your national support organization. They can provide literature or put you in touch with travel agents specializing in tours for the disabled. **VisitScotland** produces a guide, 'Accessible Scotland', for disabled travellers, and many local tourist offices can provide accessibility details for their area. A useful website is www.disabledholidayinfo.org.uk. Accessible Travel & Leisure, www.accessibletravel.co.uk, and www.disabledholidays.com specialize in organizing holidays for disabled travellers.

Useful organizations
Capability Scotland, ASCS, 11 Ellersly Rd, Edinburgh EH12 6HY, T0131-337 9876, www.capability-scotland.org.uk.
Tourism for All UK, T0845-124 9971, www.tourismforall.org.uk. An excellent source of information about travel and for identifying accessible accommodation in the UK.

Electricity

The current in Britain is 240V AC. Plugs have 3 square pins and adapters are widely available.

TRAVEL TIP
Once bitten, twice shy

The major problem facing visitors to the Highlands and Islands of Scotland during the summer months is *Culicoides impunctatus* – or the midge, as it's more commonly known. These tiny flying creatures are savage and merciless in the extreme and hunt in huge packs (it is estimated that midges cost the Scottish tourist industry nearly £300 million a year in lost revenue). No sooner have you left your B&B for a pleasant evening stroll, than a cloud of these bloodthirsty little devils will descend, getting into your eyes, ears, nose and mouth – and a few places you forgot you even had. The only way to avoid them is to take refuge indoors, or to hide in the nearest loch.

Midges are at their worst in the evening and in damp, shaded or overcast conditions, and between late May and September, but they don't like direct sunlight, heavy rain, smoke and wind. Make sure you're well covered up and wear light-coloured clothing (they're attracted to dark colours). Most effective is a midge net, if you don't mind everyone pointing and laughing at you. Insect repellents have some effect, particularly those with DEET, but those who don't fancy putting chemicals on their skin can try Mozzy Off, www.mozzy off.com, which comprises 100% plant oils, while the Thurso-made Essential Spirit, www.essentialspirit.co.uk, is also made from natural ingredients. A more radical approach is the Midegeater, a trap which emits carbon dioxide to lure the little blighters within range and then sucks them in at high speed. Those who see prevention as the best form of cure can log on to www.smidgeup.com, an online midge forecast service that gives five-day predictions of midge movements.

If you do get bitten, spare a thought for the gravedigger from Rùm. According to legend, as punishment for not burying a body properly he was stripped naked, tied to a post and left outside with only the midges for company. The poor chap eventually died of the countless bites.

Embassies and consulates

For a list of foreign embassies in London, consult www.gov.uk. Some nations, including the United States, Canada and several EU countries also have consulates in Scottish cities; these are listed at www.visitscotland.com.

Health

No vaccinations are required for entry into Britain. Citizens of EU countries are entitled to free medical treatment at **National Health Service (NHS)** hospitals on production of a **European Health Insurance Card (EHIC)**. For details, see the **Department of Health** website, www.dh.gov.uk/travellers. Also, Australia, New Zealand and several other non-EU European countries have reciprocal healthcare arrangements with Britain. Citizens of other countries will have to pay for all medical services, except accident and emergency care given at **Accident and Emergency (A&E) Units** at most (but not all) National Health Service hospitals. Health insurance is therefore strongly advised for citizens of non-EU countries.

Pharmacists can dispense only a limited range of drugs without a doctor's prescription. Most are open during normal shop hours, though some are open late, especially in larger towns. Local newspapers will carry lists of which are open late. Doctors' surgeries are usually open from around 0830-0900 till 1730-1800, though times vary. Outside surgery hours you can go to the casualty department of the local hospital for any complaint requiring urgent attention. For the address of the nearest hospital or doctors' surgery, www.nhs.com. See also individual town and city directories throughout the book for details local medical services.

You should encounter no major problems or irritations during your visit to Scotland. The only exceptions are the risk of hyperthermia if you're walking in the mountains in difficult conditions, and the dreaded midge, see box, page 475.

Insurance

It's a good idea to take out some form of travel insurance, wherever you're travelling from. This should cover you for theft or loss of possessions and money, the cost of all medical and dental treatment, cancellation of flights, delays in travel arrangements, accidents, missed departures, lost baggage, lost passport, and personal liability and legal expenses. There are a variety of policies to choose from, so it's best to shop around to get the best price. Your travel agent can also advise you on the best deals available. **STA Travel**, www.statravel.com, with branches nationwide, and other reputable student travel organizations often offer good-value travel policies. Older travellers should note that some companies won't cover people over 65 years old, or may charge high premiums. The best policies for older travellers are offered by **Age Concern**, www.ageuk.org.uk.

Points to note: you should always read the small print carefully. Some policies exclude 'dangerous activities' such as scuba-diving, skiing, horse riding or even trekking. Not all policies cover ambulance, helicopter rescue or emergency flights home. Find out if your policy pays medical expenses direct to the hospital or doctor, or if you have to pay and then claim the money back later. If the latter applies, make sure you keep all records. Whatever your policy, if you are unfortunate enough to have something stolen, make sure

you get a copy of the police report, as you will need this to substantiate your claim.

Internet

Even in the Highlands of Scotland, internet access is extensive. The vast majority of hotels, guesthouses, B&Bs and hostels will offer free Wi-Fi as part of the cost, and many cafés, bars and restaurants also have free Wi-Fi. Websites are listed where appropriate in this guide. VisitScotland and area tourist boards have their own websites and these are given on page 482.

Language

Though the vast majority of Scots speak English, to the untutored ear the Scottish dialect can be hard to understand, as many words and expressions are derived not from English but from Lowland Scots, or lallans, which is now recognized as a separate language as opposed to simply a regional dialect. In the Highlands and Islands, however, the accent is very clear and easy to understand.

Scotland's oldest surviving language is Scottish Gaelic (*Gaidhlig*, pronounced 'Gallic'), spoken by only about 2% of the population. Notably, a 2001 Census found Glasgow has the highest concentration of Gaelic speakers. Generally however, the Highlands, Outer Hebrides and Argyll have the greatest numbers of Gaelic-speaking inhabitants. Indeed, on many islands including Harris and Lewis road signs are written in both Gaelic and English. In recent years greater efforts have been made to revive the language, including the creation by the BBC of wholly Gaelic TV and radio programming, www.bbc.co.uk/scotland/alba. A good phrasebook for getting to grips with the basics of the ancient Celtic language is *Scots Gaelic, an introduction to the basics* by George McLennan (Argyll Publishing). *Macbain's Etymological Dictionary of the Gaelic language* contains a wealth of words and information, or learn online at www.learngaelic.scot. For more on the history of Gaelic, see page 453, and for a glossary of Gaelic words, see page 485.

Laundry

Most towns have coin-operated launderettes. The average cost for a wash and tumble dry is about £3-4. A service wash, where someone will do your washing for you, costs around £5-6. In more remote areas, you'll have to rely on hostel and campsite facilities. An increasing number of SYHA hostels have excellent 'drying rooms' and washing facilities.

LGBT travellers

Though Scotland is generally tolerant of homosexuality, overt displays of affection are not advised. Gay couples may also come up against subtle forms of discrimination, such as B&Bs spontaneously 'losing' bookings for a double room and being left with the option of taking 2 singles. The *Scotsgay* magazine, www.scotsgay.co.uk, is a good source of information, as is the **Stonewall Scotland** organization, www.stonewall scotland.org.uk. *The List Magazine*, www.list. co.uk, published fortnightly and available at newsagents in Scottish cities, includes listings of venues and events that may appeal to the gay, lesbian and bisexual community.

Media

Newspapers and magazines

The main British daily and Sunday newspapers are widely available in Scotland and some of them publish special Scottish editions, among them the *Scottish Daily Mail*, *Scottish Daily Express* and Rupert Murdoch's notorious scandal sheet, *The Sun*.

The Scottish press produces 2 main 'quality' newspapers, *The Scotsman*, published in Edinburgh, and *The Herald*, published in Glasgow, which is the oldest daily newspaper in the English-speaking world, dating from 1783. The biggest-selling daily is the *Daily Record*, a tabloid paper. The

Press and Journal, published in Aberdeen, also enjoys one of the highest circulations in the country. The weekend equivalents of the dailies are *Scotland on Sunday* from the Scotsman stable, the *Sunday Herald* and the *Sunday Mail*, published by the Daily Record, while *The Sunday Post* tends to be popular with the older generation. Provincial newspapers are widely read in Scotland. The main Highlands varieties are the weekly *Oban Times* and the radical, crusading *West Highland Free Press*, published on Skye.

TV and radio

There are 5 main television channels in Scotland; the publicly funded BBC 1 and 2, and the independent commercial stations, ITV, Channel 4, Channel 5. The main commercial TV network in Scotland is STV, providing national coverage. There is also a vast array of digital channels on offer. BBC1 and 2 were joined by 3 and 4, the former now being online only and aimed at younger viewers and the latter on more serious documentaries and foreign TV series. BBC1 broadcasts many regional programmes as its BBC Scotland incarnation, including regular local news, and Scotland has its own variant of ITV, which is STV. There is also a dedicated Gaelic channel, BBC Alba.

The BBC network also broadcasts several radio channels, most of which are based in London. These include: Radio 1 aimed at a young audience; Radio 2 targeting a more mature audience; Radio 3 which plays mostly classical music; Radio 4 which is talk-based and features arts, drama and current affairs; and Radio 5 Live which is a mix of sport and news. Radio Scotland (92-95FM, 810MW) provides a Scottish-based diet of news, sport, current affairs, travel and music. It also provides an ever-expanding Gaelic network in the northwest, and local programmes in Orkney and Shetland. There are also a number of local commercial radio stations, stretching from Shetland in the north to the Borders.

Money For up-to-date rates, visit xe.com.

The British currency is the pound sterling (£), divided into 100 pence (p). Coins come in denominations of 1p, 2p, 5p, 10p, 20p, 50p, £1 and £2. Bank of England banknotes are legal tender in Scotland, in addition to those issued by the **Bank of Scotland**, **Royal Bank of Scotland** and **Clydesdale Bank**. These Scottish banknotes (bills) come in denominations of £5, £10, £20, £50 and £100; regardless of what you are told by shopkeepers in England, the notes are legal tender in the rest of Britain.

Banks

The larger towns and villages have a branch of at least one of the big 4 high street banks – **Bank of Scotland**, **Royal Bank of Scotland**, **Clydesdale** and **TSB**. Bank opening hours are Mon-Fri from 0930 to between 1600 and 1700. Some larger branches may also be open later on Thu and on Sat mornings. In small and remote places, and on some islands, there may be only a mobile bank which runs to a set timetable. This timetable will be available from the local post office.

Banks are usually the best places to change money and cheques. You can withdraw cash from selected banks and ATMs (or cashpoints as they are called in Britain) with your cash and credit card. Though using a debit or credit card is by far the easiest way of keeping in funds, you must check with your bank what the total charges will be; this can be as high as 4-5% in some cases. In more remote parts, and especially on the islands, ATMs are few and far between and it is important to keep a ready supply of cash on you at all times. Some guesthouses and restaurants in the remoter reaches of Scotland will still request payment in cash. Outside the ferry ports on most of the smaller islands, you won't find an ATM. Your bank will give you a list of locations where you can use your card. **Bank of Scotland**, **Clydesdale** and most building society cashpoints are part of the Link

network, the largest cash machine network in the UK. For a list of all Link cash machines, visit www.link.co.uk. See also Credit cards below. In addition to ATMs, bureaux de change can be used outside banking hours. These can be found at the main airports and train stations. Note that some charge high commissions for changing cheques. Those at international airports, however, often charge less than banks and will change pound sterling cheques for free. Avoid changing money or cheques in hotels, as the rates are usually very poor.

Currency cards

If you don't want to carry lots of cash, prepaid currency cards allow you to preload money from your bank account, fixed at the day's exchange rate. They look like a credit or debit card and are issued by specialist money changing companies, such as **Travelex** and **Caxton FX** as well as the **Post Office**. You can top up and check your balance by phone, online and sometimes by text.

Credit cards

Most hotels, shops and restaurants accept the major credit cards such as **MasterCard** and **Visa** and, less frequently, **Amex**, though some places may charge for using them. They may be less useful in more remote rural areas and smaller establishments such as B&Bs, which will often only accept cash or cheques.

Visa card holders can use the **Bank of Scotland**, **Clydesdale Bank**, **Royal Bank of Scotland** and **TSB** ATMs; Access/MasterCard holders, the Royal Bank and Clydesdale; Amex card holders, the Bank of Scotland.

Money transfers

If you need money urgently, the quickest way to have it sent to you is to have it wired to the nearest bank via **Western Union**, T0808-234 9168, www.westernunion.com, or **Money Gram**, www.secure.moneygram.co.uk. Charges are on a sliding scale; ie it will cost proportionately less to wire out more money.

Cost of travelling

The Highlands and Islands of Scotland can be an expensive place to visit, and prices are higher in more remote parts, but there is plenty of budget accommodation available and backpackers will be able to keep their costs down. Petrol is a major expense and won't just cost an arm and a leg but also the limbs of all remaining family members. Expect to pay up to 15p per litre more than in central and southern parts of Scotland and never pass a fuel station in the Highlands and Islands if running low as the next one might be hours away. Accommodation and restaurant prices also tend to be higher in more popular destinations and during the busy summer months.

The minimum daily budget required, if you're staying in hostels or camping, cycling, and cooking your own meals, will be around £25-30pp per day. If you start using public transport and eating out occasionally that will rise to around £35-40. Those staying in slightly more upmarket B&Bs or guesthouses, eating out every evening at pubs or modest restaurants and visiting tourist attractions, such as castles or museums, can expect to pay around £70-80 per day. If you also want to hire a car and use ferries to visit the islands, and eat well, then costs will rise considerably and you'll be looking at least £100-120pp per day. Single travellers will have to pay more than ½ the cost of a double room in most places, and should budget on spending around 60-70% of what a couple would spend.

Trust for Scotland (**NTS**), T0131-458 0200, www.nts.org.uk. National Trust properties are indicated in this guide as 'NTS', and entry charges and opening hours are given for each property.

Historic Environment Scotland (**HES**), Longmore House, Salisbury Place, Edinburgh EH9 1SH, T0131-668 8600, www.historicenvironment.scot, manages more than 330 of Scotland's most important castles, monuments and other historic sites. Historic Scotland properties are indicated as 'HES', and admission charges and opening hours are also given in this guide. Historic Environment Scotland offers an **Explorer Pass** which allows free entry to 70 of its properties including Edinburgh and Stirling castles. A 3-day pass (over 5 days) costs £31, concessions £24.80, child £18.60, family £62, and a 7-day pass (over 14 days) costs £42, concessions £33.60, child £25.20, family £84. It can save a lot of money, especially in Orkney, where most of the monuments are managed by Historic Envirnoment Scotland. For details of the **Orkney Explorer Pass**, see page 373.

Many other historic buildings are owned by local authorities, and admission is cheap, or in many cases free. Most fee-paying attractions give a discount or concession for senior citizens, the unemployed, full-time students and children under 16 (those under 5 are admitted free everywhere). Proof of age or status must be shown. Many of Scotland's stately homes are still owned and occupied by the landed gentry, and admission is usually between £8 and £12 per adult.

Museums, galleries, historic houses

Most of Scotland's tourist attractions, apart from the large museums and art galleries in the main towns, are open only from Easter-Oct. Full details of opening hours and admission charges are given in the relevant sections of this guide.

Over 100 of the country's most prestigious sights, and 75,000 ha of beautiful countryside, are cared for by the **National**

Opening hours

Businesses are usually open Mon-Sat 0900-1700. In towns and cities, as well as villages in holiday areas, many shops open on a Sun but they will open later and close earlier (for further details, see page 28). For **iCentre** opening times, see page 482. Those visiting the Outer Hebrides need to be aware of the strict observance of the Sabbath on those islands.

Post

Most post offices are open Mon-Fri 0900-1730 and Sat 0900-1230 or 1300. Smaller sub-post offices are closed for an hour at lunch (1300-1400) and many of them operate out of a shop. Post offices keep the same ½-day closing times as shops.

Stamps can be bought at post offices, but also from vending machines outside, and also at many newsagents. For more information about Royal Mail postal services and prices, call T03457-740740, or visit www.royalmail.com.

Safety

Incidences of serious crime in Highlands and Islands tend to be the exception rather than the rule and are so rare that they always make front page news. In fact, if someone failed to say 'good morning' – heaven forfend – it would provoke such an outcry that locals would be talking about little else for weeks to come. Orkney, for example, has the lowest crime rate in the UK. In most island communities, even sizeable ones such as Tobermory on Mull, people don't even lock their doors at night. The major safety issue when visiting the Highlands and more remote parts relates to the unpredictable weather conditions. Everyone should be aware of the need for caution and proper preparation when walking or climbing in the mountains. For more information on mountain safety, see www.mountaineering.scot/safety.

Student travellers

Discount passes

There are various official youth/student ID cards available. The most useful is the **International Student ID Card (ISIC)** which gains you access to the world of student travel with a series of discounts, including most forms of local transport, cheap or free admission to museums, theatres and other attractions, cheap meals in some restaurants and discounted fares on certain ferry, rail and even Scotland tour operators. For details of discounts and cost of the various types of card, see www.isic.org. You'll also receive the ISIC handbook, which ensures you get the most out of services available. ISIC cards are available at student travel centres. US and Canadian citizens are also entitled to emergency medical coverage, and there's a 24-hr hotline to call in the event of medical, legal or financial emergencies.

If you're aged under 26 but not a student, you can apply for an **International Youth Travel Card (IYTC)**, which gives you much the same discounts. These discount cards are also issued by student travel agencies and hostelling organizations, see page 35.

Studying in Scotland

If you want to study in Scotland you must first prove you can support and accommodate yourself without working and without recourse to public support. Your studies should take up at least 15 hrs a week for a minimum of 6 months. Once you are studying, you are allowed to do 20 hrs of casual work per week in the term time and you can work full-time during the holidays. In North America full-time students can obtain temporary work or study permits through the **Council on International Education Exchange (CIEE)**, www.ciee.org. For more details, contact your nearest British embassy, consulate or high commission, or the **Foreign and Commowealth Office** in London, T020-7008 1500, www. gov.uk. See also UK Visas and Immigration, T0300-123 7000.

Telephone *Country code +44.*

Useful numbers: operator T100; international operator T155; directory enquiries T192; overseas directory enquiries T153.

Roaming charges for smartphones and tablets have come down drastically and the EU has banned mobile roaming charges (this unfortunately won't apply to the UK after 2019). Sightings of public payphones are about as frequent as Nessie, so don't rely on being able to find a payphone wherever you go. BT payphones take either coins (20p, 50p and £1) or phonecards, which are available at newsagents and post offices displaying the BT logo. These cards come in denominations of £2, £3, £5 and £10. Some payphones also accept credit cards.

For most countries (including Europe, USA and Canada) calls are cheapest Mon-Fri between 1800 and 0800 and all day Sat-Sun. For Australia and New Zealand it's cheapest to call 1430-1930 and 2400-0700 every day. Area codes are not needed if calling from within the same area. Any number prefixed by 0800 or 0500 is free to the caller; 08457 numbers are charged at local rates and 08705 numbers at the national rate. To call Scotland from overseas, dial 011 from USA and Canada, 0011 from Australia and 00 from New Zealand, followed by 44, then the area code, minus the first zero, then the number. To call overseas from Scotland dial 00 followed by the country code. Country codes include: Australia 61; Ireland 353; New Zealand 64; South Africa 27; USA and Canada 1.

Time

Greenwich Mean Time (GMT) is used from late Oct to late Mar, after which time the clocks go forward an hour to British Summer Time (BST). GMT is 5 hrs ahead of US Eastern Standard Time and 10 hrs behind Australian Eastern Standard Time.

Tipping

Believe it or not, people in Scotland do leave tips. In a restaurant you should leave a tip of around 10% if you are satisfied with the service. If the bill already includes a service charge, you needn't add a further tip. Tipping is not normal in pubs or bars. Taxi drivers will expect a tip for longer journeys, usually of around 10%; and most hairdressers will also expect a tip. As in most other countries, porters, bellboys and waiters in more up-market hotels rely on tips to supplement their meagre wages.

Tour operators

There are many companies offering general interest or special interest tours of Scotland. Contact **VisitScotland** for a list of operators. Also worth checking for a list of professional guides and tour operators is the **Scottish Tourist Guides Association**, T01786-447784, www.stga.co.uk. You can book a tour guide directly through the STGA on T01786-451953.

In the UK

About Argyll Walking Holidays, Letters Lodge South, Strathlachlan, Argyll, T01369-860272, www.aboutargyll.co.uk. As its name suggests, this operator specializes in offering guided and self-guided walking trips of Argyll and the islands.

c-n-do Scotland, 32 Stirling Enterprise Park, Stirling, T01786-445703, www.cndoscotland.com. A highly reputable walking holiday specialist with diverse itineraries across the Highlands and Islands, including a 4-day walk in Perthshire to a 14-day wilderness experience in the far northwest of Scotland.

Haggis Adventures, 60 High St, Edinburgh EH1 1TB, T0131-557 9393, www.haggisadventures.com. Award-winning operator specializing in a variety of day and week-long tours for independent travellers, including backpackers.

Heart of Scotland Tours, T0131-228 2888, www.heartofscotlandtours.co.uk. Runs 1-day coach tours departing from Edinburgh city centre. Loch Ness and highland castles are among the guided itineraries.

Macbackpackers, Edinburgh, T0131-558 9900, www.macbackpackers.com. Well-established tour operator for independent budget travellers with 2- to 5-day minibus tours ranging from £69-165 of the Highlands and Islands that depart from Edinburgh and use a network of hostel accommodation.

North-West Frontiers, Viewfield, Strathpeffer IV14 9DS, T01997-421474, www.nwfrontiers.com. Offers a good range of guided and self-guided hiking and walking tours across north of Scotland and islands including a trip focused on Assynt's world-renowned geology.

Rabbie's Trail Burners, 207 High St, Edinburgh, T0131-226 3133, www.rabbies. com. Tours from Glasgow, Edinburgh and Inverness, 1- and multi-day, minibus based tours of the Highlands and Islands for independent travellers.

Ridgway Adventure, Ardmore, Rhiconich, by Lairg, Sutherland IV27 4RB, T01971-521006, www.ridgway-adventure.co.uk. Whether you want to spend a weekend sea kayaking and climbing, or a week trekking the wilds of northwest Scotland, this acclaimed operator offers bags of adventure for families and individuals.

Scot Mountain Holidays, Fraoch Lodge, Boat of Garten, PH24 3BN, T01479-831331, www.scotmountainholidays.com. The owners of this lodge have expanded their business to include family-focused homestays and self-guided mountain biking breaks. Andrew Bateman is a qualified mountain guide who can offer bespoke walking trips and cycling advice to guests.

Scottish Cycling Holidays, 87 Perth St, Blairgowrie, T01250-876100, www.scotcycle. co.uk. Perthshire-based operator that for over 30 years has offered guided and self-guided 2-day to 8-day pedal-powered trips throughout Scotland.

Timberbush Tours, 555 Castlehill, Edinburgh, T0131-226 6066, www.timber bush-tours. co.uk. Award-winning, family-run operator offering a variety of 1- to 3-day guided coach tours around the country.

Walkabout Scotland, 5 Rose St, Edinburgh EH2 2PR, T0131-243 2664, www.walkabout scotland.com. Day, weekend and week-long walking tours around Scotland including day jaunts up Ben Lomond or Ben Lawers.

Wilderness Scotland, T01479-420020, www. wildernessscotland.com. Specialist adventure tour operator offering excellent walking, climbing, kayaking, hiking and photographic trips into Scotland's wild places, plus tailor-made and self-guided trips.

Tourist information

Tourist information centres

Tourist offices – called **iCentres** – can be found in the main tourist centres though many offices have closed in recent years. Those that remain open are listed in the relevant sections of this book. Opening hours vary depending on the time of year, and many of the smaller offices are closed during the winter months. All tourist offices provide information on accommodation, public transport, local attractions and restaurants, as well as selling books, local guides, maps and souvenirs. Many have free street plans and leaflets describing local walks. They can also book accommodation for you, for a small fee.

Finding out more

The best way of finding out more information for your trip to Scotland is to contact **VisitScotland** (aka the Scottish Tourist Board). Alternatively, you can contact **VisitBritain**, the organization that is responsible for tourism throughout the British Isles. Both organizations can provide a wealth of free literature and information such as maps, city guides and accommodation brochures. If particularly interested in ensuring your visit coincides with a major festival or sporting event. Travellers with special needs should also contact **VisitScotland** or their nearest **VisitBritain** office. If you want more detailed information on a particular area, click through to the specific tourist boards via the **VisitScotland** website, www.visitscotland. com. Brochures can be downloaded from their website and also accommodation bookings can be made.

Useful websites

Useful websites for specific regions are given in the relevant sections at the start of each chapter.

www.aboutscotland.co.uk Online resource for information on accommodation.
www.scotland-info.co.uk Good for local information on hotels, shops and restaurants.
www.undiscoveredscotland.com Another good online source of information for details about villages and towns across the country including their history and with recommendations for accommodation.

Visas and immigration

Visa regulations are subject to change, so it is essential to check with your local British embassy, high commission or consulate before leaving home. Citizens of all European countries – except Albania, Bosnia Herzegovina, Kosovo, Macedonia, Moldova, Turkey, Serbia and all former Soviet republics (other than the Baltic states) – require only a passport to enter Britain and can generally stay for up to 3 months. Citizens of Australia, Canada, New Zealand, South Africa or the USA can stay for up to 6 months, providing they have a return ticket and sufficient funds to cover their stay. Citizens of most other countries require a visa from the commission or consular office in the country of application.

The **Foreign and Commonwealth Office (FCO)**, T020-7008 1500, www.gov.uk, has an excellent website, which provides details of British immigration and visa requirements. Also the **Home Office UK Border Agency** is responsible for UK immigration matters and its website is a good place to start for anyone hoping visit, work, study or emigrate to the UK: www.ukba.homeoffice.gov.uk.

Citizens of Australia, Canada, New Zealand, South Africa or the USA wishing to stay longer than 6 months will need an Entry Clearance Certificate from the **British High Commission** in their country. For more details, contact your nearest British embassy, consulate or high commission, or the **Foreign and Commonwealth Office** in London.

Weights and measures

Imperial and metric systems are both in use. Distances on roads are measured in miles and yards, drinks poured in pints and gills, but generally, the metric system is used elsewhere.

Women travellers

Travelling in Scotland is neither easier nor more difficult for women than travelling in other parts of the UK. Generally speaking, Scots are friendly and courteous and even lone women travellers should experience nothing unpleasant. However, common sense dictates that single women would do well to avoid hitching on their own in the middle of nowhere. In the main cities and larger towns, the usual precautions need to be taken and you should avoid walking in quiet, unlit streets and parks at night.

Working in Scotland

In today's economic climate and with ever more stringent immigration rules it's not easy picking up work in Scotland. Most citizens of European Union (EU) countries can live and work in Britain freely without a visa, but non-EU residents need a permit to work legally. This can be difficult to obtain without the backing of an established company or employer in the UK. Rules and regulations for working in the UK are constantly being updated by the government so if you are unsure of your visa status you should check the government website, www.gov.uk, for the latest information.

Volunteering

See www.volunteerscotland.net.
National Trust for Scotland, T0131-458 0200, www.nts.org.uk, is among a number of Scotland-based charities that offer volunteering opportunities.

Footnotes

Glossary 485
Index 486
Acknowledgements 495
Credits 496

Glossary

Scottish terms

ben	hill or mountain
bothy	farm cottage/mountain hut
brae	hill or slope
brig	bridge
burn	brook
clan	tribe bearing same surname
crannog	Celtic lake or bog dwelling
croft	small plot of farmland and house
dram	small measure of whisky
factor	manager of estate/landlord
firth	estuary
ghillie	personal hunting or fishing guide
howff	traditional pub/haunt
kirk	church
lade	mill stream
laird	landowner/squire
Mac/Mc	prefix in Scottish surnames denoting 'son of'
machair	sandy, grassy coastal land used for grazing
manse	vicarage
merse	saltmarsh
Munro	mountain over 3000 ft
provost	mayor
Sassenach	literally 'Saxon', ie English
sept	branch of clan
Wee Frees	Followers of the Free Church of Scotland
wynd	lane
yett	gate or door

Useful Gaelic

abhainn	river
aonach	ridge
aros	dwelling
ault, allt	stream
bagh	bay
bal, baile	town or village
ban, beinn	mountain
bealach	mountain pass

beg, beag	small
cairn	heap of stones marking a spot
camas	bay or harbour
ceilidh	social gathering involving singing, dancing and drinking
cnoc, knock	hill
coll or coille	wood or forest
corran	point jutting into the sea
corrie, coire	hollow in mountainside or whirlpool
craig, from creag	rock, crag
drum	ridge
dubh	black
dun	fort
eas	waterfall
eilean	island
fin or fionn	white
gare, gear	short
garv, garbh	rough
geodha	cove
glen, glean	valley
inch, innis	meadow or island
inver, inbhir	river mouth
kyle, caolas	narrow strait
liath	grey
loch	lake
more, mór	great, large
rannoch	bracken
ross, rubha	promontory
sgeir	sea rock
sgurr	sharp point
sheiling	shepherd's hut
strath	wide valley
tarbet, tairbeart	isthmus
tigh	house
tir, tyre	land
torr	hill, castle
tràigh	shore
uig	shelter
uige	water

Index

Entries in bold refer to maps

A

Aberfeldy 122
Aberfoyle 129
Abernethy Forest RSPB Reserve 146
accident and emergency 473
accommodation 32
  price codes 32
Achamore Gardens 67
Acharacle 214
Achgarve 240
Achiltibuie 250
Achmelvich 251
Achnacarry 187
Adroil 334
Aigas 175
Aird of Sleat 305
airport information 466
air travel 465, 469
alcohol 40
Allasdale 360
Allathsdal 360
Amhuinnsuidhe Castle 338
Amulree 123
animals 457
An Lanntair Arts Centre 324
An Sgurr 308
An Tairbeart 340
An Taobh Tuath 344
An Teallach 249
Ant-Ob 344
Aonach Eagach 208
Aonach Mhor 201
Aoradh 99
Appin 54
Applecross 232
architecture 443
Ardbeg 97

Ardfin 104
Ardgarten 71
Ardgay 272
Ardgour 212
Ardlanish Bay 81
Ardmeanach Peninsula 81
Ardnamurchan Peninsula 213
Ardnave Point 100
Arduaine Gardens 56
Ardvasar 305
Ardvreck Castle 251
Argyll 44
Argyll Forest Park 71
Arichonan 64
Arinagour 91
Arisaig 219
Armadale 305
Armadale Castle 305
Arnol 330
Arnsidale 226
Aros 285
Aros Castle 78
Arrochar 71
arts and crafts 454
Auchindrain Township 62
Auldearn 173
Auld Lang Syne 445
Aurora Borealis 263
Aviemore 139

B

Badachro 239
Bàgh a Chaisteil 359
Bagh a Tuath 360
bagpipes 451
Baile a Mhanaich 352
Baile an Trùiseil 327
Baile Mór 88
Baile Na Creige 360
Baile Sear 349

Baille nan Cailleach 353
Bain, Ally 451
Balephetrish Bay 92
Balephuil Bay 92
Baleshare 349
Balevullin 92
Balfour Bay 81
Balfour Castle 397
Balivanich 352
Ballachulish 207
Ballantrushel 327
Ballater 148
Balloch 135
Ballygrant 101
Ballymeanoch Standing Stones 63
Balmaha 135
Balmavicar 68
Balmoral 148
Balmoral Castle 149
Balnakeil 258
Balnakeil Craft Village 258
Balquhidder 131
Balranald Nature Reserve 348
Balranald RSPB Reserve 349
Balvicar 55
bank holidays 473
banks 478
Banks, Iain 450
Barabhas 327
Barcaldine Castle 53
Barnhill 104
Barony Mills 384
Barpa Langass 349
Barra 358
Barrie, JM 447
Barvas 327
Battle of the Braes 294
Bays 344

B&Bs 34
Bealach na Bà 232
Bearnaraigh 334, 351
Beauly 175
Beauly Firth 175
Beauly Priory 175
beer 40
Beinn Alligin 235
Beinn Dearg 245
Beinn Eighe National Nature Reserve 236
Beinn Ghulean 68
Beinn na Faoghla 352
Benbecula 352
Ben Hope 259
Ben Lawers 124
Ben Macdrui 145
Benmore 71
Ben More 81
Ben More Assynt 249, 251
Ben Nevis 198, **199**
Ben Nevis Distillery 192
Ben Wyvis 276
Bernera Island 55
Berneray 351
Berriedale 267
Bettyhill 259
Bharraigh 358
Bhatarsaigh 358, 360
Big Sand 239
birdwatching 20, 257, 311, 348, 349, 415, 420, 425
Birks of Aberfeldy 123
Birnam 113
Birsay 384
Black Isle 277
Black Watch Museum 110
Blair Atholl 118
Blair Atholl Distillery 117

Blair Castle 118
Blairgowrie 126
Blairmore 253
Boat of Garten 146
Böd of Gremista
  Museum 409
Bonar Bridge 272
Bone Caves 251
Bonnie Prince Charlie
  357, 440
Book of Kells 88
books 445, 462
Boreray 366
Borgh 360
Bornais 355
Bornish 355
Borreraig 295
Borve 360
Bosta 334
Bostadh 334
Bowmore 99
Bowmore Distillery
  99
Bracora 220
Bracorina 220
Brae 422
Braemar 149
Braemar Castle 149
Braemar Gathering
  149, 150
Braemar Highland
  Heritage Centre 149
Braeriach 145
Braes, The 302
Bragar 330
Brahan, Seer 278
Branklyn Garden 111
Breacleit 334
Breaclete 334
Breadalbane 131
Bressay 410
Bressay Lighthouse
  410
Bridgend 99
British Tourist
  Authority 482
Broadford 301
Brochel Castle 302

Broch of Gurness 385
Broch of Tirefour 54
brochs 443
Brodie Castle 173
Brough of Birsay 384
Brown, George
  Douglas 448
Brown, George
  Mackay 448
Bruar 119
Bruce, Robert 66, 433
Bruce, William 444
Buachaille Etive Mór
  208
Buchan, John 447
Bun Abhainn Eadarra
  338
Bunavoneadar 338
Bunnahabhain
  Distillery 101
bureaux de change
  478
Burns Night 19
Burns, Robert 445
Burra 413
Burray 390
bus travel 467, 470
Bute 73, **75**
Butt of Lewis 328

C

Cairndow 71
Cairn Gorm 145
Cairngorms 138
  National Park 144
  Reindeer Centre
  139
  Ski Area 144
  skiing 144
  Sled-dog Adventure
  Centre 139
  walking 145
Cairn Toul 145
Caithness 263
Calanais 332
Calanais Standing
  Stones 332

Caledonian Canal
  Heritage Centre 181
Calgary Bay 80
Callander 130
  Toy Museum 130
Callander Crags 131
Callanish 332, 429
Camas Mor 239
Camas nan Geall 214
Camasunary Bay 299
Cambus o' May 150
Campbeltown 68
camping 36
Canisp 249
Canmores 432
Canna 313, **314**
Cannich 176
canoeing 20, 148, 203
canyoning 21
Caolas Scalpaigh 340
Caol Ila Distillery 101
Cape Wrath 258
Carbost 298
car hire 471
Carinish 350
Càrlabhagh 330
Carloway 330
Carnach 340
Carnasserie Castle 63
Carradale 69
Carrbridge 146
Carrick Castle 71
Carrick House 398
Carsaig Bay 81
car travel 468, 470
Castle and Gardens
  of Mey 262
Castlebay 359
Castle Coeffin 54
Castle Maol 301
Castle Menzies 123
castles 443
Castle Stalker 54
Castle Sween 64
Castle Tioram 215
Castle Urquhart 179
Cathedral of
  St Moluag 54

Cawdor Castle 172
Ceann a Deas na
  Hearadh 343
Ceann a'Mara 92
Ceann a Tuath na
  Hearadh 338
ceilidhs 452
Chanonry Point 278
Charles II 436
church, early 430
Churchill Barriers 389
Cia-Aig Falls 187
Cille Choirille 188
Civil War 435
Clachan 71, 302
Clachtoll 252
Clan Cameron
  Museum 187
clans 435
Claonaig 69
Clava Cairns 171
Cleadale 308
Clearances 55, 80,
  185, 186, 212, 220,
  259, 267, 272, 302,
  355, 414, 440, 454,
  456
Clickimin Broch 409
Cliff 334
climate 17
climbing 71, 144,
  175, 203, 234, 297
Cliobh 334
Clyde Coast 70
Clynelish Distillery
  268
Cnip 334
coach travel 467, 470
Cobbler, The 71
Cock Bridge 147
Coire Walk 236
Colbost Folk Museum
  294
Coldbackie 259
Coll 91
Colonsay 94
Colonsay House 94
Contin 275

Copinsay 389
Corpach 193
Corran 226
Corran Ferry 213
Corryvreckan
  whirlpool 104
Covenanters 435
Cowal Highland
  Gathering 70
Cowal Peninsula 70
Craignish Peninsula
  56
Craignure 78
Craigston 360
crannogs 443
Craobh Haven 56
Crarae Gardens 62
Crathie Church 149
Creag Meagaidh
  National Nature
  Reserve 188
Crianlarich 131
Crinan 64
Crinan Canal 64
crofting 329
Cromarty 277, 444
Cromarty Firth 275
Cruachan Power
  Station 60
Cubbie Roos Castle
  396
Cuillins, The 297
Culbin Sands 173
Culla Bay 353
Cullipool 56
Culloden 171
Culloden, Battle of
  172
Culrain 272
currency 478
customs and duty
  free 473
cycling 22

D

Dail Beag 330
Dalavich 61

Dalbeg 330
Dalmally 60
Darién Scheme 436
Davaar Island 68
Deerness 389
deer stalking 25
Deeside 148
  walks 150
Dervaig 80
Destitution Road 239
Devils Staircase
  205, 208
Dewars World of
  Whisky 122
Diabaig 235
Dingwall 275
Dingwall Museum
  275
disabled travellers
  474
diving 22
dolphins 29
dolphin watching 28
Dores 181, 182
Dornoch Firth 270
  cathedral 270
Doune Carloway 331
Doyle, Arthur Conan
  447
Drumbeg 252
Drumnadrochit
  176, 179
Duart Castle 78
Duirinish Peninsula
  294
Dukes Pass 129
Dulsie Bridge 173
Dun 366
Dunadd 63
Dunaverty Castle 68
Dun Bharpa 360
Dun Caan 302
Duncan 431
Duncansby Head 263
Dùn Chàrlabhaigh
  Broch 331
Dundonnell 249
Dunkeld 113

Dun Mór (Argyll) 64
Dun Mor (Tiree) 92
Dunnet Head 261
Dunollie Castle 49
Dunoon 71
Dunrobin Castle 268
Dunsgaith Castle 305
Dunstaffnage Castle
  49
Duntulm Castle 290
Dunvegan 293
Dunvegan Castle 293
Dunyvaig Castle 97
Durness 257
Dwarfie Stone 394

E

Eadar Dha Fhadhail
  334
Easdale 55
Eday 397
Eday Heritage Walk
  398
Edderton 272
Eddrachillis Bay 252
Edinbane 293
Edradour Distillery
  117
Egilsay 396
Eigg 308, **309**
Eilean Ban 301
Eilean Donan Castle
  226
Eilean Garbh 67
Eilean Mor 101
Eirisgeidh 357
electricity 474
Elgol 298, 299
Ellenabeich 55
Elphin 250
embassies and
  consulates 475
Enlightenment, The
  440
Eòlaigearraidh 360
Eoligarry 360
Eòropaidh 328

Eoropie 328
Eriskay 357
Erraid Island 81
Errogie 182
Evanton 275
events 18
everburgh 344
Evie 385

F

Fair Isle 420
  birdwatching 421
Fair Isle Bird
  Observatory 421
Fair Isle knitting 454
Fairy Glen 289
Fairy Knowe 129
Falls of Bruar 119
Falls of Leny 131
Falls of Lora 53
Falls of Measach 249
Falls of Moness 123
Falls of Shin 272
Fanagmore 253
Fergusson Gallery 111
festivals 18
Fetlar 425
Fetlar Interpretive
  Centre 425
Fingal's Cave 80
Fionnphort 81
fishing 23, 82, 144,
  148, 175, 270, 395,
  414, 415
Five Sisters of Kintail
  225
Flannan Islands 334
Flora MacDonalds
  Monument 290
Flotta 393
Flow Country 259
folk 452
Ford 61
Forsinard 259
Fort Augustus 180
Fort Charlotte 408
Fort George 171

Fortingall 123
Fortrose 278
Fort William 191, **193**
Foula 415
Foyers 181
Fyrish Monument 275

G

Gaelic 453, 476
Gairloch 238
Gairloch Heritage Museum 238
Gairlochy 187
Gallan Head 334
Galmisdale 308
game reserves 24
Ganavan Sands 49
Garenin 330
Gearraidh Bhailteas 355
Gearrannan 330
geography 457
George Waterston Memorial Centre 421
Giant Angus MacAskill Museum 294
Gigha 67
gin 42
Glen Affric 176
Glenborrodale 214
Glen Brittle 298
Glen Coe 203, **204**
   climbing 207
   Massacre 206
Glencoe ski centre 208
Glencoe village 207
Glendale 294
Glenelg 226
Glenelg Brochs 226
Glen Esk 150
Glen Etive 208
Glenfinnan 217
   Station Museum 218

Glenfinnan Games 218
Glen Garry 186
Glen Kinglas 71
Glen Lonan 60
Glen Lyon 124
Glenmore Forest Park 145
Glen Moriston 180
Glen Nevis 198
Glen Ord Distillery 175
Glen Roy 188
Glen Shiel 225
Glen Sligachan 298
Glen Strathfarrar 175
golf 23
Golspie 268
Gometra 80
Gott Bay 92
Grantown-on-Spey 146
Gray, Alasdair 449
Great Bernera 334
Great Glen Way 193
Grey Cairns of Camster 264
Grimsay 350
Griomasaigh 350
grouse shooting 25
Gruinard Bay 240
Gruinard Island 240
guesthouses 34
Gungstie 410
Gunn, Neil 267, 448
Gylen Castle 53

H

haggis 38
Hallaig 302
Handa Island 252
Haroldswick 426
Harris 337
Harris Bay 312
Harris Tweed 28, 324, 340

health 475
Helensburgh 72
Helmsdale 267
Hermaness National Nature Reserve 426
Highland Folk Museum 153
Highland Games 18
Highland House of Fraser Kiltmaker Centre 163
Highland Museum of Childhood 275
Highland Park Distillery 378
Highland Wildcat Trails 268
Highland Wildlife Park 153
Hill House 72
Hill of Fearn 273
hillwalking 23
Hirta 366
Historic Scotland 479
history 429
hitching 471
Hogg, James 446
Holm of Papay 403
horse riding 26
hostels 35
hotels 33
   price codes 32
Houbie 425
Housay 424
House of Bruar 119
Howe of Hoxa 391
Howmore 355
Hoxa Tapestry Gallery 391
Hoy 393
   walking 394
Huisinis 338
Huntingtower Castle 111
Hushinish 338
Hynish 93
hyperthermia 476

I

iCentres 482
Inchcailloch 136
Inchmahome Island 129
Inchmarnock 75
Inchnadamph 251
Inchnadamph National Nature Reserve 251
Industrial Revolution 440
insurance 476
internet 476
Inveraray 62
Inveraray Castle 62
Inveraray Jail 62
Inverarish 302
Inverarnan 135
Inverawe Smokehouses 60
Inverewe Garden 240
Inverey 149
Inverfarigaig 181
Invergarry 185
Invergordon 275
Inverie 186, 222
Inverinan 61
Inverlochy Castle 193
Invermoriston 180
Inverness 160, **162**
   castle 161
Inverness Museum and Art Gallery 161
Inverpolly National Nature Reserve 250
Inversnaid 135
Iona 77, 87
Iona Abbey 87
Islay 97, **98**
   malts 100
Islay Ales Brewery 99
Isle of Bute 73
Isle of Mousa 417
Isle of Raasay 302
Isle of Scalpay 301

Isle of Ulva 80
itineraries 11

J

Jacobite rebellion 438
Jacobs Ladder 49
James VI 434
Jarlshof 419
Jenkins, Robin 449
John o'Groats 263
Jura 103, **98**
Jura Distillery 103

K

Kailyard 448
kayaking 20
Keen of Hamar National Nature Reserve 425
Kenmore 123
Kentra Bay 214
Keppoch Murders 185
Kerrera 53
Kerrycroy 75
Kilchattan Bay (Bute) 75
Kilchattan (Colonsay) 94
Kilchoan 214
Kilchoman Distillery and Visitor Centre 101
Kilchurn Castle 60
Kildalton Cross 97
Killiecrankie 118, 438
Killin 131
Killinallan Point 100
Kilmartin 63
Kilmartin Glen 63
Kilmory Knap Chapel 64
Kiloran Bay 94
Kilravock Castle 173
Kilt Rock 291

Kincardine 272
Kincraig 153
Kingussie 153
Kinloch 311
Kinlochbervie 253
Kinloch Castle 311
Kinlochewe 237
Kinloch Hourn 186
Kinlochleven 204, **204**
  walking 205
Kinloch Rannoch 119
Kinnoull Hill Woodland Park 111
Kintra 97
Kintyre 66
Kirkwall 376, **377**
Kisimul Castle 359
kitesurfing 26
Knapdale 64
Knap of Howar 402
Kneep 334
Knock Castle 305
Knockvologan 81
Knoydart Peninsula 222
  walking 222
Kyleakin 301
Kyle of Lochalsh 227
Kyle of Sutherland 272
Kylerhea 301
Kylesku 251, 252
Kyles of Bute 72

L

Lagavulin 97
Laggan 185
Laide 240
Laidhay Croft Museum 267
Lairg 273
Lairig Ghru 145
Lake of Menteith 129
Lamb Holm 390
Landmark Forest Theme Park 146

language 476
Laphroaig 97
Largiebaan Bird Reserve 68
laundry 477
Laxford Bridge 253
Leakey's Bookshop 163
Lealt Falls 291
Ledmore 250
Leodhas 319
Lerwick 408, **409**
  town hall 408
Letterewe Estate 237
Lewis 319
Lews Castle 323
LGBT travellers 477
Liathach 235
Lingarabay 344
Lingreabhagh 344
Liniclate 353
Linklater, Eric 448
Lionacleit 353
Lismore 54
literature 445
Lochailort 218
Lochaline 213
Loch an Eilean 140
Loch Arkaig 187
Loch Assynt 251
Loch Avich 61
Lochawe 60
Loch Awe 60
  walking 61
Loch Baghasdail 354
Loch Barnluasgan 64
Lochboisdale 354
Lochbuie Stone Circle 82
Loch Carron 232
Lochcarron village 232
Loch Coille-Bharr 64
Loch Coruisk 298
Loch Druidibeag Nature Reserve 355
Loch Dunvegan 294
Lochearnhead 131

Loch Eriboll 259
Loch Etive 60
  walking 61
Loch Eynort 355
Loch Faskally 117
Loch Finlaggan 101
Loch Fleet 270
Loch Gamhna 140
Lochgilphead 64
Lochgoilhead 71
Loch Gruinart 99
Lochinver 250, 251
Loch Katrine 129
Loch Kernsary 239
Loch Kishorn 232
Loch Laggan 188
Loch Lochy 185
Loch Lomond 127, 135
Loch Lubnaig 131
Lochmaddy 348
Loch Maree 237
Loch Mhorand 182
Loch Moidart 215
Loch Morar 219
Lochnagar 150
Lochnagar Wildlife Reserve 149
Loch na Keal 81
Loch nam Madadh 348
Loch nan Uamh 218
Loch Ness 178
  boat tours 184
Loch Ness Monster 178, 181, 460
Loch Oich 185
Loch Quoich 187
Loch Tay 122, 123
Loch Torridon 235
Loch Trollamarig 340
Losgaintir 343
Lost Valley 207
Luing 55
Luskentyre 343
Luss 135
Lyness 393

M

MacAlpin, Kenneth 430
MacAskill, Angus 294
Macbeth 87, 431
MacDiarmid, Hugh 448
Macdonald Aviemore Highland Resort 139
MacDonald, Flora 161, 355
Machir Bay 100
Machrie Golf Course 99
Machrihanish 68
MacKenzie, Compton 360
MacKinnons Cave 81
Mackintosh, Charles Rennie 72
Maclean, Sorley 302
MacQuarrie Mausoleum 78
Maes Howe 381, 385, 443
magazines 477
Mallaig 220
Mallaig Heritage Centre 220
Mamores 206
Mam Ratagan Pass 226
Mangersta 334
maps 472
Markwick Head 384
Mavis Grind 422
Maxwell, Gavin 226, 301
McCaigs Tower 49
McDiarmid, Hugh 424
McIlvanney, William 449
Meavaig 338
media 477
Mellon Udrigle 240
Melvaig 239
Melvich 259
Mendelssohnn, F 80
Miabhag 334, 338
Miavaig 334
midges 475
Midhowe Broch 396
Midhowe Cairn 395
Midtown 239
Mid Yell 425
Milton 355
Mingary Castle 214
Minginish 297
Mingulay 358, 360
Mitchell, James Leslie 448
Molinginish 340
Monach Isles 349
money 478
Morar 219
Moray Firth 171
Morrone 150
Morven 267
Morvern 213
mountain biking 22, 26, 138, 144, 148, 191
mountain safety 21
Mount Stuart 74
Muck 310
Muckle Flugga 426
Muir, Edwin 396
Mull 78, **79**
    walks 81
Mull Museum 79
Mull of Oa 97
Munro-bagging 458
Museum of Abernethy 111
Museum of Islay Life 101
music 451

N

Na Baigh 344
Na Fir Bhreige 349
Na Hearadh 337
Nairn 173
Nairn Museum 173
National Trust for Scotland 479
Neil Gunn Trail 267
Neist Point 295
Neptune's Staircase 193
Ness 327
Nevis Range Ski Centre 201
newspapers 477
Nigg Bay 275
Nis 327
Noltland Castle 401
Norman Conquest 432
North Ballachulish 204
Northbay 360
North coast 257
North Coast 500 14
North Cuan 55
Northern Lights 263
North Harris 338
North Laggan 185
Northmavine 422
North Ronaldsay 403
Northton 344
North Uist 348
    excursions 349
Noss 410
Nunton 353

O

Oa, The 97
Oban 49, **51**
    Distillery 49
    Marina 53
    Sealife Centre 54
    War and Peace Museum 49
Old Byre Heritage Centre 80
Old Man of Hoy 393
Old Man of Stoer 252
Old Man of Storr 291
Oldshoremore 253
Onich 204
opening hours 479
Opinan 240
Ord 305
Ord Hill 273
Orkney 371, **374**
    Fossil and Vintage Centre 390
    Museum 377
    scuba-diving 388
    Wireless Museum 378
Orkneyinga Saga Centre 386
Ornsay 304
Oronsay 94
Orphir 386
Orwell, George 104
Ostaig 305
otters 29
Outer Hebrides 316
Out Skerries 423

P

palaces 444
Papa Stour 416
Papa Westray 402
Paps of Jura 103
Pennyghael 81
Pentland Firth 262
Perfume Studio 240
Perth 110, **112**
    Museum and Art Gallery 110
Perthshire 109
phone codes 481
photography 30
Pier Arts Centre 382
Pierowall 401
Pitlochry 117
    walking 117
Plockton 227
Plodda Falls 176
Pobull Fhinn 349
pony trekking 26
Poolewe 239

Port Appin 54
Port Askaig 101
Portavadie 72
Port Charlotte 101
Port Ellen 97
Port Mór 310
Portnahomack 273
Port Nis 327
Port of Ness 327
Portree 285, **286**
post 480
Puffin Dive Centre 52
Pulteneytown 267

Q

Queen Elizabeth
  Forest Park 129
Queen of Scots, Mary
  434
Quendale 419
Quinag 249
Quiraing 290
Quoyness Chambered
  Cairn 399

R

Raasay 302
Raasay House 302
radio 477
Rae, John 376
rafting 20
Rankin, Iain 450
Red Point 239
Reformation 434
Reilig Odhrain 87
Reinigeadal 338, 340
religion 456
restaurants 43
  price codes 32
Restoration 436
Rhenigidale 338
Rhiconich 253
Rhidorroch Estate
  244
Rhue Lighthouse 244
Rhue Peninsula 219

Ring of Brodgar
  381, 385
Rinns of Islay 99
Road to the Isles 217
Rob Roy 130
Rodel 344
Ròghadal 344
Roinebhal 344
Rosemarkie 277
Rothesay 73
Rothiemurchus
  Estate 140
Rousay 395
Rowardennan 135
Roy Bridge 188
Rùm 311, **312**
  walking 312
Ruthven Barracks 153

S

Sabhal Mor Ostaig
  305
Saddell Abbey 68
safety 480
  on mountains 21
Salen 78, 213
Saligo 100
Sanaigmore 100
Sandaig 226
Sanday 313, **314**, 399
Sandness 415
Sand of Wright 391
Sandwick 384
Sandwood Bay
  24, 258
Sanna Bay 214
Scalasaig 94
Scalloway 413
Scalloway Castle 413
Scalpaigh 340
Scalpay 340
Scalpsie Bay 75
Scapa Flow Visitor
  Centre 394
Scarba 104
Scaristabeg 344
Scarp 339

Schiehallion 119
Scone Palace 111
Sconser 301
Scoor 81
Scottish Tourist
  Board 482
Scottish Youth Hostel
  Association 35
Scott, Sir Walter 445
Scourie 252
scuba-diving
  388, 422
seals 29
sea travel 468, 471
Seil 55
Sgarasta Bheag 344
Shader 327
Shapinsay 397
Shapinsay Heritage
  Centre 397
Shawbost 330
Shell Beaches 67
Shetland Folk Festival
  18
Shetland Islands
  405, **407**
Shetland Museum
  and Archives 408
Shiel Bridge 186, 225
Shieldaig 235
shopping 28
Siabost 330
Siadar 327
Sinclair and Girnigoe
  Castle 267
Singing Sands
  215, 308
Skaill House 382
Skara Brae 381, 382
Skerryvore
  Lighthouse 93
skiing 27, 138, 147,
  148, 149, 203
Skipness 68, 69
Skye 283
Skye Museum of
  Island Life 289
Slaggan 240

Slate Islands 55
Slatrach Bay 53
Sleat Peninsula 304
Sma Glen 123
Small Isles 307
Smoo Cave 257
Soay 366
Solas 349
Sollas 349
Southend 68
South Glen Shiel
  Ridge 225
South Harris 343
South Lorn 55
South Ronaldsay
  389, 390
South Uist 354
South Walls 394
Spark, Muriel 449
Spean Bridge 187
Stac Pollaidh 250
Staffin Bay 290
Standing Stones of
  Stenness 381, 385
Stanley Mills 113
Stanydale 415
St Blanes Chapel 75
St Boniface Kirk 402
St Columba 68, 89
St Columbas Shrine
  87
St Conans Church 60
Steall Falls 200, **200**
Stenness 385, 429
Steòrnabhagh 322
Stevenson, Robert
  Louis 426, 447
Stewart dynasty 433
St Kilda 364
St Magnus 396
St Magnus Cathedral
  376
St Magnus Church
  384
St Margarets Hope
  390
St Martins Cross 87
St Ninians Isle 419

St Ninians Point 75
Stoer Lighthouse 252
stone circles 63, 82, 333, 349, 385, 443
Stone of Setter 398
Stornoway 322, **323**
    Museum nan Eilean 323
Stratherrick Valley 182
Strathglass 176
Strathnaver Museum 259
Strathpeffer 275
Strathspey 138
Stromness 381
Stromness Museum 382
Stronsay 400
Strontian 212
student travellers 480
studying 480
Suilven 249
Sula Sgeir 327
Sumburgh 419
Summer Isles 250
surfing 27

T

Tain 271
Talisker 298
Talisker Distillery 298
Tangasdale 360
Tankerness House and Gardens 377
Taransay 343
Tarasaigh 343
Tarbat Discovery Centre 273
Tarbert (Harris) 340
Tarbert (Kintyre) 66

Tarskavaig 305
tartan 28
Tattoo 451
Taynuilt 60
telephone 480
Three Sisters 207
Thurso 261, **262**
Tighnabruaich 72
Timespan Heritage Centre 267
time zone 481
Timsgarry 334
Timsgearraidh 334
Tingwall 414
tipping 481
Tiree 92
Tobermory 78
Tobermory Distillery 79
Toberonochy 56
Tobha Mòr 355
Toddun 338
Toe Head 344
Toft 422
Tokavaig 305
Tòlstadh 328
Tolsta North 328
Tomb of the Eagles 391
Tomdoun 186
Tomich 176
Tomintoul 146
Tonque 259
Torosay Castle 78
Torridon 234
Tourist Information Centres 482
tour operators 481
Tràigh Mhòr 360
train travel 466, 469
transport 465-472

Treasure Island 426, 447
trekking 23
Treshnish Isles 80
Trondra 413
Trossachs 127, 128
Trotternish Peninsula 289
Trumpan 293
Tyndrum 131

U

Udale Bay 277
Uibhist a Deas 354
Uibhist a Tuath 348
Uig 289
Uig Peninsula 334
Uisken Bay 81
Ullapool 243, **245**
Ulva 80
Union of Crowns 434
Unst 425
Unst Boat Haven 426
Unst Heritage Centre 426
Up-Helly-Aa Exhibition 409
Upper Killeyan 97
Urgha 340

V

Varick Castle 259
Vatersay 358, 360
vegetarians 43
Victoria Falls 237
Vikings 430
Vinquoy Chambered Cairn 398
visas 483
Voe 422

W

walking 23
walking guides 462
Wallace, William 432
Ward Hill 393
Wars of Succession 432
Waternish Peninsula 293
weather 17
websites 483
Weisdale 414
Wester Ross 232
West Highland Museum 192
West Highland Railway 218
West Highland Way 131, 135, 205, 208
Westray 401
    walking 401
Westray Heritage Centre 401
whale watching 28
Whalsay 423
whisky 41, 42, 100
Whitehall 400
Wick 266
Wick Heritage Centre 267
wild camping 36
wildlife 28
windsurfing 26
women travellers 483
working 483
Wyre 396

Y

Yell 424
Yesnaby 384

Features

A böd for the night 416
After the goldrush 268
A stab in the back 206
Battle of Culloden 172
Better red than dead 130
Close encounters of the bird kind 418
Croft conversion 329
Death of the clans 439
Dolphin cruises 176
Faithful Flora 291
Five great short walks 24
Gaelic spread 302
Gaelic writers 446
Gatliff Trust 331
Go green 474
Great Monster Hunt 181
Great Scots 450
How St Kilda was killed off 365
Islay's malts distilled 100
Law of the land 299
Learning the lingo 378
Mountain safety 21
Munros, Corbetts and Grahams 458
Music to your ears 332
Never on a Sunday 328
Old as the hills 186
Once bitten, twice shy 475
On the buses 468
Packing for the Highlands and Islands 466
Piscine cuisine 61
Raising standards 220
Riding the rails 218
Right to buy 341
Scandinavian settlements 383
Shopping on the Isle of Skye 288
Take no prisoners 290
The end of an era 308
The graveyard of Scapa Flow 390
The Great Glen Way 180
The Hebridean Way 324
The story of St Columba 89
Things to do on Skye when it's raining 295
Tight little island 358
To dive for 388
Turn water into whisky 41
We are most certainly amused 150
What's in a name? 435
Which whisky? 42
Wild camping 36

Acknowledgements

A huge number of people need to be thanked for helping with this new edition. Firstly, a big thank you to the dedicated staff of the tourist offices throughout the Highlands and Islands of Scotland who answered my many, many questions with patience, politeness and a smile (always). Thanks also to the good folk at Historic Environment Scotland, Caledonian MacBrayne, and to Alan Hendry for his invaluable contributions on the North Coast 500 route.

A massive shout to all the people who tirelessly strive to improve Scotland's reputation as a first-class tourist destination by continually raising the bar for standards of food and accommodation. I hope you're all mentioned in this guidebook. If I've missed you then please email or write and tell me about it.

Thanks to everyone at Footprint for their support, especially to my editor, Felicity, whose steady hand guided the ship through the stormy seas of authorial oversight and inconsistency.

Finally, and most importantly, to my wife, Philippa, for her selfless and unstinting help, support and love, and for putting up with many rain-soaked family holidays in the Scottish Highlands. Without her this book would not exist.

Credits

Footprint credits
Project editor: Felicity Laughton
Production and layout: Emma Bryers
Maps: Kevin Feeney
Colour section: John Hendry

Publisher: John Sadler
Marketing: Kirsty Holmes

Photography credits
Front cover: Sergejus Lamanosovas/
Shutterstock.com
Back cover top: Miledy/Shutterstock.com
Back cover bottom: Scott Jessiman Photo/
Shutterstock.com

Colour section
Page 1: Targn Pleiades/Shutterstock.com,
Lukassek/Shutterstock.com, Ludovic Farine/
Shutterstock.com. **Page 2**: Steve Bower/
Shutterstock.com. **Page 3**: travellight/
Shutterstock.com. **Page 4**: SergeBertasius
Photography/Shutterstock.com, Peter McBride/
Superstock.com. **Page 5**: Federica Violin/
Shutterstock.com, Frederic Maillard 49/
Shutterstock.com, evenfh/Shutterstock.com.
Page 6: mountaintreks/Shutterstock.com, John
A Cameron/Shutterstock.com. **Page 7**: Swen
Stroop/Shutterstock.com, Alistair MacLean/
Shutterstock.com. **Page 9**: corlaffra/Shutterstock.
com, Evgeniy Kurochkin/Shutterstock.com,
Pecold/Shutterstock.com. **Page 10**: Petr Jelinek/
Shutterstock.com. **Page 11**: Antonin Vinter/
Shutterstock.com. **Page 12**: Spumador/
Shutterstock.com. **Page 13**: trotalo/Shutterstock.
com. **Page 14**: Dave Head/Shutterstock.com.
Page 15: jpatava/Shutterstock.com, Northern
Wild/Shutterstock.com. **Page 16**: Ysbrand Cosijn/
Shutterstock.com.

Duotones
Page 44: Stephen P Baker/Shutterstock.com
Page 106: Targn Pleiades/Shutterstock.com
Page 156: Susanne Pommer/Shutterstock.com
Page 280: Nataliya Hora/Shutterstock.com
Page 316: happylights/Shutterstock.com
Page 368: Pecold/Shutterstock.com

Publishing information
Footprint Scotland Highlands and Islands
7th edition
© Compass Maps Ltd
June 2018

ISBN: 978 1 911082 57 6
CIP DATA: A catalogue record for this book
is available from the British Library

® Footprint Handbooks and the
Footprint mark are a registered
trademark of Compass Maps Ltd

Published by Footprint
5 Riverside Court
Lower Bristol Road
Bath BA2 3DZ, UK
T +44 (0)1225 469141
footprinttravelguides.com

Every effort has been made to ensure that
the facts in this guidebook are accurate.
However, travellers should still obtain advice
from consulates, airlines, etc about travel
and visa requirements before travelling.
The authors and publishers cannot
accept responsibility for any loss, injury
or inconvenience however caused.

Printed in the UK
Print and production managed by
Jellyfish Solutions

Footprint Mini Atlas
Scotland Highlands & Islands

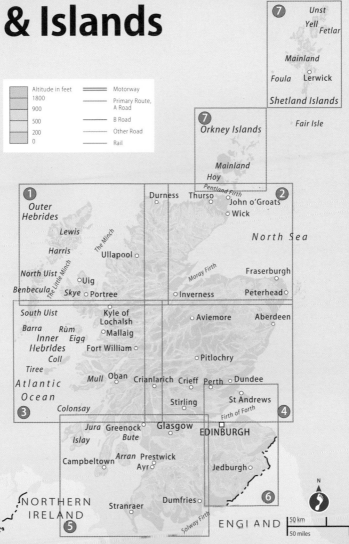

Altitude in feet		Motorway
	1800	Primary Route, A Road
	900	B Road
	500	Other Road
	200	
	0	Rail

7 Unst
Yell Fetlar
Mainland
Foula Lerwick
Shetland Islands
Fair Isle

7 *Orkney Islands*
Mainland
Hoy
Pentland Firth

1 *Outer Hebrides*
Durness Thurso John o'Groats
Wick
2
Lewis
The Minch
North Sea
Harris
Ullapool
The Little Minch
North Uist
Uig Moray Firth Fraserburgh
Benbecula Skye Portree
Inverness Peterhead

South Uist Kyle of Lochalsh Aviemore Aberdeen
Barra Rùm Mallaig
Inner Eigg
Hebrides Fort William
Coll Pitlochry
Tiree
Atlantic Mull Oban Crianlarich Crieff Perth Dundee
Ocean
Stirling St Andrews
Colonsay
3 *Firth of Forth*
4
Jura Greenock Glasgow
Islay Bute EDINBURGH
Campbeltown *Arran* Prestwick
Ayr Jedburgh

6

NORTHERN
IRELAND Stranraer Dumfries
5 *Solway Firth* ENGLAND
N
50 km
50 miles

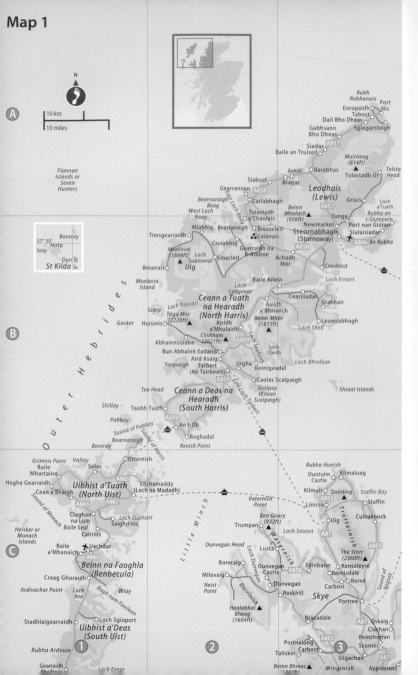

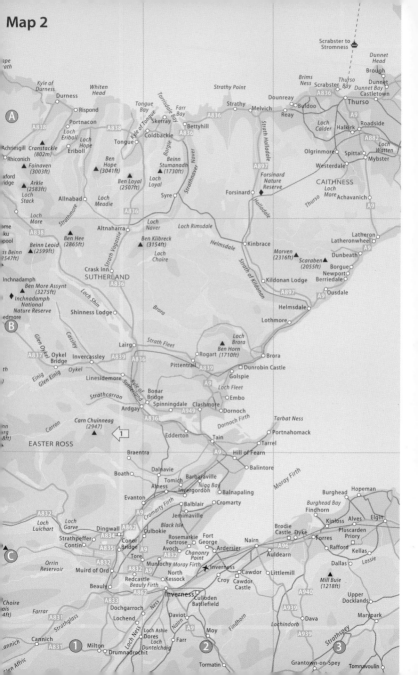

Map 2

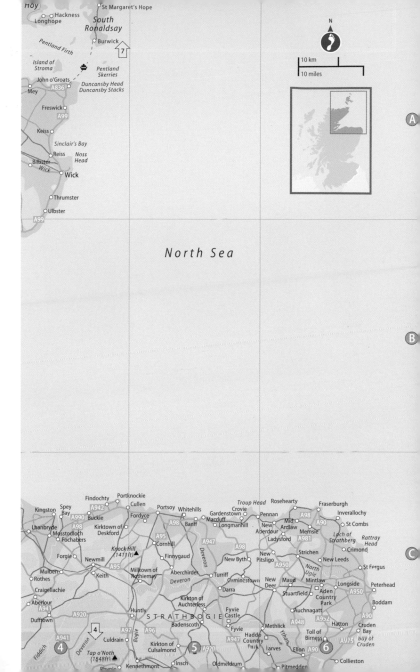

Map 3

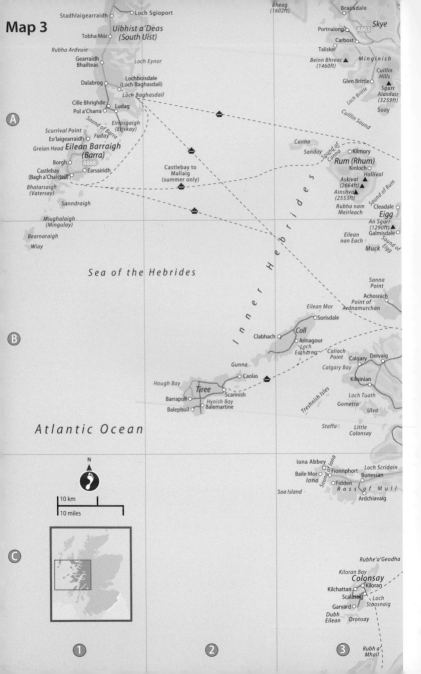

Stadhlaigearraidh ○ ○ Loch Sgioport

*Uibhist a'Deas
(South Uist)*

Tobha Mòr ○

Rubha Ardvuie

Gearraidh ○
Bhailteas

Loch Eynor

Dalabrog ○ ○ Lochboisdale
(Loch Baghasdail)
○ Loch Baghasdail

Cille Bhrighde ○
Pol a'Charra ○ ○ Ludag

A

Scurrival Point
Eo'laigearraidh ○
Greian Head **Eilean Barraigh
(Barra)**

Eirosgaigh
(Eriskay)
○ Fuday

Sound of Barra

Borgh ○ A888
Castlebay ○ ○ Earsairidh
(Bagh a'Chaisteil)

*Bhatarsaigh
(Vatersay)*

Sanndraigh

*Miughalaigh
(Mingulay)*

Bearnaraigh

Wiay

Sea of the Hebrides

Castlebay to
Mallaig
(summer only)

B

Hough Bay

Barrapoll ○
Balephuil ○

Tiree

Hynish Bay
Balemartine

○ Caolas
Gunna

Scarinish

Atlantic Ocean

N

10 km
10 miles

C

*Bheag
(1602ft)*

Bracadale

Portnalong ○ A863 **Skye**
Carbost ○

Talisker ○

Minginish

Beinn Bhreac ▲
(1460ft)

Glen Brittle ○

*Cuillin
Hills*

Loch Brittle

▲ Sgurr
Alasdair
(3259ft)

Soay

Cuillin Sound

Canna

Sanday

Sound of Canna

○ Kilmory

Rum (Rhum)
Kinloch ○
Hallival ▲

Askival ▲
(2664ft)
Ainshval ▲
(2553ft)

Sound of Rum

*Rubha nam
Meirleach*

○ Cleadale

Eigg
An Sgurr ▲
(1290ft)
Galmisdale ○

*Eilean
nan Each*

Muck

*Sound of
Eigg*

*Sanna
Point*

Achosnich ○
*Point of
Ardnamurchan*

Eilean Mor

○ Sorisdale

Clabhach ○ **Coll**
Arinagour ○
*Loch
Eatharna*

*Caliach
Point*

Calgary ○ Dervaig ○

Calgary Bay

Kilninian ○

Loch Tuath

Gometra ○

Ulva

Treshnish Isles

Staffa

*Little
Colonsay*

Iona Abbey □ □ Iona
Baile Mor ○ ○ Fionnphort
Iona ○ Bunessan
○ Fidden
Ross of Mull
Soa Island ○ Ardchiavaig

Sound of Iona

Loch Scridain

Rubhe'a'Geodha

Kiloran Bay
Colonsay
Kilchattan ○ ○ Kiloran
Scalasaig ○
Garvard ○ ○ *Loch
Staosnaig*
*Dubh
Eilean* ○ Oronsay

*Rubh a'
Mhail*

1   **2**   **3**

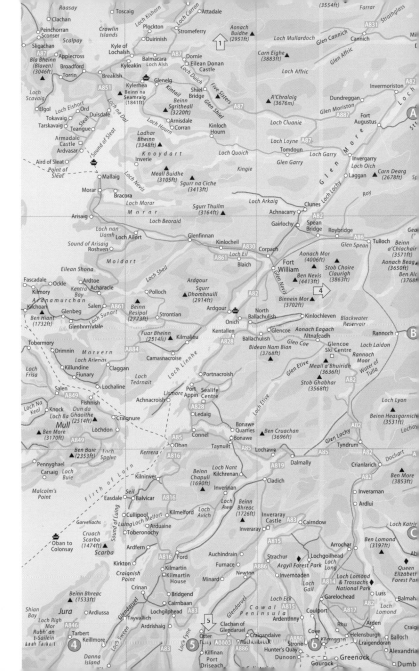

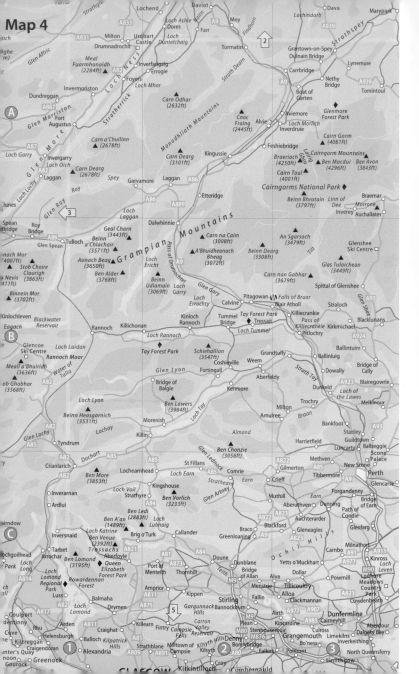

Map 4

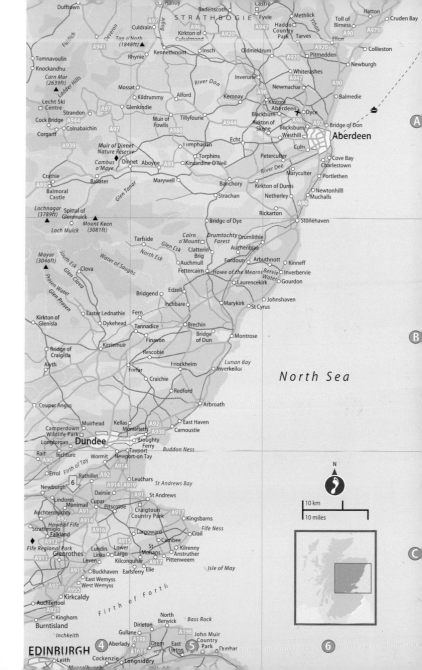

Map 5

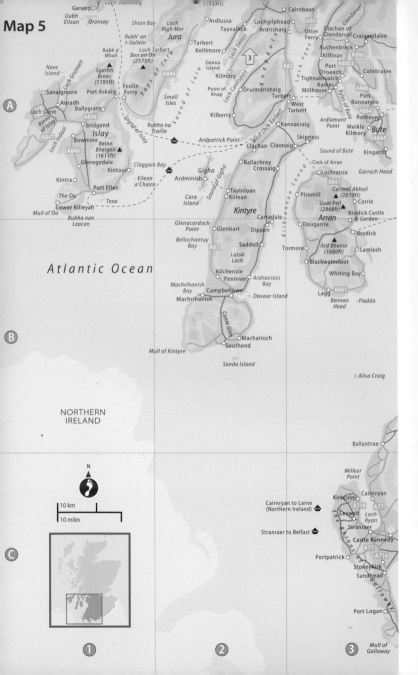

Garvard · Loch Staosnaig
Dubh Eilean · Oronsay
Shian Bay · Loch Righ Mor · Jura
Rubh' an t-Sailein
Rubh a' Mhàil
Nave Island
Sgarbh Breac (1195ft)
Sanaigmore
Aoradh · Loch Gruinart
Ballygrant
Feolin Ferry · Ben an Oir (2575ft)
Port Askaig
Loch Indaal · Bridgend · Islay
Bowmore
Rinns of Islay
Glenegedale
Kintra · Kintour
Kintour
Port Ellen
The Oa · Texa
Lower Killeyan
Mull of Oa · Rubha nan Leacan

Atlantic Ocean

NORTHERN IRELAND

Cairnbaan
Ardlussa · Lochgilphead · A83
Tayvallich · Ardrishaig · Otter Ferry
Clachan of Glendaruel · Craigandaive
Tarbert · Loch Sween · Auchenbreck
Keillmore · Kilfinan · A886
Danna Island · Port Driseach · A8003 · Colintraive
Kilmory · Tighnabruaich · Kames
Point of Knap · Loch Caolisport · Druimdrishaig · Millhouse
Tarbert · A88 · Kyles of Bute · Port Bannatyne
Kilberry · West Tarbert · Ardlamont Point · Rothesay
Kennacraig · Meikle Kilmory · Bute
Ardpatrick Point · Clachan · Claonaig · Skipness · A844
Rubha na Traille · Ballachroy · Cock of Arran · Kingarth
Crossaig · Lochranza · Sound of Bute · Garroch Head
Gigha · Pirnmill · Casteal Abhail (2819ft)
Ardminish · Tayinloan · Killean · Goat Fell (2868ft) · Corrie
Cara Island · Kintyre · Carradale · Dougarie · Brodick Castle & Garden
Glenacardoch Point · Glenbarr · Dippen · Arran · Brodick
Bellochantuy Bay · A83 · Saddell · Tormore · Ard Bheinn (1680ft) · Lamlash
Lussa Loch · Blackwaterfoot · Whiting Bay
Kilchenzie · Peninver · Ardnacross Bay
Machrihanish Bay · Campbeltown · A841 · Lagg · Bennan Head · Pladda
Machrihanish · Davaar Island
Conie Glen · Macharioch · Southend
Mull of Kintyre · Sanda Island

Ailsa Craig

Ballantrae

Milleur Point
Cairnryan to Larne (Northern Ireland)
Kirkcolm · Cairnryan
Leswalt · A718 · Loch Ryan · A77
Stranraer to Belfast
Stranraer · Castle Kennedy
Portpatrick · A77 · A716
Stoneykirk
Sandhead
Port Logan · Mull of Galloway

N
10 km
10 miles

A · B · C
1 · 2 · 3

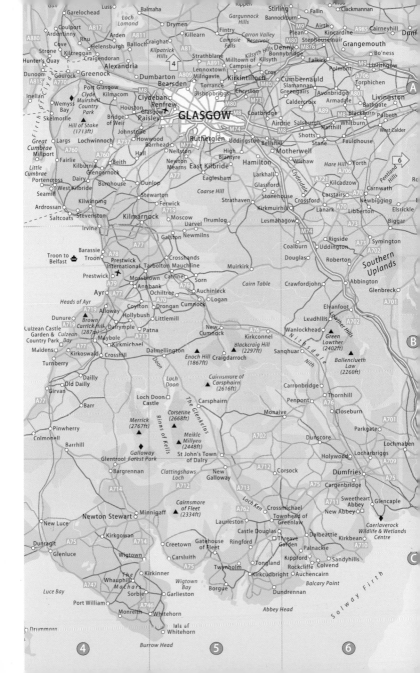

Map 6

Perth · Glencarse · Errol · Firth

Newburgh · Leuchars · St Andrews Bay
Path of · Abernethy · A912 · Lindores · Dairsie · A919 · St Andrews
Condie · Auchtermuchty · Monimail · Cupar · A91
Glenfarg · Strathmiglo · A92 · Pitscottie · Craigtoun · Kingsbarns
· Falkland · A914 · A916 · Country Park · Fife Ness
Milnathort · Palace · Glenrothes · Largoward · Crail
· Fife · A912 · A915 · Cambee
· Regional · Kilconquhar · St · Kilrenny
Kinross · Park · Kilconquhar · Monans · Anstruther
Loch Leven · A911 · Leven · A917 · Pittenweem
Lochore · Buckhaven · Elie · Isle of May
Meadows · A915
Country · East Wemyss
Park · Cowdenbeath · Kirkcaldy
Lochgelly · A92 · A955
A823 · Auchtertool
Dunfermline · Aberdour · Kinghorn · Firth of Forth
Cairneyhill · Burntisland · Inchkeith
Limekilns · Inverkeithing · North · Bass Rock
South · Dalgety · Berwick · Auldhame
Queensferry · North Queensferry · Gullane · Dirleton · Auldhame · John Muir
Lauriston · Aberlady · A198 · Country · Dunbar
Castle · Cramond · A198 · Drem · Park
EDINBURGH · Cockenzie · A1673 · Longniddry · East Linton
Leith · & Port · A1
Edinburgh · Musselburgh · Prestonpan · Haddington · Stenton
Whitecraig · Tranent · Macmerry · A6093 · Bolton · Garvald · Cockburnspath
Water of Leith · Loanhead · Dalkeith · Ormiston · Pencaitland · Gifford · St Abb's
Scald Law · Bilston · Bonnyrigg · Humbie · Lammermuir Hills · Head
(1900ft) · Roslin · Rosewell · Whiteadder Water · St Abbs
Pentland · A6094 · Gorebridge · Meikle · Ecclaw · Grantshouse · Coldingham
Hills · Penicuik · North Middleton · Says Law · Eyemouth
Regional · Gilston · A68 · (1756ft) · Duns · Auchencrow · Reston
(1844ft) · A702 · A701 · Leadburn · Heriot · Dirrington · A6105 · Burnmouth
Carlops · Oxton · Westruther · Great Law · Chirnside · Foulden
West Linton · Blackhope · Gala Water · Lauder · A6105 · Swinton · Ladykirk · Berwick-
Dolphinton · Scar · Houndslow · Greenlaw · A6112 · upon-Tweed
Romannobridge · (2137ft) · Stow · Gordon · A697 · Eccles · Coldstream
Elsrickle · Blyth Bridge · Eddleston · Leader Water · A6089 · Stichill
A72 · Peebles · Colquhar · Windlestraw · Galashiels · A6105 · Greenlaw · Floors
Stobo · (2613ft) · Innerleithen · Abbotsford · Melrose · Castle · Kelso
Broughton · Tweedale · House · Newtown St · Kelso · Town
Traquair · Minch Maw · Melrose · Boswells · A698 · Yetholm
House · (1861ft) · Abbey · Selkirk · A699 · Eckford · Morebattle
Tweedsmuir · Dun Rig · Yarrow · Midlem · Nisbet · Kirk
Broad Law · (2439ft) · Mountbenger · Lilliesleaf · Bonjedward · Oxnam
(2758ft) · Black Knowe · Hassendean · A698 · Jedburgh
Glenbreck · Capplecleuch · Head · Ettrick Water · Jedburgh · Abbey
White · Hawick · Chesters · Camptown
Coomb · Ettrick · Roberton · Bonchester · Carter Bar · Cheviot Hills
Hart Fell · Bridge · Southdean
Capplegill · (2652ft) · Teviothead
Moffat · Loch Fell
Beattock · (2258ft) · Hermitage
Castle
Eskdalemuir · Roan Fell
Boreland · (1861ft) · Newcastleton
Lochmaben · Locherbie
Langholm
Ecclefechan
M74 · Waterbeck · Canonbie · ENGLAND
Eaglesfield
Kirkpatrick- · Blacksmith's
Fleming · Shop · Gretna
Annan · Eastriggs

N

10 km
10 miles

A · B · C

1 · 2 · 3

Map 7

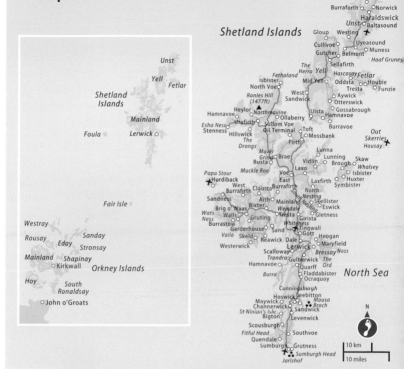

Index

A
4 A6	Aberdeen
4 B2	Aberfeldy
4 A5	Alford
3 B5	Appin
1 C4	Applecross
1 C4	Ardnamurchan Peninsula
3 B5	Ardgour
5 A3-B3	Arran, Isle of
4 A3	Aviemore

B
4 A4	Ballater
4 A4	Balmoral Castle
4 A4	Balmoral
4 A5	Banchory
3 A1	Barra
2 C1-C2	Beauly Firth, The
1 C1	Benbecula
1 B1	Berneray
2 C2	Black Isle, The
4 B3	Blairgowrie
4 A3	Boat of Garten
4 A3	Braemar
3 A4	Broadford
2 C3	Brodie Castle
2 B2	Brora
5 A3	Bute, Isle of

C
5 B2	Campbeltown
3 A3	Canna
4 A3	Carrbridge
2 C2	Cawdor Castle
3 B3	Coll
3 C3	Colonsay
3 B5	Connel
5 A3-A4	Cowal Peninsula
3 C5	Crinan Canal
2 C1-C2	Cromarty Firth, The
2 C2	Culloden

D
4 A4-A6	Deeside
4 A4-A5	Don Valley, The
4 A2	Dores
2 B2-C2	Dornoch Firth, The
2 C1	Drumnadrochit
2 C4	Dufftown
2 B3	Dunbeath
2 A3	Dunnet Head
5 A4	Dunoon
1 A6	Durness

E
3 A3-B3	Eigg
3 A5	Eilean Donan Castle
3 A1	Eriskay

F
4 A1	Fort Augustus
2 C2	Fort George
3 B6	Fort William

G
1 C4	Gairloch
5 A2	Gigha
3 A6	Glen Affric
3 B6	Glen Coe
3 A6	Glen Garry
3 B6	Glen Nevis
4 A1-B1	Glen Roy
3 A5	Glen Shiel
1 C6	Glen Strathfarrar
3 A5	Glenelg
3 B5	Glenfinnan
4 B3	Glenshee
2 B2	Golspie
4 A3	Grantown-on-Spey
1 B5	Gruinard Bay

H
1 B2-B3	Harris
5 A4	Helensburgh
2 B3	Helmsdale
2 C5	Huntly

I
3 C6	Inveraray
4 A1	Invergarry
4 A1	Invermoriston
2 C2	Inverness
4 A5	Inverurie
3 C3	Iona
5 A1	Islay

J
2 A4	John o'Groats
5 A1-A2	Jura

K
3 B5-C5	Kerrera, Isle of
3 C5	Kilmartin
4 A2	Kingussie
3 A5	Kinloch Hourn
1 A5	Kinlochbervie
1 C5	Kinlochewe
5 A2-B2	Kintyre
3 A5	Knoydart Peninsula
3 A5	Kyle of Lochalsh
1 B5	Kylesku

L
4 A5	Lecht Ski Centre
1 A3	Lewis
3 B5	Lismore, Isle of
3 A5-A6	Loch Arkaig
3 C5-C6	Loch Awe
3 B5-B6	Loch Etive
1 C4	Loch Kishorn
4 C1	Loch Lomond
4 B2	Loch Tay
3 A1	Lochboisdale
1 C4	Lochcarron village
3 C5	Lochgilphead

M
3 A4	Mallaig
2 C2	Moray Firth, The
3 B4	Morvern
3 B3	Muck
3 B3-4, C3-4	Mull

N
2 C2	Nairn
1 A3	Ness
1 B2	North Harris
1 C1	North Uist

O
3 B5	Oban

P
4 C3	Perth
4 B3	Pitlochry
3 A5	Plockton
1 B4	Poolewe
2 B2	Portnahomack
1 C3	Portree

R
3 A3	Rùm

S
1 A5	Scourie
3 C4-C5	Slate Islands
3 A4	Sleat Peninsula
1 B2	South Harris
3 A1	South Uist
3 B6	Spean Bridge
2 C3-C4	Speyside
1 B3	Stornoway

T
2 B2	Tain
4 A5	Tap o' Noth
1 A3 5 B2	Tarbert
2 A3	Thurso
3 B2	Tiree
4 A4	Tomintoul
2 A1	Tongue
1 C4	Torridon
4 C1-C2	Trossachs, The
1 C3	Trotternish Peninsula

U
1 B2	Uig Peninsula
1 B5	Ullapool

W
2 A4	Wick

Aviemore

Distance chart

	Aviemore	Campbeltown	Crianlarich	Crieff	Durness	Edinburgh	Fort William	Glasgow	Inverness	John o'Groats	Mallaig	Oban	Perth	Portree	Thurso	Uig	Ullapool
Campbeltown	190																
Crianlarich	95	107															
Crieff	90	142	35														
Durness	132	298	226	222													
Edinburgh	126	189	88	65	258												
Fort William	61	129	51	86	169	132											
Glasgow	140	138	56	49	272	46	107										
Inverness	31	193	116	121	104	157	65	170									
John o'Groats	148	313	242	237	93	273	185	286	119								
Mallaig	100	171	93	128	179	174	43	149	104	223							
Oban	105	87	41	76	213	122	44	97	109	228	86						
Perth	85	160	52	18	217	43	104	59	116	232	143	93					
Portree	142	238	160	195	187	230	109	216	113	212	48	153	192				
Thurso	138	303	232	227	74	263	175	276	110	20	213	219	220	201			
Uig	157	252	175	210	202	251	124	231	128	227	63	217	168	207	16		
Ullapool	85	240	162	175	67	210	111	224	57	130	112	155	167	119	120	134	
Wick	131	297	219	221	94	257	168	271	103	16	207	212	216	196	21	209	114

Distances in miles   1 mile = 1.6 kilometres

Map symbols

- □ Capital city
- ○ Other city, town
- ⟷ International border
- ⟼ Regional border
- ⊖ Customs
- ⬭ Contours (approx)
- ▲ Mountain, volcano
- ⇌ Mountain pass
- ⟶ Escarpment
- Glacier
- Salt flat
- Rocks
- ⤙⤙⤙ Seasonal marshland
- Beach, sandbank
- ⟨⟩ Waterfall
- ⌒ Reef
- ═══ Motorway
- ─── Main road
- ── Minor road
- ╌╌╌ Track
- ⋯⋯ Footpath
- ── Railway
- ⊢■ Railway with station
- ✈ Airport
- ⊟ Bus station
- Ⓜ Metro station

- ---- Cable car
- ╫╫╫╫ Funicular
- ⛴ Ferry
- ══ Pedestrianized street
- ⊃ ⊂ Tunnel
- ⟶ One way-street
- ⬚⬚⬚ Steps
- ⇌ Bridge
- ▂▂▂ Fortified wall
- Park, garden, stadium
- ⬤ Sleeping
- ➊ Eating
- ➊ Bars & clubs
- Building
- □ Sight
- ♰♰ Cathedral, church
- 🏯 Chinese temple
- 🛕 Hindu temple
- 🗼 Meru
- 🕌 Mosque
- △ Stupa
- ✡ Synagogue
- ℹ Tourist office
- 🏛 Museum
- ✉ Post office
- Ⓟ Police

- Ⓢ Bank
- @ Internet
- ♪ Telephone
- 🏪 Market
- ➕ Medical services
- Ⓟ Parking
- ⓟ Petrol
- ⚐ Golf
- ⁘ Archaeological site
- ♦ National park, wildlife reserve
- ❈ Viewing point
- ⊼ Campsite
- ⌂ Refuge, lodge
- 🏰 Castle, fort
- ⤷ Diving
- 🌲 Deciduous, coniferous, palm trees
- ⇧ Hide
- 🍇 Vineyard, winery
- △ Distillery
- ⤓ Shipwreck
- ✕ Historic battlefield
- 1 Detail map
- 1 Related map

About the author

Alan Murphy

As a journalist living in Dundee, Alan Murphy enjoyed many opportunities to explore the glories of the Scottish Highlands before leaving his native country to travel in South America. During a stint working for the English-language *Bolivian Times* in La Paz, Alan met the editor of the legendary *South American Handbook* and was invited to write a new series of Footprint guides to *Bolivia*, *Peru*, *Ecuador* and *Venezuela*. But the pull of his homeland proved too strong and he eventually returned to write the new Footprint guides to *Scotland*, *Edinburgh*, *Glasgow* and *Scotland's Highlands and Islands*. Work opportunities once again pulled him away, this time to the wilds of West Yorkshire, where he now lives with his wife, three children and dog.